And the light shineth in darkness: and the darkness did not comprehend it.

John 1:5 (Douay-Rheims)

The light itself, which shines in the uncomprehending darkness, no longer understands itself within the darkness; that it still shines is its irrevocable obedience to the paternal sun.

Hans Urs von Balthasar, *Leben aus dem Tod*, 40

LIGHT IN DARKNESS

*Hans Urs von Balthasar
and the Catholic Doctrine
of Christ's Descent into Hell*

Alyssa Lyra Pitstick

WILLIAM B. EERDMANS PUBLISHING COMPANY
GRAND RAPIDS, MICHIGAN / CAMBRIDGE, U.K.

Published 2007 by
Wm. B. Eerdmans Publishing Co.
2140 Oak Industrial Drive N.E., Grand Rapids, Michigan 49505 /
P.O. Box 163, Cambridge CB3 9PU U.K.

Printed in the United States of America

11 10 09 08 07   7 6 5 4 3 2 1

Library of Congress Cataloging-in-Publication Data

Pitstick, Alyssa Lyra.
    Light in darkness: Hans Urs von Balthasar and the Catholic doctrine
of Christ's descent into Hell / Alyssa Lyra Pitstick.
        p.   cm.
    Includes bibliographical references.
    Cloth ISBN 978-0-8028-0755-7
    Paper ISBN 978-0-8028-4039-4
    1. Balthasar, Hans Urs von, 1905-1988. 2. Jesus Christ — Descent into hell.
    3. Catholic Church — Doctrines.   I. Title.

    BX4705.B163P58   2007
    232.96′7 — dc22
                                                      2006019378

www.eerdmans.com

Dedicated to

Our Lady of the Rosary

under the patronage of

St. Catherine of Siena and
St. Thérèse the Little Flower

Contents

Acknowledgments

This book is a revised version of my doctoral dissertation, *Lux in tenebris: The Traditional Catholic Doctrine of Christ's Descent into Hell and the Theological Opinion of Hans Urs von Balthasar* (S.T.D. diss., Pontifical University of St. Thomas Aquinas, 2005). The footnotes have been reduced in content and the text tightened by this additional round under the knife.

The publication of this book so soon after my defense of it as a dissertation gives me the happy opportunity to thank publicly once again all those who assisted me in its original completion. My particular gratitude goes above all to those who prayed for me; to my mother Penelope Pitstick; the William E. Simon family; Jacques Servais, S.J., and the residents of Casa Balthasar in Rome; Sr. Aurelia Spendel and the Dominican community of St. Ursula in Augsburg, Germany; the Rev. Peter Waters; William Harbig; Wolfram Hoyer, O.P.; and my moderator, Charles Morerod, O.P. I add here my thanks to the Rev. Richard John Neuhaus for his proactive encouragement of the present publication.

Finally, I wish to acknowledge with all seriousness the United States government, without whose academic loan program my studies would not have been possible. Certainly I will not be able to forget this assistance for quite some time.

Abbreviations

i. Works by Hans Urs von Balthasar

Crown	*You Crown the Year with Your Goodness*
"Desc"	"The Descent into Hell," *Expl IV*
"DescHell"	"The Descent into Hell," *Chicago Studies*
Dare	*Dare We Hope "That All Men Be Saved"?*
Expl I	*The Word Made Flesh*, Explorations in Theology, vol. I
Expl II	*Spouse of the Word*, Explorations in Theology, vol. II
Expl III	*Creator Spirit*, Explorations in Theology, vol. III
Expl IV	*Spirit and Institution*, Explorations in Theology, vol. IV
GloryI	*Seeing the Form*, vol. I, *The Glory of the Lord*
GloryVI	*The Old Covenant*, vol. VI, *The Glory of the Lord*
GloryVII	*The New Covenant*, vol. VII, *The Glory of the Lord*
MP	*Mysterium Paschale*
ThDrI	*Prologomena*, vol. I, *Theo-Drama*
ThDrII	*The Dramatis Personae: Man in God*, vol. II, *Theo-Drama*
ThDrIII	*The Dramatis Personae: The Person in Christ*, vol. III, *Theo-Drama*
ThDrIV	*The Action*, vol. IV, *Theo-Drama*
ThDrV	*The Last Act*, vol. V, *Theo-Drama*
ThLogII	*Wahrheit Gottes*, bd. II, *Theo-Logik*
ThLogIII	*Der Geist der Wahrheit*, bd. III, *Theo-Logik*
Th'l Anth	*A Theological Anthropology*
"Vicarious"	"On Vicarious Representation," *Expl IV*

ii. Other Works

CCC	*Catechism of the Catholic Church*
CF	Dupuis, Jacques, ed., *The Christian Faith*
DS	Denzinger, H., and A. Schönmetzer, eds., *Enchiridion Symbolorum*
ICR	*Communio: International Catholic Review*
IKaZ	*Internationale katholische Zeitschrift: Communio*
Mansi	Mansi, Giovanni Domenico, *Sacrorum Conciliorum nova, et amplissima collectio*
PG	Migne, *Patrologia . . . : Series graeca*
PL	Migne, *Patrologia . . . : Series latina*
RITC	*Rivista internazionale di teologia e cultura. Communio*
ST	St. Thomas Aquinas, *Summa theologiae*

Editorial Conventions

A. Citations

The texts cited throughout this work were written by Hans Urs von Balthasar except when indicated otherwise.

B. Quotation Marks

A standard governing the use of quotation marks was necessitated by the variety of conventions used in different languages and in different editions of Balthasar's works. Generally, in English texts, a distinction may be made between double quotation marks (" "), used to report another person's words, and single ones (' '). Besides indicating material quoted within another quotation, single marks may signify a word or short phrase is used in an unusual way, as a special term, or loosely. The latter function of single quotation marks does not exist in German; the normal quotation mark („ " or, in the editions of Balthasar's Johannes Verlag, « ») is used for the functions of both kinds of marks. A problem arises due to the fact that Hans Urs von Balthasar used German quotation marks around single words or short phrases with unusual frequency. In addition, he does not provide a citation for every individual quotation, but typically marks only the last quotation in a series. Moreover, there is no standard practice in *English translations* of Balthasar's works regarding which quotation marks to use for the single words and short phrases he encloses in German quotation marks: Some translators leave all marks double, while others offer an interpretation and change some marks to single. There is also no standard practice in *English secondary works* about Balthasar's theology. Invariable use of double marks may obscure Balthasar's original meaning, while the use of single marks leaves it unclear whether it was Balthasar or the secondary author who intended to loosen the word's meaning. These problems are compounded when a translation or a secondary source must be quoted by a third author, such as in the present work, since double quotation marks within a quoted text would normally be changed to single, and vice versa. By this point, any differentiation suggested by the context of Balthasar's original is lost, the inconsistency among the translations and secondary sources is perpetuated, and the interpretative replacement of a German mark with a single quotation mark is lost upon the reader in a blizzard of inverted commas.

To provide some order in this confusion, I have adopted the following rules of usage. In general, the English convention is retained, except that the function of single inverted commas to indicate an unusual use of a common word is transferred to double inverted commas when the term thus used has its origin in a particular author. Hence single quotation marks indicate a term should be taken ironically or loosely (e.g., '*kenosis*' signifies something like *the so-called kenosis*), or is a special term in wider use (e.g., a technical word).

Because the English convention is generally retained, most readers will not note anything unusual, and the following rules will not be of interest. For those who have struggled with the problems summarized above, however, they may be helpful. They also serve to indicate I have not taken arbitrary liberties with the work of others, but have tried to incorporate their work into my own as accurately as possible.

1. Quotations within a quotation from a text in a language other than English retain their original marks.
2. Additions to quoted texts made for the sake of summary, or minor changes made for the sake of grammatical connection with the surrounding text, are indicated by square brackets ([ ]). The omission of text is indicated by an ellipsis (. . .).
3. Text is enclosed in *double* quotation marks (" ") in the following cases, all of which aim to identify the author of the text quoted:
   a. Text longer than a word or short phrase by another author, followed by a citation.
   b. When not appearing within a wider quotation, text quoted by one author that is clearly attributed to another, followed by a citation.
   c. *Common words or terms redefined* by an author or used in a particular way by him, *when used in his particular sense*, followed by a citation

upon the first use. Afterward, changes in case, number, or tense are made as necessary, but are not indicated by square brackets within the double quotation marks.

    d. *Special terms* introduced by an author upon first use. Thereafter, they are *not* enclosed in marks.

4. Text is enclosed in *single* quotation marks (' ') in the following cases:

    a. Text, *originally in either single or double quotation marks,* quoted within a wider quotation of a translation or secondary source.

    b. Common words used as a special term (e.g., 'second death').

    c. Colloquial idioms.

    d. The ironic or loose use of a word.

5. Text is *not* enclosed in marks in the following cases:

    a. My own text.

    b. Extended quoted material indented from the margins.

    c. Special terms in common theological usage (e.g., *kenosis*).

    d. Special terms introduced by an author after their first use.

6. When I quote material that itself contains a quotation, the text is considered first to be standardized according to the above rules and then enclosed within double quotation marks, which changes the now-standardized double marks to single, and vice versa.

C. Non-Roman Alphabets

Some editions, translations, and secondary sources of Balthasar use Greek characters, while others transliterate his Greek into Roman letters. To avoid suggesting a distinction where none is intended, all Greek is standardized with Greek characters.

D. Capitalization

The following conventions regarding capitalization are adopted:

1. The abodes of the dead are not capitalized when used according to their common meaning: heaven, purgatory, the limbo of the Fathers, hell, sheol, hades, gehenna, etc. When used according to Balthasar's signification, *sheol* is capitalized thus: Sheol.

2. When not qualified with identifiers such as *Christ's* and *His,* the mysteries of Christ's life are capitalized in order to distinguish them from the events

considered in general. Hence, *the Resurrection* refers to Christ's resurrection, but *the resurrection* refers to the raising of the dead in general.

3. The personal pronouns *he, him,* and *his* are capitalized in reference to God. Relative pronouns (e.g., *who*) are not, however, because their antecedent is already clearly identified by name, title, or a personal pronoun.

4. *Person* is capitalized to identify someone divine when not preceded by a personal pronoun that serves this function.

5. When I quote an English translation, the translation's capitalization is retained.

CHAPTER ONE

Introduction

Christus descendit ad inferos. This article of the Christian Faith, most often translated into English as "He descended into hell," is increasingly an object of interest in contemporary theology, and even more so since the writings of Hans Urs von Balthasar last century. The article is very brief in many formulations of the Faith, including the Apostles' Creed, while it appears only implicitly in others, such as in the Nicene Creed. Yet this mystery of faith is by no means insignificant, though it is often overlooked. Its very presence in the creeds indicates that it is tied in a peculiarly intimate way to the revelation of God, and in particular to the Person of Christ and His redeeming work. Every theological investigation of the Descent into hell reveals this close relation, explicitly or implicitly.

Traditionally, Christ's descent has been seen as the beginning of the manifestation of His triumph over death and the first application of the fruits of redemption. Gloriously descending to the holy souls in the abode of the dead called *the limbo of the Fathers,* Christ bestowed upon them the beatific vision and gave them the fullness of freedom. The multivalent *Anastasis* icon of the Eastern Catholic Church, as well as Catholic artistic representations in the West, portrays this doctrine visually. There one sees Christ freeing Adam and Eve from their graves, and the broken gates of hell beneath His feet. In the West, this doctrine of a triumphal Descent of Christ was held universally until the Protestant Reformation, and then also afterward by the Catholic Church. It remains, then, part of the heritage of Christians of all denominations.

The writings of Hans Urs von Balthasar, however, suggest that this doctrine does not do justice to the depths to which Christ went for man's redemption nor, consequently, to His love. Instead, Christ must have suffered after His death the full force of what would have awaited mankind without the Redeemer. Although Balthasar would agree that Christ's descent should be called triumphal and glorious, his theology gives these words a sense similar to that in which Christ's crucifixion is said to be His triumph and glory.

The theological explication of Christ's descent, including the sense in which it was triumphal, is of no mean significance. What one says about this mystery of Christ's work must be consistent with the manner in which the Person of Christ and His two natures are conceived. Accordingly, the doctrine of Christ's descent into hell uniquely reveals and safeguards something true about Christ. It is by no means superfluous.

The ultimate aim of the present work is to consider whether a triumphal descent by Christ or a descent to suffering is the true expression of the Catholic Faith. Now the Catholic Faith is not something arbitrarily constructed though human ingenuity. Rather it is received through divine revelation as this is handed on and interpreted by a specific tradition. Consequently, our first task is to discover whether there is a consensus on the interpretation of this credal article in authentic sources of Catholic Tradition and to summarize this understanding. Theological sources to be drawn upon include Scripture and commentaries upon it, statements of the Magisterium, liturgical texts, sacred art, catechisms, writings of the saints and Doctors of the Church, and the creeds themselves.

This first part is also necessitated by two historical circumstances. First, there is a lack of contemporary catechesis on the Descent, whether in homes, in Catholic schools, or from the pulpit. Over the past few years, in my conversations about the Descent with others in the United States and Europe, a line of demarcation became evident: Catholics of my mother's generation know the doctrine, and they all describe it along the lines of Christ's descent to the holy dead. In contrast, when Catholics of my own generation heard I was studying Christ's descent into hell, they frequently asked me in a disturbed, hesitant, or incredulous tone, "Do we believe in that?"

The second circumstance that calls for a demonstration that there is indeed a Catholic doctrine about Christ's descent concerns Catholic theologians. From the treatments of the topic I have seen, there appears to have been a shift in approach sometime in the third quarter of the last century, i.e., roughly during the 1950s to 1970s. Generally I found that Catholic theologians before this period hold the doctrine of Christ's triumphal descent to the limbo of the Fathers; in contrast, with a few exceptions, those after it either appear hesitant to set forth this doctrine as true and defend it from error, or seem unaware of its existence. Some make vague allusions to the traditional doctrine, reinterpreting it in symbolic or psychological language, while others appear to be trying to come up with a doctrine from scratch. Neither fulfills adequately the mandate of Vatican II:

> While adhering to the methods and requirements proper to theology, theologians are invited to seek continually for more suitable ways of communicating doctrine to the men of their times. For the deposit of faith or revealed truths are one thing; the manner in which they are formulated without violence to their meaning and significance is another.[1]

In other words, there are two generation gaps, so to speak, in catechesis and theology. Christian Duquoc rightly draws attention to the fact that it is a modern emphasis to limit the *descensus* article to a profession in Christ's death and then to reflect upon it in anthropological, existential terms.[2] These elements were not absent from the early centuries, but were clearly not the focus. The Fathers, and the Catholic Tradition after them, moved on from the mere fact of Christ's death to the significance of the living God Himself, by means of the flesh, being in the realm of the dead. The existential aspect was reflected in the Christian's distinct attitude towards death and experience of it. It seems likely that the causes for the shift noted by Duquoc are the 'anthropological turn' in general, the propagation of new doctrines of a descent to suffering by Martin Luther and John Calvin, and the 'demythologization' of Christian beliefs. In particular, the face of death in the twentieth century — conditioned by philosophical and social alienation, the great wars, and atheism — often figures noticeably in the new interpretations of Christ's death and descent proposed by the later group of theologians. However, as Vatican II suggests, such pastoral exigencies can only be adequately met with God's revealed truth, proclaimed anew to a changed audience, not by the molding of doctrinal content to the image of human horror in any age.

In this second group, one theologian stands out in particular: Hans Urs von Balthasar. In contrast to the other theologians of the second group, Balthasar both clearly knew the traditional Catholic doctrine on Christ's descent and firmly proposed something different as more in line with the Catholic Faith. In Part Two, the major features of his theology of the Descent will be presented and key differences from the traditional interpretation noted.

Here, no doubt, someone will raise an objection. Perhaps even more than during his life, after his death some few days before being elevated to the cardinalate in 1988, Balthasar has a name as a *Catholic* theologian. Biographical comments about him highlight his intelligence, erudition, extensive reading in literature and theology, special interest in patristics, and prolific writing. In addition, in many of his works on the Descent, a hypothetical or suggestive tone may often be noted. Have I then been fair to him by claiming he both knew and rejected the traditional Catholic doctrine?

The reader will have the opportunity to judge for himself. Besides the exposition and argument in the main body, the footnotes provide abundant citations for this purpose, as well as occasional quotations and comments. The latter are not necessary to follow the main line of exposition and argument, but are provided for readers with particularly detailed interest. Given Balthasar's reputation and style, I have chosen to err on the side of excess in documentation, rather than deficiency.

Notwithstanding the differences between Balthasar's theology and that of others who hold that Christ suffered after His death, two factors in particular commend the consideration of this doctrine's compatibility with the Catholic one by focusing on Balthasar's work. First, his theology as a whole is uniquely conditioned by his theology of Christ's descent. He has thus made explicit some of the possible theological consequences that follow from holding such a theology of the Descent consistently. Since an exhaustive treatment of this part of his theology would almost be equivalent to an estimation of his theology as a whole, I concentrate on his theology of the Descent in its more narrowly Christological and Trinitarian aspects. Its relevance to his views in other areas of theology will be sketched in Chapter Nine, but not considered in equal depth. Secondly, Balthasar's influence among the second group of theologians is readily discernible. Here one often finds echoes or explicit developments of his outlook, methodology, and conclusions.

In general, there are few treatments of Balthasar's theology of the Descent. Most of these are brief summaries in the context of a larger work focusing on some other aspect of his theology, on his work in general, or on the history of theological treatments of the Descent. Others focus on the comparison and contrast of Balthasar's position with that of another author. And still others simply use Balthasar's theology of the Descent more or less uncritically as the foundation for the examination of another topic or for developing his thought. As for general works on Christ's descent, those written in the last century are primarily historical in character, or have very specific exegetical interests; I know of only one full-length treatment from the second theological period I proposed that argues on the basis of multiple *loci theologici* for the existence of a traditional Catholic doctrine of the Descent.[3]

In contrast to what is available in both these areas, I set Balthasar's theology of the Descent in a dogmatic context. Our interest here does not focus on historical relationships of development, neither within Balthasar's own corpus nor even within the history of Catholic doctrine. There is a strong consistency in Balthasar's thought on this topic over the decades.[4] In one of his last major works, the *Theo-Logik,* he feels it necessary to distance himself explicitly on only one point from his earlier expositions of the Descent; in other words, he has nothing similar to St. Augustine's *Retractions.* Similarly, notwithstanding typical developments in theological precision, there is also a very consistent Catholic doctrine about Christ's descent to the holy dead in the limbo of the Fathers. Indeed, this Tradition is both so old and so unusually constant that the task before us may seem pointless to historians of the theology of the Descent, to whom the contrast between the two doctrines is readily evident. For example, Markwart Herzog comments that "A real change in the Roman Catholic doctrine has approached under the influence of Hans Urs von Balthasar's 'Theology of Holy Saturday.'"[5] Herzog's remark is particularly significant because he focuses on monographs about the Descent since the sixteenth century but deliberately eschews an in-depth consideration of Balthasar's theology.[6] In other words, he finds that the Catholic Tradition after the Reformation is constant, but concludes — and this on the basis of a much more limited reading than that done for the present work — that Balthasar's opinion constitutes a "real change" from the traditional doctrine.

To judge by the majority of the works produced on the Descent in the second theological period mentioned above and by those texts written about Balthasar's theology or based upon it, however, this contrast does not seem to be apparent either to contemporary Catholic theologians in general or to those who focus their studies on Balthasar. What is lacking is an assessment of Balthasar's theology of Holy Saturday in its wider dogmatic context; hence, we will compare the work of one who saw himself as a Catholic theologian with the traditional doctrine of the Church he strove to serve, according to his lights, until his death. Balthasar thought he apprehended an aspect of the truth of the Catholic Faith that had been overlooked and misinterpreted in the course of history. Are his arguments sound? And what is at stake in relinquishing or radically reinterpreting the old doctrine?

While the existence and authority of an authentic Tradition concerning Christ's descent would be sufficient to answer our overall inquiry, the additional standard of Christology is drawn upon in Part Three. Such a Christological consideration will both reveal the degree of weight of the argument from authority and serve as an additional criterion of judgment. I will assume that any traditional consensus about the Descent is compatible with traditional Christology, since the two developed alongside each other. Reciprocity between Balthasar's Christology and his *descensus* theology is clearly manifest in his position that the Descent entails a "suspension, as it were, of the Incarnation"[7] as the result of Christ's total gift of self. If Balthasar's differing theology of the Descent yields problematic implications in the light of necessary principles of Catholic Christology, there will be even stronger grounds on which to reaffirm the traditional doctrine of Christ's triumphal descent. On the other hand, a conclusion that Balthasar's theory does not result in such difficulties would contribute to its possible incorporation into the Catholic intellectual and spiritual milieu. In Part Three, I will also examine some of Balthasar's arguments that could not be considered in the course of the exposition of his thought, as well as certain points of his methodology. The results of this study, although focused specifically on the compatibility of Balthasar's doctrine of the Descent with that of the Catholic Tradition, would be relevant to other doctrines of a descent to suffering.

PART ONE

The Catholic Tradition

CHAPTER TWO

Creeds and Catechisms

If theology is "faith seeking understanding," as St. Anselm says, then the theologian must know what is to be believed before attempting to penetrate it further according to the power and limitations of the human intellect. Indeed, if he would have a supernatural light by which to consider what is beyond his natural ability to know, namely, the Revelation of God, then he must not only know what is to be believed, but believe it as well. Even more, he ought to have that living faith that works through charity (Gal 5:6).

It makes sense, then, to begin a theological investigation of the meaning of an article of the Faith with an examination of the article itself as presented in the creeds. As authoritative expositions of the Faith professed in the creeds, the official catechisms of the Catholic Church should also be considered, as well as other magisterial statements relevant to the subject at hand.

The Creeds

An examination of the creeds reveals varying expressions of the article of Faith that Christ descended into hell. The most obvious difference among the creeds is that the Descent is explicit in some, and seems not to be present at all in others. This apparent absence is not alarming, however: No authentic creed could deny by omission what another explicitly affirms. Christ's descent into hell is always present implicitly in the articles concerning His death and burial: As Christ truly died, His soul was separated from His body, and each went to its proper place after death, the body to the tomb, and the soul to the abode of the dead.[1] The Descent is also implicit in the article on the Resurrection, since it is from both the tomb and the abode of the dead that Christ arose.

Most details concerning the history of individual creeds fall outside our present interest in what can be gathered about Christ's descent from these varied credal forms themselves. Suffice it to say that an article about the Descent was present in the orthodox (i.e., Catholic) Creed of Aquileia before the beginning of the fifth century: The Aquileian *descensus* article was accepted as authoritative by the time Rufinus mentions it c. 404 in his commentary on the Apostles' Creed of Rome.[2] What is striking here is that the Apostles' Creed does not contain an article explicitly on the Descent, as the Aquileian creed does. Rufinus holds that the Aquileian *descensus* clause has the same implications as the profession of Christ's burial, which appears in both creeds: "The force of the article . . . seems to be the same as in that which treats of the burial."[3] This comparison is generally treated as if it means that the Descent signifies nothing other than burial. I would argue instead that Rufinus intends the force of the comparison to go in the other direction, i.e., he is not suggesting the descent means burial, but rather that the burial means descent. This reading is more in line with Rufinus' interest in the Roman creed and deference to it: If the Aquileian creed is orthodox, it cannot say more than the Roman one and hence what it professes explicitly must already be implicit in the creed of Rome. Thus Rufinus is saying that when the Christians in Rome profess Christ was buried, they are professing His descent as well. The burial and descent are necessarily linked through the ancient conception that a descent to the abode of the dead was the natural consequence of death: As the body was buried, so did the soul go to the realm of the dead. Hence, when commenting on the article of Christ's burial in the Apostles' Creed, Rufinus provides Scriptural testimony for Christ's *descent* immediately after that for His burial.[4]

It is noteworthy (though not surprising) that the Descent's presence in Western creeds is probably due to influence from the East, even though official creeds from the East lack the article.[5] The presence and acceptance of such influence suggests a commonly held belief in both East and West, which took official form in the Western creeds. Whatever the reason the article was not incorporated into more universal oriental creeds, it cannot have been disbelief in the doctrine itself, because there is ample Eastern evidence to the contrary. Because the article did not enter the creeds through specific conciliar action, however, the reason for its inclusion at the particular time it appeared is unknown. In any case, the *belief* in Christ's descent necessarily predates its appearance in the creeds, and may in fact be traced back to apostolic times.[6] What then do the forms of the profession tell us about Christ's descent?

The creeds that do not explicitly mention the Descent into hell may be divided into two groups based on the different formulations of the Resurrection article. In both we will find that Christ's descent is implicit in the profession of His resurrection. One group may be represented by the Niceno-Constantinopolitan Symbol, which says, "And He rose on the third day, according to the Scriptures."[7] One may ask, "From where did He rise?" The answer is simple, "From the tomb and from where a soul goes after death." The text cannot refer only to the resurrection of Christ's body from the tomb. To say "He rose" is to refer to the Person, not just His body. Although separated from each other in death, both the body and soul of Christ remained united to the divine Person of the Word.[8] But Christ's soul was not 'where' His dead body was, but separated from it; otherwise, His body would still have been alive. Therefore, since the creed says, "He rose," and *He* refers to the Incarnate Word, it professes that Christ rose in both His body and His soul.

Now, because separated souls are purely immaterial substances, strictly speaking they are not in a place after death the same way a body is always in a place, i.e., as situated and bounded by dimensive quantity. Hence to ask where a separated soul was, or from whence this soul arose to be reunited with its body, is to use these spatial terms analogously. This use of spatial analogy is not merely a way of thinking necessitated by our condition as embodied creatures; in this case, it also reveals something metaphysically true. For the soul of a living person is in fact located where it acts, i.e., coextensively with his body. We can see how the soul is located by its acts by considering that a person's soul no longer acts in an amputated finger, and so must no longer be present to it. Likewise, a separated soul is located where its powers are in act, and so it can rightly be said to be in that place. In contrast to a body, however, a soul is more properly said to contain its place than to be contained by it: The soul as immaterial is not limited by the material dimension of place; rather the soul's extension is determined by its own power to act.[9] Since a soul is a finite creation, however, it is not omnipotent and cannot act everywhere at the same time. Thus it is not omnipresent, as only the infinite God is.[10] Hence, without being able to say exactly where, in corporal terms, a separated soul is, we can nevertheless truly say it is in some place, namely, where it is in act. In contemporary treatments of the Descent, the authors frequently insist that the souls of the dead are not in a place, but in a condition.[11] If *place* is taken analogously to be determined by the act of the soul, instead of taken properly as determined by the location of a body, *place* and *condition* imply each other and should not be opposed.

Keeping in mind then that *where* is used analogously with respect to Christ's soul, one can ask "From where did He rise?" in relation to the Word united to His body, the Word united to His soul, and the Word united to His body and soul reunited on Easter. In the first and third cases, the answer is,

"From the tomb," but in the second case the answer is, "From where a soul goes after death."

In contrast to creeds in this first group, other creeds without an explicit profession of the Descent qualify the statement on the resurrection further, saying *resurrexit . . . a mortuis.*[12] Again it is professed that Christ rose, but more specifically that "He rose from the dead." Now the English word *dead* here translates the Latin substantive adjective *mortuis,* which means *those who are dead,* and not *the state of being dead.* (The difference in signification can be seen in English if one contrasts the meaning of the word *dead* in the examples, "We pray for the dead" and "He is dead.") Thus these creeds implicitly profess that before His resurrection, Christ was 'where' other souls of the dead were, and that it is from among them that He rose.

The professions of faith that explicitly mention Christ's descent likewise differ in their wording of that article of Faith. Some say, *descendit ad inferna,*[13] others, *ad infernos*[14] or *ad inferos.*[15] There is testimony from the fourth century for both the forms *ad inferna* (DS 16) and *ad inferos* (see notes to DS 76); *ad infernos* appears to be a later and rarer form. As the three terms have similar functions in the creeds, they appear to be fairly interchangeable in this context; hence we will not here examine details of their individual histories. The standardization of *ad inferos* after the Council of Trent, however, would suggest this form is the most authoritative.

All three words, *inferna, infernos,* and *inferos,* refer in their stems to something *lower* or *below.* The plural neuter noun *inferna* is to be understood as a place or regions "below," whereas *inferni* and *inferi* are plural masculine nouns, i.e., those individuals who are "below," thus paralleling the *mortuis* of the resurrection articles. These root meanings give rise to derivative connotations of *the dead, the underworld,* or *hell,* the three words variously used in English translations of this credal article. Of these three translations, which is the most accurate?

Since place with regard to immaterial substances does not refer so much or immediately to a location but rather to the spirits themselves, the most accurate translation of the article would be, "He descended to those below" in the sense of those *who* are below, instead of those *which* are below: Christ's action terminates with the spirits, not so much with the places where they are. The disadvantage of this translation is its reference to spirits in spatial terms; however, this connotation is present in the originals as well.

In parallel to the articles on the resurrection, one might also translate the article as, "He descended to the dead." This translation excludes reference to spirits other than separated souls. However, the terms translated are generic enough they could include beings of an angelic nature 'below,' i.e., demons.

This second translation therefore is more restrictive than the original term. It is a legitimate translation in that it is certain Christ descended at least to the dead, because He Himself was dead and He rose from among those who are dead *(resurrexit . . . a mortuis)*. However, the meaning of the *descensus* article cannot definitively be restricted in this way on the basis of the wording of the creeds alone.

This problem of apparently premature limitation can be avoided by translating the article, "He descended into hell." In this case, when one takes *hell* in the generic sense as all or any of the abodes to which the dead might go other than heaven, this translation has the advantage of including possible reference to the demons, since the hell where the devils are punished is the same as that where any damned souls suffer. (Hence, "He descended to the dead" could be said to admit reference to the demons obliquely, if "the dead" includes the damned, but that is not evident, since "the dead" is indefinite.) However, to translate the masculine nouns *infernos* and *inferos* as "hell" requires the substitution of a place name for the spirits who are actually mentioned, whereas to render the neuter noun *inferna* that way, though justifiable grammatically, is misleading to the modern ear, because the Latin need not suggest the "everlasting fire" (Mk 9:42; Mt 25:41) currently evoked by the English word *hell*. This connotation of eternal punishment is essential to many theologies that hold Christ suffered in His descent. Since we are examining the nature of Christ's descent in this work and since *hell* is also the most common translation used in English, it is the translation we will use here.

However, it is still important to be clear about which translation is the most accurate. We are left with two possibilities: "He descended to those below" and "He descended to the dead." The first translation is the most accurate, and preferred; the latter can be admitted with qualifications. In either case, "those below" and "the dead" referenced are indefinite; that is, whether Christ descended to all those below (or to all the dead), or only to some of them is not specified. This question must be answered on the basis of other sources of doctrine.

The creeds tell us at least this much then about Christ's descent into hell: After dying, the soul of Christ went to a 'place' of spiritual substances where human souls were. The natural question that follows on this conclusion is, "Which human souls were these?" Or, if the place may be named from the spirits who are there, "To where did Christ descend?" This question is answered by the Church's catechisms, which expound the creed.

The Catechisms

Drawing on Scripture and Tradition, the teaching of the Church in her catechisms makes clear that what is translated "hell" is a differentiated place. The
netherworld, or hell taken generically, is characterized by not being heaven; that
is, the inhabitants do not behold God in eternal bliss.[16] Hell as a whole may be
differentiated into at least three species: gehenna, purgatory, and sheol; according to a long-standing theological view, there is also a limbo (from the Latin
limbus, meaning *edge* or *threshold*) for unbaptized children, the *limbus puerorum.* Although it may sound strange to the contemporary ear, one can use the
generic name in reference to each species: the hell of the damned (gehenna),
the hell of purification (purgatory), the hell of the Fathers (sheol), and the hell
of the children. Though these four abodes of the dead are very different in character, *hell* in all these cases can be represented with the generic Latin neuter,
infernum. It should be noted that heaven is not one of the *inferna,* nor was it an
abode of the dead before the redemption accomplished by Christ made it possible for souls to go there.

Gehenna is hell proper, the place of eternal fire for the punishment of the
damned, whether angelic or human. Hell proper receives this Greek name in allusion to the valley southwest of Jerusalem, where human sacrifices to the idol
Molech, particularly sacrifices of infants, were burned in Old Testament
times.[17] In the New Testament, the name is stripped of geographical reference
by the significance of Jesus' words (e.g., Mt 18:9; Mk 9:42-48; Lk 12:5) and refers
to the place appointed by God for the eternal punishment of the unrighteous.

The second species of hell, purgatory, is a place of temporary purification
for the souls of men and women who die united to God by charity, but without
having satisfied for their sins or having been fully freed of disordered attach-
ments.[18] Purgatory will be abolished at the Last Judgment, after which mankind will be divided simply into the damned and the blessed.

Rarely mentioned in contemporary treatments, but no less real, is the
third abode, "into which the souls of the just before the coming of Christ the
Lord, were received, and where, without experiencing any sort of pain, but
supported by the blessed hope of redemption, they enjoyed peaceful repose."[19]
This abode is sheol, named from the Hebrew parallel of the Greek underworld
hades. Like the English *hell,* the Greek *hades* is both a generic and a specific
name, but unlike *hell, hades* refers most properly not to a place of punishment,
but to the nondescript afterlife of most souls according to the common ancient Greek belief. In fact, the English word, *hell,* and its German ancestor,
Hölle, originate from *hel,* the Old Norse equivalent of the Greek *hades*
proper.[20] Since the New Testament was written in Greek, it uses *hades* as both a

generic and a specific term. Due to the very different religious context, however, its meaning is not identical to the classical pagan Greek understanding.
To demonstrate this contrast would be something of a digression; more of interest here is to note the general development of the word's meaning within
the Judeo-Christian context.

In the Old Testament, sheol, like hades proper, is a shadowy and lethar-
gic abode to which all the dead, good and bad, go down.[21] If in the Old Testament, particularly in some of the oldest books which have a more historical
focus, there is not always a clear sense of a distinct fate or reward for the just
and retribution for the unjust, this belief grows over time under the continuing pedagogy of God's revelation: The weight of individual responsibility and
the consciousness that merely temporal retributions are not appropriate to
the divine justice gradually become explicit, transforming the generic sheol
into a place of passage, an abode of waiting for the definitive end,[22] although
the passageway, so to speak, will only be completed through the Descent of
Christ. The effect of this development is a certain ambiguity in the concepts
of death and the fate of the dead in the Old Testament. In the intertestamental period, the vocabulary of *gehenna* and *paradise* to designate respectively the place of punishment of the wicked and of repose of the just appears
in various Jewish apocalyptic works, but their relation to sheol is not rigidly
defined; sometimes they are distinguished from sheol, other times included
as a part of it.[23] "The term *sheol* becomes very ambiguous and, in certain
cases, 'to descend into hell' ultimately corresponds to 'to mount up to paradise'!"[24] The ambiguity of the term *hades* remains to an extent in the New
Testament.[25] At the far end of this pedagogy, later Christians would settle on
a precision in terminology, understanding the character of sheol in a significantly different manner from a generic shadow existence and calling it "the
bosom of Abraham" from Christ's parable about the beggar Lazarus (Lk
16:22ff.). Though the rich man is said to be suffering punishment in hades, it
is reasonable that hades proper, or sheol, acquired the specific significance of
the peaceful bosom of Abraham precisely in contrast to gehenna, because the
torments of the rich man embody Christ's warnings about gehenna. However,
the most common theological name in Catholic theology for sheol is "the
limbo of the Fathers." The Fathers in question are the saints of the Old Covenant, men and women, Jews and non-Jews, who believed in the coming of the
Savior and died in a state of grace; they are all the holy men and women who
died before the death of Christ.

This limbo of the Fathers must be carefully distinguished from the limbo
of the children. The children referenced here are those who die without committing any actual sin, but also die without faith, and so without grace and with

original sin. As one's state after death depends on one's degree of guilt or of charity, the limbo of the unbaptized children could reasonably be without physical pain and characterized by the attainment of an end appropriate to rational nature, but not the supernatural end of beatitude. The assumption of the existence of this *limbus puerorum* is made on the basis of the doctrine that those who die with original sin are excluded from the beatific vision, complemented by the fact that a difference in personal guilt entails a corresponding difference in punishment.[26] The limbo of the children remains a topic of unresolved theological understanding.

The Ecumenical Councils of Lyons II and Florence refer very clearly to heaven, purgatory, hell proper, and the limbo of the children, without necessarily naming them as such;[27] because their teachings concern the souls of the dead after the time of Christ, they do not treat the limbo of the Fathers, which ceased to exist after Christ's descent. However, the *Catechism of the Catholic Church* refers to the parable of Lazarus and the rich man, and cites the passage from the *Catechism of the Council of Trent* quoted above (marked with note 19), when teaching that, though all the dead at the time of Christ were "deprived of the vision of God," yet that "does not mean their lot [was] identical. . . ."[28] The differentiation of hell (the *inferna*), including the existence of the limbo of the Fathers, is unequivocally part of the Church's Tradition and confirmed in her magisterial teachings.

The generic character of the word *hell*, and the differentiation of the reality that hell is, are stressed because these points are directly relevant to the question at hand, "To where did Christ descend?" In other words, if hell is differentiated, did Christ descend to all of the abodes of hell or only to some? If He descended to all, did He descend to them all in the same way or not? How did He experience this descent? And, if the Word became flesh 'for us and our salvation,' what role does the Descent have in the redemptive work of Christ? That is, why did He descend into hell?

The *Catechism of the Catholic Church* answers the above questions on Christ's descent in this way:

> Jesus, like all men, experienced death and in his soul joined the others in the realm of the dead. But he descended there as Saviour, proclaiming the Good News to the spirits imprisoned there.
>
> Scripture calls the abode of the dead, to which the dead Christ went down, "hell" — *Sheol* in Hebrew or *Hades* in Greek. . . . Jesus did not descend into hell to deliver the damned, nor to destroy the hell of damnation, but to free the just who had gone before him.[29]

The *Catechism* refers the reader to Scripture, the *Catechism of the Council of Trent,* two councils, and the declarations of two popes in connection with the various parts of this teaching.[30] It continues:

> Christ went down into the depths of death so that "the dead will hear the voice of the Son of God, and those who hear will live." [Jn 5:25; cf. Mt 12:40; Rom 10:7; Eph 4:9] Jesus, "the Author of Life," by dying destroyed "him who has the power of death, that is, the devil, and [delivered] all those who through fear of death were subject to lifelong bondage." [Heb 2:14-15; cf. Acts 3:15]
>
> . . . In his human soul united to his divine person, the dead Christ went down to the realm of the dead. He opened heaven's gates for the just who had gone before him.[31]

In brief, the *Catechism of the Catholic Church* answers that Christ descended to sheol, but in a manner unlike other men, that is, as Savior, in order to free the just who had died before Him, admitting them into heaven. Before the *Catechism*'s publication, the traditional teaching about Christ's descent had been reiterated by Pope John Paul II in his General Audience of January 11, 1989. The *Catechism* and the pope present this doctrine in declarative statements as facts, without suggesting any uncertainty or ambiguity.

The *Catechism of the Council of Trent* elaborates on the character of Christ's descent and its purpose, saying, "Christ the Lord descended . . . not to suffer, but to liberate the holy and the just from their painful captivity, and to impart to them the fruit of His Passion."[32] The "pain" of "the holy and the just" was to be "deprived of the vision of God, and . . . tortured by the delay of the glory and happiness for which they yearned,"[33] that is, the pain of charity desirous of union with God. This *Catechism* gives two reasons why Christ descended into hell, namely, "to liberate the just" and "to proclaim His power."[34] Both these ends were accomplished in a glorious way:

> Christ the Lord descended into hell, in order that, having despoiled the demons, He might liberate from prison those holy Fathers and the other just souls, and might bring them into heaven with Himself. This He accomplished in an admirable and most glorious manner; for His august presence at once shed a celestial lustre upon the captives and filled them with inconceivable joy and delight. He also imparted to them that supreme happiness which consists in the vision of God, thus verifying His promise to the thief on the cross. . . .[35]

In regard to Christ Himself, it is to be noted that His soul is in a state of heavenly glory, and He communicates this glory to the holy dead.

Representing the consensus of saints and drawing upon his intimate familiarity with the writings of the Fathers, St. Thomas Aquinas' answer to "Whether Christ went down into the hell of the lost?" provides scientific structure to the traditional teaching. Because St. Thomas is singularly preeminent as a theologian and Doctor of the Church,[36] his theological exposition bears special weight:

> A thing is said to be in a place in two ways. First of all, through its effect, and in this way Christ descended into each of the hells, but in [a] different manner. For going down into the hell of the lost [gehenna] He wrought this effect, that by descending thither He put them to shame for their unbelief and wickedness: but to them who were detained in Purgatory He gave hope of attaining to glory: while upon the holy Fathers detained in hell solely on account of original sin, He shed the light of glory everlasting.
>
> In another way a thing is said to be in a place through its essence: and in this way Christ's soul descended only into that part of hell wherein the just were detained [sheol]; so that He visited them *in place,* according to His soul, whom He visited *interiorly by grace,* according to His Godhead. Accordingly, while remaining in one part of hell, He wrought this effect in a measure in every part of hell, just as while suffering in one part of the earth He delivered the whole world by His Passion.[37]

The Church's doctrine of Christ's descent into hell can be summarized by four points. First, Christ descended in His soul united to His divine Person only to the limbo of the Fathers. Second, His power and authority were made known throughout all of hell, taken generically. Third, He thereby accomplished the two purposes of the Descent, which were "to liberate the just" by conferring on them the glory of heaven and "to proclaim His power."[38] Finally, His descent was a glorious one, and Christ did not suffer the pain proper to any of the abodes of hell. The elements of this doctrine go back to patristic times,[39] reach particular systematic integrity in the scholastic period, are reaffirmed as the Catholic doctrine in the *Catechism of the Council of Trent* after the Protestant challenges to it during the Reformation, and are reiterated in the twentieth century in the *Catechism of the Catholic Church.*

Other Magisterial Statements

The Catholic doctrine of Christ's descent as professed in the creeds was considered above via the creeds themselves and the catechisms of the universal Church instead of through a historical survey of magisterial documents. This approach conveys the doctrine in a clear and succinct, yet authoritative, form. It allows the doctrine itself to stand out without occasioning debate about the dogmatic weight or particular limits of individual documents, or about the authority or relevance of individual councils. What is scattered with diverse emphasis through history is united and explicated in its organic whole by the catechisms.

Particular papal and conciliar statements of varying magisterial weight lend their support to the doctrine. Although it could be revealing to consider these statements in their particular historical circumstances, such issues shall not be considered here. We must also bear in mind that the doctrine of Christ's descent did not enter the creed as the result of a solemn decision that ended a theological controversy; hence, one cannot expect the same sort of magisterial statements as are found concerning, e.g., the single Person and two natures of Christ.

In 447, Pope St. Leo the Great wrote a letter to Turribius, a Spanish bishop, in which Christ's descent is mentioned as certain doctrine: "I marvel that the intelligence of any Catholic labors, as if it were uncertain, whether after Christ descended into hell, his body rested in the tomb. As it was truly both dead and buried, so it was truly revived on the third day."[40] Note here the implicit affirmation of death as the separation of body and soul.

In a letter of 521 to the Emperor Justin, Pope Hormisdas wrote of the Son of God that

> the same is indeed God and man, not by the introduction of a fourth person
> as the unfaithful say, but the Son of God is Himself God and man, the same
> one power and infirmity, humility and majesty, ransoming and sold, fixed to
> the cross and granted the rule of heaven, being thus of our infirmity that He
> might destroy it, being thus of unbegotten power He could not be consumed
> by death. Just as that one was buried, who willed to be born man, just so He
> who was like the Father rose: suffering wounds and the savior of the
> wounded, one of the dead and the giver of life to the dead, descending into
> hell [*ad inferna*] and not leaving the bosom of the Father. Hence also the life
> which He set down according to the common condition, He soon resumed
> according to His singular excellence and admirable power.[41]

Something similar, though less elaborated, is found in a letter of Pope Hormisdas' predecessor, Symmachus: "Thus Christ truly is perfect God and perfect man, as when He was conceived, so when He dwelt in time, when He suffered, when He was among those below [*apud inferos*], when He was raised. . . ."[42]

The early papal statement of Pope Hormisdas is wholly consistent with the developed theology used earlier to summarize the Church's teaching, even if not stated in a similarly explicit manner. To be noted here is the affirmation that Christ died a real human death (He was "one of the dead," "according to the common condition") and truly descended into the realm of the dead. He is not "consumed" or overpowered by death as other men, however, because He is not only man but God. He remains in "the bosom of Father" during His descent. Although this statement applies first to Christ in His divinity, its lack of limitation allows it to suggest the idea that, in His human soul, Christ did not suffer the pain proper to any abode of the dead, all of which relate to separation from God. Finally, it should be noted that He gives life to the dead at the same time as He Himself is dead.

There are other magisterial statements testifying to the reality of Christ's descent in His human soul to the abode of the dead. The Council of Sens (1140), confirmed by Innocent II in the same year, condemned the error attributed to Peter Abelard (1079-1142), "that the soul of Christ per se did not descend to those who are below [*ad inferos*], but only by means of power,"[43] i.e., that Christ had an effect on the dead without joining them in His soul. The teaching of the Fourth Ecumenical Lateran Council (1215) also confirms the reality of Christ's descent in His soul.[44] Though the Council may well have had the debate over Abelard in mind, the Cathars in general and the Albigensians in particular were also of contemporary concern.[45] The Cathars held that Christ descended into hell, but understood *hell* to be this earthly world, while since the Albigensians denied the reality of Christ's death, it is logical they also denied His descent to the dead.[46] Hence, in the face of these denials, the Lateran proclamation is a reaffirmation of the reality of Christ's descent into the realm of the dead as understood by the earlier Catholic Tradition. The fact of Christ's descent appears again later, in the acts of the Second Council of Lyons (1274) under Pope Gregory X, when the Emperor Michael Paleologus' acceptance of a creed (prepared earlier by Pope Clement IV) was read before the Council Fathers.[47]

In regard to what occurred in Christ's descent, the Fourth (633) and Sixteenth (693) Councils of Toledo approved texts that state explicitly Christ descended to liberate the holy elect.[48] The Sixth Council of Arles (813) would take up the text of the influential Fourth Council of Toledo.[49] By specifying the beneficiaries of Christ's descent, these statements appear to exclude the extension of this liberation to any others, i.e., the damned. This reading would be consistent with papal documents that appear before and after these councils. Earlier, in 597, Pope St. Gregory the Great had reproved a priest named Georgius, writing,

> Nothing else are you to hold but what true faith teaches through the Catholic Church: that descending to those who are below [*ad inferos*] the Lord only rescued from the prisons of hell [*ab inferni claustris*] those whom He preserved in faith and good works through His grace during their life in the flesh. . . . For he who separated himself from God by evil while alive, could not be drawn to God after death.[50]

Later, in 745, a council held in Rome under Pope St. Zachary condemned the teaching of another priest, Clement, which was similar to that of Georgius.[51] Later yet, Pope Benedict XII (1334-1342) indicated the Armenians must renounce errors of faith before he would ally papal forces with them against the Saracens.[52] Among these were the ideas that those liberated from hell *(ab inferno)* in virtue of Christ's passion had been detained there, not due to original sin, but due to the grave personal sin of Adam and Eve; and that Christ's passion totally destroyed hell *(destruxit totaliter infernum)*.[53] The Armenians responded in 1342 to Benedict's successor, Clement VI, and said that they rejected those who held damned sinners believed in Christ during His descent and were justified in hell.[54] The pope did not find their responses wholly satisfactory, and communication on the various matters continued until some ten years later, when Clement wrote to ask for clear answers to particular questions of faith. In this letter, he also indicated his great surprise that the respective Armenian authority had removed from one of the letters — an action suggestive of disagreement — that "Christ, descending to those below [*ad inferos*], did not destroy the lowest hell [*inferiorem infernum*]."[55] From the papal statements in this exchange, it seems implied that, contrary to the first listed error, those liberated from hell were detained there due to original sin. Moreover, it is clear that Christ did not destroy the lowest hell in His descent. These two positions together are practically equivalent to those of the above-mentioned Councils of Toledo, Pope St. Gregory, and the Roman council under Pope St. Zachary, i.e., that only the righteous were liberated in Christ's descent.

Also in regard to what occurred in Christ's descent, mention must be made of the examination Pope John XXII commissioned in 1333 of Durandus' *Tractatus de statu animarum sanctarum postquam resolutae sunt a corpore.* Among the theses found to be erroneous by the commission and confirmed as such by the pope are two concerning the Descent: "that in the limbo of the holy fathers there was no penalty other than the *pena damni,* which is the lack of the vision of God"; and "that Christ could not liberate the souls of the holy from the pit of hell and from their chains, except by giving them clear vision according to the divine essence."[56] The first of these neglected the "captivity, local detention, and privation of liberty"[57] suffered by the holy dead as they awaited Christ, while the second contradicted the power of Christ, either in general or specifically His divine omnipotence.[58] One notes that the *Catechism of the Council of Trent* is consistent with the doctrine made explicit by the condemnations, in that it distinguishes the liberation of the holy dead and the conferral of the beatific vision by mentioning them separately, though always in conjunction: Christ liberates the holy dead in granting them the beatific vision, though there were other possible ways to have set them free from the limbo of the Fathers.

In this context, it is worth recalling that only heaven (and not also hell) was closed before the accomplishment of redemption. Hence in the Constitution *Benedictus Deus,* Benedict XII differentiates the moment of the beginning of eternal bliss for those who died before Christ from that of those who came after Him, but he does not so differentiate in regard to those who die in mortal sin.[59] These, the Constitution says, "go down into hell immediately *(mox)* after death and there suffer the pain of hell."[60]

In more recent times, Pope John Paul II gave a catechesis on the Descent in his General Audience of January 11, 1989. Above all, the pope emphasizes the reality of Christ's death, which he equates with the separation of His body and soul (##4, 5); the glorified state of His separated soul (##4-7); and the salvific effects His descent brings to the holy dead (##5-7).

The Question Refined

The foregoing papal and conciliar evidence confirms our proposed summary as an accurate representation of the Catholic Church's doctrine of Christ's descent. It is worthwhile to note that Hans Urs von Balthasar would agree the summary presents the Church's traditional doctrine.[61] For example, in one place he writes, "If we then ask, where the dead Jesus descended, according to Christian tradition, the answer is unequivocal: to *sheol,*"[62] in the sense of "the antechamber of hell for those whom Jesus intended to redeem shortly,"[63] i.e., the limbo of the Fathers. In the same place, he also indicates the uniformity of the doctrine in patristic, liturgical, and artistic sources.

Moreover, our summary could even be read to represent Balthasar's own theology of Christ's descent if qualified in two essential ways. First, as we will later see, his writings suggest that the doctrine of Christ's descent in soul only to the limbo of the Fathers does not do justice to the extent to which Christ went for man's salvation. Second, Balthasar's texts would give to each sentence of the summary a meaning other than its face value, since he argues that the Descent is glorious in an indirect sense, as Christ's death on the cross is said to be glorious. Consequently, the question before us becomes, "How is one to understand the teaching of the Church on this article of the Faith: in an open sense, or in the more veiled way Balthasar proposes?" In other words, in what sense was Christ's descent glorious?

To proceed, it becomes necessary to consider briefly how the word *glory* is used, and what its proper sense is. We speak of glory in three ways: first, when the appearance and recognition of splendor or triumph coincide with reality, as when a king entering his capital is greeted with rejoicing after a final and conclusive victory in war; secondly, when triumph is present without recognition, as when the pivotal battle of a war is finished, whether it was won in a straightforward manner or deliberately lost; and thirdly, when the appearance of glory is present without true cause, as when an impostor pretends to the throne or to great wealth. Which of these three senses is the most proper use?

As the proper sense of a word is its meaning in reference to its prime analogate, we must ask what is the prime analogate of glory and in which sense the word *glory* is imposed in that case. The prime analogate of a word is that to which the word most properly refers. Now it should be indisputable that glory is most proper to God. That is, the prime analogate of glory is glory in God, just as God the Father is the prime analogate of fatherhood (Eph 3:14-15).[64] In God's glory, however, appearance and recognition coincide with reality. The Son is the image of the Father's splendor (2 Cor 4:4-6), the three Persons of the Trinity know perfectly the full truth of each other, and this truth comprehends every perfection. Even if one wanted to prescind from the Trinitarian perspective, God knows His own perfection. Thus, *glory* is most properly used in the first sense listed above, even if said of something other than God.

This usage is also the first imposition of *glory*. The first imposition is the way in which a word is first and most naturally used. The word is to be understood in this open or ordinary sense, and will be so understood, unless it is made clear from the context or from an explanation that it is intended in a different sense. Since our use of words is based on experience, we first know glory in situations of the coincidence of reality, appearance, and recognition. Triumph in seeming defeat is recognized as glorious not in itself but in its effects and hence some time afterward, whereas the appearance of splendor without any substance is also called *false glory*. Thus, in contrast to the first imposition of *fatherhood*, which is human fatherhood and not that word's most proper sense, we see that the first imposition of the word *glory* is also its most proper sense.

A further precision is required: *Glory* refers most properly to the reality itself that appears and is recognized, and not to the appearance, the recognition, or even the coincidence of all three. For when we say, "We beheld the glory of the king," we do not intend to signify primarily our recognition of glory, the appearance of glory, or even the reality *as* thus recognized; instead our interest is to say *what* we beheld, namely, the king. We aim to point to the reality itself. In this way, the first imposition indicates what is glorious in itself (and likewise in the prime analogate), namely, the reality. It is the reality's own being that is its glory, not the recognition given it. Nonetheless, any reality that exists in such a way that it can be predicated as glorious according to the first imposition will, precisely as such, appear and be recognized; the properly glorious reality is ultimately inseparable from the coincidence of reality, appearance, and recognition.

It is in this first and proper sense of *glory,* when appearance and recognition coincide with real splendor or triumph, that Christ's descent is traditionally understood. In contrast, the Incarnation and Christ's death on the cross are glorious according to the second imposition, a triumph in seeming defeat: In the Incarnation, the Son emptied Himself (Phil 2:7) and the living God humbly accepted human death, even the shameful death of the cross (Phil 2:8), in order to redeem mankind. However, the Incarnation and Passion are fully recognized as the strongest signs of God's love for us (see Jn 3:16) and the means of God's victory over sin and death only after Christ's resurrection.

Hans Urs von Balthasar could reasonably be expected to concur with the foregoing discussion of the nature of glory.[65] He opens his consideration of the New Testament understanding of glory with the coincidence of the same three elements mentioned above as essential to an ordinary use of the word.[66] He likewise acknowledges glory as most properly a property of God.[67] And he points out that *glory* can be applied accurately to such seemingly unlike events as Christ's death on the cross and His resurrection.[68] According to Balthasar, this last consideration is the "genuinely decisive" one in relation to the glory of God.[69] However, he does not distinguish the glory in Christ's death and resurrection as, respectively, analogous and proper. Rather he thinks the one glory of God

> would not be a statement about God unless it were the expression of his hiddenness just as much as the expression of his manifestation, possessing dimensions enough to make itself known in Cross and death just as much as in Resurrection and 'return in glory.'[70]

Thus it "can *integrate* even contradictions into the statement as a whole."[71] At first glance, it may appear that Balthasar is not saying here anything other than that *glory* is said of some of God's acts according to the first imposition, and of others according to the second, depending upon how He chooses to reveal the splendor of His being. In fact, however, Balthasar instead means to conflate these two impositions in the case of God, such that the contradiction between the cross and the proper imposition of glory becomes the essence of the one glory of God, for "what God's glory in its good truth is, was to be revealed in Jesus Christ, and ultimately in his absolute obedience of Cross and Hell."[72] In other words, according to Balthasar, God's glory is in fact most perfectly present and openly apparent (and so to be most recognized) in that moment when it would seem to be most hidden or obscured. The reason for this position will become clearer after the exposition of Balthasar's theology of the Descent in Part Two. For now, it is sufficient and necessary to point out that Balthasar takes the second imposition of *glory*, and not the first, to be its proper sense.

Balthasar also sees a fourth element in glory, namely, the communication and impression of the reality's form on the beholder, not just intellectually (i.e., in recognition), but in his being.[73] Effectively, his complete definition of glory includes the rapture of the one who beholds the manifestation of God's deeds of love. Balthasar would perhaps think this element applies also to the Godhead as the prime analogate of glory, in that the single divine form, existing in the Father (the reality), appears in the Son when the Son receives the divine form and knows the Father as His origin. The difficulty here is that, in the case of the Son, the appearance of the reality and the act of acknowledgment are logically dependent on the configuration. This order is the reverse of the general order Balthasar sees between the three, in which configuration is dependent on recognition, and recognition on appearance.[74] Hence the Trinity cannot be the prime analogate for *glory* if it must have the four elements Balthasar describes; the causal order between them cannot be irrelevant.

However, it must also be said that this configuration, even if related to glory as a possible effect, does not belong essentially to it. Precisely as a configuration to what is apprehended, such a result indicates a distinction between the splendor beheld and the beholder. Hence the effect is indicated as *other* than what is glorious *in itself*.

This conclusion holds true also in the Trinity, in which the Persons are distinct from one another and so can behold, so to speak, the glory of the divine nature in the others. If the configuration of an image to the appearing reality is necessary to glory, only the Father would properly be glorious, for the Father alone has an image in the Person of the Son. Neither Son nor Holy Spirit has such an image, and hence would only be glorious in an improper sense. The failure to find configuration with respect to one divine Person, not to mention two, is sufficient to show this configuration is not essential to glory.

Nevertheless, one might renew Balthasar's proposal by claiming God is glorious insofar as this configuration exists in the Trinity as a whole, namely, in the Son. To do so ascribes glory to God in virtue of the relations, however, not in virtue of the essence. No single Person could then be said to be glorious in Himself, but only the three Persons considered together. It would be false, for example, to say, "The Holy Spirit is glorious," for this statement is not intended to ascribe glory to Him under the aspect of His unity with the Father and the Son, but as He is considered in Himself, which is clear from the lack of qualification.

The consideration of further details of Balthasar's fourth aspect will reveal still other obstacles to regarding it as essential to glory. According to Balthasar, this configuration to the reality sometimes requires the assent of the thing configured; it is required precisely in the case in which Balthasar is most interested, namely, the configuration of rational creatures to God's Trinitarian life.[75] Of course, such consent cannot be given apart from God's action of configuring.[76] Nevertheless, the configuration does not occur without this consent, and hence it is dependent upon a response from the creature, just as the vesting of a soldier in the personal livery of the king depends upon his accepting to be a member of the king's household, even if this acceptance itself follows on an offer from the king. The proposed fourth aspect of glory is then more precisely seen to be a positive response following upon recognition of the reality that appears and including two elements: first, acknowledgment of what has already been done on one's behalf (which goes beyond recognition because it takes account not only of the deed, but of its benevolent character and of oneself as the intended recipient);[77] and, secondly, permission that one be configured to the reality.[78] This latter is required since the possibility of refusal must be taken seriously.[79]

These precisions reveal new difficulties in trying to see God as the prime analogate of glory in Balthasar's sense. If each Person beholds the glory of the divine nature in the others, does the Son grant the Father permission to beget Him as His image? It seems Balthasar would say so — indeed, as we will see later, he speaks of the Son's "antecedent consent"[80] to His generation. Might the Son refuse to be generated? This possibility ought not to be ruled out in Balthasar's theology, particularly as he says "there are no inbuilt securities"[81] in the Trinitarian relations. Other questions may be raised: If each Person is glorious in Himself, where does configuration come in? What form do the two elements of consent (God's configuring action that enables consent and the recipient's consent itself) take? If it makes no sense to speak of such configuration in the case of a single divine Person, it again appears that glory is not an essential divine attribute, but one somehow predicated only of the relational complex of the Trinity, and not of the Persons individually.

On the other hand, if there are adequate reasons to doubt that configuration through affirmation is essential to glory as Balthasar proposes, why was recognition originally said to be necessary? Is not recognition similar to configuration in being an effect that implies the one who recognizes is other than what is glorious in itself? Let us approach this objection from our analogy of the king. If he reflects upon his own majesty, the king takes himself as a conceptual object. There is then a logical relation, and so a logical distinction, between himself as beheld and himself as beholding, even though there is no real difference in the king himself. There is distinction, but no real other-ness. The king who beholds himself and the king beheld are identical. Even less is other-ness or difference entailed in the apprehension of the divine glory by the three Persons, whose single act of being is their single act of self-knowledge. For the same reason, recognition by the three Persons is not only inseparable from the reality of the divine glory, but identical with it.

Due to the simplicity of God, however, the divine love is also inseparable from the divine glory. Moreover, love, which has its perfection in the Trinity, has a certain likeness to configuration insofar as the lover's love unites him to his beloved. Might not adequate ground for Balthasar's criterion of configuration be found here? Again, no, for configuration between two persons or things is not possible to the extent to which they are already the same. In the case of the divine Persons, whose essence and love is not merely the same in kind but identical in number, the only point of 'configuration' would be the relations. However, to configure, e.g., the Son to the Father in this way would be to make the Son identical to the Father, thereby obliterating the Son completely.

In short, recognition is oriented toward the reality that appears. It is the reality's own being that is its glory, not the recognition given it. In contrast, a response of affirmation or rejection refers to the object beheld in its significance for the beholder. It puts the object in orientation to the beholder. Since the response in the beholder does not change the object's own reality, however, to speak of configuration means we are no longer talking about the glorious object in itself, but about the beholder.

Configuration (or affirmation) can then only belong to glory said in an improper sense, because affirmation does not pertain to glory in the prime analogate. If configuration through consent or affirmation were an essential element of glory as Balthasar holds, our glorification of God's deeds and configuration to Him would add something to His glory (contrary to Ps 15:2 and Sir 42:21); they would even be necessary for it. And indeed, though Balthasar denies (at least in part) that any change on God's part is entailed, he does assert that God gains something from the salvation of souls. First, "something in the *internal* life of God has become different":[82] His wrath of judgment has been changed to love through the atonement completed by the Son.[83] Second, the participation of those saved in the Trinitarian life consists in their receiving and returning the divine life as a gift.[84] No essential change occurs in God, because, in the first case, God's wrath is always only an expression of His love (when it is rejected) and, in the second, saved creatures have simply been taken up within the Trinitarian life, which has always been this giving and receiving.[85] Thus Balthasar carefully says that "the work of the *oikonomia* . . . actually does 'enrich' God in a particular respect, without adding anything that is lacking to his eternal life."[86] It should be noted that both these cases treat only the question of addition to God; they do not answer the concern that the configuration of creatures to God is necessary for His glory.

Conclusion

In this chapter, an analysis of credal formulations was supplemented with material from the Church's official catechisms, as well as papal and conciliar statements about Christ's descent, to arrive at a reliable summary of the doctrinal content of this article of Faith. St. Thomas Aquinas' synopsis of the doctrine, consistent with the magisterial texts, was also put to use. Our summary states,

> First, Christ descended in His soul united to His divine Person only to the limbo of the Fathers. Second, His power and authority were made known throughout all of hell, taken generically. Third, He thereby accomplished the two purposes of the Descent, which were "to liberate the just" by conferring on them the glory of heaven and "to proclaim His power."[87] Finally, His descent was a glorious one, and Christ did not suffer the pain proper to any of the abodes of hell.

It was remarked that Hans Urs von Balthasar would agree this summary accurately presents the Church's Tradition and, moreover, that he could agree with the doctrine as stated, *if the statements were given an interpreted reading.* Since his reinterpretation turns largely on what is implied by *glory,* an investigation of the proper meaning of this term was undertaken.

The foregoing discussion of *glory* served to show several important things. First, Balthasar agrees that glory requires a splendid reality that appears and is recognized. Second, he thinks that the splendor of this reality, or the manner in which it appears, is not so much like that of Easter Sunday, but like that of Good Friday. In other words, he holds that the proper sense of *glory* is its second imposition, not its first. He will thus be able to *assert* Christ's descent is glorious, as the Church does, but he will mean something very different. Third, he adds to glory's three aspects of reality, appearance, and recognition a fourth, namely, configuration. We have rejected this addition as not being essential to glory, because it does not derive from the prime analogate.

Bearing in mind this similarity and these differences, we can now proceed to consider the glory of Holy Saturday, both in the traditional doctrine of the Church and in that of Balthasar. That the brief consideration in this chapter indeed summarizes the Catholic Faith regarding Christ's descent, and that the Descent's glory should be understood according to the first and proper meaning of *glory*, will become yet clearer in the chapters immediately following, in which the testimony of Scripture and Tradition are examined. Once the various sources of Catholic doctrine have been examined, Balthasar's theology of the Descent will be set forth and considered in light of them. This order is taken in keeping with the principle that faith goes before understanding. It respects the precedence of the universal Faith over private theological reflection, as well as the priority of the first, proper, and traditional sense of a word over other uses.

CHAPTER THREE

Scripture and the Traditional Doctrine of Christ's Descent

In this chapter, we consider the Scriptural nature of the Church's doctrine of Christ's descent as understood in the open sense. In other words, approaching Scripture from the Tradition's doctrine, we will see what Scriptural foundation this doctrine claims. After all, the Church's teaching on the Descent has always been the offspring of both Scripture and Tradition. One must question the possibility of the opposite approach, i.e., seeing what doctrine the Bible gives 'by itself,' because every reader of the Bible stands already in a history, hence in a doctrinal tradition, which influences, if not determines, his principles of Scriptural interpretation. For example, many books and articles list verses possibly about the Descent, but predominantly such lists are drawn only from the New Testament. This limitation sometimes reflects an interest in considering whether the New Testament's human authors had Christ's descent explicitly in mind when a particular passage was written. Although works with this limited intention may be helpful, by themselves they cannot be an adequate examination of the Scriptural basis for the doctrine of the Descent. The restriction overlooks, for example, all the Old Testament passages that were used as the doctrine crystallized, and hence ignores part of the doctrine's claim to a Scriptural foundation.

Such works approach the traditional doctrine from Scripture and aim to judge whether particular passages teach the doctrine. In contrast, we will here approach Scripture from Tradition, to see something of how the Tradition itself saw Scripture supporting it. This chapter is by no means intended to be an exhaustive exposition and evaluation of the Scripture passages relevant to Christ's descent. The wealth of Scriptural material that relates explicitly to the Descent, typologically prefigures it, or is otherwise taken to refer to it by *loci theologici* is too vast. The fact that the relevance of some individual passages to the Descent is heavily debated only makes such a project more imposing. Hence our examination of this material will be limited by our present aim, which is to see whether the Church's Tradition indeed holds Christ's descent to have been glorious in the first imposition.

Since there is no Bible 'by itself' and since we desire to know the Tradition's Scriptural basis for the doctrine of the Descent, the *locus theologicus* particularly drawn upon in this chapter is Scriptural commentaries. Commentaries on the creed are also relevant insofar as the authors were interested to show the Scriptural basis for the article on the Descent.

Of particular importance are those commentaries written by saints since it may be argued that a consensus of the saints has unique authority. As is well known, the consensus of the Fathers has great authority in the Church, for through it the Faith of the Apostles is transmitted.[1] However, these early saints believed the same perennially true Faith as the saints who followed them, each with the theological precision appropriate for his time and status in life.[2] In the consensus of all the saints, early and late, the same belief is professed across different times and cultures, by persons united in an eminent way with God, the ultimate object of faith. This consensus plays an important role in the transmission and clarification of the Faith received through the Fathers. Hence such a consensus is a preeminent expression of the *sensus fidelium* and an invaluable theological source, bearing a particular authority, albeit different from that of the Fathers. The consensus of the saints is necessarily identical with the Church's Tradition. As a consequence, when the concern is to establish with certainty the Catholic doctrine, the works of the saints through the ages must have pride of place over theologians not yet canonized. This reserve is an appropriate safeguard, and does not necessarily imply a judgment on the ability or sanctity of those in the latter group, unless the Church herself has made such a determination, e.g., by excommunicating someone.

On the other hand, however, the saints were limited by their theological environment even as many of them made great strides in developing it. Diversity of opinion arose among them in regard to some matters not yet clearly expressed by the Church in their day. They were human, and not all were trained in the precisions of theology as a science. Their sanctity and the illumination it shed grew and increased in the course of their lives. They themselves would be the first to admit the limitations of their intellects in understanding the truths of Faith, and of their words in expressing them. Thus, their writings must ever be put in relation to the whole nexus of the mysteries of the Faith as taught by the Church. As Jesus Christ Himself is the Way, the Truth, and the Life (Jn 14:6), the believing theologian's question is always, "What is the Truth of the matter?"

31

The question, "Who said it?" is relevant insofar as it aids the former, since it is proper to this science that arguments from authority are the strongest.[3]

Given these two factors — the unique authority of the saints and its limitation to their expressions consistent with the wider Tradition — the interpretations of Scripture presented here were selected for their ability to illustrate the Church's traditional doctrine. Isolated statements may be found in the works of individual saints that do not coincide perfectly or in the most explicit way with the Tradition; such as these have been set aside for the time being. On the other hand, often a non-canonized writer has made a point more aptly or insightfully than many saints; such as these have been included. In some places, I have consolidated a number of commentaries into a single composite statement.

In keeping with the choice of our principal sources and their character, our consideration of Scripture in this chapter will not focus on modern exegesis nor employ its methodology. Our sources were not inattentive to issues of linguistics or the history of religions, but placed a different weight upon them and put them to different use. Moreover, full-length contemporary works considering the relationship between Scripture and the Descent generally focus narrowly on a few verses,[4] whereas our interest is broader.

Our order is determined not by a particular passage, but by the doctrine of Christ's descent, and we proceed on the basis of two perennial theological principles necessary for the sound interpretation of Scripture. As both were fundamental to the development of Catholic doctrine from apostolic times, they should likewise guide contemporary reflection on Christ's descent. These principles will first be presented and Christ's descent considered in a general way in light of them. Afterward, Scriptural support specifically for each of the four points of the Church's doctrine will be brought forth. The controversial passage 1 Pet 3:18–4:6 will then be briefly considered, due to its especial role in the history of the doctrine of the Descent. Finally, the chapter will close with a select list of Scriptural references relevant to the Descent, which is far more expansive than those found in most works on the topic today. This fact reflects my differing sources and differing principles of interpretation. The relevance of the verses may be debated, some more than others, some with more cause than others. As the list's purpose is merely to indicate something of the breadth of the loci of interest, I will not here evaluate objections or make definitive affirmations.

Scriptural references are to the Douay-Rheims Version (DRA) as a more literal translation of the Vulgate, the version used by most of the authors considered here. I have occasionally substituted the Revised Standard Version (RSV) when the vocabulary or grammar of the Douay-Rheims was overly archaic, provided there was no significant difference in meaning; such instances are indicated by adding RSV in parentheses after the Scriptural citation.

The Incarnation, Typology, and Christ's Descent

The first perennial principle of Catholic theology that must be kept in mind constitutes a profession of the economy of the Incarnation. It derives from the doctrines that Christ has two natures, and that the salvation of mankind is accomplished by means of the Incarnation. As one Person in two natures, Christ always acts in accord with both His human nature and His divine nature. Furthermore, all His actions were directed to the end of making possible man's salvation, which requires faith in Jesus Christ as God. Thus, in all the works of Christ, and especially the most significant, both His humanity and His divinity may be apprehended (though sometimes one is more apparent than the other) in order that we might believe this man is God. For example, Jesus Christ was born of a woman, thereby indicating He had a true human nature, but His mother remained a virgin in His birth, thereby showing His divinity.[5]

Considering the Descent in light of this first principle, we recall that the *Catechism of the Catholic Church* teaches that "Jesus, like all men, experienced death and in his soul joined the others in the realm of the dead. But he descended there as Saviour, proclaiming the Good News to the spirits imprisoned there."[6] "Like all men," Christ experienced death, thereby manifesting His true humanity. "But He descended [to the realm of the dead] as Saviour," in which His divinity is apparent. As St. Gregory of Nyssa says, "In the *fact* of this death we must contemplate the human feature, while in the *manner* of it we must be anxious to find the Divine."[7] St. Thomas Aquinas points out this manner more precisely in his sermons on the Apostles' Creed. There he says that Christ took on the full punishment of sin, i.e., both the death of the body and the descent of the human soul to hell (*infernum,* neuter singular, thus hell taken generically), but in a way unlike others. Both Christ's death and His descent were undertaken with power and at will *(cum potestate et sponte),* for the Son of Man had power to lay down His life (Jn 10:18). In contrast, all other men are constrained by necessity to die on account of original sin, and can do nothing to prevent eventually dying.[8] The great analogy of Rufinus illustrates the same application of this theological principle to the mystery of the Descent:

> It is as if a king were to proceed to a prison, and to go in and open the doors, undo the fetters, break in pieces the chains, the bars, and the bolts, and bring forth and set at liberty the prisoners, and restore those who are sitting in darkness and in the shadow of death to light and life. The king, therefore, is said indeed to have been in prison, but not under the same condition as the prisoners who were detained there. They were in prison to be punished, He to free them from punishment.[9]

Rufinus uses this analogy to show that Christ died of His own power (for the king has free access to his own prison), and enters the realm of the dead in authority and power to loose those detained there. This analogy is notable for its orthodoxy, compact accuracy, and consequent influence. Rufinus's testimony is also key, because his commentary is the earliest extant witness to the Descent article in an orthodox creed.

Another principle, the second considered here, that must guide a Catholic theology of the mystery of Holy Saturday is that persons, things, and events in salvation history sometimes prefigure, or typify, the life of Christ, who is the fulfillment, perfection, or archetype of the types that preceded Him. Because God desires man's salvation and works for it through His revelation in history, He provides the means to understand what He does through a divine pedagogy. One of these means is typology's analogy of being, which binds together the Old Covenant, the life and passion of Christ, Christian life, and eschatology. Typology reflects both the power of God to create things with particular natures and His providence in working through them as secondary causes. For example, both the fall of manna from heaven in the desert and Christ's miraculous change of water into an exceptional wine at the wedding feast in Cana prefigure the institution of His sacramental Presence in the Eucharistic species. Incorporated into Christ through baptism, the Christian is strengthened by this heavenly food as he is conformed to the cross in preparation for the eschatological banquet. Thus as the types of the Old Testament prepare for the coming of the Messiah, so Christ's whole life is a preparation for His Passion and prefigures what will happen afterward in Christian life and in the end-times.

The Old Testament types relevant to Christ's descent are of two kinds. One group asserts that Christ's death on the cross is the ultimate locus of redemption. This affirmation implies that Christ's work in His descent is an *application* of the fruits of redemption, and not a work *meritorious* of man's redemption. The wood on which Isaac was to be sacrificed (Gen 22:6-10), the wood of Noah's ark (Gen 6), the bronze serpent in the desert (Num 21:8-9) to which Christ compares Himself (Jn 3:14), Moses ensuring the success of the Israelites' battle as long as he stands with his arms outspread (Ex 17:8-13), the wood of his staff splitting the waters (Ex 14:16), and the many other life-saving miracles wrought through wood during the Exodus (e.g., Ex 15:25; Num 20:11; Josh 3:13) — these passages all typologically highlight the cross as the pinnacle of Christ's redeeming work. As the Council of Trent put it,

> The meritorious cause [of justification] is the beloved only-begotten Son of God, our Lord Jesus Christ who . . . merited for us justification by His most

holy passion on the wood of the Cross . . . and made satisfaction for us to God the Father.[10]

Our death then is conquered by death, not by the Descent, even as man is redeemed by man, i.e., the God-Man. As St. Bede says, "The first Adam by sinning brought death into the world, the second Adam by dying destroyed death. . . ."[11]

Now the descent of a soul to the hell of the damned may be called the death of the soul insofar as the souls there lack charity, which is the life of the soul. It cannot be said, however, that Christ experienced this death or that such a death accomplished mankind's redemption. Charity is only lost through mortal sin and Christ never sinned (Heb 4:15). Hence, though He died in the flesh, He remained living in the Spirit (1 Pet 3:18).[12] Furthermore, Christ is the source of all human charity and indeed Love itself, since God is love (1 Jn 4:8). Thus it is Christ's death in the flesh, and not a death of the soul impossible and blasphemous to ascribe to Him, that conquers both the death of the soul and the death of the body to which man is subject. As St. Augustine put it,

> The death of our Lord Jesus Christ was not in the soul, but in the flesh alone: our death however is not in the flesh alone, but also in the soul: in the soul due to sin, in the flesh due to the punishment of sin. Because He did not commit sin or have it in His soul, however, He was not dead except as regards the flesh; and this by means of the likeness to the flesh of sin which he bore from Adam. . . . [A]nd He submitted to His one death of the flesh, and dissolved our two.[13]

Three Scriptural passages frequently cited as referring to Christ's descent in documents of the Church and in the writings of the Fathers and other saints also point to the definitive power of Christ's death on the cross. Zechariah 9:11 prophesies, "Thou also by the blood of thy testament hast sent forth thy prisoners out of the pit, wherein is no water."[14] It is in virtue of Christ's blood shed on the cross that the souls of the holy dead are released. Hosea 13:14 is quoted particularly often: "O death, I will be thy death; O hell [in the Vulgate, *inferna,* neuter plural], I will be thy [sting]. . . ."[15] On this passage, St. Thomas Aquinas observes that Christ destroyed death, but only stung or bit hell, since not all those in hell were freed in His descent.[16] Finally, Colossians 2:13-15 is also a noteworthy example in this context:

> And you, when you were dead in your sins, and the uncircumcision of your flesh; he hath quickened together with him, forgiving you all offences:/ Blotting out the handwriting of the decree that was against us, which was

contrary to us. And he *hath taken the same out of the way, fastening it to the cross:* [emphasis added]/And despoiling the principalities and powers, he hath exposed them confidently in open show, triumphing over them in himself.

Perhaps the most significant Scripture passage of all with regard to Christ's death on the cross as the locus of redemption is His final word from the cross, *Consummatum est* (Jn 19:30), "It is finished," or better, "It is completed" or "It is consummated." A dying man has no need to announce the moment of his death. Moreover, Christ, as God, lays down His human life at will (Jn 10:18), and He does this "knowing that all things were now accomplished" (Jn 19:28), fulfilling the Scriptures (Jn 19:28-30), and saying, "It is completed." Thus these words of Christ from the cross must refer to the completion of something other than merely His human life, namely, to the consummation of His redemptive work.

The second group of Scriptural types relevant to Christ's descent explicitly characterize the time between His death on the cross and the resurrection. The seminal example in this group is the creation of man on the Sixth Day and God's rest on the Seventh. As God gave life to Adam and Eve on the Sixth Day, so mankind is recreated in the fullness of the divine life of grace in virtue of Christ's crucifixion on the sixth day of the week. Likewise, God rested after perfecting His work of creation with mankind and Christ rested after returning the possibility of perfection to humanity, having conquered sin and death through His own guiltless death. St. Bede the Venerable writes,

> Fitly was our Saviour crucified on the sixth day, and thus fulfilled the mystery of man's restoration. But on the sabbath, resting in the tomb, He was waiting for the event of the resurrection, which was to come on the eighth day.[17]

Jonah's sojourn without harm in the belly of the whale is similarly a rest after a redemption, one which Christ applies to Himself, saying, "For as Jonah was in the whale's belly three days and three nights: so shall the Son of man be in the heart of the earth three days and three nights" (Mt 12:40). In order to save his shipmates (Jon 1:12-17), Jonah voluntarily allowed himself to be thrown overboard to an apparently certain death in the tempest-tossed sea, itself a Scriptural image of death and of the realm of demonic powers.[18] To save His brothers according to human nature, Christ voluntarily allowed Himself to be handed over to the death of the cross, an apparently certain, final, and total defeat. As the just Daniel was like a New Adam among the lions in their den (Dan

6:16-23),[19] and as the sacrificed Jonah lived in the belly of the whale in the depths of the sea, however, so Christ was unharmed and at ease in His stay in the abode of the dead. The *Catechism of the Catholic Church* summarizes this typological understanding of the Descent as Christ's rest, teaching that

> The state of the dead Christ is the mystery of the tomb and the Descent into hell. It is the mystery of Holy Saturday, when Christ, lying in the tomb, reveals God's great Sabbath rest *after* the fulfillment of man's salvation, which brings peace to the whole universe.[20]

The Israelites' own rest on the Sabbath commemorates their redemption from their slavery in Egypt by God (Deut 5:15), a rest also connected by the Ten Commandments (Ex 20:11; see also Ex 31:16-17) to God's rest on the Seventh Day (Gen 2:1-3). As the sign of the covenant between God and His chosen people is the observance of the Sabbath (Ex 31:16-17; Ezek 20:6, 12, 20), He who is the fulfillment of the covenant keeps it perfectly even in His death, both in regard to its timing and how this time is passed. First, "every Friday, at dusk, . . . the faithful [Jews] enter into the delights of the Sabbath, wherein they remain until the next day, Saturday, after nightfall."[21] The period between Christ's death on the cross and His resurrection is marked by similar boundaries: There is the unnatural darkening of the sun before His death (Mt 27:45; Mk 15:33; Lk 23:44) and the tomb is empty by the time the women arrive at dawn (Mt 28:1; Mk 16:2; Lk 24:1) or "while it was still dark" (Jn 20:1). Christ enters into the Sabbath rest before the Jews themselves do: He immediately after His death on Good Friday, they after His burial (Mt 28:1; Mk 16:1; Lk 23:56; Jn 19:42). Second, keeping the Sabbath has a double feature, that of abstention from work and praise of God for the wonders He has worked in creation and in salvation history.[22] Thus Christ rests from the work of redemption completed in the blood of His cross on Good Friday, but also announces the good news of salvation to the holy dead (1 Pet 3:19). But it is worth noting that Easter (and so all its commemorations) is not the extension of Christ's Sabbath to Sunday: The time of waiting for the Messiah and the blessings of His time, represented by the cycle of weeks, is over; in Christ, the Sabbath is fulfilled and transcended.[23] Sunday is not the seventh, but the eighth day. Christ's resurrection will anticipate, even begin, the Final Resurrection of the Last Day, in which the just, in virtue of their union with Christ (see Mt 27:52-53) enter body and soul the day of eternity which has no setting sun. Before that, however, His rest in the tomb and conferral of the beatific vision on the holy dead prefigure the state of holy souls before this Final Resurrection.

The parallels between type and archetype in these examples also point to

Christ's two natures and thus serve to illustrate our first theological principle. What is indicated by diverse types, however, is united in the Person of Christ and His descent. Thus the descent of Christ's human soul is typified in Jonah's sojourn in the belly of the whale, the tranquility of His sinless soul is prefigured in the safety of the just Daniel among the lions, and the indissoluble union of the divinity of the Word with the soul of Christ on Holy Saturday parallels the Creator's rest on the Seventh Day.

Balthasar seems to suggest several other episodes of the Old Testament as prefigurations of Christ's descent. These "descents into hell"[24] include the flood, as well as the destruction of Sodom, Samaria, Tyre, Egypt, Nineveh, and Babylon.[25] Balthasar mentions these examples, because all show the blaze of God's wrath kindled against the people who have been dissatisfied with Him and His covenant, and unfaithful as a result.[26] Anticipating somewhat the work of later chapters, we note here that the archetype to which these figures would point for Balthasar is the destruction of the sins borne by Christ, which are to be consumed by God's wrath in Christ's descent into hell. However, although the flood or rather the flood *with* the ark is sometimes used as a prefiguration of baptism and its *saving* effects,[27] I know of no authoritative Catholic source for the interpretation Balthasar gives of this and the other Scriptural events; he himself does not cite any.

Prefigurations of the Descent in Christ's Life and Their Fulfillment

Following our two theological principles, we have considered how some events in salvation history prefigure Christ's descent, simultaneously manifesting the Incarnation of the Word. Similarly, earlier events in Christ's own life may shed light on later ones. For example, Christ's power and authority over the spirits of the underworld is frequently manifested during His life in His expulsion of demons and the obedience they show Him (Mt 17:17; Mk 1:23-27; 5:6-13; 9:24-26; Lk 4:33-35; 8:23-32; 9:43), while the saving (as opposed to meritorious) character of His Holy Saturday rest among the dead is mirrored in the miracles of healing He works on the Sabbath (Mt 12:10-13; Mk 3:1-5; Lk 6:6-10; Jn 5:1-47; 9:1-41; and especially Lk 13:10-16 and 14:1-5). Even as it was most appropriate that the daughter of Abraham be liberated from her long subjection to Satan on the Sabbath (Lk 13:10-16), and liberated immediately (Lk 13:12; see Lk 14:5), so it was fitting that, during Christ's Sabbath in the tomb, Abraham and his children in faith should be freed to enter the rest of God after their long detention from it. This delay had subjected them to Satan both because he had desired man's separation from God and because the justice of such detention was the result of his original temptation.

The rich mysteries of the finding of the child Jesus in the Temple and of Jesus' baptism in the Jordan are two events in Christ's own life that merit particular attention in this context. The typological relationship between the finding of the child Jesus in the Temple and His paschal mystery has not been investigated adequately, if at all. Nevertheless, the parallels between them suggest a peculiarly close bond. Both events occur at Jerusalem at the time of the Passover. The Holy Child is in the Temple, three days hidden and lost to the sight of His mother and foster father, who fear He may be dead. Christ is three days in the tomb, hidden and lost to His disciples, His family in grace, who know without doubt He is dead. After three days, the Child will be found in the Temple, while after three days Jesus will be found once again in the temple of His body (Jn 2:19-22). The Child will be found near the place of the figurative sacrifices of the Old Covenant, while Christ will be found near the place of the definitive, archetypal sacrifice of the Cross, for "there was in the place where he was crucified a garden: and in the garden a new sepulchre" (Jn 19:41), in which He was buried. When Mary and Joseph find the child Jesus at last, His mother asks, "Son, why hast thou done so to us? Behold thy father and I have sought thee sorrowing" (Lk 2:48), and the Christ Child answers, "How is it that you sought me?" (Lk 2:49). The angel's response to the women who come mourning to the tomb and who will later find the resurrected Jesus is the same, "Why seek you the living with the dead?" (Lk 24:5). For, as the Child explains, "Did you not know that I must be about my father's business?" (Lk 2:49). Now the Father's business, which is given into the hands of the Son (Jn 3:35; 13:3; 16:15), is nothing other than judging and the giving of life to the dead (Jn 5:17-30) — and the Father is always working, and likewise the Son, even on the Sabbath made for man (Jn 5:17-18; Mk 2:27-28; see also the references given above to Jesus' healings on the Sabbath). Thus the Christ Child teaches in the Temple with the authority of His wisdom, and the light of His doctrine shines upon those still dead in ignorance and sin. Similarly, descending in soul to the limbo of the Fathers, Christ sheds the light of His glory upon the souls of the just sitting in the shadow of death, raising them to the fullness of life. Christ thereby also exercises His power and authority of judgment, ending the reign of the strong man in his own house (Mt 12:29; Mk 3:27; Lk 11:21-22).[28] As the Holy Child sat in the House of God, Christ went in soul only to the abode of the dead where God dwelt in His saints, i.e., only to sheol. In the end, the significance of the typological relation between the finding of the child Jesus in the Temple and Christ's descent into hell is that the prefiguration indicates its fulfillment as one of authority and wisdom recognized, that is, of glory according to the first imposition.

Whether the foregoing link I propose between the two mysteries is legitimate may be debated; in contrast, there is an undeniable link between Jesus'
baptism in the Jordan and His descent. The purification of the waters — abode
of evil powers in the biblical view — by Jesus in His baptism has its parallel in
His descent into the house of the strong man to despoil him. Living, Jesus descended into the waters of the Jordan and living He rose from them. The heavens were opened, and the Trinity revealed in the one who had been baptized,
the dove, and the voice (Mt 3:16; Mk 1:9-11; Lk 3:22; see also Jn 1:32). Jesus is the
ever-living Word, one of the Most Holy Trinity, who descended from heaven
into mortal nature (Phil 2:7-8). Living in the flesh and the spirit, i.e., having a
living human body and soul further enlivened by the Presence of God that is
grace, He went down into the river waters and came up from them. Likewise,
Christ descended into the waters of death. Entering them through His death,
He descended into sheol, dead in the flesh but "enlivened in the spirit" (1 Pet
3:18). Christ, the "just" one (1 Pet 3:18), to whom the Father is ever-present (Jn
16:32), who with the Father breathes forth the eternal Spirit, lives in the Spirit
always, even when dead in the flesh. Christ is Himself substantial Life (Jn 14:6)
and, though living also in a composite nature of matter and form, being wholly
guiltless He is not subject of necessity to that death which in fact only entered
the world through sin (Rom 5:12). Thus death cannot hold Him, and He rises
with the fullness of life, body and soul, on the third day. Thus also Christ, the
Holy One of God (Mk 1:24; Lk 4:34), had no personal need for any baptism and
John the Baptist protests against it (Mt 3:14).

In His baptism, Jesus provided a model and example for sacramental
baptism. In contrast to Christ's baptism, the baptismal candidate is living to the
flesh, in the sense of the world and sin (Rom 7:5; 8:1-2; Gal 5:17, 24; Col 2:13), before his reception of the sacrament. With the pouring of the water and the saying of the baptismal formula, by the power of the Holy Spirit, he is baptized in
Christ and in His death (Rom 6:3), and so rises from his baptism alive in the
spirit of Christ, dead to sin, and fit for heaven.

This typological link between baptism and the death, descent, and resurrection of Christ is reiterated in Scripture and Tradition.[29] For example,
Romans 6:3-4 relates baptism to Christ's burial and hence, to the Descent:

> Know you not that all we who are baptized in Christ Jesus are baptized in
> his death?/For we are buried together with him by baptism into death: that,
> as Christ is risen from the dead by the glory of the Father, so we also may
> walk in newness of life.

The second verse does not say so much Christians are "buried . . . into death," but rather they are buried with Him by "baptism into death," i.e., baptism into Christ's death. In other words, being crucified to the world and having died to sin in sacramental baptism, the Christian is buried with Christ. Buried with Him, nonetheless he is truly alive, though dead to the world. With Christ, the Christian is truly alive, whether he lives or dies (Rom 14:8). Thus, from the perspective of different mysteries, one can say both that, buried with Christ, Christians await the resurrection of the body, and that, already truly alive in the resurrected Christ after having been raised from the waters of baptism, they await the resurrection to come.

Given the typological connection between Christ's baptism and the Descent, and hence between sacramental baptism and the Descent, many Old Testament types of baptism can conversely shed light on the Descent. For example, the Israelites crossed the Red Sea dry-shod, fleeing Pharaoh and following Moses, himself a type of Christ. They passed living through what would have been waters of death for them without the intervention of God, water that instead proved to be the death of the enemies of God, Pharaoh and his army (Ex 14:15-29). Likewise, the Israelites followed Joshua behind the ark of the covenant into the Promised Land as they cross dry-shod the Jordan (Josh 3:11-17), the same river in which Christ is baptized. Similarly, in the fulfillment of these types, Christ descends without harm into the abode of the dead, passing through which He leads those true Israelites, ethnically Jews or Gentiles, who had the faith of the uncircumcised Abraham (Rom 4:11-13; 9:6-8), into the Promised Land of heavenly rest.

Standing in the early stages of an interpretative tradition that will become widespread by the fourth century, St. Melito of Sardis links Christ's baptism and descent together with the ancient image of the sun submerged in the sea: Christ, the rising sun, was baptized in the Jordan and shed light on both the dead in hades and mortals living on earth,[30] i.e., in His descent and resurrection. In the ancient world, the West symbolized the setting of the sun, death, and the grave, while the East represented dawn, life, and resurrection.[31] The sun's setting was therefore considered as its descent into the shadowy realm of the dead, imagined as under the earth, with its entrance in the extreme West.[32] However, even as the sun was not extinguished in the sea but burned on, unconquered,[33] so St. John Chrysostom says that, upon Christ's death, "the Sun of Righteousness descended and shed light upon [the darkness of Hades] and made Hades into heaven. For where Christ is, namely there is heaven."[34] Here, Isaiah 9:2 *(DRA)* is relevant: "The people that walked in darkness have seen a great light: to them that dwelt in the region of the shadow of death, light is risen." Likewise, the gospels employ imagery of Christ as the light of the world, e.g., John 1:5 *(RSV*[35]*)*: "The light shines in the darkness, and the darkness has not overcome it." By the fourth century, the image of the setting sun as Christ's death and descent, and that of the rising sun as His resurrection, was widespread.[36] At the same time, the Descent was commemorated in prayer at the twelfth hour after sunrise, i.e., more or less at sunset.[37]

Christian Baptism as Participation in Christ's Descent

In this context of the typology of baptism and the Descent, it is appropriate to flesh out how the individual Christian's baptism unites him to Christ by being a sacramental participation in His descent. Sacramental liturgies are the preeminent mode of participation in the mysteries of Christ's life, death, and resurrection. In them, the Church is configured to her Head by the action of Christ in a real though veiled way.[38] In virtue of this union, she participates in the perfect cult of glory He gave to the Father throughout the mysteries of His life and death,[39] and which He continues to give.

In the most ancient liturgies, the events of Good Friday, Holy Saturday, and Easter Sunday were not commemorated separately. This liturgical unity reflected the unity of the paschal mystery itself:[40] Christ's death was not a simple end, but a passover to perfect life. Conversely, His resurrection is necessarily a resurrection *from the dead*. Given this intrinsic interrelation, the unity of these mysteries as emphasized by the single ancient commemoration is not fundamentally ruptured when the liturgies of the days of the Triduum and Easter each re-present and contemplate one aspect more than the others, as they do today.

The distinct feature of the liturgy of Holy Saturday, including the current practice of having no celebration of the Eucharist until the Easter Vigil, is the contemplation of the death of the Lord. By *death* is here meant not His sacrificial dying on the cross (commemorated on Good Friday), but His sojourn in the abode of the dead. What is this sojourn, and what is its significance for mankind? First, the profession that Jesus was buried or, more specifically, descended to those below indicates simply that Jesus was dead. He partook of the general human fate. The simplicity of this observation masks its importance: The confession of Jesus' death is also a confession that He is really human, i.e., it is a specific affirmation against heresies that deny this fundamental truth of faith. More specifically yet, the profession of Jesus' death means He descended to those who died before Him: The abode of the dead has no passage out until Christ Himself makes one. His descent is to open the way to heaven, to the Father's bosom. Still more specifically, because He was perfectly just, He descended to the abode of the holy dead. Christ's descent will then address the concern, motivated by charity, of whether any were saved from among those who died before Christ instituted the sacraments and established the Church, the ordinary means of salvation. At the same time, to those who hope to join the holy dead in the presence of the Father, death need no longer be a terror.

All that has been said thus far considers the true humanity of Christ, and the specific character of the general human fate of death He underwent. As Christ is also God, however, the significance of His descent cannot be limited to the normal possibilities of human fate: Christ is mankind's Savior, and descends to the dead having redeemed mankind in the blood of His cross. Hence, in descending to the holy dead, He does so to apply to them the fruits of this redemption. Here another reason is seen why Christ descends in His soul only to the holy dead: In view of the redemption wrought by Christ, God gives every man the grace necessary for salvation, whether he died before Christ's coming or was born after it. The fruit of salvation is then fitting only to those in whom the divine life of grace took root, lived, and flourished.

It is particularly significant that among these holy dead is Adam, the first human lord of creation but also the cause of the Fall that affected all creation. As a result of his sin, paradise was closed. If heaven is now opened to him, it is, as it were, a return to paradise (albeit an infinitely more perfect one): As suggested by the presence of the Good Thief in some artwork depicting Christ's descent, this new paradise is wherever Christ is.[41] The whole order of creation is re-established in virtue of the New Adam's salvation of the old, and creation is set free from the slavery of Satan to celebrate the eternal Sabbath.[42]

The incorporation of the individual man into this new order of creation, with its passage to heaven, is accomplished through baptism.[43] The sacramental baptism of the New Testament is the Christian's bridge from the prefigurations and shadows of the Old Testament to the eschatology already begun in grace, though yet to be perfectly fulfilled in the final resurrection. Baptism is a passage from death to life, with Christ and in virtue of the archetypal passage made by Him.[44] The person baptized not only dies (sacramentally), but dies specifically the death of Christ and is buried with Him, in order that he may rise with Him. Thus baptism exhibits the same essential unity as the entire paschal mystery, as seen earlier in the quotation of Romans 6:3-4. From this unity derives the possibility and legitimacy of emphasizing links between baptism and the individual mysteries commemorated from Good Friday to Easter Sunday. Generally speaking, Christ's sacrifice on the cross is the definitive *origin* of the sacrament and its efficacy:[45] From the side of the paschal Lamb (Ex 12:46; Jn 19:36), blood and water flow forth as a purifying nuptial bath for the Church (Eph 5:25-27), the Bride of the Lamb (Rev 21:9).[46] The *effect* of the sacrament is seen in connection to Easter Sunday: a new life in God, dead to sin and the world, free from death and the devil. The *sacrament itself*, however, is typified in connection to Holy Saturday. The Scriptural images for baptism are those connected in the Catholic exegetical tradition to Christ's descent, because baptism *is* a sacramental participation in Christ's descent.[47] Here is the passage through the waters of death, the Exodus from slavery to freedom through the Red Sea,[48] the entrance into the Promised Land through the waters of the Jordan where Jesus will be baptized,[49] the washing of the bridal bath that cleanses the sullied image of God.[50]

The catechumen who dies with Christ in baptism hopes to rise with Him in glory after the end of his earthly life. This desired passage to glory was made already by the holy men and women who were dead with Christ in the flesh but alive in the Spirit. By the sacrament he is about to receive, the catechumen passes from the general fate of mankind to that of Christ and of those conformed to Him by faith. Olivier Rousseau summarizes five principal themes of the primitive catechesis of the Descent that find their echo in the one baptized into Christ:[51]

First, Christ descends into the realm of death, and likewise the catechumen descends into the waters. The waters of death, cleansed by Christ's baptism, now mean death to sin.

Second, He illuminates the holy dead, and also the catechumen. Developed out of Scriptural language about the sons of light (e.g., Jn 12:35; Eph 5:8; Heb 6:4; 1 Thess 5:5), a very early name for baptism was φωτισμός *(enlightening)*.[52] Baptism as an illumination is imaged in the Easter Vigil, the premiere celebration of baptism in the liturgical year. During the Vigil, the Easter candle is lit for the first time and its base plunged into the water that will be used for baptism. The candle represents the column of fire that led the Israelites through the desert by night, so that, in the words of the Exultet, sung at the Easter Vigil, "The night will be filled with light as the day."[53] In fact, Christ's triumphal descent into hell is one of the standard illustrations found on medieval Exultet scrolls.[54]

Third, Christ vivifies the holy dead in His descent, and in baptism gives the catechumen the new, divine life. Like the holy dead awaiting Christ, the catechumen is disposed by faith and hope to receive the new life Christ brings.[55] This life was glory for the holy dead and is grace for the baptized. Baptism is a return to paradise:[56] Like the miracles of physical healing that are signs of the spiritual healing brought by Christ, resurrection from the death of sin through the life of grace means one is captive no longer to the death that entered the world through sin; baptism and the new life it brings thus are a prelude to the final resurrection of the body.[57] Note here the eagerness, so to speak, of God to share the gift of His life: In virtue of Christ to come, men after the Fall did not have to wait for His actual coming before living again the life of grace. Similarly, although the holy dead awaited Christ's descent, they did not have to await the end of time before entering essential beatitude. Likewise, the one living in grace now already has a foretaste of glory.

Fourth, Christ triumphs over the strong man in his own realm. Through His perfect human obedience unto the death of the cross, Christ reversed the defeat of mankind through the temptation of the devil that had death as its result. Consequently, He enters the realm of death as victor. The catechumen shares in Christ's victory in the form of the catechumen's renunciation of Satan, his pomps, and works; the baptismal exorcism; his reception of the 'arms' of God (Eph 6:12-18); and his being ordered by baptism to the ultimate victory.[58]

Fifth and finally, Christ rises again, and so too the new Christian is raised from the waters. Christ's resurrection reveals its ultimate archetypal form in the Ascension, when He goes to the Father, body and soul; the baptized who abides in the life of God will follow Him.[59]

Thus, in its connection to Holy Saturday, the baptismal descent into the water symbolizes not only dying, but also death as the entrance into the abode of the dead and a sojourn there; the triple immersion recalls the three days before the resurrection; and the coming up from the waters in the new life of grace mirrors the liberation from death of those who belong to Christ.[60] The one plunged into the water and blood from Christ's side through baptism or martyrdom is cleansed in the nuptial bath of the Church.

Again we see why Christ liberated only the holy dead in the limbo of the Fathers: Only they had washed their garments in the blood of the Lamb (Rev 7:14), and hence were fit to partake in the wedding feast itself (Mt 22:11-13). As the Descent was the efficacious application of the redemption wrought by Christ on the cross to the individual for the sake of eternal life, so is baptism. Conversely, as baptism is the passage to the new life of grace for the living united to Christ by faith, Christ's descent meant passage to the new life of glory for the dead united to Him by faith. The profession of faith solemnly made at baptism and during the liturgical vigil of Easter is also relevant in this connection: Those who believe and are baptized reject the slavery of the devil and, being freed from it, are made sons and heirs of the kingdom.

The unity of the paschal mystery, the role of the Descent, and the participation of the faithful in it may be illustrated in a summary way by the Eucharistic liturgy of the Ethiopian Catholic Rite. In the Anaphora of the Apostles, the priest prays just before the Consecration,

> He extended His hands to the passion; suffered that He might deliver (redeem) the sufferer who trusted in Him. He offered up Himself of His own

will to the passion that He might overcome death, break the bonds of Satan, trample upon hell, lead forth the saints, establish the covenant and reveal His resurrection.[61]

It is by participating in the mysteries of Christ, by being assimilated to Christ as one's archetype, that one comes to bear the name Christian:[62] Earlier, at the proclamation of the Gospel, the congregation offers praise to Christ, saying,

> Who is like You, O Lord, among the gods? . . . You manifested Your might to Your people and You saved them with Your saving arm. You went into the nether world and set free those who were in captivity. You delivered us once again, for You came and saved us.[63]

Hence to commemorate the Descent is to commemorate not only this mystery of Christ as it reveals His true humanity and divinity, but also its significance for the individual Christian in his baptism, for the larger Church in the salvation of the holy dead, and for the universe in general which, in those liberated by Christ, tastes the first fruits of redemption.[64]

The Scriptural Basis for the Summary of the Church's Doctrine

The biblical texts were written within the community of the Church and, vice versa, the Church's Tradition developed in reflection upon Sacred Scripture. Consequently, Scriptural support for the elements of the traditional doctrine of the Descent is a rich topic, one which we will briefly sketch in this section. Recall that, according to this doctrine, Christ descended in His soul united to His divine Person only to the limbo of the Fathers. His power and authority were felt throughout all the abodes of hell, although differently in each one. His descent accomplished two purposes, the liberation of the just and the proclamation of His universal power. Finally, in this glorious descent, Christ did not suffer the pain proper to any of the abodes of hell.

First of all, the existence of the limbo of the Fathers itself is indicated in the passages about the deaths of the patriarchs, who "sleep" with their fathers (Gen 15:15; 25:8; 25:17; Deut 31:16; 1 Kings 2:10; see also Dan 12:13), and in Christ's parable about the pleasant repose of the beggar Lazarus in Abraham's bosom (Lk 16:22). The language used in these passages stands in sharp contrast to that which describes the fate of the rich man in the parable of Lazarus, and to Christ's warnings about a place of eternal pain (Mt 25:46), fire (Mt 3:12; 5:22;

18:9; 13:42; 13:50; 25:41; Mk 9:42, 46-47), and the worm (Mk 9:41-47), which place He identifies as *gehenna* (Mt 5:29; 10:28; 25:15; 25:33; Mk 9:43; 9:45; 9:47). St. Augustine explains that the limbo of the Fathers is called "the bosom of Abraham" by Christ, "not that it is [Abraham's] alone, but because he is the father of many nations and placed first, that others might imitate his preeminence of faith."[65] Since Abraham's faith was accounted to him as justice (Gen 15:6; Rom 4:3), the bosom of Abraham is the resting-place of all the holy dead before Christ. Nevertheless, because original sin was not yet expiated, these souls suffered the delay of perfect union with God prior to the accomplishment of Christ's redeeming work of atonement[66] — prior, because after the work of Christ the just may go straight to the bosom of the Father if they have no need of purification in purgatory. The holy dead had to await the 'opening of heaven' both because its 'closure' was part of the penalty of original sin, still unexpiated at that time, and because they were to receive salvation through Christ, even as the living do. The fact that no movement is possible between the bosom of Abraham and the hell of the rich man indicates how far righteousness is from unrighteousness, how meriting and thus movement toward heaven ceases with death, and finally how God's mercy respects His creation to the degree that He does not override His free creatures' voluntary rejection of Him.

Second, that Christ descended in His soul only to the limbo of the Fathers and in order to liberate them, is supported by John 5:25: "The hour cometh, and now is, when the dead shall hear the voice of the Son of God, and they that hear shall live." These words of Jesus are multivalent, and may be understood both in regard to those dead in their sins but living on earth, and to those physically dead but living by grace and awaiting the perfection of the life to come. Thus Christ says, "The hour cometh" to both groups, but the hour "now is" to whomsoever hears this word of His, in His own time on earth and in the present. Commentaries of the saintly ecclesiastical writers in the *Catena Aurea* mostly take John 5:25 as spoken to listeners in the present life, and so referring to the future resurrection of the body, the dead people Christ miraculously raised, or the life of faith. The *Catechism of the Catholic Church* (#634), however, quotes it as a major text specifically referring to Christ's descent.

The liberation of the holy dead as part of the purpose of Christ's death and descent is also indicated by Hosea 13:14, "I will deliver them out of the hand of death. I will redeem them from death: O death, I will be thy death; O hell, I will be thy [sting]."[67] The liberation of the holy dead from the limbo of the Fathers would mean the end of their waiting for the Christ and of their longing for the fullness of life with God. Thus, descending to them in His soul united to His divinity, Christ reveals the Gospel and its fulfillment in Himself to them, but more, He reveals Himself. At Jesus' death on the cross, the Temple veil was torn in two from top to bottom (Mt 27:51; Mk 15:38; Lk 23:45), revealing the Holy of Holies, the seat of the Presence of God. Likewise, Christ's human nature veiled His divinity; with this torn in two by the separation of body and soul in death (see Heb 10:19-20), Christ reveals Himself in the glory of His separated soul united to His divine Person, to the just who are dead with Him. He is now truly known as Emmanuel, God-with-us. The liberation of the Fathers from limbo is nothing other than the commencement of the beatific vision in them, for eternal life is this: to know God personally, and Jesus Christ whom He sent (Jn 17:3). It is the bringing of them forth to heaven, that is, to the Father's house, the Father's bosom, through the only-begotten Son who is ever in the bosom of the Father and who alone has seen Him (Jn 1:18; 8:29; 16:32).

That Christ's power was made known and had effects throughout all the abodes of hell is supported by Hosea 13:14, quoted in the previous paragraph, and Colossians 2:15, quoted in the previous section, as well as by Acts 2:24, Philippians 2:8-10, Revelation 1:18, and the parable of the plunder of the strong man's house in Matthew 12:29, Mark 3:27, and Luke 11:22; compare also Isaiah 49:24-25a.[68] On Matthew 12:29, St. John Chrysostom comments, "He proves that not only daemons, yea but the prince also of daemons He hath bound. . . ."[69] St Jerome concurs, "The strong man is bound and chained in tartarus [i.e., hell proper], bruised by the Lord's foot."[70] And likewise St. Augustine, "He has bound the strong man, in that He has taken away from him all power of hindering the faithful from following Christ, and gaining the kingdom of heaven."[71]

Finally, that Christ did not suffer the pain proper to any of the abodes of hell (i.e., eternal fire, purification, or charity's longing for union with God) is supported by the typological 'rests' examined earlier, the parable of the strong man, and also, for example, by Psalm 23 (24):7-10:

> Lift up your gates, O ye princes, and be ye lifted up, O eternal gates:
>> and the King of Glory shall enter in.
> Who is this King of Glory? The Lord who is strong and mighty:
>> the Lord mighty in battle.
> Lift up your gates, O ye princes, and be ye lifted up, O eternal gates:
>> and the King of Glory shall enter in.
> Who is this King of Glory? The Lord of hosts, he is the King of Glory.

This psalm is found with unusual frequency in the saints' treatments of Christ's descent. It is interpreted as the gates of hell opening before the soul of Jesus in recognition of His authority both as Creator and as the Christ.[72] Also particularly relevant to the Descent, Psalm 15 (16):8-10 is a song of praise and trust in God:

> I set the Lord always in my sight: for he is at my right hand,
>> that I be not moved.
> Therefore my heart hath been glad, and my tongue hath rejoiced:
>> moreover my flesh also shall rest in hope.
> Because thou wilt not leave my soul in hell; nor wilt thou give
>> thy holy one to see corruption.

Said in the Person of Christ, this passage may be read to affirm His continual possession of the beatific vision ("I set the Lord always in my sight . . ."). It refers to His unfailing confidence in God ("for he is at my right hand, that I be not moved"), implying no despair may be attributed to Christ. Finally, it indicates that the Descent of Christ, "the holy one," did not extend to gehenna, the pit of "corruption." These topics will receive more attention during the discussion of Balthasar's theology of the Descent.

The Interpretation of 1 Peter 3:18–4:6

One final Scripture passage requires more extended individual consideration at this point, namely, 1 Peter 3:18–4:6. The passage seems to refer explicitly to Christ's descent by saying that Christ preached to the spirits in prison (3:19) and that the Gospel was announced to the dead (4:6).[73] Strong arguments can be made in support of this application.[74] However, St. Augustine, St. Thomas Aquinas, and others have raised questions and objections to what might seem to be such a straightforward interpretation.[75] In his *Epis. ad Evodius*,[76] St. Augustine suggests a figurative interpretation. St. Thomas Aquinas mildly says it is better to understand it along the lines of St. Augustine, and presents a similar interpretation (*ST*, IIIa q. 52, a. 2, ad 2). Because 1 Peter 3:18–4:6 is not the only passage in Scripture relevant to the Descent, this long-standing exegetical debate need not be resolved conclusively here. Nevertheless, the passage merits brief discussion due to its long history of association with the doctrine of the Descent. It will not be used in any way, however, that would make our overall investigation concerning the character of Christ's descent dependent upon one or another interpretation. Moreover, no attempt will be made to eliminate interpretations that do not apply the passage to Christ's descent. Due to God's providence, passages of Sacred Scripture can bear the weight and convey the light not only of multiple senses (literal, allegorical, anagogical, tropological) but also of multiple interpretations in one particular sense, provided they are indeed sound interpretations. Thus, the treatment here will be limited to responding to four major objections against understanding the passage in reference to the traditional doctrine of Christ's descent into hell. As we shall see, understanding 1 Peter 3:18–4:6 in this way does not seem excluded by any conclusive objection.

St. Augustine found it deeply puzzling why, if 1 Peter 3:18–4:6 refers to Christ's descent in soul after His death, St. Peter should refer only to those who had been unbelieving at Noah's time (1 Pet 3:20), and not to other unbelievers who died after Noah but before Christ.[77] He therefore suggests that Christ's coming in the spirit does not refer to the descent of His soul to hell, but to His divine activity of instructing souls through the preaching of the Church, represented by Noah's building of the ark. Those unbelieving at the time of Noah are thus a figure of those who hear the Gospel at any time, but refuse to believe.[78]

Rather than being a figure, however, one might suggest they are a part that stands for a whole, e.g., for the souls in purgatory at the time of Christ. St. Robert Bellarmine proposes that the reason only those unbelieving at the time of Noah are mentioned is that there was particularly great doubt about whether any who had been so punished by the flood attained eternal salvation. According to St. Robert, the text of 1 Peter indicates some of those who did not believe Noah did penance (i.e., repented) at the end of their lives. They still died in the flood, and thus were "judged in the flesh" because they seemed damned as far as human judgment could go, but they lived "according to God," that is, died in a state of grace and ultimately attained heaven. St. Robert draws upon St. Jerome in his interpretation, referring to St. Jerome's comment that, although God punished many in a temporal fashion through the flood, He was not bound necessarily to punish them eternally.[79]

Those who die now with similarly imperfect charity go to purgatory, which is preparatory for heaven. It is reasonable to believe that purgatory existed also prior to the accomplishment of Christ's redeeming work, but was preparatory for the limbo of the Fathers so long as heaven was closed. Thus, since even a perfect act of contrition does not necessarily satisfy for the temporal punishment due to sin, perfectly repentant souls who did not have time to perform adequate penance would either have been in purgatory or, after being purified, in the limbo of the Fathers at the time of Christ's descent. Though Christ did not descend in His soul to purgatory, the souls there (and likewise the souls of the damned) would have been able to know of His coming, even as the rich man beheld Lazarus in the bosom of Abraham.[80] Now the 'preaching' of Christ need not be an exhortation, but may be the announcement that redemption has been accomplished through His death on the cross, i.e., a proclamation of a fact.[81] Hence, because Christ descending to the souls of the just brought tidings of great joy to them, namely, of the completion of the redemption, the souls in purgatory would also have rejoiced in His descent, although the time when they might savor the fruit of that redemption would have had to be postponed until their purification was complete.

St. Augustine's figurative interpretation of the Petrine passages can thus be integrated with the traditional doctrine of the Descent along the lines proposed by Jean Galot:[82] Noah's generation is mentioned to indicate that even the worst of sinners have received the call to salvation (and hence its possibility), even if this call came only through the voice of conscience. For those souls who responded to this call, Christ brought to fulfillment in His descent the interior work He had begun earlier, or, in the case of the souls in purgatory, announced its imminent fulfillment.

If St. Jerome, St. Robert, and those who follow their interpretations are right in believing some sinners repented perfectly before dying in the flood, one can also respond to St. Augustine's puzzle by asking what other situation in the Old Testament has a group of sinners who repent and yet die. In the Old Testament, repentance is usually the key to the continuation of life and the prevention of death, thereby prefiguring the revival of the life of grace through repentance and the forgiveness of sins. Thus, given the different aim of the author of 1 Peter, namely, to point to the death of baptism, he seems not to have made a strange choice, but the perfect one.

Another more direct, if very different, solution may be proposed. Those in all the abodes of the dead were aware of Christ's descent, yet had different reactions: The just and those in purgatory rejoiced, while the damned were ashamed "for their unbelief and wickedness"[83] and the demons must similarly have been dismayed at this indication of their ultimate defeat. In this case, the imprisoned spirits would not be those who repented, but rather precisely those who died in their disbelief and sins at the time of Noah, despite the ample time God gave them to reconsider entering the ark after its completion and before the beginning of the flood (seven days: Gen 7:4, 10). These sinners typify all the unrepentant and hence to mention them is to include all who would have been ashamed before Christ in His descent. Similarly, the "spirits in prison" may also include the demons, insofar as one interprets "the sons of God" in the passage leading up to the story of Noah (Gen 6:1-4) to be fallen angels. That these spirits, human and angelic, are mentioned in particular as the recipients of Christ's 'preaching' indicates His dominion extends over the entire domain of hell, including its depths. The consternation of the damned angels and souls is an effect, however, not the ultimate end, of His descent. Christ descends as a result of His real human death and in order to proclaim His sovereignty as the Incarnate Word over death by the liberation of the holy dead and by His own resurrection. 1 Peter may then refer specifically to the time of Noah in order to allow the reference to Christ's announcing His triumph in the abode of the dead to be not only a statement of a fact, but also a figure of the Church's preaching to those still dead in sin prior to baptism (1 Pet 3:21).[84]

Such an interpretation has certain advantages. It takes the disobedient spirits simply as such, without postulating the conversion of at least some of them before their death in the flood. It integrates St. Augustine's figurative interpretation, which is relevant to the living readers of the exhortations in 1 Peter about baptism. Even more important, it is consistent with the typology of Noah, the ark, and the flood that, as Jean Daniélou has indicated, stands in the background of the Petrine letters.[85] Daniélou sets 1 Peter 3:18 in the context of another Petrine passage concerning Noah, namely, 2 Peter 2:4-9:

> For if God did not spare the angels when they sinned, but cast them into hell and committed them to pits of nether gloom to be kept until the judgment; if he did not spare the ancient world, but preserved Noah [the eighth person, the preacher of justice], when he brought a flood upon the world of the ungodly; . . . then the Lord knows how to rescue the godly from trial. . . .[86]

This passage shows a clear opposition between the just Noah and the ungodly world destroyed in the flood, thereby suggesting that a similar contrast may be being drawn in 1 Peter. In addition, as the eighth person, Noah represents the end of one age and the beginning of a new one, even as the eighth day is the first day of a new week. As Daniélou draws it out,[87] this early Christian exegesis is the foundation for a Scriptural typology of Christ as the New Noah, with His cross as the ark. By baptism, the Christian's sins are destroyed just as the disbelieving impious underwent judgment in the flood. The one configured to Christ by baptism is, as it were, one of Noah's family inside the ark, now the Church, awaiting the final judgment of God upon the world. It would seem implicit in Daniélou's presentation that even as Noah, Christ, and the Church urge men to conversion before the judgments respective to their times, this 'preaching' continues after that judgment in the form of salvation made evident, i.e., in the manifestation of an accomplished fact: The ark rose above those drowning in the flood, Christ manifested Himself free and sovereign in the realm of death, and the Church with her Head will stand triumphant in glory at the end of time. What was proclaimed as the truth will then be seen to be the truth; what was previously apprehended by some by faith will then be apprehended by all. Given that 1 Peter is generally accepted to have been connected with a liturgical celebration of baptism, likely even at an Easter Vigil,[88] such a typological opposition between the just and the unjust would probably be closer to the first meaning of the text, although St. Robert's solution remains an interpretation compatible with Catholic doctrine.

Another question that arises in the interpretation of 1 Peter 3:18–4:6 with reference to Christ's descent is how the dead can be judged in the flesh (1 Pet 4:6), from which they are separated prior to the resurrection of the body.[89] Could Christ's preaching in order that the formerly unbelieving might live in the Spirit suggest the possibility of conversion after death?[90] St. Augustine thinks this proposed interpretation is contrary to the Faith, and likewise the suggestion that the Gospel might still be preached in hell,[91] for it should not be concluded "that what the divine mercy and justice granted to some had been granted to all."[92] Even if one does not agree with St. Augustine's reason, one would have to agree with his conclusion: If those who die in mortal sin go to hell immediately *(mox)* upon their death (DS 857, 1002, 1306) and their punishment is eternal (DS 72, 76, 411, 780, 801), there is no possibility of their conversion after death. Indeed, St. Augustine finds the ideas of conversion after death and the ongoing preaching of the Gospel in hell to be ridiculous, since they militate against the necessity and charity of preaching the Gospel in this earthly life.[93]

The verse need not be understood to suggest conversion after death, however. This judgment of the dead according to the flesh can refer to death itself as a judgment, suffered as the effect of original sin. Death can also be the judgment of particular men, such as those who failed to go aboard the ark, insofar as it directly results from personal sin.[94] A third possibility for interpreting the verse is the one St. Robert suggests, that this judgment in the flesh according to men is the error-fraught human assessment that a terrible death indicates someone is damned.

However, if judgment in the flesh refers to physical death, why does it say Christ preached to them *in order that* they might be judged in the flesh?[95] Moreover, death is more the execution of judgment than a judgment itself. Thus, the first and second possibilities just mentioned seem ruled out. The verse then must refer to the judgment of these souls according to their deeds in the flesh,[96] even as all are so judged both by God and by man. Though all the souls unbelieving at the time of the Flood were mistakenly judged damned according to human judgment, some lived in the spirit after death according to God's judgment of their repentance — and it is only the divine judgment that is the definitive passage to life in the spirit. Thus, in Christ's announcement of the Gospel in His descent, those of these souls in the limbo of the Fathers received the definitive judgment that is the reception of their eternal reward, while those in purgatory were assured of it. At the same time, the salvation of those who had disbelieved Noah but perfectly repented humbles human judgment and reaffirms God as the ultimate and unique Judge, thereby indicating Christ's supreme dominion over heaven, earth, and hell, a dominion exercised in His descent. Such an interpretation eliminates any need to interpret the verse as suggesting the conversion of souls after death.

This interpretation also can satisfy another query, namely, "In what sense did Christ preach to [the physically dead] *in order that* they might live?"[97] As discussed earlier, Christ 'preached' to the holy dead by announcing the redemption in His blood and giving them the beatific vision, the fullness of life.

Finally, the question may be asked how else is Christ's being made alive in the spirit (1 Peter 3:18) to be understood other than in regard to His resurrection in the body, since His soul was subject neither to the death of the soul that is sin nor to the 'second death,' which is damnation?[98] William J. Dalton in particular understands 1 Peter 3:18 in reference to Christ's bodily resurrection, and thinks the key mistake made in interpreting the entire passage 1 Peter 3:18–4:6 is to read it in light of a soul-body dichotomy he characterizes as Greek and foreign to the anthropology of the New Testament.[99] Interpretations of the passage in this supposedly faulty light apparently tend toward a figurative (St. Augustine) or historical (St. Robert Bellarmine) understanding, which Dalton rejects for an entirely different interpretation.

In response, however, it may be said that Christ's being made alive in the spirit can be understood in a way similar to God's indwelling and providential care of His adopted children during their earthly life. In other words, Christ's being made alive in the spirit is not in contrast to some point of physical or spiritual death, but simply indicates the continual preservation of the human life of Christ in the fullest possible state of grace and union with the Godhead. It may also indicate the glorification of His entire soul after the crucifixion, i.e., the end of the sorrow and pain suffered during the Passion and the overflow of the joy of the beatific vision — which Christ always possessed in His intellect and will — to all the powers of Christ's soul.[100] Although an alternative interpretation of the whole passage might be offered for evaluation, as Dalton does, to deny application of the passage to the Descent on the basis that the soul-body distinction is foreign to the Old or New Testament is not convincing. The purportedly "Greek" anthropology is already important in the *Old Testament* theology of the afterlife.[101] In venerating the tombs of the patriarchs while also speaking of *sheol,* the people of both Testaments (which would include the early Christian audiences of 1 Peter) indicate an understanding of these two principles of the human person, in practice if not also in systematized belief. In addition, since God is the principle of all truth, philosophical and theological, nothing prevents Him in His providence from inspiring the human authors of Scripture to write something the fuller truth of which will be better understood by later generations.

Four questions about the interpretation of 1 Peter 3:18–4:6 were raised in this section: Why are only the souls unbelieving at the time of Noah mentioned? How are the dead to be judged in the flesh? How are they judged in order that they might live? And, finally, how is Christ made alive in the spirit? The obstacles they posed to understanding the passage with reference to Christ's descent were removed in light of a developed understanding of the traditional Catholic doctrine of the Descent. In the resulting interpretation, Christ's preaching to the just dead is the announcement of the good news of their imminent salvation, i.e., the conferral of the beatific vision. This announcement could include the explanation of how God worked the redemption for which the just dead had waited in faith, hope, and charity, i.e., through the sacrifice of Christ, the fulfillment of the Old Testament prefigurations.[102] Furthermore, Christ's triumphal descent would give a new vigor to the hope of those in purgatory, for they would know the redemption had been accomplished and they were destined for salvation.[103] In contrast, the damned would realize the gravity of their sins even more as they beheld the triumphal presence of Christ and the glorification of the just. Thus Christ's descent spreads the Gospel message to men of all times and places.[104] The emphasis on Christ's announcement of this message at the particular point in 1 Peter in which it comes is consistent with the general aim of the letter, namely, the encouragement of Christians in the face of persecution. Conformed to Christ through baptism with its typological links to His death, descent, and resurrection, Christians may join their sufferings to His in order that they may share in His glory. They may be confident that the enemies of God will suffer ultimate defeat even as Christ has already decisively disarmed them.

This developed interpretation of 1 Peter 3:18–4:6 and the responses given to the objections against interpreting the passage with reference to Christ's descent into hell preserve the fruitfulness of Christ's descent, as well as the doctrines that Christ descended in soul only to the faithful and that conversion is not, and never has been, possible after death. In addition, such an interpretation eliminates neither the figurative interpretations of St. Augustine and St. Thomas, nor what may be gained from Dalton's exegetical attempt to clarify the human author's primary intention. These other interpretations are subject to evaluation in their own right. Although St. Augustine doubts the application of the verse to Christ's descent to the dead, he raises his perplexities as questions, thereby indicating a certain openness.[105] St. Thomas does not deny the application, but only says the figurative interpretation is better. This treatment, coupled with the early origin of the interpretation and its persistent recurrence with various nuances up to the present time (including, e.g., in the *Catechism of the Catholic Church*) suggests the interpretation of 1 Peter 3:18–4:6 with reference to Christ's descent is still both an open and a reasonable possibility.

Scriptural Passages of Interest concerning the Descent

The Scriptural basis of the doctrine of the Descent is then the subject of some little debate, as has been seen in the case of 1 Peter. A selected list of other loci of interest appears below. The purpose of this list is merely to suggest the wide variety of passages drawn upon by different sources as Scriptural foundation for the traditional doctrine of the Descent; hence, it is neither exhaustive nor definitive. It focuses more narrowly on Christ's descent, rather than, e.g., the characterization of sheol. Some verses are truncated, because only the part here quoted was used by the Tradition. The exact extent and importance of the context of the verses is itself sometimes open to debate.

All references are to the Vulgate and Douay-Rheims versions; when different, the numbering of more modern versions is indicated in parentheses. Occasionally, when there was no significant difference in meaning, I have substituted the *RSV* when the vocabulary or grammar of the Douay-Rheims was overly archaic.

> Gen 2:2-3: God's rest after creation
>
> Deut 5:15; Ex 20:11: The Sabbath rest in commemoration of God's rest and of His liberation of His people from Egypt
>
> Ex 3:7-8: The Lord's intention to descend to lead His people into the land of milk and honey
>
> Ex 14:21-29: The Israelites' crossing of the Red Sea and the destruction of Pharaoh's army
>
> Josh 3:11-17: The Israelites' entrance into the Promised Land behind the ark
>
> Job 38:17: "Have the gates of death been opened to thee, and hast thou seen the darksome doors?"
>
> Ps 15 (16):7-11 *(RSV):* "I bless the Lord who gives me counsel; in the night also my heart instructs me./I keep the Lord always before me; because he is at my right hand, I shall not be moved./Therefore my heart is glad, and my soul rejoices; my body also dwells secure./For thou dost not give me up to Sheol, or let thy godly one see the Pit./Thou dost show me the path of life; in thy presence there is fullness of joy, in thy right hand are pleasures for evermore."
>
> Ps 23 (24):7-10: "Lift up your gates, O ye princes, and be ye lifted up, O eternal gates: and the King of Glory shall enter in./Who is this King of Glory? The Lord who is strong and mighty: the Lord mighty in battle./ Lift up your gates, O ye princes, and be ye lifted up, O eternal gates: and the King of Glory shall enter in./Who is this King of Glory? The Lord of hosts, he is the King of Glory."

Ps 67:19 (68:18): "Thou didst ascend the high mount, leading captives in thy train, and receiving gifts among men. . . ."

Ps 73 (74):12-13 *(RSV):* "Yet God my King is from of old, working salvation in the midst of the earth./Thou didst divide the sea by thy might; thou didst break the heads of the dragons on the waters."

Ps 87:6: One who is free among the dead

Sir 24:45: "I will penetrate to all the lower parts of the earth, and will behold all that sleep, and will enlighten all that hope in the Lord." (This verse, missing in some translations, is retained in the Neo-Vulgate.)

Is 9:2: "The people who walked in darkness have seen a great light; those who dwelt in a land of deep darkness, on them has light shined."

Is 25:8-9 *(RSV):* "He will swallow up death for ever, and the Lord God will wipe away tears from all faces, and the reproach of his people he will take away from all the earth; for the Lord has spoken./It will be said on that day, 'Lo, this is our God; we have waited for him, that he might save us. This is the Lord; we have waited for him; let us be glad and rejoice in his salvation.'"

Is 42:6-7: The servant of the Lord will bring "out of prison those who sit in darkness."

Is 45:2 *(RSV):* Destruction of the "doors of bronze" and "bars of iron" before the Lord's anointed (Cyrus)

Is 49:8-9 *(RSV):* "Thus says the Lord: In a time of favor I have answered you, in a day of salvation I have helped you; I have kept you and given you as a covenant to the people, to establish the land, to apportion the desolate heritages;/saying to the prisoners, 'Come forth,' to those who are in darkness, 'Appear.'"

Is 60:1-2: "Arise, be enlightened, O Jerusalem: for thy light is come, and the glory of the Lord is risen upon thee./For behold darkness shall cover the earth, and a mist the people: but the Lord shall arise upon thee, and his glory shall be seen upon thee."

Dan 3:23-28: The three young men in the furnace with the one like a son of God

Dan 6:16-23, 14:30-42: Daniel in the lions' den

Hos 13:14: "I will deliver them out of the hand of death. I will redeem them from death: O death, I will be thy death; O hell, I will be thy [sting]. . . ."[106]

Jonah 1:15–2:10: Jonah in the belly of the whale

Zec 9:11: "Thou also by the blood of thy testament hast sent forth thy prisoners out of the pit, wherein is no water."

Zec 14:7: "And there shall be one day, which is known to the Lord, not day nor night: and in the time of the evening there shall be light."

Mal 4:2-3: "But unto you that fear my name, the Sun of justice shall arise, and health in his wings: and you shall go forth, and shall leap like calves of the herd./And you shall tread down the wicked when they shall be ashes under the sole of your feet in the day that I do this, saith the Lord of hosts."

Mt 3:16; Mk 1:9-11; Lk 3:22: Jesus' baptism

Mt 12:29; Mk 3:27; Lk 11:21-22: The plundering of the strong man

Mt 12:39-40; 16:40: The sign of Jonah

Mt 22:32; Mk 12:27; Lk 20:38: The God of Abraham, Isaac, and Jacob "is not the God of the dead, but of the living."

Mt 27:52-53: After Jesus' death, "the graves were opened, and many bodies of the saints that had slept arose,/and coming out of the tombs after his resurrection, came into the holy city and appeared to many."

Lk 1:79 *(RSV)*: The prophecy of Simeon that Jesus will "give light to those who sit in darkness and in the shadow of death."

Lk 13:10-16: Jesus heals on the Sabbath (and the other works that show Jesus is Lord of the Sabbath: Mt 12:11-13; Mk 2:23–3:5; Lk 14:3-5; Jn 5:10, 16; 9:14, 16)

Lk 23:43: Jesus' promise to the good thief

Jn 5:25-26: "Amen, amen, I say unto you, that the hour cometh, and now is, when the dead shall hear the voice of the Son of God: and they that hear will live./For as the Father hath life in himself, so he hath granted to the Son also to have life in himself."

Jn 8:12: Jesus, the light of the world

Acts 2:24-31: The application of Ps 15 (16):8-11 to Christ by St. Peter

Rom 10:6-7 *(RSV):* "But the righteousness based on faith says, Do not say in your heart, 'Who will ascend into heaven?' (that is, to bring Christ down)/or 'Who will descend into the abyss?' (that is, to bring Christ up from the dead)."

Rom 14:9: Christ, Lord of the dead

1 Cor 15:55: "O death, where is thy victory? O death, where is thy sting?" (Allusion to Hos 13:14)

Eph 4:8-10 *(RSV)*, an adaptation of Ps 67:19 (68:18): "Therefore it is said, 'When he ascended on high he led a host of captives, and he gave gifts to men.'/(In saying, 'He ascended,' what does it mean but that he had also descended into the lower parts of the earth?/He who descended is he who also ascended far above all the heavens, that he might fill all things.)"

Col 1:18: Christ, first-born from the dead

Heb 2:14-15: "Therefore because the children are partakers of flesh and blood, he also himself in like manner hath been partaker of the same: that, through death, he might destroy him who had the empire of death, that is to say, the devil;/And might deliver them, who through the fear of death were all their lifetime subject to servitude."

1 Pet 3:18–4:6: Christ's going to the spirits in prison and the preaching of the Gospel to the dead

Rev 1:17b-18 *(RSV):* "I am the first and the last,/and the living one; I died, and behold I am alive for evermore, and I have the keys of Death and Hades."

Conclusion

In this chapter, the testimony of Scripture about the character of Christ's descent was considered in light of two essential principles of orthodox Catholic theology: the revelation of Christ's two natures in His works and the typological character of Sacred Scripture. This typological relation is extended into Christian life through the relation between the Christian and his archetype Christ. In light of these two principles, the elements of the Church's doctrine on Christ's descent were found to have a broad Scriptural foundation. Those who aim to study the Scriptural foundation for the doctrine of Christ's descent but limit their investigation to New Testament passages that explicitly mention it have mistakenly truncated their field of research. Moreover, the Scriptural evidence indicates the Descent to have been triumphal, an interpretation reflected in the commentaries of the saints and succinctly illustrated by Rufinus' analogy of the king liberating the prisoners. This chapter thus indicates the Scriptural basis and support for the open sense of the Church's teaching on Christ's descent into hell.

Although little attention has been paid to ascertaining the original intentions of the human authors and developments in theological precision have not been discussed, as typical in contemporary Scriptural exegesis, the premise for this procedure is simple: All the authors considered desired to speak the truth God has revealed and confided to His Church. They themselves would have been the first to desire their works be used and interpreted in accord with the faith of the Church, especially in those cases where they did not see the truth as fully or clearly as those who followed them. This having been said, the texts employed for this chapter were selected for their clarity and orthodoxy.

This chapter was not intended as a conclusive demonstration of the

Church's doctrine. For not only must Scripture be read in the Church's Tradition, but the interpretation that results must be consonant with other authentic expressions of that Tradition. Thus, having seen the compatibility of the summary of the magisterial doctrine in its open sense with Scripture as read in the Church's Tradition, we turn now to the testimony about Christ's descent into hell given in certain other *loci* of Catholic Tradition.

CHAPTER FOUR

Magisterium and *Sensus fidelium:* Liturgy and Art

The twin mouths of the single wellspring of divine Revelation are Scripture and Tradition.[1] The life-giving water of God's Revelation has been handed down to the present day through both, in modes appropriate to their differing characters. Tradition especially is preserved through multiple modes. This multiplicity does not detract from the unity of its content, just as the same color tone may be found in diverse media, such as paper, ceramics, and textiles. The pre-eminent expression of apostolic Tradition is the liturgy of the Church. *Lex orandi, lex credendi:* The rule of prayer is the rule of belief.[2] In investigating the Catholic Faith with respect to Christ's descent into hell, it is important then to probe the liturgies and prayers, both Eastern and Western, connected to the commemoration of this mystery. In this context, one should also examine the Eastern icons of the relevant liturgies. In addition, art other than the liturgical icons can express the belief of the faithful. Certain caveats, however, must be observed in examining such non-liturgical art for this purpose, given its greater remove from the life of the Church and the flexibility of its artistic canon.

The aim of the present chapter is twofold: to consider what the liturgy of the Church, including the relevant liturgical icon, teaches about Christ's descent into hell, and to examine the testimony of non-liturgical sacred art. An exhaustive consideration of these sources of evidence cannot be attempted here. Such comprehensive treatment is not really necessary, however. The Church cannot contradict herself in her various liturgies: The rich diversity of expression in different Eastern and Western rites must be reconcilable in substance, else the Church would profess in one liturgy what is incompatible with the Faith professed in another, thereby ceasing to be a sure guide to divine truth. At the same time, the witness of non-liturgical sacred art is strikingly uniform. The specific texts and works of art examined in this chapter appear for their importance (e.g., the liturgy of the day) or because they are representative of a group of works unified by their depiction of Christ's descent. Relevant selections from the Eastern and Western liturgies will be considered first. A valuable theological source in itself, their eloquence regarding the Church's understanding of the Descent also provides the foundation for objective readings of the representations of the Descent in Eastern and Western art. The icon itself will then be examined. The chapter closes with an investigation of the testimony of non-liturgical sacred art from the West.

From His incarnation to His second coming, the saving mystery of Christ has a great unity, a unity that is likewise found concentrated in the central paschal mystery of His passion, death, and resurrection. This unity is not homogeneity, however, and so distinctions within this unity can be observed. Otherwise some aspect of the mystery (one of the 'days') would be redundant and superfluous. All theological fonts emphasize the unity of the mysteries in certain places, highlighting the distinction in others. Now, generally speaking, unity is presumed until a positive distinction is found. Hence, in ascertaining the particular relationship between Good Friday and Holy Saturday, it is not the greater unity of the paschal mystery that is at question, but the distinction between these two elements of it. Thus the consideration here is based upon a reading particularly attentive to the liturgical and artistic expressions that assert or imply a distinction.

Christ's Descent into Hell according to Liturgical Texts

The mystery of Christ's descent into hell may seem overshadowed by the visibly dramatic events of the first Good Friday and Easter. It is certainly true that the Descent can only be approached by faith because it occurred beyond sensory experience. The faithful seeking to penetrate something of this mystery are greatly helped by the liturgical texts for Holy Saturday, the day on which Christ's descent is commemorated, because these texts are expressions of Tradition and suffused with Scripture. Ideally the Holy Saturday texts would be considered in the context of those for Good Friday and Easter; in doing so, the differences among the three mysteries would become yet clearer. It would also be relevant to consider liturgical prayers for the dead, as well as baptismal rites. Nevertheless, the examination here is limited to the texts of Good Friday, the Feast of the Exaltation of the Cross as a companion to Good Friday, and Holy Saturday, since the question at hand is whether the Descent is triumphal specifically in contrast to Christ's death on the cross. The texts selected are rich enough to require limitation. Liturgical texts from a variety of historical periods would also ideally be considered, but we limit ourselves here to contemporary texts: What is even clearer in many of the more ancient texts is still today *lex orandi.*[3]

These liturgical texts never assert that Christ's expiatory suffering continued in His descent into hell. If stretched and interpreted against the more explicit statements to the contrary, a few individual lines may admit of ambiguity, but only ambiguity. When taken in context, however, the liturgical texts as a whole make unambiguously clear the differing natures of Good Friday and Holy Saturday: On Good Friday, by His death on the cross, Christ redeemed mankind; on Holy Saturday, by His descent to hell, Christ opened heaven to those who had been awaiting His redemptive death in the limbo of the Fathers. In theological terms, this difference corresponds to that between the objective redemption by which Christ made salvation possible, and the subjective redemption, by which an individual is actually saved, i.e., enters eternal beatitude (or is assured of it in purgatory) after death. Subjective redemption is salvation in the most proper and strict sense.

Let us now examine several representative liturgical texts, considering first texts from the East and then texts from the West. First, from the Byzantine Matins for Great and Holy Friday (Good Friday), consider the hymn that follows the proclamation of the twelfth Gospel reading:

> Thou hast redeemed us from the curse of the Law by Thy precious Blood: nailed to the Cross and pierced by the spear, Thou hast poured forth immortality upon mankind. O our Saviour, glory be to Thee.[4]

This hymn indicates that the price of mankind's redemption is Christ's blood. The significance of the blood of the Lamb may be seen in a plethora of other liturgical texts, writings of the Fathers, magisterial teachings of the Church, and Scripture, including typological prefigurations.[5] For example, 1 Peter 1:18-19 *(RSV)* says, "You know that you were ransomed from the futile ways inherited from your fathers . . . with the precious blood of Christ, like that of a lamb without blemish or spot." The great Latin hymn of thanksgiving, the *Te Deum,* beseeches God, saying, "We therefore entreat you to assist your servants whom you have redeemed with your precious Blood."[6] Innocent III wrote in 1201 to Humbert, Archbishop of Arles, that "the Kingdom of heaven . . . remained closed for all till the death of Christ. . . . [Its] gate the blood of Christ mercifully opened to his faithful."[7] And in the Jubilee Bull *Unigenitus Dei Filius* of 1343, Pope Clement VI teaches that "immolated on the altar of the cross though he was innocent, he did not merely shed a drop of his blood — although this would have sufficed for the redemption of the whole human race because of the union with the Word — but a copious flood."[8]

The redemptive value of Christ's mental and emotional anguish before His death is not diminished by this doctrine of the centrality of His blood. The suffering of the soul and that of the body are not separated from each other as long as the body and soul are united in the living person. Rather, spiritual sorrow is proportionately indicated by corporal suffering due to the concomitance of the soul with the body during life. In contrast, when the body and soul are separated after death, what is said to affect the soul cannot be said to affect the body, or vice versa; they are, after all, separated from each other. Although both Christ's body and separated soul remained united to the Person of the Word, this general situation is no different in His case, for the hypostatic union did not change human nature in Him. Were it otherwise, His death would not have been a real human death, for human death is precisely the separation of the person's body and soul. Thus, because Christ's descent into hell is a descent not of His body, but of His soul, the redemptive ransom of mankind with Christ's blood cannot be prolonged into His descent.

It is worth noting that, when the Byzantine hymn says immortality was poured forth from the pierced side of Christ, the liturgy cannot be taken to teach that eternal life (i.e., subjective redemption) was universally granted at that moment. There are still people who have yet to pass through bodily death to their eternal recompense. Thus, because "mankind" is indefinite, it indicates some (i.e., the holy dead) received eternal life. However, since the blood and water that came forth from Christ's side are understood not only to have been real blood and water, but also to signify the Church and the sacraments, the hymn's use of "immortality" here is also to be understood in reference to the possibility of attaining eternal life (i.e., the objective redemption), as well as the means of doing so.

Another noteworthy text is the exapostilarion after the proclamation of the eighth Gospel reading: "O Lord, this very day hast Thou vouchsafed the Good Thief Paradise. By the Wood of the Cross do Thou enlighten me also and save me."[9] The seed of eternal life, grace, is granted the sinner when he is justified and thus he is 'saved' already in this life. But no one is definitively saved until after final perseverance.[10] Since the person praying the exapostilarion is still living, the "save me" refers then most essentially to the moment of death, especially given the parallel text makes with the Good Thief's entry into paradise. However, the desired salvation requires that one be illumined in the present by the cross, that is, freed from the darkness of sin and joined to Christ, who is repeatedly described in terms of light in the texts preceding this exapostilarion and is indeed the Light of the world (Jn 1:9). When the necessity of final perseverance and the reality of death as the separation of body and soul are kept in mind, then, two conclusions may be gathered from the hymn and exapostilarion, which are representative of the Matins as a whole. First, it is Christ's death on the cross that is redemptive. Second, salvation is something actually granted after death.

The Byzantine liturgical texts for the feast of the Exaltation of the Cross give an even clearer exposition of the mystery of the Crucifixion. They refer to the destruction of the power of death, the resurrection of the dead, the vanquishing of demons, and the freeing of creation from corruption as effects of Christ's death upon the cross.[11] Especially significant is the additional attribution that all grace comes through Christ in virtue of His death on the cross, as both the culmination and summit of Christ's lifelong redeeming work, and as the specific event through which grace becomes available to mankind.[12] Two conclusions may be drawn from the feast's characterization of the Crucifixion. First, the texts amount to a liturgical statement of the doctrine that no meriting is possible after death. If all grace is merited by Christ, but all grace comes from His death on the cross, then Christ did not merit grace by His descent. This position is consistent with the doctrine that one receives eternal reward or punishment based upon one's deeds in the flesh, and that this recompense is received immediately after death, except when the eternal reward is delayed for the completion of purification in purgatory.[13] Since Christ was sinless, the Descent then entails the *application* of those merits. Though not meritorious, Christ's descent nevertheless remains an integral part of the objective redemption: The souls in the limbo of the Fathers cannot take heaven for themselves after Christ's death. They must be conducted there by Christ, the definitive Judge and their good Shepherd, who visits them in His soul for that purpose. Secondly, if death's power was destroyed and the demons vanquished by Christ on the cross, then His descent must have been triumphal, or glorious, in the proper sense. How could a conqueror be subjected to the power of the enemy he had just vanquished?

In this context, however, the most significant feature of the Byzantine liturgical texts for the feast of the Exaltation of the Cross is their complete silence on the Descent into hell. Everywhere the liturgy exalts the cross itself as the very instrument of Christ's victory, of redemption, and of sanctification. The cross, not the Descent, is held up as the fulfillment of all the Scriptural types of redemption, and this victory on the cross is repeatedly stressed to be a complete one. Nowhere is the cross treated as the gateway to the Descent, as if victory by the cross signifies victory by invisible suffering in hell after death on the cross; or as if victory through the cross indicates the cross is hailed as victorious because it is the means of Christ's death, in virtue of which He will descend to accomplish a definitive victory in hell. As the texts make repeated reference to Christ's resurrection, it is not the case that they do not mention the Descent simply because they are texts for a feast of the cross; if that were the reason, they should likewise not refer to the resurrection. Rather the silence of the liturgy points to the very different characters of Holy Saturday and Good Friday. Christ's death on the cross is the consummation of man's objective redemption, to which the Descent does not essentially contribute, since Christ descends in consequence of His death and to bring the fruits of the accomplished redemption to those who were awaiting it in sheol.

Yet here St. Thomas Aquinas seems to differ from the Church's liturgy. In his commentary on the Apostles' Creed, St. Thomas Aquinas writes that the first reason Christ descended into hell was "to undergo the entire punishment of sin, and thus to expiate all guilt."[14] If the Descent is expiatory, must it not also have been meritorious and have continued Christ's work on the cross? As St. Thomas would be understood consistently with the Church in her liturgical tradition, however, it seems one must distinguish between Christ's death as perfect expiation in that it accomplished man's redemption, and Christ's descent as expiatory insofar as it is essentially connected to that perfect expiation. The distinction may be seen by considering the Descent's twofold connection to Christ's expiation. First, the Descent is the necessary consequence of His death. Because death is essentially the separation of body and soul, Christ's death would not have been a true human death without His soul separating from His body and going to an abode of the dead. Thus, without His descent, Christ's death would not have expiated the guilt of sin or destroyed death, because it would not have been a real death. However, His death, which is thus expiatory in a causal way, is the moment or instant of separation; death is not the descent of the soul, just as it is not the placing of the body in the tomb.

Secondly, the Descent is connected to Christ's expiation insofar as it was an assumption of a punishment of the soul. Mankind became subject to death through the sin of Adam. This subjection entailed not only the separation of body and soul, but also the deprivation of the vision of God after death. Due to the stain of original sin, not even the most holy or most innocent souls could enter heaven before Christ accomplished the redemption. Christ did not have original sin, however, and was perfectly innocent and holy when He died. His soul deserved to enter heaven immediately on His own merits. Instead, however, He descended in His soul into limbo. He did not suffer there the delay of the vision of God, however, for Christ always possessed the beatific vision. In this way, Christ assumed the punishment for sin in a way that manifested both His humanity (in His descent to the abode of the just dead) and His divinity (in His continual possession of the beatific vision). The descent of the ineffable Word in His human soul, free among mankind's helpless dead (Ps 87:6, 5), is no dishonor to His divine dignity — a concern of some ancient objectors. Rather it glorifies God through the manifestation of the Incarnation, i.e., that *God* became man. It ought indeed to excite our awe, wonder, and thanksgiving that the innocent soul of Christ descended to the limbo of the Fathers to bring them with Him to the bosom of the Father.

The essential difference between the mysteries of Good Friday and Holy Saturday is indicated by the Byzantine texts for Good Friday and the Exaltation of the Cross. This difference is made even more evident in the liturgical texts for Holy Saturday itself. Matins of Holy Saturday, also known as the Office of the Burial of Christ, similarly testifies to the *redemptive* nature of Christ's death on the cross and the *salvific* character of His descent. Perhaps the clearest statement is in the Melkite-Byzantine rite of the Blessing of New Light. It speaks first of the crucifixion, "But You, O Lord, . . . submitted Yourself to death . . . in order to lead us back to that former glory and light from which we had fallen away."[15] Then it turns to the Descent,

> For the sake of us transgressors of Your divine law, You accepted to be buried, to go down into Hades, to the depths of the earth. Then, O Lord, You destroyed the gates of death, delivering and raising up those who had been chained in its darkness; You filled our human nature with the light of your resurrection; . . .[16]

Man is led back to his former glory through the cross, but clearly is not yet filled with the light of the resurrection; that is the state only of the souls in heaven. The descent into hell is seen to be the bringing of salvation, the bringing of that light, to the just who had died before Christ's redemptive death on the cross. As St. Thomas Aquinas says,

> Christ's Passion was a kind of universal cause of men's salvation, both of the living and of the dead. But a general cause is applied to particular effects by means of something special. Hence, as the power of the Passion is applied to the living through the sacraments which make us like unto Christ's Passion, so likewise it is applied to the dead through His descent into hell.[17]

Though not so common, there are some texts that indicate more explicitly the distinct characters of Crucifixion and Descent. For example, there are the following verses from three hymns: "By dying, O my God, Thou puttest death to death though Thy divine power";[18] "Wrapped in a winding-sheet, O Saviour, and buried in a tomb, Thou hast loosed the prisoners . . .";[19] and "How great the joy, how full the gladness, that Thou hast brought to those in hell, shining as lightning in its gloomy depths."[20] Again death is vanquished by the Cross, whereas Christ's descent brings actual salvation to the just who died before Him and who would rejoice in His coming. Another verse from the same eulogies of the buried Lord is likewise clear: "O Life, how canst Thou die? How canst Thou dwell in a tomb? Yet Thou dost destroy death's kingdom and raise the dead from hell."[21] The first clause of the response answers the first question, as the second half addresses the second question: The death of God in the flesh means the destruction of the reign of death, and His sojourn among the dead means their resurrection to life.

Other texts refer to the completeness of the redemptive work of Good Friday, in contrast to Holy Saturday as the fruit of that work, in terms of the Scriptural typology of God's rest:

> Moses the great mystically prefigured this present day [Holy Saturday], saying: "And God blessed the seventh day." For this is the blessed Sabbath, this is the day of rest, on which the only-begotten Son of God rested from all his works.[22]

As God rested after creation in the beginning (Gen 2:2-3), so He rests *after* the re-creation of man. In the West, the Office of Readings for Holy Saturday makes the same connection between Holy Saturday and a rest for God in the selection of Hebrews 4:1-13 for the First Reading.[23]

Throughout the Byzantine texts, the unity of the redemption wrought by Christ and the original unity of the ancient liturgical celebration of what is now the Triduum and Easter is reflected in the lack of sharp distinctions. A single sentence may unite allusions to two, or even all three, of the events of Christ's crucifixion, descent, and resurrection. Not only are the historical events and witnesses referenced, but also often their continuing significance and reflection in the life of the Christian participating in the liturgy. The following verse is a relevant example: "Willingly, O Saviour, Thou hast gone down beneath the earth, and Thou hast restored the dead to life, leading them back to the glory of the Father."[24] This text most directly refers to the entrance into beatitude of the holy dead at Christ's descent. It may allude as well to the dead who came out of the tombs with the resurrection of Christ (Mt 27:52-53) and ascended with Him into heaven (taking one interpretation of Mt 27:53 and Eph 4:8). More remotely, there is an echo of the work of Christ in the life of the Christian who desires to be joined with the holy dead in the life of faith and in ultimate blessedness.

In addition to such explicit statements as those discussed above, frequent references are made in the Byzantine liturgical texts for Holy Saturday to Christ's radiance in His descent.[25] Christ descends into hades like the setting sun,[26] an ancient image seen in the previous chapter, and "the lights of heaven hide their radiance, when Thou, the Sun, art hidden beneath the earth."[27] Although the sun's darkening is expressive of creation's horror at Christ's crucifixion,[28] it also appears connected with Christ's burial as a sort of 'sympathetic' parallel to Christ's descent as the setting of the Sun of Righteousness.[29] If the archetype of Light is in darkness, its image ought likewise to be so. The earth is similarly shaken to hold Him who cannot be contained, and the realm of the dead is rocked to receive the Giver of Life.[30]

> The angelic choirs are filled with wonder, beholding Him who rests in the bosom of the Father laid in the tomb as one dead, though He is immortal. The ranks of angels surround Him, and with the dead in hell they glorify Him as Creator and Lord.[31]

Having considered the theological significance for Christ's descent of some representative liturgical texts from the East, let us now look at some key characteristic texts from the West. The liturgies of the Roman Rite for Good Friday and Holy Saturday are consistent with the conclusions drawn from the examination of the Byzantine texts above.

Consider first the Divine Office for Holy Saturday. In the Office of Readings, the psalms speak of the secure and peaceful rest of the one who trusts in God (Ps 4:1-5, 8; and Ps 15 [16]), as well as God's ruling majesty (Ps 23 [24]:7-10 or Ps 94 [95]). Similarly, the First Reading of the Office, Hebrews 4:1-13, refers both to God's rest from His work and to His universal governance. Given their place in the liturgy for Holy Saturday, these texts point to the traditional teaching that, though Christ suffered death, He did not suffer the pains proper to any of the abodes of hell. Rather His descent was glorious in the common sense of the word, a manifestation of light and power.

The Second Reading is the climax of the Office. This selection from "an ancient homily"[32] tells of the profound stillness that settles over the world after Christ's death, and the great drama that continues in the underworld as Christ calls Adam and his just descendants among the dead to Himself. The homily reiterates the two purposes of the Descent, to liberate the just and proclaim Christ's universal power: "God slept in the flesh and raised up those who were sleeping from the ages. . . . [A]nd the underworld has trembled."[33] "Holding his victorious weapon, the cross,"[34] Christ goes in to where Adam and Eve are. Whereas before Christ's death, the cross could only be an emblem of shame and torture, it is now a "victorious weapon," because on it the Redeemer has accomplished the victory over sin, death, and the devil. Christ says to Adam,

> I am your God, . . . who for you and your descendants now speak and command with authority those in prison: Come forth, and those in darkness: Have light, and those who sleep: Rise.[35]

This passage makes explicit that Christ exercises His authority over the underworld even in His descent and not only after His departure. Taking up Luke 4:18-19 and Isaiah 61:1-2,[36] the homily shows Christ proclaiming the Gospel, and fulfilling both it and the Old Testament, in the abode of the dead as He did in the land of the living. He does so in a way appropriate to the different situation, however: Christ is no longer on earth preaching to the living who look forward to redemption and salvation. The redemption having been accomplished, He announces this good news to the just dead and brings them the light of heaven. The homilist goes on to end a long description of how Adam was recreated through the wounds of the Passion and the Cross with these words in the Person of Christ:

> My [wounded] side healed the pain of your side; my sleep will release you from your sleep in Hades; my sword has checked the sword which was turned against you.[37]

Like the response of half a monastic choir to the other in the chanting of psalms, the wounds of the Passion are seen in the West as in the East to be the source of the healing of the wound of sin, while Christ's descent (His sleep) has the purpose of releasing the just dead. This joyful healing and liberation is possible because Christ's "sword," the "victorious weapon, the cross," "*has* checked" the sword of sin, death, and banishment turned against Adam and his descendants. The Office's selection from the homily closes with Christ's command and invitation to go with Him to the Father's house, indicating He descended to bring the just dead into the kingdom of heaven.

The Responsory that concludes the Office of Readings is explicit, as well, and does not require elaboration:

R. Our shepherd, the source of living water, has departed. At his passing the sun was darkened, for he who held the first man captive is now taken captive himself. *Today our Saviour has shattered the bars and burst the gates of death.

V. He has torn down the barricades of hell and overthrown the power of Satan. *Today our Saviour. . . .[38]

The other Offices of Holy Saturday are consistent with these explicit texts.

This brief consideration of Western liturgical texts relevant to the Descent cannot conclude, however, without mention of three great Latin hymns. The *Crux fidelis* and the *Vexilla regis*, both composed sometime between A.D. 530 and 600, are particularly instructive. The *Crux fidelis* echoes in the *Pange, lingua*, a hymn from the Office for the Feast of Corpus Christi written by St. Thomas Aquinas, hence in use from the Middle Ages.

The *Crux fidelis* explicitly shows Christ's sacrifice on the cross as the fulfillment of three important Scriptural types: the tree, the lamb, and the ark.

> Sing, my tongue,
> The victory of the glorious battle
> And over the trophy of the Cross
> Sing a noble song of triumph:
> How the world's Redeemer,
> Though slain, was victorious.
>
> For the sin of our first parent,
> When with a bite of the fatal fruit
> He rushed headlong into death,
> The Maker, deeply grieving,
> Himself then chose the tree
> To undo the other tree's harm.

. . . .

> When he had completed thirty years,
> Finishing the period of his mortal life,
> The Redeemer, committed to the Passion of his own free will, is
> Lifted up upon the trunk of the
> Cross as the sacrificial lamb.
>
> Having drunk of the gall, behold he swoons!
> With thorn, nail and spear
> They have pierced his tender flesh,
> Blood and water flow forth
> In whose stream the earth, sea,
> Stars and world are washed clean.

. . . .

> You alone were worthy
> To carry the Victim of the world,
> And as an ark, a harbor to prepare
> For a shipwrecked world.

You, the sacred Blood anointed,
Poured forth from the Body of the Lamb.[39]

The *Pange, lingua* recalls the *Crux fidelis* both by using the same first line and by teaching the same doctrine of the salvific value of Christ's sacrifice on the cross:

Sing, my tongue,
The mystery of the glorious Body
And of the precious Blood
Which, as a ransom for the world, the King of nations,
Fruit of a noble womb, poured out.[40]

Finally, since its composition in the sixth century, the *Vexilla regis* has been used as a processional hymn for both Good Friday and the Feast of the Triumph of the Cross:

The standard of the King appears,
The mystery of the Cross shines forth
On which Life endured death
And from death brought forth life.

Life, wounded by the lance's cruel point
So as to wash us clean
From the stains of sin,
Poured forth water and Blood.

Fulfilled were the events that
David prophesied in his unerring song
Addressed to the nations:
God has reigned from the wood.

O gleaming and beauteous tree,
Decked out with the royal purple,
Chosen from a worthy stock
To touch the sacred limbs of God.

Blessed tree, on whose arms   (*Beata, cuius brachiis*)
Hung the ransom of the world: (*Pretium pependit saeculi:*)
Weighed his Body on your balance   (*Statera facta corporis*)
Which carried off the spoils of hell. (*Tulitque praedam tartari.*)

Hail, O cross, our only hope:
    For the Triumph of the Cross:
  In the glory of the triumph
    For Good Friday:
  In this time of Passion
Give added grace to the faithful
And forgive sinners their offenses.

May every spirit together praise you,
O Trinity, spring of salvation:
And to those whom you grant the victory of the Cross,
Give also its reward. Amen.[41]

The two holy days on which this hymn is used are intimately connected, because Christ's triumph on the cross took place on Good Friday. They celebrate the same thing, but in complementary ways: While on Good Friday Catholics mourn that their sins have crucified their loving Creator in the human nature He assumed, they rejoice on the Feast of the Triumph of the Cross that He has redeemed them from sin by laying down His life on the cross. The hymn's appearance on both of these days, which differ so much in character, reinforces the message it proclaims with awe: The cross, an instrument of torture and death, is made the instrument of mankind's redemption and new life. It is the cask in which the sacraments were perfected in efficacy and then poured out upon the world. The cross is called the throne of the King of the universe, and from it Christ reigns with as much power as from the throne of heaven, though here His throne bears the royal purple of His blood, and there the light of glory. And *Statera facta corporis,* that is, the balance of Christ's dead Body having been taken, the cross is lauded as that in virtue of which He carries off "the spoils of hell." The *Vexilla regis* beautifully expresses the doctrinal differences between Good Friday and Holy Saturday that have been discussed in this section on liturgical testimony: the redemptive efficacy of Christ's cross and the salvific effect of His descent.

As may be seen from the unified liturgical testimony of East and West, the glory of God is present in both the mysteries of Good Friday and Holy Saturday, but in very different ways. The glory of Christ crucified is seen only by the eyes of faith, and only in light of His resurrection. The glory of Christ in His descent is that very resurrection light shining in the underworld, infusing the holy dead with the light of glory.

The glorious descent of Christ into hell is nevertheless also the continuation of the Son of God's self-emptying in His incarnation, called His kenosis (see Phil 2:5-8). In this humbling of Himself, Christ assumed a created human nature, and moreover assumed it with certain *defectus*, i.e., without certain perfections to which He would have been entitled in principle as God Incarnate. These defects were passibility and mortality; i.e., Christ could suffer and die. If the Word had assumed human nature with the preternatural gift of immortality, He would not have died, and His body and soul would never have been separated from each other. In His death, however, Christ 'emptied' Himself of the body that was His by His assumption of human nature. (Strictly speaking, Christ 'emptied' Himself of the unity of body and soul; the body and soul themselves always remained united to the Person of the Word.) He then descends to the farthest depths to which a just man can, the abode of the holy dead.

That the profession of Christ's descent is an implicit profession of the reality of His death[42] may seem like a statement of the obvious. In fact, it is extremely important and part of the scandal of the cross. The article of the Descent is a profession unacceptable to those who would deny Jesus died (e.g., docetists, Muslims). Even as the Incarnation testifies to the extravagant love of God (Jn 3:16), so this continuation of Christ's kenosis in a human death and descent reveals the depths of God's love for man: "To earth hast Thou come down, O Master, to save Adam: and not finding him on earth, Thou hast descended into hell, seeking him there."[43] However, unlike other men, Christ descended at will and with power,[44] and moreover His death had vanquished death prior to His descent. Thus, His descent into hell is the limit of Christ's kenotic condescension in the Incarnation for He left nothing undone that could or needed to be done. At the same time, it is the beginning of His glorification in the proper sense of the word.

The liturgical texts make a clear contrast between Good Friday and Holy Saturday. One might ask, however, what happened to Christ after His death, yet before Holy Saturday. It is important to remember that Holy Saturday is the day on which Christ's descent is commemorated, but there was no interlude for Him between His death on the cross and His descent into hell: "When the Saviour shut his eyes upon the cross,/light shone in hell."[45] Thus, as Orthodox theologian Paul Evdokimov rightly says,

> For the earth, [Good Friday] is the day of pain, the burial service, and the tears of the mother of God, but in Hades, on Good Friday, it is already Easter. Christ's power dissipated the darkness in the heart of death's kingdom.[46]

Icons and Tradition

The Church's liturgical texts proclaim her Faith in words. The visual expression of that Faith is found in her liturgical icons. Since the Christian art of iconography is indeed one of the ways in which Tradition is preserved and expressed, icons have dogmatic content and force. Examination of a particular icon, therefore, can lead to understanding something of the truth of the mystery of faith represented in it. However, before we examine the liturgical icon of Christ's descent, the way in which authentic icons preserve Tradition, can be taken as doctrinal statements, and are safeguarded from doctrinal error should be briefly investigated.

According to a pious tradition, the first icon is attributed to St. Luke.[47] If this attribution were more than a legend, icons diligently copied from this model might bear a peculiar relation to apostolic Tradition. It might even be suggested that successors to the apostles could paint icons in an exercise of their teaching office. Yet if copies of the alleged Lucan icon received their authority in a way similar to translations of the Bible, i.e., from being accurate representations of the original, the attribution of one icon to an evangelist is insufficient to justify the multitude of different iconic themes in the Church's history. As for the exercise of the episcopal office through painting, one notes the general absence of bishops who paint with this intention. Hence the connection of icons to Tradition must be sought elsewhere.

Now if an artist intends to paint an image to represent some reality, the resulting work will reflect what he understands to be the truth about that reality. Similarly, aside from admiration based simply on technique or historical interest, a piece of art is appreciated by its viewer because it illustrates some truth, i.e., it reflects something the observer thinks is true. In this way, icons witness to the Faith of those who painted and venerated them. Just so, some images have been officially forbidden by the Church, because they reflect doctrinal confusion or can be interpreted in a seriously misleading way. These prohibitions are not an abstract set of norms that specify every possible aberration, but responses to particular problematic forms as they appeared. Consequently, given the responsive character of magisterial prohibitions in the area, the non-magisterial origin and use of icons, and their ability to express the Faith, it seems safe to say that authentic icons preserve and express apostolic Tradition not so much as exercises of the Magisterium, but rather as expressions of the *sensus fidelium.*

This conclusion does not throw open the door to uncertainty. The Church is *infallibilis in credendo* as well as *in docendo.*[48] These two aspects of the Church's infallibility never authentically conflict with each other, but rather always support each other. In the case of icons, the *sensus fidelium* preserved and expressed in them receives a certain approbation by the Magisterium through their prominent role in Eastern liturgies, which are public prayers of the Church. *Lex orandi, lex credendi.* Insofar as they are public, liturgies are corporate expressions of faith and moments of preaching, falling under the care of the bishops. Of course, not all *objets d'art* used in liturgies are *de facto* approved by the Magisterium. Icons of the Eastern rites are a unique case: They have roots in early Christianity, enjoy almost ubiquitous use in the East, and aim at continuity with the greater Tradition.

The most important continuity at issue is not that of time or style, though these may be significant, but of apostolic Faith: Does the icon preach the truth of the Gospel? The Eastern Fathers of the Church frequently compare icons to books, expressing truth visually through images instead of audibly through words. Hence the Fourth Ecumenical Council of Constantinople decrees that they are to be given the same veneration as the book of Gospels,[49] which transmits God's revelation through words. By representing Christ in the way proper to visual images, through color and form, authentic icons also re-present Christ, and so reveal Him. As a vehicle in the service of Revelation, this preeminent form of Christian art thus has as its subject the figures and events of salvation history, both as recorded in Scripture and as lived by the saints. The very instruments of salvation God Himself used are made present again through their images. Icons thus follow the divine pedagogy of revealing the invisible by means of the visible.

Insofar as icons are intended to preach the Gospel and express the *sensus fidelium,* and insofar as their mode of expression has a certain kind of magisterial approval (i.e., certain forms are allowed in liturgies, others are forbidden to be painted), they may be considered as doctrinal statements. The defenders of icons during the iconoclastic controversies of the eighth and ninth centuries understood very well that icons are doctrinal in nature, not only with respect to the visual elements of an icon, but most especially in regard to the very orthodoxy of representing the Incarnate Word and of venerating Him and His saints through images. Icons reveal the truth of the divine mysteries. The iconophiles fought not for a school of art, but for the true Faith. Thus those who died in their defense are said to have been martyred, not just killed, while the liturgical feast of the victory of Nicaea II over the iconoclasts of the eighth century is called "the Triumph of Orthodoxy."

The preservation of Tradition in these visual doctrinal statements is aided by the relatively strict iconographic canons of color, features, etc., that developed over time as a sort of theological vocabulary of icons. These conventions help safeguard icons from conveying error as long as the viewer knows how to read their visual language. The readings of the day or liturgy during which the icon is given particular prominence also guide the viewer in understanding the meaning of an icon. These texts preach in words the truth revealed in the icon, as the icon reveals visually the truth of the Gospel.

Icons thus have an objective reading. Precisely as her official prayer, the liturgies of the Church are public professions of her Faith. Since these professions of Faith accompany the icons, the liturgical texts state in words the objective content of the icon. In examining the icon of Christ's descent into hell for its doctrinal meaning, one must therefore attend to both the liturgical texts as we have done in the previous section, and to the artistic canon. The liturgical texts are of first importance since some flexibility exists within the artistic canon.

The Icon of the *Anastasis* and Christ's Descent into Hell

Particularly relevant to the Catholic doctrine of Christ's descent into hell is the liturgical icon of the *Anastasis,* which means *resurrection.*[50] Its name and subject matter make evident it is an Easter icon, that is, an icon belonging to the celebration of Christ's victory over sin and death. The name, then, can suggest Christ's own resurrection and that of the saints who rose with Him (Mt 27:52-53), His raising of the holy dead into eternal life during His descent into hell, and the resurrection of the body on the Last Day. This visual multivalency parallels how the Byzantine liturgy knits Descent, Resurrection, and Christian life closely together, as seen earlier. The icon is most frequently interpreted to picture, however, Christ's authoritative action in the limbo of the Fathers. It reveals the same mystery as do the words of the liturgy.

Images of Christ's crucifixion, burial, and resurrection developed only as a result of the resolution of the Christological controversies of the first eight centuries. As early as the beginning of the second century, however, the Fathers were preaching about Christ's journey to the underworld, the reasons for His descent, and how He rose from the dead. By the late fourth century, the doctrine was embodied in poetry, the creed, and the liturgy. As for images, in the sixth century, both the Descent and the Resurrection were suggested by the image of light bursting forth from Christ's tomb.[51] This representation clearly reflects the patristic theology of Christ's sojourn in the realm of the dead. For example, St. John Damascene echoed the metaphor of the setting sun we have seen earlier, saying that, as Christ was "the Sun of Righteousness" for those on earth, so also He would "bring light to those who sit under the earth in darkness and the shadow of death."[52] And St. Athanasius pointed out the dead Christ's undiminished power and freedom, writing, "Christ could not possibly be kept under the bonds of Hades."[53] The stock features of visual representations of the Descent were firmly established by the early eighth century, and individual exemplars from yet earlier are known.[54]

The *Anastasis* icon generally has three groups of figures: Christ drawing forth Adam and Eve from their graves in the center; several identifiable saints, including David, Solomon, and John the Baptist; and a group of unidentifiable holy individuals. Like other icons of events, some *Anastasis* icons show only the most central elements of the mystery while others include more details. The central group of the *Anastasis* icon is clearly the most important, and the discussion here will be restricted to it. Individual icons may vary in some points (e.g., sometimes only Adam is represented as being drawn forth), but these differences do not affect the conclusions that can be drawn from *Anastasis* icons as a genre. The following description is based upon the *Anastasis* image in the church of the Monastery of the Holy Savior in Chora (Istanbul), arguably the finest exemplar ever made; it is depicted on the cover of this book.

In the icon, Christ is dressed in luminous white garments, with a stole upon His arm. He is surrounded by the mandorla of divine glory, a radiant halo encompassing His figure. The drama of His posture bespeaks energy, power, and activity. He grasps Adam and Eve by the wrists, pulling them upwards toward Him. Their limp hands show they are utterly powerless even to assist Him. Christ stands over the shattered gates of hell. Scattered impotently beneath them are emblems of the now-broken power of death and the devil, such as chains, shackles, nails, and keys. Christ's clothing, activity, and mandorla in this icon are in unmistakable contrast to the naked, limp, and apparently merely human Christ in icons of the Crucifixion. On the cross, He suffers; in hades, He acts, and with power.

Adam and Eve are also significant figures in the icon. Adam is dressed in a muter white than the garments of the New Adam. Christ, the "Father of the world to come" (Is 9:6), is Adam's source and exemplar in both the order of creation and of grace. In a parallel fashion to the figure of Adam, Eve's red mantle over blue inner garments is reminiscent of the New Eve, the Blessed Virgin Mary, who is most often represented with similarly colored clothing in other icons. Eve, "the mother of all the living" (Gen 3:20), is by nature the mother of all mankind. At the same time, her figure represents the New Eve, Mary, who is herself a type of the Church and mother by grace of the Church's members. On the Last Day, the Church will be coterminous with Adam and Eve, and those of their descendants who are also Mary's. Thus, by pulling Adam and Eve out of their graves, Christ seems to be taking the Church in hand and raising her as His spotless Bride into the light of His glory.

The multivalent character of the figures of Adam and Eve is further suggested by the fact that both of them wear mantles over blue inner garments. Blue is symbolic of the divine life. For example, in Rublev's well-known icon of the Trinity, the three angels are established in a self-contained community by the light blue under their wings. To suggest how intimately human nature is joined to the divine Person of Christ, other icons usually show Him garbed in a blue mantle over red inner garments (the red representing human nature), when not portrayed in the white of glory. The Blessed Virgin Mary is customarily dressed in the opposite manner, with red over blue; she received the divine life first intimately in her soul through faith and then also in her womb. The corollary in the rest of the children of God, including Adam and Eve, is the presence of God in the soul through grace. Those who are sons in the Son (see 1 Jn 2:29–3:1; Rom 8:16; Gal 4:6) share in the divine life through the inner life of grace, which has its perfection in the beatific vision. The blue inner garments of Adam and Eve hence show they are alive in Christ (Rom 6:4; 1 Cor 15:22) through charity. Furthermore, they see the glory of God, Christ triumphant and surrounded by the mandorla. Garbed in garments of typological significance, the first human parents thus point to the New Adam and the New Eve, and also to all those living the divine life. Between the figures of Adam and Eve, the interior space of the icon opens up to the reader, much as the Rublev icon of the Trinity does, making him a participant in an inviting and, it is to be hoped, anticipatory way.

In other versions of this icon, Christ is depicted holding a cross or a scroll in His left hand, while with His right He pulls Adam out of his grave. The scroll is the "symbol of the preaching of the Resurrection in hell, in accordance with the words of Apostle Peter"[55] (1 Pet 3:19), while the cross is the newly made symbol of victory over death. These variations again indicate the triumphal character of Christ's action in hell.

Non-Iconic Representations of the Descent

Like the Eastern icons, visual Christian art of the West also reflects the traditional teaching of the Church concerning Christ's descent, frequently called in English, "the Harrowing of Hell."[56] Works of Western sacred art do not have the prescribed relation to the liturgy as do the icons. Nevertheless, the uniformity and universality of Western representations of Christ's descent, as well as their harmony with the liturgical icon of the East, indicate an authentic expression of the *sensus fidelium*. Again, the difference of detail among individual works, e.g., "whether Christ holds both Adam and Eve or neither of them, does not matter. These are different ways of visualizing essentially the same thing."[57] The artistic concern is not the photographic representation of an unseen event, but the significance of an article of Faith; this substance remains constant. In Western representations, Christ is usually garbed in the same manner in His descent as in His resurrection: either completely dressed in white, or half-robed with the wounds of His Passion revealed. As in the Byzantine icons, the state of greater and richer dress in comparison to the crucified Christ points to the difference in His situation in the Descent. Light shines forth from Christ, and He has a halo with an inscribed cross.

This description also matches typical representations of Christ at the Last Judgment and, except for the wounds, at His Transfiguration. The common representation indicates a like revelation of glory, quite different from that of the crucified Christ. Images of these three theophanies are differentiated by Christ's posture, among other elements. Christ usually stands in the Transfiguration and sits at the Last Judgment. In the Descent, however, He is more dramatically active: He tramples the devil and pulls Adam forth, while His feet are separated so as to suggest His entrance into hades or His departure.

In the Western representations of the Descent, Christ very frequently carries the standard of the cross, a long and narrow triangular white flag emblazoned with a red cross. Sometimes He wields instead a long, thin, staff-like cross. He usually stands only just inside a doorway, the gate of hell, indicating that His soul did not descend to its farthest depths, gehenna, but only to the holy dead whom He is shown drawing forth. As in the Byzantine icon, Christ grasps the wrist, or occasionally hand, of Adam, drawing him forth from hell, represented by the walls of a fortress, a cave, or the mouth of a large beast. Behind Adam are visible the souls of the just, often depicted with halos and in a posture of supplication. In more elaborate representations, the damned are seen in torments and distinctly separated from the souls Christ leads forth. Again as in the icon, the broken gates of hell are frequently represented, indicating Christ's power, authority, and victory. The image of the defeated devil, shown bound or crushed under Christ's feet, serves a similar purpose.

The *Holkham Bible Picture Book,* an illuminated manuscript from the fourteenth century, affords a stunning example of an elaborate *Harrowing of Hell.*[58] With masterful balance and detail, the artist represents all the major features, but the image is particularly striking for the delicately filigreed limbo of the Fathers. This gazebo-like structure contrasts dramatically with the hellmouth behind it, which holds a simmering cauldron of damned souls. The Holkham representation also belongs to the subset of images that represent Christ in the midst of freeing the just souls, rather than at the beginning with Adam. Adam and Eve already stand behind Christ, on the side away from the various domains of hell, while Christ draws yet another soul forth from the group of praying saints who wait inside the gazebo.

Whatever the relation between the development of the genre in the West and the earliest icons in the East, all the standard elements are present in a non-iconographic style at least as early as the *Tiberius Psalter* of 1050.[59] The *Psalter's* image is particularly noteworthy in its representation of Christ. His long, graceful figure is nearly four times larger than all the others, and he bends down to take the hands of the souls reaching up to Him. Not only are His power and authority thereby manifested, but also His mercy, condescension, and faithful love. The fact that this unique posture of Christ is not copied in other representations suggests first that Christ's stance in the *Tiberius Psalter* is an original feature. Secondly, the lack of duplication implies that other artists recognized it precisely as original and thus not as part of the strict canon of the image. This fact, coupled with the likeness the *Tiberius* image bears to later images in utilizing most of the common features described above, suggests that it stands already as a late descendant in a long lineage. If so, the Western canon was already well established prior to the time of the *Tiberius Psalter*. Indeed, a relief on a silver container of Pascal I (817-824) merely shows Christ with the cross on His shoulder, leading a man dressed similarly to Himself toward an open door. This abbreviated representation indicates the artist's confidence of being understood and thus also a widespread diffusion of similar images.[60] It is important to bear in mind that means of mass reproduction of artwork, including even printing, were still centuries away at the time of both these images. The Church, however, linked the diverse parts of the world and was the font of learning and culture. Thus the universality of the image must be attributed to the universality of the Church's teaching and belief.

Western representations of Christ's descent are not confined to painted media. The same elements appear in illuminated manuscripts, stone reliefs, and poetic, dramatic, and prose representations. For example, in the fourth century, St. Ephraim the Syrian makes clear the triumphal character of Christ's descent to the dead in his *Nisibene Hymns,* particularly Hymns 35-68. His refrains stress Christ's cross as the source of all redemption: "Blessed is He Who has broken the sting of Death by His Cross!" (Hymn 37), "Blessed is He Who has quickened the dead of Sheol by His Cross!" (Hymn 38), "To Thee be glory, Watcher, that didst come down after them that slept: and utter the voice from the Tree, and waken them!" (Hymn 66).[61] The fluidity between the events of the Crucifixion, Descent, and Resurrection observed earlier in the Byzantine liturgical texts is present also in St. Ephraim's works, but likewise there are some verses that are more defined: The "Evil One" sings in Hymn 60 that "I rejoiced when I crucified Him: and I knew not that He was crucifying me, in His crucifixion,"[62] while the refrain of Hymn 65 runs, "To Thee be glory who didst descend and plunge, after Adam: and draw him out from the depths of Sheol, and bring him into Eden!"[63]

After the early centuries of Christianity, of which St. Ephraim's *Hymns* are not the only possible examples, Christ's triumphal descent appears more and more frequently in literary representations. The same major doctrinal features are found in each age, though naturally not found in each work. Individual theological aberrations are not picked up by the stream of artistic consensus. The rejected universalism of the Alexandrian school would be an example: In art of the Descent, the holy dead saved by Christ are clearly separated from the souls of the damned, if these latter are shown at all. An Anglo-Saxon poem bears the same message about Christ's descent as Dante's *Divine Comedy* centuries later, as do plays all across Europe in the intervening years, and even afterward, for example, in seventeenth-century Ukraine.[64] Differences in the mode of expression, or even

> the mythical and fantastic accretions to this doctrine of the Descent over the centuries have nothing to do with its substance . . . — the glorious and revelatory presence of Christ among the dead which brings about the entry of the righteous into glory and testifies to the power of Christ's glorious life over all.[65]

For example, Christ's use of His cross to pin the devil down or to open the gates of hell has symbolic, not literal, significance. The dramatic elements associated with artistic representations of the Descent are intended to show the spiritual reality that Christ, Life itself and the Sun of salvation, cannot be dominated by sin, death, or the devil — and neither are those who are united to Him and participate in His death through baptism and a holy life. This freedom and victory has already been revealed as true in the case of the holy dead at the time of Christ; it is the hope of Christians of all time.

Both the standard Western and Eastern representations of the Descent are consistent with the distinct purposes of the Descent indicated in the magisterial fonts treated in Chapter Two: The drawing forth of Adam and Eve from their graves or from limbo indicates the liberation of the holy dead as a liberation *from* sin, death, and the devil. Yet it is Christ who draws them forth, and He pulls them toward Himself: Here their liberation is seen in its aspect of the beginning of heavenly communion. Finally, the manifestation of Christ's power over the devil is represented in some icons by the figure of a chained devil in the black pit under the graves of Adam and Eve, while in the Western images he is more often prostrate under the feet of Christ.

The voice of non-liturgical art is astonishingly consistent, if not unanimous, in representing Christ's descent. Such unanimity is not the result of a lack of imagination: The astonishing and grotesque torments of damned souls depicted in representations of Christ's descent or the Last Judgment indicate no lack of artistic imagination or willingness to provoke audiences. Artists could have represented Christ suffering in hell — if they had believed it. It seems not to have crossed their minds, at least not up until around the time of the Protestant Reformation. (Even then, references to either extant or lost representations of Christ suffering in hell are extremely rare; I have heard of no more than five.) Nor does it seem artists were mindlessly copying a stock theme that held no resonance for the hearts and minds of their audience. Such sterility would have resulted in the quick death of the genre itself. In fact, differences among the various visual and literary representations suggest that artists understood that some features were of the essence of the genre and were not to be changed, whereas they were quite free with others. For example, dramatic representations of Satan range from portraying him as an almost comic fool to a swaggering braggart. These characterizations reveal something true, but are irrelevant to the Church's teaching on Christ's descent. Such variations are accidental to the content of the work of art, and do not affect the essence of the message.

The message itself is twofold: First, there is reference to a specific act in the course of time, namely, Christ's deliverance of the holy dead from the limbo of the Fathers. Secondly, a representation of the harrowing of hell "signifies Christ's salvation of mankind from sin and death, and it is a statement of a timeless fact, and not a transient scene."[66] According to this second aspect of the message, the believer presently observing the artistic representation of the Harrowing of Hell is invited to make the concrete event his own; i.e., through faith and hope, he desires that he too will one day receive ultimate liberation from sin and death through participation in Christ, even as the holy dead were liberated through the Descent of Christ:

> The beatific vision thus has a special relevance to the harrowing of hell. It was in the Descent into limbo that God revealed His beatific essence to man and the Descent into limbo is the only subject in the life of Christ which can illustrate that most desirable revelation.[67]

The connection between the Descent and the beatific vision is reinforced by the representation of the Good Thief Dysmas in some images of Christ's descent. Christ had promised him, "This day thou shalt be with me in paradise" (Lk 23:43). Hence the image of Dysmas

> reminds us that Christ's presence is paradisiacal, that whoever is with Christ is in paradise, and thus his presence serves the same function as the

gold striations around Christ . . . ; but whereas the glory emphasizes Christ's divinity the companion emphasizes His humanity.[68]

The elements of the Western 'canon' we have examined remain essentially unchanged at least until the mid-sixteenth century, after which representations become much more scarce. In the Catholic world, the decrease of artistic attention does not reflect a change in Catholic doctrine but appears to reflect a change in devotional emphasis.[69] By the Baroque period, one may note a shift in the focus of religious art to Scriptural events that were witnessed, e.g., to Christ's Passion; even depictions of the Resurrection were less favored than images of the post-resurrection appearances of Christ.[70] In addition, the theme of the salvation of the souls in purgatory had became increasingly popular with the Counter-Reformation; viewers of images with this subject matter could identify by faith and hope with those represented much in the way they did earlier in regard to the holy dead in images of Christ's descent.[71]

Conclusion

The similarities between the Eastern iconic representations and the non-liturgical artworks of the West are unmistakable. The agreement is striking, given the great span of time involved and the vast diversity of countries, cultures, and media. Such unanimity, together with its harmony with official Church teaching, strongly suggests that in these works the *sensus fidelium* speaks. The mystery of the triumphal character of Christ's descent penetrated the lives of orthodox Christians down through the ages and across cultural boundaries, to announce itself again and again through diverse media. These works then are truly Christian art, for they preach the Gospel.

According to the testimony of the *sensus fidelium* expressed in these works, Christ's descent is more the beginning of the glory of Easter Day than the continuation of the suffering of Good Friday. Most important of all, the liturgies of the Church testify to the same, thereby also confirming reading the Eastern icon in this way.

Throughout Part One, representative examples from the various *loci theologici* have been examined to determine whether a traditional doctrine of the Descent exists, and what its content is. Such a determination is an essential foundation for the consideration of the work of any individual theologian. As the Second Ecumenical Council of Nicaea states, "Anyone who does not accept the whole of the Church's Tradition, both written and unwritten, *anathema sit.*" From the work of Part One, we may conclude that the creeds, magisterial teaching, Scripture, the liturgy, the consensus of the saints, and the *sensus fidelium* expressed in sacred art speak with one voice and testify that the mystery of Christ's descent was glorious in the first and proper sense of the word. As a consequence, as far as the consensus of these sources goes, interpretations of the Descent that contradict this conclusion are excluded.

Hans Urs von Balthasar's Theology of Christ's Descent into Hell

CHAPTER FIVE

The Descent Event

Hans Urs von Balthasar's presentation of Christ's descent into hell is quite complex. He has few extended treatments, but even these supplement each other and are incomplete individually. Key details are found scattered throughout his corpus. Most often one finds oblique references that only reveal their full significance when read in light of his principal theses. Consequently, the task of Part Two is to introduce these characteristic features. The more thematic consideration in Part Three will address the compatibility between Balthasar's theology of the Descent and Catholic doctrine, particular attention being paid to overarching issues of Christology and methodology. But since it is good to have some idea of the solidity of one step's foundation before taking the next step, questions related to details of his thought are raised along the way of our exposition here in Part Two. Precision demands they be treated in direct conjunction with the quotations used or the position summarized.

Balthasar's principal theses on the Descent fall into three groups. The first treats what happened to Christ in His descent in a general way. The second group sets forth the differing involvement of the Father, Son, and Holy Spirit in the Descent event. In the final group, the significance of this Christological and Trinitarian event is applied to other major branches of theology. Part Two is structured according to these three groups: Chapter Five corresponds to the first group, Chapters Six through Eight to the second, and Chapter Nine to the third.

With regard to what happened to Christ in the Descent, three points repeatedly appear in Balthasar's treatments of Christ's passion and descent. First, His descent is a continuation of His cross. Second, the expiatory suffering

Christ undergoes in His descent surpasses that of the cross. Finally, Christ is definitively "made sin" (2 Cor 5:21) for man's redemption in His descent experience. Because Christ's descent is particularly important for Balthasar as a descent of the *Son,* i.e., as a Trinitarian event, the full import of these themes and their basis in Balthasar's texts will become more evident in Chapters Six to Eight. But already in this chapter the differences between his theology of the Descent and the traditional doctrine will be clear. As we shall see, he himself makes the contrast explicit.

The Descent as Continuation of the Cross

As we saw in Part One, the traditional Catholic doctrine holds that the redemptive suffering of Christ on the cross gives way to the glorification of His whole soul in His descent and the manifestation of His glory to the holy dead. In contrast, the first key characteristic of Balthasar's theology of Christ's descent into hell is that he understands the Descent as a continuation of Christ's cross, both in terms of suffering and in terms of its redemptive value. Christ's sojourn in the realm of the dead "should be conceived as the efficacious outworking in the world beyond of what was accomplished in the temporality of history."[1] This formulation may sound as if Balthasar is referring to the application of the fruits of redemption as in the traditional doctrine, but the Descent for him seems to be the 'fruit' of the Cross only insofar as it follows upon Christ's crucifixion and is made possible by His death. He develops the relation between the two in a very different way: The Descent is the same reality as the Cross, but under a different aspect, what will be called a "moment."[2] What Christ did in time and place on the cross, He completes outside the time and place of the living after His death.

Cross and Descent are distinguished according to opposing features, something like the back and front of a coin. The Passion of the living Christ is called "subjective and active," whereas the experience of the dead Christ is "contemplative and objective (passive)."[3] In this context, "subjective" and "active" are basically synonymous; they signify the agency of a subject, his acts. In contrast, what is "objective" happens to someone who is passive in the face of the event. This passivity is characterized by receptivity, as opposed to agency. In this reception, the passive subject contemplates, as it were, an event or the action of another.

Balthasar employs these contraries, albeit in a sense somewhat different from their normal use, to stress that death drastically changes the subject's capacity for action. For him, death "signifies in the first place the abandonment of all spontaneous activity and so a passivity. . . ."[4] "Forms of activity that are new and yet prolong those of earth" are categorically not to be ascribed to the dead.[5] Holy Saturday thus is a "contemplative . . . moment," a vision passively experienced by the soul,[6] for activity has ceased in the powerlessness of the grave.[7]

Balthasar thus rejects the verb *descend* as giving to the mystery "the unintended and unexamined meaning of an action such as, at root, only a living man, not a dead one, can perform."[8] *Descend* may also misleadingly suggest that the realm of the dead is located "below" in a physical way.[9] Finally, as Christ was passive in His "going to heaven"[10] (i.e., in His resurrection and ascension), because "the active agent is God (the Father),"[11] so His parallel going to the realm of the dead should likewise be understood to have been passive. Thus, argues Balthasar, "Should we not be content, rather, to speak of a '*being* with the dead'?"[12] "Being dead" has "absolute passivity."[13]

It should be noted that, with respect to certain interior acts, Balthasar will not maintain this contrast between *active* and *passive* strictly. For example, obedience out of love "is anything but 'passive,'"[14] even though it entails the determination of one person by another in some respect: The person is active formally in willing to obey, but he is passive materially in that what he wills is determined by another. This passivity is heightened when his obedience means letting something be done to him. In this latter case, he is receptive both to the will and to the act of another.[15] Obedience then is "consenting passivity."[16] Hence Jesus' passivity in death is dependent upon His prior (active) choice to give Himself up obediently to it.[17]

Balthasar protests the "active" portrayal of Christ's descent in "liturgical, speculative and rhetorical-popular theology,"[18] i.e., in the sources seen in Part One. In the same place, he also raises the interesting question of how Jesus' descent was different from all other mythic or Scriptural 'descents' (e.g., "from Orpheus and Odysseus to Enoch, John, Aeneas and Dante"[19]). His answer is that all these others go down alive, but Jesus is truly dead in His descent. He therefore concludes that He cannot be active as the living are, but His condition must be that of the dead: "lifeless, powerless, without effect, and above all without contact with God or thus either with his fellow human beings."[20] Balthasar's eye has caught a fascinating contrast among the 'descents,' literary and real. Based upon the Catholic Tradition of Christ's descent, however, a different conclusion can be drawn: All others but Christ can only go down to the dead if they are alive, because if they were dead, they would not be "free among the dead" (Ps 87:6), as the dead Christ was. This conclusion is consistent with the principle that in Christ's works are manifest both His humanity and His divinity. He descends because He is truly human, but the manner of His descent (active and in power) reveals His divinity.

With his critique of the use of *descend*, Balthasar stresses that the significance of the mystery of Holy Saturday lies in what happens in the realm of the dead itself, and not so much in the transition to this abode from that of the living. This emphasis is correct, since death is the common term, or cusp, between life and the state of being dead. It is not a third moment between the two, for one is dead only when one has ceased living completely. *Dying*, after all, is the tending toward imminent death, but by a person who is still living. Like Balthasar in this regard, Catholic Tradition concerns itself with Christ's sojourn in the underworld, not His going there. (Although some dramas and poems depict Christ's soul *approaching* the gates of hell in a bright light, this literary technique merely extends the dramatic time for manifesting events and their significance; the 'approach' still relates to events *in* the realm of the dead, since only the dead come to those gates.) Thus our earlier chapters stressed the necessity of understanding the *inferos* of the credal article, not the *descendit*. Whether Balthasar is correct to protest against the active implications of *descend* in this context depends in part upon whether the Descent was actually glorious in the first imposition or not. Perhaps he is being somewhat overly strict, however: As he himself points out, the going to the dead "is taken for granted, and identified, simply, with what it is to be genuinely dead. . . ."[21] One is either dead or alive. Balthasar's rigor in this case largely reflects his prior commitment to the passivity of Christ in His descent. In any case, his portrayal of the passivity of Christ after death contrasts explicitly with the power and authoritative action of Christ in the underworld traditionally ascribed to Him.[22]

Balthasar is also right to emphasize that death effects a drastic change in a subject's capability for acting. However, what this change is and whether it is detrimental are questions of metaphysical and anthropological analysis that Balthasar does not undertake in treating of Christ's death. Balthasar's approach to death is largely existential and literary.[23] One difficulty with this approach is that one cannot reason with necessity from one person's existential experience to that of another. The only feature common to all deaths, and hence necessary in the death of Christ, is the separation of body and soul (and whatever may stand in necessary connection to this separation, such as the soul's going to an abode of the dead, i.e., its continued existence separate from the body). Moreover, other than the possible value of near-death experiences, which Balthasar does not invoke, testimony about the experience of death is actually testimony about the experience of *dying*, or else the construct of literary imagination. A more certain basis of argument is necessary. Still, Balthasar asserts, "The condition of being dead, and not the 'separation' [of body and soul], is what is essential. . . ."[24] In context, Balthasar is directing his reader's attention away from the question of how the body and soul of Jesus continue to subsist in the Word, despite being separated from each other. For Balthasar, this question is not of interest (or even of importance); rather attention should be given to Jesus' state of being dead, by which he means not the separation of body and soul (which is one way to speak of His condition of being dead), but rather Christ's subjective experience of that state.

In Catholic anthropology, however, it makes no sense to oppose the condition and the separation for they are defined in terms of each other.[25] Balthasar characterizes this identity as one of Greek anthropology, which "evades the essential issue,"[26] "for this truly being dead is a function of the total surrender of the Son."[27] We have already had cause in Chapter Three to argue that the body-soul distinction is also Scriptural. Regarding whether the separation of body and soul is "essential" or not, it would be well to recall that the Catholic Faith proclaims the saving *death* of Christ. That death happens on the cross, and is not the same as His state of being dead, since death is exactly the boundary between that state and the state of life. If there is a real hiatus in the paschal mystery, it is the instant of Christ's death, not His being dead. Hence, if Christ's death is of eminent importance, and death is the separation of body and soul, then this separation itself must be worth considerable attention.[28]

Balthasar does not deny in general that death is the separation of body and soul;[29] it is just that he does not generally consider the implications of this separation for Christ other than to assert that it means absolute passivity for Him. Note that this position implies the body is the key principle that enables a man's activity. This conclusion is supported by the fact that Balthasar characterizes the Passion of the living Christ as active in contrast to the passive Descent, despite often stressing how Christ is passively burdened with sin, whipped, crucified, etc. Identifying the body as the principle of activity in turn calls into question, e.g., the soul's being able to love after death. The possibility of activity for a separated soul in general, and for the soul of the Incarnate Word in particular, is not discussed by Balthasar. Perhaps as a result of his reluctance to consider at any length death as the separation of body and soul, Balthasar rarely speaks of the Son descending in His human soul, or of the reunion of Christ's body and soul in His resurrection. Balthasar most commonly speaks about "the Word" or "the Son," sometimes about "Jesus," and occasionally about "Christ" in this context. As we shall see, this usage is consistent with his doctrine of the Descent as the most perfect expression of the Son's *Trinitarian* personality. Balthasar treats Christ's death so much in this way that the factual separation of His human body and soul apparently does not merit much consideration. Balthasar's reluctance to consider Christ's death in relation to this separation will become notable. If act flows from being — and the Descent is precisely an expression of the God that the Son is, according to Balthasar — then the extent to which the separation of His body and soul conditions the Son's activity in His human nature is not irrelevant. That is, not unless His humanity in general is.

Since Balthasar does not examine death from the perspective of a metaphysical anthropology, his idea of the passivity of being dead must derive from some other principle. This principle appears to be his concept of the abode of the dead in Scripture. According to Balthasar, the realm of the dead up until the death of Christ was uniformly the Sheol of the Old Testament, as understood prior to any pagan influences that led to expecting diverse fates for the just and the unjust.[30] (As is more or less customary in English translations of Balthasar's work, *sheol* will be capitalized when it is to be taken in Balthasar's sense rather than the traditional one.) He rejects the division of the underworld prior to the consummation of Christ's redemptive work. "As for a Hell of infants, of that we know nothing,"[31] he says, while it is only Christ's own experience of Sheol that gives both purgatory and the hell of the damned definitive existence:[32] Christ is the first to move from the abode of the dead to heaven, and only afterward does purgatory as a state of transition make sense.[33] Similarly, eternal punishment is only possible after Christ has taken possession of the knowledge of Sheol as the fate of man without a redeemer, in order that He may thereby judge in light of it.[34] Since the differentiation of the underworld is the result of Christ's sojourn there, an abode of the holy dead existing up until the time of Christ's descent does not make sense in Balthasar's scheme, unless perhaps as a milder form of the Sheol Christ undergoes.[35]

The single realm of the dead, Sheol, is characterized by darkness and powerlessness (hence passivity).[36] It is the place where, without Christ, humanity would have been weighted down with the penalty for which original sin, not to mention actual sin, is sufficient, namely, the "deprivation of the vision of God."[37] It is the exclusion from God's eternal Life.[38] Hence there is a great solitude,[39] for "in death, every communication ends, not only with men, but also with God."[40] Sheol is "the summation of everything that resists God's sway, that cannot be united to God and is, as such, rejected by God."[41] Instead of eternal bliss, there is eternal sinfulness, a "second 'chaos'"[42] of human freedom run amok that fiendishly apes in the end that chaos out of which God brought order in the beginning. Note that exclusion from God's life necessarily implies the lack of grace. Balthasar does not explain such Scriptural texts as Psalm 139:8 *RSV* ("If I make my bed in sheol, Thou art there!") and Matthew 22:32 (in which Jesus says, in relation to the dead patriarchs Abraham, Isaac, and Jacob, that God is "not the God of the dead, but of the living").[43]

But Sheol, as an abode of the dead, is not a place in the spatial sense. Based upon the "existential . . . tenor"[44] of the Old Testament texts and the subsequent fluidity with which theologians switch between the themes of place and condition,[45] Balthasar considers Sheol really to be a "psychic" or "spiritual" condition.⁴⁶ His concern is to avoid any suggestion of the "mythical three-storey world-picture,"⁴⁷ which surely has an influence on his view of "Christ's 'descent' into (we do not say the 'place,' but) the 'state' of perdition."⁴⁸

According to the traditional Catholic doctrine, Christ did not experience the pain proper to any of the abodes of the dead. In contrast, Balthasar essentially argues that, if Sheol is a spiritual condition, Christ must experience that condition in Himself. In His incarnation, the Son became a true man and thus also died a true human death; He "was really dead,"⁴⁹ as Balthasar takes great pains to emphasize. Being truly dead means that, even as Christ "was in solidarity with the living, so, in the tomb, he is in solidarity with the dead"⁵⁰ in their condition. But if Sheol is an undifferentiated condition for all the dead and if Christ is solidary with the dead, then He also experiences the same condition of gloom, powerlessness, and radical solitude. Indeed, more than that, because "for the death of Christ [by which, Balthasar is speaking of His state of being dead] to be inclusive, it must be simultaneously exclusive and unique in its expiatory value."⁵¹ That is, if Christ's being dead is to be efficacious for the salvation of all, it must be a being dead that goes beyond all others (and is thereby "exclusive and unique").

> Christ's ability to do this [encounter the underworld in a salvific way] is owing to his unique being and mandate. According to the Christian understanding, this uniqueness implies the mystery of the Trinity. . . .⁵²

That is, the specific character of His descent derives from the fact that the Person of Christ is one of the Trinity.

Three features here are particularly striking: first, the expiatory value of Christ's descent, which will be considered in this section; second, the greater intensity of Christ's experience of Sheol, which will be treated in the next; and third, the claim that Christ's Trinitarian personality makes this experience possible. This final, specifically Trinitarian characteristic will receive detailed treatment in the following chapters, particularly Chapter Seven. All three features will reveal continuity and intensification in the movement from Cross to Descent.

Let us see now how this is so with regard to the first. According to Balthasar, Christ's being dead is expiatory. Traditionally, His descent was understood as the first application of the fruit of salvation, now available through the perfect expiation of the cross. And although Balthasar says Christ's work of redemption remains "fundamentally finished *(consummatum est!)* on the Cross,"⁵³ he nevertheless argues,

> ["]Now the penalty which the sin of man brought on was not only the death of the body. It was also a penalty [that] affected the soul, for sinning

was also the soul's work, and the soul paid the price in being deprived of the vision of God. As yet unexpiated, it followed that all human beings who lived before the coming of Christ, even the holy ancestors, descended into the *infernum*. And so, in order to assume the entire penalty imposed upon sinners, Christ willed not only to die, but to go down, in his soul, *ad infernum*.["][54] . . . [T]his act of sharing constituted the term and aim of the Incarnation. . . . [For] only what has been endured is healed and saved.[55]

Balthasar's argument here concludes that Christ's sharing in the experience of being dead, i.e., His descent, is the ultimate goal of the Incarnation. The argument is founded on two premises: The first, that Christ descended into hell to assume the general penalty imposed on the soul after the Fall, comes from St. Thomas Aquinas. The second, "Only what has been endured is healed and saved," Balthasar attributes to St. Irenaeus. This latter attribution, however, is not correct; the cited text does not mention the maxim and I do not know what other part of St. Irenaeus' work Balthasar may have had in mind.

Elsewhere Balthasar credits a similar principle to St. Gregory Nazianzen, namely, "What was not assumed was not redeemed."[56] Here the attribution is correct: In an anti-Apollinarian letter (Ep. 101), St. Gregory wrote, Τό γὰρ ἀπρόσληπτον, ἀθεράπευτον. The English translation *redeemed* is an accurate rendition of the corresponding word in Balthasar's German version of St. Gregory's principle ("Was nicht übernommen wird, wird nicht gerettet"), but would be a rather free translation of *atherapeuton*, which is better translated *healed*. More important, note that St. Gregory used the verb ἀπρόσληπτον (assume),[57] but the principle Balthasar wrote and attributed to St. Irenaeus has "endured" ("das Erlittene"[58] in the original German). All significations listed in the extensive entry s.v. προσλαμβάνω in Lampe's *A Patristic Greek Lexicon* (Oxford: Clarendon, 1961) are related to the taking up of something, and none to *endure*. The situation is the same in the entries of derivative words. The anti-Apollinarian context of the maxim confirms this reading, even if there were no doubt about the word itself. Thus both the natural reading of the word and its context militate against translating it as "endured."

The maxim stated by St. Gregory is frequently found in patristic theology. In contrast, it would appear Balthasar's second premise, the one he attributes to St. Irenaeus, is a principle of Balthasar's own, i.e., it does not have the patristic authority Balthasar suggests it has. The importance of the substitution of *endured* for *assumed* cannot be overestimated. Balthasar's principle takes suffering as the *formal* principle of Christ's redemptive work:[59] Christ's experience in Sheol must be like the suffering unredeemed man deserved to experience there and His endurance of this state is expiatory. In contrast, it would be more along patristic lines to see Christ's suffering as a *material* principle of redemption, made efficacious through union with the Divinity; or, as St. Thomas Aquinas would say, it was made meritorious through the formal principle of charity.[60]

We must ask then, what does Balthasar mean when he says that Christ's redemptive work was "fundamentally finished . . . on the Cross," yet argues that it nonetheless continues *ad infernum?* The Catholic Faith is unambiguous that it is the sacrifice of the cross that accomplishes the redemption of man.[61] When Balthasar says "fundamentally finished," does he mean 'mostly finished' such that Christ's work in the underworld is merely a nonessential accessory to the main action and resolution that has already taken place? The importance Balthasar gives to Christ's sojourn among the dead would alone preclude this interpretation.

Rather, in Balthasar's view, the cross is the locus of man's redemption insofar as the sins of the world are fully transferred to Christ hanging upon it. "It is possible to distinguish between sin and the sinner,"[62] he says, "distinguish" here being used not in the sense of conceptual analysis, but in the sense of a real separation. "Because of the energy that man has invested in it, sin is a reality, it is not 'nothing.'"[63] Thus this reality of sin, which is not merely a defect, may be separated from the sinner and loaded upon another.[64] Sin "has been isolated from the sinner";[65] it "has been separated from the sinner by the work of the Cross."[66] The burden of all the world's sin began to be loaded upon Christ in the Garden of Gethsemane, but upon the cross, this transfer is complete.[67] Thus at this point, even before Christ's death, all mankind is truly freed from guilt. Their sins and guilt are no longer theirs, but have been loaded upon Christ, since "nothing would be achieved by men unloading their sin if the one onto whom they load it were incapable of receiving it in its totality, as *what it is.* . . ."[68] Thus Balthasar can identify Redeemer and sinner, saying, "God in human form died the death of a redeemer (that is, of a sinner)."[69] It is due to this personal assumption of the world's sin by Christ that His work of liberating man from his sin and guilt is "fundamentally finished . . . on the Cross."

Christ's *work* is also finished on the cross because, through it as the instrument of His death, He descends to His passive experience in the realm of the dead, in virtue of which the actual reconciliation of God to the fallen world will be accomplished. "Here lies the 'unfathomable' (Eph 3:8) mystery of the Cross, in the momentum of the collision of the entire burden of sin with the total powerlessness of the kenotic existence."[70] This "collision" defines Christ's experience in the realm of the dead, as we shall see in the following chapters. It is the "key to the interpretation of the event of the Cross,"[71] which will grant access to the "'unsearchable riches' (Eph 3:8) [that] lie 'hidden' (Col 2:3)" in it,[72] that is, in Sheol. The Cross "shows nothing any longer of its glory, but nevertheless *contains* the whole of the glory to which the signs [in the Gospel of John] are pointing."[73] Thus it is "the embodiment and summing up of the entire lifework of Jesus"[74] in that it is the *visible* sign of the perfect accomplishment of Christ's mission which culminates in His descent, out of sight of all human eyes. In this way, the Descent is the continuation of the Cross as its invisible counterpart and peak.

The unity of Balthasar's work requires that any references to the centrality of the Cross be read with its unity with the Descent in mind, since the Cross is incomplete without the Descent, as is explicit when Balthasar speaks of "Good Friday, with death's Holy Saturday in it."[75] The Descent is the continuation of the Cross insofar as the reconciliation of God with the world, begun on the Cross, is completed in Sheol, a reconciliation manifested in Christ and applied personally to Him through His being raised from Sheol to new life. At the beginning of a section focusing on soteriology in the *Theo-Drama*, Balthasar makes the breadth of "the Cross" as a specialized term clear, saying, "Here and in what follows, the 'Cross' is always used in the Pauline-Johannine sense — which is also that of the Synoptics — that is, including the Resurrection."[76] "The Cross" thus often signifies what Balthasar also calls the "hour" of Jesus, which begins with His agony in Gethsemane and lasts until His resurrection.[77] It is in this expanded sense of the Cross as an event that includes Holy Saturday that many of Balthasar's references to it must be taken.[78] Thus, for example, "the event of the Cross" from which "the final epiphany and δόξα [glory] of God's Word spreads forth"[79] is not the Cross in isolation from the Descent, but in its unity with it.[80] The peak of the "hour" and of "the event of the Cross" is not the Crucifixion, however, but the Descent. This claim and the distinction made here between the redemption of mankind on the Cross and the ultimate reconciliation of God through the Descent may seem premature, but they will be seen to be an accurate representation of Balthasar's thought as his theology of Christ's descent is elaborated in what follows. Although some of his statements on the Cross are susceptible of a different interpretation if read in isolation from his theology of the Descent, this ambiguity gives way to the clear distinction made here when they are read in the context of his corpus.

The Expiatory Suffering of the Descent Surpasses That of the Cross

The second central thesis of Balthasar's *descensus* theology is that the expiatory suffering Christ undergoes in His descent surpasses that of the cross in virtue of His more intense experience of Sheol. As Balthasar sees it, Sheol is a condition of the soul after death, characterized by darkness and powerlessness. But this description is still very much an external one. To understand the essence of Sheol, one must bear in mind that, if man had not been redeemed, Sheol would have been the eternal punishment for sin through the deprivation of the vision of God. Through sin, death entered the world (Rom 5:12) — not only physical death, but also the death of the soul (see Ezek 18:20), which is the loss of God's life of grace. Since physical death and spiritual death are linked intimately together, Balthasar stresses they should not be distinguished from each other in texts such as Romans 14:9, "For to this end Christ died and lived again, that he might be Lord both of the dead and of the living."[81] Likewise, in 1 Peter 3:18-20, "physical death and spiritual death are inseparable."[82] If they are not distinguished, then "the interior death of sin . . . is the *terminus a quo* of the common Resurrection, both Christ's and that of those who are dead 'because of their misdeeds,'"[83] i.e., of all other men. Again, the scars in Christ's risen body reveal His "unique experience of death that is both spiritual and bodily."[84]

Now the state of grace, which is the life of the soul as a participation in the life of God, entails the presence of God, who is wholly present wherever He is, even if participation in God's life is perfected for a soul only in the state of glory. Thus it seems that, in Balthasar's view, the deprivation of the vision of God necessarily entails the loss of the interior presence of God, i.e., grace. Indeed Balthasar presents a dialectical problem: On the one hand, "hell, the eternal exclusion from the presence of God,"[85] accrues as a penalty to original sin, not to mention actual, personal sin.[86] This penalty would exclude hope, for hope as a theological virtue informed by charity is already a true anticipation of the vision of God, a participation through grace in His life. Possession of hope (and likewise, faith and love) would seem to weaken both the force of the penalty and any sense of waiting for Christ as not yet present.[87] Hence Balthasar effectively denies Christian faith, hope, and charity to the dead Old Testament fathers, saying, "as long as the bonds of death have not been broken through, [faith, hope, and charity] are limited in the Old Covenant to earthly and mortal life. . . ."[88]

> On the other hand, before Christ there was already . . . an order of salvation oriented towards Christ which in some way makes it possible, in cooperation with the grace of God, to be 'just' and thus, in the midst of the *poena damni*, to await 'redemption.'[89]

Balthasar then suggests a solution that would preserve both poles without "naively"[90] opting for one or the other: "If through the grace of Christ, working by anticipation, those who lived before Christ in love did not experience the entire, truly merited, *poena damni* (since they waited for him in the light of faith, hope and charity),"[91] — and yet this penalty of the soul must be endured in order to be expiated,[92] — "who then did really experience it save the Redeemer himself?"[93]

According to Balthasar, Christ's abiding in Sheol is both a more intense and a more extensive experience of Sheol than that of the souls awaiting Him there. As Franco Giulio Brambilla summarizes,

> Such a movement through which the Descent of one alone into the abyss is transformed into the ascent of all presupposes the "for all" of the Descent, that He may be the prototype of the resurrection: and exactly for this reason it is salvific.[94]

If then through physical death, one's soul is inducted into the spiritual death that is the punishment for sin — and if not everyone experiences this punishment to the full extent, that is only because the Redeemer did — the Redeemer's abandonment by God before death must not only continue but intensify after His death, and must be far worse than anyone else's experience of the abode of the dead. This argument actually supports both the expiatory value of Christ's descent and the extremity of His suffering in it — and it means Christ in His descent is solidary with sinners "in their — ultimately hopeless — separation from God."[95]

Balthasar's position contrasts with the traditional consensus, which holds that Christ did not experience the pain proper to any of the abodes of hell and that His descent was not meritorious, but rather in it He conveyed beatitude on the holy dead. In consequence of his position, Balthasar will also deny that Christ had the beatific vision, particularly on the cross or in His descent, as this would render "innocuous"[96] Christ's redemptive physical death on the cross and His experience of the spiritual death of Sheol.

Let us now examine this penalty in more detail. For Balthasar, just as the first descent — from heaven, in the Incarnation — ended with the death of the body, just so Christ's second descent — in soul to the state of being dead — culminates with death, the death of the soul. This 'second death' is the "term and aim of the Incarnation"[97] since it is the "utmost pitch"[98] of the Son's obedience and hence of His mission. It therefore will definitively accomplish man's redemption and establish Christ as eschatological judge.[99]

What is this 'second death' that Christ must experience in Sheol, this death of the soul due to sin? It has been said that the relationship between mortal sin (with its loss of grace) and death (which would necessarily be followed by hell, were it not for the Redeemer) means spiritual and physical death need not be sharply distinguished, at least not before the resurrection of Christ. A conceptual link is thus established between the (negative) exclusion from the presence of God, including the lack of grace, and the (positive) terrors of hell. To characterize the experience of its horror, Balthasar draws upon Nicholas of Cusa, pointing out that Nicholas spoke "of a vision of the (second) death, a *visio mortis.*"[100] Balthasar says "Nicholas of Cusa was fundamentally right,"[101] referring to a passage he had quoted:

> The vision, *visio,* of death by the mode of immediate experience, *via cognoscentiae,* is the most complete punishment possible. . . . Christ's suffering, the greatest one could conceive, was like that of the damned who cannot be damned any more. That is, his suffering went to the length of infernal punishment *(usque ad poenam infernalem).* . . . He wanted to experience the *poena sensus* like the damned in Hell for the glorifying of his Father. . . .[102]

It is worth noting that Nicholas of Cusa, at least in the passage that Balthasar quotes, attributes explicitly only the *poena sensus* to Christ. Balthasar will go beyond this, however, in his own theology. He had, after all, only said Nicholas of Cusa was *"fundamentally* right." Balthasar characterizes Christ's experience in Sheol in two ways: In one, he stresses hell as the absence of the presence of God;[103] in the other, he emphasizes the *visio mortis* of Sheol.[104] Since the abandonment by God experienced by Christ makes possible His *visio mortis,* and His *visio mortis* entails His union with what is contrary to God,[105] these two presentations cannot be set over against each other as if they conflicted. Setting aside any questions about the nature of being, not-being, and the contrary of being, the unity of the two approaches might be expressed thus: Where God is not, there is what-is-not-God, in the sense of what-is-contrary-to-God.

"God has redeemed us," Balthasar reminds his reader, from "nothing less than hell, the eternal exclusion from the presence of God."[106] Our Savior, "conformed to his brethren even in this,"[107] descended into it, suffering it vicariously for the redemption of the world. If the Son is to bear the sin of the world as His own, out of solidarity with sinners He must also experience the separation from God that is the essential consequence of sin.[108] He will go "into ultimate perdition" and the "estrangement from God of hell" such that "he experiences the complete godlessness of lost man."[109] As the Redeemer, Christ experienced this reality of the abandonment by God inherent in sin and that of dying "into the darkness of eternal death . . . more deeply and definitely than any mere creature can experience such things."[110]

This *visio mortis* that Christ has in virtue of His being dead helps explain how His being dead is a "contemplative and objective (passive) moment."[111] Being dead is "objective," i.e., passive, because the dead are powerless[112] and the "vital activity" of the living has ceased.[113] Christ descends "in an obedience that has been humiliated to the point of being pure matter, the absolutely cadaver-like obedience that is incapable of any active gesture of solidarity. . . ."[114] In His perfect obedience, Christ becomes absolutely passive to the point of suffering-as-thing: He disposed Himself completely to be wholly disposed by another even to the point of being disposed of in the "sewer" of Sheol, the refuse incinerator of "Gehenna."[115] (Note Balthasar is explicit: Using the traditional distinction of the abodes of the dead, he says, "Christ descended not merely to *sheol* but to *gehenna* in a purely objective victory, which he would experience subjectively in his final abandonment by God."[116]) Passivity as a receptive suffering-as-thing would explain Balthasar's use of *objective* as a synonym for *passive*. Indeed, he not infrequently describes Christ as the "object" of God's wrath, which is to be understood not merely in the sense of *that toward which something is directed,* but also in the sense of *a thing:* Christ is, as it were, the target board that is the target of God's wrath.[117] Over against His passivity stand the active wrath of the Father and the seething horror of the *visio mortis:*

> In this solitude [of the abandonment of the Cross (and *a fortiori* that of Sheol)], he is not left alone, for 'terrors are turned' actively and aggressively upon him (Job 30:15).
>
> The true subject who acts on the Cross is therefore God [the Father], and the instrument he employs in acting is sin,[118]

which the Father "loads"[119] upon the Son.

Note here that Balthasar preserves Christ's "vital activity" insofar as He is still capable of intellection and volition: Christ knows the contents of the *visio mortis* and He continues to obey and love the Father. Moreover, for a subject with a will and the power to prevent his suffering, to suffer-as-thing requires the continual will not to resist and such willing is a vital activity. What Balthasar wants to deny is the sort of "vital activity" ascribed to Christ in the traditional doctrine, i.e., the furthering of a goal by action rather than passion.

Being dead is "contemplative" both because the soul is passive, and because it is subject to images.[120] *Image* indicates both the reality apprehended and its intimacy with the knower in the *visio.*[121] The representation that characterizes Sheol is the *visio mortis,* the infernal vision that substitutes for the *visio Dei* in the soul deprived of it by sin. This vision, like the beatific vision, is no external matter; it is experienced by the soul in the most intimate way. "The reality of the *poena damni* is spiritual and can be experienced only spiritually."[122] As St. Thomas says that God unites Himself to the human intellect in the beatific vision,[123] so Balthasar says that the extremity of contemplative powerlessness of the soul in Sheol

> can and must be one with the object of his vision: the second death which, itself, is one with sheer sin as such, no longer sin as attaching to a particular human being, . . . but abstracted from that individuation, contemplated in its bare reality as such. . . . The object of the *visio mortis* can only be the pure substantiality of 'Hell' which is 'sin in itself.'[124]

This condition is specifically that of Christ's soul in Sheol, for He alone is to experience its full force.

Sin is no longer "attached" to individuals in the *visio mortis,* because Christ took all sins from all men in order to be "made sin" (2 Cor 5:21) and assume them on the Cross. Each individual's sins are assumed by Christ, in order that each individual may be redeemed as such.[125] "In this amorphous condition, . . . in [this] separation between sin and the living man," sin in Sheol "is then precisely the product of the active suffering of the Cross."[126] As was said, mankind is fundamentally redeemed by the crucifixion, but the work of redemption remains to be perfected in Sheol through Christ's experience of the *visio mortis.* Christ thus contemplates in Sheol the triumph of the Cross, says Balthasar, though not from the perspective of the Resurrection, but through "the one and only condition which allows such immediate contact [with it], namely, the absolute emptying of life," physical and spiritual, "which he knew as the Dead One."[127]

The "contemplative" nature of the *visio mortis* stresses its immanence: "The experience of the abyss he undergoes is . . . entirely in him (insofar as he comes to know in himself the full measure of the dead sinner's distance from God)."[128] "Sin in itself" and this "distance" is not simply "in Him" as the object known is in the knower when he sees something outside himself; more, it is "in him" because He is conformed to it in His being, He is "literally 'made sin' (2 Cor 5:21)."[129] Christ identifies Himself not only "with the *status* of sinners," but also "ultimately with the sin of all sinners."[130] If not, if the *visio mortis* were to remain only an external object apprehended, mankind would still be in its sins;[131] Christ's Passion would be a brief physical event from which His spirit remains essentially detached;[132] His descent experience would amount to a mere intellectual knowledge; and the "distance" of sin would not be taken into the "distance" between the Trinitarian relations or consumed in the fire of the divine love.[133] No, what is called for is "an *inner* appropriation of what is ungodly and hostile to God, an identification with that darkness of alienation from God into which the sinner falls as a result of his No."[134] "In him" thus indicates the formal aspect of His *visio mortis*. The material aspect — the deprivation of the *visio Dei* and the presence of the *visio mortis* of "sin in itself" — has already largely been described, though Balthasar also characterizes it as the self-alienation of the divine Son, "because what he experiences is utterly foreign to him (as the eternal Son of the Father)."[135] The *visio mortis* thus is both "entirely in Him" and "entirely outside of Him."[136] Note that *in* and *out* are not used as real contraries, but *in* describes the formal aspect of how Jesus is "made sin," and *out* the material aspect of what this being "made sin" consists. Jesus must undergo from the inside out all that had alienated mankind from God in sin and anti-godly acts without distancing Himself from it, so that, as Balthasar interprets St. Paul, He may literally be "made sin" for us.

According to Balthasar, then, Christ's experience of Sheol surpasses the living physical pain of the cross since only in virtue of His being dead can He come into intimate contact with the reality of sin abstracted from men as the product and triumph of the Cross. His agony in Sheol goes beyond the *poena sensus* of which Nicholas of Cusa spoke. It is ultimately not even simply the *poena damni*, since Christ's *visio mortis* goes far beyond the *visio mortis*, the *poena damni*, possible to any other soul. Adding still more to the extreme painfulness of Christ's *visio mortis* and to its intimacy, however, is the *mode* of His suffering. This mode is *compassio*.[137] Balthasar quotes St. Bonaventure to establish a distinction between the pain of physical suffering, *passio*, and the spiritual pain of "co-suffering," *compassio*, which is greater than that of *passio*.[138] Balthasar goes on to say,

> This spiritual suffering was the more intense, because its ultimate cause was so much deeper — offence against God and our separation from God, and also because Christ's excess of love made him the more inclined to suffer. The stronger love is, the more painful are the wounds of co-suffering.[139]

The especial torment of Christ in Sheol, His spiritual *visio mortis*, is to be experienced in the mode of *compassio*, i.e., the spiritual sharing in the suffering of the beloved by the lover out of love. *Compassio* is by nature more painful, intimate, and intense than *passio*, both because it concerns a graver matter and because love actually inclines one to this suffering, pressing the hand, as it were, to the brazier. Moreover, Christ's *compassio* in the *visio mortis* is all the more intense, because He is the God-Man: God alone knows fully the gravity of sin, while His omnipotent love makes possible the most intimate experience of the *visio mortis.*

Insofar as Christ's suffering in Sheol by *compassio* expresses love, it points to a final characteristic to be mentioned here: His freedom. Christ alone freely suffered for all men. The Son was able to determine the extent of His suffering: He chose to give Himself as Incarnate wholly to it in the mode of *compassio*,[140] and He chose to embrace all humanity in His suffering.[141] His freedom means His suffering is not something forced upon Him, but rather a work of love, which is free because it acts from its own desire. Freedom is ever an important concept for Balthasar. Here it distinguishes Christ's sacrifice from that of other men, including martyrs. Most men suffer against their will and are unable to prevent their anguish; their "suffering is constrained"[142] in these ways. Further, even if martyrs suffer voluntarily despite their ability to prevent their agony by escape or apostasy, constraint is not merely a matter of will and power, but also of extent and efficacy. Christ's suffering is distinguished from the martyrs' by its extent and efficacy: The extent is the full weight of all sin in its abstracted reality as contrariety to God, whereas its effect will be the redemption of mankind.

For Balthasar, then, the Descent is a continuation of the cross. It is a continuation of expiation and it is a continuation of suffering. Indeed, it is the completion and perfection of both of these, for only in Sheol is the redemption accomplished. Christ suffers more in Sheol than He suffered on the cross, more than the souls awaiting Him there. Through His physical death on the cross, Christ is inducted into Sheol's state of spiritual death, in order to take upon Himself the spiritual penalty of mankind's sins and thereby expiate them. In Sheol, Christ voluntarily suffers by *compassio* what all men (taken cumulatively) should have suffered. In the spiritual intimacy of contemplation and the pliability of perfect passivity/object-ivity, He suffers the most extreme form of the *visio mortis*: He suffers the full import of sin known to God alone. Hence Christ's suffering in Sheol is incomparably greater than that of the Cross and immeasurably greater than the *poena damni* of any and all other sinners. His agony in Sheol was the definitive experience of hell, for not only did He assume the penalty of the *poena damni* for all sins, but He went beyond it.

Christ "Made Sin" for Man's Redemption

The precise reason why Christ suffers what He does, in the way He does, and with redemptive efficacy is that He Himself was "made sin" (2 Cor 5:21) for the salvation of mankind. Over and over, these words of St. Paul's are foundational to Balthasar's exposition of the mysteries of the Cross and the Descent.

The stage is set by Balthasar's asking,

> Could Jesus somehow mysteriously adopt the world's guilt — without having incurred it — and experience [the essence] and its effects in that "hour" which is both the Father's hour and the "hour of darkness"? Did the Redeemer so identify himself with his brothers, the sinners, that he will not distinguish himself from them in the presence of God, with the result that, like a lightning rod, he draws the judgment of God — a judgment upon the reality of opposition to God in the world — onto himself?[143]

Balthasar answers "Yes" to both questions.[144] Jesus freely allowed the guilt of all sin to be loaded upon Him on the Cross. In having identified Himself with his fallen human brothers in this way, His *visio mortis* will be the judgment of God upon sin: In it, the full truth of sin is known by Christ and condemned in His person ('judged'), while mankind's guilt is expiated through His undergoing its punishment (the 'judgment'). In Balthasar's theology, then, Christ is "made sin" in three ways: by taking to Himself the guilt of all sin, by suffering their punishment through the *visio mortis* of these sins, and by thus being made an offering for all sin.[145]

The first way was introduced earlier: All sin is separated from sinners and loaded upon Christ on the cross, who is passive in this matter. It is not He, or the Trinity as a whole, but the Father who is active, "who loads on him the burden of the reality that is 'the sin of the world,' or, in other words, that is 'the wrath of God,' made concrete in everything that arouses this 'wrath.'"[146] Strictly speaking, God's wrath is His absolute and forceful rejection of sin and His abandonment of the sinner in consequence. It is His "categorical 'No'" to sin,[147] "the manifestation of . . . righteous governance which aims to destroy injustice."[148] Insofar as sin necessarily provokes God's wrath, Balthasar says this wrath may be called sin-in-itself, with which Christ is united in His *visio mortis*. Sin and wrath are necessarily linked: Where there is one, there is also always the other. Seen together, they are judgment: In Christ's passively being "made sin" (through the transfer of sin to Him on the Cross and in His *visio mortis* in Sheol) and the Father's rejection of sin as such in Him, judgment against sin itself is pronounced.[149]

Regarding the second, recall that Sheol is not a place such that its punishment is brought to bear from the exterior of those who suffer there; Sheol is an interior spiritual condition of the one who is dead. Whatever the gloomy and solitary experience of Sheol had by those who died before Christ, He alone is to experience it in its essence. 'Vice is its own punishment,' so to speak, in Sheol, where the ego-centrism of sin is experienced in the full force of its reality, in both its (positive) repulsiveness, and its (negative) self-imposed isolation from God. Its repulsiveness is paralleled by God's condemnation and rejection of sin, while the sinner's self-isolation is mirrored by God's abandonment of the sinner as the consequence of His condemnation. The reality of the dead sinner is thus defined by the reality of sin, not so much in the sense of *conditioned* by his acts, as Dante has a sinner's agony linked to his sins, but more in the sense of *identified with* sin as a state. This description, however, would apply also to hell. Hence, if the Son's being dead is to be "exclusive and unique in its expiatory value,"[150] it must go beyond hell. He must suffer self-repulsion and -isolation, as likewise God's condemnation and abandonment (in the Person of the Father), but Christ alone is to be the one definitively "made sin."

Through the contemplative nature of the *visio mortis,* Christ identifies Himself "ultimately with the sin of all sinners."[151] In having all sin loaded upon Him on the cross, Jesus "takes on total identity with 'the flesh of sin' (Rom 8:3)."[152] In Sheol, He is "literally 'made sin,'"[153] the sin of all men, but as abstracted from them, i.e., sin-in-itself.[154] Through the *visio mortis,* He is to be *identified* with the reality of separated sin and to bear the punishment of the condemnation and abandonment of the Father against Himself as against sin-in-itself, i.e., without anything that could call for mercy. One must read Balthasar again: "What is damnable in [the sinner] has been separated from him and thrown out with the unusable residue that is incinerated outside the gates of the Holy City."[155] In other words, sin is separated from the sinner and, in the Person of Christ, cast into Sheol, which is deeper than gehenna, where the fire of God's wrath will consume it in the Person of Christ.

The Father's "loading" of sin on the Son while simultaneously abandoning Him is the proximate cause of His death: "Jesus dies of the sin that murders him but . . . he also dies because God forsakes him."[156] As this God-forsakenness reaches its perfection in Sheol, the continuity Balthasar sees between "Cross and Hell" is based not only upon the fact that being dead is the consequence of the event of death, but upon the Father's continuing abandonment of the Son unto sin, and of the Son's death and being dead in the consenting passivity of obedience.

Finally, regarding Christ's being "made sin" as an offering for sin, God's wrath must be seen in the context of God's love, and as an expression of it, lest one take this wrath with both its aspects "as a punitive raging of divine anger against the innocent victim (as the Reformers tended to do)."[157] Out of love for the world, the Father sends His Son into the world to overcome its sin by suffering, dying, and being dead vicariously for mankind. He also sends Him out of love for the Son, who desires the salvation of the world. Likewise, the Son offers Himself for this mission with all it entails out of love for the Father (that He might be glorified) and for the world (that it might partake of the divine life). Hence *obedience*, or "consenting passivity,"[158] more than *vengeance* will be the keyword for the redemptive event.[159] The Holy Spirit, who is sent invisibly with the Son and through Him, will make possible this mission unto Sheol out of love by being a substantial link of love between Father and Son even in the opposition of wrath against sin-in-itself. Thus God's wrath is directed against sin due to His love, both His love for the sinner and His love for His own justice.[160] This "necessary unity of love and anger" is uncovered through the revelation of the Trinity in Jesus' mission.[161]

The timeless decision and self-offering of the eternal Son is reflected in Jesus' free self-offering and His acceptance of His death, including His "being dead."[162] From this perspective, "made sin" might be rendered as *to be made to be an offering for sin*. The notion that Christ was "made sin" in the sense that He offered His life as a sacrifice to atone for sin has a long history in the Church's Tradition. According to Balthasar, this interpretation laid emphasis particularly on the sacrificial aspect (offered Himself *as a sacrifice*), to show its connection with the Law; Balthasar's presentation emphasizes more especially the spontaneity of this offering (*offered* Himself as a sacrifice).[163]

Of course, for Balthasar, Christ's being an offering for sin is identical with His being literally identified with the sins of all mankind, as abstracted from the individuals who committed them, and suffering the Father's wrath as punishment for them. "Such a real assumption of the sinful being of all sinners"[164] and, through it, the expiation of all sin, is possible only in virtue of Christ's identity as the God-Man. In virtue of His humanity, Jesus has "real communication (solidarity) . . . with the reality of humankind as a whole and its eschatological fate."[165] But more especially His identity as the Son of God is key. This Trinitarian foundation will be treated in depth in Chapter Seven.

That Christ was "made sin" for man's redemption comes from 2 Corinthians 5:21, which runs in full, "Him, who knew no sin, he hath made sin for us: that we might be made the justice of God in him." In an attempt to put to rest any conflict between the "made sin" part of 2 Corinthians 5:21 and the first part that testifies Christ was "Him, who knew no sin," Balthasar glosses the first part with reference to Hebrews 4:15, saying,

> God is solidary with us not only in what is symptomatic of sin, the punishment for sin, but also in co-experiencing sin, in the *peirasmos* [experience of trial] of the very essence of that negation — though without 'committing' (Hebrews 4,15) sin himself.[166]

To be precise, "committing" is not in Hebrews 4:15, but is supplied by Balthasar. The Greek is χωρὶς ἁμαρτίας, i.e., *without sin,* and makes clear a noun, not a verb, is intended. "Without sin" includes the notion of "not committing sin," but is wider than it, for "without sin" also excludes any state of sin such as, e.g., original sin. Compare 1 John 3:5: "In him there is no sin." Hence Balthasar's interpretation limits the content of the original Greek.

In Balthasar's understanding (as indicated by his gloss on Heb 4:15[167]), although Christ most intimately experiences sin, He remains innocent in that He did not commit any sins Himself; on the other hand, He is fully guilty of all sins, in ascribing them to Himself as if He had committed them and letting them be "loaded" upon Him on the Cross. In other words, He did not commit the acts, but the actual guilt is truly transferred to Him. Balthasar does not mean *guilt* in the sense of *the result of guilt,* as *sin* is sometimes taken to mean *the effect of sin* with respect to Christ; rather, he means the actual guilt of all individuals.[168] Thus Balthasar stresses the singular personal pronouns: "God allows his Son to make expiation for our, for your and my sin, . . . Christ takes on himself my and your guilt in his death in abandonment by God. . . ."[169] Each person can then say, "I am the one whom God has so loved that he gave his Son for me who took my guilt upon him and took it with him into his death. . . ."[170] Jesus' solidarity with all mankind leads Him to this extreme:[171] the assumption of the guilt of all men on the Cross, and the expiation of the penalty for the sin of all men by undergoing it in Sheol. This is what the *pro nobis* of Christ is in its perfection: being in the place mankind deserved, on behalf of mankind.[172] The guilt of sin is His from the Cross, the punishment is His in Sheol. Balthasar is careful: Christ is not punished *because* He committed sin, rather He suffers the punishment due to others for their sins *as if* He had committed them. In Balthasar's soteriology, Christ undergoes the punishment due to sinners (objective factor), experiencing it punitively as if He Himself had committed their sins (subjective factor), but His suffering of what is objectively punishment is not objectively punishment *of Him,* since He Himself did not commit any sin.[173] It is only because Christ is "so truthful in himself" that He is able to see the full truth of "the lie" of sin, "to acknowledge the full negativity of this 'No': . . . to experience it, to bear it, to suffer its deadly opposition and melt its rigidity through pain."[174]

The Christological *pro nobis,* understood as *vicarious representation,* is open to a variety of interpretations: Christ as Head represents His Body; Christ dies a death like that which each man deserved; Christ was treated as if our sins were His, etc. Balthasar integrates these into his own interpretation of the *pro nobis* as subordinate concepts, while its definitive essence remains clear over and above their muted influence: The *pro nobis* indicates a real (i.e., literal) "exchange of places,"[175] the assumption of an "alien fate in place of one's own (or as one's own)."[176] The place exchanged, the fate assumed, is Sheol.

For Balthasar, then, Christ's redemption is accomplished through a *penal quantitative substitution in Sheol.*[177] Christ is "made sin" for the redemption of sinners through His union with their sin through His *visio mortis* in Sheol. This position is certainly different from the traditional Catholic understanding of the redemption through Christ's death on the cross as being satisfactory in virtue of the preeminent qualities of His person, i.e., His divine dignity and His human charity.[178] Redemption as satisfactory entails substitution as well, but neither a quantitative nor a penal one; that is, Christ did in human nature what man could not do for himself, but He did not suffer the punishment that all cumulatively would have suffered without His redemptive work.

Something Balthasar wrote, however, may be taken as an explicit attempt to deny his doctrine depends on quantitative substitution:

> Sin's impatience . . . is finally exhausted in comparison to the patience of the Son of God. His patience undergirds sin and lifts it off its hinges. Of course: it is not quantities that stand here as rivals over against each other but qualities. The quality of the loving obedience of the Son toward the Father (who wills to overcome sin from within in precisely this way: through the incarnate Son) is not to be compared with the quality of the hate that surges over him.[179]

This inflowing surge of hate is an aspect of Christ's Passion that pertains more to Good Friday, Balthasar tells us, than to Holy Saturday.[180] The scourging, the driving of the nails, all the physical blows of the Passion represent the assaults of sin. Interpreted along these lines, the "lifting of sin off its hinges" is the removal of sin from men and the loading of it upon the crucified Son. A second aspect of Christ's Passion pertains more to the event of Holy Saturday, i.e., His "solidarity in nontime with those who have been lost to God" through the definitiveness of their own choice for self and the definitiveness of death.[181] His being dead with them in their twofold death, but out of *self*less*ness rather than selfishness, is to make the definitiveness of both deaths conditional. Heaven thus is opened (though it is not the certain end of all).

In this argument, the qualities of love and of solidarity out of love in both the aspect of Good Friday and that of Holy Saturday are taken as the contraries of hate and isolation and — if quantity is not important, but only quality — assumed to outweigh their contraries if they are present. The problem is that something prevails over its contrary *only* if it is greater than the other; love may be 'greater' than hate in being better than it, but it need not always overcome it.

One subject's hate diminishes to the extent his love for the same object grows, but the love of one person in the face of another's hate may not cause that person to relinquish his hate, but may only provide the occasion for that hate to grow. Balthasar frequently points out this latter situation in regard to the provocation Jesus' presence provides.[182] Moreover, if quantity were in no way relevant with regard to love, it would be equally meaningful to say God's love is infinite, or is a thousand times greater than ours, or is less than ours, because they would all be equally meaningless. Finally, other principles in Balthasar's corpus contradict his claim that quantity in the matter of Christ's solidarity is unimportant, for he insists over and over again that the only way the sins of all can be expiated is for love to go to the end of Sheol with its *visio mortis.* Thus he says that "the Son underwent death *in and through* each individual sin that makes up the totality of the world's evil, insofar as the holy God cursed (and so banished) in him everything hostile to the Divinity."[183] Again,

> The condition of timelessness undergone by the Son on the Cross . . . must have sufficient 'space' for the (infernal) experience of sinners abandoned by God, in two aspects: the intensity of the Son's forsakenness on the Cross and its worldwide extension.[184]

Or, finally, "In the Passion Christ transformed us into himself in taking our sins into himself."[185]

Redemption through Christ being made possible for men either in virtue of His Headship of the Church as the New Adam (what Balthasar calls "physical solidarity"[186]) or through "imputation"[187] of all sin to Him "are subordinate individual aspects," he says, "that are taken up into the synthesis of the unique work of love, which encompasses them and makes use of them."[188] Though Balthasar tries to integrate Catholic and Protestant traditions in this way, both modes of redemption remain explicitly subordinate to his own proposal and ultimately ineffective without Christ's suffering in mankind's place the quantitative punishment that accrued for all sins:

> The aspect of *the voluntary self-offering of the guiltless one,* indeed his self-sacrificing (Heb 7:28) in the role of a high priest who is simultaneously the lamb of sacrifice (1 Cor 5:7), *is not at all sufficient:* the 'paschal lamb' is indeed 'slain' *(ibid.),* but *not* by himself. When the slaughtering is going on, the lamb can only endure, without opening its mouth (Is 53:7). . . . Here lies the 'unfathomable' (Eph 3:8) mystery of the Cross, in the momentum of the collision of the entire burden of sin with the total powerlessness of the kenotic existence.[189]

In short, Balthasar denies the quantitative nature of substitution in his doctrine on the basis that sins are expiated through the Son's descent experience in virtue of His undergoing of it in obedience, that is, in the divine love.[190] In this way, love is decisive; mere suffering is not sufficient. Nevertheless, this love must have a certain content, and that content is the passive suffering of each and every sin in itself in Sheol. Thus it seems either his doctrine, or his denial, must fall.

Conclusion

In this chapter, three of Balthasar's major theses about Christ's descent into hell were introduced. First, the Descent is a continuation of the redemptive efficacy and suffering begun on the Cross. The reconciliation of God with the world is not complete with Christ's death on the cross. Man is redeemed by the Cross insofar as the guilt of his sins is there actually transferred to Christ. These sins remain to be expiated in Sheol through Christ's suffering the punishment due to them. Second, Christ's suffering in His descent surpasses that of the Cross. In Sheol, He suffers the repulsive self-alienation of sin, as well as God's condemnation and abandonment due to the sin ascribed to Him. He is literally the object of God's wrath. He suffers voluntarily in the mode of *compassio* what all men would have suffered, as well as the full import of sin through a *visio mortis* of universal extent in place of the *visio Dei*. His agony thus is immeasurably greater than the *poena damni* of any and all other sinners. Finally, because Sheol is a condition of the one therein and the *visio mortis* is an intimate spiritual reality, Christ is literally "made sin" in Sheol. His descent experience will thus complete mankind's redemption, because the punishment of God's wrath due to their sins has been expiated through Christ's undergoing this punishment Himself.

These elements of Balthasar's theology depend upon his principle, "What is not endured is not healed." This maxim resembles the patristic principle, "What is not assumed is not healed," but is significantly different and captures the emphasis of Balthasar's theology on suffering. They also depend upon his interpretation of Sheol in the Old Testament and his reading of 2 Corinthians 5:21.

In Chapter Two, the traditional Catholic doctrine was summarized in this way:

First, Christ descended in His soul united to His divine Person only to the limbo of the Fathers. Second, His power and authority were made known throughout all of hell, taken generically. Third, He thereby accomplished the two purposes of the Descent, which were "to liberate the just" by conferring on them the glory of heaven and "to proclaim His power."[191] Finally, His descent was a glorious one, and Christ did not suffer the pain proper to any of the abodes of hell.

It is now evident that Balthasar explicitly disagrees with the first and fourth points, whereas his theology would interpret the second and third points in a veiled sense: According to Balthasar, Christ does not descend in soul to the limbo of the Fathers, because there is no diversified abode of the dead before Him, but rather only Sheol. His suffering is not replaced by the glorification of His whole soul and the manifestation of His glory, but rather His agony continues and intensifies. In contrast to the traditional doctrine, Balthasar holds that Christ suffered the pain proper to the abode of the dead. His being able to undergo the full extent of Sheol reveals His divine power, as we will see more explicitly in Chapter Seven. Moreover, rather than His descent being the first application of the fruit of salvation, it is expiatory. As expiatory and because Christ suffers Sheol in our place, His descent may be said to liberate souls. The passivity of His suffering there contrasts with the authoritative action traditionally ascribed to Christ. Finally, whereas the received tradition holds that Christ's death on the cross was satisfactory in virtue of the preeminent qualities of His person, Balthasar's interpretation of the Descent depends upon quantitative penal substitution.

Balthasar himself is fully aware that his opinion about the Descent differs from the historically prevalent one, that is, from the traditional Catholic theological understanding. He argues that pagan myths and Jewish apocrypha involving journeys to the underworld greatly influenced "the Christian apocalyptic," which

> developed a lively interest in this literary genre and produced those fantastic journeys into hell by Jesus that eventually led from [various Christian apocrypha] to the corresponding patristic sermons, the medieval descent plays and culminat[ed] in Dante's *Inferno*.[192]

He then goes on to say, "All of this takes us far from the biblical message. . . ."[193]

In Chapter Two, our question about the relation of Balthasar's theology of the Descent to the traditional doctrine was also couched in terms of the way in which Christ's descent was glorious. Balthasar too thinks the Descent was glorious, but we have not yet seen how he understands its glory, or why he thinks a sense other than that of the traditional doctrine would do more justice to the depths of God's love. These matters will become evident in the next three chapters, in which the Descent as Balthasar sees it will be examined from the perspective of each of the divine Persons. One might say the Descent has been considered from a distance in the present chapter; in the following ones, we look more closely at its inner structure, which is Trinitarian. This examination will reveal important new features of Balthasar's theological opinion. Simultaneously it will further clarify and support what we have already seen. After considering in some detail the involvement of the Father, Son, and Holy Spirit in the Descent event, we will then step back in Chapter Nine to look at the centrality of the Descent to Balthasar's theology as a whole.

CHAPTER SIX

Christ's Descent in Light of the Trinity:
The Father, Active Inflictor of the *Visio Mortis*

In the theology of Hans Urs von Balthasar, the Trinity is the origin of Christ's descent. This statement may appear odd, because, as the Descent of the Word Incarnate, the Descent would seem to be adequately characterized when examined from the perspective of Christ, as sketched in the previous chapter. Moreover, the doctrine of appropriation would suggest a Trinitarian treatment of the Descent is irrelevant.

According to this doctrine, all works of the Divine Persons *ad extra* (i.e., dealing with creatures and thus also with the economy of salvation) are accomplished in common. Although each Person has a proper mode of acting due to His existence as a subsisting relation (i.e., the Father acts through the Son in the Holy Spirit, the Son acts from the Father in the Holy Spirit, and the Holy Spirit acts from the Father and the Son), their divine acts are not multiplied as acts proper to the individual Persons, but are identically one single act common to all three. I say "divine acts" here, because the human acts of Christ are proper to the Word in the same way the acts of other men are proper to them; i.e., the essence, presence, and power of all three divine Persons are the creating and preserving cause of His human potentialities and human acts, which are proper to Him insofar as He is man (and not proper to Him as God).

As a mode of speaking, however, some divine works *ad extra* are attributed to individual Persons of the Trinity due to a likeness to one of the personal properties.[1] For example, according to this doctrine, the cosmos is *in fact* created by the three Persons as one God, but is *attributed* to the Father, because it is fitting to speak of the principle of the Trinity also as the principle of the cosmos. Likewise, the redemption of mankind is *in fact* accomplished by the entire

Trinity, although it is *appropriated* to the Son, because only He became incarnate for the accomplishment of that work. Similarly, men are *in fact* sanctified by the indwelling of all three Persons of the Trinity, but our sanctification is *attributed* to the Spirit. Finally, the Son is *in fact* incarnated by the Trinity as a whole, but the Incarnation may be fittingly *appropriated* to the Holy Spirit, in light of the words of the Gospel (Lk 1:35) and due to the Holy Spirit's being regarded in a special manner as the Giver of life.[2] Given the doctrine of the common work of the Trinity *ad extra,* then, the Trinity may be said to be the origin of the Descent in the sense that the created nature and action of the Word Incarnate in His descent are created, preserved, and made efficacious both naturally and supernaturally by the entire Trinity. The doctrine of appropriation rules out, however, the consideration of the Descent for any real differences in the work of the individual Persons, except that the human nature of Christ subsists in the Son, and not in the Father or Holy Spirit.

Hans Urs von Balthasar rejects the doctrine of appropriation just presented,[3] and his understanding of its foundation (the common work of the divine Persons *ad extra*) is significantly different: "Everything temporal takes place within the embrace of the eternal action and as its consequence (hence *opera trinitatis ad extra communia*)."[4] The key word here is "hence," and its significance becomes more apparent if the phrasing of the sentence is reversed: The works of the Trinity *ad extra* are in common *because* they occur within the ongoing divine action and as its consequence. Creation, for example, is then a common work because its prototype is the Trinitarian life, which involves both existence and distinction, and it occurs within that life (for where else can something be, than in God?).[5] *Opera trinitatis ad extra communia,* which was classically an assertion about the identity of the *action* of the three Persons *ad extra,* has become an assertion about the specific *condition* for the possibility of the existence of the *ad extra.*

Balthasar will thus understand the Trinity as the origin of Christ's descent in a way different from that suggested above. In the economy of Christ's mission, the Persons of the Trinity will have proper acts reflecting their personal properties. To examine Balthasar's theology of the Descent from a Trinitarian perspective thus enables a fuller characterization of it. Two additional essential elements will thereby be revealed: In abandoning the Son, the Father inflicts the *visio mortis* on Him, while the Holy Spirit preserves their loving unity despite the abandonment.

In this chapter and the following two, Christ's descent will be considered from the perspective of each of the three divine Persons. We will begin with the Father, who is the *agent* that corresponds to Christ's passive reception of the *visio mortis.* In this chapter, four aspects of the Father's role in Christ's descent will be examined: His "loading" of sin on the Son, His abandonment of the Son,

His wrathful "crushing" of sin in the Person of the Son, and His active infliction of the *visio mortis*. Due to the unity between "Cross and Hell" in Balthasar's thought, the demarcation among these four should not be maintained too strictly: The "load" of sin, together with the Father's simultaneous wrath, "crushes" the Son until He has the *visio mortis,* all of which reflects and is effected by the Father's abandonment of Him.

The Father Actively "Loads" Sin on the Son

Christ's descent is characterized by the "consenting passivity" of obedience, as observed in Chapter Five. This passivity characterizes His entire mission: Consistent with his rejection of the doctrine of appropriation, Balthasar says that the Son passively gives Himself in His incarnation to the Holy Spirit, who alone actively incarnates Him.[6] The Holy Spirit drives Him along the paths of the Father's will during His life.[7] In the events leading up to His descent, Christ is also passive: He does not take the burden of sin unto Himself, but lets it be loaded on Him in the Garden of Gethsemane and on the cross. It is as if sin is too great a burden to be lifted, but if it is loaded on Him by the Father from above, it will lie on His shoulders until it crushes Him to the ground, i.e., into Sheol. Such passivity to God is required if His mission is to attain more than that possible to human action.[8] In addition, to take this burden up actively would be too self-assertive, as if He were sure of His own strength to conquer it.[9] His existence as one who wholly disposes Himself to the will of another would thereby be contradicted.[10]

But to assert the Son's passivity in the unified event of Good Friday and Holy Saturday is to imply the activity of another Person. Thus Balthasar says, "The true subject who acts on the Cross is therefore God, and the instrument he employs in acting is sin";[11] "the Father . . . loads on [Jesus] the burden of the reality that is 'the sin of the world.'"[12] Balthasar does not specify *how* the reality of sin may be separated from men and "loaded" upon Christ such that the guilt is truly transferred to Him.

The Father Abandons the Son

In bearing the world's sins, which are essentially isolation-in-self, Christ is cut off from unity with all men; He alone is now 'the guilty one.'[13] At the same time, because it is *sin* He bears, Christ is cut off from unity with God.[14] Because sin can have no place in love, sin (personified in the Son) is cast into the outer darkness of hell.[15] Thus He is left utterly alone in His death and His being dead,[16] and this, when undergone from a previous state of loving intimacy,[17] is abandonment.[18] The theological virtues do not exist in Sheol, thus neither does grace in the soul of Jesus. Balthasar goes so far as to say that "it is no longer God who holds sway over him, but the enemy."[19]

But the God-forsakenness of Christ in Sheol is not merely that of a creature in the state of sin vis-à-vis God, but of the divine Son abandoned by His Father.[20] It not only embraces what Balthasar calls "human God-forsakenness,"[21] but also entails divine God-forsakenness. In giving Himself up, Christ will not only give up His human life in the sense of surrendering Himself to the death of the cross, He will give up His "whole existence."[22]

> The forsakenness that prevails between the Father and his crucified Son is deeper and more deadly than any forsakenness, temporal or eternal, actual or possible, that separates a creature from God.[23]

In other words, the Father abandons Christ not only as man, but *as Son*.

This ultimate abandonment as Son, undertaken for man's salvation, is the principle to which Balthasar subordinates theologies of imputation and of solidarity in Christ due to common human nature. As mentioned earlier, they are subordinated to a "unique work of love, which . . . makes use of them."[24] Balthasar says,

> We must ask whether the notion of mere "substitution" is adequate, or whether this concept, when applied to Christ, does not automatically include an element — a trinitarian element — that lifts it above the mere physical or legal plane. This implies that the Bearer of the world's sin does not simply suffer "hell" in our place: something unique is going on here that cannot be comprehended by the notion of a mere exchange of places.[25]

What this is, he reveals a little later:

> The Crucified Son does not simply suffer the hell deserved by sinners; he suffers something below and beyond this, namely, being forsaken by God in the pure obedience of love. Only he, *as Son*, is capable of this, and it is qualitatively deeper than any possible hell.[26]

In other words, having been "made sin" in Sheol, the Son *qua* Son is forsaken by the Father in an abandonment that is exactly proportionate to their prior intimacy[27] — and it is the suffering of this greater abandonment out of love that will ultimately break open the realm of the dead. Given these two theses, the reason for Balthasar's insistence that physical and spiritual death not be separated for Jesus becomes clearer: His physical death inducts Him into the spiritual death of God-abandonment, begun already on the cross through the transfer of the world's sin to Him.

Moreover, even as the Father generates the Son, the Father actively *sends* the Son into the God-forsakenness of Sheol. Thus Balthasar writes,

> The Son's "God-forsakenness" on the Cross cannot be interpreted one-sidedly as something felt solely by the dying Jesus; if God is objectively forsaken here, then we must say that God is forsaken by God: this is still an *economic* form of the personal relationship within the *immanent* Trinity.[28]

If the God-forsakenness in the economy expresses the processions in the Trinity, then the Father is just as much involved in the drama of salvation as the incarnate Son.[29] Because the Father-Son relationship is reciprocal, the Father's abandoning of the Son has consequences also for the Father. Out of love for the world, the Father will give His Son up, not only to being killed, but to being dead in Sheol. The Father gives Him up for lost, in order to gather in the lost.[30] He spares His most beloved Son nothing as He lets Him go to this extreme, and thus also spares Himself nothing.[31] The God-forsakenness of Cross and Sheol is double-sided: In losing His beloved Son by abandoning Him in Sheol, the Father also experiences the loss of intimacy.

Perhaps Balthasar has the following argument in mind: In the immanent Trinity, what is true of the Son, He has from the Father. But the economic Trinity reveals the immanent Trinity. Thus, if the Son is abandoned *as Son,* it implies the Father has a reciprocal experience that mirrors the Son's abandonment.[32] The Trinity is experienced as destroyed, at least by the Father and Son.[33] Balthasar, however, does not further specify the Father's experience.

The Holy Spirit does not experience abandonment in any parallel way, however, because Balthasar considers Him as the bond of unity between the Father and Son in both the economic and immanent Trinity. Because the Holy Spirit unites Father and Son substantially and by reminding them of the mission unto God-forsakenness they chose, all three divine Persons will be revealed through the Father's abandonment of the Son in Sheol. More will be said of the Holy Spirit's role in Christ's descent in Chapter Eight.

"Abandonment" as "Distance"

Balthasar sees the abandonment of one divine Person by another in the economy of salvation as possible due to the distinction of Persons in the immanent

Trinity, and as a manifestation of it. Hence to characterize the Father's abandonment of the Son, and the Father's reciprocal loss, we must here examine certain elements of Balthasar's Trinitarian theology, which will also be relevant to the following chapters on the Son and Holy Spirit. Balthasar discusses the distinction of divine Persons under the notion of "distance."[34] For him, "distance" is identical in content to kenosis, but "presupposes an explicit trinitarian thinking."[35] In other words, whereas kenosis might be interpreted as referring strictly to the Son's becoming incarnate and being obedient in human nature even unto death (Phil 2:7-8), Balthasar refers kenosis also to the processions in the Trinity. "Distance" is kenosis as carrying this Trinitarian emphasis.

As Balthasar uses it, "distance" properly refers to the distinction among the divine Persons as this arises from the divine nature. Given the singularity of the divine essence, one may ask how there can be three divine Persons. Balthasar's answer is that the divine nature is, in its essence, self-surrender.[36] Thus the "eternal *being*" should be seen as "eternal *event*."[37] It can even be seen as eternal becoming, without ascribing change to God, since it is "the coming about of something that has always been."[38] "This 'happening' is not a becoming in the earthly sense: it is the coming-to-be . . . of something that grounds the idea, the inner possibility and reality of [an earthly] becoming."[39] The "eternal event" is the intra-Trinitarian kenosis of the divine nature in virtue of which the Persons are distinguished. The Father, who is His own being, gives that being perfectly to the Son; He empties Himself, so to speak, in the generation of the Son and in order that the Son be generated.[40] Thus the Son receives His existence from the Father. But the existence received is existence as self-surrender.[41] Thus the Son also eternally empties Himself, so to speak, back toward the Father in love and, Balthasar says, "gratitude."[42] The Son's "gratitude" is matched by "gratitude" on the part of the Father, for the Father only is insofar as He gives the divine essence to the receiving Son.[43] The Holy Spirit proceeds in the mutual 'emptying' of Father and Son out of reciprocal love.[44]

Now, although the Father and the Son are equally self-surrender, they stand in complete opposition insofar as the Father is self-surrender without origin, but the Son is self-surrender as wholly received. Both surrender and reception are perfect: The gift is both total and without 'strings attached,' so to speak. The one who gives, does so without obliging the other, and the one who receives, does so without demanding more.[45] Thus "there are no inbuilt securities,"[46] but neither do the Persons "cling"[47] to one another. The perfection of the spontaneous gift of the divine essence on the part of the Father leaves the Son in a like perfect freedom in His receiving. This being wholly and freely the other as the result of the perfect surrender of all that the one is, is "distance." The "distance" of this other-ness admits even the Son's economic obedience *as*

Son to the Father with whom He is one, up to His being abandoned by the Father with whom He is one.[48] Unity is nonetheless maintained in the abandonment, because the Son receives all *what* the Father is, i.e., the divine essence. In addition, the Person of the Holy Spirit is a substantial bond of union between Father and Son precisely due to the "distance" between them: He proceeds from them both insofar as He proceeds from the one (the Father) together with the other (the Son).

As nothing has existence without having its prototype in God, this intra-Trinitarian "distance" makes possible every form of creaturely existence. Since creatures are not God, they are other than God, and this other-ness requires a foundation in God, which is the other-ness of the divine Persons.[49] The Son's return as the other in self-surrender out of "gratitude" (His *"eucharistia"*[50]) "is the precondition for every possible and real world"[51] of creatures originating from God and standing in right order to Him. The kenoses of God in creation, the covenant, and the Incarnation (by which He successively makes Himself 'weaker' in "restricting"[52] Himself with the authentic freedom of rational creatures, the promise of the covenant, and the limitations of human existence and death, respectively) derive their possibility and actuality from the first kenosis of the Father to the Son.[53] Thus God's very omnipotence (i.e., His divine essence, including His power to create) is His being weak (i.e., self-surrender and self-emptying, or perfect dependence in receiving, either within the Trinity or in the *economia*).[54]

Since the intra-Trinitarian "distance" is the foundation for creation, it is also the foundation for all "distances that are possible within the world of finitude, *including the distance of sin.*"[55] That

> God the Father can give his divinity away in such a manner that . . . the Son's possession of it is "equally substantial." . . . implies such an incomprehensible and unique "separation" of God from himself that it *includes* and grounds every other separation — be it never so dark and bitter.[56]

Likewise,

> This Son is infinitely Other, but he is infinitely Other *of the Father.* Thus he both grounds and surpasses all we mean by separation, pain and alienation in the world and all we can envisage in terms of loving self-giving, interpersonal relationship and blessedness.[57]

The "God-lessness" of the divine love "undergirds" sin,[58] "embrace[s]"[59] it, "renders it possible and goes beyond it."[60] The greatest suffering and forsakenness (and so all lesser sufferings) are also embraced by the Trinitarian "distance" and have their archetype in God.[61]

Note that both sin and suffering are conceived here as positive realities. In contrast, suffering is classically seen as a potentiality of human nature, but not one that it is essential to human nature to have actualized. Created in the state of grace, man would never have suffered, but for the Fall. In this view, suffering is a defect, since it is a result of the loss of original justice.

To return to Balthasar: Having its origin in God as the Trinity means the created world reveals the existence of God, not only that He is, but also what He is. The world — and recall that Balthasar has explicitly included in this the separation from God that is sin — must reflect the dynamic "trinitarian life of love."[62] The world is always "in"[63] God, even if its existence is something other than God. As much as it is founded on the primal other-ness in God, it is also founded on the single being of God; if its existence is not "in" God, where else could it be?[64] For

> the distance between the Persons, within the dynamic process of the divine essence, is infinite, to such an extent that everything that unfolds on the plane of finitude can take place only *within* this all-embracing dynamic process.[65]

The world's unity in God and distinction from Him thus are founded upon, and reflect, the intra-Trinitarian unity and distinction. Balthasar's different understanding of the *opera trinitatis ad extra communia* is at work here: Rather than the creation of the world being a common act of the three divine Persons because it is a single act, it is a common act because it is founded upon the distinctions among all three Persons.[66]

The definitive revelation in creation of God as Trinity will be accomplished through the mission of the Word Incarnate. The Word's descent into the flesh unto His being dead in Sheol is one continuous revelation of the Trinity: In His state as creature (hence, *a fortiori* in His descent), Christ's

> experience of distance from God . . . is as such the expression of God's experience of himself within the Trinity in the distance of distinction between Person and Person.[67]

Jesus reveals the one God to be three Persons most perfectly when their opposition in unity is most clear, and that occurs in His being dead.[68] There, at the "utmost pitch"[69] of His mission, the greatest other-ness pertains between Jesus and the one He calls "My Father," when the Father, in His infinite righteousness, abandons the Son "made sin" in the farthest depths of Sheol.[70]

Because the divine God-lessness and the God-lessness of sin are opposed, however, they are not identical, even if the former is the foundation of the latter.[71] They also cannot be identical because Balthasar considers both the divine essence and sin-in-itself as positive realities. The opposition between God and sin is employed for the revelation of the opposition of relations within the Trinity. As Balthasar sees it, the Father's abandonment of the Son precisely into what is anti-divine is essential to reveal the Trinity. The divine essence, which subsists in opposite relations (Father and Son) united in relation to a third (the Holy Spirit), will receive its most perfect economic expression in the Son's being conformed to what is (positively) most unlike God.[72] He must go specifically to that extreme. Then the Son's being "made sin" will stand in perfect opposition to the rejecting force of the Father's righteousness, yet the two of them will remain linked by the Holy Spirit's mediation and His affirmation of their common will for the salvation of the world, the Son's will to offer Himself and to obey the Father, and the Father's will to let Him go and to send Him.[73] In other words,

> "Of course, one cannot say that death, as an end, is in any sense in God, since his eternal life is unending. But if death is understood to mean the sacrifice of life, then the original image of that sacrifice is in God as the gift of life flowing between Father and Son in the Spirit. . . ."[74] "This 'living death' is the absolute opposite of the death of sin,"[75] in which man closes himself to self-surrender and hence to eternal life. . . . The Son's mission was therefore to take "sinful death" up into his death of self-surrender, which thus meant that his death would involve abandonment by God.[76]

Despite the extreme opposition and separation between the righteous Father and the Son "made sin," the divine unity persists in several ways. Father and Son are united in the act that occurs in the event of Good Friday and Holy Saturday, in that the Son is the object of the Father's action. They are united in a single purpose of will, to redeem the world, in which the Son obeys the Father, and the Father accepts the Son's self-offering.[77] They are united by the Person of the Holy Spirit, who mediates this will between Father and Son.[78] They are united in that Christ's abandonment in Sheol by the Father is the way in which He goes to the Father,[79] or, what is the same, in that the Father's sending of the Son is the Son's obedient descent into Sheol.[80] They are united in the continuing generation of the Son by the Father.[81] They are united in the identity of the divine nature.[82] In all these ways, they are united by their love of each other.[83]

It is with reference to these various types of union, and especially to the Holy Spirit as the substantial bond of unity, that one must read Balthasar's very occasional qualifications that the Son "*appears* to have lost the Father."[84] The appearance accurately represents the reality: The Son *is* abandoned by the Father to sin in Sheol. Nonetheless, the reality may be described as an appearance insofar as the abandoned Son still has the Father in a sense, i.e., *in* the Holy Spirit, even as the one sending is present in the mission of the one sent. These qualifications do not mitigate the reality of sin as such in Sheol, or the Son's experience of the *visio mortis* and abandonment, or the real fact that the Father has let the Son go — indeed, sent Him — into everything that stands against God in order to take sin into Himself. They only imply that the Father and Son are still united in the ways mentioned above.[85]

Unity in the greatest "distance" of abandonment in Sheol will thus reveal that the three Persons involved are divine, because "only God Himself can go right to the end of the abandonment by God. Only he has the freedom to do this."[86] Or, equivalently, it reveals that God is triune.

It may be helpful, and would do justice to the unity of Balthasar's thought, to recap this notion of "distance" in terms previously introduced, namely, obedience and passivity. As we have seen, obedience according to Balthasar is the active willing of one to fulfill the end he passively receives from another. Such obedience will be the defining personal characteristic of the Son; the Son's 'letting be' in the passivity of the Passion is only the expression of His prior Trinitarian state.[87] However, a like concurrence of activity and passivity occurs with regard to all the Persons within the Trinitarian "distance." Here the pair of contraries used is "letting go" and "letting be."[88] The Son eternally "lets Himself be" begotten by the Father. This "antecedent consent" of the Son, what Balthasar also refers to as a "passive *actio*," is a necessary condition of the "active *actio*" of the Father,[89] who eternally "lets the Son go" in His act of generation. Thus Balthasar says, "The Son even cooperates in his begetting by *letting* himself be begotten, by holding himself in readiness to be begotten."[90] A like situation attains in the case of the Spirit vis-à-vis the Father and Son.[91] In the Father's reception of the Son's and the Spirit's "antecedent consent" and consequently of His own actual paternity, for which He has "gratitude,"[92] the Father also has a certain passivity, even in His primal "active *actio*."[93] His passivity will be manifest, like the rest of Trinitarian life, in the economy: Since the Father gives everything He is away to the Son in His love, the Father has nothing, is nothing, except this giving away of Himself. Thus He is dependent on the Son for the accomplishment of His works, and it will be the Son's work to reveal this extravagant love of the Father.[94] This revelation is accomplished through the Son's mission unto Sheol, where He will give Himself wholly away, like the Father does: "The Son's self-surrender . . . is the 'economic' representation of the Father's trinitarian, loving self-surrender."[95]

The "letting go" and "letting be" within the Trinity describes what Balthasar also calls "super-death":

> This total self-giving [of all the Father is], to which the Son and the Spirit respond by an equal self-giving, is a kind of "death," a first, radical "kenosis," as one might say. It is a kind of "super-death" that is a component of all love and that forms the basis in creation for all instances of "the good death." . . .[96]

This archetypal "death," "kenosis," or "love" (all of which are equivalent to each other and, for the Son, to "obedience") in the Trinity are the ground and measure for the second "kenosis" of creation, and for creaturely love, obedience, and death.[97] Hence "super-death" necessarily characterizes Christ's existence, both from the perspective of His divinity and from that of His perfect human love, obedience, and death. Being identical to the Trinitarian life of self-surrender, this "super-death" is the cause and substance of God's beatitude.[98] Hence, as long as Christ's death is formally characterized by "love" and "obedience" (and it must be, since it is essential to His Trinitarian personality), all His suffering is objectively joy, even if His subjective experience is literally worse than hell.[99]

It is debatable whether this explication accurately replicates the Catholic belief that the Son remained unchanged in heaven, possessing its bliss, even in His incarnation and passion. One must note it also effectively means the redemption is accomplished as an expression of the Trinitarian processions, and the Son's human nature has relatively little, if any, essential role to play. In addition, in his proceedings, Balthasar neglects to give adequate attention to the fact that, although all God's attributes are simple and identical in Him, they are not so to us when we name them. Thus, his continual identification of concepts that normally carry highly different meanings begins to hinder clear thought, rather than serve it.

A number of problematic theological consequences follow from Balthasar's theology of the Father's abandonment of the Son, or are embedded it. First, Balthasar posits the Trinitarian "distance" as necessary for two reasons: to maintain the distinction of Persons, and "in order to establish the basis within the Trinity for what, in the economic Trinity, will be the possibility of a distance that goes as far as the Son's abandonment on the Cross."[100] Since discussion of the distinctions among the Persons must always be balanced by the topic of their mutual indwelling, Balthasar's intention to maintain the distinction of Persons should be considered in connection with what he writes about the Trinitarian perichoresis:

> If there is to be this reciprocal indwelling, however, it follows that *what is specific to each Person* must not be withheld from the others. . . . [O]ne of

the Persons can, by way of the divine "economy," embody and represent the qualities of the others.[101]

With this idea, Balthasar dissolves the distinction that the concept of "distance" was to preserve, for if the personal properties can be shared, the distinction of Persons is lost along with any meaningful sense of *proper* (or "specific"). Moreover, recall that Balthasar thinks the individual Persons have proper acts reflecting their personal properties. Since these acts would be "specific" to them, his theology of the Trinity admits that a divine Person can *change* to take over an act proper to another Person. The second reason Balthasar gives for his concept of "distance" reveals that his understanding of the Son's abandonment *conditions* his doctrine of the Trinity. The point is worth stressing:

> Balthasar develops his theology of the Trinity *out of* his conviction of what it meant for Jesus to become cursed for our sake and experience the condemnation of the Father in hell.[102]

The question whether his theology of Holy Saturday is true thus also has implications for his Trinitarian theology.

Second, act flows from being, whether the hypostasis originates the act, or whether it is passive as one of its potentialities is brought into act by another agent. Consequently, it makes no sense to speak of an "antecedent consent" of the Son, or of the Second Person "letting Himself" proceed, or of the Father's "passivity" (i.e., dependence) vis-à-vis the Son in this way (or likewise in regard to the Spirit's relation to the Father and Son). It is impossible for a subject to will anything before it exists; thus the Son cannot have a consent antecedent to His being begotten. Nor can this consent be given co-eternally with His being begotten, because He can only "consent" and "let be" inasmuch as He already subsists: Any "consent" He gives is logically and ontically dependent on His existence. Hence, it is never "antecedent" to that existence, i.e., an "antecedent consent" is a contradiction in terms.

Problems arise also in that such an "antecedent consent" would mean that a volitional cause conditions the Father's generation of the Son and, in consequence, conditions the existence of the Father Himself, who is supposed to be the principle without a principle.[103] In addition, in conditioning the Father's generation, the Son's "antecedent consent" likewise conditions His own existence, thereby making the Son His own Father in a certain respect; i.e., despite Balthasar's strong characterization throughout his works of the Trinitarian relations as pure opposites (notably with regard to the Father's total giving and the Son's total receptivity), his speaking of the Son as in some way "passive" (in "letting be") and in some way "active" (in "letting") is like saying the Son is partly Son of the Father and partly Father of Himself: He is Son of the Father insofar as He is that "which is from" the Father, but He would be Father of Himself insofar as that "from which" He proceeded was, in part, His own active consent.

One might try to interpret Balthasar to mean that the Son's consent is received from the Father just as much as the rest of Himself, and hence it does not condition His generation. The Father's receptivity (or passivity) then means only that He is open to the Son who proceeds, not that He is dependent upon His consent. I do not see how to reconcile this suggestion with Balthasar's assertions. Even granting it, the Father's receptivity would differ in kind from that of the Son and Holy Spirit. Hence, even if receptivity were a perfection, it would not be a perfection identically common to all three Persons, with tri-theism (or bi-theism) as a result.[104]

In any case, the divine essence — even when considered in the Father's eternal act of generating — only exists insofar as it subsists in all three divine Persons at once. "Relation really existing in God is really the same as His essence and only differs in its mode of intelligibility."[105] Hence there can be no 'time' when the Son was not, such that He gave a consent "antecedent" to His procession.

Therefore, it seems there are reasons to hesitate about Balthasar's doctrine of "consent" and passivity within the Trinity, as well as parallel aspects of his Trinitarian theology expressed in different words, e.g., the "giving" and "receiving" of the divine nature. The same critique would also apply to Jesus' "passivity" and "obedience" *as Son* throughout His incarnate mission, and in His mission as a revelation of His procession (to be seen in the next chapter), since these are merely aspects of His being begotten:

> We see the Son "letting things happen" and are inclined to think of it as passivity — for instance, he allows himself to be carried by the Holy Spirit into the womb of the Virgin[106] — but this is only the "economic" expression of the fact that, in God, he, the "Eternally Begotten," ceaselessly allows himself to be begotten;[107] in his perfect, divine freedom he regards the execution of the Father's will as the best expression of his filial love.[108]

Third, note that, on the basis of Balthasar's principle that the intra-Trinitarian "distance" is the archetype for creation, a God who was not triune seemingly could not create. The (triune) divine nature is also apparently insufficient, if considered in abstraction from the distinction of Persons, i.e., if creation is considered a common work of the three Persons in virtue of the common divine power. With this observation, we return to Balthasar's unusual interpretation of *opera trinitatis ad extra communia*. In addition, if creaturely distinction has its archetype and its possibility in the personal distinctions within God, as Balthasar sees it, then given the existence of distinction in creation, it seems revelation is not necessary to know there is more than one Person in God.[109] Moreover, Balthasar's language of God 'restricting' Himself in order to 'leave space' for creatures and finite freedom is significantly different from a theological approach that sees God's omnipresence as the necessary condition for the existence of creatures and the exercise of their powers.[110] Whether he intended it metaphorically or not, Balthasar's language carries metaphysical implications. Even if his language were only metaphorical, one must ask how it is compatible with a metaphysics of God's omnipresence, and why Balthasar uses a metaphor that suggests the exact opposite of the reality. Again, God's liberty is not limited by human liberty because human liberty enters into the salvific will of God.[111]

Finally, although Balthasar denies that the Trinitarian "super-kenosis" is the archetype of sin,[112] it is difficult to see how his assertion (and it is only that) can be consistent with other essential aspects of his own theology, such as his positions that sin is not nothing, but a reality,[113] and God is the source of all being; that sin entails opposition, and the opposition of relations in the Trinity is the archetype of all created difference. Similarly, Balthasar denies that the Trinitarian self-giving should be called *death, kenosis,* or *abnegation,*[114] in contradiction to his own use of these terms or similar ones in his corpus. But why cannot the Trinitarian life be called *death* if death has a likeness to it,[115] since archetypes are called analogically by the names of their types? And if physical death has its archetype in the Trinitarian "super-death," why does Balthasar refuse spiritual death its own archetype in God, with its God-forsakenness being an analogue of that by which the Father 'forsakes' Himself to beget the Son?[116] An archetype is the model for both its good and bad images, which differ not in what they are (e.g., death) but in how well they reflect the archetype (well, or badly). If the Trinity is not sin's archetype, what is?

In fact, numerous passages imply the existence within God of sin or that the intra-Trinitarian kenosis is its archetype. Some need refer merely to sin being in God insofar as the sinful creature is in God (though they are open to more extreme readings).[117] Also, according to Balthasar's soteriology, sin is necessarily "in" God in the course of the redemption of mankind, as we shall later see. Others, however, go beyond these possibilities, as does the following: Jesus undergoes "every possible remoteness and alienation from God. Such distance is possible, however, only within the economic Trinity" — at this point, sin seems excluded from God, but then its archetype is in God, given how Balthasar continues — "which transposes the absolute distinction of the Persons in the Godhead from one another into the dimensions of salvation history, involving man's sinful distance from God and its atonement."[118] Or again, more clearly yet: "The

Son's eternal, holy distance from the Father, in the Spirit, forms the basis on which the unholy distance of the world's sin can be transposed into it, can be transcended and overcome by it."[119] Again, the divine God-lessness "must not be confused with the godlessness that is found within the world, although it undergirds it, renders it possible and goes beyond it."[120] The intra-Trinitarian "distance" is the foundation for all "distances that are possible within the world of finitude, including the distance of sin."[121] The creature's *no* is located within the Son's *yes* as a "restriction" and perversion of the divine self-giving,[122] and the divine freedom of self-giving is aped by finite freedom's "calculating, cautious self-preservation."[123] Moreover, the Son's abandonment has a "basis within the Trinity"[124] in the "distance" between the Persons — the incarnate Son "traverses . . . the realms of forsakenness that, as God, he has already (and has always) traversed"[125] — but this abandonment is greater than that between one in the state of sin and God. There is, as well, Balthasar's statement that "all apparently negative things in the *oikonomia* can be traced back to, and explained by, positive things in the *theologia*."[126] Sin might be excluded here because it is not just "apparently negative," but actually so; the only problem that remains is for Balthasar to explain where this negativity comes from if it is a positive reality, as he holds, rather than a defect in being. God as the archetype of sin is again raised by Balthasar's insistence that physical and spiritual death not be separated, at least not in the key case of Christ,[127] whose mission is His procession, while claiming at the same time that death has a likeness in God, which necessarily means its archetype. Balthasar's denial of sin in the Trinity is inconsistent with the logic of his thought and he provides no argument for it.[128]

A thorough evaluation of Balthasar's Trinitarian theology cannot be undertaken in this context, which considers his Trinitarian theology only in order to aid an exposition of his theology of Christ's descent. As it is the *Word* Incarnate who descends, however, such an examination cannot prescind absolutely from Trinitarian theology. We limited our consideration of these matters to their relation to the *Word Incarnate*, since the proximate cause of the Word's descent is His incarnation, while His procession in the immanent Trinity is a more remote cause.

The Father "Crushes" the Son in His "Wrath"

Out of "wrath" against sin, the Father abandons the Son whom He "loads" with sin. This simultaneous "loading" of sin and "wrathful" abandonment by the Father will "crush" the incarnate Son into the depths of Sheol, as we will see in this section.

God's wrath indicates His judgment against sin and His consequent abandonment of the sinner as such.[129] Hence, the Father's wrath is specifically directed against Christ, who has assumed the sin of the world.[130] This wrath is expressed in the economy but must be seen in the context of the Trinitarian love. Out of love and obedience, the Son identifies Himself with the sin of sinners. Out of love and wrath, the Father strikes Him instead of them. Nonetheless, Father and Son are united in this common work of supreme love in which they both relinquish what they love most — each other — out of love for each other's will and for the world.[131] The anger is for the sake of love, and hence it is more love than anger, though one must not empty it of the reality of the wrath.[132] The unity of will and the bond of the Holy Spirit, who is the Father and Son's substantial love, precludes the "crushing" that results from this wrath (to be discussed shortly) from being sadism.[133]

In the case of the Father's wrath, this Trinitarian basis deepens the horror of Christ's *visio mortis*. He knows that it is none other than God who has rejected and abandoned Him, God the All-Holy, the All-Good, who is to be loved above all and in all.[134] What hope can there be for Him then?[135] In a twist on St. Paul, one might say if God is against Him, who can be for Him? The full gravity of this alienation is appreciated only by recalling that the one in Sheol is the Son: If no one knows the Father but the Son, then surely no one knows what the loss of the Father means but the Son, and for no one can this loss be worse.[136] But until the Father's wrath has exhausted itself, so to speak, there is nothing in Christ "literally 'made sin'" to recommend Him to the Father anymore. He took on "total identity with 'the flesh of sin' (Rom 8:3), in order to be only a free space against which the will of the Father may make its colliding impact."[137] And precisely here, "'hidden' (Col 2:3)"[138] in the deep, "lies the 'unfathomable' (Eph 3:8) mystery of the Cross, in the momentum of the collision of the entire burden of sin with the total powerlessness of the kenotic existence,"[139] a collision that sends Christ to Sheol, crushing Him into its depths.

On the one hand, in Balthasar's treatments, this crushing wrath of God is said not to be an emotion, but a categorical rejection of compromise or complicity with evil.[140] It is a way of expressing the fact that God does not remain uninvolved in the world, but takes action for good and against evil. On the other hand, if one takes seriously how Balthasar integrates his positive exposition of the work of Abraham Heschel into his own position, this "wrath" is not just a mode of speaking about God's acts, since God also "experiences delight or grief, shows agreement or indignation, knows reciprocal love or its opposite, namely, that 'suspended love'[141] that is anger."[142] God's wrath then would not be "anthropomorphic,"[143] but neither would it (or its lack) be an "'immutable quality'[144] of God."[145]

The Pain of God

How Balthasar might think God can experience (non-anthropomorphic) wrath may be inferred from one of his treatments of "the pain of God."[146] Balthasar begins by noting the use of emotive expressions with respect to God in the Old Testament and as these expressions are developed in rabbinic writings.[147] From the New Testament, he points out Jesus' emotions and suggests that these may reveal something about God Himself, and must not be too quickly restricted to Christ's human nature.[148] In reaction to the mythologies, philosophies, and heresies of the time, the patristic period saw the development of Christian principles regarding the impassibility of God.[149] As Balthasar presents it, these principles aimed at denying any πάθος to God, where πάθος is understood as either an "external misfortune, contrary to a person's will,"[150] or as having "a necessary connection to sin."[151] In Christ, therefore, God freely chooses (i.e., rather than being forced) to undergo the natural πάθη (i.e., those flowing from human nature as such, but not those implying guilt).[152] Consequently, "God (and this applies to the Incarnate One also) can only be 'passive,' subject to *passio*, if this accords with some prior, 'active,' free decision."[153] Note Balthasar here extends the principle evident in Christ to God as such.[154] Hence, it would be consistent for Balthasar to say that God can "experience delight and grief," as also anger, in His divine nature because He freely wills to do so from all eternity. In this way, God's immutability, power, and freedom are preserved even as His πάθος is asserted: His will to experience these things manifests His sovereign freedom over Himself, but since His will is eternal, He remains immutable. As Balthasar says elsewhere,

> We cannot postulate any alteration *as this is found in creatures,* nor any suffering and obeying *in the manner proper to creatures.* . . . [I]t will be necessary to posit an incomprehensible freedom in God that allows him to do more, and to be other, than the creature would suppose. . . .[155]

Balthasar clearly does not want to ascribe suffering *equi*vocally to God as God, because he wants to attribute something *like* creaturely suffering to God: He claims there is something in God that is that foundation for creaturely suffering, yet different from it. Neither does Balthasar ascribe suffering *uni*vocally to God as God, because God's suffering *transcends* creaturely suffering as the in-finite transcends the finite. While avoiding the heresy of patripassianism, Balthasar wants instead to ascribe suffering to God *analogically.* In other words, there *is* a divine alteration, suffering, and obedience, which is the foundation of those characteristics that go by the same name in creatures, but which also escapes our concepts of it. (Note that, in this case, suffering would be *proper* to God.) However, if to speak analogically of God means to affirm of God some truth found in creatures, albeit with a difference that cannot be defined positively (since to do so would require comprehending God's essence), one may legitimately ask what conceptual content *suffering, alteration,* and *obedience* have in regard to God if Balthasar denies all content pertaining to creaturely reality. Do they have any meaning at all?

Again, in trying to find the pain in God that is the archetype for creaturely pain, Balthasar writes, "We have no name for it: in contrast to our suffering and grief, it implies no imperfection; we can perhaps speak of it as 'the triumphant seizing, adopting and overcoming' of pain, even of death."[156] But this description is no help: First, an analogy requires the same concept in each of the terms,[157] whereas here whatever is 'pain' in God is put in opposition to pain in the world. Second, human beings also can triumphantly seize and adopt their pain (or at least some of it), but the act of doing so is not identical to the pain itself that is overcome. Thus, pain and its overcoming are *in fact* seen as opposites in the creaturely world, not analogues. The possible perfection is the approach to pain, not the pain itself. Moreover, if everything has its archetype in God the way Balthasar sees it, this triumphal act must have its own archetype in God, and creaturely pain another.

As for patripassianism, it may appear that Balthasar has adequately avoided the pitfall of attributing suffering to God by rejecting a univocal attribution in favor of an analogical one. Yet I would argue that the Catholic Tradition not only has a problem with ascribing suffering to God as God univocally, but rejects attributing it to Him as God absolutely — whether univocally, equivocally, or analogically. The Council of Chalcedon opposed those who said the divine nature of the Son is subject to suffering,[158] and this without any qualification such as Balthasar has added. But if suffering in the divine nature is ruled out without qualification in the case of the Son, it is also excluded from the Father and Holy Spirit, because the Son's divine nature is identically one with that of the Father and Holy Spirit. This absolute rejection does not rule out that "One of the Trinity suffered for us." One of the Trinity did indeed suffer for us — but *in the flesh.* Already before the Council of Chalcedon, but authoritatively at least since then, the Catholic Church has carefully insisted that God suffered *in the flesh.* Hence, to say Christ suffered for us is to attribute suffering to Christ in exactly the same way it is attributed to other human beings, i.e., it attributes suffering to Christ *in the flesh.* It does not attribute suffering to God *as God* at all. Moreover, suffering is ascribed to the Son (and only to the Son) *only* in virtue of the communication of idioms, that is, only because the flesh in which Christ suffered subsists in the Person of the Word. The Word's divine nature as absolutely impassible remains unchanged by the hypostatic union, and hence also by the fact that the communication of idioms is possible. Much confusion about God's impassibility could be avoided by recalling that a person suffers *in a nature*. If one were to say the immaterial God chooses to suffer *as God* out of love for His creation, His perfection, eternal 'fate,' and happiness have been made dependent on creation. Under the same supposition, one must question why the Son became incarnate. God could have suffered as God for our redemption without doing so.

Balthasar's presentation of the Greek and patristic notion of ἀπάθεια is only half the picture. To attribute ἀπάθεια to a subject was to deny of it the possibility of one or more of the following: that something evil could be done to the subject; that the subject could be aroused in response (i.e., have passions, in the Aristotelian sense); that the subject could experience pain; and that the subject could be disturbed by the event, his passions, or his pain (i.e., would judge the event negatively).[159] Moreover, the Greek concept of divine impassibility was essentially linked with the concepts of simplicity, immutability, and incorporality.[160] Hence, God's divine ἀπάθεια rules out not only suffering as something undergone against one's will, as in Balthasar's presentation,[161] but also as any *pain* whatsoever, because pain implies a lack of happiness, and hence finitude and imperfection. Theologians have no more business wielding words such as *impassibility* in ways heedless of their specific signification than a chemist has of putting alcohol in a bottle marked "Distilled Water." The result can only be confusion, eventual disaster, and lack of credibility.

With this absolute denial of suffering in God as such, goes a similarly absolute assertion that suffering as such is always an evil, since it is a defect, or lack, of a good both in its objective cause and in the consequent subjective reaction of pain. Even the medical wound *as wound* is an evil, and moreover it is never a *medical* wound without the evil of an illness. Likewise, a suffering accepted out of love has love for its remote cause and its good is only this love; the cause of the suffering and the suffering itself considered abstracted from this love are evils. In contrast, Balthasar seems to ascribe a positive value to suffering and death in themselves in virtue of their likeness to the suffering Redeemer, not to mention the Trinity.

To communicate the impression he has of the Father's activity in Christ's descent, Balthasar employs the metaphors of momentum, impact, crushing, and the like. In the passivity of His obedience, Jesus is the object of God's wrath: The Father's wrath "collides" against Him.[162] Bearing the inconceivable "load" of all sin and being thrust away from the Father unto absolute abandonment as a result,[163] He will thus be "crushed by the momentum of obedience."[164] "The whole momentum of the curse of the sin of the world . . . crashes against the one who bears it," leading to a death that is "definitive."[165]

It appears this "crushing" action is the counterpart in the Father to the Son's *compassio* during the Descent. Balthasar does not make this connection explicitly, but it is a reasonable inference, given his method of reflecting on the Trinitarian relations with the use of images involving reciprocity, such as "distance," and "giving" and "receiving." As we have seen, the *visio mortis* attains its peculiarly intense character not only from its intimate union with the person experiencing it (and here recall that Balthasar does not limit the subject of the *visio mortis* to the soul of Christ), but also from the mode of *compassio* in which Christ undergoes it. On the part of Christ, *compassio* powerfully inclines Him toward the *visio mortis;* on the part of the Father, His wrath "crushes" the Son up against it. In both cases the force of momentum, so to speak, is added to the *visio's* impact.

The union of the Son's *compassio* and the Father's "crushing" of Him is also indicated by the fact that Balthasar sees the motive of the Descent event as the Trinitarian love.[166] The Father begets the Son out of love; or, in Balthasar's terms, He gives Himself so completely that the Person of the Son proceeds. This begetting love of the Father's self-giving necessarily continues in the Son's incarnation. But the Father gives forth His beloved Son in the Incarnation and gives Him up to the 'second death' out of love for the world and for the Son, who desires to save the world in this way.[167] Thus, because the Incarnation reaches its term in the absolute separation of Father and Son in the Son's descent, not only does the Father's love for the world have its fullest expression there, but also the Father's original begetting love for the Son.[168] The like may be said of the Son's love for the Father and the world, out of which He obediently descends into human nature all the way unto having the *visio mortis* in the mode of *compassio* in Sheol:[169] "Jesus dies *out of love:* He dies essentially 'for' us,"[170] but this death is "a death *for love of* the Father, for the implementation of his will. . . ."[171] Hence both the Father's "crushing" and the Son's *compassio* derive from their love for each other and for the world, and express it. Thus the Father's love is imaged in the *compassio* of the Son, and the synonymous metaphors of momentum, crushing, etc., are actually analogies between the economy of salvation and the Son's procession.

Note that, given the identity between the Father's generation and His "crushing" of the Son, the Son's *visio mortis* corresponds to an insight, through the analogy of the created world and specifically that of the 'second death,' into His own generation by the Father.[172] Building upon the treatment of Robert Nandkisore,[173] we can summarize that, in virtue of Christ's super-obedience (i.e., His hypostatic obedience that is His existence as Son), He experiences a

God-abandonment beyond that due all sin, because it is proportional to His divine filial intimacy with the Father. In doing so, He enters the "darkness reserved to God [the Father] Himself."[174] This darkness is twofold: the sins of the Father's creatures in the form of sin-in-itself, and the Father's primal kenosis, which is the origin of the Son upon whose model creation is formed. The problem here is precisely the role of sin, and an ambiguity in notions of otherness and selflessness: The selflessness of the Father in generating the Other-in-God (the Son) is supposed to be imaged in the selflessness of the Son in being "made sin," i.e., in becoming what is the other-than-God (in the sense of what is anti-God). In becoming what is contrary to Himself, the Son is self-less in a sense. The analogy reads

> Father : Other than Father as Father (Son) : :
> Incarnate Son : Other than Son as God (Sin),

which interestingly enough makes the eternal Son analogous to sin.

The "crushing" effect of the Father's "wrath" serves to stress anew the passivity of Christ's descent, because He is borne down to Sheol under the Father's wrath:

> Since the momentum of the Father's will, which loaded the world's guilt onto Jesus' kenotic *fiat,* in the truest sense 'crushed' the sufferer (Is 53:10), we have here no active descent — far less, a triumphant descent. . . .[175]

Still — or, rather, precisely in this way — Balthasar sees it as a 'glorious' descent:

> The 'radiance' of the trinitarian love, which has disclosed itself in the New Testament as the truth of the *kabod* of God, is a radiance that has its source only in the momentum of the obedience on the Cross.[176]

Kabod, Hebrew for *glory,* has *weight* as its most fundamental signification. The glory *(kabod)* of God then is His inner life of love, which is extended in His love of the world. The weight *(kabod)* of this glory bears the Son down into Sheol. Vice versa, the momentum of Christ's mission and being dead reveals the glory of God, indeed is the glory of God's act.[177] The Father's glory shining through Jesus has the weight of a hammer that crushes Him in the place of the hardhearted who resisted the force of His love.[178] God's love in act derives its force from its absolute character, from its in-finitude, the proper response to which is the perfect obedience of filial love as exemplified by Jesus.[179] After the Father raises the Son from the nadir of His descent,[180] the Holy Spirit will make manifest to Jesus' disciples the significance of the Cross as the revelation of the Trinity in its kenotic love and unity.[181] And, through the Spirit, the Church will continue to live the sacrificial love and obedience of Christ.[182]

> With this threefold setting-forth of the *kabod*-momentum of the Cross of Jesus — through the Father, through the Spirit, through the Church — as *kabod*-glory, the entire horizon of the meaning of the cipher δόξα [glory] in the New Testament has been staked out.[183]

Already known in the Old Testament, the momentum (*kabod*[184]) of God's wrath is thus incorporated and overtaken by the momentum of His love, manifested in the New.[185]

The manifestation of the "glory" of the divine love through the medium of the "crushed" Son is also a revelation of the divine omnipotence. The Father's power is seen in His "crushing" of sin in the Person of the Son, while the Son is simultaneously shown to be divine in His ability to bear this burden.[186] But since the economic casting out of sin in the Person of Christ is to be identified with the Father's eternal begetting of the Son in love, the divine omnipotence is identical to the Father's and the Son's kenoses: The Father gives Himself away in begetting the Son (power, kenosis) but also experiences a reciprocal loss when He abandons Him (powerlessness, kenosis). The Son empties Himself in becoming man unto the point of descending into Sheol (powerlessness, kenosis), but also sustains the Father's "crushing" and gives Himself back to the Father such that the Spirit proceeds (power, kenosis). Omnipotence is both power and powerlessness, these two being identified for Balthasar.[187]

In short, Balthasar thinks the Descent is glorious insofar as the Father's "crushing" of the Son in Sheol is an act of the divine omnipotence/powerlessness that manifests the kenotic Trinitarian love. However, Balthasar is unable to use the second imposition of *glory* consistently as its proper meaning. He repeatedly resorts to using the first imposition as *glory*'s proper sense in order to discuss his doctrine of the Descent. For example, at the climax of *The Glory of the Lord,* he writes:

> In this sense [in that the Son, obedient to the Father in His mission, has the passive *visio mortis*], the Son therefore contemplates his own work too in what is absolutely opposed to God, in an objective "triumphal procession" (Col 2:15) that is as far remote as possible from any sentiment of victory. *It is "glory" in the uttermost opposite of "glory,"* because it is at the same time blind obedience, that must obey the Father at the point where the last trace

of God seems lost (in pure sin), together with every other communication (in pure solitariness).[188]

Here, glory is said to appear in its opposite in Sheol; that is, obedience to the All-Holy is manifested using the anti-divine's refusal to obey (i.e., sin-in-itself) and its abandonment in the utmost solitude (which is contrary to the implicit unity and communication of obedience). The qualifier *seems* (in "the last trace of God seems lost") does not diminish the reality of this sin or the abandonment, but alludes to the Holy Spirit, who unifies Father and Son in the Descent event, but of whom the Son in Sheol is unaware and whose grace He does not possess, since He does not have the theological virtues.

We must ask how Balthasar uses the word *glory* in this passage, and why he puts it in quotation marks when he is not quoting anyone. First, observe that *glory* is used twice and with the same meaning in both cases. If not, there would not be opposition between "glory" and the "opposite of 'glory.'" Next, notice that "'glory'" is used in parallel with obedience to the divine ("It is 'glory' . . . , it is blind obedience"), which Balthasar consistently values as an extremely positive characteristic. In contrast, the "opposite of 'glory'" parallels sin and the rejection that is its worst consequence ("in the uttermost opposite of 'glory,' . . . where the last trace of God seems lost," etc.). Setting aside the single quotation marks for a moment, this second parallel equates the opposite of *glory* with what is anti-divine. It follows that *glory* properly signifies the divine. Given both parallels, however, *glory* does not refer here to the divine as hidden under the assumption of the anti-divine, but rather to the divine as apparent in holy obedience, when the two opposing features of sin and solitude are removed. In other words, the proper sense of *glory* actually used here is its first imposition. The single quotation marks then serve to indicate that Balthasar regards *glory* in this sense as only a so-called glory, i.e., a glory not truly proper of God.

The same use of quotation marks is seen when Balthasar says that the *visio immediata Dei in anima Christi*

> at the very least . . . may fluctuate between the mode of manifestness (which befits the Son as his "glory") and the mode of "concealment" (which befits the Servant of Yahweh in the hiddenness of his Passion). . . . [T]he second mode here is derived from the first: a living faith is content to stand before the face of the God who sees, whether or not one sees him oneself.[189]

The first sentence only makes sense if *glory* is taken according to the first imposition and the quotation marks indicate Balthasar's opinion that the first imposition is improper. Note that the mode of hiddenness is *derived* from the mode of manifestation, suggesting the latter is more fundamental. Observe also that Balthasar here inverts the perspective of glory: If glory elsewhere belongs to the subject that is its cause, here it is ascribed to its viewers. The Father's manifestation is the glory *of the Son* who sees the Father (just as the Father's concealment is the faith of the Son).

To consider a third example:

> This power ["to give comprehensible and appropriate expression to the utter otherness of his being" through God's revelation in the Word Incarnate] that dwells in the glory is most clearly seen where God's revelation takes account of, and overcomes, man's guilty turning-away, which has led to the "loss of δόξα" for all sinners (Rom 3:23): this he does through the superior power of his grace (Rom 5:15, 16:20f.), but in such a way that this power of grace is displayed in the event of the Cross as the sheer momentum of the judgment over sin. *God shows that this sheer momentum is at the same time the absolute power of glory, when he,* as "the Father of glory," through "the power of the force of his might" *raises Jesus,* who has died for all sinners, from the dead, so that thus he makes known to us "the immeasurable greatness of his power" (Eph 1:17-20).[190]

"This power that dwells in the glory" serves to point to glory as a sort of prime attribute of God, one expression of which is His power. This phrase, however, is not the one that merits attention in the present context. Despite its length, the entire text has been quoted, so the reader can see that Balthasar says the power of God acts as judgment against sin in the Cross event (which includes Christ's descent into Sheol), while the manifestation of that same power and event as glory must wait for the Resurrection. Until then, the presence of glory in the Crucifixion and Descent was not evident. The *full* manifestation of glory then is not a glory hidden in seeming defeat but when recognition is present. Balthasar here implicitly acknowledges the first imposition of *glory* as its proper signification.

Fourth, we should consider Balthasar's assertion that "what the Son experiences on the Cross as total night is in God's sight the Son's ultimate obedience and hence his highest glory."[191] Here Balthasar is trying once again to show that the summit of glory occurs in the darkest moment. But, in fact, he does not seem to have observed that a fundamental shift of perspective prevents the attainment of his objective. The proper meaning of *glory* is supposed to be how glory exists in God. In his statement, Balthasar is speaking of the "highest glory" as *seen by the Father.* And what is it that is seen? The Son's obedience.

Hence glory is not ascribed to the "total night," even undergone in obedience as it is, but rather to the perfection of obedience itself in the Son as a reality that appears and is recognized by the Father.

Fifth, Balthasar writes, "New Testament δοξάζειν no longer has the δόξα of God as its object, but as its inner principle."[192] As long as man is not divinized so as to become a self-subsisting Person — and Balthasar wants to preserve the unity-in-distinction of perfected creaturely freedom in relation to absolute freedom[193] — God's δόξα in him *as a principle* implies a distinction between δόξα and its effect such that the effect (configuration) does not in fact pertain to the δόξα itself. This conclusion holds even though the effect of God's δόξα is to grant a participation in its form and even though a thing is its form, because man does not become the glory of God substantially as God is His glory. Man receives a participation, which is the divine life of grace and the indwelling of the whole Trinity, but it is yet only a participation, as evident from that fact that man remains what he is, a creature.

Finally, it is telling that, despite his explicit assertions that a new ideal of divine glory must replace the "original sense"[194] such as found in the Old Testament,[195] Balthasar himself is unable to maintain this new usage in his own theology. At the same time, his willingness to adapt *glory* stands in curious contrast with his insistence upon retaining the Old Testament *Sheol* (in his understanding of that term) as the abode to which Christ descends: In effect, he is saying the Old Testament as a whole had the wrong idea of glory despite God's theophanies, but that a limited part of it had the most precise idea of the afterlife despite the lack of anyone returning from the dead before Christ. Balthasar treats both *glory* and *Sheol* alike, however, in that both receive their definitive (and new) meanings with the Descent of Christ: Glory is the powerlessness of God in His surrender of self,[196] and Sheol will be transformed into heaven, purgatory, and hell by Christ's experience of its most extreme *visio mortis*.

The Father Actively Inflicts the *Visio Mortis* on the Son

The final aspect of Christ's descent as seen from the Father's perspective is the Father's active infliction of the *visio mortis*. Christ's *visio mortis* is made worse not only by the mode of *compassio* in which He experiences it, but also by the fact, known to Him in His descent experience, that it is God Himself (in the Person of the once-beloved and once-loving Father[197]) who actively inflicts the *visio mortis* upon Him.[198]

The Father inflicts it in two ways. First, by abandoning the Son, the Father permits the Son's utter deprivation of the *visio Dei*, or anything remotely related to it. In the Father's withdrawal, the Son experiences the separation from God essential to mortal sin, a profoundly sickening, enslaving, and eternal solitude. All the Son 'sees' is rejection and punishment: He no longer has the intimate knowledge of the Father that came from His mission, nor does He know His mission as a sending and a going motivated by love. He no longer has the life of grace that knows God through faith, hope, and love. Much less then does He have the beatific vision of God and perfect happiness in it.

This absence of the *visio Dei* is no mere lack, however, but characterized positively by its punitive counterpart, the *visio mortis*. Because sin as such is a reality and not a "nothing," the *visio mortis* must be brought to bear on the Son by someone other than Himself, for He is strictly and absolutely passive in His being dead. The agent may be easily inferred. On the cross, and *a fortiori* in Sheol, "'terrors are turned' actively and aggressively upon him (Job 30:15),"[199] as the Father "loads" sin upon the Son. *Sin* here is not just guilt, much less a merely intentional reference to the sins of others; it is sin as a positive reality, sin-in-itself. But sin as such is precisely the content of the *visio mortis*. Thus, as the Father actively "loads" sin on the Son, who lets Himself be burdened with it in consenting passivity, so the Father actively inflicts the *visio mortis* upon the Son, who is passively conformed to it through the union of contemplation in His being dead.

It can now be seen that the wrath of the Father is both a 'pulling away' from the disgraced Son, and a 'pushing away' of Him, i.e., it is punitive both privatively (the Father's withdrawal in rejection of sin in the Person of the Son and the consequent deprivation of the *visio Dei*) and positively (the "crushing" infliction of wrath and the *visio mortis* as just punishment). The Son is abandoned, "crushed," and afflicted by the *visio mortis*; His horror is made complete by His knowledge that it is the All-Holy Father who thus rejects Him.[200] We see here the radical revaluation of the sense in which the Father did not spare His only Son (Rom 8:32): Rather than 'not sparing' Him by not preventing His death at the hands of men,[201] the Father does 'not spare' Him because He Himself inflicts the punishment for sin. The Father does not spare the rod, but applies it to the just Son for the sake of the unjust, as an act and expression of the divine love.

Conclusion

In summary, the Father is the active agent in the Descent event. He "loads" sin on Christ. He rejects sin in the Person of Christ and abandons Him in consequence. The Father's "wrath" against sin "crushes" Christ into the depths of

Sheol as the just punishment for the sins He bears. These aspects of the Father's involvement are not separable acts, but facets of the Father's relation to the Son in the Descent. Hence the Father must also be the one who actively inflicts the *visio mortis* on the Son in Sheol. The Father's participation in the Descent event is not without consequences for Himself, however. His reciprocal relation to the Son means that the Father Himself experiences loss when He abandons the Son in Sheol.

It is important to observe that implicit in Balthasar's characterization of the Father's activity and Christ's passivity in the Descent event is his idea that the divine Persons have proper acts in the economy. The Father, and only the Father, "loads" sin on the Son. The Son, and only the Son and (as will be shown in the next chapter) *as the Son*, is conformed to sin in the *visio mortis*. The Holy Spirit, and only the Holy Spirit, incarnates the Son and mediates to Him the Father's will that this burden be placed on Him.

CHAPTER SEVEN

Christ's Descent in Light of the Trinity:
The Son, Mission as Expression of Procession

The driving force in Balthasar's theology of the Descent considered from the perspective of Christ as God the Son is the close connection Balthasar sees between the economic and immanent Trinities: The character of the Son's procession determines the character of His mission. As a result, the Son's Trinitarian personality will be most perfectly revealed at the point when His mission reaches its "utmost pitch" in Sheol. But as the Son's procession implies His relation to the Father and Holy Spirit, the Descent will also be the supreme revelation of the entire Trinity: If a Son is revealed, then the Father implied by this sonship must also be revealed, and the love between them.

We will proceed in five steps: First, the relation between the Son's procession and mission will be generally set forth. Second, the specific way in which the procession continues in the mission or, equivalently, the way in which the mission expresses the procession, will be examined. The intra-Trinitarian kenosis of the procession continues and is imaged in the Son's "deposit[ing]"[1] of divine attributes with the Father in order to become man. The divine kenosis reaches its supreme economic expression in the Son's sacrifice of His humanity in His being dead. Hence, more precisely, our second topic will be the conditions for the possibility of this "depositing." Its actuality as seen in the important example of the "depositing" of the divine knowledge will be our third, while its ultimate perfection in the "suspension, as it were, of the Incarnation"[2] will be our fourth. Christ's descent (Chapter Five) and the Son's descent (the present chapter) will then be briefly connected through the use of Balthasar's characterization of death, which specifies the way in which the Son's kenosis unto Sheol is redemptive. The chapter closes with a summary of the Descent in terms of kenosis as love, because the Trinitarian love of the divine Persons for each other and for the world is both the motivation for the Descent event and is revealed in it.

From Procession to Mission, and Back Again

To begin, Balthasar sees the Incarnation of the Son as nothing other than the procession of the Word into human nature. The divine relation of being begotten continues into human nature with the conception, life, and death of Christ: "His *missio* is the appearance in this world of his *processio* in God."[3] One might say that, according to Balthasar, Jesus is the word of God in the language of human nature. This expression might seem to be merely a metaphor at first glance, yet it goes far toward capturing Balthasar's understanding of the Incarnation. When a concept is spoken as a word, or if a word is translated perfectly from one language to another, the word that results *is* nothing other than the original despite its different *appearance.* Because the original conceptual content remains unchanged, what the word expresses and the essential function it therefore has (e.g., as a noun) do not change. Likewise, the Son's Trinitarian *eucharistia* of gratitude and return to the Father in self-surrender will be reflected in His economic mission,[4] while the unity between obedience and the freedom of love in His human life will manifest this feature of His divine Person, which is the Son's *qua* Son.[5] Moreover, the Trinitarian "distance" of simultaneous distinction and unity within the freedom of love is mirrored in the union of the distinct natures in the Person of Christ, and in the union of love between God (the Father) who commands and the man (Jesus) who obeys.[6] The Incarnate Word thus is to become the archetype for finite freedom's being united with infinite freedom without being absorbed into God, rather than rebelling against Him.[7]

If the characteristics of the procession determine the features of the mission, then they determine the particular content of the human life of Christ, that is, His actions and His experiences.[8] The Incarnation is not perfected as a static condition,[9] but is inseparably identified with what the Incarnate Word did. The Son became incarnate for a reason, His human life had a purpose, and He directs all He says and does toward this end. This goal is the reconciliation of the world with the Father, and it will ultimately be accomplished through Christ's descent. The mission of the Son is comprised by this purpose and all by which He accomplishes it (i.e., the Word's being incarnate as well as all Christ does and suffers). Since the Son as God is "eternal event," which is His divine glory,[10] His mission will reveal in act the glory *(kabod)* of the Trinitarian life of love and, on the ground of this divine "distance" (a union that admits distinction), make possible fallen finite freedom's union with infinite freedom in the same Trinitarian life. Following the metaphor of language, it may be said that the Word is known when expressed in speech, i.e., action and passion.

So the procession of the Son is, or continues as, the mission of Christ. As the Son is event, Jesus' mission is event. As the event of the Son reveals the Father's love, the event of the Son's mission will do likewise. Jesus is the procession of the Word into human nature, and His human existence perfectly expresses the content of the Word. This content, however, is the being that the Son receives from the Father. The Father gives Himself perfectly to the Son; i.e., He gives perfectly *what* He is, namely, the divine nature. It is due to this perfect correspondence between the being of the Father and the being of the Son, as well as the perfect expression of the Son *qua* Son in Jesus, that the actions, words, and sufferings of Christ reveal the Father.[11] In our analogy of language, the speaker is revealed in his word. The transcendent perfection in Jesus of those qualities that have the Son as their archetype will manifest Him as Son. In doing so, because the Son is nothing but what the Father has given Him and because the Father gives what He Himself is, Jesus makes known the Father (and simultaneously, His own divinity as Son).[12] A passage from *The Glory of the Lord* illustrates the Incarnation of the Son as the embodiment of His filial personality particularly well, especially as it manifests how the revelation of the Son in the mission of Jesus also reveals the entire Trinity:

> This man, who is obeying even as he "makes" himself into a God [by what He says], is a God who is obeying even as he makes himself into a man. For the former, taken by itself, would clearly be ὕβρις [insolence] and impossible to comprehend in terms of human obedience. For the surest thing that can be said of man is that he is not God. Thus, he [Jesus] must already be obedient even as God, and his human obedience unto death must be the epiphany of a divine — that is, trinitarian — obedience. In the Son of Man there appears not God alone necessarily, there also appears the inner-trinitarian event of his procession; there appears the triune God, who, as God, can command absolutely and obey absolutely and, as the Spirit of love, can be the unity of both.[13]

Before continuing, we must suggest in general how Balthasar attempts to avoid the implication of multiple wills in the Godhead despite his notion of a divine obedience. In discussing Jesus' self-consciousness and His consciousness of His mission, Balthasar is particularly concerned to resolve the following dilemma:[14] If Jesus is to have a mission, it means He must be sent, but to be sent necessarily implies a sender. On the one hand, the existence of a sender raises the specter of heteronomy, threatening both freedom and unity. On the other hand, if the mission does not involve heteronomy, how can it remain a sending of one by the other? The problem is solved in a way that parallels Balthasar's discussion of Trinitarian "distance." The freedom of the Son, His *distinction* in unity, is preserved in that it is His own will to be sent. The *unity* between Father and Son is maintained, as also the existence of Jesus as a mission, in that the sender is present to the one sent in the very sending.[15] In other words, the mission is a type of perichoresis between Father and incarnate Son: The Son identifies Himself with His mission. But His mission is to do the will of the Father. Thus the Son can be said to remain in the Father even as sent and even when abandoned in Sheol, because His existence is defined by the Father's will at every moment.

The problem of heteronomy is particularly pressing for Balthasar because he insists Jesus obeys *as Son*. He writes, "There is no question of Jesus as man obeying himself as God; nor does he obey the Trinity: as Son, in the Holy Spirit, he obeys the Father."[16] It might seem that Balthasar has lost the advance made by St. Maximus the Confessor, namely, since faculties flow from natures, Jesus obeys with His human will the single divine will of the Father, Son, and Holy Spirit.[17] In contrast, Balthasar wants to say that Jesus humanly obeys the Father, but in doing so, He obeys *as Son*.

It seems the only way to understand this *de facto* inconsistency with St. Maximus' teaching and to reconcile the Son's obedience with the single divine will is from the perspective of Balthasar's understanding of the Incarnation. If the mission *is* the procession, and Jesus is the Word *become* man, then His human will is the only will He has. No "supratemporal contents" are present in Jesus, for the whole Word must become flesh,[18] and this principle — if it is to be a principle — cannot apply only to His intellectual knowledge, but must apply also to His will. In other words (and the foundation for this conclusion will be seen in detail in the next section), the human will of the Son is in accord with the divine will not as two separate powers that intend the same object but because His divine will becomes and has always intended to become His human will. The Son's human will is *also* His divine will since the object willed is the same (generally, if not in detail), since the Person willing is the Son, and since the Son must continually will His kenosis in the flesh. Thus Balthasar says it is the Son's eternal will to obey in time, and it is His temporal will to hold fast to this decision, without these two decisions being separated in time.[19] Though the Son does the Father's will both in emptying Himself and in His acts, His obedience then is not the weaker part of a heteronomy, but is His own autonomy in communion with the Father.[20] He Himself wills what the Father wills.

Being sent from the Father, He empties Himself in kenosis, but His own nature is this self-surrender. He obeys the Father in virtue of the Spirit communicating to Him His mission's specific content, i.e., the task of the moment, but this Spirit is also His own.[21]

We see here that Balthasar maintains with St. Maximus the essential aspect of obedience as submission to the will of another, albeit in a very different way. In a theology following St. Maximus, this submission involves a distinction of subjects in every case but one. In Christ alone can the subject obey Himself, because He alone has two wills. With His human will, He submits to what He Himself wills with His divine will; or, what is the same, He as man obeys Himself as God. From St. Maximus' principle that the number of wills depends on the number of natures, it also follows that there can be no obedience in the Trinity; the divine nature being one and simple, there is only one single divine will, identical in power and not only in content in all three Persons. On this basis, the assertion, "The Son obeys the Father," can only be true with respect to the submission of the human will of the Son to the divine will of the Father, which is identical to the divine will of the Son. For Balthasar, on the other hand, the Son obeys already as Son. The divine obedience of the Son is His reception of His own will from the Father, but since it is received by Him, this will is His own and His acts are voluntary. Thus the Son can "obey" the Father already within the immanent Trinity, and the *incarnate* Son can still obey as *Son*. Balthasar thus effectively takes the number of wills as flowing from the number of hypostases, not the number of natures. As a consequence, Balthasar often speaks as if the divine will were one in the thing decided as the result of a sort of consensus,[22] an impression strengthened by his notion of the Son's "antecedent consent." But if the Son gives "antecedent consent" to His generation, and His consequent reception of Himself is His obedience, does He not then ultimately obey Himself rather than the Father? Consequently, it does not seem that Balthasar adequately avoids the implication of multiple wills in his Trinitarian theology.

Acknowledging that the problem remains inherent in Balthasar's conception of the Son's obedience, we return to our consideration of the revelation of the Son and the Trinity in the mission of Jesus. If the Son is to reveal the Father and His love perfectly in His mission, and if this divine love goes to the extreme of utter self-surrender, then likewise the Son's mission must entail the greatest possible self-surrender. Only then will revelation and mission be adequate to the reality revealed. Only when the Son's self-giving has gone to the utmost extreme in Sheol will He be perfectly transparent to the Father, who is the original self-surrender. In other words, the Incarnation of the Word is ordered not merely to His death — for greater love no man has, than to lay down his life for his friends (Jn 15:13) — but to His being "made sin" in Sheol, since physical and spiritual death are not be distinguished for Jesus in Balthasar's theology.[23] The following passage points both to this revelation of the Trinitarian nature of God in the Descent event and to the way in which the Son's being dead in Sheol atones for all sin:

> The world as a multiplicity (which, as such, cannot be God) only becomes intelligible in terms of a free creation; free creation gives creatures genuine freedom and implies necessarily the risk of their going astray; such a risk can only be assumed responsibly if the God of love is able to gather in such lostness into himself. This is possible in no other way than by God's going in powerlessness to share in man's lostness, but out of obedience to God; and so God must be triune: For the divine omnipotence cannot deal with the rebellious powerlessness of creaturely freedom from above and from outside. . . . Only if we presuppose a (possible) incarnation of God — to the point of death, abandonment, hell — can we continue . . . to uphold the universal religious principle that God must be all in all (even in the godlessness of rebellious freedom). For only if an obedient love, out of its pure compliance to love itself, allows itself to be sent into lostness can the creature in his freedom be saved, and that not by being overwhelmed from outside but by being gathered up into the abyss of absolute love which embraces all abysses.[24]

Balthasar's argument here runs something like this: As creator of finite freedom, God Himself must stand as its guarantor. As guarantor, He must provide a means of that freedom being restored when it rebels. But as guarantor of *freedom,* God must ensure this restoration is done from within finite freedom itself. Thus, in saving the world, God must take upon Himself the limits of creaturely freedom. As free, however, it is specifically finite freedom's real possibility of rebelling that must be set aright, which means exactly this aspect of it must be taken up and transformed. Hence, God must assume the limits of finite freedom out of obedience and go into the depths of creaturely rebellion without rebelling Himself.[25] In thus re-establishing the negative extreme of creaturely freedom's rebellion within its positive extreme of obedience under the worst circumstances possible, and both extremes within Himself, He provides a way whereby the fallen creature can be brought to restoration. A single-personed God could not do this, because obedience must precede the acceptance of creaturely freedom: If a single-personed God became incarnate, His obedience would follow after the existence of His human nature, and hence His very being human would not be characterized by obedience.[26] Hence there must be a divine Person who is obeyed, a divine Person who obeys even unto ultimate separation, and a third divine Person who maintains their unity in this extremity. Thus the descent into Sheol of the Word Incarnate is the supreme revelation of the Trinity.

The fact that this revelation is made most manifest when swathed from every eye in absolute darkness is itself revelatory of the divine nature, indicating the ultimate "incomprehensibility" of the divine love.[27] The revelation of the Trinity thus has a glory that testifies to God's sovereign "hiddenness"[28] in His transcendence, even as it preserves it. It is not only the extremes of self-giving to which the divine Persons go for each other and for the world that make this love incomprehensible, however. What is also incomprehensible is that this self-giving exists within God Himself:

> *This* is where God is an absolute mystery for us, precisely in his revelation. . . . This is what is absolutely incomprehensible to us, that in God relation-to-self and relation-to-other, eternal repose-in-self and eternal striving and loving can be identical.[29]

The mystery is twofold: first, that the one God is Trinitarian, giving Himself so utterly that other Persons proceed yet without His unity being destroyed; and second, that this extreme is *made known* to us in the extremity of the Descent event *without losing its incomprehensibility.* What is brought to light in the darkness of Sheol remains darkness to man, this darkness itself revealing that God is always greater than human concepts. The proper human response then can only be to let Him be what He wills to be.[30] If Christ's descent is the supreme revelation of the Trinity in the way Balthasar describes, the proper signification of glory *must* be its second imposition. The very fact that this imposition is second would point to how slowly the human mind comes to grasp the true nature of God and His glory.

Procession into the "Form of a Slave" through "Depositing"

As seen in the previous section, the procession of the Son continues in His mission. Since the Son's procession is His kenosis in grateful self-gift back to the Father, a like emptying of self will initiate His becoming man and continue during His mission until His return to the Father through the Descent. In other words, Christ's existence is necessarily kenotic because it is the procession of the Word in human flesh and the Trinitarian processions are kenotic by nature.[31] Hence the mission of the Incarnate Word may be identified with the Word's kenosis.

But the Son's procession in the economy must continue within the possibilities of created human nature. However seemingly impossible, the entire divine revelation to be made must be manifested in this flesh, without the flesh becoming something other than it is. God will not appear in the flesh as God — Balthasar thinks this would result in monophysitism — but as a creature:[32] "The absolute not only irradiates finitude but actually *becomes* finite."[33]

> No supratemporal contents, nor contents from another period of time, may be put into it (although they might suggest themselves in the case of this existence), for this would mean that at most a fraction of the divine Word would have become flesh.[34]

In other words, the Word must not bring with Him attributes of the divine essence ("supratemporal contents") or give His human soul exceptionally extensive knowledge ("contents from another period of time"), if the *Word* is really to *become* flesh and if the flesh, without change, is really to be the Word. Hence the importance for Balthasar of saying the (divine) procession is the (economic) mission. The Word will thus have to empty (κενόω) Himself of His divine attributes in becoming man, what Balthasar will also call His "laying aside"[35] or "deposit[ing]"[36] of the divine attributes.

The "depositing" will also make the Incarnation kenotic in a derivative sense in that it is the humbling of the divine Son. The humiliation is that God is now man:

> The humiliation is precisely the passing over from being in the one actual form to being in the other . . . which means more than a simple addition of a second nature to a first. It would be no humiliation if, in passing over to the being of a slave, he ceased to be God. . . .[37]

There is no humiliation in a man being exactly what he was made to be. Nor would the Incarnation be a humiliation if God retained or lost all His divine prerogatives. It is only a humiliation if God has man's finite form. He must remain God in some way, "but the entrance on the form of a slave must nonetheless be seen as a real movement, an event for him too, a becoming and an 'emptying' (Phil. 2:5-8)."[38]

How is such a "'surrender' of the *forma Dei*"[39] possible "for the God of whom we cannot postulate any alteration *as this is found* in creatures, nor any suffering and obeying *in the manner* proper to creatures"?[40] First, this real "'surrender' of the *forma Dei*" is possible due to the divine omnipotence: God is free "to do more, and to be other, than the creature would suppose of him on the ground of its concepts of 'God.'"[41] He can, if He wills, dispose of His own nature: "God is not only by nature free in his self-possession, in his ability to do what he will with himself; for that very reason, he is also free to do what he will with his own nature."[42] But this giving away of His nature is fully in accord with it. The absolute *bonum diffusivum sui* can give its very self, because its very being is giving.[43] Thus there is no real change, loss, or contradiction.[44]

Note that Balthasar's recurrence to God's freedom to 'explain' what would seem to be an impossible divesting of His nature suggests he sees reason's concepts of God as *distorting* due to the limit of their finitude. Such a position contrasts with a view that sees these concepts as apprehending something true of God, though without comprehending His essence. For example, in his discussion of God's omnipotence in the *Summa theologica*, St. Thomas Aquinas reasons there are things God cannot do, because they involve a contradiction in terms.[45] St. Thomas is not thereby limiting the divine omnipotence, because he would admit man cannot positively set forth the limits of God's power, as this would require comprehending the divine essence.[46] Such a positive definition cannot be given, but what may be given are both an analogical definition, which says something positively true of God's power, and a negative definition, which says what things are not part of that power. In contrast, Balthasar seems to think that explanations like that of St. Thomas amount to the imposition of a limit by a creature's reason on reason's Creator. In Balthasar's view, because God is greater than His creature, He can transcend reason's limits for the higher truth that He actually is. By definition, reason can never grasp this truth or the act in which God transcends reason's concepts. Thus contradictions (Balthasar prefers the word *paradoxes*) will arise frequently in the course of God's involvement with man. His very doing of such things proves He is God.[47] The choice of a contrast with St. Thomas's presentation of the divine *omnipotence* is apropos to Balthasar's use of the divine *freedom* here, because freedom and power are essentially linked for Balthasar. One is free to the extent he is able to do what he wills.[48]

God's omnipotence to do what He will with His nature is also expressed in Balthasar's connecting God's "ever-greaterness" and His "going to the end" or "going to the extreme."[49] These coincide in the extremity of Christ's descent, in which "he plumbed the abyss of our death far more deeply than we could ever do."[50] Thus Balthasar says, "The Cross is raised up at the end of evil, at the end of hell."[51] Here there is a play on the word *end:* The end of evil and of hell is both its furthest extent, its worst fury, which Christ suffers in His descent, as well as the termination of their power as a result of Christ's expiation.

Secondly, the real "'surrender' of the *forma Dei*" is possible, because the divine Persons are kenotic by nature: "It is only because the Son in very truth possesses the 'form of God' (μορφῇ θεοῦ, Phil 2:6), . . . that he can 'empty him-self' and take 'the form of a servant.'"[52] The kenotic "depositing" in the econ-omy is nothing other than the kenotic "giving back" of the divine essence in self-gift by the Son to the Father. He will retain His filial divine form as obedi-ence, but this consenting passivity exists now in the flesh. Insofar as the divine nature is self-surrender of the divine essence, and it is precisely through the surrender of the divine attributes that He descends into the flesh, this new form of existence does not change Him in this most ultimate sense and hence He can still be said to exist in the divine nature. He is divine precisely in the perfection of His giving away of what He is.

> Christ's μορφή [form] exists within a tension unique to it . . . : it is an emp-tying out (κένωσις) of the form proper to God (μορφὴ θεοῦ), and hence presents itself primarily as its opposite and as the uttermost concealment of this divine form

— This description applies not only to the Son's incarnation in finite, creaturely human nature, but even more so to His conformity to sin-in-itself in Sheol —

> but it is equally the bringing near and making visible of the divine form, since the humiliation (ἐταπείνωσεν ἑαυτόν) and the submission even to the Cross (ὑπήκοος μέχρι θανάτου . . . σταυροῦ) are precisely the human real-ization of the divine disposition of Jesus Christ,[53]

that is, utter self-gift and obedience.

Third, the "'surrender' of the *forma Dei*" as well as "alteration," "suffer-ing," and "obeying" are possible because the *economia* is an analogue of its ar-chetype, the *theologia;* more, the economic Trinity is itself the immanent Trin-ity, it is the divine essence in a different mode.[54] Balthasar's insistence is to be taken in the strictest sense when he says that Christ's "mission from God (*missio*) . . . is identical with the Person *in* God and *as* God (*processio*),"[55] i.e., with the Son as a subsisting relation ("the Person *in* God") and with the Son as divine ("the Person . . . *as* God"). The mission *is* the procession: The "becoming man"[56] (and all His actions as man) is the "becoming the eternal Son"[57] in that both are the giving back of the divine essence.

> We could put it this way: the Son's *missio* is his *processio* extended in "eco-nomic" mode; but, whereas in his *processio* he moves toward the Father in receptivity and gratitude, in his *missio* (thanks to the "trinitarian inver-

sion"),[58] he moves away from him and toward the world, into the latter's ultimate darkness. In fact, since all is obedience, he *is* moving toward the Father through this utter estrangement, but for the present [while He is in this estrangement] he must not be allowed to know this.[59]

As His mission is His procession, and His task obedience, thus His abandonment by the Father can be a mode of His intimate relation to Him, and His kenosis to the point of being "literally 'made sin'" can be an act of His supreme kenotic love within the Trinity.[60]

To illustrate Balthasar's doctrine of the Incarnation, we can build upon the ancient analogy of the sun, which illustrated the consubstantiality of the Father and the Son. In this analogy, the sun generates a ray of light that has the same nature as the sun. Now let us say this sunbeam exposes some photographic slide film as the ray dramatically pierces the clouds just after the sun sinks below the horizon. The image on the film testifies to the sunbeam, which testifies to the now-hidden sun. However, the sunbeam in the photographic image appears no longer in the nature of light, but in the nature of the physiochemistry of the film. The Father is the sun, the Word is the sunbeam, and Jesus is the ray that appears on the photographic film. Jesus' mission reveals the Word's procession, which in turn reveals the Father. When the Word receives back His divine attributes in the resurrection of Jesus, it is as if the slide is held up to the sun the next morning: Light streams through the image of the ray, and the ray now possesses both its original attributes and the physiochemical ones of the film image.

This Balthasarian "depositing" is not just a matter of not using the divine power (as in the account of Jesus' arrest in the Gospel of John), or of not manifesting a concealed majesty (as in the Transfiguration). In becoming man, the Word actually divests Himself of divine attributes. Instead of thinking Jesus could have come down from the cross, but did not do so out of love for mankind, Balthasar says it is "the profound truth of the cross, that the doctor who helped others *cannot* now help himself. . . ."[61]

> The event by which he consents to be transferred from the form of God into the "form of a servant" and the "likeness of men" (Phil 2:6f.) affects him as the eternal Son. . . . We can call it *kenosis,* as in Philippians 2, but this does not imply any mythological alteration in God; it *can* express one of the infinite possibilities available to free, eternal life: namely, that the Son . . . "lays up" and commits to God's keeping the "form of God" he has received from him. He does this in order to concentrate, in all seriousness and realism, on the mission that is one mode of his procession from the Father.

There is nothing "as if" about this: the outcome is that he is forsaken by God on the Cross. Yet this "infinite distance," which recapitulates the sinner's mode of alienation from God, will remain forever the highest revelation known to the world of the diastasis (within the eternal being of God) between Father and Son in the Holy Spirit.[62]

Nor is the Word's going "from the form of God into the 'form of a servant'" just a mode of speaking in which the grammatical subject is the Person in whom human nature comes to exist rather than the human nature that actually comes to be; instead, His kenosis "affects him as the eternal Son." But the "distance" of *absolute* opposition between Father and Son means the "distance" between infinite freedom (the Word) and finite freedom (the incarnate Word) is a relation that was always in God, at least as a possibility (i.e., *in potentia*) [63] Though the second "distance" is also infinite, it is less, so to speak, than the absolute "distance" between Father and Son.[64] It thus can be established as a reality — which, like all reality, exists "in" God — without change in God Himself.

Thus does the procession continue into the mission. Thus does the flesh fully express and "comprise within itself the full [divine] freedom and the full [filial] personality of the active Word."[65] Thus is Jesus true God and true man: true man because His humanity is not compromised by divine or exceptional attributes, true God because the self-emptying required of the Son to descend into flesh is a continuing act of divine kenosis. Thus is "the lamb which was slain from the beginning of the world" (Rev 13:8). Indeed,

> the Lamb can only ride out to battle as the 'Lion of Judah' (Rev 5:5) and tread 'the wine press of the fury of the wrath of God the Almighty' [i.e., drink the cup of the Father's "wrath" and be "crushed" in Sheol] *because* he stands on God's throne as the 'slain' and 'slaughtered' Lamb,[66]

pouring Himself out in self-gift from eternity. Due to the divine omnipotence (or freedom), the Son's personal property of obedience, and the identity between His procession and mission, the Son can kenotically "deposit" the divine attributes with the Father, yet continue existing as the pure relation of the filial hypostasis,[67] now with human attributes. "The hypostatic obedience of the Son of God, his *kenosis* or *diastasis* [distance]"[68] — all three are equivalent.

In short, as a result of his theology of "depositing," Balthasar's reiteration that the Son's (divine) procession is His (economic) mission takes on clearer significance. The hypostasis of the Son does not retain His divine attributes (otherwise, He would not be wholly incarnate[69]), but through the Incarnation has a new mode of existence, i.e., in the flesh instead of in the divine nature (taken as the divine attributes): Thus the procession (the hypostasis of the Son) *is* the mission (the man Jesus, i.e., this person with these human attributes).

Before examining the "depositing" of the divine attribute Balthasar most singles out, it should be noted that the Son's consenting passivity (i.e., obedience) is vitiated in proportion to the real extent to which He "deposits" the divine attribute of power in order to become weak as man. Because one can only act, or choose not to act, in virtue of one's present potential for this act, Christ's active "letting be" becomes meaningless and nonexistent if He lacks the actual power, say, to come down off the cross, as Balthasar had said.[70] This objection can be resolved neither by Balthasar's identification of the divine power as its powerlessness in the kenosis of self-gift,[71] nor by his assertion that God is "ever-greater" than power or powerlessness.[72]

It should also be noted that Balthasar takes up the Thomistic concept of the divine Persons as self-subsisting relations — I take it this is what Balthasar is getting at when he describes them in terms of giving and receiving, speaks of "opposition" between Father and Son, etc. — but he understands the concept in a significantly different way. For St. Thomas, *relation* necessarily signifies both *esse* and *ratio*, that is, both being and reference to another.[73] However, since the *ratio* is that in virtue of which this being is a *relation*, Balthasar appears to have understood *self-subsisting relation* as a comportment to another (the *ratio*) that exists simply as this reference. He seems to have overlooked the necessity of the *esse* as a specific nature. For Balthasar, the *ratio* can therefore be found in various natures without change in itself.[74] Thus we find in his theology such terms as "pure 'relationality'"[75] and "hypostatic obedience."[76]

The idea represented with these terms can be illustrated by a container, since a container is what it is solely by reference to another, namely, something to be contained. For example, a glass is what it is in order to hold liquids, it can hold an endless variety of such, and its own nature is not changed by the kind of liquid it contains. Likewise, as a *self-subsisting* relation (understood as the *ratio*) from and back to the Father, the Son can lay aside His divine attributes and become man without changing His own nature as a relational *ratio*, i.e., His person, or hypostasis. If this "movement"[77] is undertaken in obedience (the personal property of His hypostasis), the divine contents, so to speak, may be exchanged for human ones without the nature of the Son *qua* Son changing. And similarly the human ones can give way to His being "literally 'made sin.'" Thus, for Balthasar, the divine nature is the glass (the self-subsisting relational *ratio*), not this glass with a necessary content (namely, the divine attributes). What is truly divine about God is not *what* He is, so to

speak, but *how* He is, i.e., His self-giving, which constitutes the personal relations.[78] As a consequence, it goes far toward capturing Balthasar's Christology
to say the content of Jesus is human, but the form carrying that content is divine.

One might object to this analogy by pointing out how Balthasar asserts
that "the Giver (whose act of giving is eternal) does not lose what he gives, that
is, himself."[79] He then quotes the Fourth Lateran Ecumenical Council (DS 805),
which teaches that the Father does not give His substance to the Son so as not to
retain it Himself. Balthasar continues from there, saying,

> We need to hold the two things simultaneously and affirm their identity:
> the genuine, active giving that involves the entire Person who gives, and the
> eternal Being of the Person that remains constant throughout this act of
> self-giving.[80]

Even when Balthasar's formulations here are assumed to be in accord with the
Council, however, the "identity" is difficult to maintain in Balthasar's theology,
if not impossible. In another place, Balthasar again states what can be read as
the Lateran doctrine in other words, but then develops it in a way in which its
orthodoxy turns on an ambiguous reading of "himself."[81] For Balthasar, however, the "himself" of the Father is ultimately His person alone, not His person
with His divine attributes, since it is only His person ("the *act* of giving") that
He cannot give away.[82] Also consistent with the glass analogy are passages in
which Balthasar says the Father's generation of the Son "leaves the [Father's]
'womb' empty"[83] and those in which God's wealth is His giving the divine essence away, as opposed to having it.[84]

The analogy of the divine Persons as glasses is consistent with Balthasar's
theology and sheds light upon it. For example, regarding the Son's Incarnation,
he says,

> It is not that God, in himself, changes but that the unchangeable God enters
> into a relationship with creaturely reality, and this relationship imparts a
> new look to his internal relations. This is not something purely external, as
> if this relationship *ad extra* did not really affect him: rather, the new rela-
> tionship to worldly nature, which is hypostatically united to the Son, high-
> lights one of the infinite possibilities that lie in God's eternal life.[85]

Let us reread this passage using the analogy. If one replaces *glass* with *divine
hypostasis* in the 'translation' that follows, one sees just how well the analogy fits
Balthasar's doctrine of a divine Person as a self-subsisting relational *ratio*:

"It is not that God, in himself, changes"	The three glasses of Father, Son, and Holy Spirit are not changed. . . .
[in the Incarnation]	by the fact that the (divine) content of the glass of the Son has been replaced with a different (human) content.
"but that the unchangeable God enters into a relationship with creaturely reality,"	To contain this new (human) content is a new relationship, one that was not actual before.
"and this relationship imparts a new look to his internal relations."	As a consequence, the (optical) relations among the three glasses have changed.
	Though the new content does not penetrate the glass itself of the Son and the natures of the two thus remain unmingled (the doctrine of Chalcedon [DS 302]),
"This is not something purely external,"	nevertheless the new relationship is not wholly external;
"as if this relationship *ad extra* did not really affect him: rather, the new relationship to worldly nature, which is hypostatically united to the Son,"	it does affect the glass of the Son, because this new (human) content is in His glass, not in the glass of the Father or Holy Spirit.
"highlights one of the infinite possibilities that lie in God's eternal life."	The fact that the Son can contain this new (human) content shows it is one of the infinite varieties of content that could lie within the three glasses of Father, Son, and Holy Spirit.

Because the Son remains God in this event that "affects Him"[86] without changing Him "in Himself,"[87] it is apparent that the essential divine nature is not the divine attributes but rather hypostatic self-giving, i.e., not the glass's contents or the glass with a particular content, but the glass itself. This conclusion is not contradicted, but again confirmed, when Balthasar says that "the perfect obedience of the Son . . . is both the means and the content of his eternal relationship with the Father."[88] Obedience is "the means" in that His being is received from the Father (through the Father's self-gift as God), and it is "the content" in that His being is to be self-abnegation for the other (the Son's self-gift as God). "The content" here is not the contents of the glass in the analogy, but the glass content, i.e., its being a glass made of glass like the glass of the Father. "The means" of obedience cannot be shown precisely with this analogy; the closest one could come would be to say the Father pours the divine attributes into the glass of the Son, who exists in "antecedent consent"; in doing so, the glass of the Son is actually generated and filled with the divine contents, ready to empty itself back toward the Father. In the mutual emptying of Father and Son toward each other, the third glass of the Holy Spirit — also with "antecedent consent" — is spirated. The internal establishment of the relationship (i.e., the hypostatic union with its consequences for Jesus' obedience *as Son* to the Father) is possible without change, because it was always there *in potentia*, the "distance" between God and man in Christ being less than the "distance" between Father and Son, and imaging it.[89] Thus Balthasar says, "It is only *because* the Son in very truth possesses the 'form of God' . . . that he can 'empty himself' and take 'the form of a servant.'"[90] In other words, it is because the Son is a divine glass big enough to hold the divine attributes and is indeed filled with them that He can pour Himself out and be filled with human nature, which is something less (being finite) than the divine attributes. If He were not filled with divine attributes, He would not have anything to pour out in emptying Himself. However, this divine content is not what makes possible His kenosis, but the fact that He is a divine glass. God, after all, is "free to do what he will with his own nature,"[91] pour it out or retain it. But whether He pours out the divine attributes or retains them, He remains unchanged as a glass.

A second, simpler, example provides additional confirmation of our interpretation. Balthasar says that, in the Resurrection, "the Son receives himself — with body and soul, with divinity and humanity — back from the Father."[92] Although the reception of the Son's divinity could be taken to refer in general to His generation by the Father, here it must refer more properly to the divine attributes. Since it is these that He "deposited" with the Father, it is these He can receive "back." This reading is consistent with Balthasar's speaking of "the sacrifice of [the Son's] *divinity*,"[93] which occurs "finally and definitively"[94] in the Cross event.

Balthasar's way of handling the idea of a self-subsisting relation, in conjunction with his theology of "depositing," implicitly results in the undoing of the Trinity even as the Incarnation is accomplished: If the Father's generation of the Son is to be meaningful, then the Son must receive from Him both the divine nature and His filial relation, both the divine attributes and the divine essence as self-gift, both His *esse* and His *ratio*. Thus, if "the Son, who has every-thing from the Father, 'lays up' . . . the 'form of God' he has received from him," He would have to lay aside not only His divine attributes but also His hypostasis.

The Divine Wisdom's "Depositing" of the Divine Wisdom

Balthasar especially singles out the divine knowledge among the attributes the Word "deposits." The "depositing" of this attribute and its implications for the Word's knowledge as man are particularly important to Balthasar's theology of the Incarnation and of Christ's mission. Consequently, they are central to his theology of the Descent.

Within the Trinity, the Son's self-awareness as God (i.e., as a subsisting re-lation of the divine nature) is inseparable from His obedience (i.e., as the rela-tion of being begotten). This fundamental self-identity persists in His mission. Thus, even as His divine personality is wholly determined by another through the reception of the Father's perfect self-gift, so also from the very beginning of the Son's incarnation, He is disposed to be disposed of, and is so disposed of, by another, this time the Holy Spirit, who actively brings about the Incarnation.[95] Continually letting oneself be determined by another in this way requires the greatest self-possession, and thus is a form of activity even in the perfection of its passivity.[96] However, the identity of self-awareness and obedience in the Son's procession and mission is not only ontological, but also cognitive. In other words, as the Son knows Himself to be the one from the Father, Jesus' un-derstanding of Himself and of His mission are defined in terms of each other: "Jesus' fundamental intuition concerning his identity [is] 'I am the one who must accomplish this task.'"[97]

This self-understanding is not, "I am God, and the Son of God," because the plenitude of divine knowledge has been "deposited" with the Father as part of the Son's self-emptying in becoming incarnate. Since kenosis is self-abandonment toward an increasing passivity,[98] the Word becomes ignorant in becoming man.[99] Instead of knowing His mission in advance, He must *receive* the will of another (the Father) through another (the Spirit).[100] The Holy Spirit mediates the will of the Father to Jesus, revealing it to Him over time.[101] Christ always has this will as His own in that He is sent and in that He is sent "in the *form* of his readiness to obey,"[102] but the *content* of what He is to do, He receives from the Spirit. This "'economic' ignorance"[103] makes clear that *His mission is kenotic*,[104] while His reception of knowledge through the Spirit shows that *His kenosis is a mission*, i.e., from another.

The extent of His knowledge is determined by two principles: First, His acceptance of His mission does not occur after coming to realize He is, or can be, the Messiah, but His mission is based upon a free decision prior to the Incarnation.[105] The decision about His mission prior to the Incarnation thus parallels the Son's "antecedent consent" to His procession. Thus He has always known that He has a mission,[106] and although He does not know the details of what it will entail, He is "adequately aware of its universality."[107] As a result, "Jesus knew of his identity as the Son of God right from the start," but "the awareness of this identity only came to him through his mission, communicated by the Spirit."[108] In other words, His knowledge of His divine Sonship comes through His knowledge that He is the "one sent."[109] This knowledge is "qualitative,"[110] deriving from the mission's universal scope, of which He is aware, even if He does not comprehend its details.[111] As mentioned in the previous section, if the Word is to *become* flesh, His humanity may not possess "supratemporal contents, nor contents from another period of time."[112] In short, Balthasar denies Christ's possession of the beatific vision, at least as traditionally understood, or of any preeminent infused knowledge of the past or future.

Second, Christ's mission is the measure of His knowledge, in that He knows what He needs to know when He needs to know it, but no sooner.[113] Everything is on a 'need to know' basis. The specific content of what He knows at any one time is determined by the needs of His mission; it is "successively revealed"[114] and changes over time,[115] being manifested to Him "step by step"[116] with greater or lesser clarity.[117] He is ignorant sometimes of the full significance of what He does and what happens to Him.[118] He grows in knowledge over time,[119] and He Himself, in consenting passivity (i.e., in obedience), does not attempt to anticipate what is coming, most especially not the "hour."[120] Prayer and faith will hence be essential parts of His life.[121] Experience is necessary for Him to know certain things. For example, if Christ did not actually suffer the sinner's separation from God, He "would not have known all the phases and conditions of what it means for man to be unredeemed yet awaiting redemption."[122] From this growth in knowledge of His mission follows a like growth in His knowledge of His self-identity.[123] He comes to know His own divine kenosis through His human humility,[124] or obedience.

Christ's knowledge can also decrease. His ignorance increases enormously in His Passion and descent: "The suffering Jesus, at particular moments of his Passion . . . [may be given] a clear awareness that he is suffering on our behalf — an awareness that, with equal necessity, is then withdrawn."[125] He is then "blind"[126] in the 'hour,' to the point of no longer knowing Himself.[127] He will think His mission is futile, that is, He will be ignorant of its ultimate success.[128] He must experience the darkness of the world, which includes meaninglessness, and His ignorance makes this sense of futility possible.[129] This sense of futility is necessary because His mission is to end in death, which (according to Balthasar) must be characterized by futility if it is to be a death like that of other men.[130] His ignorance also serves to increase His agony: Knowledge of the purpose or success of His mission would mitigate His pain.[131] For this same reason, He must be ignorant of the exact time of the 'hour' itself.[132] Balthasar does not explain Jesus' predictions of His resurrection. Christ's ignorance with its implications of agony and a sense of meaninglessness is necessary because His is a real inner appropriation of the state of sinners.[133] What distinguishes Him is the obedience that is the measure of this ignorance and its effects. The "depositing" of His knowledge and hope reduces Him to obedience out of love alone.[134]

Note that here ignorance is taken as the presupposition for the reception of knowledge. Hence, if Christ's earthly existence is to manifest His eternally receptive (i.e., filial) personality and the other Persons by implication, He must be ignorant so that He may receive.[135] The kenosis of the Incarnation *qua* kenosis entails that Christ receives knowledge of His divinity rather than possessing it from Himself.[136] In contrast, if one maintains the perfection and distinction of the two natures in Christ, He as man may receive this knowledge from His divinity. Kenosis and the perfection of wisdom need not be mutually exclusive.

Note also that, because Jesus knows His mission is universal in a general way, but does not comprehend its precise extent, He does not offer His death immediately for all men, knowing them and their sins individually, but gives His life for His mission, which has significance for all men. In this view, and because Balthasar effectively rejects Christ's possession of the beatific vision, Christ does not appear to have known each individual sinner He was redeeming. Nor would He have known each sin for which He was atoning, at least not until He was conformed to sin-in-itself through the *visio mortis* in Sheol. Due to their multitude and their dispersion across centuries, these things would be simultaneously knowable to one who is truly man only in seeing God, i.e., in the beatific vision. Indeed, Balthasar would seem to agree, since he both rejects the beatific vision and thinks Christ's knowledge does not attain the level of detail just described.

Christ's Faith

Balthasar's understanding of Christ's faith must here be considered in some detail because possession of faith reflects ignorance, and ignorance is, as we will see, essential to Christ's experience in His descent. Because Christ obeys perfectly in the darkness of ignorance, in Him is found the perfection of the proper attitude of man toward God, namely, faithfulness despite not seeing. According to Balthasar, this attitude is called *faith* in the Old Testament,[137] of which Jesus is both exemplar and fulfillment. Indeed, He more than fulfills it, since there is a particular qualitative difference between His faith and the faith of all other men. The "difference between his faith and ours is this: we only receive our mission on the basis of our coming to faith, whereas Jesus always has and is his mission."[138] In other words, the difference is that the mission of men other than Jesus is consequent to their faith and hence distinct from their existence; in contrast, Jesus' existence is His mission, which is eternal loving self-surrender. His creaturely obedience is one with His Trinitarian obedience and procession.[139] Mission, existence, and faith thus are synonymous in Jesus. The human faith of Jesus and the faith of other men are alike, however, in the character of the struggle it entails to be faithful without full knowledge.[140] Thus Christ's kenotic existence in faith will be the Christian form of life for His disciples.[141] Because Jesus is God incarnate, however, He manifests not only the perfect attitude of man toward God, but also the perfect attitude of God, namely, the fidelity of love.[142]

Both the human faith and the divine faith(fulness) of Jesus find their most perfect expression in His descent into Sheol. There, in utter blindness, He persists in obedience out of the enduring love of God that goes to the greatest extreme. Because Christ's faith and His faithfulness derive from the Trinitarian "distance,"[143] which entails both separation and union, Christ can remain united to the Father through obedience even though He is separated from Him (and from His own knowledge of His filial divinity) by ignorance.[144] The incomprehensibility of God's love, manifested by the fact that the greatest revelation of the Trinity occurs through the darkness of the Son's abandonment by the Father in Sheol, has here an echo in the ignorance, faith, or incomprehension of the Father by the Son Himself during His incarnate life and especially in His being dead. His incomprehension will be likewise mirrored in the life of faith others have in Christ,[145] since He is the model for the insertion of creaturely life into the Trinitarian life.

Before turning to Balthasar's specific arguments for his understanding of Christ's faith, it should be noted in general that his notion of faith results in certain inconsistencies. First, he elsewhere insists the theological virtues, including faith, do not exist in Sheol and he explicitly denies them of Christ Himself there.[146] How then can Christ have faith there?[147] Or, how then could He be faithful, i.e., obedient, there? Second, if there is a *qualitative* difference between His faith and ours, they are ultimately different things. But Balthasar argues that Christ's death, in order to be representative of mankind (i.e., *pro nobis*), must have the characteristics of the common experience of death, e.g., ignorance of its hour,[148] a sense of futility, etc. If then the faith of Jesus and that of other men are ultimately different, and if His mission is executed in an exceptional abandonment to the guidance of another in utter trust and ignorance, one must ask how the life and death informed by His faith are representative of the rest of men. Finally, as Balthasar presents it, *faith* as used in the Old Testament is to be distinguished and even opposed to *faith* as used in the New Testament,[149] even if the New Testament fulfills the Old.[150] As he sees it, faith is fidelity in ignorance according to the Old Testament,[151] while in the New Testament, πίστις (faith) "means holding the announced kerygma to be true as well as the individual statements either contained in it or implied by it."[152] Jesus does not have this kind of faith, but is its content[153] or makes it possible.[154] This opposition suggests the object of the Old Testament trust is something other than the object of the New Testament profession. But, in fact, God, including the Son of God, is the object of both. Balthasar himself is unable to maintain his contrast: He reads the central New Testament text for definitions of *faith* (Heb 11:1) as revealing the same attitude of absolute trust he had characterized as Old Testament faith.[155]

Balthasar gives seven arguments in support of his view that Christ had ignorance and faith. The strength of these arguments is also relevant to the strength of Balthasar's concept of "depositing" in general. First, such limitation on Christ's knowledge is necessary because otherwise the *whole* Word did not become flesh.[156] That is, a 'part' of God (His omniscience) would not have become man. Such an objection is only intelligible in light of Balthasar's theology of the Incarnation, i.e., his understanding of *how* the Word became flesh through divesting Himself of divine attributes.

Second, if the Word is to be "like us in *all* things but sin,"[157] He must live in ignorance and the darkness of faith. This principle alludes to Hebrews 4:15,[158] but Balthasar does not limit its interpretation to its original reference to Christ's temptations or to the generic features of human nature, but invokes it also with regard to the conditions of fallen nature. The difference between this argument and the former is that there Balthasar is concerned about the entire Person of the Word becoming man, whereas here he is concerned about the kind of man He becomes. However, Balthasar's insistence upon Jesus' intimate knowledge of His mission and exceptional abandonment of self to the Spirit contradicts Balthasar's application of the principle, as does Jesus' personal sinlessness. Since it is one thing to know the will of God and another to choose it, Christ must have received at every moment not only the grace to know the will of the Father for that concrete situation, but also the actual grace to do it. But these graces are something other than sin, and hence would contradict Balthasar's application of the principle from Hebrews 4:15. Note also that if Christ had faith as other men have it, then He did not know Himself to be God, but only believed it. There is an exhaustive division between faith and the beatific vision, between seeing "in a mirror darkly" and "knowing even as we are known" (1 Cor 13:12). These are the only two modes of human knowledge of divine Revelation. One cannot have both, and there is no intermediate reality, no *tertium quid*. Hence, as it is a matter of revelation that Jesus is God, Christ as true man either knew He was God by the beatific vision, or He only believed Himself to be God, with the darkness of faith. Finally, observe that Christ's faith differs in two essential respects from that of other men: The Son has faith as a result of His having freely chosen not to know. In contrast, our faith is the initiative of God, not ours; and for us faith is a coming to knowledge, not a falling away from it.

Third, Christ's ignorance is necessary because not knowing is required for obedience.[159] Balthasar does not explain why obedience is not the virtue that would also govern the fulfillment of a given task in full knowledge of its scope and difficulty. Even if the merit of faith comes from not seeing, this need not be so for the merit of obedience.

Fourth, ignorance is necessary in order that Christ experience futility, which would be impossible if He had foreknowledge of the ultimate victory of His mission of obedience. This argument depends on the premise that Christ should have experienced futility. Note that the result of the necessary connection between ignorance and the sense of futility is that Christ's ignorance is often not simple lack of knowledge, but actual error.

Balthasar makes a fifth argument implicitly, namely, that ignorance is necessary for a normal (i.e., typical) life: Christ led "a simple human life with nothing exceptional about it save an ardent love for the Father and for men, a life of work and teaching, ending in poverty and disgrace."[160] One must wonder then: What about the miracles? And the casting out of demons who acknowledged Him? And who did they go out in great crowds to see? Moreover, how is it He led a normal life, if He had a faith that was not 'normal,' being qualitatively different from that of other men?[161]

The sixth argument is also implicit, namely, that ignorance is necessary for any meaningful use of Christ's human powers. He does not find His mission "ready-made"[162] or "prefabricated."[163] It is not "an object of contemplation,"[164] nor does He know the Father or Himself as Son through an "'objectivised' vision."[165] Rather, "he must fashion [His mission] out of himself in utter freedom and responsibility, indeed, in a sense, he even has to invent it."[166] It is not evident how Balthasar sees the exercise of Jesus' darkened understanding in the "invent[ion]" of His mission to be compatible with His reception of a sufficiently clear, unmistakably recognizable, and inerrant directive from the Father through the Spirit.

Balthasar's seventh argument derives from the fact that, although on the one hand he presents faith as a solution to ignorance in earthly life,[167] he also presents ignorance (and hence faith) as a perfection. "Faith . . . not only is an attitude of expectation . . . but also is *the definitive messianic attitude itself.* It is the co-perfecting of the Messiah's form of existence."[168] Ignorance and faith are a part of the life of the saints in heaven,[169] imaging the divine life from which surprise and wonder are not absent.[170] An

> "all-knowing" attitude . . . eviscerates the joys of expectation, of hope and fulfillment, the joys of giving and receiving and the even deeper joys of finding oneself in the other and of being constantly over-fulfilled by him; and finally — since we are speaking of God — it destroys the possibility of mutual acknowledgment and adoration in the Godhead.[171]

There is "no end to being surprised"[172] within the Trinity. Indeed, God even wonders at His own Trinitarian nature:

> To himself, God is never "just there" in the Positivist sense: rather, he is always the most "improbable" miracle in that the utter self-surrender of the Father-Origin truly generates the coeternal Son and the encounter and union of both truly cause the one Spirit, the hypostasis of all that is meant by "gift," to proceed from both.[173]

This wonder among the three Persons is a result of the intra-Trinitarian "distance." Together with the unpredictable ways in which one Person reveals His love to the others,[174] it constitutes a "primal faith within the Trinity"[175] that is the basis for the faith of men. God's fidelity of love within the Trinity thus has the same character of faithfulness in ignorance that human faith should manifest vis-à-vis God. One must ask whether these suggested aspects of divine love do not result in a sort of process theology in which God is continually discovering Himself. If the divine knowledge is identical with the divine essence, the surprise of one Person by another means the one surprised grows in knowledge of what the other is; hence He grows in knowledge of what it is to be God, and hence in divinity itself.

To be complete, we must note a few passages in which Balthasar appears to contradict the conclusions here that Christ was truly without the theological virtues in His descent and also sometimes during His life and passion. Whenever an assertion of Balthasar's appeared to contradict the majority of his corpus, I took it that such apparent inconsistencies are to be resolved in favor of the position he asserts more often and explicates in more depth, since the seeming contradictions afforded by the minor positions are dissolved by the spin Balthasar puts on them in his more detailed treatises. Thus, e.g., Christ knows of His triumph — but this knowledge is veiled in His Passion. Or, when Balthasar says in one place that it was necessary for Christ to have known for whom He was dying, because otherwise He would not have done it,[176] one is to understand that He knew He was dying for all men, insofar as He knew His mission had universal significance — lest the Father's request alone be insufficient, and Balthasar's usual insistence on Christ's absolute and hypostatic obedience to the Father be contradicted. Or, again, Christ's sense of futility does not eliminate His hope,[177] because confidence in the Father is essential to Christ's being as Son. Or, Balthasar does not deny the theological virtues to Christ on the cross, but rather only His apprehension of their existence and hence of their efficacy.[178]

Regarding this last, to affirm the objective presence of the theological virtues while denying Christ's subjective experience of them would seem to allow Balthasar his understanding of Christ's abandonment without it following that Christ succumbed to the sin of despair. But the solution is only apparent. If the theological virtues exist in a person, they incline him to acts of faith, hope, and love. But the intellect and will are self-reflexive, i.e., human acts of the intellect and will are necessarily known to the knowing and loving subject of these acts. Hence the human subject possessing the theological virtues knows his acts of faith, hope, and love because it is he who knows and wills, even if he does not necessarily know this particular act has a supernatural principle. Thus if Christ had the theological virtues objectively and He did not act against them, then He subjectively experienced their acts, which is to experience both their existence and their efficacy. In fact, Balthasar himself goes on to deny also their objective presence when he describes Christ's redemptive abandonment and mystic desolation in terms of "the privation of *this* light," i.e., "God's light in faith, love, and hope in the very depths of the soul."[179]

The foregoing presentation of Balthasar's notion of Jesus' faith is not intended to be an exhaustive consideration, but rather to show that Balthasar intends *the "depositing" of divine attributes not just as a way of speaking, but as an actual reality*, with significant effects. This "depositing" must be as real as the Trinitarian procession of the Son, since it simultaneously reveals His divinity (for only God has such absolute freedom over Himself) and manifests in this image the Father, who is the divine origin that gives itself wholly away. One may make the reasonable connection here that the limits of Jesus' knowledge, as mediated by the Spirit, can "allow every possible variation,"[180] from detailed understanding to vaguer intuition,[181] without diminishing His "immediacy"[182] with the Father, because His kenotic existence as a finite man, and hence His finite, variable knowledge, is one of "the infinite possibilities of divine freedom [that] all lie *within* the trinitarian distinctions."[183] If the Son's "depositing" were not real, it would suggest the divine kenosis of the Father was also only apparent. The "depositing" of the perfection of knowledge is taken as our example, because Balthasar himself singles it out, giving numerous arguments for it. The perfect divine knowledge of the Word need not affect or impinge the human ignorance of Jesus if the Word gives up this attribute in becoming man.

Doctrines that attribute to Christ a beatific vision embracing all details of the economy of salvation and persisting without interruption from His conception are thus incompatible with Balthasar's theology,[184] because they would be incompatible with his understanding of the Incarnation and Christ's descent to the *visio mortis:* "Christ's divinity being 'laid up' in God . . . is the *precondition* of the Incarnation."[185] *A fortiori*, it is the precondition of the *visio mortis:* "Any admixture of divine knowledge would be like an anesthetic preventing him from experiencing human suffering to the limit."[186] This particular example of "depositing" thus is absolutely central to Balthasar's theology of the Descent. As a result, however, Balthasar must provide a new theology of the beatific vision of Christ.

Beatific Vision *or* Visio Immediata?

In speaking of "Christ's 'descent' into (we do not say the 'place,' but) the 'state' of perdition,"[187] Balthasar provides a footnote very relevant to his theology of Christ's beatific vision. He writes,

> Of course, this does not mean approval of Calvin's doctrine, for the reason that the continuous *visio immediata Dei in anima Christi* makes his experience of hell wholly incommensurate with any other, gives it an "exemplary," soteriological and trinitarian significance.[188]

Note that he says *"visio immediata Dei in anima Christi,"* and not *beatific vision.* Although the two normally would be identified, Balthasar's choice of terminology suggests a distinction, and the identification should not be immediately assumed.

Can the *visio immediata Dei* of Balthasar's theology be identified with the *visio beatifica?* Balthasar says both that the *visio immediata Dei* is "continuous" and, in contrast, that Jesus' peculiar intimacy with the Father need "not mean that his spirit must already enjoy a perpetual *visio beatifica*."[189] In other words, the *visio immediata* is "continuous," but the *visio beatifica* might not be. But if Christ undergoes death as Balthasar understands it to be expressed in the Old Testament, i.e., "as the loss of the living relationship to God,"[190] then the *visio beatifica* is not "perpetual," but must be suspended at least in His descent. Balthasar is more explicit when he says that Jesus' awareness of His divinity "only came to him through his mission, communicated by the Spirit. This would exclude the 'beatific vision' of God, at least for periods."[191] Ultimately, he says, "Jesus does not see the Father in a *visio beatifica* but is presented with the Father's commission by the Holy Spirit, that is, his awareness of his mission is only indirect."[192] Observe that the *visio beatifica,* which was *possibly* "perpetual," was then held to be intermittent, and finally ruled out altogether.

What then is the "continuous *visio immediata*"? This *visio* intensifies Christ's suffering in His descent and elevates its significance, making His experience "wholly incommensurate with any other." These factors suggest that the *visio immediata Dei* is, or derives from, Christ's divine relation of Sonship, since it is this relationship that gives Him His peculiar intimacy with the Father and a proportional agony when that intimacy is withdrawn in the Father's wrath, and it is this relation that makes His being dead redemptive. As Balthasar says,

> No one could utter this cry ["Why hast thou forsaken me?"] more intensely than he whose life it is to be everlastingly generated by the Father and, *in this generation, to see the Father.* Now he, too, experiences what it means to lose God, to know him only as the far-away Judge.[193]

This passage makes clear that the procession of the Son is correlative with His knowledge of the Father, as just suggested, while Christ's loss of God, by which He knows the Father only as Judge, illustrates the actual decrease in His knowledge. One must assume it is due to God's very nature as self-gift that the Son's procession is not impaired by His decrease in knowledge of the Father, given their correlation. The Son's 'glass' remains intact, even if emptied of its contents.

Balthasar later points out that the *visio immediata Dei*

> at the very least . . . may fluctuate between the mode of manifestness (which befits the Son as his "glory") and the mode of "concealment" which befits the Servant of Yahweh in the hiddenness of his Passion). . . . [T]he second mode here is derived from the first: a living faith is content to stand before the face of the God who sees, whether or not one sees him oneself.[194]

Whereas the first quotation about "the continuous *visio immediata Dei*" pointed to the Son's Trinitarian procession, this one connects it to Jesus' faith, or at least to the variable knowledge that is an essential aspect of His faith. In this dual orientation of the *visio immediata*, His faith is once again seen to be an economic counterpart of His procession.

As a result of this connection, the nature of the *visio immediata Dei* is made still clearer in another place. Balthasar points out that this "immediate vision of the Father"[195] pertains to Jesus "as the God-man,"[196] i.e., because, notwithstanding His humanity, He also is divine.

> It is an indispensable axiom that the Son, even in his human form, must know that he is the eternal Son of the Father. He must be aware of the unbreakable continuity of his *processio* and his *missio*. . . . Nonetheless the Son, insofar as he is man, must be able to experience faith. . . .[197]

Hence, "in the Lord's Passion his sight is veiled";[198] indeed, "on the Cross, Jesus is deprived of the sight of the Father."[199] Nonetheless, "his obedience remains intact, and to that extent we must also say that Christ has a real 'faith.'"[200] Hence, because obedience is the characteristic proper to the Son's Trinitarian personality and because that divine obedience is the source of His obedience in the flesh, we find again that Jesus' faith is the economic mode of His procession. In addition, a sort of content-form distinction in the *visio immediata* is made evident, in which the content of Jesus is human, i.e., ignorance, while His form is divine, i.e., obedience. This distinction is reminiscent of the analogy of the divine Persons as glasses and similar to Jesus' obedient reception of the details of His mission through the Spirit. It remains unclear, however, how Jesus can know He is the Son of the Father (which He must, according to Balthasar's "axiom" above) when He loses sight of the Father and of His own identity on the Cross and in Sheol.[201]

In summary, in the first text, Balthasar's use of a descriptive tag *(visio immediata Dei in anima Christi)* normally associated with the beatific vision implies the two are the same. He goes on effectively to deny Christ's possession of the beatific vision, however, by radically changing the conceptual content of the words of the tag. We see here an attempt to retain the vocabulary of the theological tradition (and thus verbal agreement with Church doctrine) while replacing its conceptual content. Consequently, henceforward in this work, *beatific vision* refers to this as traditionally understood, whereas *visio immediata* refers to Balthasar's version. The hints in the first text about the *visio immediata* giving Christ's descent experience "trinitarian significance" were confirmed by the passages that were examined afterward. Christ's filial intimacy then is *visio* because it implies knowledge; *immediata Dei* because it is, or is linked with, His divine relation to the Father; and *in anima Christi* because Jesus is the divine relation of the Word in human nature. Any *visio* of God other than His living relation to the Father through the execution of His mission under the guidance of the Holy Spirit is excluded from Jesus' understanding.

In other words, an intellectual *visio* in which the intellect beholds God in His essence and the will rejoices in union with Him is denied.

> Jesus willed out of love to experience only the judicial character [of the redemption], and therefore to renounce everything that would have comforted him and strengthened him.[202]

In His passion and descent, Jesus experienced, and hence knew, only the punitive wrath of God. As suggested by His experience of the Father's wrath and the futility of His own death,[203] He did not have any sense of the Father's love for Him or of the triumph that would be His and, through Him, available to mankind. If so, He was not only ignorant, but erred.

Insofar as the *visio immediata Dei* is identical with Christ's consciousness of Himself as God, which changes as the Spirit manifests it to Him through His mission, the content of this *visio* also increases, changes, and decreases over time. Christ's actual mission determines, and is, its only content. "No supratemporal contents, nor contents from another period of time,"[204] no "purely theoretical content, over and above his mission"[205] at any particular moment can be part of it.

Though there is no beginning to Jesus' consciousness of His universal mission and, through it, of His divinity, His knowledge of both is limited for the sake of His mission:

> Insofar as, from all time, he fully embraces and affirms his mission (which does not mean that he has a total and detailed view of it), he is a *comprehensor;* but the mission itself sets him upon a path, and, to that extent, he is a *viator.*[206]

(This passage is a still clearer example of Balthasar's attempt to maintain the vocabulary of the theological tradition, but endow it with different meaning within his own theology.) In short,

> Jesus is aware of an element of the divine in his innermost, indivisible self-consciousness . . . but it is limited and defined by [His] mission-consciousness. It is of this, and of this alone, that he has a *visio immediata. . . .*[207]

The limited knowledge of His own divinity is paralleled by a limitation of His knowledge of the Father, inasmuch as the latter likewise comes through His mission. This limitation peaks during His abandonment in Sheol, when He knows only the Father's wrath. Nonetheless, "the one who sends . . . is always present *in the mission itself*,"[208] and "the Son . . . always behold[s] *in his mission* the Father who sends him."[209] Thus the Son, even though He has deposited His divine attributes and is abandoned in Sheol, can still be said to be always with the Father insofar as He always does the Father's will.[210] However, that the *Son* beholds the Father, not directly, but "in his mission," the knowledge of which changes over time, indicates again the reality of the "depositing" of the divine attribute of knowledge; it is not just a question of the possible extent and influence of the beatific vision in the *human soul* of Christ.

Of course, the beatific vision does not pertain only to the intellect, but also to the will. The knowledge that perfects the intellect is paralleled by the will's rest and joy in its possession of the divine object desired in love. Hence, because Balthasar effectively denies the one, likewise in his theology of Christ's *visio immediata Dei* there is a suffering in the will of Christ that parallels the darkness of His intellect. He suffers the loss of the object of His human will both in being forsaken by God (the Father) and in believing His mission would be futile. As that intellectual darkness corresponds to the Son's filial receptivity and obedience, this suffering is also to be an expression of a divine reality, more specifically, the divine bliss: "God's blessedness consists in his *being* self-surrender. . . . [T]he eternal life . . . *is* perfect self-surrender, manifesting itself ultimately in suffering and death."[211] In other words, the definitive 'second death' of the Son in Sheol is an image (and the supreme one) of that "super-death" in the Trinity which is the divine relations of love. As "on the Cross, the lived reality of [human] death, objectively, is [trinitarian] life; so extreme suffering, objectively, is joy."[212] Hence the Son may be said to have an objective joy in doing the will of the one He loves, in offering Himself for the creatures He loves, and in sharing in the Father's joy in receiving this gift.[213] Nonetheless this joy is not subjective (He does not know or 'feel' it), and His suffering is not diminished by it in the least.[214] Indeed, His definitive suffering presupposes this divine bliss,[215] because the intensity of His pain derives from the loss of His previous intimacy with the Father,[216] and is proportionate to it. Finally, because the perfect fulfillment of the will's desires in God explains why those who have the beatific vision cannot sin, we will need to examine how Christ's sinlessness may be explained without it in the context of Balthasar's theology, but this topic is deferred until the following chapter.

We note here that, for both Balthasar and St. Thomas Aquinas, Christ's knowledge is measured by His mission, but St. Thomas understands this measure very differently from Balthasar. For St. Thomas, Christ has the beatific vision without interruption from the moment of His conception.[217] The perfect knowledge He has through the beatific vision is finite (i.e., He does not comprehend the Divine Essence), even as His human soul is finite.[218] Its measure is His mission; i.e., He knows everything that pertains to Him as the head of all creation,[219] including the sins and ultimate destiny of all men. Hence, although both Balthasar and St. Thomas see Christ's mission as universal in scope and effect, St. Thomas's understanding of the mission as the measure of Christ's knowledge differs from Balthasar's at least in regard to its relation to time and its content. If Christ had the beatific vision in the way St. Thomas thought, then the knowledge He had through it did not change over time and was perfect in extent. On the other hand, according to Balthasar, Christ's knowledge through the *visio immediata* changes over time as the Spirit reveals His mission to Him moment by moment; sometimes ignorance rather than knowledge is essential for this mission; and Christ is always ignorant of some things pertaining to His mission, such as whether it will be successful. Hence, in Balthasar's view, the whole mission is the mission of the moment for Christ, whereas in St. Thomas's, the whole mission is present to Christ in the moment.

It is clear then that the *visio immediata Dei* attributed to Christ by Balthasar is not the beatific vision, neither with regard to the intellect nor in respect to the will.

Objections to Christ's Beatific Vision

In support of his theology of Christ's faith and *visio immediata*, Balthasar raises a variety of objections specifically against the traditional understanding of Christ's beatific vision. First, after asserting that the Holy Spirit's communication to Jesus of His mission excluded the beatific vision, Balthasar quotes "J. Guillet on the baptism scene": "It is not said that Jesus, with his human eyes, saw the Father but only that he saw the heavens opened and the Spirit descending upon him."[220] Since this quotation is brought forward not only in support of Jesus' mission being communicated to Him by the Spirit, but also against His possession of the beatific vision (because He did not see the Father "with his human eyes"), it suggests a possible misunderstanding of the beatific vision on Balthasar's part. Since the souls of the just enjoy this vision before the resurrection of their bodies,[221] it is not a vision of God by means of "human eyes." Moreover, the dichotomy Balthasar establishes between the Holy Spirit's communication of the mission and Christ's possession of the beatific vision is false — it is only in the Holy Spirit that one has the beatific vision. Second, Balthasar characterizes a "mysticism in which self-consciousness and God-consciousness coincide" as "Eutychian."[222] Although this statement is not related in its context explicitly to the doctrine of Christ's beatific vision, it suggests Balthasar may have thought Christ's beatific vision implied some sort of monophysitism. However, the doctrine (at least as formulated by St. Thomas) did not ascribe the omniscience of God to the human soul of Jesus. Third, Balthasar is particularly concerned to deny of Christ "an 'objectivised' vision which is separated from his own reality."[223] The love of God "is not an object that one could contemplate (thereby 'objectivising' it) from an impartial stance; it is seen to be what it is, only when one is oneself seized by it."[224]

> Eternal life in God cannot consist simply in "beholding" God. In the first place, God is not an object but a Life that is going on eternally and yet ever new. Secondly, the creature is meant ultimately to live, not over against God, but in him. Finally, Scripture promises us even in this life a participation — albeit hidden under the veil of faith — in the internal life of God; we are to be born in and of God, and we are to possess his Holy Spirit.[225]

In this objection, it appears that Balthasar misunderstands the beatific vision developed in Catholic theological tradition as something like a movie,[226] and not at all as the union of God with the soul in the most intimate and living communion. Thus Balthasar contrasts it with Jesus recognizing the divine love from inside, from experiencing it in act. Fourth, Balthasar makes the following, similar contrast: "Eternal blessedness can by no means consist of a mere *visio*, but must involve genuine, creative activity."[227] To Balthasar's credit, he wants to assert the vital nature of beatitude, i.e., of the beatific vision. To do so, however, he rejects perfection of knowledge as contradictory to vitality, rather than seeing them as compatible.[228] This opposition conditions his Trinitarian theology, as manifested by his idea that the divine Persons surprise each other. It likewise appears in his Christology and soteriology under the notions of the *visio immediata Dei* and of Christ's faith. It influences his ecclesiology and eschatology since the blessed in heaven, conformed to their divine archetype, also experience surprise.[229] His emphasis on creativity and surprise together with his negative characterizations of the *nunc stans* and of the objective nature of the beatific vision suggests he sees life and freedom as perfected in unpredictable exercise rather than in a determined form.[230] The objective nature of a movie-like vision, with the attendant questions about the role of Christ's human powers to which Balthasar alludes, seems more implicated in Balthasar's own idea that the Spirit communicates the Father's will to Jesus as a rigid rule that may at times even go against reason. Indeed, the analogy of a movie might fit well Balthasar's descriptions of heavenly bliss, which is essentially characterized by sequential revelation.[231]

The previous objections all relate to Balthasar's (mis)understanding of the traditional concept of the beatific vision. Balthasar also raises certain Christological objections to it. He asserts that the most that can be said of Christ's human experience of God is that his experience of distance from God, which in him constitutes the archetypal *fides,* is as such the expression of God's experience of himself within the Trinity in the distance of distinction between Person and Person.[232]

Balthasar comments in a footnote to this claim,

> And this must suffice. Whoever would say more will either judge Christ's experience of God by the laws of ordinary human psychology, which cannot grasp the hypostatic union; or, starting abstractly from Christ's vision of God, he will no longer make Christ's human psyche credible, or, finally, he will no longer be able to unite Christ's different *scientiae* into one unified life of the soul.[233]

Here, two additional objections to Christ's beatific vision are presented: first, that Christ would not really be human (His human psyche would no longer be credible); and second, that the extreme differences among the divine *scientiae* (Christ's knowledge as Son) and the human *scientiae* (Christ's knowledge as man, including experiential, infused, and beatific knowledge) would result in a split consciousness if they were to coexist in one soul without the divine (and beatific?) overwhelming the others. Similar concerns are implicit when Balthasar says his theory of the unity of Christ's consciousness of His divinity with His consciousness of His mission means

> we shall no longer need regretfully to banish "direct vision" in Jesus' consciousness to the "uppermost region of the soul," lest it should endanger the life of his normal human soul.[234]

But one might ask, if Jesus' human soul is quite "normal," why does it lie outside the purview of "ordinary human psychology"? Or, on the other hand, if human psychology is not helpful in understanding the hypostatic union, as Balthasar says, then neither can it be claimed on the basis of human psychology that the beatific vision makes Christ's human psyche not "credible," not human, or divided. A metaphysical anthropology would likewise be limited. The resolution of the question properly pertains to Christology.

These objections concerning the relationship between the divine and human in Christ, and those specifically about Jesus' unified psyche, reappear as corollaries to Balthasar's most common objection against the beatific vision, namely, its seeming incompatibility with His suffering. Because this vision of God is the defining feature of perfect beatitude, it can be difficult to see how Christ suffered at all, not to mention suffered more than anyone else. Perhaps one must choose between Christ's peerless suffering and His beatific vision. Given the centrality of suffering in Balthasar's theology, it is not surprising that he opts for the former and rejects the latter. To respond to this last and most important objection, we must examine Balthasar's reasons for his choice. Doing so simultaneously sheds light on the specific question of Christ's suffering or triumphal descent, and on the question's fundamental Christological boundaries.

Balthasar is above all concerned to preserve the unique *degree* of Christ's suffering, which must be greater than that of any other person. In arguing that Christ experiences "what it means to have lost contact with God,"[235] he says,

> If the experience of being forsaken by God on the Cross had not gone to the very extreme, the suffering of the "Servant," of Job and of the Lamentations would have been more profound than that of Jesus. For in those cases the whole horizon between heaven and earth is shrouded in total blackness, the burden of suffering is boundless and seems completely meaningless and unfruitful.[236]

Since "the experience of being forsaken by God on the Cross" continues and is perfected in the Descent, as shown in Chapter Five, Balthasar's comparison here applies also to Christ's experience in Sheol. If the Redeemer "suffered what the sinner deserved"[237] in order to make reconciliation between God and this individual sinner possible,[238] how could anyone suffer more in hell than the Redeemer suffered in Sheol? But if Christ made possible the reconciliation of all sinners in this way, He must have suffered the cumulative punishment of all. By insisting upon the unique degree of Christ's suffering, Balthasar is then also implicitly concerned to preserve its redemptive efficacy.

In the context of the quotation above comparing Jesus' agony to cases of suffering in the Old Testament, Balthasar does not offer a strict argument for why it would be problematic if anyone suffered more than Christ. He does raise rhetorical questions, however, that suggest three other concerns that relate to this one: First, "should the poet's 'nothing human is foreign to me' not apply to him?"[239] In other words, if Christ possessed the beatific vision, His experience of the human condition would be deficient, thereby calling into question the perfection of His assumption of human nature. The earlier objections about the unity of Christ's psyche and about the general relation of the human and divine in Christ are embraced by this concern. The Incarnation, we recall, is not a static condition, but a human life under the conditions that pertain after the Fall. Balthasar objects to Christ's beatific vision because he thinks it would prevent some part of Christ from being configured to the situation the sinful world experiences, diminishing thereby the perfection both of the Incarnation and of Christ's suffering.[240] This concern reflects Balthasar's application of the principle that the Word became "like us in *all* things but sin"[241] to the specific conditions of fallen nature. Implicit also are his overarching concerns to preserve the degree of Christ's suffering, and suffering as the formal and efficacious principle of redemption in his theology.

Second, if others went beyond Christ's knowledge of human guilt and pain, "how could he say that he is 'the first and the last,' that he has 'the keys of death and hell' (Rev 1:18)?"[242] In other words, Christ's primacy in the order of glory seems jeopardized.

Finally, Balthasar says, "Only now, having passed through the dark terrain, the chaos of human sin, has Jesus gained complete knowledge of man."[243] This statement, which appears in a work on Christ's knowledge of men and of the human condition, suggests that Balthasar thinks it would be a deficiency in the perfection of Christ's knowledge if His suffering were not supreme. This last concern may seem to contrast strangely with Balthasar's rejection of Christ's beatific vision in favor of His faith and sense of futility, both of which entail ignorance. In fact, however, the two positions are completely in line with each other, since the perfection of knowledge Balthasar wants to preserve is that of the knowledge that comes through personal experience of the fallen human condition.

In summary, Balthasar objects to Christ's possession of the beatific vision for the following reasons: First, he sometimes appears to have misunderstood its nature, in particular characterizing it as if it were a movie, as we have seen. His other objections, however, cannot concern such an "objectivised" vision, since if the beatific vision were thus externalized and not identified with the divine life in the human subject, its possession would not be incompatible with the suffering Balthasar thinks Christ should have undergone. This is his primary concern, to preserve the unique degree of Christ's suffering. In his view, if this is lost, so is the truth of His human nature, the unique efficacy of His suffering, His primacy in the order of glory, and the perfection of His knowledge of the human condition.

Before considering how effective these objections are, it would be well to look briefly at how Balthasar understands the suffering that Christ's must surpass. He approaches Christ's suffering in this comparative way through possible foreshadowings of it in the Old Testament and through mystical participation in it after Christ. From the Old Testament, he considers both God's abandonment of the whole people of Israel due to their idolatry, and the abandonment of representative individuals, such as Job and the Suffering Servant.[244] In each case, the anguish of abandonment is particularly characterized and intensified by the fact that God has not only withdrawn Himself, but rejected those to whom He had been uniquely present:[245] This "active aversion on God's part" is worse than mere death, "deeper than Sheol" even, and later gives rise to the notion of gehenna.[246] According to Balthasar, Christ will know this abandonment and rejection in the most definitive way:

> If, in his "hour," Jesus comes to experience the nature of sin from the inside, the center of the Passion lies not only in his perfect death . . . , but equally in his experience of mortal anguish and of being forsaken by God. Here, genuinely in our place, he experiences in his own person the right and necessary judgment of God upon evil.[247]

A few observations should be made about Balthasar's use of the Old Testament cases. First of all, the Israelites were abandoned by God because and insofar as they sinned. The fact that Balthasar sees their abandonment as a prefiguration of Christ's reveals just how strongly he regards Christ's redemption as a substitutionary, rather than satisfactory, one. That is, it is not enough that Christ took upon Himself the generic punishments of passibility and death due to sin, that the Divine Word humbled Himself to suffer in the flesh and this in the most horrific way. Rather, for Balthasar, Christ must suffer the sum total of the punishment due to sin. Christ is literally "made sin" — every sin — in order to be charged with and experience the cumulative punishment for all these sins and thereby reconcile the world with the Father.[248] Being "made sin," He draws the judgment of God upon Himself: Jesus Christ, the Word made flesh, "experiences *in his own person* the . . . judgment of God *upon evil*."[249] Whether this view is properly a Catholic one is questionable. Secondly, Balthasar says that Christ's passion is "pre-experienced"[250] in the case of Job, who "experiences the absolute disproportion between guilt and punishment. . . ."[251] Yet Job himself insists upon his innocence and rejects the solution that his suffering is a punishment (Job 1:21; 2:10; 6:2, 25; 7:22-23; 10:3, 7; 13; 16:18; etc.), although he acknowledges no one is just in the sight of God (Job 7:20). Balthasar's interpretation of Job as guilty therefore seems skewed, and his inductive argument about the character and necessary connection of God-forsakenness to sin is consequently weakened by the loss of one of his major examples. Finally, is it not the case that divine reprobation is something *from* which Christ saves people by His death, and not something *to* which He who always does the Father's will (Jn 5:30) is brought? But if He only saves by being brought through that punishment Himself, as Balthasar argues, then the substitutionary character of Balthasar's theology again becomes apparent.

The suffering that Christ's must surpass is particularly characterized by Balthasar in reference to the experiences of Christian mystics, specifically the spiritual 'dark night.'[252] "Again," he writes, it is unthinkable that people following Christ should have had to go through more terrible experiences than their Lord himself; their experiences can only be a muted echo of the unique and incomparable burden which the God-Man endured.[253]

As with the examples he draws from the Old Testament, Balthasar considers the experience of the mystics to be especially relevant, because "only the person who has truly 'possessed' God in the Covenant, knows what it means to be truly abandoned by Him."[254] In summarizing these mystical experiences,[255] Balthasar stresses the sense of God-abandonment, of its timeless and definitive character, of the justice of the punishment, of willingness to remain in the condition as long as it pleases God, and of desire to suffer with Christ. He emphasizes how these experiences are denoted in terms of *hell*. He also points out that they were variously understood as struggles against demons, tests, purifications, the experience of a more perfect spiritual state, or encounters with the "radiant darkness"[256] of God.

Because Balthasar does not examine these experiences in much detail or provide much context for the texts he quotes, an adequate assessment of how well they support his conclusions cannot be made on the basis of his representations. A separate investigation of his sources would be required, but this is beyond our present scope, which concerns the doctrinal content of Balthasar's theology of the Descent in relation to the traditional one. Moreover, I will note here that the experiences he invokes were not considered as fonts for the summary of the Church's doctrine in Part One for three reasons. First of all, mutual reference may be observed among the fonts actually used in Part One, but such reference is not made to such experiences. For example, one sees the saints invoking magisterial documents in their works of theology and, conversely, the teaching authority of the Church utilizing elements of their work. However, the *loci theologici* considered in Part One that are clearly authoritative do not invoke such individual experiences in reference to characterizing Christ's descent. Vice versa, these experiences do not make reference to the well-known traditional doctrine, at least to judge by the excerpts Balthasar presents. The significance of this *de facto* lack of mutual recognition merits reflection, but would seem to imply at least that the experiences are irrelevant to Christ's descent. Second, there is the necessity of discerning the authenticity of these experiences, as Balthasar himself would agree.[257] Only experiences of clearly divine origin would be sound sources. Those psychological in origin would be highly questionable, while it cannot be forgotten that unusual phenomena may be the result of demonic influence. In other words, the evaluation of these experiences and their worth would be an extended task, with unsure potential for a worthwhile outcome. Finally, these experiences are, at best (i.e., when not of psychological or demonic origin), private revelations. They are not necessary for the sure knowledge of divine truth, for which Scripture (as read in the Church) and Tradition suffice. Hence one could not call for a change in the traditional doctrine of the Descent on the basis of such experiences without implying new public revelation.

So much being said, given that it is Balthasar's postulate that these experiences are participations in Christ's descent, one would expect the strongest possible case for this interpretation to be found in his treatments, if anywhere. What one sees there, however, invites caution concerning his conclusions. The experiences he mentions are quite diverse, as is the authority of the individuals involved. His grouping of them nonetheless together suggests a greater similarity among them than perhaps is warranted. Also, to support his idea that Christ must suffer something worse than the extremity of hell in order that His sufferings exceed those of anyone else, Balthasar assumes that mystical experiences of hell do not differ from the actual pains of hell; this assumption is debatable. Further, Balthasar prescinds from considerations of authenticity. Whatever discernment of spirits he made is not indicated. Hence, from what may be gathered from his own presentations, his selection appears to be based only upon similarity of description of some experience. This criterion would invite questions of literary criticism, including the question of the possible difference between a mode of expression and the reality actually experienced. Finally, some of the experiences from which he quotes are not understood by the person involved as a participation in Christ's descent, but in connection with punishment for sins. Their application to Christ's descent thus depends upon Balthasar's postulate, and cannot be invoked in support of it.

Having seen something of the sufferings that Christ's must surpass, we return now to consider the efficacy of Balthasar's objections to Christ's possession of the beatific vision, since these are relevant to the question of a triumphal Descent or a Descent to suffering. The overarching argument is that, if one accepts on principle that Christ ought to have suffered more than anyone else and if some people suffered experiences of hell, then surely Christ had the definitive experience of hell (which, as definitive, would be worse than any participations in it). This position entails the rejection of Christ's possession of the beatific vision during His life and descent in order to preserve the unique degree of His suffering, which in turn is seen as necessary to preserve the truth of His human nature, the unique efficacy of His suffering, His primacy in the order of glory, and His perfect knowledge of the human condition.

In other words, in order not to jeopardize these four last truths, it is held *as a principle* that Christ's suffering must have been the greatest, and greater than hell. This principle is chosen over Christ's possession of the beatific vision, which may be understood to follow from other truths of faith, such as the hypostatic union, His fullness of grace, etc. Secondly, again *as a principle,* it is held that the beatific vision is incompatible with the greatest suffering, and so Christ's possession of it while suffering more than anyone else is also rejected.

Evaluation of Objections

But are the four truths Balthasar is concerned to preserve jeopardized in fact by the traditional doctrines of the Descent and of Christ's possession of the beatific vision?

First for that matter, is the beatific vision incompatible with suffering? Balthasar writes, "Any admixture of divine knowledge would be like an anesthetic preventing him from experiencing human suffering to the limit."[258] Note the emphasis here on the quantitative nature of Christ's suffering. Is Balthasar correct?

This question must be considered with respect to the different powers of the soul according to which a person suffers. The beatific vision is traditionally understood to be apprehended in the 'superior reason,' that is, the intellect and will directed to the *bonum increatum.* As with all suffering, suffering in these faculties arises from a lack or excess of the faculty's proper object.[259] Now the proper object of the intellect is to know God, even if not to see Him in His essence, while the proper object of the will is to cling to Him. But these objects do not admit of excess when man is lifted above his natural powers by the aid of grace to the beatific vision. Nor in Christ do they admit of defect since He was "full of grace and truth" (Jn 1:14), and always did the will of His Father (Jn 4:34; 5:30). Thus Christ's possession of the beatific vision would rule out suffering in His rational faculties, i.e., the suffering described by Balthasar as caused by Christ's ignorance and sense of futility. This incompatibility is reflected in Balthasar's rejection of the beatific vision specifically to preserve these latter two characteristics.

Yet since the rational soul can know the same thing under different aspects, Christ could rejoice in His own possession of the beatific vision and the possession of it by those who would be saved, even as He sorrowed over the sins of men and the loss of beatitude by those who would damn themselves. With this consideration in mind, the beatific vision would actually seem to increase the spiritual suffering of Christ since, through it, He would see the full truth and full extent of the rejection of God by man. One suffers at the sight of sin in proportion to one's love of goodness.[260] As the beatific vision perfects Christ's human knowledge and charity, His hatred of sin and anguish at its commission would be similarly intensified. In other words, one may argue contrary to Balthasar that possession of the beatific vision did not diminish Christ's suffering, but rather perfected it. Only in seeing the infinite goodness of God and His extravagant love for mankind can the offense of sin be understood in the full truth of its horror: to see the lover loving — even more, to be the very lover loving — , to see the beloved spurn that love, and to see the agony that will result for the beloved.

Now, since man's end is God, if he attains this superabundant good, one may expect the whole man to be fulfilled, and not only his intellect and will. Even in this world, when a person attains a difficult but much-desired good, he often does not feel his physical fatigue in the joy of his triumph. Such satisfaction of the whole person in the possession of the good of the intellect and will might be expected in the case of Christ's possession of the beatific vision, thereby 'overriding' His physical and emotional anguish. However, because God alone is the cause of this intimate union, and because the natural relation between Christ's body and soul was subject to His divine will, there was no necessity for His beatific vision to affect the lower powers of the soul,[261] i.e., His 'inferior reason' (intellect and will as by nature directed to the *bonum creatum*), His emotions, or His body.[262]

Now Christ permitted each nature and each faculty to do what was proper to it.[263] Each faculty has a different object and thus there is no contradiction in two faculties simultaneously having differing relations to their individual objects. In the case of Christ, He would have been in anguish with respect to His body and emotions, and likewise His will insofar as He considered His injuries and men's sins, all the while His rational powers were confirmed through grace in the joy of beholding God. Unlike the merely apparent suffering taught by the docetists, Christ's possession of the beatific vision then jeopardizes neither His real suffering nor His real assumption of human nature. But if it does not jeopardize these two, neither can it jeopardize the unique efficacy of His suffering, His primacy in the order of glory, or the perfection of His knowledge of the human condition, insofar as one ties these three to the former two.

Balthasar does not like the distinction made between the 'upper,' or rational, part of the soul (in which the beatific vision is received), and the 'lower,' or sensitive and vegetative parts of the soul, because it seems divisive.[264] Moreover, he argues that blessedness in this world is to be on the right way with God, not to feel blessed. However, in both these objections, he has fundamentally made the same distinction as the scholastics: First, he points out that the sufferer should rejoice in the joy to come, but that the present suffering as such is no cause of joy.[265] This position parallels the scholastic doctrine that the beatific vision concerns the intellectual soul as directed to the Final Good. Secondly, the question of what a person feels (as in whether he feels blessed) relates to the sensitive part of the soul.

The theological explanation offered here for the compatibility of Christ's beatific vision with His suffering does no violence to the unity of His soul: The fulfillment of one power of the soul even as the person suffers according to a different power is commonly experienced,[266] with no threat to personal unity. For example, a man aware of his hunger may nonetheless be enjoying his work. For the sake of His redemptive work, Christ permitted each power of His human soul to exercise its proper function, just as the operations of His divine and human natures were unchanged. He could suffer anguish even while possessing the beatific vision, and this without jeopardizing either His human nature or psychological unity. Hence, to deny the beatific vision in Christ because it supposedly vitiates His humanity is not to affirm human nature, but to misunderstand it.

The distinction among the various modes of possible suffering is important, for it reveals in what ways Christ, as true man, could suffer before and after His death. Before His death, Christ could suffer corporally, emotionally, and in His rational faculties insofar as these concern the goods of this life for Himself, and the goods of both this life and the next for others. After His death, however, His soul being separated from His body, it was impossible for Him to suffer in these ways. If then one wants to maintain that Christ suffered after death, He could only have suffered in His rational faculties insofar as these concern the eternal good, and such suffering after death is the suffering of waiting, purgation, or damnation, according to God's just judgment of the soul of the dead person. None of these pains makes sense with respect to Christ without injustice on the part of God — unless, of course, the Holy One of God actually became evil Himself.

Balthasar's second objection raises the question whether Christ's possession of the beatific vision would jeopardize the efficacy of His suffering. The answer to this question depends on what determines that efficacy. Linking the *degree* of Christ's suffering with its redemptive efficacy indicates suffering is taken as the formal principle of redemption. Redemption is then not a work of merit, in which a good is awarded in proportion to a good done, but rather simply the most extreme case of utilizing a mode open to all. Christ simply does to an outstanding degree what others (such as Job, the idolatrous Israelites, and martyrs who offer themselves for others[267]) did, namely, suffer. In contrast, according to a soteriology based on merit, Christ accomplishes a uniquely good work, when no one else was even capable of a good work (except through grace in virtue of Christ's work to come).

Balthasar's insistence that Christ's death be "qualitatively different"[268] does not contradict so much as confirm the conclusion that suffering is the formal principle of redemption in his soteriology. According to Balthasar, Christ suffered *our* death *("pro nobis")*. It is made "qualitatively different" because Christ is divine, which means (for Balthasar) the abandonment of the incarnate Son can be "ever-greater." Hence, in the end, the real difference of 'quality' is one of degree. One might counter by noting that Christ's abandonment is in proportion to the closeness of His relation to the Father, whereas the experience of Sheol other men deserved would have been a factor of their sinful distance from God. In this case, however, redemption is seen clearly to be a factor of Christ's divinity, and His human nature is irrelevant. In addition, as failures to correspond with grace, men's sins put their sinfulness in proportion with their (potential) closeness with God, whereas Christ's closeness with the Father is diminished to the extent He really takes men's sins upon Himself. Thus, in the end, the real difference of 'quality' is again one of degree.

Suffering as such has no intrinsic value. It becomes a potential bearer of eternal value only due to the charity of Christ (or, as Balthasar would say, His obedience). But if charity (or obedience) is the principle of merit rather than suffering, one drop of Christ's blood would have been sufficient for the redemption of the world. Hence, the efficacy of His suffering would be increased by the beatific vision to the extent to which it would perfect His charity (or obedience) by enabling Him as man to know God better, know the individuals He was saving by name, fulfill the divine will more consciously, and love both God and His human brethren more fervently. Just so the saints insist the value of their good works is not based upon what they do but upon with how much charity they do it. Balthasar, however, considers the possibility of Christ redeeming the world with a drop of blood as "free-wheeling speculation in empty space," caused by a "foolishness" that neglects God's "actual deeds."[269]

Third, would Christ's possession of the beatific vision jeopardize His primacy in glory because its possession would mean He did not suffer the most? It has already been argued the beatific vision and suffering on earth are not incompatible. Moreover, it should be noted that, as the previous objection took pain instead of charity as the principle of redemptive efficacy, this one has the same preference in regard to the principle of heavenly reward or primacy. In these two regards, the objection has been answered by earlier considerations.

So much being said, it may be noted that suffering need not be taken as the formal principle of redemption to say there is a certain fittingness to the extremity of Christ's suffering. By means of the lengths to which God in Christ went for man's salvation, His great love is shown: "Greater love than this no man hath, that a man lay down his life for his friends" (Jn 15:13). In addition, Christ's patient suffering can thereby serve as an encouraging example to all other men.[270] Finally, His extreme anguish indicates the gravity of sin, not just cumulatively considered, but even of any individual sin, since the single sin of

Adam and Eve was sufficient for God to have cause to promise a redeemer (see Gen 3:15).

That Christ's pain in His passion was indeed the greatest ever in the present life is proposed by St. Thomas Aquinas for four reasons: first, the extent and degree of His bodily and interior pain; second, the perfection of Christ's body and soul, and their extreme sensitivity due to the fact that their union was not damaged by original sin; third, the fact that each faculty was allowed its proper function, and pain in one did not distract from pain in any other; and fourth, the fact that Christ embraced His agony to deliver men from sin and thus there was a certain proportion between them.[271] Nevertheless, St. Thomas is careful to point out that Christ did not endure all sufferings in any cumulative sense, since some sufferings are mutually exclusive. However, He did suffer every generic human suffering, i.e., from all kinds of men, in His entire body, and of every kind (in His soul, body, reputation, etc.).[272] If one wished to do so, Christ's primacy in the order of glory with respect to His suffering could then be established on the basis of the reasons given by St. Thomas, which remain unchanged by Christ's possession of the beatific vision.

The distinction St. Thomas makes between generic types of suffering undergone according to an individual's circumstances (e.g., death, humiliation, betrayal), and the specific types of suffering (e.g., death by crucifixion, death by beheading) is relevant also to Balthasar's question, "Should the poet's 'nothing human is foreign to me' not apply to him?" This first objection suggested Christ's assumption of human nature would be deficient if His experience of human suffering were not the greatest. Balthasar's question can now be answered by saying both that no human suffering is foreign to Christ generically speaking, though not specifically, and that the degree of His suffering in these generic ways was the greatest. It is ultimately this last that Balthasar is interested to preserve, since he cannot take exception to the exclusion from Christ of most specific kinds of pain without having to explain why Christ's lack of undergoing decapitation, for example, does not jeopardize His full experience of the human condition.

Extending the application of the distinction, however, note that if Christ suffered generic punishments for sin *according to His individual circumstances* (e.g., He died by being crucified, not beheaded), He did not suffer the cumulative individual punishments for sin on earth *or after death*. At most, Balthasar could argue that Christ suffered Sheol generically, i.e., adapted to His personal guilt. But if all suffer the same in Sheol, then Christ's experience there could have been *no greater* than anyone else's.

Balthasar's fourth objection concerns whether the beatific vision jeopardizes the perfection of Christ's knowledge by preventing His experience of some aspects of the human condition. Before considering this objection, it is noteworthy that, although Balthasar insists Christ must fully know man, Balthasar does not similarly insist that Christ — who is the Word — must fully know God. This emphasis suggests Balthasar's Jesus is more man than God, as also indicated by the Word's "depositing" of the divine attributes.

Balthasar's objection is the rejection of the definitive perfection of knowledge in favor of a lesser perfection, that of knowledge acquired through experience, because the two are held to be incompatible. However, since knowing something through a more perfect cause does not change the fact that one may know it also through a less perfect cause,[273] the perfection of knowledge Christ had through the beatific vision would not have been incompatible with the perfection of His experiential knowledge, generally speaking. If one knows something in virtue of one argument, so to speak, to know the same conclusion on the basis of another does not remove the validity of the first. The beatific vision would, however, be incompatible with the experiential knowledge of ignorance (including faith).

Although Balthasar thinks Christ had faith and erred, i.e., had those experiences, he denies that Christ sinned. Christ's perfect knowledge of men's sins comes not through experience, but through the *visio mortis,* which He experiences as if He Himself had committed all sins. Although knowledge of sin through the *visio mortis* is not the same as knowledge through personal experience (i.e., through commission of sin), Balthasar would exempt Christ from this latter by reference to the principle that Christ was "like us in all things but sin (Heb 4:15)."[274] Now Hebrews 4:15 actually reads that Christ was "*tempted* in all things like as we are, without sin." In alluding to the verse in a truncated form like Balthasar does, the Council of Chalcedon extends its significance, but in the clear context of affirming Christ's true and whole human *nature.*[275] In contrast, Balthasar alludes to the verse to make a claim about Christ's *experience.* Since act follows on nature, and experience would be dependent upon act, it would seem one could use the Council's application in support of Balthasar's. However, nature does not necessitate the experience of any particular free act of intellect and will; if it did, human freedom would be only an illusion. Moreover, one observes there are universal experiences that are not sin and yet which Christ did not have, e.g., remorse for personal sin. If Christ felt remorse for the sins of others as if He had committed them Himself, such vicarious remorse is the same as remorse for personal sin only generically: It is remorse, but not the same kind. Hence one may induce that likewise Christ's ignorance need not concern the same things as that of other men. His possession of the beatific vision, coupled with His ignorance of the things possible to God that will never be,[276] would satisfy Balthasar's way of applying Hebrews 4:15.

It remains to consider Balthasar's overarching argument that Christ's sufferings exceeded that of the saints (or, more accurately, of the mystics), some of
whom had experiences they described as hell. As pointed out earlier, no attempt
is made here to consider these experiences on their own terms; instead they are
approached through Balthasar's representations of them. As he describes them,
some of these experiences are simple visions of hell that do not entail any sort
of experience of it, even if great sorrow accompanies or results from the vision.
These cases are irrelevant to the question of Christ's comparative suffering because they do not bear sufficient likeness to the interior *visio mortis*, or experience of sin and Sheol, that Balthasar argues Christ experienced. There remain
visions of that abode of the dead with some experience of it, and the mystical
'dark night' that is likened to hell.

Regarding visionary or mystical experiences of hell (as opposed to the
'dark night'), we note first the caution recommended by St. Thomas Aquinas:

> The pain of a suffering, separated soul belongs to the state of future con-
> demnation, which exceeds every evil of this life, just as the glory of the
> saints surpasses every good of the present life. Accordingly, when we say
> that Christ's pain was the greatest, we make no comparison between His
> and the pain of a separated soul.[277]

In other words, since there is no basis for proportionate comparison between
sufferings before and after death, actual condemnation in hell cannot be meaningfully compared to the sufferings of either Christ or the mystics. Secondly,
note also that it would seem no one can experience the actual reality of hell before his death without involving God in the injustice of punishing precipi-
tously; the visionaries may have experienced something like hell, but not its full
reality. Third, no one will ever have as intimate a union between body and soul,
or such perfection of body and soul, as Christ did. Therefore it is possible that
His suffering before His death exceeded any mystical or physical sufferings.
Finally, such mystical experiences do not claim to be comprehensive, i.e., any
one experience is the experience of a single case of punishment, not the punishment of all souls and perhaps not even the punishment of the worst. Hence, if
Christ's suffering must exceed the visionary experiences of hell, it need only exceed that of the worst single instance; it need not be the *visio mortis* appor-
tioned to the sins of all mankind.

As for the mystical 'dark night,' it would be worthwhile to recall briefly
what this night is. St. John of the Cross, the spiritual doctor of the 'dark night'
to whom Balthasar most often refers, distinguishes three nights that plunge the
soul into darkness, the night of the senses, of faith, and of God:

The first has to do with the point of departure, because the individual must deprive himself of his appetite for worldly possessions. This denial and privation is like a night for all his senses.

The second . . . [is] the means or the road along which a person travels to this union [with God]. Now this road is faith, and for the intellect faith is also like a dark night.

The third . . . [is] the point of arrival, namely, God. And God is also a dark night to man in this life.[278]

The darkness of the latter two nights is not caused by deprivation like the first, but rather by the presence of a light that surpasses the natural capacities of the soul.[279] God is by nature beyond the soul (the third night), but faith is also (the second night), since it is the only proportionate means of union with God in this life.[280] It should be noted that St. John of the Cross is referring to that living faith informed by charity, not to the faith of a soul without the third theological virtue.[281]

Now God is not dark at all to Christ, nor does He have faith, according to His divine nature. The like must be said according to His human nature on account of the hypostatic union. There are three differences between the hypostatic union of Christ and the union of the saints with God in the 'dark night': the kind of union, the perfection of the means to the union, and that fact of the union's being accomplished or yet being perfected. First, Christ's human nature is "full of grace and truth" (Jn 1:14; see also Col 1:19; 2:9), because it is united to the divine Word in His person. At the moment of Christ's conception, His human nature was united with God in the most intimate and perfect way possible. This unity far surpasses the unity granted to souls in the 'dark night,' which lacks even the unity of vision. Second, the union in Person surpasses the union of vision, which in turn surpasses the union of the 'dark night,' so Christ's natural faculties must have been strengthened by grace to a higher degree, and so to a higher end, than other souls. In other words, not only was Christ's union with God greater and more perfect, but His apprehension of that union was greater and more perfect. Finally, while the saints proceed toward greater union with God during their life on earth, Jesus was God always. There is no greater union with the divine to which human nature could be brought than the hypostatic union.

These three factors suggest that Christ's knowledge and experience of pain must have differed essentially from that of all others, even of those in the 'dark night,' even of those most conformed to Him and to His cross. One must question whether Christ possessed the conditions for the possibility of the 'dark night.' This difference does not affect Christ's true humanity or His real human pain; it merely reminds us that Christ is not only human but also divine, and so His actions (including His suffering) are determined not only by His humanity, but also by His divinity.

If the differences between Christ and the saints of the 'dark night' invite caution about using the 'dark night' to characterize Christ's sufferings, the joy frequently manifested by saints in the midst of their agonies bears a certain likeness to Christ's possession of the beatific vision during His Passion.[282] This joy is often observed in saints subjected to fierce physical torments; St. Lawrence's jesting while being roasted is a prime example. The extreme fasts and penances of saints who were not martyrs would also be relevant. If the cause is not a grace of ecstasy, the martyrs' and ascetics' calm disregard of pain and approaching death might be attributed to the natural forgetfulness of other faculties during intense engagement of one power, augmented by grace. The supernatural joy of saints suffering more spiritual agonies cannot be explained in the same manner. In all cases, however, the essence of this supernatural joy is not to be confused with sensory or emotional pleasure, satisfaction, or delight. St. John of the Cross's frequent warnings about what a mistake it is to take these for spiritual joy indicates how very different they are. Hence it is not that the saints' seeming unawareness of physical agony gives reason to call into question again the compatibility of Christ's beatific vision with His agony, since He permitted each power its proper operation. Instead, the firm commitment to God despite pressing physical, emotional, or spiritual demands is faith's foretaste of the definitive rest of the will in God through the beatific vision. In this connection, it is significant that the saints' union with God in the 'dark night' is not interrupted, however isolated they feel, but is growing. This parallel of faith to the beatific vision is manifest in common spiritual direction, where inner peace of the heart (meaning, the will) reflects acceptance of God's will and can confirm particular decisions, even if the emotions sometimes remain or become disturbed at the challenging character of this decision.[283]

In his apostolic letter *Novo millennio ineunte*, Pope John Paul II draws on the mystical experiences of the saints precisely for insight into the mystery of Christ's beatific vision even in (or especially in) the moment of His abandonment on the cross:

> His eyes remain fixed on the Father. Precisely because of the knowledge and experience of the Father which he alone has, even at this moment of darkness he sees clearly the gravity of sin and suffers because of it. He alone, who sees the Father and rejoices fully in him, can understand completely what it means to resist the Father's love by sin.[284]

The pope goes on to use words St. Catherine of Siena heard from God the Father to describe the state in which joy and suffering can be present together in holy souls: "Thus the soul is blissful and afflicted: afflicted on account of the sins of its neighbor, blissful on account of the union and the affection of charity which it has inwardly received. These souls imitate the spotless Lamb, my Only-Begotten Son, who on the Cross was both blissful and afflicted."[285]

Finally, the pope quotes St. Thérèse of Lisieux as a witness of the possibility of simultaneous bliss and affliction:

"In the Garden of Olives our Lord was blessed with all the joys of the Trinity, yet his dying was no less harsh. It is a mystery, but I assure you that, on the basis of what I myself am feeling, I can understand something of it."[286]

In conclusion, there are reasons to doubt the strength of Balthasar's argument that Christ's sufferings must include those of hell in order that His suffering be the greatest and surpass the saints' or mystics' experience of something described as hell or in terms of it. The simple visions of hell are not sufficiently like the definitive experience Balthasar claims for Christ. The visions of hell with some experience of it lack a basis for meaningful comparison. The mystical 'dark night,' sometimes described in terms of *hell*, is a night of purgation, inapplicable to Christ, while even in the midst of that night, the saints are not abandoned by God, but are growing in union with Him. Finally, the saints have a supernatural joy or peace in their sufferings, which is analogous to Christ's beatific vision during His passion.

We lack space here for a positive exposition of a Catholic psychology of Christ, but note, first, that Balthasar's objections to the beatific vision suggest in general that he thinks the beatific vision threatens, rather than perfects, the life of the human soul. Second, it is a mistake to ask how Jesus as man knows He is God, if one intends by doing so to abstract from the hypostatic union with its attendant gifts of grace. Taken absolutely, the subject of Christ is the Person of the Word, who knows He is God by the divine act of being. To the subject taken insofar as He is man, the divinity of Jesus is as much beyond His human powers as it is beyond those of any other man, and hence He as man would require the beatific vision to know, as man, His own divinity. Third, to assert that Christ's abandonment was the loss of His beatific knowledge would mean that the same subject would both know He is God (by the divine knowledge) and believe it (by faith). It is at this point that the unity of Christ's consciousness is truly threatened. For it is impossible for the same subject to know and to believe the same thing.[287] Even though a subject knows in virtue of a nature — and so as

Christ has two intellectual natures, He has two acts of knowing — the subject of knowing is a hypostasis, not a nature. As Christ's hypostasis is single, *He* (i.e., as a unified subject) cannot both know and believe the same thing — just as He cannot love a person with one will and hate him with the other. Besides sundering the unity of Christ's consciousness, if Christ both knows and believes the same thing, it could suggest His human nature has been made into a person. Fourth, to say Christ's incarnation or abandonment entailed the loss of His *divine* knowledge also has problematic consequences. God's knowledge and His act of knowing are identical to His nature, because He is absolutely simple; they are thus also identical to each Person of the divine nature.[288] It is an essential operation for the Word to know Himself; if the divine knowledge is lost, the Person is lost. Thus to assert that Christ loses His divine knowledge of the Father or of Himself as the Son means His loss of the Godhead. In his encyclical letter, *Sempiternus Rex* (1951), Pope Pius XII denounced the "kenotic theory" according to which "in Christ the divinity of the Word is lost."[289] Of course, as I have tried to explain, Balthasar does not hold that the Word's divinity was wholly lost in the Incarnation: The Word retains the perfection of the divine essence as self-gift, even as He "strips" Himself of the divine attributes. But Pius XII goes on to quote Pope St. Leo, "The true God . . . was born with the complete and perfect nature of a true man; he is complete in his [divine] nature and complete in ours."[290] Hence Pius XII's censure applies also to the Word losing *any* of the divine attributes in becoming incarnate since the divine nature is utterly simple; i.e., the "complete" divine nature includes *all* the divine attributes. Again, the attribution of ignorance to the Son through the "depositing" of His divine omniscience introduces a difference *in content* (not simply mode) between the incarnate Son's consciousness of Himself as God, and the Father's and Holy Spirit's. The single divine act of knowing is thereby splintered, which likewise means the incarnate Son ceases to be God.[291] Both arguments indicate the *de facto* destruction of the Trinity and of the hypostatic union as the union of the unconfused divine and human natures in the divine Person of the Son. Since there must yet remain someone with human nature who does not know he is God, however, and as this person cannot be God since God's knowledge and His act of knowing are identical to His nature, which is identical to each Person, there must have been two persons in Christ from the beginning, which is Nestorianism; or if the Word was transmuted into man, which is monophysitism; or if the Word remained a hypostasis without the divine nature but with a human nature of unusual value, and thus was neither God nor man, which is basically Arianism. In this context, we add that Balthasar's theology of the Descent attributes suffering to God as such, both in regard to the Father's sense of loss in abandoning the Son and to the Son's experience of

Sheol.[292] Finally, if indeed Christ's abandonment by the Father in Sheol is the ultimate term of the Word's incarnate kenosis, and if His whole life and death are one unified work, then His conception in the flesh must be understood as the beginning of abandonment by God, and this effectively is Origenism (though we will see that the Son 'falls' not so much into human nature as through it).

In summary of this subsection, Balthasar considers the Word's "depositing" of the divine knowledge necessary in order that His mission correspond to His kenotic procession and in order that He truly become "like us in all things but sin" in His incarnation. As a consequence of the "depositing" of this divine attribute, Christ has faith (and the ignorance essential to it) instead of the beatific vision. In place of this latter, Balthasar describes a *visio immediata,* which amounts to Christ's consciousness of His mission as mediated by the Spirit. Christ's faith and *visio immediata* permit Balthasar to ascribe to Christ a supreme degree of suffering, which he thinks would be incompatible with the beatific vision. In light of this example and its significant role in Balthasar's theology of the Descent, the "depositing" of the divine attributes in general is seen to be a reality, and not merely a mode of speaking.

The "Depositing" of the Word's Humanity

In the previous section, the Word's "depositing" of His divine attributes was seen through Balthasar's preeminent example, the "depositing" of the divine knowledge. The "depositing" of the divine attributes follows from Balthasar's view of the real continuation and expression of the kenotic intra-Trinitarian procession of the Son in His economic mission. The entire mission of the Word is characterized by His "giving back" all He is to the Father. This mission is perfected not in the simple fact of the Word's incarnation, however, but in His acts: The Word's kenosis, or "depositing," does not cease with the fact of His becoming man, but will continue through His human life. He continually and actively holds Himself passive in the hands of the Spirit and, when it is the Father's will, in the hands of human beings. He lives in physical poverty and in the spiritual poverty of prayer, faith, and not disposing of Himself.[293] Finally, through His death and in His being dead, He gives back to the Creator Father even this creaturely existence and the very humanity He originally received from Him through the Holy Spirit. This "depositing" of His humanity, so to speak, results in the "suspension . . . of the Incarnation"[294] in Sheol. It is, in fact, the term of His whole mission. Let us carefully examine how Balthasar indicates this final kenosis.

In general, kenosis is self-abandonment on behalf of the other.[295] The

Word abandons Himself, so to speak, by "depositing" His divine attributes and becoming what He is not in Himself, namely, a creature.[296] After becoming man, He abandons Himself psychologically by not disposing of Himself but letting the Holy Spirit dispose of Him, i.e., by putting His entire life at the disposal of the Father and of men. Even as the Son's kenotic procession is an "eternal event," His incarnate kenosis continues throughout His life. Ultimately, He even abandons His very self that is being man.

For this goal to be met, the totality of the common human existence that the Word takes upon Himself must be utterly at His disposal. It is, as it were, passive and object-ive to the Son in His descent into the flesh, as the Son is passive and object-ive to the Father in His descent into Sheol.[297] Because the final deed of death seals the meaning of everything that preceded it,[298] the Son's existence in kenotic obedience would not be perfect unless, precisely in His death and being dead, He gives up the humanity He entered, and in which He lived, in such obedience.

Balthasar says that Jesus

> lets his entire formless and therefore wordless existence (as "flesh") be yielded up in an ultimate gesture, so that it may become something that God's hand can form in its entirety, including his mother's womb and his burial, into "the Word of God."[299]

Balthasar is speaking here in a vocabulary he has developed throughout the text that precedes this quotation, and so its meaning is not immediately evident, when removed from its context. Jesus' existence is "formless" and "wordless," because He has "deposited" the divine attributes ("form") of the Word. He thus exists "as 'flesh.'" This existence from its beginning to its end, including those extremes of "his mother's womb and his burial," must also be "yielded up." In this way and only in this way (because if the whole is required, no part alone will suffice), the entirety of His existence can be revelatory of God, i.e., can be formed "into 'the Word of God.'" "God [the Father]'s hand," not His own, determines the content and expression of this revelation: Out of love for the Father and to reveal the Father's love,[300] the Son becomes "only a free space against which the will of the Father may make its colliding impact, . . . a uniquely suitable medium for this power of the Father as he gives himself expression."[301] This "ultimate gesture" must occur in His death and being dead for two reasons. First, the "entirety" is required and this whole is only present at the end. Second, as this consummate moment, death can definitively determine the meaning of the entire life that went before it.[302] If the Son had refused to give up His humanity in the end, His self-giving would not have been total.

Moreover, He would have personally participated in the godless *no* of refusal to give one's self in acknowledgment of the ultimate other (God) as the source of one's existence.

Not much later in the same work, Balthasar writes,

> Jesus has "authority" to "give himself up" (Jn 10:18). Here, the "giving up of self" certainly means in the first place death, but it is quite essentially a phrase that includes the whole existence in itself, as the directive that the believers must "give themselves up" for their brethren shows (1 Jn 3:16). The "authority" to "take back" what has been given up is not the revocation of the self-abandonment, but its inner completion, inasmuch as the going out into the final dispossession of self-abandonment belongs to the original "authority," which thereby distinguishes itself from every other human authority, even that of a prophet.[303]

We must first note that Balthasar is *interpreting* John 10:18 when he says "give himself up," not *quoting* it, even though he uses quotation marks.[304] The original phrase ἐγὼ τίθημι αυτὴν ἀπ' ἐμαυτοῦ[305] is closely translated into English by the Douay-Rheims, "I lay it down of myself." The feminine pronoun αὐτὴν in John 10:18 refers to its antecedent in John 10:17, ψυχήν. The context of the good shepherd who gives his ψυχήν for his sheep (Jn 10:1-18, especially verses 11 and 15) makes clear ψυχήν in verse 17 means *life*. If it were not just Christ's physical life that He would lay down but His very self, as in Balthasar's interpretation, the Greek should have the *masculine reflexive* pronoun ἐμαυτὸν, instead of the *feminine personal* pronoun αὐτὴν.

If we allow Balthasar his interpreted reading of John 10:18 in order to follow his thought, we see that he goes on to state his interpretation explicitly: Jesus not only goes to His death, but He gives up His "whole existence." Balthasar then makes an analogy: There should be a like "giving up of self" in Jesus, as is required of His followers. At this point, it seems difficult to say that Jesus' "whole existence" is more than His physical human life, since it is impossible for Christians to give up more than their lives in the flesh. There is a tension between Jesus' "giving up" something more than just His physical life (i.e., "himself," His "whole existence") and the illustration Balthasar has provided. It is resolved in the final sentence: Jesus' going into "final dispossession" belongs to His superior "original 'authority.'" This authority is, of course, His divine authority, by power of which He is "free to do what he will with his own nature."[306] Hence, as He is free to "deposit" divine attributes with the Father, He is free to dispossess Himself also of His human nature. The comparison with the sacrifice made by Jesus' disciples simply falls short — as it must, since Jesus' giving up of self is the archetype of their "giving up," and qualitatively superior to all other kenoses.

The Word's dispossession of His human nature during His kenotic mission into self-abandonment is made yet clearer in the following passage:

> If "man" is the living and mortal being composed of body and spirit in a unity whom we know and if *this* man ceases to be in death (whatever might become of him after death), {then Jesus has gone to the end of his being human and, having become human, he has gone to the limits in his surrender of himself (Jn 10:17). And in his being dead with the dead, the attitude and stance of the divine Logos has been stripped away, as it were. For it was in the extremities of this death that the Logos found the adequate expression of this divine stance:} letting himself remain available for the Father in everything, even in the ultimate alienation. The stripping away [*Entblößung*] of the man Jesus is the laying bare [*Bloßlegung*] not only of Sheol but also of the trinitarian relationship in which the Son is entirely the one who springs forth from the Father. Holy Saturday is thus a kind of suspension, as it were, of the Incarnation, whose result is given back to the hands of the Father and which the Father will renew and definitively confirm by the Easter Resurrection.[307]

Our consideration of this significant text must begin with several corrections to the translation. The text that appears in braces above is the translator's rendition of the original German, which runs

> so ist Jesus in der Hingabe seiner selbst (Jo 10, 17) bis an Ende seines Menschseins und Menschgewordenseins gegangen, und in seinem Totsein mit den Toten entblößt sich gleichsam jene Haltung und Gesinnung des göttlichen Logos, der in diesem Äußersten ihre[n] adäquaten Ausdruck fand.[308]

Balthasar says here quite clearly that "in his offering of himself (Jn 10:17), Jesus has gone to the end [*bis an Ende*] of his being man and his having become man [*seines Menschseins und Menschgewordenseins*]." In the official translation above, however, three violent changes have been made to his meaning. First, this compound genitive has been split and represented as a single genitive ("of his being human") and an adverbial participle ("having become human"). Whereas Balthasar said Jesus went to the end of both, the translation has Him going only to the end of the one: "Jesus has gone to the end of his being human." Next, the translator duplicates the German verb "ist . . . gegangen," translating it as "has gone . . . has gone." This repetition in itself is not a problem.

Likewise, it is not problematic in itself (i.e., abstracted from the context) that Balthasar's single "bis an Ende" is duplicated, and translated first with "to the end," then with "to the *limits*." What is problematic, however, is that the "to the limits" is modified with the phrase "in his surrender of himself." In contrast, in the original, the adverbial phrase "in der Hingabe seiner selbst" in no way modifies "bis an Ende." Finally, the adverbial participle "having become human" created by the translator modifies the duplicated verb in the translation, whereas "seines . . . Menschgewordenseins" cannot and does not modify the verb in the original; nonetheless, we are given "and, having become human, he has gone." The change of the genitive modifying "bis an Ende" to an adverbial phrase modifying "has gone" together change what was an offering of His very being human to His reaching of the limits of human self-surrender.

Continuing on, we see that the present active "entblößt sich" has been translated with the perfect passive "has been stripped away." The translator appears to have made this choice in order to maintain in the English translation Balthasar's connection between "entblößt sich" here and his later use of "Entblößung," translated as "stripping away." The change from present active to perfect passive diminishes the nature of Christ's being dead as a personal 'event' of self-surrender that continues and expresses His eternal intra-Trinitarian self-surrender. More important, since the Logos *is* nothing other than His "attitude and stance," the official English translation incorrectly implies that it is the Logos Himself that is stripped away, rather than His humanity. It would have been more accurate to say that "that attitude and stance of the divine Logos strips itself [*entblößt sich*] as it were." The primary meaning of *sich entblößen* is *to remove one's clothes;* this is *to expose oneself* in the exhibitionist sense.[309] *To strip* (as opposed to *to strip away*) thus would be a reasonable alternative that captures both these senses of removal and revelation.

These more technical matters have already gone far in revealing Balthasar's thought in this passage. Only one more such technical issue need be raised, namely, whether it is just to translate *entblößt sich* as *strip itself*. Some might want to translate "entblößt sich gleichsam jene Haltung und Gesinnung des göttlichen Logos" as "the attitude and stance of the divine Logos as it were *reveals* itself," because *uncover,* and hence *reveal,* is a secondary meaning of *entblößen*.[310] The corrected translation I proposed ("strips itself" in the exhibitionist sense) nonetheless seems preferable and more accurate, for several reasons. First, *to strip oneself* is the primary meaning of *entblößen; to reveal oneself* is a secondary, derivative meaning. Second, the secondary meanings usually require that *entblößen* be transitive, while here it is reflexive, which is the typical construction when the primary meaning of *to strip oneself* is to be understood. Third, Balthasar uses the substantive *(Entblößung)* of the same verb two sentences later exactly in distinction to *Bloßlegung. Bloßlegung,* translated "laying bare" in the English, would admit the wide sense of *revealing.* Hence Balthasar could have used its verbal form *(bloßlegen)* if his intention had been to speak of the revelation of the Logos' stance without implying also its removal (stripping away) of something in self-exposure; however, he did not. Fourth, the corrected translation I proposed is wholly consistent with the concept Balthasar is expressing in the paragraph as a whole, for he goes on to speak of this revelation of the Logos in the very "stripping away [*Entblößung*] of the man Jesus"[311] and of Holy Saturday as "a kind of suspension, as it were, of the Incarnation." In contrast, the translation "reveals itself" has lost this sense, so much a part of Balthasar's thought in this passage. Finally, an advocate of the rendition "reveals itself" would have to explain why Balthasar says "*as it were* reveals itself." "As it were" suggests it is not a true revelation, but Balthasar is explicit in the same passage that the definitive revelation of the Son, and so also of the Trinity, occurs in the Descent.

Our ultimate interest here is not mere analysis of a translation, however, but exposition of Balthasar's thought. The preceding selected considerations were necessary due to the significant and misleading changes made by the translator. At the same time, discussion of the necessary corrections has served to make Balthasar's thought here clearer. In the Word's descent to the dead, He "strips" Himself in an exhibitionist sense, an action that parallels His "depositing" of divine attributes with the Father in the descent of His incarnation. It appears Jesus thus goes to the end of his being man in two senses: First, His *Menschsein* ("being man") comes to an end in the sense that the separated body and soul do not constitute the substantial unity signified by *man.* He "strips" Himself of His "being man," namely, a unity of body and soul. The two are separated from each other by death, and hence the Word is no longer man, in a highly technical sense. Second, His *Menschgewordensein* ("having become man") comes to an end (is "stripped away") in the sense that the Word empties Himself even of His very humanity. Balthasar cannot mean to imply here that God undoes the past, because the Word could not undo the past of His "becoming man" in the Incarnation without undoing the very revelatory and redemptive act for which He became man. No, the Word does not revoke His mission, but pursues it to the utmost end. Since the Son's mission consists in His utter self-emptying, beginning with the divine attributes, and since He has the power and self-possession to surrender Himself in this way, it seems that "the end . . . of his having become man" means He empties Himself of His human nature, even as He emptied Himself of the divine;[312] the power to do the one enables Him to do the other. Otherwise, He could not be merely "a free space" for the Father. Otherwise, His self-giving would not be perfect. Otherwise, He would not really have gone to the "end,"[313] or really have surrendered everything of Himself, of His "whole existence."[314] Indeed, Balthasar says that in this stripping the Word "adequately" expresses Himself. But if He as Word is absolute self-giving back to the Father, then this stripping must likewise be a perfect return of self if it is to be an expression proportioned to its content and hence "adequate." Thus His existence as a hypostasis of the self-surrendering God is 'exposed.' Precisely this extreme "stripping" in the realm of death is the "adequate expression" of His divine "attitude or stance."

This "stripping" is "the laying bare . . . of Sheol" in that the cumulative sin-in-itself of the world will be definitively comprehended by the Word through His being conformed to it and "literally 'made sin'" in the *visio mortis*. At the same time, it is the "laying bare" of the Trinity, because the Son now appears only as the divine hypostasis sent by the Father to the farthest extremity possible from Him (i.e., physical and spiritual death in Sheol), thus signifying the perfect opposition within the Trinity between Father and Son *qua* Father and Son. "Holy Saturday is, thus a kind of suspension, as it were, of the Incarnation,"[315] of Jesus' "being man and of his having become man."[316] This "suspension" raises the question, to which we shall return, of whether Christ's humanity as such has any importance at all in mankind's redemption.

The necessity of the "stripping" away of the Incarnation within Balthasar's thought may be considered from another angle. Balthasar says that, in the tearing off of Jesus' garments, the Bridegroom appears naked before the world.[317] This nudity on the cross is to show in human flesh, and through nakedness as a sign of corporal love, two things: First, it is the unveiling on the cross of the self-surrendering divine love. Second, it is the sign that creaturely love is to become elevated to the divine love through a similar self-surrender,[318] through a "stripping" of self, one might even say. In Christ's death, the character of true life (whether divine or human) as self-surrender is manifested:

> What is involved is a double, reciprocal dispossession: of God into the human form and of man into the divine form, and this double dispossession contains the most concrete possible life: the life of man, which attains its form by letting itself be shattered to become the form of God; the life of God, that gains man for itself by renouncing its own form and, obedient unto death, pouring itself into the form of existence unto death.[319]

That is, in the Incarnation, the Word relinquishes the divine form in becoming man, while his human nature is "dispossessed" of its strict creatureliness by being elevated in this assumption. The human nature of all men consequently has the same normative end as its archetype: to let itself, through self-surrender, be elevated to being more than what it is. The Word will "pour" Himself out into the 'second death' of Sheol, but because He is also man, His human life must also be "shattered." Whereas for all other men such a "shattering" involves the transcendence of self in self-surrender through incorporation into Christ and the growth of the Spirit, the Word alone is a self-subsisting relation that, if He can do what He will with His own divine nature, can do what He will with His human nature. Thus, His human nature is "shattered" in Sheol by "a certain 'stretching apart' . . . which remains physiologically indescribable."[320] It is ultimately "stripped" from Him, leaving Him only as that "free space for the collision of the sin of the world."[321] In short, if the revelation of the divine love is signified on the cross by the stripping merely of Jesus' clothes, then even more so in Sheol, where this revelation reaches its utmost expression, must His human nature be "stripped" away.

For final confirmation and clarification of Balthasar's doctrine of the "suspension" of the Incarnation, we read,

> Thereby, with the removal of the whole superstructure of the Incarnation [*nach Wegziehung des ganzen inkarnatorischen Überbaus*], the eternal will of the Son within the Trinity to obedience is exposed, as the substructure that is the basis of the entire event of the Incarnation: and this is set face-to-face with the hidden substructure of sinful existence, exposed in Sheol, as the state of separation from God, the "loss of his glory."
>
> Now it is precisely this face-to-face confrontation between the "naked" God and "naked" sin that shows that Jesus' solidarity even with the utter lostness of sinners presupposes the uniqueness of his condition: the "inclusive quality" of his being with the dead rests upon something "exclusive" that he alone possesses.[322]

Here the Incarnation is a "superstructure," while the divine will of the Son to obey is the Incarnation's "substructure." This will to obey is also His kenosis: "The whole structure of his being and his time is built upon the foundation of the free act of obedience that is his kenosis."[323] This "substructure" of obedience "is set face-to-face" with a different "substructure" in Sheol, namely, that "of sinful existence, . . . the state of separation from God." God is "naked" in Sheol, because the Incarnation "superstructure" has been "removed," while sin is "naked" there, because it exists as sin-in-itself, having been removed from sinners and loaded upon Christ. The "confrontation" that occurs between these two reveals ("shows") that Jesus' being dead in utter abandonment by God and man depends upon His divinity, which is "the uniqueness of his condition." This "he alone possesses" among men, because He is the only God-man. Only God has the freedom to go into utter abandonment by God,[324] that is, into sin-in-itself. Only a divinity this free can die a death, physical and spiritual, that is "inclusive" of all other deaths. In addition, His being dead depends specifically upon His divinity *as Son*, for the Son alone as the obedient other among the divine Persons is the archetype for the creaturely existence in which the Trinity can be revealed through obedience unto death, and He alone is incarnated in obedience for this revelation.

This last passage makes Balthasar's thought about the "removal of the whole superstructure of the Incarnation" in Christ's descent sufficiently clear. It serves also to confirm our reading of the passage with the debated translation. It would not do Balthasar justice to overlook the connections he has woven in these passages using the ideas of dispossession, self-abandonment, and alienation; of stripping away, removal (of Christ's garments, of the "superstructure of the Incarnation"), yielding up, and giving up; of stripping, nakedness, and self-exposure; and of exposure, laying bare, and revelation. Christ's garments having been removed, His nakedness on the cross will be the corporal sign of the metaphysical "nakedness" to come when the "superstructure of the Incarnation" is removed in Sheol. The unified event of "Cross and Hell" will thus lay bare the "naked" hypostatic obedience of the Son, who in turn is the revelation of the Father.

If Balthasar's position has been accurately portrayed, it becomes evident why he does not consider the separation of Christ's body and soul to be particularly important.[325] In dying, the Word's human body and then His entire human nature are just other attributes He "gives back" and "deposits" with the Father, to receive back in the Resurrection. One might say that, in His Passover to the Father, the Son 'passes through' human nature; or that, in eternally falling in love with the Father, the Son falls into and through human nature all the way into the deepest pit of Sheol, since *descend* would suggest something active, as Balthasar has said,[326] but a *fall* is purely passive "letting be." Balthasar speaks of "a step, a fall through the depths of hell into the bosom of the Father."[327] Marek Pyc summarizes using the same image:

> Jesus is before all else he who is handed over by God; the men in contrast are only instruments within this action of God. God pushes him into the arms of the powers of corruption. . . . In front of us is revealed a super-tragedy of extreme abandonment of God, of a fall into the hell of the loss of God. On one side is the Father, who makes the Son fall into the abyss of hell . . . and, on the other, is the Son who, impelled by the Spirit, lets himself fall into this bottomless abyss, placing himself in the hands of the Father. . . .[328]

Here, Pyc's language of the Father pushing the Son parallels Balthasar's expressions of the Father "crushing" Him. If the "pushing" or "crushing" is the economic expression of the Father's generation, then the fall corresponds to the Son's procession: The mission is the procession. There, in Sheol, His "corporality" undergoes "a certain 'stretching apart' . . . which remains physiologically indescribable."[329] In the end, even this attenuated humanity does not remain, but in the extremity of the Word's total self-giving, He has become just "free space for the collision of the sin of the world."[330]

Light is shed here on how God redeems through the Descent event. As this "free space," i.e., without the limiting attributes of either the divine or human nature, the Son can be "literally 'made sin'"[331] through conformity to sin-in-itself in the *visio mortis:* By committing sin, sinners invested it with reality. But this sin — a reality — was transferred to Christ upon the cross and, in consequence, the Father's "wrath" against *sin* "crushes" *Christ* in Sheol. But it is the "naked" hypostasis of the Son that experiences the *visio mortis* in Sheol, while its intimate nature means the Son is conformed to the object of His vision. In effect, *the Son becomes the hypostasis of sin-in-itself.* For the rebellion of finite freedom must be taken up into the intra-Trinitarian "distance" "from within"[332] by God in perfect obedience (that is, in utter self-giving) if it is to be set aright. By being taken up in the Person of the Son, it is taken up within the Trinitarian relations of love and thus overcome through the "ever-greater" divine love.

Hence the *visio mortis* is ultimately experienced by Christ in relation to and as a result of His divine nature. "The condition of being dead, and not the 'separation' [of body and soul] is what is essential; for this truly being dead is a function of the total surrender of the Son."[333] In other words, in contrast to the being dead of other men, Christ's being dead ("*this* truly being dead") is not so much a function of human nature, but a function of His Trinitarian Person, of the kenosis of divine attributes that continued in the kenosis of human attributes. The Son of God is dead, not so much because He has joined to Himself a human nature and in His human soul He descends to an abode of the dead, as the traditional doctrine has it, but more because He is the filial hypostasis of obedient and complete self-gift who has given away what He is to be "literally 'made sin.'" Hence, He likewise undergoes the *visio mortis* precisely insofar as He is the Son, and hence insofar as He is God, since *as Son,* He is God:

> The perfect *self*-alienation of the experience of hell is the function of the incarnate Christ's obedience, and this obedience is once more a function of his free love for the Father.[334]

Self, we note, here refers not to a nature but to a Person and, as the Person of the Son, Christ is God. This clarification is confirmed by Balthasar's theology of the Incarnation and the Trinitarian context of the above quotation.

The *visio mortis* is precisely an alienation of the Son from Himself and thus, necessarily, also from the Father, because the Son is Son only in relation to the Father. In obedience to the Father, the Son accepts "from within"[335] and unites to Himself the experience of everything that is against God and so, of everything God is against. "The path is one of total self-alienation, for the triad of death-Hades-Satan is the summation of everything that resists God's sway, that cannot be united to God and is, as such, rejected by God."[336] But *He Himself is God,* and He is God *in relation to God* the Father.[337] Thus, the *visio mortis* is "perfect self-alienation" for the Son *as God:* He accepts what is most alien to Himself, sin, "from within," i.e., in virtue of His Trinitarian personality and into it. It is also "from within" in the sense that He takes it and its consequences as His own. As a result, He is alienated from the Father, in relation to whom is His whole existence. The self-alienation is perfect in being a complete acceptance of what is most unlike Himself and a total rejection by what is most similar to Him, and both of these alienations are to be the supreme expression of His love.

For Balthasar, this extremity of alienation and abandonment most perfectly reveals God:[338] "He can reveal his life precisely even in death, his Trinitarian communion precisely even in abandonment."[339] "God himself has proven to be the Almighty who is able to safeguard his identity in nonidentity, his being-with-himself in being lost."[340] The god of Balthasar's theology of the Descent does not proclaim "I am who am," but rather "I am when I am not." He is most "yes" the closer he unites the "no" of what is anti-God to himself.[341] Although Balthasar writes, "Nor . . . can [Christ's work on our behalf] be interpreted as an identification of the Crucified with the actual No of sin itself,"[342] this one passage does not contradict what has been said here, because the passage merely intends to indicate that Christ does not commit personal sin and that, even united to sin-in-itself in Sheol, His hypostatic obedience remains. But if a hypostasis is named by the nature it possesses, and Christ in Sheol no longer has the divine or human attributes but only the divine essence that is self-gift, which is His hypostasis, then He is God when He is Sin.

At this point, certain hesitations may have arisen in the reader. For one, does not the Son's "depositing" of His divine attributes import change into the Godhead or make Christ monophysite? To respond on Balthasar's behalf from the perspective of his principles, I would propose the following explanation: Because the Son's Trinitarian existence is kenotic, the kenotic character of His incarnation and descent does not effect real change in Him or the Trinity.[343] He willed from all eternity to empty Himself in this fashion, which is in accord with His eternal nature; hence He does not change. Likewise, Christ is not monophysite, at least not as commonly understood, because His form remains kenotic obedience. Consequently, far from impairing the Son's divinity, the Son's kenosis in "depositing" His divine and human attributes is an act of divine power and freedom, revealing Him to be God.[344] It also reveals the Trinitarian nature of God, since

> the poverty of the Son, who sought only the glory of the Father and let himself be robbed of everything in utter obedience [i.e., kenosis on behalf of the other], was the most exact expression of the absolute fullness [i.e., divinity], which does not consist of "having," but of "being = giving."[345]

In other words, if absolute being is absolute giving, there must be an absolute recipient that is the object of the Son's act of absolute self-gift in His mission; i.e., there must be another Person in God. His kenotic "depositing" of the form of God thus ushers in a new ideal of glory as renunciation of self, because it shows that the most essential aspect of the divine nature — and hence of *glory*'s prime analogate — is self-renunciation.[346]

Another concern arises because the Incarnation was never interrupted, and will never cease.[347] It seems in line with this lack of interruption that Balthasar says the Descent involves "*a kind of* suspension, *as it were*, of the Incarnation,"[348] thereby suggesting some (unspecified) qualification. On the other hand, the passages above and their content as set forth are consistent with the rest of his thought. The whole weight of his theology of God as self-gift and Christ's descent to the *visio mortis* drives toward a real suspension of the Incarnation. Indeed, he himself makes the point explicitly. It is tempered with the ambiguous "a kind of" and "as it were" only once in all the passages I found on this topic. Is some reconciliation of these three factors possible?

It seems implausible that Balthasar could have been ignorant of the Church's teaching, but I know of no place where he explicitly attempts to reconcile his notion of this "suspension, as it were, of the Incarnation" with the Church's teaching. One might surmise, however, that the qualification "as it were" is meant to serve this function, though this qualification without further clarification is scant acknowledgment for a doctrine of such importance. I would propose the following explanation: If the Son "strips" Himself of His humanity just as He "deposited" His divine attributes with the Father, then also His humanity was "given back" *to the Father*. If His absolute freedom lets Him do the first, it must also let Him do the second. The Son will receive the attributes of both natures back in His resurrection, which is the proper work of the Father.[349] In the Resurrection, God (the Father) draws Him back "into his divine life,"[350] which is multivalent for Jesus: As the Son abandoned in Sheol, He returns to the Father; as conformed to sin-in-itself, He returns to grace; as the Incarnation having been "suspended," He is returned to His body and soul, and the two reunited. In the meantime, however, after His death and before His resurrection, the Word may still be said to be united to His human nature inasmuch as He is united to the Father in the Holy Spirit.[351] This Trinitarian unity makes Sheol heaven,[352] and hence the Word in Sheol can also be said to be where His human nature is. Similarly, *He* is with the Father insofar as He has deposited *His* divine and human attributes with Him.[353] He can also always be said to be with the Father insofar as He always does the Father's will.[354] Therefore He can always be said to be with the divine and human attributes He "gave back." Moreover, the human nature He has wholly "given back" is still His in that it is *His* human nature that has been deposited with the Father, and no one else's. The "as it were" would also indicate the inability of the human mind to comprehend this mystery, which amounts either to a hypostasis without a nature or to the hypostasis of the Word with the nature of sin-in-itself; as Balthasar says frequently, what happens in Sheol is indescribable,[355] is indeterminable,[356] or remains in the darkness of God's inner mystery.[357]

I admit that this explanation does not achieve the integrity of the Church's doctrine, which is that Christ's human nature remains subsisting without interruption in its perfect entirety in the Person of the Word from the moment of His conception; nevertheless it the only one I see possible given the framework Balthasar has established. Of course, Balthasar's thought must be taken as he presents it, and so it must be granted that Balthasar may not have desired to reconcile his idea with the Church's. After all, he regarded the testimony (discussed in our first four chapters) of over 1500 years of "liturgical, speculative, and rhetorical-popular theology"[358] on the Descent, including the patristic sermons, as "folk myths,"[359] "lead[ing] far from the biblical message."[360] If he rejects the Church's doctrine of the Descent, there are bound to be consequences for his Christology. Reading Balthasar's "a kind of suspension, as it were, of the Incarnation"[361] more attentively in this light, his qualifications (the only instance of such) suggest not a hesitation to assert a real hiatus in the Incarnation, but simple dissatisfaction with the word "suspension." The other texts examined indicate there is ultimately nothing "as it were" about the "suspension . . . of the Incarnation." According to the Council of Chalcedon, on the other hand, the union of the two natures in the Person of the Word is "without separation," that is, it has continued permanently from its beginning and it will continue so forever. Hence, the Incarnation can in no way be suspended, for it is nothing other than the hypostatic union.

To summarize, Balthasar sees the Word's divine existence, His incarnation, and His mission unto being dead in Sheol informed by a kenosis (a consenting passivity, or obedience). This kenosis is "the self-abandonment of [His] whole existence,"[362] i.e., an abandonment by Christ of His self. "If God is objectively forsaken here, then we must say that God is forsaken by God":[363] The Father abandons the Son that Christ is, the Father is 'abandoned' by the Son insofar as the Father feels the loss of the Son when He abandons Him, and the incarnate Son abandons Himself both by "depositing" His divine and human attributes, and by assuming sin as such into Himself. The Father's utter kenosis of His nature in generating the Son but without losing Himself is imaged in the Son's kenosis in becoming man and being "made sin" without losing His divinity or His sinlessness,[364] indeed, it is an exercise of His divine obedience, of His filial personality. The archetypal God-forsakenness in the Trinity is thus manifested in the analogue of the sinful world through the definitive God-forsakenness of Sheol.[365] The Son abandons His divine attributes in "depositing" them with the Father through the Incarnation, and He abandons His human attributes in His descent, abandoning Himself as hypostasis to the *visio mortis* of sin-in-itself. Conformed to all that is contrary to Him as God and as a sinless man, "he is himself entirely alienated from himself."[366] Only in Sheol does Christ's "total-self-giving" reach its perfection and reveal "the essence of the pure 'relationality' ('fluidity') of the second divine person. . . ."[367] In other words, what is revealed in Sheol is the "naked" Son of God, the relation without any nature except the act of kenosis. By implication, the Father and Holy Spirit are also revealed. "With this the Greek axiom of the *bonum diffusivum sui* is fulfilled beyond anything conceivable. . . ."[368]

Death and "Super-Death"

The key themes of Balthasar we have seen (glory as act, specifically as self-gift; death; obedience; and love) are united in a supreme way in the Descent considered from the perspective of the Son, as evident when the following quotation about death is applied to Christ:

> Death is a final *deed,* with many facets, but it is always a self-suspension, a deed that is so all-embracing that it can only be performed by the investment of one's whole existence. It is related to, or identical with, absolute love, which ultimately calls for the suspension of the isolated self; it can consist in atonement (required by others or undertaken by oneself) for some transgression that cannot otherwise be expunged; finally, it can be representative, where one person dies on behalf of someone else or even takes over the latter's terrible manner of death.[369]

Only after the Son's death (physical and spiritual) has been contemplated with Balthasar can this text resonate its full implications for Christ in His descent, with its "suspension" of the Incarnation and His redemptive, substitutionary self-alienation. However, not these features, but a more general characterization of death with its fulfillment in Christ requires our present attention. This consideration will specify further the link between suffering as the formal principle of redemption in Balthasar's theology and Christ's death.

To summarize Balthasar's general characterization of death then, one may say that man finds himself bound to death as a general fate against his will. In the face of its inevitability and usually in the event itself, man undergoes death, and thus is largely passive in it. Death may be endowed with a character as deed, however, insofar as man strives to make something of his life, ever conscious of his end such that the close of his life will cap it rather than be wholly foreign to it. This character as deed is preeminently found when the person chooses his particular death as his last act; here Balthasar most frequently has in mind a death undertaken for the good of others, if only in atonement for one's own past evil.[370] Life's meaning is derived from the giving of oneself wholly for a cause or a person, and this attitude of being for another culminates in the utter "letting go" of oneself that is death.[371]

Jesus must freely take His death upon Himself, then, if His death is to be endowed with redemptive meaning.[372] On the other hand, if it is to be representative, He must share the common human experience of death:[373] its futility,[374] its unknown hour,[375] terror at its approach,[376] the attack which one is ultimately powerless to fend off,[377] the condition of being dead.[378] His death will then overcome death, for "how can an annihilator be annihilated unless by itself?"[379]

If death's power is to be destroyed, it must lose its character as an inevitable and futile fate.[380] Insofar as the Son voluntarily accepts His death, it can be endowed with meaning, i.e., with the purpose for which He freely accepts it. The voluntary character of Jesus' death will contradict death's general inevitability. Death's futility, its ending in ruin, will be overturned by the fact that He takes it upon Himself out of love, which seeks to give to the other rather than retain for oneself. Indeed, by linking the utter surrender of self in death to its archetype in the Trinitarian love, Christ will endow death's very futility *as such* with meaning.[381]

> He wants to share not only finitude, with all its happiness and sorrow, but also the human demise, human collapse and death. This being the case, existence will not be able to complain that its own intrinsic significance has been overlooked.[382]

The suggestion here that creaturely existence receives its significance from death, i.e., the termination of its existence, is striking.

But because Balthasar links physical death and spiritual death so closely together (so as not to distinguish them even in Rom 14:9[383]), Christ's particular death must be union with the *visio mortis*. He undergoes it, however, not as the result of personal sin but out of obedience, since His death is a continuation of His procession, that first and most radical kenosis, the Trinitarian "super-death," which is a "more radical form"[384] of death than even the 'second death.' The Son's incarnate existence begins with His offer to become man:

> [Jesus'] existence itself rests on a kenotic act of obedience that moved him to let go of the "form of God" and embrace the "form of a slave." The final goal of this kenosis was the particular death of Jesus, designed to outstrip and "conquer" death itself. Death, therefore, is uniquely immanent in this act of self-emptying and what flows from it, in his creaturely existence before the Father.[385]

As a result of this unique derivation from the prototype of all death, Christ's life will necessarily bear closer than normal links with creaturely death, physical and spiritual; indeed, "the whole direction of his existence progresses towards a death . . . which is understood to be the quintessence of his mission."[386] The Word's kenosis as humiliation (or obedience) — as letting Himself be disposed of, rather than disposing of Himself — reaches its perfection in His abandonment in Sheol.

Christ's death there as the ultimate death to self for the good of another will destroy the reign of sin, which is the living death of living for one's self and as if from one's self. The state of sin lacks humble recognition of one's dependence upon another and has no transcendent, perfecting orientation toward the other, both of which the Son has with regard to the Father in the eminent and archetypal way.

> Beyond death and hell — that is, beyond final distance from God, He surfaces with these scars into the light. That without an exit has an exit. And not only that: that without an exit . . . turns out itself to be precisely the way in the end. . . . Through a deeper *yes*, to seize the form of the *no*, suffering, from beneath and to revalue it as an expression of love.[387]

Note the general conflation between the act of sin (the "no" itself), the state of sin, suffering as a consequence of original sin, suffering as a consequence of personal sin (one's own or someone else's), and hell or damnation as punishment for sin. The major exception is that Balthasar indicates Christ commits no sin, though He suffers the state of abandonment that is sin's result.

Since Christ's death is the utmost death undertaken out of the absolute love, it will be the deed of greatest glory. His death, and His being dead, are thus to reveal the "super-death" within the Trinity. Since both death and love involve "suspension" of the self, death "is related to, or *identical* with, *absolute love....*"[388] The death of Christ will be a death for love, both in intention and in form: He will die for love of the Father and for love of the world, and He will die in self-abnegating obedience to the other for the good of the other, i.e., in consenting passivity to the Father and to men, for the Father's glorification and men's salvation.[389] It will be a death for love in content as well: Since love calls for the "suspension" of self, so to speak, the Son will take upon Himself in His obedient death what is utterly foreign to Him, namely, "the guilty death that is our fate."[390] The perfect love of His death is its power,[391] because perfect death ("super-death") is the divine, all-powerful ("ever-greater") love.

Because Christ's being dead is undergone out of the absolute love, Balthasar denies his soteriology is based on quantitative substitution, because it is the obedience of Christ that overturns the death of sin.[392] In fact, however, Christ's obedience, even unto dying on the cross (see Phil 2:8), is insufficient in Balthasar's theology for the efficacious reconciliation of God to the world: The material content of the *visio mortis* is essential. Christ's obedience must embrace *specifically* the 'second death' accruing to the sins of all men in order to have its universal transformative and redemptive effect; only then can the Trinitarian relations "include and embrace all distance between the sinner and God."[393] Only then can one go to God through alienation from Him and through death.[394]

If it were otherwise, Balthasar might have given a different answer to his question, "How can an annihilator be annihilated unless by itself?"[395] The annihilator can be overcome by its opposite. Then self-subsisting Life, dying in the human nature He united to His person and descending to the realm of death as a result of His physical death, would overthrow the reign of death. Such destruction of death by its opposite is reflected, e.g., in the homiletic tradition from patristic times, as suggested by the image of Christ as the Sun of Righteousness that brightens the realm of hades in its descent. In fact, Balthasar's requirement that Christ experience Sheol *in obedience* indicates that the death proper to selfish sin is only annihilated by its opposite: "The central fact ... is that Jesus by his obedient death takes over the guilty death that is our fate. This, and this alone, can undermine death from within and draw its sting."[396] The *visio mortis* then ought not to be necessary, as Balthasar says it is.

This last quotation comes in a context in which both obedience and

Christ's "unique death" are said to be the "inner form" of His life.[397] The latter seems to have preeminence, however: Although Balthasar effectively treats what Christ experienced in Sheol as a material principle transformed by obedience, which is the formal principle of His being dead, the material principle in His being dead (the suffering of sin-in-itself) is the formal principle of *redemption.* The incarnate Word's existence, including His descent, is an act of filial obedience (a.k.a., death to self), but "the final goal of this kenosis was the particular death of Jesus. . . ."[398] Now Christ's "*particular* death" is distinguished by its union with the *visio mortis* more so than by its obedience, because self-offering may be a feature of death in general, but only He experienced the full brunt of Sheol. Again, the priority of the type of Christ's death (i.e., the cumulative *visio mortis* under the "wrath" of the Father) over His love or obedience can be seen from the following:

> *The aspect of the voluntary self-offering of the guiltless one,* indeed his self-sacrificing (Heb 7:28) in the role of a high priest who is simultaneously the lamb of sacrifice (1 Cor 5:7), *is not at all sufficient:* the "paschal lamb" is indeed "slain" (ibid.) but *not* by himself.[399]

His obedience is not sufficient; He must be passively "crushed."

One might object that the issue at hand is not the priority of the material principle of Christ's death over the formal, but a difference in qualities. Earlier Balthasar was quoted, saying sin "is finally exhausted in comparison to the patience of the Son of God. . . . Of course: it is not quantities that stand here as rivals over against each other but qualities."[400] But how he continues makes clear the difference in "quality" is not the redemptive factor:

> The quality of the loving obedience of the Son toward the Father (who wills to overcome sin from within in precisely this way: through the incarnate Son) is not to be compared with the quality of the hate that surges over him.[401]

Certainly the "rivals" are not comparable qualitatively, in the sense that they are not identical and one is better than the other. Can we say more? Can we say the "quality" of the Son's loving obedience *as such* "exhausted" sin and hate, and not some quantitative difference between Christ's *visio mortis* and the sins of all men?

In fact, we cannot: The Father does not will to destroy the death of sin through its difference, simply speaking, in comparison to the quality of "loving obedience" (the annihilation of the annihilator by its opposite). The means used by love to triumph over sin is precisely sin's form: The Father willed to destroy sin *"from within in precisely this way: through the incarnate Son,"* i.e., through Christ's being "literally 'made sin.'" The Son "makes fluid the boulders of sin . . . and dissolves them in that experienced godforsakenness of which they secretly consist."[402] Again, Balthasar is not working with contraries here, but rather with one term of an analogy and its "ever-greater" counterpart, according to his understanding of analogy. When death is engulfed by a greater death, it is consumed by this "super-death" and taken up into it. The redemptive turn occurs, so to speak, by a physical mechanism or as a natural event. Thus the annihilator is annihilated by itself,[403] i.e., by the Son undergoing the full quantitative spiritual death mankind deserved. Indeed, more: The degree of suffering should not be overlooked. Christ not only assumed the eternal deaths all men deserved, but an eternal death surpassing them, one in proportion to His filial intimacy with the Father: "The forsakenness that prevails between the Father and his crucified Son is deeper and more deadly than any forsakenness, temporal or eternal, actual or possible, that separates *a creature* from God."[404] (Hence, if one follows Balthasar's principle about the annihilator strictly, one should be able to say sin can only be annihilated by "ever-greater" sin within the Trinity. To object to describing the Trinity as this "super-sin" is to recognize that sin and self-gift *are* not death, even if Balthasar calls them that analogically. In turn, this recognition reveals that sin and self-gift are not called death in relation to the same characteristic, as would be required if they really were analogues of death and each other.)

We must consider another place in which he claims the redemptive factor is a difference in quality:

> Death, therefore, must be stripped of its fate-character, or the latter must be so changed that its sting is drawn. . . . A qualitatively different and more profound kind of fate must be found in order to overcome the deadliness of death from within.
>
> Thus, without noticing it, we have come close to the theology of Anselm. He too was looking for a death that was unmerited, undergone by someone entirely guiltless and that, as such, was not subject to fate. In addition, this death was to be accepted freely *(sponte)* by the most precious person imaginable, thus outweighing all the fate-bound deaths incurred through guilt. Anselm's approach was correct, but he did not take it far enough; he compared only the external value of the two kinds of death, not their inner quality. We must remember this: if Jesus' atoning death is to be really representative ("for us"), he must share the experience we have of fate; he must comprehend and embrace it. Death as fate must be overcome from within, by something more deadly than itself. . . . Insofar as death is overcome in this struggle, we can speak of a duel between life and death *(mors et vita*

duello conflixere mirando), but equally, and at a deeper level, it is a duel between death and itself, a duel between two forms of death. The more intensive, more radical form vanquishes the other and then takes it over. This
differs from and complements the Anselmian version.[405]

The character of Christ's death as a death of obedience and love is in the background here — Balthasar will say that, to one in sin, the self-sacrificial death of
love is "deadly"[406] — as well as the insertion of man's death of sin into the divine "super-death" through Christ's death; nonetheless it is rather the 'second
death' of Sheol that he has particularly in mind here as being "more deadly"
than death.[407] For, he says, a "representative" death is necessary, and this death
is precisely a guilty one, not an obedient one. Thus Christ's death must be of the
same kind as ours, yet also "more profound," "more deadly," "more intensive,"
"more radical." Such a (guilty) death can only be the 'second death' in Sheol. It
is "qualitatively different" because only He ever experienced the full weight of
punishment due sin. Only He was completely conformed to sin-in-itself in virtue of His divinity. Only He experienced Sheol in utter God-forsakenness. Anyone else who goes to hell finds God there with him, at least inasmuch as the Son
Himself has been there, indeed has been in a more profound abyss.[408]

One might also counter that Balthasar says Jesus "experiences [the load of
the world's guilt] as something unbearable that can only be borne *in obedience*
to the Father's will. This is the crucial word."[409] However, this passage merely
points to the necessity of obedience, but says nothing of its sufficiency. Obedience is necessary so that Christ may be conformed *passively* to sin-in-itself
rather than actively taking it upon Himself in a self-assertive way that might
mimic sin. Obedience is not sufficient, however: Balthasar considers the possibility of Christ redeeming the world with a drop of blood as "free-wheeling
speculation in empty space."[410]

A final example makes the point clear. Balthasar writes,

> The poverty that has no means of exercising control over oneself is one with
> Jesus' obedience in total self-abandonment. That is what the hymn at Phil
> 2:7 calls kenosis. In this, the one who has abandoned himself can be utterly
> and completely determined by the will of the Father, who loads on him the
> burden of the reality that is "the sin of the world" or the reality that is "the
> wrath of God," made concrete in everything that arouses this "wrath."[411]

Jesus' existence in kenosis *enables* His being "loaded" with sin and the Father's
"wrath." In other words, His obedience is *for the sake* of being "literally 'made
sin.'" Again, the latter has priority over the former.

Obedience itself is insufficient then, even obedience embracing great suffering. According to Balthasar, what is required is obedience *unto a particular term*. This term, and only this term, perfects Christ's redemptive work. "The 'means of atonement' (Rom 3:25) [is] the hypostatic obedience of the Son of God, his *kenosis* or *diastasis* . . . his yielding-up of himself,"[412] but, for Balthasar, *obedience* in its soteriological signification points not to obedience commonly so-called, but to the Son's going into self-alienation, His becoming what is anti-divine, His being "literally 'made sin'" in Sheol as a continuation of His Trinitarian procession. Let us read Balthasar again, and attentively: "*Insofar* as death is overcome in this struggle, we can speak of a duel between life and death . . . , *but* equally, and *at a deeper level*, it is . . . a duel between two forms of death."[413]

Christ's being "made sin," then, is treated as a material principle that is transformed through being informed by His loving obedience. In fact, however, the material principle is the decisive redeeming factor. Hence, though Christ's suffering the 'second death' in Sheol is the material principle of His *descent*, it is the formal principle of *redemption* in Balthasar's soteriology. The formal redemptive principle of suffering was seen earlier (Chapter Five) in Balthasar's principle, "Only what has been endured is healed and saved."[414] Only if sin itself is endured can it be expiated.

Conclusion

This chapter on the Descent from the perspective of the Son must conclude with a summary in terms of kenosis as love, for two reasons. First, Balthasar approaches his topic from multiple angles, which mutually illuminate each other, but this concept underlies and unites them all. Second, much has been said about the Father's "wrath" (Chapter Six) and the Son's suffering (Chapters Five and Seven). But both the motivation of the Descent event and the heart of the revelation that occurs there is the Trinitarian love of the divine Persons for each other and for the world. What does this love tell us about the Descent, and does love 'make it all better'?

This question must be approached from the kenotic nature of the Descent. The Descent is kenotic because it is a continuation and a revelation of the Son's procession, that is, of the intra-Trinitarian kenosis of the Father. It is also kenotic because it is a humiliation of the Son insofar as He actually gives up His divine attributes and becomes man. Finally, the Descent is kenotic because the incarnate Son is passive from His incarnation to His resurrection, and in particular during His experience of the futility of death and abandonment by God in Sheol.

Throughout His incarnate existence, as a result of His own active will, the Word remains utterly at the disposal of the Father through the mediation of the Holy Spirit, as well as at the disposal of men in His passion.[415] The Son lets the Spirit incarnate Him and reveal the Father's will to Him, and then He does it. He lets men condemn and crucify Him. He lets Himself be abandoned by the Father and by mankind;[416] and if His Mother does not abandon Him at the foot of the cross, He abandons her and finds her presence not a support, but the occasion for questioning the necessity of His agony and hence an intensification of it.[417] He Himself thinks all is futile. In all these kenotic elements, the Word's self-abnegating passivity of not being at His own disposal in obedience to another is the underlying characteristic of His kenosis.[418]

In fact, in His intra-Trinitarian procession as well as in His kenotic mission, the self-subsisting relation of the Son may be characterized as obedient, i.e., as consentingly passive: As Son, He actively *lets* Himself *be generated* by the Father; as incarnate, He *lets* the content and progression of His mission *be given* to Him from the Father through the Holy Spirit. Such coincidence of activity and passivity constitutes obedience.

However, these features characterize His kenosis only in reference to its term (as complete, and not partial) and to its relative character (obedience and humiliation, rather than self-aggrandizement). What is kenosis itself, and how does the Son's mission unto Sheol reveal the *love* of the Father?

Kenosis as such (i.e., as it is in its prime analogate, the Trinity) is love, because God is love, and love Balthasar understands essentially as the gift of self.[419] Thus, in His giving of *Himself* (i.e., what He is, the divine nature as love and the divine attributes), the Father begets the Son. In this *giving* of Himself, He loves the Son. The Son, being what the Father is, likewise loves by giving Himself (and, once incarnate, this self-giving includes His human nature). He gives Himself back to the Father, and His giving is His love, while what He gives are His natures. The bond constituted between the Father and the Son through their mutual divine self-gift to each other is the Holy Spirit.

From this Trinitarian perspective, we are able to understand how the kenosis of the Son reveals the Father and His love. This revelation may be described in terms of kenosis both as gift of self and as obedience, because together these two characterize the Son's divine Person. The gift of self is the inalienable essence of all the divine Persons, whereas obedience is the personal property of the Son.

In terms of kenosis as self-gift, the revelation of the divine love may be summarized this way: The Son, receiving Himself from the Father, gives Himself back to the Father out of love-as-self-gift. This substantial relation of the Son to the Father (i.e., the Son's procession) continues in the Incarnation (i.e., His mission). Thus the Word "deposits" His divine attributes with the Father (i.e., gives Himself to the Father) to become true man. Balthasar especially singles out the Word's perfect knowledge among these "deposited" attributes. Insofar as it constitutes a neglect or, indeed, effectively a real loss of the divine prerogatives, this "depositing" characterizes the Incarnation as humiliating. The kenosis of divine attributes is perfected in the Son's descent into Sheol. There, despite being abandoned by the Father, He continues to give more and more of Himself up in the self-gift of love until there is nothing left to give and He exists solely as conformed to the *visio mortis*. In having perfectly given Himself up, He perfectly reveals the Father, who, in perfectly giving Himself to the Son, is the ultimate origin of the Son's self-gift. The content of the Word, His revelation, is that God's being is His giving of being; His wealth is not His having or retention, but His giving all away; His omnipotence is His 'powerlessness.'[420]

The revelation of the Trinitarian love in the Son's kenosis may also be approached in terms of obedience: The Son obeys the Father so perfectly as to be just an open space or medium for the Father's self-expression,[421] i.e., He is and does only what the Father gives Him. It is by this very giving to the Son that the Father loves Him, however, just as it is by His very obedience that the Son loves the Father.

The final giving in Sheol is the moment of most perfect love of the Son for the Father. There the Son is giving Himself out of the purest obedience, a blind obedience of faith, because He no longer 'sees' the Father, who has abandoned Him. The self-abnegation of obedience in the Son reveals the self-abnegation of the Father's self-gift.[422] Obedience as the property of the Word's filial personality reciprocally points to the corresponding relation of the Father as the one who is obeyed. For Balthasar, then, the Descent is the fullest expression of the Son's Trinitarian personality, that is, of the Son *qua* Son. The Son *qua* Son is the divine relation of being begotten. But in Balthasar's theology it seems that the Son *qua* Son refers to the Person of the Son *qua* Person, i.e., in a certain sense as abstracted from the divine nature, because the nature has reference to all three Persons, not just one in particular.[423] Having given *what* He is (i.e., the attributes of the divine and human natures) back to the Father perfectly, the Son in Sheol thus remains existing *qua* the self-existing relation of giving back to the Father, i.e., *qua* Son, i.e., *qua* Person without divine or human attributes and thus is the hypostasis for the *visio mortis* — and this without essential change in either the divine nature, which is essentially self-gift, or in the Person of the Son, who is essentially self-gift back to the Father.

The Descent event is also the moment of the Father's most perfect love for the Son. The 'command' obeyed by the Son corresponds to the Father's generation and sending of Him. The Father's counterpart to the Son's kenosis in the economy is His withdrawal. In Sheol, the Father has given divinity so perfectly to the Son that the Son is both free and able to go into what is contrary to divinity without the Father selfishly, as it were, keeping Him back with Him. The Father selflessly sends the Son away in order to redeem the world. The Father loves the

Son so much that He makes the Son's supreme act of love possible by withdrawing Himself. By abandoning the Son on the cross and in Sheol, the Father gives the Son 'space' to give Himself up wholly.[424] Thus He does not spare Himself the loss of His beloved Son, but loves the Son, so to speak, more than Himself.

In the extreme to which the Father and the Son go, each of them giving away all He has, the divine love as self-surrender will be revealed,[425] and hence the Trinity: Christ's *descent reveals His mission* in that He is the one sent to complete this task, a task completed not outside of Him, but in Him insofar as mankind's sins are taken into the Trinitarian love in virtue of the *visio mortis* being enhypostasized in the Son. Due to the perfect correlation between His mission and His person, and that between His consciousness of His mission and His consciousness of His identity, His *mission reveals His procession,* indicating He is nothing other than one who is always going forth from another.[426] His *suffering is essential* to this mission because the extremity of His passivity reveals His Trinitarian personality to be the one completely at the disposal of another:

> If it is possible for one Person in God to accept suffering, to the extent of God-forsakenness, and to deem it his own, then evidently it is not something foreign to God, something that does not affect him. It must be something profoundly appropriate to his divine Person, for — to say it once again — his being sent *(missio)* by the Father is a modality of his proceeding *(processio)* from the Father.[427]

(This suggests, of course, that neither the Father nor the Holy Spirit could become incarnate, or, at the very least, it would be highly unfitting if one of them did.) Finally, the Son's *procession reveals the Trinity,* because if He is one who comes from another and is wholly at the disposal of another, there must be this other; at the same time, if He goes into utter separation from this other, there must be yet another who unites them in the mutual distancing of His coming forth and being disposed.[428] In short, Christ's descent reveals His mission, which reveals His procession, which reveals the Trinity. In His person and in His human life and death, Jesus reveals both that God is love, and what the nature of this divine love is, namely, voluntary self-sacrifice, or kenosis: "Jesus is the witness for the Truth that he is."[429]

The divine revelation that peaks in the Descent is revelatory also *to* the incarnate Son. According to Balthasar, creation out of chaos is the proper work of the Father. The Father 'risks' creating a finite freedom, however, only because He trusts that the Son's love will make good any abuse of His paternal love by creatures.[430] The reality of creaturely abuse of the Father's love is experienced by Christ in Sheol. The 'second chaos' of sin created by the Father's creatures is apprehended there precisely as such an abuse of the paternal love, since the God-abandonment of the Son-made-sin in Sheol is proportional to His filial intimacy with the Father. Hence the *visio mortis* amounts to an experiential insight by the Son into the Father's "personal mystery" not only as Creator but as Father.[431] Hence, too, in this revelation of the Father's "personal mystery," the Son receives insight into His own filial procession. (This ultimate revelation imparts new significance to Balthasar's idea that the incarnate Son comes to know His divine procession through His humility.) In other words, the darkness of Sheol is not only the darkness of God-abandonment, justly deserved due to the sins Christ carries, but also a twofold darkness formerly known to the Father alone:[432] the extreme consequences of the Father's creation of finite freedom (i.e., sin-in-itself), and the Father's primal kenosis, which is the origin of the infinitely free Son upon whom creation is modeled. Hence the God-abandonment in the economy is itself based upon and expresses the utter self-surrender of the divine essence of the Father to the Son, and of both to the Holy Spirit. Only if the wrath of the Father *is* His generation of the Son can this wrath be as real as Balthasar insists; can the Father and Son continue to spirate the Spirit as His joint principle despite their mutual abandonment; and, for that matter, can the Father continue to generate the Son out of love.

We close this chapter on the Descent from the perspective of the Person of the Son with a few questions and final words of caution. First, it is worth asking why self-surrender on behalf of another is *love*. Taking love as self-surrender to another absolutely rules out any legitimate self-love; even if one takes oneself as a logical other, one cannot surrender oneself to oneself. The command to love one's neighbor *as oneself* (Mt 19:19; 22:39; Mk 12:31; Lk 10:27) then becomes opaque, if not meaningless or wrong-headed.

Moreover, one can legitimately ask *why* one should surrender oneself to another. To answer, "Out of love," begs the question, since it is claimed self-surrender is love. If one should surrender oneself because it is good to do so, then love (including in "God is love") has a more fundamental description than surrender of self. If the good is the motive for this self-surrender, and is attained in the self-surrender, and no further reason can be given, then the *good* is this more fundamental description.

This good must be for the agent, and not only for the recipient, because no agent will act against himself unless he also thinks it is better for himself in a more important respect. If self-surrender as such (i.e., regardless of the good for agent and recipient) sufficed for love, it would be an act of love for the Father to surrender Himself such that He ceased to exist, for example, or for the Son to surrender Himself in His state of having been "made sin," i.e., to give this state as such to another. In both cases, however, the self-surrender does not do good — in the one case, for the 'agent' Father, in the second, for the recipient of the Son's 'gift.' And *because they do not do good,* they are easily dismissed as not being love, as unworthy of God (because "God is love"), and hence ridiculous. Hence, it appears the good is more foundational to love than self-surrender, and Balthasar has not addressed it adequately. Or, since Balthasar considers the good to be the central concern of the *Theo-Drama,*[433] one could say he did not fail to address the good, but that he effectively reversed the order between the good and self-surrender.

Second, given Balthasar's insistence on the Son's "depositing" and the necessary role it plays in his theology of the Incarnation, I cannot agree that this "depositing" is to be taken as a metaphor, as some authors represent it.[434] The work of this chapter demonstrates that in Balthasar's theology the Son's "depositing" is as real as His procession. In any case, even if these other authors were right, a metaphor is used to point to a reality, and one must ask what reality Balthasar intends with the 'metaphor'? One should also not forget that things can be *said* which cannot *be.*

Finally, in his connection of the immanent and economic Trinities, and particularly in his linking of the procession of the Word with the mission of Christ, Balthasar would appear to mirror the doctrine of St. Thomas Aquinas in some respects, although Balthasar uses very different terminology. We have already seen Balthasar's differing understanding of the divine Persons as self-subsisting relations, discussed at the beginning of this chapter.[435] The Thomistic ring of Balthasar's identification of the mission and procession is also misleading. According to St. Thomas,[436] the missions of the Son and Holy Spirit signify the processions with the addition of the temporal effect. Hence mission and procession could not be identical without importing the temporal effect into God as such. If Anne Hunt is correct to say that, for Balthasar, "it is the missions rather than the relations of origin in the immanent Trinity that play the predominant role in distinguishing the divine persons,"[437] the consequence is a sort of modalism, for then the Persons are distinguished *from each other* by their temporal effects. Moreover, if one assumes the identity of mission and procession as Balthasar asserts, events of the economy such as the suffering of Christ cannot be held at arm's length from the immanent life of the Trinity by describing them as analogies, expressions, or modalities of that life; if they are identical, they must be that life. *Kenosis* then becomes a univocal term. Hunt asserts Balthasar's analogical predication of kenosis, saying the economic form is the Incarnation ordered to the Descent, while the immanent form is the procession,[438] but she has not seen that the economic kenosis is a kenosis of the Son as such, one that at the same time corresponds to His eternal filiation.

To take another example, St. Thomas teaches that no change occurs in the Person of the Son when human nature is assumed to the Word in the Incarnation.[439] This doctrine is incompatible with Balthasar's doctrine of "depositing," although it might seem to be stated by Balthasar in terms of the Word being perfectly expressed as the man Jesus, and his denial of anything other than the Word as Word being expressed. Balthasar does not indicate, however, how the finite human nature of Jesus could express the Son as infinite, or what aspects of the Word are expressed by such essential characteristics of human nature as digestion and sneezing. Balthasar says, "*Everything* human in Christ is a word, an image, a representation, and an expression of the Father."[440] As seen earlier in our discussion of Christ's wills, Balthasar considers Christ's humanity itself as the manifestation of His divinity under a different form. To avoid the conclusion that sneezing, e.g., is revelatory of the divine nature, one might limit this quotation (and similar ones) to refer only to Christ's deliberate human acts as opposed to His acts of man. This solution, however, implicitly divides Christ's human nature into a part that is not so much human but animal and a part that is not so much human but (analogically) divine, whereas, in fact, human nature is the *integrated* union of the corporal and the spiritual. Hence there are three possibilities: first, to destroy Christ's human nature as just described; second, to take Balthasar at his word, in which case also Christ's acts of man are revelatory of God; or, third, to follow the traditional theology of theandric acts, according to which Christ always acts both in His divine nature and in His human nature, but sometimes the reality of one or the other nature is more clearly revealed in the theandric act (the conjoined divine act and human act) that is apprehended. In the last case, both Christ's divinity and His humanity are manifested as such in His acts, i.e., they are manifested precisely *as divine* and *as human,* even if the human nature instrumentally reveals the divine Person.

These difficulties, and others touched upon in the course of this work, suggest incompatibility between Balthasar's and St. Thomas's doctrines of the Incarnation. It is beyond the present scope to determine its precise extent. This incompatibility is merely mentioned at this point as a word of caution against assuming the support of the Common Doctor for Balthasar's doctrine on the basis of what can appear to be the same thought merely expressed differently. Each case of apparent equivalence would require, and merit, adequate examination before such a conclusion would be warranted. Even then, Balthasar's other doctrines or the changes he makes in what he has from St. Thomas often invest what he retains from him with a largely different meaning. It is due to the seeming likenesses with their associated implications of St. Thomas's singular authority that positions of his serve as a sort of foil during our exposition and evaluation of Balthasar's doctrine, not to mention the insightful precisions one may bring to bear from St. Thomas's theology.

CHAPTER EIGHT

Christ's Descent in Light of the Trinity: The Spirit, Bond of Love, Bridge of Separation

The Descent from the perspective of the Holy Spirit has already been touched upon in the foregoing chapters on the Father and the Son, so that the relations between the Persons could be more easily seen. Since the whole Trinity is involved in the Descent, apprehension of its significance would be impeded were its unity fractured by separating the involvement of one Person too much from that of the others. Our consideration of the Descent specifically from the perspective of the Holy Spirit is made somewhat shorter as a result.

As has already been seen, the Holy Spirit is the subsistent bond of love that results from the mutual love of Father and Son. Their mutual gift of self to each other is so perfect that it constitutes another divine Person. Because the Spirit proceeds from two others insofar as they are both distinct and united in their mutual love, He bridges, so to speak, the separation that is the absolute opposition of the relations of the Father and of the Son. This separation has three faces: within the Trinity, between the Father and Christ in general, and in the Father's abandonment of Christ in Sheol. As the Spirit bridges the first opposition, He likewise can bridge that between God and man in Christ, and that between God and fallen man,[1] preeminently the Son "made sin" in Sheol. In this chapter, the Spirit's unifying work in these three forms will be examined.

Bridge between Father and Son

In the context of his soteriology of the Descent, Balthasar focuses primarily on Christ's experience, and secondarily on His relation to the Father, saying comparatively little about the Holy Spirit directly. Typically, after elaborating on these other two elements of the Descent with greater or lesser emphasis, Balthasar will close with only the briefest mention of the Spirit in relation to the Father and the Son. Balthasar's use of opposite reciprocal terms for the relations of the Father and Son does not leave him vocabulary for a third Person. Hence Balthasar is generally not very clear about the procession and role of the Holy Spirit in his soteriological discussions, which form the basis for the present work. He usually just asserts the Holy Spirit's existence as "bridge" of the "distance" between Father and Son, or "bond" and "seal" of their love, or their "We" without integrating these metaphors in relation to the terms he uses for the Father and Son (e.g., "giving," "receiving"). Indirect references, however, can be found in those passages in which he discusses the relationship *between* Father and Son, as opposed to the relationship of one *to* the other.

For example, Balthasar says that the "double love [between Father and Christ] is, so to speak, a bracket that includes everything that takes place within it as the event of reconciliation,"[2] which is nevertheless "not to be neutralized and transfigured because of the bracket of love that surrounds it."[3] The Holy Spirit Himself is this "bracket," since His hypostasis is spirated precisely in the mutual love of the Father and the Son, and since He unites the Father and the Son in their very real abandonment.[4] As obedience is the personal property of the Son, union is the mark of the Holy Spirit. Father and Son "exist, from their uttermost origin, in a substantial fellowship of love."[5] That this fellowship is "substantial" and coeternal with the Father and Son points to this "fellowship" as the Person of the Holy Spirit Himself: He is the substantial "We"[6] of the Father and Son, "the realized union"[7] of their love.

As has been seen, however, the divine love is "not an object,"[8] but a life, an "event." The Holy Spirit is, as it were, an "event" between Father and Son. He lives due to their ongoing mutual surrender. He is "the 'personified handing-over,' the 'gift.'"[9] The Spirit is the fulfillment of the love between Father and Son, and in Him creation also has its fulfillment:[10] Through participation in the life of the Spirit (in virtue of the redemptive reconciliation wrought by God), man is "seized"[11] and brought into the life of Father and Son,[12] i.e., into the whole "eternal event"[13] of Trinitarian life, the "single mystery, that of the love *between* Father and Son."[14]

As the subsisting love between Father and Son, the Spirit "maintains," "seals," and "bridges"[15] the intra-Trinitarian "distance" between them. Because Balthasar does not elaborate overmuch on these descriptive terms in his treatments of the Descent, one might propose that they be understood in the following way: The Spirit "maintains" the "distance" insofar as the reciprocal self-gift of Father and Son would be in danger of collapsing, so to speak, without His procession as a third Person: "The distance/distinction between these two is eternally confirmed and maintained ('kept open') by the Hypostasis who proceeds from them."[16] Given the Son's "antecedent consent" to His generation in virtue of which the Father receives His actual paternity, it would be difficult to distinguish the first two Persons without the procession of the Spirit. In addition, the image of two points collapsing into one another suggests the violation of love, which requires that the beloved be allowed a realm of personal mystery.[17] The Spirit *as love* would "maintain" this "distance" of respect. He "seals" the "distance" between Father and Son insofar as He is their definitive fruit; there is no other. As a "seal" closes or joins two things together, He shows the unity of the Father and Son's love.[18] He is the embrace, as it were, that closes and "seals" the circle formed by the arms of the Father, open in self-gift, and by those of the Son, open in receptivity and grateful return of the gift. Finally, the Spirit "bridges" the "distance" between Father and Son insofar as He unites them despite their absolute opposition as Father and Son (though also as a result of it). Of the three terms, this final one appears most frequently in Balthasar's soteriological treatments and seems the most comprehensive. The image of a bridge spanning the two banks of a river captures all three functions well: The arch of the bridge can be thought of as a mode of union between the two banks, but also as a spring that holds at bay the collapse of one bank toward the other.

Before considering how the Holy Spirit "bridges" the "distances" in the economy, a few concerns should be mentioned. First, Balthasar says the Holy Spirit is the "We" of Father and Son. If the Father and Son spirate the Holy Spirit *as a single principle*, however, then they constitute a corporate "We" over against Him as a hypostatic "We." It is as this "We" that they spirate Him, and He is not this "We," unless He is both Father and Son, and spirates Himself. In other words, to speak of the "We" of Father and Son is ambiguous. The "We" that they *are* is the corporate "We" by which they spirate the Holy Spirit. The so-called "We" that is the Person of the Spirit is "of Father and Son" in the sense of *from Father and Son*, not in the sense of *comprised of*, as *we* normally is. Karl Josef Wallner explains that, insofar as the Holy Spirit is a divine Person who proceeds from Father and Son, the personal "We" that He is, is something "more" than the joint "We" of Father and Son.[19] Although I think this exposition is helpful and just to Balthasar, it also sets the problem anew before us: As something more, i.e., as *a* Person proceeding, the Holy Spirit is another *other* in the Trinity, not a "We." In short, Balthasar calls the Holy Spirit a "We," because His principle is a "We," but this name does not actually reflect what He Himself is. In any case, there is reason for caution in describing Father and Son as a "We" in spirating the Spirit. They spirate Him as a single, or corporate, principle, not a collective one, as "We" may suggest. It is not as though the Father and Son both have some 'power' of spiration that they simultaneously exercise, a power which the Father gives the Son, a power which the Son can "deposit" and receive again, a power which the Holy Spirit does not have. Only *with the Son* can the Father spirate the Spirit. It is vis-à-vis this single principle that the Holy Spirit is another divine Person in distinction to the other two.

Secondly, the Holy Spirit is said to be the substantial love between Father and Son. But the essence of love is self-gift, according to Balthasar. Hence the love of the Father for the Son — indeed, the Father Himself — is the Father's surrender of Himself to the Son; and vice versa for the Son. What is between Father and Son then is nothing other than the relation of the Father to the Son (i.e., the Father) and the relation of the Son to the Father (i.e., the Son). If the Holy Spirit is the substantial love *between* Father and Son, He is Himself again not a third Person, but both the Father and the Son.

To prevent this identification, the Holy Spirit is said to be a bond constituted by the actual reciprocal love of Father and Son. In this case, however, He is not love in the way in which Father and Son are love (as self-gift), but love in a different way (as a realized union). Balthasar takes this love-as-union to be the personal distinction of the Holy Spirit, as contrasted with the primal giving of the Father, and the Son's giving back. This proposition does not change the fact that the Holy Spirit is not love as the Father and Son are, i.e., as self-gift. Does that mean He is not divine, if "being = giving"?[20] That the Spirit is different, and not merely distinct, from Father and Son is made further evident by the fact that, if He were self-gift, a fourth person should proceed from His surrender back to the Father and Son in response to their surrender to Him, even as the Spirit proceeds from the Son's surrender back to the Father as the Father surrenders Himself to the Son. Balthasar says that "eternal freedom eternally gives itself away and *thus* generates the Son."[21] Here the divine self-gift is linked with the procession of another divine Person as its necessary consequence, i.e., in this very giving, a Person proceeds. If the Spirit is no less "eternal freedom" than the Father, and if He too gives Himself, another Person should likewise proceed in His gift. Finally, this difference of the Holy Spirit's Person is manifest in the *necessity* of the Spirit to unite the Father and the Son in the Descent. The Spirit does in the economy what the Father and Son *cannot* do in their respective wrath and abandonment. The unity achieved by the Holy Spirit, and the necessity for it, must be as real as the wrath and abandonment, the actuality of which Balthasar takes such great pains to stress. But the economy is only an image of the immanent Trinity, and hence this necessity likewise pertains within the Trinity from eternity.[22] Again, we find there are proper acts of the Persons in Balthasar's theology, not just proper modes of acting.

Third, Balthasar's calling the Holy Spirit "love" bears a verbal likeness to the teaching of St. Thomas, but a wholly other doctrinal content. For both Balthasar and St. Thomas, God is love, and also each of the three Persons, and the Holy Spirit in a particular way. For St. Thomas, however, *love* is a proper name of the Holy Spirit because He proceeds in a way *analogically* like the way in which love proceeds in a rational subject.[23] In contrast, for Balthasar the Holy Spirit has this name because He *is* the love (as union) between Father and Son. This identification perhaps clarifies why Balthasar speaks so little of the Holy Spirit: It is sufficient to speak of the Father and the Son, and their love. What is said of their love can then be said of the Holy Spirit.

Bridge between God and Man, i.e., between the Father and Christ

The second opposition "bridged" by the Holy Spirit is that between the divine and human, a union based upon the intra-Trinitarian one. The unity the Holy Spirit effects here is relevant to the hypostatic union, to the unity between the Father as God and the Son as incarnate, and to the unity between God and the man in right relation to Him. The Holy Spirit first "bridges" the "distance" between the divine and human insofar as it is proper to Him to be the active principle of the Son's incarnation, as mentioned earlier.[24] In this section, we will focus on the continuation of this active priority of the Spirit over the incarnate Son, which reflects the unity achieved between the divine and the human in Christ's conception and is the model for the unity to be achieved in Christian life.

The Holy Spirit's proper work of incarnating the Son begins what Balthasar calls the "trinitarian inversion,"[25] i.e., the "economic reversal of the relation between Son and Spirit."[26] This inversion establishes the Spirit as an authority over Christ, thereby making apparent the distinction of the three Persons in that the rule in Jesus is the will of another, i.e., the Father, and communicated to Him by another, i.e., the Spirit. As the Son's passivity to the Spirit in being incarnated ensures His economic mission is characterized by obedience to the Father from its beginning,[27] so the Trinitarian inversion continues the Spirit's active role vis-à-vis the incarnate Son. The Spirit is "above"[28] the incarnate Son, enabling Him to receive His mission in faith (trusting obedience despite ignorance),[29] but all heteronomy is prevented because the Spirit is also the Son's own *qua* Son, such that the Spirit is "within"[30] Jesus.

It is the work of the Holy Spirit, then, to communicate the Father's will to Jesus. "Jesus does not possess his mission as if it were his own property," and His mission "is not given once for all but is revealed and can be realized in a new and surprising way by the Holy Spirit at every moment."[31] The Spirit "mediates the Father's will to the Son."[32] It is revealed to Him with greater or lesser clarity,[33] from moment to moment,[34] but nonetheless the mission is presented to Him "in the form of a *rule* that is unconditional."[35] To reject it would be to reject the Spirit, and the Father whose will He reveals; this alone is the unforgivable sin.[36]

In the previous chapter, we saw that Balthasar's rejection of Christ's possession of the beatific vision meant he would need to provide another explanation of Christ's sinlessness. Exposition and examination of his proposal was postponed for the present chapter, since the Holy Spirit's communication of the Father's will to Christ with adequate clarity and moral force would seem to serve this purpose. Consequently, our consideration of the Holy Spirit's cognitive and moral communication of the Father's will to Christ will proceed with particular attention to the sinlessness of Christ. Does Balthasar's solution work?

To begin, Balthasar says the temptation of Christ is

> only possible if, with his entire task in his mind's eye, he has to use his own freedom to search for ways of implementing it in detail; for only then can there be any attraction in the suggestion that he avoid the hard path . . . by taking the short-cut put forward by human calculation. As man, he must continually measure the partial values that present themselves against the totality of the mission, of his Father's will; when he does this, the direction he is to take — the hardest course — becomes luminous. He sees the totality of the Father's will, and hence of his mission, shining forth from this partial value — which may be of no value at all in terms of all that human beings strive for; and such luminous radiance is only possible within his total, free availability. It is then that, although he cannot sin, his obedience is meritorious.[37] His merit is that he himself anticipates nothing; thus no particular success can obscure the mission's universality.[38]

In short, Jesus knows the universal good that is the goal of His mission. Against it, He weighs the various possible particular goods of the moment, as means to this end. He always chooses the universal good, which is the Father's will for Him and represented in the most difficult option, over other limited particular goods that tempt Him.

How do we arrive at such an interpretation? The assertions here that Jesus sees "his entire task" and "the totality of the mission, of his Father's will" appear to contradict Balthasar's extended discussion and emphasis on His faith, which entails ignorance. To reconcile this seeming contradiction, we note that the mission as the Father's will can be taken in two senses: in a general, or universal, sense; and in a particular, or momentary, sense. The apparent contradiction is resolved in that Jesus always knows He has a universal mission, but He does not know what it will demand of Him in detail. In the first sense, this mission is the reintegration of lost finite freedom into proper relation with infinite freedom through perfect self-gift, or the redemption of fallen mankind through the In- carnation, Cross, and Hell. In this first sense, insofar as He knows He is to rec- oncile the world with God,[39] He knows the totality of His mission, which is the Father's will. In the second sense, however, Jesus does not know His mission, because He does not know the details of how this reconciliation will come about; instead the Father's will is moment by moment revealed to Him by the Spirit as an unconditional rule.

The "partial values" to be measured against the mission as a whole are the finite options of the moment. Some of these offer a "particular success," i.e., present an end with a more limited scope and value than the universal mission the Father desires. As Jesus considers His various options, He discerns which is the most difficult and He is given to understand this possibility is the one He must pursue. One may surmise the hardest option is the best because it requires the most self-abnegation (kenosis) and perhaps also because it entails the most suffering. This choice would not be possible if He "anticipate[d]" the future, i.e., formed specific goals or ideas about it Himself. Such plans would necessar- ily be finite, because human. Hence also they would be His own, and not part of a mission received from another.

The "total, free availability" that makes possible this ignorance of details combined with certainty of the Father's will regarding the moment is the Son's Trinitarian personality as perfect consenting passivity (i.e., obedience). The fact that this filial obedience, which determines everything about His being human, is His divine freedom simultaneously rules out both actual sin (i.e., disobedi- ence) and any heteronomy that would diminish His personal liberty. Christ's merit then is that He always obediently chooses the universal good over the particular good.

This interpretation preserves Balthasar's assertion that Christ can both have "his entire task in his mind's eye," but also need "to use his own freedom to search for ways of implementing it in detail." "The totality of the Father's will . . . shining forth from this partial value" then does not indicate that Christ's knowledge is perfect in extent and detail, or that He knows how the choice of this particular means conduces to His mission. Rather it indicates that the full force of the Father's authority is present in this means — and, if the Father's will is present, also the mission in general is. In short, Christ knows the end, but not the means, not until the Spirit reveals them to Him.

This passage, taken in the context of Balthasar's theology already seen, implies certain difficulties with Christ's sinlessness, however. First, it makes evident that Balthasar thinks one must know the end if one is to choose means toward that end: Jesus knows, or is "adequately aware,"[40] of His mission's universality and He "measures" the possibilities of the moment against the ultimate end of His mission. Now mere knowledge of the right end is not sufficient for sinlessness, as there are multiple means to the same end. One can sin not only with respect to the choice of one's intended end, but also with respect to the means to that end. Hence the Holy Spirit must reveal to Jesus the right means, and at every moment. The problem is that means are not chosen only in relation to the ultimate end, but also in relation to more proximate ends; i.e., the means of the present moment are chosen in relation to the means of the future moment. If I wish to fly from Los Angeles to Rome, I will not accept a flight through Atlanta if no flights continue from Atlanta to Rome. In Jesus' case, each partial value that presents itself can only be chosen or rejected in its known relation to the universal value, but this relation entails likewise its relation to other partial values in the proximate future. Hence either Jesus must know the details of His universal mission, including its proximate ends, through a beatific vision, or He must be given infallible knowledge of the best partial value among those present at the moment. To preserve his doctrine of Christ's faith, which follows from his doctrine of the Incarnation, Balthasar opts for the latter. However, if Jesus is never to anticipate the future, but always rests in consenting passivity in the present, He will often be required to choose things that go against His human reason, thus contradicting the dignity of His human finite freedom. He must sometimes choose things that would not appear to conduce to His mission's goal. Hence the inflexibility and the unconditional character of the Spirit's communication become necessary.

Second, and as implicit in the foregoing, it is not clear how the Spirit's moderation of Jesus' knowledge and the rigid character of the mission as it is presented to Him are conceived to be compatible with His human creativity and freedom, which Balthasar also wants to preserve: Jesus "must fashion [His mission] out of himself in utter freedom and responsibility; indeed, in a sense, he even has to invent it."[41] Even though finite freedom is most free when it transcends itself in relation to God,[42] finite freedom normally exercises itself without such an inflexible rule as Balthasar presents in the case of Jesus, even in the case of the artist "who is so possessed by his vocation that he only feels free, only feels totally himself, when he is able to pursue this task that is so much his own,"[43] to whom Balthasar compares Jesus. Though in every situation, there is certainly one thing that is best to do, fallen man usually does not know what this absolute best thing is. God speaks to every man in his conscience and His voice there is binding, but this voice is not always clearly identified due to the effects of original sin. Moreover, there may be other possibilities that are good, even if not the best. If man chooses one of these lesser, but nonetheless good, possibilities, he still does good, and does not sin.

Here again, we find another implicit choice of Balthasar's. He writes, "Since he is free, [his mission's] implementation will under certain circumstances need to be considered, planned, and tested."[44] Now if a mode of implementation must be tested, it suggests it is open to correction. Here a choice must be made: Either Jesus never makes a mistake, or sometimes He does. In the first case, if no action is ever corrected (i.e., the action chosen was always the best for the situation), it implies infallible knowledge on the part of the agent. It then becomes rather meaningless to speak of Him 'testing' an option for His mission's implementation. The second option simply means Jesus errs with regard to what is best in some particular moments — and hence also possibly sins. As the perfect, if limited, knowledge of the first option is certainly not what other men have in life, one would expect Balthasar not to choose this option in order that Jesus be like his brethren in everything; however, this first option is Balthasar's position.

Third, both the clarity and moderation of Jesus' knowledge, as well as the force of the moral obligation it imposes upon Him, seem to conflict with Balthasar's principle that Christ be like fallen man in everything except sin. If human nature is to be endowed with the dignity of a free cause, albeit a secondary one, its causality must be effective without the continuous gift of unusual graces. Balthasar writes,

> The Son experiences his mission on earth, now as something more personal, now as something more impersonal. Knowing himself to be identical with this mission, he sometimes sees the generating and sending Father in it more immediately; at other times, he worships the Father in a more veiled, objectified form and "believes" — albeit in a unique sense that goes beyond all analogies.[45]

Note that the Son sees the Father, not directly, but in His mission — and that this is the best-case scenario. In addition, if the Son's experience is sometimes "more personal" and sometimes less, with a corresponding change in His apprehension of the Father, then His experience of Himself (and not only His knowledge as mediated by the Spirit) should likewise vary since His mission-consciousness is His self-consciousness. What such change would mean is unclear: Would He experience Himself as "something more impersonal" at times? Moreover, as Christ's loss of His knowledge of the Father and the Father's love contributes a great extent to His suffering, the mission "experience" mediated by the Spirit is not only cognitive, but also affective, even if only indirectly. This affective component is essential to Christ's agony in His descent. Because the Spirit possesses full knowledge of the divine plan of redemption (indeed, He must 'remind' the Father and Son of it in the height of their respective wrath and abandonment[46]), the affective consequence must be willed by the Spirit inasmuch, and just as much, as He wills to mediate the cognitive revelation. In other words, Jesus knows what the Spirit gives Him to know, feels what the Spirit causes Him to feel, and does what the Spirit drives Him to do. This state also does not seem to be the one common to finite freedom, even finite freedom perfected in relationship with God.[47]

Fourth, Christ must not only know what is the right action for the moment, He must also never fail to do it. His sinlessness consists precisely in this latter, rather than in the perfection or limitation of His knowledge. If Christ possessed the beatific vision, His sinlessness in the face of temptation would follow necessarily: Resting in His ultimate end, He would not desire, and so would not choose, any lesser good above it. However, not even the unconditional character of the Father's will, presented to Jesus as a rule according to Balthasar's theology, suffices to explain Christ's sinlessness: From the time of Adam and Eve, men and women have chosen to act against the demands of their knowledge of the good. The weight of authority behind a particular demand does not ensure compliance with it. The will of the one commanded must submit. It may be that this obedience is secured through the Holy Spirit being "within" Jesus. However, in Balthasar's Christology, Jesus obeys the Father *as Son,* and the Holy Spirit is "within" Jesus *because He is the Son.* Hence, again, Christ's obedience is an expression of the Son's divine Trinitarian personality.

'Hardwired' Obedience, or Freedom as Nature

The identity between Christ's self-consciousness and His mission-consciousness is the ultimate reason for His sinlessness: The Spirit's revelation to Christ of His mission is the Son coming to know Himself through the gift of the Father. That is, His mission-consciousness (through the Holy Spirit) is His self-consciousness (as Son). His mission is His procession. To go against the mission given to Him by the Father through the Holy Spirit then would be to go against His own Person, against what He is in Himself: "It is not the Father who compels him . . . but the mission itself, which *coincides* with his filial freedom."[48] One might say His mission is hardwired into Him. *It* is what *He* is. The Son, also when incarnate, is always the hypostasis of obedience to the Father.

If He as Son is the perfect response to the Father, then He as the Son become flesh must still obey the Father perfectly if He is to remain what He is as Son. The passivity and pliability of the Son's human existence make possible the intended revelation of the divine in the human.[49] That this Person, for whom obedience is His very existence, can be tempted reflects His lack of the beatific vision and His indirect awareness of His mission.[50] His sinlessness then only makes sense if He is determined to the fulfillment of this rule, that is, if to act against His mission is to act against Himself, against His person, against His (divine) nature, against what He is, against His 'hardwiring.' Balthasar can deny that Christ's hopelessness on the cross constitutes (the sin of) despair,[51] because Christ dies as He does *out of obedience,* His Trinitarian property. The assertion of Jesus' sinlessness prevents a contradiction in terms: Hypostatic obedience to the Father *cannot* sin. Thus we find that Balthasar does not give a general argument for Jesus' sinlessness; he simply asserts that "'being able to sin' is not part of his freedom."[52] Balthasar cannot account for why this sinlessness is a *perfection* of finite freedom. Note too that Christ's inability to sin violates Balthasar's principle that Christ be like the rest of mankind except in not committing personal sin, as also the fact that this inability is a physical one, i.e., one of nature. For the rest of mankind, the *possibility* not *to sin* is one of grace — and likewise for Christ, according to a more traditional Christology.

The foregoing quotation with its reference suggests, however, the ultimate reason why Balthasar concludes Jesus is sinless. In his reference, Balthasar quotes three sentences, one each from St. Augustine, St. Anselm, and St. Thomas Aquinas. Like his own statement, all link freedom and the impossibility of sinning. Because Balthasar does not mention the reasons for their statements — reasons that for St. Thomas at least have a necessary connection to the beatific vision[53] — or take account of them in his discussions of Christ's sinlessness and *visio immediata Dei,* it appears Balthasar cites the three saint-theologians only because they too think that the one who cannot sin has the greater liberty. That is, he references their consensus and authority only with respect to this limited conclusion, without any implicit reference to their reasons or to any corollaries (such as Christ's beatific vision) they see following from the conclusion, because in these latter matters he differs from them. These quotations stand as an argument in support of his assertion only given the absolute value he places on freedom. For Balthasar, freedom is the absolute good, as made clear by a section title in the concluding volume of the *Theo-Drama,* "The Absolute Good: Freedom."[54] Christ's freedom from the possibility of sin must then be affirmed in order to affirm the maximal freedom of the incarnate Word.

Because the essential feature of God is self-gift, an ultimate freedom to do what one wills even with one's own nature, Balthasar need not address the question of the end for which freedom exists, or how this freedom comes to be perfected as it pursues this end: If the absolute good is freedom, freedom requires no end, no justification, other than itself. If the absolute good is freedom, freedom is desirable for its own sake. If the absolute good is freedom, freedom is not perfected by something other than its own exercise. God then is the absolute good, *because* He is infinite freedom: The principle of God's *diffusivum sui* is His freedom.

The Holy Spirit is this divine freedom in a particular way.[55] Freedom is self-possession, or the capacity to dispose of oneself — and this is the mark of being a person.[56] Hence the Holy Spirit is freedom in a particular way because His spiration is the result and sign of the Father's freedom to do what He will with His own nature to the point of generating another divine Person who, allowing the Father to dispose Him, spirates the Spirit with the Father. That the Spirit is freedom itself indicates His divinity.[57] But that the "seal" of the Spirit is freedom means the love between Father and Son is not only fulfilled in their unity by which He is spirated, but also that this love is opened up.[58] There is simultaneously perfect fulfillment and openness.[59] The Holy Spirit's procession does not close the Trinity in on itself,[60] but indicates its continuing *pro* character. The divine nature as freedom, as self-disposal, as self-gift, as love is *essentially* 'open' to an other.[61] Its essence is the positing of a real other who is capable of freely loving in return, and who actually does so. The problem of an unlimited number of divine processions may seem ruled out here by the 'closure' of the love between Father and Son with the "seal" of the Spirit, and by the Spirit's orientation to creatures to engender new sons in the Son.[62] But it is not so: If proof of a Person's divinity is self-gift such that another divine Person proceeds, as in the case of Father and Son, the Holy Spirit would not be divine, since the extension of the temporal effect of the Spirit's procession in the hearts of the faithful is not equivalent to the mutual self-gift of the Father and Son that generates another divine person.

Revelation is particular to the Spirit,[63] since the Father and Son's mutual outward gift of self is made manifest in His procession. His revelation of the other Persons is at the same time a self-revelation:[64] The revelation of the Persons in their distinction entails the revelation of the love that unites them. Thus, the point of maximal economic revelation, the point of maximal self-gift in kenosis, must especially involve the Holy Spirit:[65] Christ in Sheol remains united to the Father in the Spirit, and this unbroken union in the substantial love that is the Spirit accomplishes the redemption of mankind. Note that if the Holy Spirit is freedom, His presence "within" Jesus to communicate the Father's desires in a clear, compelling way may be said to *increase* Christ's freedom.

Balthasar's position that the principle of God's *diffusivum sui* is His freedom contrasts with one in which God is perfectly free, because He is the absolute good.[66] Then it is the *bonum* that is *diffusivum sui*, not *libertas*. If the goal of everything is actual perfection and God as First Cause is infinite act, then the end of freedom is union with God, and the means is union with God — even, so to speak, for God Himself. Or, what amounts to the same, the end of freedom is union with the good, this end is sought because the good is good, and the means is union with the good through being good, which being good is itself the perfect act. Freedom's value comes from its being a mode to reach the good; if it did not do so, freedom itself would not be desirable. Balthasar says that it is "freedom that most makes you similar to your Creator."[67] But it seems instead that goodness does, and not only for man, but for all creatures. The intellectual and volitional freedom of rationality does distinguish, it is true, man from other bodily creatures by this greater likeness to God — but precisely as a good intended for a particular good end. For evil deliberately and voluntarily done makes man more unlike God than irrational creatures. The fact that evil freely done is said not to be true freedom indicates that freedom's fundamental reality is the good, and not vice versa. Thus the absolute good cannot be defined as freedom, because the Good is the last end and hence the concept of it is ultimate.

In terms of freedom from the possibility to sin, the infallible clarity and effective moral force of the mission of the moment received by Christ through the Holy Spirit (i.e., union with divine freedom) — which is an economic form of the Son's hypostatic obedience — effectively substitutes in Balthasar's theology for the beatific vision (i.e., union with the divine good). It is noteworthy that, having rejected the beatific vision, Balthasar develops something very like it (despite the radical differences) insofar as his substitute is both cognitive and moral, and is essential to Christ's sinlessness. In this context, note also that although Balthasar had said obedience is faithfulness *despite* not seeing and, for this reason, rejected Christ's beatific vision so that His faith would be like that of other men and their archetype, Christ is in fact obedient *precisely to the extent* to which He knows the Father's will. In other words, in Balthasar's theology, Christ is ignorant of many things and, despite not knowing everything about His mission, He is faithful to it. His fidelity, however, takes the concrete form of His doing exactly what the Spirit *reveals* to Him to be the Father's will, i.e., Christ's obedience effectively depends on His knowledge, not upon His ignorance.

The foregoing considerations largely concerned the implications for Christ of the Spirit's communication of the Father's will. This mediation itself merits reflection: It is not clear how the Spirit can *mediate* between Father and Son if these two together are a single principle in spirating Him. Balthasar denies his doctrine of Trinitarian inversion changes the order of procession in God. Examination of possible arguments for the lack of change will help characterize the Holy Spirit's role in the *economia* further.

A first argument would seem to be the invocation that the mission, which is mediated by the Holy Spirit, is the procession. This principle of Balthasar's is implicit when he says that Jesus' perfect obedient consent as the God-man to the Father's will is "the economic form of their common spiration of the Spirit"[68] insofar as it points to His union as Son with the Father:

> If we may deduce this [that the Son's (and the Spirit's) eternal self-offering is as original as the Father's desire for the Son to restore creation in the way He does] from Jesus' awareness of his mission (an awareness that has no imaginable beginning) and his consent to it, it follows that this absolute, free consent between himself and the Father is the economic form of their common spiration of the Spirit.[69]

The chain of logic latent here is as follows: Jesus' knowledge of His mission and consent to it in the *economia* images the Son's eternal self-offering. This latter includes both knowledge and consent, and is His self-gift back to the Father. Because the Holy Spirit proceeds from this filial self-gift in union with the Father's self-gift to the Son, the incarnate Son's obedience to the Father's will is the "economic form" of the spiration of the Spirit.

However, what Christ's obedience reveals of His divine Person does not explain how the one whom He spirates forth with the Father can mediate to Him the Father's will in virtue of which He is obedient. Balthasar explains further:

> In "economic" terms, his reception of this power [to participate in spirating the Spirit] corresponds to the first *status* [*exinanitionis*] of the Incarnate Son, whereas the actual breathing forth of the Spirit (in conjunction with the Father) corresponds to the second [*status exaltationis*].[70]

Since this economic "reception" of power corresponds to the incarnation of the Son prior to His resurrection, the "reception" relates to the Son's humility because the power of spirating is not from Himself, but from the Father, while the actual spiration is linked to His exaltation because He exercises the power He received. Again, the mission is the procession. If the correspondence of the two *status* with the reception or exercise of the 'power' of spiration is only conceptual, such that in fact Christ always receives and always exercises this 'power,'

Balthasar's idea of how the *economia* really expresses and thus reveals the *theologia* is jeopardized. On the other hand, if the two *status* have a sequential temporal order, it is not clear how the Spirit proceeds in the time prior to the Son's *status exaltationis*.

Balthasar's reason for denying change in the order of processions eventually becomes explicit:

> For just as the Son eternally receives his entire divine being from the Father, he also eternally receives from him the ability to send the Spirit forth in conjunction with the Father. The infinite vitality of the relations between the divine Persons is so rich in aspects that one such aspect can precipitate the Son's Incarnation, and the "inversion" we have described, without requiring any change in the internal divine order. All that is required is that the Son, in his eternal origin from the Father, should go back to a point where he can receive the power of (participating in) breathing forth the Spirit.[71]

The change under discussion is prevented by the 'richness' of the divine life, i.e., by the fact that the Incarnation and Trinitarian inversion is "one of the infinite possibilities that lie *in* God's eternal life."[72] God does not change because this possibility always existed within Him.

This 'solution' evades the question, however, since it may be rephrased by asking whether it was always a possibility within God for the order of processions to be otherwise. In other words, these "infinite possibilities" seem to extend even to the processions themselves: Almost as if there might be another way for God to be, Balthasar says,

> One must ponder *the way* in which the triune God *wishes* to be almighty. He wishes to be almighty not solely by creating: by begetting and breathing forth, and allowing himself to be begotten and breathed forth, he hands over his power to the Other . . . without ever seeking to take it back.[73]

Balthasar uses "triune" here, not because the processions are necessary by nature though in accord with the *single* will of the three eternal Persons,[74] but because the Father requires the Son to breathe forth the Spirit insofar as the Son does all the Father gives Him, and both the Son and Spirit give "antecedent consent" to their processions. Hence, if God is free to do what He will with His own nature, could He just as well not be Trinitarian?

Also, it is not clear what it means for the Son "in his eternal origin from the Father, to go back to a point" of receiving the 'power' of spiration: As eternal, He always has this 'power'; hence there is no need to "go back"; as incarnate, how is He to "go back" without undoing the Incarnation? Perhaps it makes most sense to understand this second 'solution' to mean that the Son's 'power' of spirating persists in the Incarnation because He *receives* Himself as self-*gift* from the Father, as a result of which, since He is always giving Himself back, the Spirit proceeds.

However, what I proposed on Balthasar's behalf is not what he himself says. Particularly noteworthy in this context is his comment that

> Insofar as Jesus is the fruit of the Spirit's overshadowing of the Virgin, he naturally has the Spirit within him; but insofar as the Spirit is sent *down* upon him explicitly ('in bodily form') the Spirit is 'over him.' . . . [T]he Spirit in him and above him is the manifest presence of his divine mission. . . . [T]he *being* of the Spirit in him — the Incarnate One — is the economic form of the *filioque;* and the Spirit who *comes down* upon him, hovers over him and drives him is the *a Patre procedit.*[75]

This description of the Trinitarian inversion is striking, because it does not attribute the presence of the Spirit in Jesus to the (incarnate) Son's continued spiration of Him or even to the indwelling of the Spirit in the soul of Jesus according to the single will of all three Persons of the Trinity. Rather through His proper work of incarnating the Son, the Holy Spirit Himself alone is the *principle* of His presence in the incarnate Son. Hence it appears the active 'power' of spiration is another divine attribute the Son "deposits" in His becoming incarnate.

Balthasar also makes some implicit attempts to resolve the dilemma that the Holy Spirit's mediating between the Father and Christ as Son changes the immanent Trinity. First, he says, "The Spirit does not prevent the Son from receiving his mission directly but makes it possible for him to receive it obediently."[76] One wonders why Jesus could not obey the Father directly, even as the Son's immediate generation by the Father is His immanent and archetypal 'obedience.' In other words, why has mediation become necessary for obedience?

Secondly, Balthasar says that "the Spirit in him and above him is the *manifest* presence of his divine mission,"[77] as if the Trinitarian inversion is only an inverted *appearance* of the unchanged order of processions. But if the mission is to reveal the procession, then the real order of the processions (Son → Holy Spirit) would be revealed in its opposite (Holy Spirit → incarnate Son). This reversal is similar to the procession and divinity of the Son being revealed in His going into what is not-God (man, sin-in-itself in Sheol). The difficulty is, how is one to know God is opposite from His manifestation? Is the Trinitarian inversion and the Son's being "literally 'made sin'" merely how things appear or a real new way of being? In the first case, is God's credibility jeopardized or are we led back to the 'hidden God' of Luther? In the second, is it possible for God to have different modes of being? And why is the Son's divine obedience expressed in obedience as man, but the Father's generating love for the Son is expressed in His rejecting, "crushing," and abandoning Him?

Third, Balthasar says, "It is only when the Son has risen and returned home to the Father that, together with the Father he can *openly* represent a single principle of spiration."[78] The qualification "openly" suggests that the Son also spirated the Spirit prior to His exaltation; He merely appeared 'poor' before. The suggestion of the Son's poverty being merely apparent goes against Balthasar's whole doctrine of the Incarnation, however, and vitiates his teaching of God's actual poverty (in surrendering Himself) being His wealth,[79] His powerlessness being His omnipotence. The qualification "openly" should perhaps be taken then without the suggestion of contrast, and as a new appearance revealing a new reality, as likewise when we read that

> in the *status exinanitionis,* Jesus' relationship with the Spirit consists in the carrying out of his mission — expressed both in his possession of and obedience to the Spirit, both in his "claim" and in his "poverty and self-abandonment"[80] — whereas, in the *status exaltationis,* . . . the exalted Lord is given *manifest* power, even in his humanity [*dem nunmehr Erhöhten die offenbare Macht gegeben, auch in seiner Menschheit*[81]], to breathe forth the Spirit.[82]

Here, there is the additional problem that to say Jesus breathes forth the Spirit "in his humanity" implies a change in His human nature, because the spiration of the Spirit is not a power proper to human nature. Even if read in light of Balthasar's theology of the Incarnation — that the Word become flesh receives back in the Resurrection the divine (and human) attributes He earlier "deposited," and this reception pertains to His divinity since the reception of the divine attributes is as much a function of His divine Person as is His surrender of them — it is difficult to see how the passage can avoid heterodoxy. If the Word only became flesh through the "depositing" of divine attributes, to receive them back suggests the undoing of the Incarnation. Or else it suggests the change of Christ's human nature into the divine nature, since even the elevation of human nature to participate in the divine nature through grace does not confer the power to spirate the Spirit, because that power must be coeternally actual with the Spirit and no human nature, not even that of Christ, meets that requirement.[83] Made manifest here is the absolute necessity to profess that the Son became man without loss of His divine glory. Perhaps one may gloss the "manifest power" received by the Son in His humanity in the sense of another passage where Balthasar tries to explain that the economic form of the Trinity, in which Jesus possesses the Spirit yet at the same time receives *from Him* what He is to do, ceases with His Resurrection, after which Jesus disposes of the Spirit *how He wills.*[84]

It is not clear, however, that this interpretation does justice to the other texts, particularly to Balthasar's comment that "even in his perfected humanity he has become the one principle of breathing the Spirit (Lk 24:49; Acts 2:33)."[85] Here, why does Balthasar say Christ "has *become*" a principle of the Spirit unless either He received back the divine power of spiration He "deposited," or He began to spirate the Spirit also from His human nature? The choice is only between which nature changes — both options are contrary to the Council of Chalcedon (DS 302). If Balthasar means by this sort of statement that the Son does not repudiate His humanity after His resurrection but, as one who is both God and man ("one principle" referring to the hypostasis, not the natures), spirates the Spirit with the Father in virtue of His divine nature (and not in virtue of His human nature), it is not at all clear.

The same difficulties are still more clearly present when Balthasar writes,

> This *divine* commonality in the breathing out of the Spirit is first 'inhaled' by the *man* Jesus only when as a human being he has 'breathed out' his Spirit of mission and when as the Exalted One, united again with the Father and receiving from him power over the Spirit (Acts 2:33), he can send and breathe the Spirit into the Church.[86]

Who is this "man Jesus"? If Balthasar is referring to Jesus as a subject, either as a Person or as a Person with two natures, Jesus always had this "divine" unity with the Father in spirating the Spirit. On the other hand, if Balthasar is referring to Jesus with respect to His human nature, His human nature cannot receive the power of spiration without ceasing to be human and becoming divine, which, in its very becoming, would only be divine in an Arian, Nestorian, or similar sense.

Hence the problem concerning a change in the relation between Son and Holy Spirit remains, especially if one takes Balthasar seriously when he says that the Incarnation "is not something purely external, as if this relationship *ad extra* did not really affect him."[87] If the Son is affected, all the relations of the Trinity are affected by the Trinitarian inversion that brings the Incarnation about. The problem becomes even more acute since Balthasar sees the Incarnation as the actual "depositing" of divine attributes. Jesus possesses the Spirit as His own (as He must, to avoid heteronomy), but only because He is *given* to Him (as He must, if He is to be true man, and humble and poor in obedient faith). The notion that this gift is received *in His human nature* cannot be supplied, unless it is referred to the Word become flesh in Balthasar's sense. Then it is not that the Son become man receives the Holy Spirit according to grace in His human nature while spirating Him according to His divine nature; instead, the Son who is man receives the Spirit in His human nature as the result of His divine act of "depositing" His divine attributes with the Father. Only this "depositing" ensures the Son becomes true man, and no man has the power of spiration. Moreover, His "depositing" is the foundation of what Christ receives back from the Father in the Resurrection. Hence, "the exalted Lord is given manifest power, even in his humanity, to breathe forth the Spirit."[88] Now, in fact, the Son's 'power' of spiration is as much a necessary feature of His hypostasis as His relation to the Father is: The Son is the divine hypostasis that is begotten and spirates, in distinction from the Father, who is unbegotten and spirates, and the Holy Spirit, who is spirated. To "deposit" this 'power' is to destroy the Son. Nonetheless it appears as though Balthasar treats this aspect of the Son's Trinitarian personality like a common (common only with the Father, that is) divine attribute.

Bridge between God and Fallen Man, i.e., between the Father and Christ in Sheol

With this section, we stand again at the center of Balthasar's Trinitarian soteriology of the Descent. The role of the Holy Spirit in the Descent manifests how the Father's "wrath" and the Son's conformity to sin-in-itself through the *visio mortis* can be redemptive and an act of love. "The abyss of absolute love . . . embraces all abysses,"[89] including the deepest one man knows, the separation of the lost creature from God. God can "go into abandonment by God,"[90] because the one who abandons and the one abandoned remain united by the Spirit of their mutual love. In addition, when the Son becomes a "space" for the collision of the Father's wrath with the sin of the world, the Father acts "not as in an alien realm of expression but as in his very own,"[91] because He crushes *in the Person of the Son* what is contrary to God, all the while remaining united to Him *in their substantial love, the Holy Spirit.*

Given the immanence of men's sins in the Son and the abiding Trinitarian unity in the Holy Spirit, creaturely freedom *as lost* becomes established within the intra-Trinitarian "distance," since "the Son's God-forsakenness is drawn into the love relationship within the Trinity."[92] Just as the opposition of intra-Trinitarian "distance" is the presupposition of Trinitarian love as self-surrender, so the opposition, or "distance," between infinite and finite freedom is the presupposition for God's self-gift in love to the world.[93] Since it images the absolute freedom that is absolute good, this latter opposition can be "very good,"[94] but only if finite freedom, with its real and inherent possibility of failure, can be ensured a way *through its own reality* to persist in this just relation of opposition with God, or return to it, if and when it fails.[95] God, i.e., the Spirit bridging the Father and Son separated in their mutual abandonment, establishes creaturely freedom anew in a just opposition with God, all the while respecting finite freedom by not overwhelming it.[96] The Son's abandonment by the Father while being united to Him by the Spirit despite His ignorance of it "introduces everything that is called communication and communion in the eternal sense"[97] into the timeless, miserable isolation of sin. Neither Sheol, which will become hell, nor the living 'hell' of the living sinner can be the same. "No abyss is deeper than God. He embraces everything: himself and everything else."[98]

It can now be seen why the Holy Spirit does not experience abandonment in the Descent event, although the Son experiences the active abandonment of the Father in His "wrath" and the Father experiences 'abandonment' in losing His Son. The Spirit is just as much "involved"[99] as they are,[100] but in a way properly His own, namely, as the bond of unity, a bond that nevertheless does not diminish the very real "distance" or separation between them, either personally or in abandonment.[101]

The redemption of fallen man through the Trinitarian Descent event can be summed up in Balthasar's notion of God as "ever-greater."[102] As we saw in Chapter Seven, the Trinitarian "distance" between Father and Son is the foundation of all creaturely "distance," including both the "distance" of the creature in union with God (though not absorbed by Him) and the "distance" of the lost creature, separated from God by sin. The "distance" of God's intra-Trinitarian life of love is "greater" than these 'lesser,' creaturely "distances," however, because it entails a more absolute opposition. In addition, the Trinitarian "distance" is fruitful: The relationship between the Father and Son is "greater," i.e., more, than the relation of the one to the other, because the relation between them is a third Person. The fruitful aspect of God's being "ever-greater" derives from the freedom that characterizes His love, because the divine freedom makes possible the giving of the divine nature such that other Persons proceed.

As a greater physical distance can include lesser ones, God can include creatures in the "distance" of His internal life, if He freely chooses to do so out of love. But if God is "ever-greater" than Himself,[103] at least to the extent that there is a procession to union despite "distance" within the Godhead, then the 'lesser' "distance" of mutual abandonment between Father and the Son in the Descent event can be "bridged" by the "ever-greater" fruit of their love, the Holy Spirit.[104] Likewise the Holy Spirit can "bridge" the yet 'lesser' "distance" between God and the individual creature lost in sin. Because the intra-Trinitarian "distance" is simultaneously maintained *and* bridged by the Holy Spirit, both the lostness and ultimate perfection of fallen creatures can be re-established in relationship with God insofar as both are found in the Son, lost in Sheol out of perfect obedience and abandoned by the Father, but united to Him in the Spirit. In virtue of this "ever-greater" Trinitarian love, of its unity that "bridges" the most extreme "distance," i.e., in virtue of the Holy Spirit, the Son in Sheol can endure, outlast, and make impotent the fury of sin,[105] of re-bellion against God, of the selfish self-love of creatures that would hoard in the face of their archetype of self-giving love.[106] As every negative creaturely reality has in Him its positive archetype and perfection,[107] He can undergo them in their very negativity (suffering, death, sin-in-itself), but in a context (i.e., the Trinitarian unity of the Holy Spirit) that configures them to the positivity of their archetype (joy, life, obedience).

We see again that the Son of God is "made sin" in the most literal way possible. If sin only existed in the "distance" between the Persons, the Son could not fear it or suffer from it, since it would be 'less' than the divine "distance," which is the foundation of His generation in eternal bliss. In the same case, His becoming man would be unnecessary, since sin would already exist within the embrace of the intra-Trinitarian love, as does the entire creation.[108] Since, on the contrary, His terror and suffering are supreme, sin must come to be within His very self, in His hypostasis, by which He Himself is "made sin." In being in Him, it comes to be within the Trinitarian love, since He remains embraced by the Holy Spirit in His descent experience, albeit without knowing it. As has al-ready been seen, His being "made sin" in Sheol requires that His human nature undergo "a certain 'stretching apart' based upon his power to give himself (*dis-tentio* — Augustine),"[109] i.e., based upon His divine kenosis. It must ultimately be "stripped" from Him, given back to the Father with His divine attributes. As a "naked" hypostatic *ratio,* a "pure 'relationality'"[110] thus "distanced" ("alien-ated") from Himself and from the Father, He will be left to be a "free space for the collision of sin."[111] At the same time, He will remain nonetheless united to the Father in an uncomprehended communion of love through the Holy Spirit, because the divine life is precisely going to the farthest extreme of self-gift out of love. "God's act of reconciliation . . . takes as the 'means of atonement' (Rom 3:25) the *hypostatic* obedience of the Son of God, his *kenosis* or *diastasis*. . . ."[112] His *kenosis* is the Son's hypostatic obedience in the Incarnation, while His *diastasis* refers to the same thing within the Trinity, but ultimately all three are equivalent, since the *missio* is the *processio*. More than Christ meriting forgiveness, "he himself *is* the forgiveness of sins,"[113] because *in His person* they have been overtaken by the divine love. In this way, the "distances" of creaturely existence and lostness are "undergirded"[114] by the Trinitarian life in the very possibility and actuality of both lostness in sin and the re-establishment in relationship with God:[115] All are taken up into the "bracket" of the divine love.[116]

Although the "distance" of sin must both exist and be overcome within the intra-Trinitarian "distance," Balthasar adamantly denies that sin has any place in the immanent Trinity: "This [the free refusal to accept God's will] *cannot* be said to be an element that is present as a possibility in the Son's relationship with the Father."[117] Ultimately this position remains on the level of assertion. Since every reality is from God and in Him, and since sin is not nothing, sin must likewise be from God and in Him. Again, sin is a reality, according to Balthasar, and the Son is the archetype for all non-divine reality.[118] Again, because there are no guarantees in the intra-Trinitarian relations,[119] and because the possibility of sin proves the reality of the freedom of creatures,[120] and given that Balthasar cannot show why the one who cannot sin is more free,[121] sin ought also to be a possibility within absolute freedom. Again, the Son is "literally 'made sin'"[122] for the redemption of the finite freedom, but this kenotic mode of redemption is only one of the infinite possibilities that were always within the eternal life.[123]

Hence we read that God's "love can still be itself, unchanged in its true nature, and yet be in what is foreign to it, in the darkness of nonlove, in the hate of the world":[124] This text does not point to God's presence in the sinner, who is good insofar as he is. Instead, God is in sin, both in Christ's being obediently conformed to it and in the Father's wrath against Him in that state, both of which are economic modes of their eternal love. Though Christ crucified cannot be identified "with the actual No of sin itself," this is only in the sense that He Himself does not personally commit actual sin, but remains ever obedient to the Father; in other respects, "Jesus *does* experience the darkness of the sinful state," in terms of both temptation and alienation from God, but "in a deeper and darker experience."[125] Even granted that sin might not be a possibility (i.e., it is something that never happens) in the Son's relationship with the Father, the possibility for sin itself lies in the "distance" between the Son and Father.[126] Again, if sin was not "in" the Trinity before Christ's descent, it certainly is after.[127]

God's going into His opposite, or, what amounts to the same, taking His opposite into Himself, proves His "ever-greater" freedom, i.e., His divinity.[128] In demonstrating His absolute freedom, which makes possible this integration, God proves His divinity. His freedom may also be called His self-subsistence, since He, as a self-subsisting Person, is free to do what He wills with His nature. God can and does integrate such varied and extreme "distances" as divinity and sin-in-itself within Himself without being other than what He is.[129] Because the "ever-greater" character of the divine love is its character as self-gift, which is the single inalienable feature of the Godhead, and this self-existing love-as-self-gift is "ever-greater" than all else that is, including sin, the Descent event does not change the essence of the Trinity, although the Persons are truly affected by it.[130] Thus the Father can withdraw Himself and abandon the Son, and remain the Father who is essentially self-gift to the Son. Likewise the Son can kenotically give Himself back to the Father and remain the Son who is essentially self-gift to the Father. Similarly, the relation between the Son and Holy Spirit can be "inverted" in the Incarnation, and the Holy Spirit can continue to unite Father and Son in the Descent's moment of their greatest opposition, for the Incarnation effects no change in the relations of Father and Son *as relations of self-gift,* and hence none in the relation of the Holy Spirit as "bridge" between them. Since the mission of the Son is the continuation of His eternal procession and since the Incarnation does not change what He essentially is or what He expresses of the Father, it is all the same to the Spirit as far as His personal property is concerned that He is the bond of love between the Father and the Son in the eternal beatitude of their love for each other, and that He is the bridge between the Father and the Son in the Son's descent into self-alienation. For the perfect opposition between the Father as active wrath and the Son as passively being "made sin" in the *visio mortis* perfectly corresponds, in the 'language' of fallen human existence, to the perfect opposition between the eternal self-subsisting relations of the Father and Son.

Thus the Descent event is the definitive revelation of the Trinity.[131] The love of the Father and the Son is revealed in its most perfect, because most extreme,[132] form in the Descent. If it is the moment of their greatest distance, it is precisely so as the moment of their greatest intimacy,[133] because their love is complete self-surrender. The Descent is thus the locus also of the most perfect revelation, or economic expression, of the Holy Spirit, who is the substantial love of Father and Son:

> This "infinite distance," which recapitulates the sinner's mode of alienation from God, will remain forever the highest revelation known to the world of the diastasis (within the eternal being of God) between Father and Son in the Holy Spirit.[134]

Conclusion

In this chapter, we have considered the Descent from the perspective of the Holy Spirit insofar as He is the substantial bond (or "bridge") between Father and Son in the Trinity itself, in the Incarnation, and in the Descent. This investigation shed particular light on how the Descent event accomplishes the redemption of mankind through the inclusion of the fallenness of creatures in the Trinitarian love in virtue of the Son being "made sin" while remaining united to the Father by the Spirit.

Having examined the involvement of each of the three divine Persons in the Descent event, we are now able to summarize its reciprocal relation to the Trinity (founded on the principle that the mission is the procession): From the Father's begetting (His self-gift, or kenosis) proceeds the Son. The procession of the Son continues and is revealed (or expressed) in His incarnate mission. Even as the Son eternally loves the Father by giving Himself back to Him, His mission has the form of self-gift, or kenosis, back to the Father. The filial kenosis in the economy reaches its perfection in Sheol, when the Son is united to sin-in-itself through the *visio mortis*. As the subsistent bond of love that eternally results from the mutual love of Father and Son, the Spirit also bridges the separation of abandonment between the Father and the Son in Sheol. In this way, God's "ever-greater" love exceeds and embraces the "no" of all sin.[135] The Trinitarian love is most perfectly revealed in the Descent through the extremity of each divine Person's self-gift.[136]

The relations of the Trinitarian Persons in the Descent event may be illustrated by Figure 1 on the facing page. In the divine "event" of love, the Father gives Himself to the Son, who proceeds in receiving Himself (Fig. 1.a). The Father's sending forth of the Son from Himself continues in His sending of the Son in His incarnate mission, which reaches its term in the Son being "made sin" in His descent. The Father's "crushing" rejection of sin in the Person of the Son now characterizes the Father's *sending forth* of the Son as a *sending away* in rejection and abandonment (Fig. 1.b). The continuity of the Father's begetting with His "crushing" means that this punitive aspect is no less the love of the Father for the Son than His generation: They are the same act, differing only as immanent and economic perspectives of the Father's relation to the Son.

The Son receives Himself wholly from the Father (Fig. 1.a). This complete reception is the Son's "obedience." Since the economic mission of the Son corresponds to His immanent procession and expresses it, He is also perfectly obedient in His mission. Thus, out of obedient love for the Father, He accepts to be "made sin" in Sheol through the *visio mortis,* to the extent of inclining Himself to it through *compassio* (Fig. 1.b). The "momentum" of the procession of the

a. Father gives Himself to Son; Son proceeds in receiving Himself

b. Sending of Son by Father; Mission of Son
   Also: Father "crushing" Son; Son in state of *compassio*

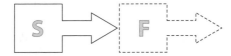

c. Son's "antecedent consent"; Father's reception of actual paternity
   Also: Son "depositing" divine and human attributes in kenosis;
   Father withdrawing in abandonment of Son

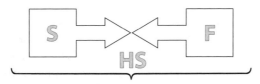

d. Son gives Himself back to Father; Holy Spirit proceeds as the mutual love
   between Father and Son
   Also: Holy Spirit unites Father and Son as Father "crushes" Son and Son "deposits"
   attributes in the Incarnation and Descent

Figure 1. Trinitarian Relations and the Descent Event

Son (i.e., the Father's generation and the Son's hypostatic obedience) thus impels Him into Sheol, to an obedience in the most extreme conditions.

In the economy of the Incarnation, the Son's self-gift back to the Father continues through the "depositing" of the divine attributes with Him in His kenosis until He is entirely "made sin" in Sheol. This "depositing" of the divine and human attributes originally received from the Father is paralleled by the Father's withdrawal as a result of which the Son experiences abandonment (Fig. 1.c). Though it is not explicit in Balthasar, we may deduce that the Father's withdrawal *is* effectively the Son's "depositing," because the Son only is what the Father gives Him. Hence if the Father withdraws, the Son must lose His attributes. Balthasar also does not make explicit the *eternal* parallel to the Father's economic withdrawing. It would seem to be the Father's grateful reception of His actual paternity due to the Son's "antecedent consent."

The Holy Spirit proceeds as the substantial bond between the perfect love of the Father and the Son for each other (Fig. 1.d), since the Son always expresses His love not only as obedience, but also as self-gift. The bond of love between Father and Son is thereby joined, even as a hand offered by one person is joined to the hand offered by another person in the clasp of a handshake. This link is something distinct from the hands themselves in their act of self-giving, but inseparable from those acts. Because the Son's incarnation, life, death, and descent merely express in time the relations that in the Trinity are eternal, the begetting, "crushing," withdrawing act of the Father is simultaneous with the Son's procession, His mission, and His kenosis in *compassio,* and both are simultaneous with the Spirit's procession and His uniting of Father and Son in eternal love and in the Descent event (Fig. 1.d). Thus the Father and Son are forever 'toward' each other in the Holy Spirit, even as the Son goes forth from the Father in His descent and as the Father turns away from the Son by withdrawing Himself (see the Son in Fig. 1.b and the Father in Fig. 1.c). The Spirit thus "brackets" the whole Descent event (Fig. 1.d). When the world's sins are assumed by the Son through the *visio mortis,* they are brought "within" this "bracket" of the Trinitarian love.

In consequence, besides the Descent's exceptional importance in Balthasar's Christology and soteriology, it is the key to understanding his theology of the Trinity, because the immanent Trinity is only known through its economic revelation, which is at its supreme concentration and clarity in the Descent. Balthasar's understanding of love as gift of self is another key, but a derivative one, since the perfection of God's gift of self (hence its essential nature) is revealed only in the Descent.

Balthasar admits Christ's descent was glorious in the sense in which glory is proper to God. We can now apprehend more clearly the significance of the entirely different meaning he gives to that proper sense: In his reading of Philippians 2:6-11, he says,

> we apprehend something like the replacing of one ideal by another: of the ideal of a divine glory that is so much the property of the only God that he can and may never rid himself of it by a new ideal which as such cannot yet bear the name δόξα, because it consists precisely in ridding oneself of what bore this name in the Old Testament in order to make ready the space of complete poverty, indeed more than this, of full abandonment of self, which holds itself open for this new splendour and glory alone. The first concept is closely tied to "power" (δύναμις),[137] the second to an utter powerlessness that will prove to be that which is genuinely glorious in its final attitude, and will perhaps absorb the first concept of glory into itself.[138]

The cautious qualifications of this passage reflect its early position at the beginning of *The Glory of the Lord*. Once one has traversed the entire argument made in the series, it is evident that Balthasar considers the self-surrender and abandonment of the Trinitarian "distance" to be the proper sense of *glory*. The remnant of the "Old Testament" concept of *glory* in "the new ideal" is its link with "power," since it is God's omnipotence that enables Him to surrender the divine nature, whether within the Trinity or in the Incarnation and Descent. Omnipotence, however, is only another way to describe the absolute freedom of God, which is His fundamental essence: because He is absolute freedom, He can give Himself away so as to subsist as Trinitarian.

CHAPTER NINE

The Centrality of the Descent
in the Theology of Hans Urs von Balthasar

The fuller characterization of the Descent from a Trinitarian perspective undertaken in the previous three chapters has revealed two additional essential features of Hans Urs von Balthasar's theological opinion: The Father is the agent of the Son's passive experience of the *visio mortis,* while the Holy Spirit proceeds as the bond of love that bridges the opposition between Father and Son in the Descent as in the immanent Trinity. The Descent is no less central to Balthasar's Trinitarian theology than to his soteriology. Since all other branches of Christian systematic theology are dependent upon these two, Balthasar's understanding of the Descent explicitly or implicitly conditions the rest of his theology.[1] Wilhelm Maas is explicit: For Balthasar, the doctrine of Christ's descent is "the center and actually the entire essential content of his theology."[2] The Descent, as distinct from the Crucifixion, is the center of Balthasar's theology.[3] Indeed, he sees it as the heart of Christian theology:

> The trinitarian love . . . proved itself to be the final thing, the *eschaton,* because in the midst of its opposite — in the "hell" of lost human freedom — it could be itself, as the Son's perfect obedience of love even in the realm of the dead. In the New Testament, then, there is one single total truth, one single dogma, which at its center is christological, but in its immediate implications is trinitarian as well as soteriological, and, indeed, soteriological (*descensus* and Resurrection) *as* trinitarian.[4]

In this chapter, we will trace the major links in the chain of this influence: Having previously seen that the Descent event reveals the Trinity as its origin, we will now see that the Descent serves as the guarantee of a responsible creation, and founds sacramentology, ecclesiology, eschatology, and Mariology. Balthasar's theology could be sketched from the perspective of a causal chain in the following way:

1. Trinitarian theology: The immanent Trinity is self-subsisting gift of self.
2. Christology, soteriology (the incarnate Descent event): Self-gift in the economic Trinity reveals the immanent Trinity, including its incomprehensibility, and establishes the possibility of creaturely participation in the Trinitarian life of self-gift. Only in virtue of the Descent can the world be created responsibly.
3. Sacramentology (preeminently the Eucharist): The soteriological self-gift is extended as the means to begin and continue the Trinitarian life in mankind.
4. Ecclesiology: The Trinitarian life in man is continued in time.
5. Eschatology: The Trinitarian life in man is perfected and continued in eternity.
6. Mariology: Mary is the exemplar of the disciple in whom Christ's archetypal life of self-gift takes form.

In this chapter, the above topics will be briefly considered in their connection with the Descent insofar as they have not been discussed previously.

The Descent and Creation

The Descent event itself (item 2) and its connection with the Trinity (item 1) have already been sufficiently elaborated. As regards creation and the Descent (mentioned in item 2), three aspects may be considered: how the Son's descent is the presupposition of creation; how creation reveals the Trinity in virtue of the Descent; and how the Descent is the supreme revelation of God in creation.

It might initially appear that Balthasar's theology of creation should influence his *descensus* theology, and not the other way around. After all, in Christ, the Word appears in the mode of human nature. Hence, what Balthasar says about the nature of creatures as finite freedom in relation to God as absolute freedom must lie in the background of his Christology. However, although it is true that the Son becomes a creature of a particular sort, His being the absolute other vis-à-vis the Father and His eternal willingness to go into utter abandonment are the preconditions for there being creatures, especially creatures with finite freedom, in the first place. In regard to His relation to creatures with finite freedom, we read:

> The world as a multiplicity (which, as such, cannot be God) only becomes intelligible in terms of a free creation; free creation gives creatures genuine freedom and implies necessarily the risk of their going astray; such a risk can only be assumed responsibly if the God of love is able to gather in such lostness into himself. This is possible in no other way than by God's going in powerlessness to share in man's lostness, but out of obedience to God. . . .[5]

This "obedience to God" refers above all to the Son's obedience to the Father in becoming a creature to share in creatures' "lostness." The Descent thus serves as a 'guarantee' of finite freedom by providing a way back to God if finite freedom falls.

The Descent simultaneously guarantees finite freedom *as such*: Obedience belongs to the very structure of creaturely existence,[6] both because creatures by their nature as finite are submitted ontologically to their creator,[7] and because their archetype is the Son, whose Trinitarian personality it is to be "obedient." When the Word exists in the form of man, His perfect creaturely obedience is given a qualitative superiority because it is founded upon, expresses, and is a form of His obedience as Son.[8] By the perfection of His obedience in human form, the Son will make finite freedom a new creation from within: "from within," because accomplished by the Word made flesh; "a new creation," because accomplished by the Word in His divine relation to the Father and Holy Spirit. Because redemption is accomplished "from within," creaturehood itself is affirmed and not treated as nothing.

In this context of the Son's descent as the presupposition for creation, we recall that, because the Son's eternal self-gift to the Father includes His self-offering for the redemption of the world, no change occurs in the divine nature during the Descent event. The whole possibility of creation (and thus the possibility and actuality of sin, the Incarnation, and Sheol) always exists within God. His presence makes the existence of things other than God possible,[9] while the absolutely opposite relations between Father and Son make possible every difference among creatures, and between God and creatures, including the "distance" of sin. The relationship between the Father and the Son, and thus also the self-existing relation of the Holy Spirit, is "ever-greater" than all else that is, since no creaturely opposition (not even that of sin) exists that is as perfect an opposition as that between Father and Son, because the Father and the Son, as opposite self-existing relations, share nothing in common. Thus the substantial love of the Father and Son as the Holy Spirit is also "ever-greater" than the Descent event, and can embrace and "bracket" the separation of Father and Son in it.

Second, creation reciprocally reveals its Trinitarian origin in virtue of the 'guarantee' provided by the Descent. If God alone truly is and if He is to be the immanent cause of all, i.e., "to be 'in' something finite, without himself becoming finite,"[10] He must be transcendently free.[11] In creating the world, He endows some of His creatures with freedom, a freedom that is genuine because it comes from His own absolute freedom, yet finite because created. But if God is "in" all that is finite and some creatures have a real freedom to choose self-damnation, which is still a mode of finite existence, God must also be able to be "in" this self-damnation while remaining the absolute good that He is.[12] Or rather, since everything finite is contained by its infinite cause of continued existence, such self-damnation must somehow be able to be "in" God.[13] This is "the only valid answer."[14] If He is to remain absolute good, however, such creaturely lostness must be able to be "in" Him not as a perversion of freedom, but as good creaturely freedom, i.e., obedience. If this obedience in perdition is to be "in" God without Him being other than He is, there must be distinction in God as such. He must be triune: one who is lost obediently in creaturely freedom, one who rejects this rebellion (otherwise the perdition is not a real loss, nor does God remain true to His own goodness, i.e., remain just), and one who can maintain the unity of the other two in being God. Given the existence of creation including finite freedom, this possibility must be an actuality.[15]

Balthasar's theology of the Descent is connected with his treatment of creation in a third way, more methodological in nature. Balthasar considers in the various fields of his reflection how the Trinity expresses itself in creation and, vice versa, what creation reveals of the Trinity. As has been seen in previous chapters, God's supreme act of self-expression is the Descent event. Consequently, it is also His supreme self-revelation through creation. Hence the Descent manifests the general features of how God's action in the created world is self-revelatory. The key here is that God reveals Himself through acts of love (i.e., self-gift), and this kind of revelation is His glory.

Creation is not a static object, but a dynamic situation: God is continually creating the world, and the world is a place of action. Thus God reveals Himself not only in the existence of the world, but also in deeds, in His own deeds on behalf of His creatures and in the deeds of the creatures themselves.[16] Hence man can meaningfully use creation, his own action, and history as a basis for reflecting upon the truth about God, including upon God's Trinitarian nature. However, human reflection upon the divinity must always admit God is "ever-greater" than what man understands by his conclusions. In His sovereign otherness, God always transcends creation and man's comprehension.

Because God cannot need creation to be what He is, i.e., self-giving love, God is Trinitarian.[17] His nature as such is revealed through His interaction with the world, most particularly with His creatures endowed with free will. Now the revelation of God's love is the aim of Jesus' life and death in a preeminent way, but its expression in Him exemplifies something true of the created world at large: Everything in creation, including the action therein and "all apparently negative things,"[18] derives from the Trinitarian "event," reflects it, and occurs "within"[19] it.[20] Thus, like all creaturely realities, the suffering of Christ has its basis in God as such, and, like the entire mission of Christ, His suffering will reveal both this basis in the divine essence and the Trinity itself.[21] God is

> the unutterable first origin from which everything that exists . . . comes forth. . . . But, as the one who lives and is free, he is present in his creatures and gifts in such a way that he distances himself from them in order to leave them a space of freedom. Therefore his power, divinity, wisdom and radiant majesty fill the universe. . . . [A]s the "glorious one," he makes known both his "being present" in the world and, united to this, his sovereign superiority to the world. It is precisely this interplay of the immanence of God's power and wisdom in all that exists in the world, and his transcendence over the creatures (as the free creator who remains free), who thereby receive a space for their own existence and freedom, that is the foundation of the biblical δόξα.[22]

This coincidence of immanence and transcendence has its perfection not in the mere existence of the God-man Jesus, but in His mission.[23] The important thing is not that God exists in the flesh, but the unified event of His "becoming"[24] man through emptying Himself, of His obeying the Father, and of His going to the Cross, to the dead, to the Father. The height of concurrent immanence and transcendence in the mission of Jesus — including the configuration of men to Him by the Spirit through faith[25] — means His mission will be the definitive glory of God in the world. As God's consummate act of loving self-gift, Christ's descent is the supreme revelation of God in creation (manifesting even the divine incomprehensibility) and it is God's preeminent glory.

We recall that, according to Balthasar, creation out of chaos is the proper work of the Father. The Father 'risks' creating a finite freedom only because He trusts the Son will make good any creaturely abuse of His paternal love. The event of Cross and Hell seems to be then not only a guarantee of God's responsibility vis-à-vis His creatures to provide them a way out of possible damnation, but also a guarantee of His own beatitude.[26]

The Descent as the Foundation of the Sacraments

God's intimate and loving involvement with His creation continues in a special way through the lasting sacramental presence of Christ. Balthasar focuses in a particular way on the Eucharist. Although instituted in anticipation of Holy Thursday before Jesus goes to His death and being dead, the Eucharist is effectively the sacrament of Holy Saturday, signifying and continuing the utter self-gift of Jesus, and causing a like selflessness in the communicant.

The Son's incarnation and passion are the kenotic parallel in the economy of the eternal gift He makes of Himself back to the Father in gratitude, called His "eucharist."[27] It is not to be forgotten that the Father and the Holy Spirit also have, or rather are, a similar "eucharist" vis-à-vis the other two divine Persons.[28] The filial eucharist in eternity and in time derives from the Father's (grateful) surrender of Himself in the Son's generation, which is manifested as His surrender of the Son to the world and sin in the economy.[29]

The Son's kenosis and abandonment out of love are continued in the sacraments. The "Eucharist of the Cross,"[30] in which the Spirit, water, and blood are poured forth, is followed by the Descent, "the fundamental act of the eucharistic self-abandonment."[31] Christ's institution of the sacrament of the Eucharist at the Last Supper thus points back to the Son's eternal "pre-sacrifice"[32] and represents in anticipation His being dead, through which God's gift of Himself to the world is realized.[33]

Even after His resurrection, Jesus' life remains "eucharistic," poured out for others out of love. Insofar as His self-giving in the Descent went "to the end," it goes also to the extreme of not asking for itself back. Because He has drunk the cup of God's wrath and been "crushed" in the wine press of the Father's fury, the Son is poured out in the Eucharist as a drink for others:[34]

> God's anger strikes him instead of the countless sinners, shattering him as by lightning and distributing him among them; thus God the Father, in the Holy Spirit, creates the Son's Eucharist. Only the Eucharist completes the Incarnation.[35]

When the Eucharist is received by the believer, the Son's kenosis attains its intended end of including man in the Trinitarian life,[36] which occurs through configuration to Christ in the self-abandonment of faith.[37] As Jesus' "corporality" undergoes "a certain 'stretching apart'"[38] in Sheol, His "earthly substance"[39] is "liquif[ied]"[40] or made "fluid"[41] in the Eucharist so that He can be divided among the faithful while remaining what He is. The Eucharist is thus the full economic representation of the kenotic Trinitarian love, extending in the spiritual creatures who receive it throughout time the Incarnation and the utter surrender of self that characterizes the Descent.[42] One sacrifice is inseparable from another in the sacrifices of the Mass (which as the sacrifice of the Church embraces the personal sacrifices of Her members), Christ's sacrifice before His resurrection, and the Father's sacrifice of His Son for the world.[43] This singular unity has ecclesiological implications, and not only for those who are part of the Body of Christ through receiving the sacrament: "The believer believes for the non-believer, he communicates for the one who does not communicate, because the Body he receives bore the sins of all."[44] Unfortunately Balthasar does not explain this extension of *sanctorum* (holy things such as faith and communion in the Trinitarian life) to the non-believer as such. I would rather say the Church is sacrament to the non-believers of the world insofar as she effects what she signifies, i.e., the conversion of non-believers to Christ and the maintenance of believers in Him.[45]

The sacrament of Confession, which is an "Easter grace,"[46] bears a particular relation to the Eucharist in that both are "life out of death."[47] The Eucharist is substantially the "ever-greater" divine life that transcends even the definitive death of sin's God-abandonment. In contrast, the sacrament of Confession is given by Jesus, resurrected into the divine life again after His death. Through the "crucifying light and . . . liberating summons to come forth from darkness"[48] that characterize this latter sacrament, "through the Lord risen from the death of sinners, the dead-to-God sinner is taken back into a life through God and for God."[49] Thus he participates in Christ's archetypal cross, on which the sins of all were confessed (in their being loaded onto Christ), and in His resurrection, in which the world is absolved (insofar as it is reconciled to the Father through the Son undergoing the Father's wrath, thereby "bracketing" these sins in the Trinitarian love).[50]

In connection with the Descent event, Balthasar focuses explicitly on the sacraments of the Eucharist and Confession. In general, however, if all sacraments cause a participation in the divine life in virtue of Christ's redeeming act, then within Balthasar's system all must derive their efficacy through the Descent.

It may be that the Eucharist's reception of its efficacy from Christ's descent contributes to Balthasar's reluctance to discuss Christ's descent in relation to the separation of His body and soul in death. After all, Jesus' body lying in the tomb did not take part in the *visio mortis*, the redemptive climax of the Descent, except indirectly if Balthasar were to say it was "deposited" as part of Christ's kenosis. In other words, if the Eucharist is the sacrament of Christ's body and blood, soul and divinity, how can this sacrament represent Christ's descent if His body and soul were separated during it?

The Descent in the Life of the Church

The union of human nature with God in Christ is the archetype for the distinction in unity ("distance") that is eventually to be established between finite and infinite freedom through the participation of rational creatures in the Trinitarian life. The Trinitarian "distance" (distinction in unity), in which the One is united to the wholly Other, is imaged in the hypostatic union, in which the divine Person of the Son (the One) is united to what is other than He is, human nature.[51] God becomes what is not-God in the sense of what is finite, i.e., man. Ultimately, in Christ's descent, He will also become what is not-God in the sense of what is anti-God, i.e., "literally 'made sin.'" Consequently, Christ's abandonment in Sheol has implications for Christian life.

The reconciliation achieved in the Descent makes possible the inclusion of men in the Trinitarian unity-in-distance through inclusion in Christ.[52] The revelation of the divine love that persists (in virtue of the Holy Spirit) despite the opposition between the Father's wrath and the Son's being "made sin" will assure the sinner that he too is loved despite his sinfulness. Christ took the world's sins unto Himself as His own and "finished" these imperfect works.[53] As a result, both the sins and the perfection of every individual are in Him and, in virtue of these, He is therefore the judge of all. Moreover, by being "in Him" through His obedience, men participate in His Sonship.[54] With respect to the world's redemption, this adoptive sonship means that men are taken into the Trinitarian life in virtue of their sins being taken into the Word. The Father's love for the Son and His just wrath against men can be reconciled, because the sinner's relationship has been embraced by the obedient Son: In loving the Son, the Father thus also loves sinners. Humanity is seen within the divine justice, because its sinfulness is within the just Son.[55]

To the extent to which the form of Christ becomes actual in believers (and in their acts, which pertain to Christ's form[56]), the glory of God is "brought into force."[57] All four aspects of Balthasar's understanding of glory are present: reality, appearance, recognition, and configuration to the reality's form.[58] The form of unity-in-distance originates in the Trinity, is embodied in the hypostatic union, and in virtue of Christ continues in the Eucharist, the Church in the world, and ultimately the eternal inclusion of the Church in the Trinity. The form of God's love as manifested in Christ thus becomes the standard for human love,[59] called to be Christ-ian love.

The redemption has been accomplished in Christ. Man can neither prevent, change, nor add to this work of God. The normative response is to accept in faith what has been done on behalf of each individual, even as Christ accepted in faith what was to be done on behalf of others. The response of faith arises within a person's interior freedom as he is convinced by the power of the love manifested; his motivation, like the motivation of Christ, is the Trinitarian love. Faith apprehends the redeeming event and in it grasps that its own nature is free obedience, like Christ's. This response is not coerced from him, however; neither can someone take this new sonship upon himself nor imitate the inimitable redemptive act of Christ.[60] By the grace of the Spirit, the human person is "disposed to follow the Lord."[61] Through faith,[62] he "may share in the fullness of Jesus' disposition of sacrifice,"[63] in virtue of which "the boundary between oneself disposing (even in faith) and being at God's disposal must disappear."[64] In a kenosis of emptying himself of the old Adam and receiving the mission of Christ-ian love, he is configured to the Son's filiation, attaining freedom and self-fulfillment as a result:[65] "'Christ in us' expresses the essential result of his mission."[66] The reception of baptism signifies this total responsive gift of himself, in which he leaves everything of his old life, even as the sacrament itself confers on him the Holy Spirit, bond to the Father, and the quality of sonship.[67]

Even as Christ's love is a double love, for the Father and the world, so the Christian's participation in the Trinitarian life of love orders him not only to God, but also to his brother, and this most preeminently in regard to the Church, the public community of brothers in Christ who precede and assist the individual's own configuration. If he is to be joined to Christ such that he will live his life in Him, he will also be joined necessarily to those who already live this life in Christ. Then, as Jesus' supreme act of love was the perfection of His kenosis in Sheol out of obedience, likewise in the members of the Church kenosis, self-surrender, obedience, love, gratitude, and freedom coincide, are expressed in acts, and find their supreme expression in the Eucharist.[68] Christian love is "eucharistic," i.e., obedience to the Father in the Spirit through inclusion in the Son, a love for the other manifested in deeds unto the death of all selfish self-love.[69] The new life in them, and which they live, will be the principle of their working greater works than their own previous capabilities, in which might be heard the echo in creatures of the "ever-greater" character of the redeeming Descent event and of the Trinitarian love.[70]

The Christian as such participates in the death of Christ:[71] He enters it through baptism;[72] communicates in it in the Eucharist; and through the sacrament of Confession, receives anew the eternal life of death to self on behalf of others. His sufferings have a place within those of Christ (Col 1:24), and like those of Christ are to bear fruit, not for himself, but for others in the kingdom of God.[73] Although the Christian participates in the life of Christ as well,[74] this life is always defined by the presence of death. Death, not life, is the more fundamental concept in Balthasar's theology, as revealed by the perfection of Christ's mission in being physically and spiritually dead in Sheol, which mission (as His procession) in turn reveals the nature of God himself as "super-death."

The disciple's configuration to Christ and His death suggests a problem, however: Even if the Christian can follow Christ unto death through martyrdom,[75] if only a bloodless martyrdom of persecution by the world, it would appear to be a problem that he cannot follow Him "to the end," i.e., into perdition in Sheol. This difficulty does not arise in a theology that sees Christ's death on the cross as the consummation of redemption. In both theologies Christ alone is the Redeemer, because He alone bears and expiates the sins of others. Likewise in both, Christians participate in that redemption subjectively and objectively (Col 1:24) in virtue of His unique act. The question is whether those whom Christ promised would do even greater things than He (Jn 14:12) can be conformed to Him not only interiorly, but exteriorly, not only in disposition, but in act; it seems "at best, we were invited to follow, but then we were left behind at the decisive point of the journey."[76]

Balthasar approaches the objection in two ways. First, Christ's being dead liberates man from something foreign to his nature (i.e., selfish self-love, or sin) and sets him free for giving himself in love,[77] thus re-establishing his creaturely freedom in the likeness of infinite freedom. Christ's utterly inimitable act then "does not alienate his brothers from themselves,"[78] but reacquaints them with themselves by revealing their real nature and making possible their re-creation according to it.

This first response only addresses an ontological self-alienation in believers, however, and actually strengthens the original objection. The tension possible between gratitude for redemption and sorrow that "we were left behind" is intensified by the acceptance of redemption, because love and faith increase the desire to follow Christ. Emotional self-alienation and an alienation from Christ are the result. This problem does not arise in a theology that sees Christ's death on the cross as the locus of redemption, because the act of giving one's physical life for others (as permitted by God) is indeed imitable, even if — or, precisely since — all imitations derive their value ('merit') from this single original act. One thinks of the martyrs, in particular of those martyred by crucifixion, such as St. Peter, St. Andrew, and St. Paul Miki and his companions. The different forms of martyrdom and of these crucifixions, and likewise St. Peter's desire to be crucified upside down out of his sense of unworthiness to be crucified like Christ, do not vitiate them as imitations of Christ's crucifixion, since an image is an image precisely as a likeness that is not identical to its archetype. Of course, the interior disposition is essential to this imitation as indicated by the difference between the two thieves crucified by Christ. In Balthasar's theology, since the Christian cannot descend to Sheol as Christ did, it then appears that

Balthasar's repeated emphasis on the interior disposition of believers is partly necessitated by the fact that they are unable to do what He did.[79] This tension is aggravated by his approving as a Christ-like love St. Paul's desire of losing God and himself for the sake of the Jews' salvation, a desire impossible to realize.[80]

The second way Balthasar approaches the objection resolves the question concerning subjective alienation and has the additional advantage of making possible the realization of the Pauline desire. Balthasar interprets the 'dark night' of the mystics as just such a participation in Christ's descent.[81] The mystical 'dark night,' however, is itself simply a more extreme case of something found in Christian life in general: Because the Christian's mission is a participation in the mission of Jesus, he participates as well in Christ's being dead. The intensity of this participation depends on the mission he receives from God. In Christian life, as God draws closer to a person, as this person's love of God grows, and as the mission he receives is greater, God reveals Himself more.[82] However, God's self-revelation includes making apparent His being "ever-greater." The Christian, and preeminently the mystic, thus experiences God's incomprehensibility and seeming distance in proportion to His actual closeness.[83] This paradoxical nearness to God despite His seeming absence in the experience of suffering fittingly has a place in the life of all Christians,[84] because it characterized the existence of Christ, the archetype of Christians. Aside from the believer's greater or lesser share in this experience of God's seeming absence, the darkness of his faith and his Christian life as death-to-self combined with the indwelling of the Trinity suffice for participation in Christ's death.[85] The Christian's suffering and death thus take on meaning in relation to Christ's.[86]

The mystical 'dark night' is a preeminent participation in Christ's mission and thus its extremity shows the features of Christian life more clearly. As in Christ's descent, there is the greatest intimacy in the greatest distance. The 'dark night' reflects Christ's God-abandonment, mirroring the unity achieved by the Holy Spirit between the wrathful Father and the Son, unaware of this bond in Sheol.

It also reflects Christ's passivity and obedience: The 'dark night' is a contemplative moment of being purely at the disposal of God, a passivity that is not quietistic but rather a readiness or anticipated acceptance of letting God do more through the person than he himself can do or bear.[87] It thus is a participation in Christ's perfect obedience as manifested in His descent.

The 'dark night' also reflects the ignorance essential to Christ's faith and its link to His experience of forsakenness. We recall that the perfection and extent of the Son's knowledge during His economic mission varies over time. Most especially, the Son in Sheol is unaware of His union with the Father through the Holy Spirit. He thus erroneously thinks He is lost forever, and this belief intensifies His torment. Similarly,

> the equally great variation found in Christian mystical experience of God — ranging from moments of illumination to the constrictions of dryness and forsakenness — can give us an inkling of the possible variety of forms of knowledge experienced by the earthly Jesus.[88]

Balthasar thus uses the mystical 'dark night' to approach the knowledge and experience of the Son in His kenosis and abandonment. According to Balthasar, the *provisional character* of the 'dark night' ceases when the soul is adapted to the object of contemplation; the *darkness* itself does not terminate, however, "but reveals to the soul night's *own* inner and superabundant light."[89] Balthasar sees here "the counterpoint to the Alexandrian and Augustinian terminology, . . . where πίστις [faith] primarily is seen as the first step to γνῶσις [knowledge]."[90] In other words, faith during earthly life gives way not so much to knowledge, but to deeper participation in the Trinity's 'super-faith,'[91] i.e., in the divine life of eternal surprise at the personal mystery of others. The increased intimacy may be considered as knowledge, but insofar as it is intimacy with the mystery of the "ever-greater" God, it is induction into infinite darkness.

Finally, the 'dark night' reflects the Descent's *pro nobis* character, that is, as suffering on behalf of the salvation of others. Balthasar sees these experiences as being tied to the widest eschatological hope precisely in their character as a participation in Christ's mission.[92] For Balthasar, the closer the union between God and the person abandoned, the greater the privation possible; and the greater the privation, the more redemptive. Hence, the Son's abandonment is both the greatest abandonment possible, and the definitive work of redemption. This topic will be touched upon again in the following section.

Before the relation between the Descent and eschatology is considered, a few observations should be made. First, in contrasting the 'dark night' and the movement from πίστις to γνῶσις, Balthasar neglects to make clear (or else holds a contrary position) that the 'dark night' is a super-rational knowing, not an ignorance. Mystic desolation is more accurately an intensification, rather than a privation, of divine light. Moreover, the darkness of faith's 'dark night' will not remain when the mystic enters heaven. The light of glory renders the saint *capax* to see God (1 Jn 3:2: "When he appears we shall be like him, for we shall see him as he is.").[93] Faith's darkness relates to the way, not to the end.

Second, Balthasar overlooks the fact that the holy mystics' creaturehood contributes to the limits to their illumination. The holy mystics participate by grace in God's nature, but they still are not God. Hence, participation in the incarnate Son's abandonment and ignorance as proposed by Balthasar is not necessary to account for those limits.

Similarly, although a connection between darkness and sinfulness is seen in Balthasar's theology, Balthasar does not give sufficient attention to the purificatory aspect of the 'dark night,' namely, that its darkness bears a relation to the soul's imperfections. Christ had the darkest experience of God-forsakenness precisely because He took all sins into Himself to be consumed by the fire of God's wrath/love. In Christ's case, this 'fire' is clearly both undergone on behalf of others and directed against Himself personally. In the mystics' experiences, Balthasar rather emphasizes the soteriological connection, and downplays the role of the 'dark night' in their personal purification, even when made by the mystics themselves.[94]

Fourth, Balthasar argues that the desire to suffer hell if it would serve the salvation of others is expressed not infrequently in the history of mysticism.[95] No single case is brought forward, however, in which this desire is fulfilled or in which the person's experience of hell is explicitly meritorious to expiate the sins of others. The cases he discusses are quite varied; of the some fifteen cases mentioned, in only three (St. Paul, St. Mary Magdalen dei Pazzi, Marie des Vallées) is there an offer to undergo damnation on behalf of others and only one of these (St. Paul) is given in his own words, as opposed to a paraphrase (St. Mary) or a quotation of reported speech (Marie des Vallées).

Finally, Balthasar himself says that if "an explicit request, directed to God, that another's damnation be taken upon oneself" is made, it should be forbidden by the person's spiritual director.[96] This counsel seems odd if the supreme manifestation of Christ's love was in fact His experience of Sheol and if the guidance of a spiritual director is sought specifically to aid one in following Christ. The prohibition contrasts starkly with the laudable act of laying down one's physical life for another (Jn 15:13; e.g., St. Maximilian Kolbe) by which *the blood of martyrs is the seed of Christians,* i.e., is actually conducive to the salvation of others. There ought to be no such contrast if Balthasar is right in not distinguishing between physical and spiritual life. If Christ sacrifices the life of His soul for the salvation of men,[97] but Christians are to be forbidden to make such an offer, as Balthasar says, do we not then need to say Christ did something that, as a rule, is immoral for men to do — and that the Father accepted precisely this immoral act as superabundantly meritorious? No comparison can be made to Abraham's willingness to kill his son (also an act immoral as a rule) at the command of God; if Abraham's obedience meant he did not sin, yet Christ's obedience in being "made sin" as Balthasar understands it implies a contradiction, for how can a soul be just in making itself unjust?

The Descent in Relation to the End-Times

Although the Church includes the blessed in heaven, both now and after the end of time, topics such as the resurrection of the body and the end of purgatory usually serve to distinguish more properly eschatological considerations from those of ecclesiology. In Balthasar's theology, however, his ecclesiology and eschatology tend to merge. Insofar as the Church is with Christ in heaven and even on earth is configured to Him in the expectation of loving (i.e., living) faith, the Church already stands in the end-times.[98] Eschatology becomes difficult to define due to this co-penetration of time and eternity,[99] a mutual inherence that has its prototype in a particular way in the Incarnation. This difficulty is intensified by the fact that the time of the Church begins with the temporal "hiatus"[100] of Christ's experience of timeless abandonment in Sheol.[101] Rather than attempting to specify further the relation Balthasar generally sees between time and eternity, including that during their most critical moment (the Descent), we shall focus here on the effect the Descent has on the afterlife.

The Son descended into the flesh and into Sheol in order to embrace fallen creaturely freedom in the Trinitarian love by outstripping it in its most extreme form. The very extremity of Christ's descent experience in its extent, intensity, and mode means that the abode of the dead can no longer be the same afterward: Christ's being dead introduces mercy into what was a place of exacting justice, because He took upon Himself the full demands of that justice out of love. In consequence, He is made eschatological judge, since He alone knows the full extent of all crime and all guilt (i.e., of all sins), and of all punishment (i.e., sin itself as the *visio mortis* that takes the place of the *visio Dei*).[102] As eschatological judge, He holds the keys of death and hell,[103] and is free to use them how He chooses. One might put it this way: Sinful creatures incurred a debt to the Creator Father through their abuse of His loving paternal gift of finite freedom. Having exercised judgment against sin in the Person of Christ, the Father has nothing more to say on the subject, but the Son who suffered that judgment might. Sinners, who were debtors to the Father, have become debtors to the Son, while judgment is the Son's because He has undergone all judgment.[104] By suffering the punishment mankind deserved, He purchased, so to speak, mankind's debt. As a result, He is free to collect it or not.

In addition, the afterlife becomes diversified. In experiencing a *visio mortis* of universal extent in Sheol, Christ takes possession also of all more limited experiences of it. Because He does so for man's redemption, He thereby makes it pass "into his own domain as the Redeemer."[105] As a result of the reconciliation of God with the world wrought by Christ, no one will ever experience definitive eternal rejection by God as the Son experienced it. Hell (as opposed to Sheol) is "a *product* of the Redemption."[106]

> In rising from the dead, Christ leaves behind him Hades [Sheol], that is, the state in which humanity is cut off from access to God. But . . . he takes "Hell" with him, as the expression of his power to dispose, as judge, the everlasting salvation or the everlasting loss of man.[107]

In hell, sinners are confronted with the greater abandonment of Christ on their behalf.[108] His own experience of the timeless isolation of sin out of solidarity with sinners, solidarity with the physically and spiritually dead, will ever after disturb that ultimate loneliness with His once-for-all communion in it.[109] The timelessness of His experience embraces anyone else's experience of hell, regardless of when it begins.[110] To the question whether Christ descended to the farthest depths of hell, Balthasar answers "Yes,"[111] as he must, since, according to Balthasar, Christ Himself constitutes and establishes hell.[112] On this point, recall the critique made by Johannes Rothkranz:[113] Although the Constitution *Benedictus Deus* differentiates the moment of the beginning of eternal bliss for those who came before Christ and for those who came after Him, it does not so differentiate for those who do not attain beatitude.[114] Unlike heaven, hell was not closed before the accomplishment of redemption.

Also as a result of Christ's descent, according to Balthasar, purgatory is erected as an encounter with Christ the Judge. The sinner lets his view of himself, his sins, and the world be conformed to God's.[115] His purification ends when he desires to suffer yet more for the world's sin and his own part in it.[116]

Finally, with Christ's resurrection, the archetype of creation has come forth from the Father in the form of a creature and returned to Him.[117] Since Christ lived the divine life of self-gift in all possible stages of earthly life, including the abode of the dead (spiritually and physically), the earthly has been made ready for the heavenly.[118] The way to the Father for sinners was opened through Christ's descent.[119]

The Descent thus has eternal consequences for God and for the world. On the one hand, God is reconciled to the world:

> As a result of the *oikonomia*, something in the internal life of God has become different: "The new and changed dimension consists above all in the fact that judgment has now been absorbed into love. . . . Life emerges out of death."[120]

Here, Balthasar says "in the internal life of God," because all creation, and thus also the world as fallen and as redeemed, is "in" Him.

This is not the only reason, however. For, on the other hand, the consequence for the world is that finite freedom is perfected in the individual members of the Church as they are conformed to Christ through self-surrender for God and for the world. Christ's return to the Father has no other meaning but to complete "the world's incorporation into the triune life."[121] This incorporation must signify, first, the indwelling of the Trinity in the blessed through their configuration to Christ, by which they are made sons of the Father in the Son and through the Spirit. Secondly, because the Trinity is an "eternal event" and not a static object, those incorporated into the Trinity through this configuration *live* this divine life as sons; i.e., a new act pertains to their existence recreated in Christ. The world is no longer *extra muros*,[122] but participates in the Trinitarian life from within the relations. The Trinity has, so to speak, expanded through the inclusion of creatures who, incorporated into the triune life, participate in the divine event. Since this event was always openness to an other, one can say no change occurs in the Trinity as a result of this inclusion:

> The fact that the Son returns to the Father richer than when he departed, the fact that the Trinity is more perfected in love after the Incarnation than before, has its meaning and its foundation in God himself, who is not a rigid unity but a unity that comes together ever anew in love, an eternal intensification in eternal rest.[123]

This participation in Trinitarian life from within is the second reason "something in the internal life of God has become different":

> What does God gain from the world? An additional gift, given to the Son by the Father, but equally a gift made by the Son to the Father, and by the Spirit to both. It is a gift because, through the distinct operations of each of the three Persons, the world acquires an inward share in the divine exchange of life; as a result the world is able to take the divine things it has received from God, together with the gift of being created, and return them to God as a divine gift.[124]

Again,

> It will not do to locate the reason for the creation of the world in God's will to procure his own ('accidental') glorification (primary goal) by leading rational creatures to share his blessedness (secondary goal). . . . [T]he final

goal of creation, the *gloria Dei (formalis)*, can only be properly reached from the trinitarian perspective. . . . [I]t follows from the fact that the creature is drawn into the reciprocal acts of love within the Godhead so that the collaboration of each Divine Person is intended to magnify the 'glory' of the Others. . . . [T]his avoids giving the impression that the creation is basically a superfluous work since God gains nothing from it toward his own perfection and blessedness: . . . [A]ll suspicion of divine solipsism is removed from the *gloria Dei* in creation, since the inner participation of creatures in the life of the Trinity becomes an internal gift from each Divine Person to the Other: this overcomes every appearance of a merely external 'glorification.'[125]

The actual union of the creature with God in love, i.e., in the Holy Spirit, attains the character of "surprising" enrichment among the divine Persons.[126]

This inclusion *intra muros* sheds light on Balthasar's statement that "the exalted Lord is given manifest power, *even in his humanity,* to breathe forth the Spirit."[127] A Thomistic theology of the Incarnation would not say the Lord breathes the Spirit forth from His humanity even if He, incarnate, spirates Him both before and after His exaltation.[128] Within Balthasar's theology, however, the Son receives His divine attributes back after His descent, but He continues to be man — and this must be in the same way in which He became flesh, i.e., in giving back what He is to the Father. In addition, as a man living the Trinitarian life, His humanity participates in the divine vitality *intra muros*. In both ways, then, He spirates the Spirit "in his humanity." In His Trinitarian relation and in His humanity, the exalted Christ is the archetype of perfected mankind, overcoming in His person the "distance" between absolute freedom and finite freedom.

Despite the inclusion of finite creatures *intra muros*, essential change in God must be ruled out, as well as in the creature. What Balthasar says of the Incarnation can reasonably be used to reflect upon this inclusion insofar as the humanity of Jesus is the archetype for such incorporation. As we read in Chapter Seven,

> It is not that God, in himself, changes but that the unchangeable God enters into a relationship with creaturely reality, and this relationship imparts a new look to his internal relations. This is not something purely external, as if this relationship *ad extra* did not really affect him: rather, the new relationship to worldly nature, which is hypostatically united to the Son, highlights one of the infinite possibilities that lie in God's eternal life.[129]

If we are right to extend this perspective to those who are sons in the Son, it would appear that "the creature's participation in the trinitarian processions"[130] likewise entails the internal establishment of a relationship in God. This new relation need not be a union in Person — "Naturally, there will be no smoothing out of the difference in level between the originating Archetype and its effect in the participants"[131] — but it can be like the hypostatic union in being a real "internal" relation. The establishment of this relation, with its corresponding giving and receiving, would be what God "gain[s] from the world." At the same time, it would not imply change in God insofar as it was always one of the infinite possibilities within Him. As Guy Mansini explains, according to Balthasar, the divine Persons are always glorifying each other and hence they do not change if they elect the inclusion of creation in the Trinitarian life as a means to do so.[132]

Creatures also remain creatures, even if they live the Trinitarian life *intra muros*. Balthasar gives an analogical explanation for their lack of change:

> It is the same ineradicable difference as between the *communio* of the immanent Trinity (where the total self-surrender of each Hypostasis to each Other — beginning with the Father's self-surrender — grounds eternal life) and that of the economic Trinity (where the Son's self-surrender [to] the Father in the Spirit remains the abiding icon of the mystery of God's essence).[133]

Unfortunately, Balthasar's explanation is of minimal help, for two reasons. First, although the immanent Trinity is "ever-greater" than *what is revealed* of it through the economic Trinity, the *Persons* remain the same; the Son's mission *is* His procession. Hence there is no essential difference between the *communio* of the immanent Trinity and that of the economic Trinity. The only difference is the mode in which the Persons surrender themselves to each other, the mode of the *immanent* Trinity being one of the "infinite possibilities" within God just as much as that of the economic Trinity, since in both cases, there remain latent all the other possibilities.

The second difficulty is that Balthasar's explanation involves him in a self-contradiction. When discussing the variation in the Son's experience of the Father through the mediation of the Spirit "now as something more personal, now as something more impersonal," Balthasar concludes,

> The important point, however, is this: when the Son has been resurrected and the economic form of the Trinity is suspended and absorbed into the immanent, there is no reversion to former conditions; nothing needs to be "inverted" once again.[134]

In other words, a difference that Balthasar had said was "ineradicable" here is said to be "suspended and absorbed." The reader then is left in the following quandary: If this difference in *communio* between the immanent and economic Trinity is indeed "ineradicable" and endures in eternity, it means that the Son forever continues to have the Father revealed to Him through the Spirit. In effect, the Son never receives back the divine omniscience He "deposited." On the other hand, if the difference is "suspended," and Balthasar's claim that Jesus receives "manifest power, even in his humanity, to breathe forth the Spirit"[135] means only that He does not repudiate His humanity after His resurrection but spirates the Spirit with the Father in virtue of His divine nature (and not in virtue of His human nature), no explanation is given for why "the difference in level between the originating Archetype and its effect in the participants" is not similarly "absorbed." Moreover, in the case of the incarnate Son, the "suspension" of the difference would mean that He would no longer relate to God in the manner that was deemed to be the *only* mode possible if His humanity were not to be compromised. Again, change in the Son's humanity is found implied: Before His exaltation, His divine attributes could not inhere in His person without vitiating His humanity; afterward, they can. If the presence of these divine attributes in His exalted state neither overwhelms His humanity, nor changes it and His divinity into some third thing, why did these concerns necessitate His "depositing" of them in order to become incarnate in the first place? Why is it a problem for the Word to retain His divine attributes from the beginning of the Incarnation if His reception of them back in the Resurrection does not compromise His humanity?[136]

In the face of this dilemma, the only option left apparently is to say, as Balthasar says, that "naturally" the difference between divinity and finitude remains even if finite creatures are taken into the inner life of God. But help is not to be had from the philosophy of nature: The Son's human *nature* has been divinized to the extent that He spirates the Spirit "even in his humanity" — and the incarnate Son is the archetype of all creaturely participation in the divine life.

The inclusion of creatures *intra muros,* together with Balthasar's understanding of the doctrine *opera trinitatis ad extra communia,* may account for why Balthasar has no difficulty with ascribing proper acts to the divine Persons. If the world is taken into the life of Trinitarian love and participates in it, the three Persons may relate to it with proper acts, even as they relate to one another in proper relations, which relations are acts.

A difficulty arises, however, because these proper acts vis-à-vis the world depend upon the prior reconciliation of the world, in virtue of which the world can participate in the divine life. How then can there be proper acts of the divine Persons with respect to the world *prior* to the Descent event, such as Balthasar says pertain in the Incarnation and Descent? On the other hand, if the world is always in God in the way Balthasar portrays it, why is the Descent event necessary to bring about participation in the divine life? It would appear that a latent attempt to solve this dilemma may be seen in Balthasar's notion of the co-penetration of time with eternity such that, in a certain way, all moments of time are simultaneous in the eternal Now of God, but discussion of Balthasar's concept of time is outside our scope here.

The Descent and Universal Salvation

Setting aside these difficulties, we ask now what is the extent of this eschatological inclusion *intra muros*? Concerning the moment when time's "movement is taken up into God's eternal super-movement," Balthasar writes,

> There comes the moment of the Son's full victory when nothing more opposes his will, when all beings are animated by his breath. The word "all" here does not mean only all men but also all the things that were created for man, and hence also for the Son. The entire creation bears the sign of the Son. . . . Men and things are differentiated from the Son only by the distance that God has put into his creation; and the ultimate form of this distance is that between the Head and the Body, whereas the distance occasioned by sin is abolished. "Then the Son himself will be subject in his turn to the One who subjected all things to him, so that God may be all in all" (1 Cor 5:28 JB).[137]

He continues, "The Son brings his mission to a close at the point where everything enters into the triune life."[138] The Son's submission of all things in Himself is a final, and eternal, act of self-surrender in obedience to the Father.[139]

By itself, the above passage indicates what Balthasar probably thought would be the actual outcome of his hope that subjective salvation would include all men, a hope he proposed as the properly Christian one.[140] As a *hope*, he considered that it did not fall under the Church's condemnation of the doctrine of apokatastasis, which he understood as pertaining to the claim of *knowledge* of universal salvation.[141] In the present context, however, we will not consider Balthasar's arguments for his hope, objections and responses, the general nature of doctrines of apokatastasis, or the extent of the Church's condemnation.[142]

What must be briefly set forth, however, is the inherent inclination of

Balthasar's theology of Christ's descent toward a doctrine of universal salvation, whether certain or as a hope. As Balthasar sees it, universal salvation (if actual) will be the result of the utter abandonment the Son undergoes. "Every contradictory *no*" by the creature to God is wiped out "not only symbolically, but also really (in the truly vicarious suffering for sinners on the cross),"[143] a suffering which reaches its perfection in Sheol. If God overcame the opposition of every *no*, if the Son took all sins with their guilt onto Himself and expiated them by suffering their just punishment in Sheol, what sin is left in virtue of which a man could be condemned? What punishment is left for him to undergo? Cross and Hell together mean the removal of sin and guilt from all sinners, their expiation, and the completion of their punishment (and more) by Christ. All that stands between the sinner and God then is his own acceptance of God's work in Christ. Whether he can maintain a refusal forever is the question, as also whether Balthasar's theology necessarily implies he cannot, even if Balthasar refuses to draw this conclusion explicitly himself. As will be seen a little later, the damned remain such as long as they reject forgiveness. The unforgivable sin against the Holy Spirit, i.e., against the Trinitarian love and inclusion in it, is effectively this refusal to accept the forgiveness wrought in Christ.

Balthasar also sees the momentum of the Descent toward actual universal salvation as implied in every protest against the loss of any single created person and in the mystical 'dark night.'[144]

> An eschatology that leaves open the outcome of the judgment . . . and renounces any final systemization . . . has always been characteristic of the eschatology of the mystics, for whom the experiences of the 'dark night' and of 'hell' always had a soteriological meaning. . . .[145]

The experiences of the 'dark night' have a soteriological, hence eschatological, meaning insofar as they involve a sense of vicarious suffering, which, like that of Christ, introduces a communion with the lost, if only a desired one.[146] Of course, not only the mystics in their sufferings, but also the 'ordinary' Christian in his own, contribute to, and partake of, the spiritual goods of the Church that aid the salvation of men through the communion of saints.[147]

Balthasar's positive regard for death also inclines his theology toward actual universal salvation. We have already seen (in Chapter Seven) how creaturely death in its ideal form of an act of self-giving love on behalf of another is modeled on the divine "super-death." Creaturely death is also both punishment for sin and an act of mercy on God's part: "God interposes death to put an end to the creature that chose sin, lest its state of guilt should persist indefinitely."[148] He does so with a view toward the redemptive death of the Son, who will complete this work of the Father: Its penal aspect will be suffered by the incarnate Son on behalf of sinners, while its character as mercy is indicated by the redemption accomplished through it, which changes death into a way for men to participate in the divine life.[149] In virtue of Jesus' unique being dead on behalf of all sinners distinct from their own disposition, "the death of sinners acquires an objective relation to Christ's death."[150] Even the death of those "who die turned away from God" receives "a totally new value."[151] If all sin and guilt were taken upon Christ and destroyed in His descent, guilt indeed does not "persist indefinitely" — as it would persist eternally in hell if, contrary to Balthasar, guilt is inalienably personal. Again, it appears that the only thing to stand between a man and his salvation is neither his sins nor his guilt, but only recognition and acceptance of the Trinity's redemptive work.

Balthasar thinks hell remains a possibility because the possibility exists for a free creature to refuse this recognition and acceptance, i.e., to reject God's desire for it.[152] Created freedom is an image of infinite freedom, hence a real freedom. On the other hand, he points out that it is truly freedom only when it orients itself beyond itself, to the ultimate other, to the absolute good, to God.[153] Obedience to God and the acceptance of redemption necessary for salvation are necessarily correlative to this perfect finite freedom. In contrast, "if created freedom chooses itself as the absolute good, it involves itself in a contradiction that will devour it. . . . This contradiction, if persisted in, is hell."[154] Hell then would be "a personal and existential question,"[155] a "condition of the damned person himself,"[156] not a place to which God actively thrusts him and which affects him by its conditions.[157] It is not essentially painful punishment, but hatred of God.[158] Insofar as this contradiction has its most extreme form when God manifests to the one under judgment his true nature and vocation as finite freedom, however, hell can be said to be in God.[159]

The question arises whether the sinner's rejection of the truth about himself and God's relation to him as Creator, Redeemer, and Sanctifier can be maintained eternally. Although man receives a real freedom to make a choice against God that seems definitive for him, *God* need not take this choice as definitive.[160] Otherwise, His absolute freedom (which is identical to His omnipotence) would be compromised.[161]

The Descent of the Son indicates that God does not in fact take man's choice as definitive, but instead reconciles the world in a way that utilizes this very human lostness. The Lord fashions alienation from God into a way to Him;[162] utilizes lost finite freedom in redeeming mankind;[163] endows death's futility as such with meaning;[164] and changes the objective value of death.[165] By no means does God take man's subjectively definitive choice against Him as binding; He did not do so before the redemptive Incarnation and Descent event

— its occurrence shows He did not — and He will not do so after: Jesus descends into the definitiveness of the choice of selfishness over selfless love in "solidarity *in nontime* with those who have been lost to God."[166] The Cross is erected at the far end of hell,[167] beyond every rejection of God, and Christ "in his dying has reached the end of the world,"[168] the end of time, by timelessly embracing all sins committed within time.

If so, the Son's subjective descent experience apparently is not limited to the objective time between His death and His resurrection, because some of these sinners whose lostness He disturbs died after the time of Christ. By not fixing the Son's experience in time,[169] Balthasar allows its extension beyond time; i.e., the Son's lostness out of love can as well affect the lostness of any sinners damned at the end of time as much as it prevented the holy dead of the Old Testament from experiencing the full impact of Sheol.[170] If hell, like purgatory, consists in the sinner's encounter with the divine fire of judgment,[171] it is not unreasonable to say that the damned sinner finds Christ in solidarity with him, suffering this same fire of wrath in "nontime" and thus disturbing his rejection of God in the very moment of judgment. The utter isolation of the sinner who has damned himself is disrupted by the presence of the God of love in that very abandonment,[172] indeed in an abandonment that exceeds that of the sinner. Balthasar describes the conversion of Raskolnikov in Dostoevsky's *Crime and Punishment* as one of several possible "metaphors"[173] for this disturbance, i.e., for

> the unimaginable process whereby man, timelessly closed in upon himself, is opened up by the ineluctable presence of Another, who stands beside him, equally timelessly, and calls into question his apparent, pretended inaccessibility. Man's shell is not hard enough, however, for it is formed of a contradiction. Perhaps the man whose shell can be broken open is not yet really in hell but only — in his rebellious attitude to God — turned toward it.[174]

Although Balthasar in this text does not explicitly assert that this disturbance provides an occasion after death for conversion, active or passive, an inclination in that direction is given. If seeing God's love go to such an extreme should convince the living sinner to follow Him,[175] and if Christ's presence marks the afterlife of the damned, then this second premise seems pointless unless it follows that dead sinners also have some way back to God. Otherwise, the presence that meant salvation for others could mean an increase in torment, rather than the tempering of Sheol as Balthasar asserts.

It seems this 'conversion' is more passive than active. The same divine freedom that stepped beyond the original human rejection of God to redeem mankind comes into play in the judgment of individuals.

> Man's verdict on himself in his relation to God cannot be the last act of the Judgment. . . . While infinite freedom will respect the decisions of finite freedom, it will not allow itself to be compelled, or restricted in its own freedom, by the latter.[176]

Metaphorically speaking, one might say God has veto power over man's refusal, or that He has a final ace to play. This 'ace' is the gift of the perfection of finite freedom.

The perfection of finite freedom is participation in the Trinitarian life of love, in which the absolute freedom of God is always both given and received. Until finite freedom finds its place there, some part of its freedom is "laid up" (or "deposited") with God in order that it may be received "as the final gift that will bring [the creature's] freedom to fulfillment."[177] If man then can only be truly free in conformity to Christ in this divine life, his power and freedom to reject God totally is not absolute as long as that life is not perfected in him:

> Hell *was* necessarily the fate of man, where he *had recognized* this vicarious deed of God but *consciously* rejected it; anyone who *has received* the *fullness* of the goods of *the end time* and 'tasted them,' yet 'falls away again,' 'cannot possibly again attain repentance,' and 'his end is to be burned' (Heb 6:4-8; *cf.* 12:25f.).[178]

A man's judgment of himself just before dying, and God's judgment of him just after, will thus necessarily differ in their finality.

Consequently, when the finite creature considers his judgment before God, and ultimately stands before Him,

> the appropriate attitude will be a hope that is not without a certain fear. For if it is true that not only a person's last moment but his entire life is to be the object of judgment, it is impossible that 'nothing worthy of damnation' will be found in him.[179]

The matter of concern is not quantitative, but

> it is something qualitative here that cannot enter into the kingdom of God. . . . Accordingly his hope can only cling blindly to the miracle that *has already taken place* in the Cross of Christ; it takes the entire courage of

Christian hope for a man to apply this to himself, to trust that, by the power of this miracle, what is damnable in him *has been separated* from him and thrown out with the unusable residue that is incinerated outside the gates of the Holy City.[180]

The sinner sees what merits damnation in him, yet he must trust that this has, already before his judgment, been removed from him and destroyed.

God, on the other hand, looks not for whether there is anything damnable, but whether the sinner's rejection of Him has been deliberate and total.

> In order to proceed to condemnation, the divine Judge would have to encounter nothing contrary to a rejection on man's part, nothing that would relativize it.[181]

> We must ask whether a negative fundamental decision, even if it is chronologically the last in a particular life, can have expressed itself in all life situations without exception. What, for example, about early and later childhood?[182]

Balthasar's theology of the Descent conditions his account of the judgment, because the Son's experience in Sheol both justifies the possibility of a 'passive conversion' (if it occurs) and brings it about: Christ's suffering of the Father's wrath for the sins of all permits this ultimate mercy without requiring a betrayal of the justice God owes Himself, while His own being dead in abandonment disturbs that of the sinner's.

Given the foregoing, actual universal salvation appears to be a necessary conclusion implicit in Balthasar's theology of Christ's descent. First, note the reversal implied by his description of God's criterion of judgment: Rather than one mortal sin at the end of life sufficing for damnation, one good act (which is not necessarily even an act of divine charity) any time in life may suffice for ultimate salvation. This act is the crack, as it were, in the shell the sinner sets between himself and God even in hell.

Second, the deliberate and total rejection such as Balthasar thinks necessary for condemnation is impossible, because a choice against God by finite freedom in this life is not a decision made in true freedom insofar as it lacks the final gift of perfection "laid up" with God. Although Balthasar writes, "A sinner might so identify himself with his No to God that Trinitarian love would be unable to loosen the resultant snarl,"[183] such rejection that leaves the sinner to experience God's love as wrath requires not only the gift of perfect freedom but also that he "resist the triune work of atonement with *full* consciousness and realization."[184] So long as his understanding of this work is partial, his rejection of it is held to be partial as well. Full realization hence seems possible only after death, when the truth of God as Trinity and His action on a person's behalf is revealed to the soul in a way surpassing even the eminent knowledge had by faith. Though Balthasar points out that "Scripture prohibits us from saying that this deliberate No is impossible,"[185] it appears at least morally impossible within his own system of thought, given his insistence on full consciousness and full freedom, both of which can only be attained after death.[186] One may wonder whether it is not impossible simply speaking within his theology: Of all men, only Christ perfectly identified Himself with His mission.[187] If other men cannot identify themselves perfectly even with that for which they were made, how can they identify themselves wholly with a rejection of God?

Third, the Descent confirms the strong possibility of universal salvation from another perspective, as well. The quality that "cannot enter the kingdom of God" is the sinful attitude of resistance toward God,[188] as well as actual sin and guilt. Recall that the Christian is conformed to Christ preeminently in his disposition of obedience and sacrifice, and that his deeds should flow from this attitude. But this attitude, and likewise an attitude of rejection, is not something that can be lived apart from particular acts.[189] Since all sinful deeds and the guilt for them have already been destroyed in the Descent event of Trinitarian love, consequently this attitude of resistance must also already have been destroyed with them (though observation indicates otherwise) — if not, no sinner could ever be redeemed. Specifically, since the Son subjectively experiences Sheol as eternal, and since its relation to time is impossible to determine, Christ's redemptive expiation can be *actual* at the moment of each sinner's judgment. His descent thus would embrace in the "ever-greater" Trinitarian love even a *final* act (or attitude) of rejection.[190]

Fourth, since every person has some sin that is borne down to Sheol with the Son, every sinner's way to perfection of life follows the Son's way to the Father through lostness, abandonment, and the fire of wrath. The futility of death (physical *and* spiritual) thus is given ultimate meaning in its conformity to the Son's being dead in utter passivity to the will of the Father as the way to enter and participate in the Trinitarian love. Christ's death gave meaning to the futility of existence *as such* and "hope to those who live under the rule of death, hope in a life with God which overcomes death."[191] But no existence is more futile than the eternal existence of the damned is to themselves. Are not they those who most definitively "live under the rule of death"? Did not Christ's being dead in Sheol mean no one shall ever have to suffer such definitive abandonment by God as He did? Thus it would seem hope and a way are provided also for those in this ultimate futility.

Fifth, Balthasar insists that God will not allow Himself to be restricted by finite freedom's choice against Him and that all sins, even those of apparently unrepentant sinners, have already been destroyed and expiated in the Descent. These two factors suggest why Balthasar's characterization of hope as "the appropriate attitude" at the time of judgment can in fact describe a hope possible to anyone, whatever the state of his soul, since no mention is made of repentance or of sacramental confession. Since every man has something "worthy of damnation" in him, each person can only hope that God will grant him the gift of perfect freedom out of His own absolute freedom and out of consideration for the imperfect character of his rejection of God. In addition, if the sins and guilt of each sinner have been consumed in the Person of Christ regardless of his acceptance of redemption, then not even justice need prevent God from granting him the gift of perfect freedom. As a consequence, however, the individual's salvation is something voluntaristic on the part of God, and the *certain* hope of Catholics in ages past — that if they persisted in the means of salvation they would be led to the Father's house in virtue of the Son's promises and merits — appears unfounded.

Finally, if the possibility of finite creatures' falling away from God binds God to provide a way back to Him, then the same argument may be brought to bear on the second chance itself. The result will be a regress necessarily ending in universal salvation, since no finite creature could freely act against the order of his being an infinite number of times.

Although Balthasar characterizes Jesus in the Gospel of John as calling for a decision for or against Him, which "absolute decision must be made in one's earthly life; in the hereafter it will be too late . . . ,"[192] if we are to preserve both his theology and agreement with this doctrine of Christ's, mustn't we say that man cannot make this ultimate decision after death, but *God* makes it for the otherwise damned with the trump of the perfection of finite freedom, in which no one can be against God? However, this gift of free choice still requires an act of decision on the part of the recipient. Such a gift and decision amount precisely to conversion after death, since the two are necessary only in the case of those who rejected God in earthly life. There are reasons then to doubt whether Balthasar is wholly in accord with Jesus' doctrine as he himself presents it.

For the reasons discussed above, as well as the fact that Balthasar's primary argument in support of hope for the salvation of all is that the eternal loss of some implies a defect in God's omnipotence, it would appear Balthasar's denials of apokatastasis are just as "rhetorical" as those for which he criticizes Karl Barth.[193] James T. O'Connor comments that, "while explicitly and repeatedly stating that a synthesis cannot be made which will give us certitude on this matter, [Balthasar] appears to make one *in practice, not in theory.*"[194] Which is to say that Balthasar verbally denies the necessary conclusions of the principles he sets forth.

Before closing this section on eschatology and the Descent, certain questions must be raised. First, in his eschatological treatments, Balthasar frequently identifies hell with hatred of God. In this way, he can deny Christ goes to hell, even while asserting explicitly that He goes to gehenna and that He there experiences something far worse than hell.[195] Balthasar's denial raises the question whether Christ is really solidary with sinners as Balthasar would have Him be. If we assume Christ takes on the guilt of all sinners as well as the objective alienation from God that is the result of sin, as Balthasar says, is Christ really solidary "from within" with sinners in their condition if He does not experience, if not sinful hatred itself, then hatred's rage against God? If the judgment of God is a punishing rather than purifying fire insofar as it is derived from and aimed at the sinner's relation to God,[196] can subjective and objective realities be separated from each other, such as when Balthasar says the Son made sin will "interpret," not the attitude of evildoers, but their experience of God?[197] If God does not thrust anyone from Him,[198] i.e., does not damn anyone, but the obstinate sinner damns himself, such that God-abandonment is on the part of the sinner, can Christ be solidary with all the dead and conform Himself to the sin separated from all sinners without being conformed to hatred of God? Can He be eschatological judge without doing so, since Balthasar has said that He must know experientially from within all the states of the fallen man He is to redeem?[199]

Second, contradictions are embedded in Balthasar's idea that Christ's descent makes Him present to the lost of all time: If hell is to lose God, or to want to lose Him, it must mean the loss of Christ, as well. In addition, since Balthasar thinks Christ's descent tempered Sheol for the holy persons who died before Him, it is not unreasonable to think the prevenient effects of His being dead should apply also to those damned before His descent. However, both Balthasar's explicit position regarding the holy dead and its corollary with respect to the damned undermine his idea that the underworld was different after the Descent. That is, by making the effects of Christ's descent prevenient, Balthasar has differentiated the afterlife prior to the Descent, something he had strenuously argued against in favor of Christ's solidarity with all the dead. Finally, if the holy people who died before Christ did not experience Sheol's full fury, where were they?

Third, the question arises whether mortal sin exists in Balthasar's theology and, if so, what it would be. Man is necessarily ordered to God by being created in the image of God and by his vocation. For such a creature to lose God would indeed be a hell of self-contradiction. But can he actually thus damn himself if, in choosing any particular good, he is implicitly seeking the absolute Good? And since no sin however grave changes this basic order of his nature, can he hold out forever if confronted with the love of God in Christ even in hell? The logic of the problem suggests that, for a sin to be truly deadly, it must destroy the principle of life in a man, namely, his likeness and orientation to the living God. If mortal sin is thus impossible, then an eternal hell as punishment of such likewise would be impossible.

Fourth, Balthasar refers to the superabundance of Christ's satisfaction, which means "God's love is stronger than any resistance to accepting it."[200] He then goes on to say, "We cannot predict which will go on longer: God's 'yes' or men's 'no.'" The difficulty with such an argument, and its metaphorical presentation, is threefold: As Balthasar himself points out with respect to hell, a possibility need not be a reality; likewise the possibility of redemption due to the superabundance of Christ's satisfaction need not become a reality for any particular individual. Secondly, the strength of God's love is not at issue, for Balthasar himself points out God's love will not force a *yes* from man. Finally, the metaphor of time 'loads the question': It invites an expectation that God's *yes* will last "longer" than man's *no*, because unlike man, God is both eternal and omnipotent. Ultimately, however, the issue is not one of the adequacy of Christ's merits, or of the fervor of God's love, or of its permanence, but rather one of sincerity, i.e., the unity of truth and life: Does not Catholic anthropology hold that the fate of the whole person, body and soul, is determined by his actions precisely as such a unity, i.e., before the separation of body and soul in death?[201] If one accepts Balthasar's characterization of God as *yes* and the sinner as *no*, does not God's *yes* confirm man's *no*, allowing man the full reality of his rejection of God? Or, from the perspective of Balthasar's principles, one may argue that, if God's "depositing" of His divine attributes to become man manifests His freedom to do what He will with His own nature, so should His free binding of Himself by the decisions of His creatures to accept or reject Him. One might ask whether Balthasar thinks God's freedom of judgment is threatened as much by faithful adherence to His commands (e.g., the Blessed Virgin Mary, or even someone who dies after receiving the final sacraments) as by the sinner's rejection. Balthasar has posed the wrong question in asking whether God will allow Himself to be restricted by finite freedom. God may not be bound by His creatures, but He is bound to be faithful to Himself (2 Tim 2:13). Hence, if God has given rational creatures a *real* but finite freedom that includes the possibility of sin, with all its consequences up to and including damnation, He *is* bound (by Himself) to accept someone's ultimate preference of something else over Him. Consequently, He is in fact *not* bound to provide any second chance, 'guarantee,' or theodicy, as Balthasar thinks He is, if He is to create 'responsibly.'[202]

A last observation must be made. Balthasar's position that man's freedom to reject God is not absolute as long as he does not participate in the perfection of finite freedom has the corollary that the blessed in heaven can turn their backs on God. This unusual doctrine receives confirmation from Balthasar: "Man can break off his relationship with heaven; even 'in death he can turn his back on the light of eternal life.'"[203] The immediate context of this quotation at first suggests that the *sinner* undergoing judgment can deny the truth of God's love that went all the way to Sheol for him, and thus cling to the sins from which he has been redeemed. The extravagance of God's mercy is too much for him, and so, since he prefers a relationship of justice, he will receive judgment, not mercy.

Balthasar continues shortly thereafter, however, with a quotation from Adrienne von Speyr, "The greater a man's intimacy with the Lord, the greater the danger that he will become estranged."[204] This general statement transcends its context first in its generality, but secondly and more importantly in that its subject is the man *intimate with the Lord*, not the man estranged from Him in sin and hence under judgment. In other words, the more free a man is through sharing in the divine life of absolute freedom, the more in danger he is of losing it. There is a likeness here in the blessed to the Trinitarian freedom that gives "without securities," and particularly to the incarnate Son, who as the most intimately related to the Father could go — and did go — into the greatest abandonment.

Earlier we saw Balthasar was not able to provide argument for his claim that Christ could not sin because not being able to sin is a greater freedom; here we see he has contradicted the basis of his own claim by asserting a greater freedom means a greater danger of estrangement. Either this principle about intimacy — to which Balthasar evidently subscribes — does not in fact hold (with consequences for those parts of his thought dependent on it) or Christ's sinlessness is merely an assertion for Balthasar, one otherwise inconsistent with his thought. The first option amounts to denying one of Balthasar's central theses, namely, that the basis of Christ's descent experience is His closeness to the Father, i.e., His own substantial divinity and absolute freedom. On the other hand, if the principle holds, it is difficult to see why Balthasar denies Christ the possibility of sinning: As the one closest to God, He should be in the greatest danger of becoming estranged from Him, not only through vicarious acceptance of the sin of the world, but also through personal sin. For "the greater the danger" does not signify so much that there is more to lose (although that is true, as well), but rather that the estrangement is more likely. Hence the Son should be the one most likely to sin (i.e., the one in greatest danger) since He is the most intimate with the Father.

The corollary we are considering has implications not only for Christ's sinlessness, but also for the final end of the blessed. Based on the example of the Son, who is creation's archetype, it can be said that finite freedom is not for a union that rests in perfect communion with God, but for a 'union' (unapprehended in its most perfect case) in abandonment by God, since intimacy with God tends proportionately toward this estrangement. Balthasar will say that the love of God in the Spirit exceeds even the estrangement of Sheol, but Christ is unconscious of the Spirit in His descent experience and, in being dead *thus*, most perfectly reveals the glory of God. St. Paul's remark of encouragement and consolation that the sufferings of the present are not worth comparison with the glory to be revealed in us (Rom 8:18) takes on the most chilling connotations in this setting. To object that this corollary for the blessed conflates the communion in self-surrender of the immanent Trinity with its economic expression as alienation and abandonment is ineffective. The quotation from Adrienne von Speyr that Balthasar has used as part of his own argument speaks in general terms and is brought forward precisely in the context of the creature about to enter the life of the immanent Trinity, or to be excluded from it.

The Descent and Mariology

The foremost example of creaturely participation in the Trinitarian life of self-giving love through Christ is the Blessed Virgin Mary. Even as the mystical 'dark night' is a more intense participation in the mission of Christ that characterizes every Christian life, Mary's participation in Christ's God-forsakenness manifests the perfection of the mystical 'dark night': First, her life embodies the union with God that has no securities yet is perfectly faithful. Her pure, definitive, and unlimited *fiat* is evidence of her sinlessness,[205] i.e., her immaculate conception and her perfect conformity to the will of God. Her *fiat* "is an act of perfect self-surrender to God in faith. Nothing is extorted from God, nor is any claim made vis-à-vis him."[206] She gives her *yes* to the Incarnation and everything that follows from it, including the Cross and ultimate forsakenness.[207]

Second, her union with God is essentially directed to self-abandonment and to abandonment by God. She says *yes* for herself, but also on behalf of all men, whether they will add their own consent to it or not.[208] Like her Son,

> she is in solidarity with [sinners], unconditionally, precisely *because* she is "immaculately conceived" and hence, in love infinitely at their disposal, infinitely available.[209]

This solidarity will necessarily mean that she too, like her Son, will be abandoned.[210] Separation between her and her Son

> is consummated on the Cross, when the Son withdraws from his mother and passes her to another: "Woman, there is your son" (Jn 19:26), thus admitting Mary into the same godforsakenness that he himself is experiencing in his separation from the Father. The intimacy of one's share in Jesus'

destiny and mission is gauged by the intimacy of one's share in his central salvific experience. Here the degree of inner participation is the degree of the experience of absence.[211]

The proximate cause of Mary's God-abandonment (and God-abandonment specifically by the Son) is, in effect, Christ's ignorance. Because the Father "has kept the Son from seeing his own redemptive achievement,"[212] Mary's sinless presence at the foot of the cross calls into question the very necessity of His agony, even mocks it. In this estrangement from her, Christ

> is forsaken *absolutely*, and the only way of fellowship with him is to take leave of him and plunge into forsakenness. He must withdraw from his Mother just as the Father has withdrawn from him: 'Woman, behold your son.'[213]

As the substantial love of the Father and Son, the Holy Spirit united the other two divine Persons in their mutual abandonment during the Descent event; likewise the Blessed Virgin Mary and Jesus are united in a "community of love and forsakenness. . . . [E]ach partner dies alone, yet death is shared."[214]

Third, her union in abandonment has soteriological consequences, in line with Balthasar's idea that the one who believes, does so on behalf of those who do not believe. Her sharing in her Son's death in utter forsakenness will make both His death and her participation in it fruitful. The new life that results is seen first of all in Mary herself as representative of the Church as a whole, but may also be seen individually in each Christian who participates in the divine life through death to self and in each mystic who participates in Christ's descent on behalf of the salvation of others and his own.

Balthasar ties Mariology to the Cross event, Christian participation in it, the Eucharist, ecclesiology, and eschatology with the language of marital sexual fertility. Under the cross, in solidarity with Jesus in being abandoned and with sinners by saying *yes* on their behalf, Mary is the "virginal Bride of the Son of God himself, who gives himself away eucharistically."[215] Due to her *fiat* of self-surrender to God, her abandonment by her Son, and her solidarity with sinners, she is 'poor' and "the only one able to receive the seed of God, eucharistically multiplied — thousands-fold — into her womb."[216] In the making of the New Covenant at the death of the Lamb, the world is judged (Jn 12:31), and

> in the midst of it, and precisely because of it, the marriage of the Lamb and his Bride and Spouse is celebrated: this union rends the "curtain" that separated God from the earth . . . (Mt 27:51).[217]

Mary's consent to her poverty and to being made fruitful by God contrast with finite freedom's sinful self-assertion, i.e., with

> man's attempt to banish God from finitude in order to avoid receiving (and conceiving) from him, his endeavor to bring forth fruit on his own . . . — attempts that are doomed to sterility.[218]

In solidarity with sinners apparently due to her condition as creature, her mission as the one to give a just response to God's redemptive action in the Incarnation and Cross event, and her preeminent abandonment by her Son, Mary stands under the cross, representing all sinners and answering *yes* for them, "whether they will receive or not,"[219] so that they are "undergirded and sustained not only by the Word of God who dies in darkness 'for them' and on their behalf but also by the response of the Church. . . ."[220]

Applying Balthasar's principles, one may surmise Mary's obedience and self-gift to God, although perfect, are insufficient to be redemptive by themselves for two reasons.[221] First, her entire existence is not kenotic. As a creature, she was not able to offer an "antecedent consent" to her existence such that her very being would only exist as a result of obedient receptivity and hence would wholly be a passive "letting be." Second, as a creature, she has not the infinite freedom of God to dispose of herself to the point of dispossessing herself of what she is. She is not a self-subsisting relation of the divine nature that is self-surrender and self-gift.

What remains unclear in Balthasar's Mariology in connection with the Cross (and Hell) event is what the elements of his metaphor of marriage are intended to indicate. For example, how can Mary or the Church effectively consent on behalf of another who is unwilling, without overriding that person's finite freedom? It is also difficult to see how Mary herself is redeemed if she had no sin, since in Balthasar's theology it is by the transfer of the actual guilt of sin to Jesus and His suffering of its punishment in Sheol that someone is redeemed. Christ cannot suffer Sheol as punishment for a sin that never was (e.g., for a putative original sin of Mary) without the Father being grossly (immorally?) unjust. In contrast, a soteriology of merit permits a gift (the Immaculate Conception) to be granted prior to the event that merits this concession. If Balthasar's soteriology of quantitative penal substitution is correct, Christ *rightly* thinks His death is unnecessary when He sees Mary at the foot of the cross: If she has true finite freedom but is sinless without anything from her being consumed in His person, the same could have been true of all other men.

Conclusion

In this chapter, the centrality of the Descent to the theology of Hans Urs von Balthasar has been traced. Man is created in the image of the Son, whose Descent is the guarantee and ultimate means of restoration for man's finite freedom. In this world, fallen man enters anew the life of self-gift through the sacraments, and attains his ultimate end in virtue of the redemptive Descent event. The most perfect example of Christian life is found in Mary. However, her sinlessness imports an ambiguity into her relationship to the redemptive event of Cross and Hell, and hence also into her ability to be representative of the rest of mankind. As has been seen, Balthasar's Trinitarian theology of the Descent is central to his reflections in the other areas of theology. In fact, it conditions them, either by means of an explicit connection (as in his Trinitarian theology, soteriology, Christology, and theology of the Eucharist) or an implicit one (as in his sacramental theology, ecclesiology, Mariology, and eschatology). In the latter case, the indirect connection to the Descent is effected through a theological element that is directly linked to it, usually his theology of the Trinity. The determining influence of the Descent on Hans Urs von Balthasar's theological reflections is like that of a rock dropped into a calm pool of water. The effects are most significant and visible in the center (Trinitarian theology and soteriology), while the influence lessens proportionately as one moves toward the periphery. Nevertheless, even the farthest shore sees at least a ripple.

PART THREE

General Comparison and Conclusion

CHAPTER TEN

Global Questions about the Theological Opinion of Hans Urs von Balthasar

In Part Two, Balthasar's theology of the Descent, its Trinitarian aspect, and its central role in other areas of his theology were set forth. Theological evaluation of his doctrine as a whole was not undertaken; rather such observations were restricted to comments intended to clarify his opinions or necessitated by their relevance to a specific detail of his theology. However, certain broad tendencies of Balthasar's theology of the Descent also raise questions and difficulties. In keeping with the Christological focus of the Descent, the topics to be considered primarily fall into two groups, one relating to the Person of the Son as such, and the other to His two natures. A third topic, relating to methodological issues, will close the chapter.

Matters concerning the Person of the Son

The first area of concern, matters concerning the Person of the Son, must be approached with reference to Balthasar's Trinitarian theology. Our questions concerning the Person of the Son take the form of questions about how Balthasar understands the divine relations in general, because the divine Persons — including the Son who descends into Sheol — are the divine relations. Already touched upon in Chapter Seven, the key problem concerns Balthasar's understanding of how the divine essence is related to the divine Persons.

As set forth earlier following St. Thomas, a relation imports both its existence (*esse*) and its reference to another (the *ratio* of this *esse*). These two aspects are not strictly separable: The reference to another only is insofar as it has existence. As an accident, a relation has its existence in another. This existence is in the mind of the knower in the case of a logical relation, but it is in the thing itself in the case of a real relation. A relation may thus generally be described as an *esse in ad*. Since a divine Person is a real relation that subsists in the divine essence, in which there are no accidents, each of the three Persons self-subsists even as the divine essence self-subsists. Put the other way around, because the divine relations are not accidents, the divine essence does not exist other than as the three divine Persons. Each of the divine Persons then is the divine *esse* (including all its essential perfections), albeit in a unique mode, i.e., in the *esse ad* of a particular relation, that of Father, Son, or Holy Spirit. Likewise, since the divine perfections such as omniscience are identical with the divine essence, again because there are no accidents in God, then they are also inseparable from the Persons. Accordingly, even if the nature of human thought requires that some propositions can be affirmed of the Persons but not of the essence and vice versa, any division or separation of the essence from the Persons *in reality* is impossible.

In contrast, Balthasar appears to understand a self-subsisting relation as a reference to another (an *ad*, so to speak) that, because it is self-subsisting and not an accident, does not exist *in* anything. Instead, the divine essence exists *in* these self-subsisting relations. Although there is a certain likeness here to what was said just above, there is also a significant difference, since for Balthasar the divine attributes are explicitly separable from the Persons. The reader will recall the analogy of the Trinity as three glasses filled with the divine attributes. This way of understanding the divine relations has several implications. First, it makes the divine essence a fourth thing in the Trinity, effectively dividing the divine Persons from the divine nature. Second, it imports real composition in the divine Persons, either because the divine nature is taken as a fourth thing or — what amounts to the same thing — because the divine nature is divided between alienable attributes such as omniscience and a single inalienable one, self-giving. Third, *the divine nature* then is an *equivocal* term as applied to the divine attributes and to self-subsisting self-gift, but refers more properly to the latter. We have already seen that "it is only because the Son in very truth possesses the 'form of God' . . . that he can 'empty himself' and take 'the form of a servant.'"[1] Possessing the form of God (insofar as this is taken to be self-surrender[2]), the Son as a divine Person empties Himself of the form of God (insofar as this is taken to be the divine attributes), in order to assume the form of a servant, namely, human nature, i.e., human attributes. Possession of the divine attributes as just one of the infinite possibilities of God's life manifests the division between Person and nature, and the equivocation of speaking of the divinity. The divine nature is more properly not the divine attributes but the hypostatic self-giving of the Persons, since this latter is inalienable, constitutes the Persons regardless of what attributes they possess, and is what all three (or at least Father and Son) have in common. Fourth, divinity becomes a species, that of self-giving hypostases, and the divine Persons become things of this certain kind. Fifth, to distinguish the members of this divine species, it becomes necessary to find a principle of individuation. This principle is still said to be the various relations among the Persons, but these relations are effectively distinguished not so much simply by being toward another in a distinct way based on origin, but by proper operations. The Holy Spirit's proper act of incarnating the Son and of being love as bond are the clearest examples.[3] Sixth, as there is then a real difference among the three Persons, their work *ad extra* becomes a matter of consensus and cooperation, instead of the operation of a single will and power. Finally, it becomes equivocal to say the Word has both the divine nature and a human nature: A thing is said to be what it is according to its nature, and natures are known through their essential attributes. These attributes are not anything other than the nature in reality but represent a composite way of thinking about it. In Balthasar's theology, Jesus is divine because He has the 'divine nature' of hypostatic self-giving, but He is man because He possesses human attributes instead of the divine attributes He deposited in order to become incarnate.[4] As Balthasar's soteriology turns on the Word, having been made man, then being "literally 'made sin'" out of obedience, the value of His human nature in the work of redemption becomes questionable.

Not surprisingly, Balthasar denies the divine essence is a fourth thing, as if it would be "aloof from the busy to-and-fro of what passes between the Persons [i.e., the processions]: no, it must be identical with it."[5] Nonetheless, it remains difficult to reconcile this one statement with his many other, more elaborated presentations of the Trinity, unless we take it to refer to the divine nature of self-gift. Indeed, in the very place where he makes this denial, a real distinction between the divine Persons and the divine nature seems latent when he says they are "identical at every point 'except where the distinct relationships [between the Persons] requires otherwise.'"[6] The distinction of Persons actually requires quite a large area in which they would not be identical, since "the divine hypostases know and interpenetrate each other to the *very same degree* that each of them opens up to the other in absolute freedom."[7] Given the unpredictability of what one will reveal to the other, and given that such surprise continues for all eternity, the realm in which the Persons do not "interpenetrate" each other must be quite large.[8] The Trinitarian perichoresis is limited precisely to the extent to which surprise exists among the divine Persons.

Consider also the following:

> The subject of the suffering is the person who is the Word (and *the Son is the Word precisely as a divine person, not as a divine nature,* which he shares with the Father and the Spirit), even if he requires human nature to suffer.[9]

Presented outside its context, this quotation could appear to be part of an exposition of the doctrine of the communication of idioms. A distinction between person and nature would be legitimate and necessary in such grammatical treatments. Balthasar is not discussing grammar, however, but rather attempting to characterize the suffering of the Son *as Son,* which he sees as a reality, notwithstanding the qualification about the necessity of His human nature. As Gerard F. O'Hanlon says, Balthasar refuses "to limit the change and suffering which Christ experiences to his human nature alone";[10] the communication of idioms is more than logical. Balthasar thus goes beyond simply asserting that the *Son* suffers in the flesh, but holds that the Son *as such* suffers. In such a context, it would have been crucial to bear in mind that, precisely as a *divine* person, the Son *is* the divine nature and that the divine nature is impassible.

A division between divine Person and divine nature is also latent in Balthasar's description of the Trinitarian processions being the result of a gift of the divine nature: "God the Father can give his divinity away. . . . He does not extinguish himself by self-giving, just as he does not keep back anything of himself either."[11] If the Father's divinity is not other than His person, then in giving His divinity away, He must also give His person away; or, if He is not "extinguished" in this gift, He must "keep back" at least His hypostasis. Balthasar goes with this latter position; hence "the Father communicates to [the Son and the Spirit] all that is his — except the act of giving, which he cannot give away."[12] Again, in the case of the Son, Balthasar says that "in his Resurrection, the Son receives himself — with body and soul, with divinity and humanity — back from the Father."[13] What receives divinity and humanity back? It appears it must be the hypostasis of the Son, which, being made sin in His being dead, existed only with the nature of sin.

Finally, consider an image of Balthasar's own:[14] "The pitcher of the Word is empty because the source in heaven, the speaking mouth, the Father, has dried up. The Father has withdrawn." Here we have the mouth, the pitcher, and (implicitly) that which they both contained. Balthasar's image parallels the patristic image of the fountain, or of the spring and river, but with a certain twist. For the Fathers, the fountain and what flows from it are inseparable and inexhaustible; similarly, neither spring nor river remains without the water that constitutes them. In contrast, Balthasar's image admits of the existence of a dry source and an empty pitcher: The spring can cease to fill the pitcher with water, while the water is separable both from the mouth from which it flows and from the pitcher into which it flows. This image reflects the way Balthasar treats the Trinitarian relations as subsisting receptacles of the divine nature.

As Balthasar divides the divine Persons from the divine attributes, he also divides the Persons from each other by ascribing to them proper operations and by treating the divine will as one in the thing decided, not as a single identical power. The existence of proper operations suggests that the English translations' frequent use of *different,* rather than *distinct,* in passages treating of the Persons in their relations to one another accurately reflects Balthasar's theology. In general, proper acts of the Persons are entailed in the notion of one Person surprising the other, and likewise in Balthasar's idea that each Person has His "own area of freedom,"[15] which the others respect or "let be."[16] That the Persons have proper operations in Balthasar's theology follows especially from his rejection of the doctrine of appropriation as traditionally understood. The situation is most noticeable in the case of the Holy Spirit.

Balthasar is clear enough that the incarnation of the Son is accomplished by an operation proper to the Holy Spirit. He asserts,

> For New Testament thought, it is impossible to hold that this Spirit who overshadows the Virgin is the "spiritual," trinitarian God in his totality and that the action would at most be appropriated to the Holy Spirit.[17]

But the rejection of the doctrine of appropriation in any one case is equivalent to a rejection of it as such, because it requires that *all* works of the Trinity *ad extra* be common.

Again, Balthasar writes,

> While he freely and voluntarily becomes man, it is not through any autonomy on his part. . . . [T]he Son's obedience does not come after an incarnation actively brought about by him: rather, his soteriological obedience starts with the Incarnation itself.[18]

In the larger context of this text, Balthasar argues the active incarnation of the Son is proper to the Holy Spirit on the basis of a grammatical analysis of the creeds and Luke 1:35 *(RSV)*, "The Holy Spirit will come upon you. . . ." Balthasar claims that the passive grammatical structure of the credal article *et incarnatus est de Spiritu Sancto ex Maria Virgine* reveals the passivity of the Son in His incarnation to be "the common Christian faith."[19] The exceptional magisterial weight he gives to the grammar of the article on the Incarnation stands in stark contrast to his dismissal of the active formulation and vocabulary of the article on the Descent, *descendit ad inferos.*[20]

Balthasar attempts to forestall objections based on Scriptural expressions suggestive of the Word's activity. First, he says the active form *taking* in Philippians 2:7 ("He emptied himself, taking the form of a servant . . .") does not contradict his claim, because

> it is directly preceded by the ἑαυτὸν ἐκένωσεν [emptied himself] that expresses his renunciation of power and because it is followed by two passives ("being born in the likeness of men," "being found in human form").[21]

One may argue to the contrary that the active form following on the alleged "renunciation of power" reveals the retention of the divine power even in the weakness of human flesh. In addition, the divine omnipresence necessarily implies the Son did not leave His celestial throne in becoming the poor babe in the manger.[22] As Pope Hormisdas wrote, Christ was "one of the dead and giver of life to the dead, descending into hell and not leaving the bosom of the Father."[23] Or to take a liturgical expression relevant to our topic: "In hell and in the tomb and in Eden, the Godhead of Christ was indivisibly united with the Father and the Spirit."[24] Note that Christ is in hades, the grave, paradise, and heaven simultaneously, not sequentially. As for the Word's "being born," the Greek form is in fact in the middle voice, not the passive, and reflects grammatical emphasis on the subject, not the mother. The construction "being found in human form" is passive, implying the activity of those who "found" Him thus, as opposed to the Word's finding Himself thus.

Balthasar's second defense is to say that the active expressions in St. John's prologue are all "governed by the central ὁ λόγος σὰρξ ἐγένετο; the latter's 'became' only indicates the new situation into which the subject enters." This assertion apparently implies that the active verbs of the prologue are emptied of their active sense simply because their context is introduced by the verb *become*. It is unclear what criteria Balthasar uses to determine that the active verbs should be understood in a passive sense, but not vice versa. In the same place, he also presents St. Irenaeus as asserting the Father incarnates the Son. Such an assertion is not incompatible with the Incarnation being an act of all three Persons. In any case, St. Irenaeus is not normative when taken in isolation.

One is struck by a text of St. Thomas Aquinas quoted by Balthasar in this context: "[The Son] is described as 'sent into the world' because he adopts a human nature."[25] Balthasar does not notice the contradiction with his own position. St. Thomas here clearly indicates that the passive *description* of the Son as "sent" is dependent upon the active *reality* of His assumption of human nature. Human nature, not the Person of the Son, is passive in the Incarnation. St. Thomas reasonably reads the passive formulation as being a mode of speaking (a 'description') of an active reality. It is most natural to human speech that the subject of a sentence be a substance. Thus, because the human nature assumed by the Word does not subsist until it comes to subsist in His Person, the hypostasis of the Son is more readily taken as the subject in a passive construction than is human nature in the abstract.

According to Balthasar, another proper operation of the Spirit is to enable men to recognize the work done by Christ on behalf of their redemption and thus to participate in it: "This is a *new* work that is *peculiarly* his own, and yet *presents* itself only as the carrying out of what had been begun by the Son."[26] The mission of the Spirit and His work of incorporation are "new" and "completely different"[27] from the mission of the Son,

> who indeed became our brother in order to bear our guilt, but — as our brother — was always the "other" *vis-à-vis* us. He was the one who did what we were unable to do. . . . The fact that this was done on our behalf, "while we were still sinners," could only leave us in an alienation.[28]

In other words, the unheard-of brotherhood of God with man through the bond of the flesh and the blood spilled for him on the cross, so frequently seen in the Church's past as impetus for the most affectionate (because Jesus is man's brother) admiration (because it is God who humbled Himself thus), is now seen as patronizing and alienating such that another (the Spirit) must be sent to overcome man's alienation from his Savior. This work is proper to the Spirit, not merely appropriated to Him nor His personal mode of acting as one with the Father and the Son.

A final example of the Holy Spirit's proper acts in the economy is His uniting of the Father and Son in their mutual abandonment. Balthasar asserts that to say "God is forsaken by God"[29] indicates abandonment of the Son by the Father, and vice versa. But why is not the Holy Spirit forsaken, if He too is God?

The Holy Spirit has proper operations not only in the economic Trinity, but also in the immanent Trinity: If the divine essence is self-gift, why does not the Holy Spirit generate a fourth divine Person, if not by Himself, at least together with the Father and the Son? If He gives Himself as fully as the others do, a divine Person should proceed from this self-gift as much as from that of the Father and the Son. This lack of active procession is unique to Him.

The same proper feature appears also from the way in which Balthasar speaks about the various Persons as love. Both the Father and the Son are love as self-gift. In contrast to both Father and Son, the Holy Spirit is not described as love as self-gift, but as love as bond. The Holy Spirit is not just love in a different mode, but is a different kind of love, since the loving acts of self-gift by the Father and by the Son are apparently insufficient to 'bond' or unite them, both within the Trinity and in the economy. Father and Son seem to require a third thing, the fruit of their act. Thus the Father and the Son give, while the Holy Spirit is the gift.

This recurring difficulty of the different character of the Holy Spirit is latent in the way in which the Holy Spirit is often simply 'tacked on' to the end of an extended soteriological discussion as the bond between Father and Son, their substantial love, their *we,* etc., despite the fact that all these ways of speaking either fail (e.g., the Father and the Son must be a *we* even prior to the Holy Spirit's spiration because they are a single principle in spirating Him) or import difference between the Spirit on the one side and, on the other, the Father and the Son.

As for the Son, His obedience effectively constitutes a proper operation, as can be seen from the fact that only the Son can become incarnate: Sin is essentially disobedience and thus must be taken up by and into a divine Person in obedience if it is to be overcome by God's essential love. As has been seen, this requires that the Person's mode of existence in itself be obedience, which is true only of the Son. Hence Balthasar says that Christ's descent into hell

> can take place in obedience (the uttermost, absolute obedience, of which *only the Son* is capable) because absolute obedience can become the economic form of the Son's absolute response to the Father.[30]

Although this absolute obedience distinguishes Jesus from all other men, it also distinguishes the Son from the Father and the Holy Spirit, and the text points precisely to this latter contrast, as evidenced by the causal phrase that references the Son in relation to the Father, not in relation to men. If Balthasar wanted to assert that any one of the Trinity could become incarnate for the redemption of the world (and it is not evident that he would), he would have to argue that the Father or the Holy Spirit could adopt the filial quality of obedience, not just in a certain likeness, but in reality.[31] Yet this very obedience is the Son's personal mode of being God,[32] and hence such a real adoption would dissolve the distinction of Persons.

In addition, a related passage indicates that the Son's being incarnated is a proper operation, i.e., not only in the sense that He alone became man, but in that He alone could become man:

> If it is possible for one Person in God to accept suffering . . . then evidently it is not something foreign to God, something that does not affect him. It must be something profoundly appropriate to his divine Person, for — to say it once again — his being sent *(missio)* by the Father is a modality of his proceeding *(processio)* from the Father.[33]

Here the reason given for the possibility of Christ's suffering is the appropriateness of this suffering to the divine Person of the Son *as Son;* that is, its possibility is proper to Him. If only the Son can become incarnated, however, Balthasar contradicts the thrust of his efforts to argue for the archetype of suffering in the Trinity, not just in the Son.[34] If the archetype of suffering pertains to each Person of the Trinity, then any one of them should be able to be incarnated. On the other hand, if only the Son can become incarnated to suffer, it seems the archetype of suffering is not common to the Trinity, but proper to the Son in a way that makes Him not only distinct, but also different, from the Father and the Holy Spirit.

Finally, according to Balthasar, the creation of the world and the resurrection of Jesus are proper to the Father. Balthasar is more explicit about the latter. He gives a grammatical argument, "It should not be overlooked that both Resurrection and Ascension are first described as a passive event: the active agent is God (the Father)."[35] Thus, in His resurrection, "the Son receives himself — with body and soul, with divinity and humanity — back from the Father."[36] Note that if the Father raises the *Son,* as opposed to the *entire* Trinity raising the *reunited body and soul of Christ,* then the Son is circumscribed if not by place, at least by condition (i.e., being dead). If He as Son is or becomes circumscribed, He is or becomes a creature.

Balthasar is less explicit regarding creation as the Father's work, at least in texts with a soteriological focus. He more often speaks of "God," but sometimes uses this word to refer both to the whole Trinity and to the individual Persons in the same passage. Nonetheless, several of Balthasar's other theses imply that the Father is the proper agent of creation. For example, although the Son's "distance" from the Father is the condition for the possibility of creaturely distinction from God, this primal "distance" is due to the Father's gift of self in generating the Son. Since Balthasar takes the economy to image the divine life in a very strict sense, as seen in the Son's descent into Sheol being an expression of His filial personality, the very coming into being of a finite other points to the Father as its source. Here, too, the explicit ascriptions of Christ's resurrection to the Father are suggestive, for the resurrection is not a return to the old life, but a new life, a new creation. It is because creation is proper to the Father that the Son's *visio mortis* of the sins of created freedom gone awry is also an insight into a personal mystery of the Father and the Son's own generation. Hence Balthasar links them thus:

> It is, then, to the Father that the initiative in the Son's Resurrection is ascribed. It is he who acts, and he acts precisely as who he is for the world, namely, its Creator who brings his creative action to its completion in the resurrection of the dead.[37]

Balthasar depends upon grammatical arguments in ascribing proper acts to each of the divine Persons. His logic seems to be that the distinct grammatical forms point to a real distinction in acts, from which one may conclude there is a real distinction of Persons. A different, more traditional interpretation of such grammatical distinction is possible, however: It highlights the distinction of Persons, but does not assert a distinction of acts. Thus, for example, Jesus may be said passively to be raised, but this formulation need not point to the *Son* as passive in the resurrection, only that the resurrection is beyond the power of His human nature, in virtue of which He is called "Jesus." In his arguments, Balthasar overlooks the fact that the meaning of Scripture and of credal formulae is determined by their context, which is the Church's understanding of them, i.e., by Tradition.[38] His arguments are not sufficiently strong to justify his rejection of the traditional theology of appropriation.

Moreover, it is questionable whether Balthasar's attribution to the Holy Spirit of the Son's incarnation and the attribution of creation to the Father are compatible with, *inter alia*, the creed of the Fourth Lateran Ecumenical Council, which professes that the Son's "incarnation is the common work of the whole Trinity" and that Father, Son, and Holy Spirit are "the one principle of the universe, the creator of all things."[39] Based upon Balthasar's use of the *opera trinitatis ad extra communia*, I surmise he would hold that the Incarnation is a "common work" insofar as all three Persons are involved in a single event, even though they have proper acts in it.

It may be that Balthasar began to recognize he was separating the Persons too much, as seen in his need to explicitly deny that the divine nature is a fourth thing and likewise in his ascription of personal properties to other divine Persons. On this latter point he says, "If there is to be this reciprocal indwelling, however, it follows that what is specific to each Person must not be withheld from the others," not only in that speaking of one Person, all three are sometimes meant, not only in reference to the single divine nature, "but — as we have already said — one of the Persons can, by way of the divine 'economy,' embody and represent the qualities of the others."[40] (The "divine 'economy'" means the immanent Trinity.) This 'solution,' however, goes to the opposite extreme and effectively dissolves the Persons.

Balthasar's difficulty in maintaining both the distinction of Persons and the identity in nature is in part the result of his choice of terms and approach. For example, having defined the divine essence as self-surrender based on the Person of the Father,[41] Balthasar must find this self-surrender likewise in the Son if the Son is to be divine. The divine self-gift of the Son is seen in His spiration with the Father of the Spirit and also in His emptying Himself of the divine attributes to become incarnated.[42] The recurring problem, however, is why the Holy Spirit is divine, since He has no similar personal kenosis — unless one wants to place the adoptive sonship of grace en par with the Trinitarian processions. Similarly, Balthasar describes the Father and Son as "(super-) masculine" because the Father begets the Son, and the two spirate the Spirit, whereas the Son and Spirit are "(super-) feminine" insofar as they consent (antecedently) to their procession from an other.[43] Though the Father can also be described as "(super-) feminine" because His fatherhood depends on their antecedent consent, Balthasar gives no way in which the Holy Spirit can be called "(super-) masculine." In both these examples, the Holy Spirit appears to be lacking a fundamentally divine attribute. Balthasar makes an attempt to provide it: The Spirit is "most active" (i.e., 'masculine') because His being spirated perfects and seals the Godhead.[44] But then His 'masculinity' is fundamentally different from that of the Father and Son — unless His role in the deification of Christians is, as we said, taken en par with the Trinitarian processions.[45]

The tri-theistic consequences that follow from Balthasar's suggestions of proper acts are not overcome by his idea that the Father gives the whole divine essence, including His will, to the Son, and the two of them give it to the Holy Spirit. To interpret Balthasar generously, if obedience is one's own willing of what another wills, the Son can be said through a certain likeness to be obedient when He receives as His own the single divine will (taken as a power and as the intention willed) from the Father. But precisely to the extent that this will is truly the Son's own (upon which Balthasar insists), He can no longer be said to be obedient to it as the Father's will, despite its origin from the Father. The long-standing view that obedience requires two separate wills returns. With it, Balthasar's theological approach is called into question, not as a matter of preference, but because it results in sundering the Trinity into three gods.

If the first way Balthasar divides the Persons one from the other is to ascribe proper acts to Them, the second way he does so is by speaking about the divine will in ways that make it sound identical only in content, not in power.[46] There is then one will between the Father, Son, and Holy Spirit as a matter of consensus. For example, he says, "Since each hypostasis in God possesses the same freedom and omnipotence, we can speak of there being reciprocal petition."[47] But if the three Persons possess the identically same power of will, in what meaningful sense can one petition the other? In contrast, the blessed petition God, even though their wills are perfectly conformed to the divine will, because this conformity is not an identity of power, but of content. There is, as well, "the unanimous salvific decision on the part of the Trinity, according to which it was resolved to send the Son."[48] Now a single will may make a resolution, but in no case is the decision of a single will said to be "unanimous." The same may be said for "cooperation," when Balthasar speaks of the Son's "primal obedience in willing cooperation and gratitude."[49] And likewise for "in concert" (somewhat mitigated by the "as if"):

> When Jesus views his mission, his gaze discerns the Father who is behind it . . . ; but it is not the Father who compels him . . . but the mission itself, which coincides with his filial freedom. . . . It is as if the Father's freedom points to the mission's necessity and as if the Son's freedom is oriented to the latter. It is as if the mission's central position indicates the 'economic' revelation of a decision freely made in concert by the whole Trinity.[50]

Or, again, Father and Son spirate the Spirit "as the expression of their united freedom,"[51] which suggests their freedom is not identical in number or identical to that of the Spirit. As a final example, observe that surprise among the divine Persons also means the act of each, and hence implicitly the will, is no longer single and identical with the act and will of the others.

But perhaps the most significant passage relating to this concern is the following:

> We must refer back to the one freedom of the divine Essence that is possessed by each Hypostasis in its own specific way; this means that the unity of the divine will is *also* the result of an integration of the intentions of the Hypostases.[52]

Multiple individual intentions and their integration are simply not possible if there is but one single divine will. From the resolution of the monothelite controversy came the axiom that, since the will is a power of the nature, the number of wills depends on the number of natures. Conversely, the number of natures is revealed by the number of wills. If then each Hypostasis has an individual intention, but an intention is only the will determined to a specific object, then each Hypostasis has an individual will. Moreover, since the divine will is to be identical with the divine nature, this position implies that each Hypostasis is a god. But as the Catholic Faith professes monotheism, not tritheism, one must conclude that the hypostases of which Balthasar here speaks are not the God of the Catholic Faith.

Balthasar gives a footnote for this problematic passage, which refers to a discussion elsewhere, but it is not clear he has provided a key that resolves this predicament. Two elements are primarily treated on the page to which he refers:[53] First there is the claim, using Speyr, that "for a will to be free, it must be part of a hierarchy," which is "freedom's primal shape,"[54] i.e., as found in the divine Persons. However, it makes little sense to say the divine will is "part of a hierarchy" just because the Persons who possess it have a hierarchical order; parts are never equivalent to the whole, and the divine will must be equivalent to the whole hierarchy of the Trinity if it is to be single. Second, there is a vague request by the Father, which the Son desires to actualize and which is made a common decision by the Holy Spirit.[55] Balthasar's formulation is extreme:

> As for the Spirit, whose *specific part it is to choose and decide in all freedom (since the Spirit is the absolute, divine will),* one might say that he embodies that reciprocal 'mode of granting requests' which is an invention of the whole Trinity, so that the decision on the part of the united Trinity (within the order of processions) is completely mutual and common to all the Persons.[56]

While the first part of this quotation makes the divine will proper to the Holy Spirit, it appears the latter half is saying each Person desires to fulfill the desires of the others, which are made known not as demands, but as requests. In the freedom and omnipotence of the divinity, which each Person possesses as His own, He grants these desires.[57] The division between petitioner and petitioned is supposedly overcome by the bond of the Holy Spirit: Even as He reminds the Father and the Son that "This is what you wanted from all eternity"[58] at the moment of their greatest abandonment in the Descent event, so His being "the absolute, divine will" may be interpreted as the Holy Spirit, choosing what the Father and Son choose but in the mode of the bond between them, and bringing this choice to a definitive state by being the substantial "we" that unites the two of them. Again, however, the one divine will is always that which is from the Father through the Son in the Holy Spirit, regardless of which Person is considered. Hence no "request," no "common" decision, no "integration of intentions" is possible within the Trinity.

Matters concerning the Two Natures of the Son

In the previous section, certain difficulties related to the Person of the Son as raised by Balthasar's theology were pointed out. The seventh one mentioned, that it appears Balthasar speaks equivocally of there being two natures in Christ, is also applicable to the present section, in which we consider some matters of concern associated with his treatment of the two natures in Christ and, in particular, the relevance of His humanity. Four broad categories emerge, relating to the distinction of the natures in Christ, the necessity of the Incarnation, the efficacy of the Incarnation, and implications for the followers of Christ.

a. Concerns Related to the Distinction of the Two Natures in Christ

As definitively taught by the Council of Chalcedon (451), the divine nature and the human nature of Christ are united in His person

> without confusion or change, without division or separation. The distinction between the natures was never abolished by their union but rather the character proper to each of the two natures was preserved. . . .[59]

Although occasioned by the monophysite and Nestorian heresies, and with an eye to that of patripassianism as well,[60] the Council's teaching is positive and definitive. Thus it cannot be limited simply to a contradiction of the aforementioned heresies, but excludes any doctrine, old or new, that jeopardizes the distinction of the natures, their perfection, and their union in the Person of Christ. Acclaimed by the Council and foundational to its teaching was the Tome of Leo, which in part reads, "For each of the two natures performs the functions proper to it in communion with the other: the Word does what pertains to the Word and the flesh what pertains to the flesh."[61] This principle would see further explication and approbation in the Third Ecumenical Council of Constantinople (680). Against monothelitism and mono-energism, this latter Council professed that the distinction of natures in the unity of the hypostasis of Christ means He has two wills and two actions, one human and one divine in each case.[62] Because these matters are essential to the Catholic Faith, it is essential to Catholic theology to maintain them as clearly as possible, both in theological content and in choice of language.

If one observes the language Balthasar uses, however, the distinction of the two natures in Christ often appears to be absent from his theology of the Descent. He frequently does not specify in virtue of which nature he affirms or denies something of Christ. This lack of specification sometimes is deliberate,[63] but it also follows naturally from his theology of the Incarnation. For example, referring to John 5:37, 12:45, and 14:9, he says, "Whoever sees Jesus, sees the Father, for Jesus is himself the Father's assumption of form, the Father's εἶδος [image]."[64] Although this sentence may sound modalist, it is not intended so. Balthasar rather seems to be thinking along these lines: The Son is the image of the Father. But the mission of the Son expresses, or is one with, His procession. The *incarnate* Word, Jesus Christ, therefore can also be said to be the image of the Father. Granting Balthasar his peculiar use of *form*, his lack of qualifying Jesus as "the Father's assumption of form" *in the divine nature* appears to be deliberate, since it is consistent with how the mission *is* the procession in his the-

incarnation, but does not emphasize one nature more than the other. The emphases of *Son* and *Jesus* are not absolutely rigid, however, because Jesus the incarnate Son has two natures; hence it is advisable to make the relevant nature explicit, given that a sufficient number of heresies can follow from a confusion of language in this matter. In Balthasar's texts, *Son* and *Jesus* are largely used interchangeably in reference to Christ, and without specification of the relevant nature. Either such usage reflects a Christology in which the unity of two *distinct* and *perfect* natures is not key, or else some of his passages are simply made more opaque than necessary by the misleading clues given by the name chosen.

For example, Balthasar writes both, "The witness of the Father constitutes the form (εἶδος) of the Son as such,"[74] and "Jesus is himself the Father's assumption of form, the Father's εἶδος [image]."[75] Both statements are to indicate that the procession of the Son as generation in self-surrender by the Father is identified with the mission of Jesus as revelation of the Father. The equivalence of the assertions, however, takes no account of the difference between the "Son as such" and Jesus, namely, the difference of human nature. The equivalence despite the lack of distinction seems permitted within Balthasar's theology, however, for two reasons. First, according to Balthasar, the incarnate *Son* can still be *said* not to be other than He is as Son, because He retains the perfection of the divine nature as self-gift (though not the perfection of the divine attributes, the lack of which is no injury to His divinity but rather a manifestation of it) and because human nature is something "in" Him as God. Second, *Jesus* can still be *said* to be the Word in human nature, as the second divine hypostasis having relinquished His divine attributes to the point that all He possesses are these finite human attributes. The same problem is implicit when Balthasar writes, "As man, [Jesus] is identical with the task given him by the Father."[76] We get the following chain of reasoning that illustrates Balthasar's peculiar Christology in which the filial hypostasis has human attributes and expresses Himself in them: Jesus *as man* = His task = His mission = the procession of the Word *as divine*.

Manifested in linguistic precision, theological clarity regarding the distinction, perfection, and unity of the two natures in the Person of Christ is essential, for to neglect what Christ is, will be to overlook what He can do or how He acts. Topics related to one or the other nature, such as death, receive their importance from this context. Thus, for example, if man is this unity of body and soul, and if death is the separation of the two, then it will not do to proceed to characterize the Descent of Christ on the assumption that "the condition of being dead, and not the 'separation,' is what is essential,"[77] since this separation affects the possibility of both action and passion in Christ according to His human nature. At best it suggests a certain lack of insight to characterize questions related to this matter as "idle."[78] They at least related to a patristic concern of which Balthasar was aware,[79] i.e., about the union of the Word with the body and soul of Jesus during their separation in death. If "one can only regret that scholastic theology . . . let itself be absorbed by the futile question as to if and how Christ, during the time of his death, remained a man and the God-Man,"[80] one might at least ask what the scholastics — a large and diverse group, and surely containing members no less intelligent than theologians after them — not to mention the Fathers, thought was so important in the issue as to merit so much attention. For one, the reality of Christ's descent itself is at stake: The question was actually raised whether Christ, the God-*man,* descended to hell *at all* if He is no longer said to be a man after His death.[81] Balthasar's refusal opens his conclusions to criticism on the basis of one of his own principles, namely, Christ's solidarity with the dead: If Christ's death and being dead are so unique that ontology can shed no light on them, how then were they a human death and a human being dead at all?

Either Balthasar's peculiar Christology or his lack of appropriate precision in how he speaks of the two natures results in ambiguities that might be expected about the two wills in Christ and His two simultaneous acts, divine and human. For example, Balthasar says that

> in the contrast between the *two wills of the Father and the Son* on the Mount of Olives, and in the *abandonment of the Son by God* on the Cross, the drastic counterposing of the divine Persons in the economy became visible.[82]

It is false to speak of "two wills of the Father and the Son" without qualification. For a Catholic theology, it would be necessary to say that there was a contrast between the Father's will (which is also the Son's divine will) and the Son's *human* will. Given that Balthasar thinks the Son *as God* is forsaken on the cross by the Father as God, the parallel between this abandonment at the Crucifixion and "the contrast of the two wills" in manifesting the distinction of Persons suggests — in the absence of other indications — that it is likewise the Father as God and the Son *as God* whose "two wills" are contrasted. Within Balthasar's theology, this multiplicity of wills may be intended to refer to the divine will in the Father as requesting, so to speak, through His generation of the Son, and the same will in the Person of the Son as being received from the Father in this way, which I take to be intended to refer to the distinct personal mode in which the Father and Son are the single, identical divine will. This distinction in personal mode is not the first thing that comes to mind if one speaks of a contrast between wills in Gethsemane, however. But if indeed Balthasar has this distinction in the *divine* will in mind, what role and what value does the human will of Christ have in this moment of crisis and agony?

Likewise, the facility with which Balthasar interchanges *Son* and *Jesus* implicitly creates problems when he says, "There is no question of Jesus as man obeying himself as God; nor does he obey the Trinity; as Son, in the Holy Spirit, he obeys the Father."[83] Is there really "no question" at all? I have supplied an analogical interpretation for the Trinitarian obedience seen in Balthasar's theology, in which obedience is the reception of the power and act of a will from another, but obedience as we know it is submission of one will to another will. In every case but one, obedience thus involves a distinction of subjects. In Christ alone can His human will submit itself to His divine will, because He alone has two wills. Conversely, if there is only one identical divine power of will, there can be no obedience in the Trinity. Seen in this light, the Son can obey the Father only with respect to the submission of His human will to the divine will of the Father, which latter is identically the same as the divine will of the Son. Difficulty arises in Balthasar's switch from "Jesus as man" to "as Son," which naturally turns the question of obedience from the human will of Jesus to His divine will. Is there "no question" because there is no human will? If we do not want to say this, we must ask whether "as Son" He obeys the Father with a human will, the divine will, or both. Balthasar frequently asserts obedience of the Son according to His divinity, and no reason is given here to think he is saying anything otherwise. But the divine obedience of the Son also raises doubts about there being "no question of Jesus as man obeying himself as God." If the Son is "obedient" to the Father in receiving the single divine will from Him, and if He possesses it as His own so that His freedom is equal to the Father's, and if the intention of this will of His is the same as that of the Father, then divine volitional power and intention are the Son's, even if received from the Father. In what sense then does Balthasar deny that Jesus as man obeys himself as God? If Jesus' human will cannot submit to His divine will, it seems we must either deny the Son possesses the divine will as His own, or else we must consider that there is only one will in Christ, i.e., the Son's divine will taking the form of a human one.

This latter option is the one consistent with Balthasar's Christology, in which the mission is the procession. It makes sense of why "Jesus as man" and "as Son" can be viewed as equivalents. It is likewise consistent with how Balthasar attempts to resolve the question of "how the Incarnate One can receive and execute this decision [of the Father] in pure obedience; for, just as eternally, it is his own decision too."[84] The solution of St. Maximus the Confessor, i.e., that Christ has two wills, is not touched upon at all. It need not be, since the Son's divine will takes the form of a human one; or, what is the same, Jesus' human will is His eternal, divine will. This conclusion follows also from another passage, namely: "When this man gives God his all, obeys him to death, he obeys but himself, his love as Son for the Father."[85] If this statement is not to stand in straightforward contradiction to Balthasar's denial that Jesus humanly obeys Himself as God, then "obeys but himself" must be taken in a broad sense, namely, that this man is not following a heteronomous command, but his own will, his own inclination. But what is that will, that inclination? His love *as Son.* This *man's* will is His will as divine Son, not in content (for that would be the admission that the human will obeys the Son's divine will), but in power. Nevertheless, this man is not then omnipotent, because the Son's divine will becomes a human will (the procession is the mission) through the "depositing" of divine attributes.

As might be expected in a Christology that sees a real transfer *from* the form of God *to* the form of man,[86] the collapse of the two wills into one is mirrored consistently in the suggestion that there are not two acts in Christ, but only one. The conflation of the wills itself suggests the lack of two distinct acts, human and divine, since an act of will is as much an act as a corporal act. Thus we read, "We would be wrong to suppose that the Son made two decisions, separated in time; that is, the first as God, in eternity, and the second as man, in time."[87] Granted time and eternity are not distinguished by some period of time, nonetheless it seems we would be right to say the Son made two decisions, "the first as God, in eternity, and the second as man, in time," if we grant that time had a beginning and that Christ as man can only act in time. But we should also read Balthasar's clarification of what he means, since he goes on to say, "The Son's eternal decision includes his temporal one, and his temporal decision holds fast to his eternal decision as the only one that matters."[88] Here the text suggests in two ways the separation to which Balthasar had just objected. Though it seems reasonable enough to say the eternal decision embraced the temporal one, the use of "decision" implies a completed act, a past point in time. This impression is reinforced by the idea that the temporal decision looks back, so to speak, to the eternal one in order to decide in accord with it. This way of speaking does not adequately indicate the divine will acting simultaneously with the human one. We must also ask why it is that the temporal, human decision does not matter vis-à-vis the eternal one? Is Christ's human self-offering irrelevant?

To take two examples that refer more specifically to acts, we read, "The mandated task is divine, its execution human, and the proportion of perfect 'attunement' prevailing between them is both human and divine."[89] If there are two natures in Christ, there should be two acts, and hence the execution of His mission should not be simply human, but also divine. Likewise, when Balthasar takes the role of prayer in the lives of human beings who are not God as the necessary model for how Christ receives and carries out the Trinitarian will,[90] he effectively limits the range of the God-man's action to human possibilities.

In these two cases regarding Christ's acts, we see a devaluation of the divine, while in the examples concerning Christ's wills, we saw a downplaying of the human intention. These emphases reflect Balthasar's Christology in which the divine procession (here, i.e., the divine will) takes the form of the economic mission (i.e., Christ's acts). The divine acts through human acts, whereas the human will *is* the divine will in a new form.

It cannot simply be said, however, that Balthasar overlooks Christ's divine nature: In his theology, it is precisely in virtue of the Son's divinity that He can empty Himself of His divine attributes such that He will, in fact, be limited to human nature, and His human nature will subsist in hypostatic obedience. This emptying includes the "depositing" of divine knowledge of the divine will. One might even say it includes the "depositing" of the divine will taken as the power to dispose of one's self, but only in the sense that the Son lets the Holy Spirit do with Him as the Spirit wills. Christ's ignorance combined with the hardwiring of obedience in His human existence (because the mission *is* the procession) would explain why Christ can be tempted yet unfailingly never sin; why Balthasar asserts Christ's impeccability without reference to any act of His divinity, explicitly denying His possession of the beatific vision[91] (which, insofar as it is the union of God with the soul, is dependent upon a divine act); and why His temporal, human decision is not one that matters. The eternal decision is revealed by the Holy Spirit to Him in prayer in virtue of the Trinitarian inversion, and since His very existence is obedience, He will cleave to it without fail.

In the end, the movement Balthasar sees in the Son's going from the form of God to the form of a servant could perhaps be compared to that of fantasy fiction's shape-shifters, who retain their personality and identity no matter what type of being they manifest themselves as. Thus the Son's "depositing" of His divine attributes to become man is an expression of His trinitarian personality, and the mission *is* the procession. "The absolute not only irradiates finitude but actually *becomes* finite."[92] The comparison seems confirmed by Balthasar's comment that he tried to introduce into theology Goethe's concept of form, such as is found in *The Metamorphosis of Plants*.[93] In Goethe's botany, the single plant can grow as the different forms of root, leaf, or flower as needed, sometimes even changing one into the other, yet the plant's identity as, say, a rose, abides and governs all these expressions.

It appears so far there is a tendency in Balthasar's theology of the Person of Christ toward division (between Person and divine nature, and between the divine essence as self-gift and the divine attributes) and a tendency toward conflation in his theology of Jesus' two natures: In being made man, the Word does not retain His divine nature as such, i.e., with all the divine attributes, but has a new mode of existence, namely, in the flesh, which is to express analogically all that the

Word is in His divinity. Thus, although everything in Christ is human except His hypostasis to the point that the Word has ignorance and faith, and even errs, we must now ask whether His humanity ultimately has redemptive value in Balthasar's theology of the Descent. This question can be considered from two angles: First, in what sense is the Incarnation necessary, or what importance *should* the human nature of the Redeemer have? And second, given this necessity, does the Incarnation actually 'work,' i.e., does it *in fact* have redemptive value?

b. On the Necessity of the Incarnation

Here and in the following section, the Incarnation is taken as Balthasar sees it, i.e., as an event that is not only the Word becoming man, but His being man, with a special emphasis on the acts of Jesus. The term thus includes the Descent, since the Incarnation is a kenosis unto Sheol. What importance does the Incarnation have such that God would join human nature to Himself, in the Person of the Son, for all eternity? In what sense is the Incarnation necessary?

In the most general terms, Balthasar thinks the Incarnation is necessary if God freely chooses to bring into being creatures with a finite but real freedom. Through the Incarnation, fallen creaturely obedience will be assured, and actually given, a path back to the Father; indeed, its very fallenness and finitude is made this path. Through the incarnate Son's life of faith and especially through His experience of abandonment by God in Sheol, He lives the life redeemed sinners are called to live and He dies the death they deserved as sinners. Undergone by the incarnate Son out of human obedience and, shall we say, divine 'super-obedience,' the spiritual death of sin's disobedience and the physical death that was its consequence are existentially made a part of the Trinitarian life of love, and so (Balthasar says) overcome. The one who is the archetype of men in their creation in this way becomes not only divinely, but also humanly, the archetype of their existence and redemption. The standard thus established in Him is not so much an exterior one, but rather demands an interior conformity. Through this configuration, man comes to participate in the archetype itself, that is, in Christ and in His return to the Father through His life, death, and resurrection. Christ's life and death are not just those of any man, however, but the life and death of God as man.

Certain problems arise, however, when this theology is considered in more detail. A first group of these problems derives from the idea that, as Balthasar asks, where else would something be, but in God?[94] But if everything can only be created and exist within the "bracket" of Trinitarian love, how then can it be necessary to bring the fallen world back into this love in virtue of the

Son's incarnation and descent? Surely the world did not fall outside of God's love through its sin. If it had, God would not have cared to redeem it. Indeed, we have seen that Balthasar gives as the motive of redemption not only the love of the divine Persons for each other, but also for the world. Hence the question remains.

It also appears the Son's incarnation and being dead are not necessary in any sense, because it seems they have no real effect: If everything that exists is created only within the "bracket" of the Trinitarian love and if sin has some real existence such that it is meaningful when Balthasar speaks of sin-in-itself, then this sin also exists within the Trinitarian love even before the Son is "literally 'made sin'" in Sheol. His descent would then be unnecessary. On Balthasar's behalf, one might respond to this objection by saying that sin exists within this "bracket" in virtue of the Cross and Hell to come.[95]

The proposed resolution is not wholly satisfactory, however. For it seems that, for Balthasar, the redemption operates in something like a physical manner: The reality of sin must be brought inside the reality of the Trinity through the Son's being configured to it in Sheol;[96] only afterward does sin exist inside the "bracket" of Trinitarian love. But, unless sin is in God from the beginning (which Balthasar denies), it is not clear how the reality of sin can exist within this "bracket" before the Descent actually brings it inside. To hold Balthasar's position requires saying that every instance of a reality (every sin) is changed before the cause of its change operates.

In contrast, this problem does not pertain to a soteriology of satisfaction. If Christ merits something such that, in virtue of the satisfaction He offered through love consummated on the cross, God will recreate grace in the soul of the repentant sinner, the change in the sinner depends on the act of God at the particular time the sinner exists and repents. God responds with love (the willing of a good) to the love (divine and human) of Christ. The meritorious act leaves the will of the one who holds the reward free. It may be unjust not to reward the act, and such injustice on the part of the one who holds the reward may be unthinkable, but nonetheless the reward remains voluntary. If so, however, it can be given freely even before the act that merits it is performed. Assuming God is omniscient, He is able to act on behalf of a particular sinner living before Christ in virtue of the satisfaction to come. Redemption is not thereby made arbitrary, but every act of God's forgiveness clearly involves His free gift to the sinner in light of the sacrifice of Christ; it involves an act of re-creation in virtue of the objective redemption. This freedom does not give the sinner reason to doubt whether God will give the gift; it only reveals that God gives it voluntarily. The repentant sinner's hope is based upon God's truthfulness, His fidelity to Himself in fulfilling His promises, and His love, which His promises manifest.

In Balthasar's soteriology, however, God's freedom figures in a different way, because his soteriology operates in a more mechanical manner. According to his theology, every man is redeemed because his sins have been physically removed from him, loaded on Christ on the cross, and 'burned' in the Trinitarian fire of love experienced by the Son in Shcol. It seems then that the change in the sinner's reality does not occur at the moment of repentance (or sacramental absolution) but at the point in time when Christ took these sins upon Himself on the cross and buried them with Himself in Sheol. As a consequence, all that stands between man and heaven is his acceptance of what has already been done. It is here that God's freedom plays a part, for He can give the gift of perfected freedom to someone after his death; He must have this prerogative, otherwise His own absolute freedom is compromised. The repentant sinner's hope is based upon God's nature as self-gift and the Son's discharge of the sinner's punishment in Sheol. Subjective redemption is more voluntaristic (almost arbitrary) in this soteriology than in one in which merit figures more prominently. On the other hand, if even God cannot act against His own nature, it also tends toward necessary universal salvation.

A second problem regarding the necessity of the Incarnation concerns whether the Incarnation and Descent have a conditional or an absolute necessity. For Balthasar, they are conditional insofar as they depend upon the free choice of God to create the world. On the other hand, they are absolutely necessary insofar as, given that choice, they are the only way in which He can create responsibly:[97] Given the type of world God chose to create (one including creatures with finite freedom), God does not create without the 'guarantee' offered by the Son, nor could He have chosen to redeem it in any other way than through His Son's becoming sin. Balthasar insists on this dual necessity of the Descent event and on its uniqueness: Given God's free decision to create finite freedom, kenosis in obedience unto Sheol is the *only* way redemption is possible and it must *necessarily* be undergone.[98] Note that the necessary corollary is that that belief is mistaken which, down through the centuries, has understood Christ's death on the cross (in contrast to a 'second death' in Sheol) as the consummation of the redemption and His descent as the application of its fruits.

The actual Descent and not merely the Son's 'offer' becomes necessary, however, because God knows creation will fall before He creates. Hence, if God will only create 'responsibly,' i.e., Himself providing an *actual* means of redemption as guarantee, and if the *only* way to redeem creation is through the Descent, then to choose to actualize the creation is also to choose that the Descent *necessarily* occur, which means not only will sin occur, but sin was inevitable. Although Balthasar calls it an extreme that would "make sin the necessary precondition for love's epiphany,"[99] merely drawing attention to a danger is not sufficient for escaping it. He suggests this necessity can be avoided by saying God could have chosen to create a different type of world. But what is this different type of world, one without sin instead of with it? Any world with finite freedom, however, requires the 'guarantee' of the Descent. . . .

Thirdly, we have also seen that Jesus' humanity undergoes an indescribable stretching apart, and ultimately is "suspended" and "stripped," before redemption is consummated in Sheol. The "stretching" of Christ's humanity and the "extension" of its possibilities calls into question the role of His humanity precisely as human, i.e., finite in the way human nature is. More, in arguing for Christ's divinity in a soteriological context, Balthasar says something very telling: "Only God himself can go right to the end of the abandonment by God. Only he has the freedom to do this."[100] The humanity of Jesus, even as the humanity of the God-man, even if extended beyond its natural capacities, must be left behind in the end. After all, because the Son's God-forsakenness is proportional to the Son's divine intimacy with the Father,[101] it is "deeper and more deadly than any forsakenness, temporal or eternal, actual or possible, that separates a *creature* from God,"[102] including therefore the created human nature of Christ. Quite simply put, all this extension of Jesus' humanity in virtue of His divinity means that neither remains perfect as it was; or, in any case, the humanity certainly changes. It also undoes Balthasar's soteriology in which creaturely obedience is supposed to be made the expressed form of the Son's divine "obedience," and hence a way of salvation for men. Such creaturely obedience is impossible in Sheol if Jesus is no longer human like other men, but has been "stretched apart" until He is "literally 'made sin.'" Rather, it is the divine "obedience" of Christ that is essential.

Again, consider that, in His economic mission, the reality of mankind's sin is "absorbed by the Son, affecting his reality as a person, who must then be condemned and expelled by God."[103] The Father-Son relationship that *is* love then exists in the mode of rejection.[104] Here, as indicated by the use of *Son*, the use of *person* without qualification, the reference to the Father-Son relationship, and the fact that the Son's rejection is proportional to His intimacy with the Father, it is the Person of Christ who is affected, not in His human nature (something that is not identical with His person), but in His person *simpliciter* (albeit this Person exists now in an economic mode).

Or again, we read,

> The sequence of the natural conditions of the Word finishes with the Man of Sorrows; the new sequence — the passion, the resurrection, and the ascension of the Word — lies in the region of divine activity, which makes use of nature and extends it beyond its possibilities.[105]

Was Christ not acting as God before the Passion then? And in the Passion and after, is Christ still man then, or some third thing? We cannot interpret Balthasar here simply as referring to how God's grace can work miracles beyond the power of nature. (In that case, the contrast would suggest Christ was without grace before the Passion and had grace during it, which contradicts Balthasar's insistence that Christ in Sheol did not possess the theological virtues, which are the necessary effects of grace.) It must be then that Christ's humanity in the Passion is no longer like that of other men.

Likewise, we read,

> For this *pro nobis* [of "the *event* of the Cross"] to be effective, the image of Christ must absolutely be true man who alone can take upon himself the vicarious experience of the sin of the world and suffer it through. But he must be more than man, more than a creature, for within the world no being can absolutely assume the place of another free fellow being. That would violate the dignity of the self-responsible person.[106]

Since (as Balthasar says) a real transfer of guilt from one man to another is not possible to human nature (much less the assumption of all the world's guilt) and since (as we have seen) Christ must be God in order to assume the place of punishment *pro nobis,* it is not clear why Christ "absolutely must be true man" to have this "vicarious experience."

But if Christ's human nature (or His being man) has no role to play at the key moment, why does the Son bother to become incarnate at all? It is the Son's kenotic existence, His hypostatic obedience, that make His death and His being dead transcend those of other men.[107] Balthasar, who began his theology of the Descent by stressing Christ's solidarity with human sinners, ends by "suspending" the Incarnation. The Descent is redemptive *only* because the Word's being made sin is undergone in divine, filial obedience and so falls within the infinite "distance" of the Trinitarian love; His charity as the holiest of men, His human virtues, and His human affections — in all the perfection these can have in a man in virtue of nature and grace — even His archetypal faith that Balthasar found so admirable have no place here.

Given Balthasar's Christology and soteriology, we must ask what in Jesus is human? If "*everything* human in Christ is a word, an image, a representation, and an expression of the Father"[108] — not as other men image the Son as their archetype, but as the adequate expression of the *divine* Son *Himself* — what in Jesus is an expression of the other-ness of His created human nature? And what is it to us men if some Thing that is no longer human or hardly divine is conformed to sin-in-itself in Sheol and suffers all the wrath of the Father? If it was truly conformed to sin in this way, it suffered nothing worse than it deserved, but perfect justice.[109] Perhaps Balthasar would respond that the Word can only enter Sheol in virtue of a fallen nature oriented to physical death and the 'second death,' since sin is not in God in any way. We have already seen that it is inconsistent for Balthasar to hold this latter condition; nonetheless, one must still ask why the God of absolute freedom needs human nature to enter the realm of death, but at the very moment He is actually made sin, He is quite capable of becoming sin without this fallen nature and indeed must strip it away. In other words, if sin is not in God, one would expect the opposite of what Balthasar holds; one would expect the assistance of human nature was not necessary for the omnipotent God to enter Sheol, but was necessary precisely at the moment the Word is made sin. Again, if at most the Son passes through human nature en route to being made sin, why does He become incarnate at all?

What Balthasar says about the suffering of God must be re-examined with the minimal soteriological role of Jesus' humanity in mind. Read in the light of his corpus, passages that earlier required careful qualification and interpretation now carry a clearer signification. For example, Balthasar writes that, anthropologically, a real exchange of places

> is only possible if *"unus ex Trinitate passus est"* both in his human nature and in his divine person. For it is only by virtue of his divine person that he can enter into the desperate situation of a free human being vis-à-vis God, in order to transform it from a dead-end to a situation full of hope.[110]

The last sentence signifies the Descent to Sheol. Since a Person suffers only in virtue of and in a nature, and if the human nature of Christ is "stripped" in the farthest depths of Sheol, and if "it is only in virtue of his divine person" that the *visio mortis* can be joined to the Son in any case (i.e., even if something of human nature remains), then Christ suffers in virtue of His divine nature, the nature of His person as such — which is perfectly consistent with Balthasar's saying the Son's suffering in Sheol is proportionate to His filial relation to the Father. To import suffering into one of the divine Persons as such is patripassianism.

Finally, one might question the necessity of the Incarnation based upon the idea that the Son's descent in obedience is to be the greatest expression and revelation of the intra-Trinitarian love. It appears Christ's humanity serves simply to make as much of this Trinitarian revelation visible (literally) as possible. Insofar as one considers Christ's humanity abstracted from His divinity, His life of charity in the flesh appears to have little, if any, importance in the redemption itself. His descent makes for fallen human nature, and of fallen human nature, a path to the Father, and His life and death are the archetype to follow, but do this life and death have any redemptive value in themselves, abstracted from the Descent? It seems only that,

> in the contrast between the two wills of the Father and the Son on the Mount of Olives, and in the abandonment of the Son by God on the Cross, the drastic counterposing of the divine Persons in the economy became *visible*.[111]

The key redemptive and revelatory moment in Sheol is beyond every eye.

c. On the Efficacy of the Incarnation

Given the unique necessity of the Incarnation as Balthasar sees it, including its character as a redemptive event, one may legitimately ask whether the Incarnation 'works,' that is, whether the redemption is in fact accomplished in a manner consistent with the reasons it was said to be necessary. Here also problems arise.

First and very significantly, how is it that Christ goes to Sheol because He must be conformed to his brethren in everything, that is, like as *they are in reality,* but *none* of his brethren go there? He is to save men through sharing their experiences, but no one other than Christ has this experience. How is Christ's being dead in Sheol a human death at all? How is it a sharing in the death that "is an essential part of our existence"?[112] After all, Christ's experience in Sheol is not simply different in degree (the merited damnation of all instead of just one person's), but ultimately of kind: He is wholly abandoned by the Father in Sheol, whereas any soul in hell will find the testimony of God's "ever-greater" love there ahead of him. Again, if the Holy Spirit maintains a bond between the Son in Sheol and the Father, how is He really dead with the human dead, with those who have died in the God-forsakenness of sin and who do not have this bond? And if His being dead remains truly human even though it differs in quality (because "He plumbed the abyss of our death far more deeply than we could ever do"[113]), why cannot His descent remain a true human death but be glorious, as the Tradition has it? Balthasar is inconsistent in arguing for the one and against the other when he holds that a glorious Descent would differ in kind from the descent for which all men were fated prior to Christ. The fact that Christ's glorious descent differed in manner from that of other men does not jeopardize the traditional soteriology that sees the cross as the *locus salutis*. In contrast, however, the difference in kind between Christ's descent and that of all other men in Balthasar's theology weakens the foundation of his entire soteriology: Christ is supposed to accomplish redemption through undergoing the punishment of the 'second death' for all sinners. Yet if this punishment was the real absence of God for all eternity,[114] it is vitiated in Christ's case by the unfelt though real presence of the Holy Spirit, who continues to unite the Son to the Father and His love. There are few options in consequence: Either Christ did not really undergo mankind's punishment and so we are still dead in our sins; He was truly abandoned by the Holy Spirit and the Father, and hence the Trinity was really dissolved in the Descent; or Balthasar was mistaken on what brought about the redemption.

Second, how is creaturely obedience made a path for man to God if Christ is no longer man in Sheol, because He has been stripped of His humanity or, at the very least, He is no longer man as other men are because His corporality has undergone an indescribable "stretching"? How indeed is creaturely obedience made a path for men to follow if Christ's perfect act is one in which He both is sin and is acting out of obedience at the same time, yet it is not possible for other men to obey and be pleasing to God in respect to the same act in which they are sinners? Though Christ's disciples share in His "disposition of sacrifice,"[115] in "being disposed to follow the Lord,"[116] i.e., to be disposed of according to the will of another, it is nonetheless impossible for them to follow or imitate Him in the most perfect expression of His love; martyrdom has only an inner likeness in disposition to Christ's death and descent.[117] What is at issue here is not Christ's undisputedly unique grace of headship, by which His redemptive act alone is the font of merit for all other good acts, but the fact that the inner likeness to Christ in disposition of the members of His mystical body has no corresponding exterior act (or passion) of the entire human person that is like His. True, Christ died, and the martyrs die, but Christ gives something the martyrs cannot give, namely, the death of His soul. The physical, which had received the increased dignity of a sacramental through the Incarnation of the Son, here is disvalued in a definitive way. For not only is the mystical body's physical participation in the death of Christ through the physical deaths of the martyrs here questioned, but likewise the meaning that the death of any Christian can have. While Balthasar interprets the mystics' experiences of hell as a participation in Christ's descent, Balthasar himself acknowledges that the inability of men to follow Christ at the key moment leaves them alienated.[118] Though Balthasar is right to emphasize the importance of the inner disposition over the exterior,[119] the union of this emphasis with his soteriology seems to lead to a devaluing of both interior and bodily imitations of Christ's life and passion, since it appears human nature has very little value both in the accomplishment of the redemption by Christ and in man's own subjective movement toward salvation: The Incarnation is dissolved at the key moment. The Descent is an expression of God's Trinitarian love, which includes a love for the world, but Christ's charity for God and neighbor is of questionable relevance; what is key here is the Son's ('interior') experience of alienation from the Father out of obedience in the Holy Spirit. His disciples also cannot imitate His self-giving in the flesh, since the flesh is "suspended" at the moment of perfect self-giving. Even a decision to reject God — which supposedly manifested the reality of creaturely freedom — need not be respected by God in the end: Balthasar insists that a total, uninterrupted, and perfectly deliberate rejection of God would be necessary for damnation. Yet such a rejection is only possible if human nature is utterly depraved, utterly disoriented from its true end. If one holds instead that human nature is deprived of its just order to God, but can still respond to the grace He always gives to seek Him, it would be morally impossible for a person always to reject grace and never to cooperate with it, since to do so would go against his very nature. Of course, if one holds this latter, more positive view of human nature with Balthasar's soteriology, universal salvation is not only something for which to hope, but something inevitable.

Third, it is difficult to see how Christ can be mankind's mediator, if He is made sin in the way Balthasar describes, even though He commits no sin personally. Balthasar himself says that a sinner cannot mediate on behalf of other sinners before God.[120] Note there is a certain inconsistency here, since he also holds the redemption is brought about not by one contrary (Life/Holiness) overcoming another (Death/Sin), but by the same thing being overcome by its ever-greater analogue: death by "super-death," the God-forsakenness of sin by the yet greater God-forsakenness of the Son,[121] etc. Taking him at his word, however, coupled with his insistence that Jesus actually takes mankind's sins upon Himself as His own, appears to end in a dilemma: If Christ's death is guilty, how can He be an effective intercessor? But if it is not guilty, how is it representative of sinners? Again, either Jesus actually takes on the world's guilt, and thus is proportionately incapable of quieting God's wrath, or else His utter sinlessness must be maintained, contrary to Balthasar's soteriology.

Balthasar's solution is to say Christ's death was guilty, but undertaken in obedience; thus it is representative of our death, but also pleasing to God.

> The perpetrator of injustice *as such* cannot appeal to God without having to expect the repudiation of his sin. . . . Only God, taking manhood in Christ, becomes in one single Person both "subject and object" of judgment and justification.[122]

Thus, according to Balthasar, Christ is still a mediator because He does not appeal to the Father on man's behalf in the same respect in which He Himself has been made sin. But the only respect in which He is not made sin is His hypostatic obedience. Thus He is mediator only with respect to His divine nature — or rather, Person — not with respect to His human nature; He is not high priest as man. Moreover, since what a thing is depends on its nature, if Christ has been "literally 'made sin'" and is only 'divine' so far as His hypostasis self-subsists, then He, the Son, *is* sin — and then He cannot be mediator with respect to His divinity either.

Fourth, it appears Balthasar separates overly much the act of sin from the guilt and loss of grace that are its consequence. Since both guilt and the loss of grace do not require that a corporal act be carried out, their cause is an act of the will. But there is no time that separates a state of indecision from decision. The decision is itself the turn from one to the other, and so grace is lost and guilt incurred in the same instant as the decision is made. Balthasar's soteriology depends on the distinction of these three, however, since Christ assumes only the guilt and the loss of grace, but without Himself committing any sinful act of the will. But if Christ brings into the Trinitarian bracket only the guilt and the loss of grace, how is it that sin itself (which is a reality only insofar as it was an act of the will) is consumed in the Trinitarian love?

Along the same lines, we must ask whether act, guilt, and consequence can really be separated as Balthasar does. The answer is negative so long as the past cannot be undone, not even by God's omnipotence: It cannot be changed that it was this particular sinner, not Christ, who committed that sinful act. Guilt (which is to be distinguished from the feeling of guilt) is the ascription of responsibility for a wrong act, and is manifested in the loss of grace. It is an acknowledgment of a reality in the sinner, namely, his injustice (past or present) before God. Guilt is not an ascription of a reality separable from the sinner like a statement of debt, which can be given or transferred to another, because sin was nothing other than this person acting in this way. Forgiveness does not undo the fact of the sinful act, i.e., it does not undo the act itself; rather, it undoes the loss of grace that is its simultaneous effect. When a sin is forgiven (or better said, when the person is forgiven for what he did wrong), guilt likewise is taken away, since the sinner recognizes he is no longer unjust, in virtue of the forgiving, justifying Word of God that effects what it says. More precisely, the guilt of the present state (i.e., guilt *in its effects*) is removed through the infusion of grace, whereas the guilt of the past event (i.e., guilt as recognition of a fact) is unchangeable in that it continues to be true to say he was the one who committed that act.

Fifth, it is difficult to understand how God, who commands no one to sin (Sir 15:21) and desires not the death of the sinner (Ezek 18:32; 33:11), could ask anyone living to God to die to Him spiritually, or why this reality would be pleasing to Him just because He asked for it.

Sixth, Balthasar had objected to the beatific vision in Christ because, as he characterized it, it left no room for human activity and spontaneity. He replaced it with the moment-by-moment revelation of the Father's will by the Spirit in the *visio immediata*. But this 'solution' in fact seems to vitiate human activity more, since human acts are chosen to reach a particular end. Yet in Balthasar's theology it appears Jesus often does not know that toward which He is advancing. Balthasar sees greater virtue in this ignorance, namely, that of faith and obedience, because faith requires ignorance and because he thinks the merit of obedience does too. But if Balthasar wanted to attribute faith to Christ in order to attribute to Him a superior motive of action than unaided human reason, one might reply that although the knowledge of God obtained through faith is superior to knowledge through human reason in a certain sense,[123] nonetheless it is not superior to the beatific vision, which is perfect knowledge of the same object that is known imperfectly by faith. In addition, Balthasar does not give convincing arguments that obedience requires ignorance. Indeed, he contradicts himself insofar as Christ fulfills His mission only insofar as it is revealed to Him, i.e., He obeys the Father only insofar as He knows what He is to do.

Finally, we must observe that the cross of Christ is emptied of its power as the definitive locus of the reconciliation of God and the world. Indeed, after stressing the importance of the Cross, treatments of Balthasar's soteriology frequently go on to discuss the *Descent,* as if the two were equivalent.[124] True, Balthasar can *say* the cross is redemptive for men because men's sins are transferred to Christ in His crucifixion, but this work of redemption cannot honestly be said to be finished *(Consummatum est!)* until God is true to His own justice and rejects these sins in the Person of the dead Son, and until what men have lost of themselves in their sins is taken up into the Trinitarian love. The crucifixion is not necessary to reveal the distinction of Persons; Christ's agony in the garden already served this purpose. His self-gift on the Cross was not even necessary as an example: Just as it was not necessary for Christ to suffer as an example to His disciples all milder trials that would have called for self-gift in obedience (e.g., a chronic medical problem), so the extreme of self-gift in obedience required for the redemption (i.e., unto Sheol) would include every lesser manifestation, including crucifixion. In the end, if it is the Son's suffering of the *visio mortis* that perfects the reconciliation of God to the world, this agony can be suffered without death by crucifixion at all. It then appears that the Cross is both insufficient for the reconciliation of God and men, and utterly unnecessary. In other words, it becomes a sadistic sort of prelude to Sheol.

d. On the Implications for Those Who Follow Christ

It has already been mentioned that Jesus' disciples can neither follow nor imitate Him in His consummate act of love, and hence the value of human nature in both objective and subjective redemption is questionable. Unlike Christ, other men cannot be sin and love at the same time. Thus they are left in alienation, which the Spirit is to overcome. It seems this situation of alienation can reappear in the spiritual life, however, but precisely as the *result* of the Spirit: A person may desire to take another's damnation upon himself. As a conscious act of self-offering, "this act would have to be forbidden, and rightly so, by his spiritual director."[125] Made "in a state of enraptured love,"[126] however, the person may be granted by God an experience of "something of the timeless hell for which, without precisely realizing the fact, [he] yearns."[127] Without entering into details of mystical theology, we must point out the questions raised by Balthasar's presentation: There are many holy acts to which someone may be inspired and which his director *may* forbid; but is it credible that the Spirit would inspire something that a spiritual director *must* forbid? Since both God and the spiritual director seek the salvation of this particular soul, if the person is inspired to an act that is truly Christ-like, how can it be something the director *must* forbid?

In addition, the minimal role of human nature in Balthasar's soteriology is again suggested: If the Father shows the Son His love by letting Him offer to go into God-abandonment and by letting Him actually do so (indeed, more: by sending Him to do so), why must the director forbid his charge from even making an analogical offer deliberately? Would not permission be an act of love with supreme likeness to the Father's love, and the offer of the person under direction an act of love similar to the Son's? Given Balthasar's prohibition, it seems rather the loss of grace is to be avoided at all costs by men — but not by the man Jesus. Thus human nature is again not respected in the Person of Christ, nor are its particular characteristics implemented in any lasting and essential way in redemption.

Finally, the justification of God-abandonment in the Trinity is the divine Persons' love for the world and for each other, manifested in their desire to grant each other His will. If love justifies the Son's going into perdition, why does not love justify someone's offer of his own damnation out of love for someone else, if such an offer were accepted by his spiritual director out of a like love? Rather, since the motive for all sins is love, albeit a disordered love, love itself is not an adequate justification for an act, nor can it make good something intrinsically evil, not even if ascribed to God.

Methodological Concerns regarding the Use of Tradition

We cannot here fully discuss the methodology that leads Balthasar to draw his problematic conclusions. In certain key instances, however, his conclusions appear dependent upon a mistaken or debatable reading of some *locus theologicus*. We will consider three such examples: Balthasar's treatment of *Benedictus Deus*, the scriptural foundation for Sheol as Balthasar understands it, and his appreciation for the traditional doctrine of a triumphal Descent. These topics were selected for the importance of the sources involved and the centrality of the theses Balthasar draws from them for his theology of the Descent.

a. The Constitution Benedictus Deus

On January 29, 1336, Pope Benedict XII promulgated the Constitution *Benedictus Deus*. In it, he positively defines that after Christ's ascension, the souls of the saints are in heaven, but already after His passion and death, they have had the vision of God's essence. The portion of the text of interest in the present context runs:

> By this Constitution which is to remain in force for ever, we, with apostolic authority, define the following: According to the general disposition of God, the souls of all the saints who departed from this world before the passion of our Lord Jesus Christ . . . — provided they were not in need of any purification when they died . . . or else, if they then needed . . . some purification, after they have been purified after death — . . . : all these souls, immediately *(mox)* after death and, in the case of those in need of purification, after the purification mentioned above, *since the ascension* of our Lord and Saviour Jesus Christ into heaven . . . have been, are and will be *with Christ in heaven,* in the heavenly kingdom and paradise, joined to the company of the holy angels. *Since the passion and death of the Lord Jesus Christ, these souls have seen and see the divine essence* with an intuitive vision and even face to face . . . ; and in this vision they enjoy the divine essence. Moreover, *by this vision and enjoyment* the souls of those who have already died are *truly blessed and have eternal life* and rest.[128]

It is important to note that the traditional doctrine of the Descent, presented in the first chapters of this work, is wholly compatible with the contrast the pope makes here. Taking into account the Constitution, the traditional doctrine could be summarized sequentially in its relation to Christ's resurrection and ascension in the following way: Christ descends in triumph to the limbo of the Fathers after His passion and death. He there confers the light of glory and the beatific vision on the holy dead. But they are not yet in heaven. (We shall see the reason shortly.) After His descent, Christ rises from the dead. Having fulfilled the proper time, He ascends body and soul into heaven. In His ascension, He leads with Him the souls of the holy dead and introduces them into heaven.[129]

Why is it important that the holy souls in the limbo of the Fathers — who possessed the beatific vision after Christ's descent — were not in heaven until after His ascension? The essential happiness of heaven is the vision of God's essence: By this vision, the souls "are truly blessed and have eternal life," as Benedict XII says. This, the *essential* happiness of heaven, the souls of the holy dead possessed *before* entering heaven. This contrast is indicated visually by the presence of Dysmas in some images of the Harrowing of Hell: The fact that he is with the glorious Christ means he is in paradise,[130] even though he is shown with Christ *in the limbo of the Fathers*. The same thing is indicated by the images when they show Christ pulling the holy dead toward Himself, i.e., into His glory, regardless of whether He stands inside or outside the gate to hell, or is shown entering or leaving it. It is from this striking separation between the essential happiness of heaven and heaven itself that the question at hand arises.

Two reasons besides the pope's definition can be given now in lieu of a fully explicated theology. First, in the Incarnation, a human nature has been irrevocably united to the divine Person of the Son. Though He is not man by His divine essence, the Son is now and forever will be man by nature, the nature He assumed to Himself. Thus to see the Son as He is — which, with the vision of the Father and the Holy Spirit, is the beatific vision — would imply also to see Him as man. But a man is this unity of human soul and body, and the holy dead beheld only His separated soul in His descent. To see the Son in His glory, divine and human, is only possible with Christ's ascension to the right hand of the Father. We see here that heaven is, in some sense, a place, since to be in heaven is linked to being in the presence of Christ's glorified humanity, body and soul. It does not seem possible to say more than this, since we lack experience of how glorified bodies are in a place.

It is to be noted, however, that this determination of heaven as the 'place' where Christ is in His glorified humanity does not change what the essential happiness of heaven is: Man's final end is still God *as God*. Without the beatific vision of the divine essence, man would not be definitively happy even in seeing the sacred humanity of Christ. Christ's humanity remains perfectly human, and no finite creation can satisfy the desire of man's heart. Thus, although the beatific vision implies the vision of Christ as man, it does not necessitate it. Hence the souls of the holy dead could have this vision fully even prior to Christ's resurrection. Nonetheless, the 'location' of heaven as a 'place' is important as a corollary of man's finitude: Though souls are not in a place as bodies are, and glorified bodies are not bound by place as bodies normally are, souls are in the finite 'place' defined by their actions. Thus, they can have the beatific vision and not be where Jesus is (after His resurrection and before the Ascension), or they can have the beatific vision and be where He (body and soul) is.

Another reason why it can reasonably be maintained the holy souls were not in heaven until after Christ's ascension, despite their possession of the beatific vision, is based on Scripture. At least Rufinus[131] and St. Thomas Aquinas[132] interpret Ephesians 4:8, "Ascending on high, he led captivity captive," to refer to the entrance of the souls of the holy dead into heaven with Christ at His ascension. Both also connect this interpretation to the doctrine of Christ's triumphal descent, Rufinus by seeing the holy dead as the victory spoils carried off from the defeat of the strong man (Mt 12:29; Mk 3:27; Lk 11:21-22). This interpretation is suggested already in a second-century homily of St. Melito of Sardis.[133] I would suggest as well that the distinction between the essential happiness of heaven and heaven as a 'place' may have a parallel in Revelation 20:4-6. There, the "first resurrection" is the entrance into definitive life with Christ in glory, i.e., heaven as the beatific vision. The period of this first resurrection lasts "a thousand years," which symbolically stands for the duration of the time of the Church before the Final Judgment.[134] The second resurrection implied in the passage corresponds to the resurrection of the body. No reference is made to the ascension of the souls with Christ to heaven as a 'place,' because the text concerns the Church in general and eschatologically, rather than the concrete past event of Christ's ascension. Study of the Scriptural foundation Benedict XII himself used for the definition is outside the present scope.

The foregoing discussion serves to show in brief the compatibility between the traditional doctrine of the Descent and Benedict XII's definition, as well as the reasonableness of this compatibility. Balthasar's theology does not demonstrate such compatibility. I found two places in which he specifically discusses the definition. In the first, he writes that the definition

> states that, *since Christ's Resurrection,* the souls of the departed after their death and the relevant purgation *attain to the direct vision* of God in heaven "before resuming their bodies and before the general judgment."[135]

In the second, he says it

> asserts that *after Christ's ascent* to heaven the souls of the righteous (having undergone the necessary purification) "*see the divine essence* intuitively and face to face . . ." (Neuner-Roos 818-19).[136]

Note that, in both these passages, Balthasar summarizes part of the definition in his own words and then quotes from the definition itself. The part of the definition quoted concerns the vision of the divine essence, while his summaries indicate when this vision first became available. But note he gives two *different* events as the key moment ("since Christ's Resurrection," "after Christ's ascent") and that both of these *differ* from what the definition itself states ("Since the passion and death of the Lord Jesus Christ").

Moreover, observe that the definition in *Benedictus Deus* is incompatible with Balthasar's theology of the Descent, for at least two reasons. First, the pope speaks of the "death" of Christ, not His being dead. If the signification of *death* here were supposed to include the period of Christ's being dead, the pope would almost certainly have used the proper expression for it, which was current at his time; he would have had to have said something like, "Since the descent *ad inferos* of the Lord Jesus Christ." Second, in Balthasar's theology, it is impossible for the souls of the holy dead to have the beatific vision until Christ's resurrection. As long as He is in Sheol, sin has not been fully brought into the "bracket" of Trinitarian love, or consumed. Hence, the souls of the dead do not have access to the Father, because the way to Him has not yet been completed. At the precise instant when this expiation is accomplished, Jesus is raised.[137] Thus the way Balthasar paraphrases *Benedictus Deus* reflects not the text itself, but the exigencies of his own theology.

b. Sheol

The second concern arising from Balthasar's methodology relates to the foundation for Balthasar's idea of Sheol. Without doubt, his idea of Sheol conditions his soteriology. If Christ has only one experience of the abode of the dead and it is to make Him solidary in condition with all the dead, then that abode cannot be differentiated. Purgatory, hell, and heaven cannot pre-exist His being dead, but are products of it, because the Descent event constitutes Christ as the universal judge: The existence of these abodes reflects a judgment, and hence they cannot exist prior to the judge's taking possession of his authority and exercising it. Hence there is only one possible abode of the dead for Christ to enter after His own death, the sheol of the Old Testament. Using primarily the Psalms, Balthasar characterizes this abode as one of darkness, powerlessness, solitude, and silence.[138] Theologically formulated, it entails the "deprivation of the vision of God."[139] To this negative characterization, Balthasar provides a positive one, describing Sheol as "the summation of everything that resists God's sway, that cannot be united to God and is, as such, rejected by God."[140] It is the realm of

317

sin-in-itself, a "second 'chaos.'"[141] Christ must go into this abode, experience it, and be conformed to it through the *visio mortis* in order to reconcile God and the world. As a result, He will be established as the eschatological judge.

The seminal Scriptural descriptions seem tame in comparison to the theology of Sheol Balthasar has established upon them, and one might ask whether they in fact assert less than he does. I have not seen any independent works that would support Balthasar's characterizations of Sheol as the realm of sin-in-itself, etc. Indeed, Alan Cooper rejects the position that "the ancient Israelites did not assert the dominance of YHWH over death"[142] as unsustainable. In contrast, Balthasar's milder descriptions of Sheol would be supported by Scriptural exegesis, but only in regard to a limited part of the Old Testament theology of the afterlife.[143] Balthasar is selective; e.g., he neglects Psalm 139:8's explicit reference to sheol *(RSV):* "If I make my bed in sheol, thou art there!" The Old Testament view of death is not as uniform as Balthasar suggests. Even if it were, the Old Testament can be understood rightly only in light of the New, and the New Testament indicates differentiated abodes of the dead, drawing upon Old Testament terms and imagery.

The matter at hand, however, does not concern interpretation, but methodology. For in order to found his theology of Sheol, Balthasar explicitly excludes certain books of Scripture. His most extensive explanation is given in a footnote to the phrase, "the classic theology of the Old Testament." There Balthasar writes,

> And it is on the basis of this theology that we must approach our consideration of the New Testament at the decisive point. The speculations which forced their way into late Judaism under Persian and hellenistic influences, concerning a differentiation of Sheol according to punishment and reward for behaviour on earth, are significant in their place, and can be traced on the margins of the New Testament too; it is significant that this should be so in Luke, in the parable about Lazarus (16:19-31) and in the word [to] the good thief (23:43). But both "paradise" and "Gehenna" remain polyvalent, and receive their theological unequivocalness only through the event of Holy Saturday. The Pentateuch, Joshua, Judges, and Kings know of no differentiation of destinies after this life.[144]

A few observations can be made on this statement of methodology. First, Balthasar implicitly contrasts the doctrinal content of the earlier books of the Bible with the later ones, i.e., with those written in late Judaism and with books of the New Testament. Second, these differences in the later books are attributed to the influence of pagan cultures. Third, these differences generally have limited significance, but they have had greater influence on the question of the afterlife, even more than they should have had. Fourth, the meaning of *paradise* and *gehenna* in the later books is determined by the event of Christ's descent. Fifth, the books of the Pentateuch, Joshua, Judges, and Kings are apparently those that embody "the classic theology of the Old Testament."

Now the authority of Sacred Scripture does not come from the culture through which it was received and passed on, but from God. Hence one wonders at Balthasar's alarm about cultural influences from the Persians and the Greeks, and his lack of it concerning the cultures of those who received the earliest revelations of God and the cultures of those lands in which they lived, such as Canaan and Egypt. Hence, if both early and late books are culturally influenced, yet they all have an equal authority from God, it is not clear why the later passages have a more limited significance simply because they are later, nor why the cultural influence on the earlier books does not merit the concern that that on the later ones does.

In addition, cultural milieux need not distort divine revelation, but may providentially aid it insofar as they provide a basis for understanding revelation (i.e., 'precomprehension'); it should require no argument that the Church does not swallow all features of the cultures she encounters, but selectively incorporates and purifies under God's guidance the elements of truth she finds in them. Against a historical-critical approach that overly dissects the Gospels, Balthasar himself insisted, "The whole Gospel is inspired."[145] Moreover, if those passages that see Sheol as differentiated are not significant in the context of the theology of death, especially that of the Old Testament, when else would they be relevant?

There is, as well, the issue of God's progressive revelation.[146] If one grants that not all the books of Scripture are equally explicit on the same topics and hence none is superfluous, then one will not look for equally clear differentiation of the afterlife in all the books, but will look rather for how what is affirmed with less specificity is compatible with what is affirmed with greater specificity. In a section on methodology outside any immediate context relating to the Descent, Balthasar himself recommends that,

> since God's entire purpose for the world is present in every phase of theo-drama . . . the entirety of the word must also be present, at all times, in the individual books and words of Scripture, however much they may characterize one particular aspect, one particular phase. . . . Therefore, if we are to proceed theologically, the individual passages can only be properly interpreted within the total context of Scripture. . . .[147]

It does not appear Balthasar follows this principle of his in regard to sheol. It is in any case debatable whether the books Balthasar favors uniformly portray

Sheol as bleakly as he suggests; the description of the death of the patriarchs as "sleep" (Gen 15:15; 25:8; 25:17; Deut 31:16; 1 Kings 2:10) would already imply there is greater variety.[148] This basis for debate acquires additional weight when it is extended to include the entire Old Testament.

As for Balthasar's statement that *paradise* and *gehenna* receive determinate meanings through the Descent, it is odd that these two concepts do not receive adequate specification prior to the Descent, but *sheol* does; that the two former words admit different readings, but *sheol* resists all nuance. Balthasar's limitation of the significance of later Scriptural books may be the cause of this rigidity: The lack of specificity could derive precisely from the elimination of the later books from consideration. The only 'polyvalency' Balthasar himself appears to draw from Scripture regards the duration of the fire of gehenna, and whether it has a purifying effect;[149] whereas his theology of God's being "ever-greater" might allow him to see an ambiguity in *paradise*, because Christ's *visio mortis* is experienced within the Trinitarian love.[150] In any case, as a result of the alleged lack of clarity from the Old Testament, Balthasar suggests that the meanings of *paradise* and *gehenna* in the New Testament must be specified in light of an exterior theology of the Descent, i.e., that no interpretative key is available in either the Old Testament (as Balthasar asserts) or in the New Testament itself (as is implied). In this case, theology determines the meaning of Scripture, not the other way around. Due to the reciprocity and unity between Scripture and Tradition, such theological dependency is reasonable and sometimes essential to eliminate false interpretations. It is only key that one applies a theology that adequately embodies the Church's Tradition. Whether Balthasar's soteriology of the Descent does so is then a question of some importance.

What is of significance just at present is not this question — Balthasar's own explicit contrast of his theology with Tradition will be seen in the next section — however, but the observation that his soteriology serves as an *a priori* principle for the interpretation of Scripture on this topic: Balthasar's soteriology determines his interpretation of Scripture, *including then his selection of which books are relevant to the nature of sheol*. If Balthasar does in fact wish to base his use of Old Testament theology on the books from the Pentateuch to Kings,[151] however, one would have to ask whether he is consistent in applying this limitation not only in regard to a theology of sheol, but also with respect to Old Testament expectations of the Messiah, for example.

In fact, one finds he is not consistent in following his own limitation even about sheol: On one occasion, he references texts from Isaiah and Daniel in regard to a *differentiated* afterlife understood "on the basis of the word of God itself,"[152] whereas in an earlier text he had used these same apparently 'late' books, even the very same chapter of Daniel, to support his characterization of Sheol as *uniformly* a place of dust, isolation, and silence.[153] In both cases, Balthasar uses books that, in his discussion of "the classic theology of the Old Testament," he treats as being of limited and questionable value due to cultural contamination.

Even more evident is the fact that he heavily depends on the Psalms to characterize Sheol, yet the book of Psalms is not on his list of books to consider. If he implicitly included Psalms with Kings insofar as the Psalms were attributed to King David, his methodology undermines his own position, for the Psalms show a much more developed theology of the afterlife than Balthasar indicates.[154] One need only cite Psalm 139:8 (*RSV:* "If I make my bed in sheol, thou art there!") as an example that would call into question Balthasar's portrayal.

Moreover, in regard to certain other topics of Old Testament theology, Balthasar explicitly asserts that Israel adopted foreign elements only insofar as they served to clarify her reflections on her own beliefs.[155] He himself also says attempts to get at Old Testament theology prior to Greek and Persian influences is foolishness, breaking up the legitimate preparation under the divine pedagogy for the New Testament.[156] If he thinks so in other cases, why not in the case of a differentiated afterlife?

What is ultimately key in Balthasar's soteriology and hence what is key in his interpretation of Scripture (since the former drives the latter) is that he sees a change in the reality of the abode of the dead between the Old Testament and the New.[157] Whereas once there was only the 'second death' of Sheol, now there is heaven, hell, and purgatory. In other words, he assumes that the earliest recipients of divine revelation had a clear and correct knowledge of the afterlife, disregarding cultural influences on them, as well as that of the natural fear of death. In contrast, the teaching of the only one who came from above, as this teaching is conserved in the New Testament (Balthasar's examples are Christ's parable about Lazarus and His word to the good thief in the Gospel of Luke), is not considered to clarify, fulfill, and go beyond what was apprehended indistinctly before, but rather is attributed to foreign cultural influences and accorded marginal relevance, if any. It is to say Christ revealed nothing of what death is, but that man knew its character rightly before His coming. This contrast is made yet stronger by the fact that no man but Christ came back from the dead with authority and it is under the inspiration of His Spirit that Scripture — including the Gospel of Luke — was written. Did Truth Incarnate misrepresent the agonizing solitude and darkness of Sheol to the good thief, by saying, "Truly, I say to you, today you will be with me in Paradise" (Lk 23:43 *RSV*)? Was He then ignorant, or malicious? Even if Sheol is paradisiacal to Balthasar, because there the Son most perfectly reveals the Trinitarian love,[158] the thief could not have understood Christ's word in this sense. At the very least, what Christ said would have given him an expectation very different from the reality awaiting him. Or was this word of Christ a misleading and erroneous addition by the evangelist? It is only a question of which author of the Gospel of Luke erred, the human or the divine?

Again, if the Old Testament cannot be understood or interpreted correctly without the light of Christ and the New Testament, as Balthasar himself asserts,[159] why does Balthasar see the case differently with the "classic theology of the Old Testament" regarding death and the afterlife? It seems rather that neither the Old Testament theology of sheol nor a portion of it should be taken as coercive to Christ's experience of death, but rather that His experience reveals what sheol was. As this event is not conserved in Scripture in the most explicit terms, dependence upon the Church's Tradition is all the more necessary to apprehend the truth of this mystery of the Faith and to prevent error. But Balthasar curiously sets Scripture and Tradition in opposition, when he says that Sheol, "in its biblical sense, is by no means the innocuous 'forehell' it has been made into."[160] Christ, however, speaking of the dead patriarchs Abraham, Isaac, and Jacob, said that God is "not the God of the dead, but of the living" (Mt 22:32 and the parallels Mk 12:27 and Lk 20:38). His words show the holy patriarchs were living to God at the time He spoke, i.e., *before* His death and descent. They reveal the reality of what was also true in Old Testament times, even though that truth was not apprehended clearly before Him.

For Balthasar, the word *sheol* defines the experience, whereas for the Tradition, the experience defines the word. Nearly 2000 years after the fact, Balthasar attempts to find the 'real' meaning of *sheol* in the Old Testament in order to say Christ went there. He then sets his conclusions against how the Church herself used and transmitted this word in the centuries after Christ. For when the living Church professed Christ's descent down through the centuries, her words were not devoid of meaning, but carried a determined doctrinal content: More than a reiteration of Christ's death, these words were a profession of the inauguration of His victory over death, beginning with a triumph in the very realm of death itself. Drawing upon her precomprehension from the Old Testament, she called the abode to which Christ went *sheol,* but did not thereby limit or define His experience according to the Old Testament descriptions, because she recognized His unique experience clarified, fulfilled, and transcended the truth in the Old Testament. In other words, Balthasar defines *sheol* and then says Christ descended there, whereas the Church believed something of Christ's descent and then called this abode of the dead *sheol.*

c. The Traditional Doctrine of the Descent

Even if one wanted to argue (and it would be difficult) that there is no traditional Catholic doctrine of the Descent, it is indisputable that a particular doctrine of the Descent has been exceptionally preeminent in the history of the Church, both theologically and in the practice of the Faith. Balthasar's comportment to this doctrine is suggestive of his valuation of the *loci theologici* upon which it is based and in which it is embodied.

The first part of the present work argued for the existence and characteristics of an authoritative traditional doctrine of Christ's descent based upon the testimony of creeds, catechisms, Scripture, Scriptural commentaries and theological explanations by saints, magisterial statements and the liturgy, and expressions of the *sensus fidelium* (as embodied in artistic representations consistent with the other sources). Most of these sources appear in various forms in Balthasar's theological treatments, as well. How does Balthasar treat the traditional doctrine of Christ's descent embodied in them?

It has been seen that Balthasar regards the active formulation *(descendit)* of the creed as misleading, in contrast to his insistence on the passive character of the Incarnation based on that article's formulation in the passive *(incarnatus est)*. Balthasar's application of his own principles of interpretation is inconsistent: He had most rigorously interpreted the passive formulations on the Incarnation in the creed, but his arguments against Scripture passages that would counter his interpretation of the passive nature of the Incarnation are tenuous and forced.[161] He did not likewise narrowly interpret the active credal formulations of the Descent, despite Scriptural support for them: When stressing the passivity of Christ's descent, he only gives the briefest footnote, "Although 1 Pet 3:19 employs an active phrase, πορευθείς."[162] The Scriptural text thus is acknowledged, together with the fact that it differs from his own understanding, but no account is given either of how to reconcile the two, or of why Balthasar preferred his own. (Note too that the passive formulation εὐηγγελίσθη of 1 Pet 4:6 also indicates an action inasmuch as a preaching to the dead presupposes the action of a preacher.[163]) Balthasar does not appear to have examined the significance of the *a mortuis* phrases in the article on the Resurrection in those creeds lacking an article specifically on the Descent. However, he develops the New Testament passages regarding Christ's resurrection ἐκ νεκρῶν (from the dead) in the direction of his sense of solidarity with the dead.[164]

As for catechisms and magisterial sources, some of the sources considered here (*The Catechism of the Catholic Church,* the apostolic letter *Novo millennio ineunte,* and John Paul II's catechesis on the Descent) were published after Balthasar's death; hence, there is no reason to expect him to have taken them into account. That is not the case, however, with earlier texts, such as *The Catechism of the Council of Trent,* the encyclical *Mystici Corporis,* or the bull *Unigenitus Dei Filius.* Earlier we saw that Balthasar paraphrased *Benedictus Deus* in accord with his theology, rather than molding his doctrine to the definition.

Balthasar's use of Scripture is ubiquitous in almost all his treatments of the Descent, though also at times arbitrarily selective, overly literal, and conditioned by debatable presuppositions. Some of his presuppositions were examined in the previous subsection on the Scriptural foundation he claims for his understanding of Sheol. Balthasar's dependence on 2 Corinthians 5:21 (on Christ's being "made sin") and Philippians 2:6-8 (on the Son's kenosis) is extraordinary. His reading of 2 Corinthians 5:21 is the most literalistic possible, and he does not seem to have anticipated the objection that these passages must be compatible with the rest of Scripture, including the whole of 2 Corinthians 5:21 (that Christ did not know sin) and, e.g., John 1:14 (on the glory of the Word "full of grace and truth" having been seen). Despite his own explicit acknowledgments of the divine inspiration of Scripture,[165] Scripture passages that would conflict with his position are either glossed into compatibility,[166] dismissed as interpretations of the human author[167] or well-meant additions to what actually happened,[168] or simply omitted.[169]

The following passage is also revealing in this context:

> That Jesus did not have many of the details of the Passion before his eyes in advance, *despite knowledge of them being attributed to him by the evangelists,* need not be disputed, precisely because he left completely to the Father the entire arranging of the time and content of the "hour" (Mk 13:32).[170]

Here, on the basis of one verse by an evangelist (and we may supply its parallel in Mt 24:36), Balthasar denies Jesus detailed knowledge of His coming passion *despite* what the *evangelists* themselves say. In other words, Balthasar sets the evangelists in opposition among themselves and then acts as the referee over them, himself determining that this one verse should be preferred to the rest of the Gospels, instead of trying to reconcile it with its broader context as part of the inspired writings. It is not unreasonable to ask what Balthasar's criteria are and where he gets his knowledge about Jesus so as to be able to judge the evangelists in this way? If the greater part of the Gospels are not trustworthy witnesses to Jesus, then what is? One must ask if it is the same source of knowledge preferred by Balthasar that led him to interpret Scriptural texts about the eschatological destruction of God's *enemies* in regard to *Jesus'* descent:

This is the plunging down of the "Accursed One" (Gal 3:13) far from God, of *the One who is "sin"* (2 Cor 5:21) *personified,* who, falling where he is "thrown" (Rev 20:14), "consumes" his own substance (Rev 19:3; "Thou hast made the city a heap, the fortified city a ruin," Is 25:2). . . . This is the essence of the second death: that which is cursed by God in his definitive judgment (Jn 12:31) sinks down to the place where it belongs.[171]

The peppering of Scriptural references suggests strong support for Balthasar's interpretation. Is it justified? The verses themselves, read together with his interpretation, speak volumes about Balthasar's use of Scripture:

Gal 3:13: "Christ redeemed us from the curse of the law, having become a curse for us — for it is written, 'Cursed be every one who hangs on a tree.'"

2 Cor 5:21: "For our sake he made him to be sin who knew no sin, so that in him we might become the righteousness of God."

Rev 20:14: "Then Death and Hades were thrown into the lake of fire. This is the second death, the lake of fire."

Rev 19:3: "Once more they cried, 'Hallelujah! The smoke from her goes up for ever and ever.'"

Jn 12:31: "Now is the judgment of this world, now shall the ruler of this world be cast out."

The 'she' referenced by Revelation 19:3 is the "great harlot" (Rev 19:2), Babylon. Balthasar elsewhere applies this same verse to Babylon "as quintessence of the sin of the world" and as the "powers of evil."[172] Here he applies it to Christ. The burning of Babylon is a symbol for the incineration of refuse;[173] in the eschatological context, this refuse is "sin, which has been separated from the sinner by the work of the Cross,"[174] and which — as it is variously described — Christ has taken to His own Person,[175] to which He is conformed by the *visio mortis,*[176] which He has "literally" been made,[177] which He embodies,[178] and which He personifies.[179] Hence we read also: "What is damnable in [a man] has been separated from him and thrown out with the unusable residue that is incinerated outside the gates of the Holy City."[180] In other words, in the Person of Christ, sin-in-itself is to be burned outside the Holy City, i.e., in Sheol.

Finally, as for the *descensus* theology of the saints, the liturgy, and the *sensus fidelium,* Balthasar groups them together in one of his more focused treatments as "the liturgical, speculative and rhetorical-popular theology"[181] of the Descent. The "rhetorical" theology refers to the presence of the doctrine in sermons, including homilies from the patristic era. Balthasar sees the theme of a triumphal Descent in these sources as the result of a large-scale incorporation of elements from midrashic, pagan, and apocryphal journeys to the under-world.[182] From this basis came "the corresponding patristic sermons, the medieval descent plays and . . . Dante's *Inferno.*"[183] He continues, "All of this" — i.e., these works from both outside *and within* the Catholic tradition up until Dante — "takes us far from the biblical message. . . ."[184] After setting forth his soteriology as one that returns to a more biblical foundation, he brings his essay to a conclusion, saying,

> So the many folk myths of the *descensus* do indeed remain significant as approaches to the mystery postulated by the riddle of human death; nonetheless, they do not *in any way* anticipate the answer to that riddle.[185]

In this essay, Balthasar treats the Descent particularly in relation to pagan, Jewish, and Christian mythology, but his conclusion is far wider. It is noteworthy that although he elsewhere refers to an extensive list of other material on the Descent, including the works of several Fathers of the Church and other ancient Christian writers,[186] he does not mention them precisely when he criticizes the whole "liturgical, speculative and rhetorical-popular theology" of the Descent, of which they form a far more authoritative part than the myths.

In general, we are reminded here of Balthasar's concern about cultural contamination in the biblical theology of sheol, and we are again puzzled by it. First, if one must strip Catholicism of anything that even resembles pagan mythology, it would be inconsistent for Balthasar to hold certain other Catholic doctrines; the virginal conception of Christ, for example, would be susceptible to this criticism.

Second, assuming the omnipotence and omniscience of God, it is reasonable to think He chose the times best suited for His revelation. Existing myths could then bear a certain influence (foreseen by God), but doctrines similar to mythic elements would only be believed by the Church if they were actually *true,* since she is *infallibilis in credendo et docendo* under the guidance of the Holy Spirit. In the case of the Descent and its representation in art and drama, one must take into account the limits and advantages of particular genres and media, in order to distinguish between the doctrine and its expression. These works are attempts to express a spiritual, intangible event in images, using a developed (sometimes exaggerated) language of symbolism, the fundamental elements of which were established in the earliest centuries and based upon Scripture. "Behind all the images . . . stands the one idea of salvation through Christ and the overthrow of the hostile power of evil."[187] The media and methodology are legitimately suited to the conditions of this earthly life, though one may, of course, debate the merits of a particular such expression. The way Balthasar expresses his concerns about the artistic representations of the Descent in general (as opposed to individual works) at times suggests that he thought people, including some of the greatest theologians, believed Christ literally used armed force to enter the underworld and physically trampled on the devil, that even in the most grossly exaggerated apocrypha and plays the moral and the medium could not be distinguished.[188]

Third, Balthasar does not conclusively show that the triumphal elements to which he objects do not have their origin in Scripture or in the beliefs of the early Christian community precisely as such, and the burden of proof rests with him. It would be undeniable that the canonical Scriptures influenced at least some of the apocryphal ones. Consequently, later works that reflect influence by apocrypha ought not to be generally dismissed as if they had no foundation whatsoever in Scripture or Tradition. Apocrypha need not be the products of heretics, madmen, or individuals merely 'baptizing' pagan myths; they are simply ancient works that arose in the Christian community and were later recognized as not having been divinely inspired. Taking into account the limitations of their literary forms, these works may be considered in general as expressions of belief; the specific details to be held or rejected as in accord with the Faith would require (and merit) consideration. Judicious use of their witness does not imply they are affirmed in every detail. The relevance of pagan myths is, in any case, debatable.[189] The Fathers of the first four centuries took 1 Peter as the chief witness to the doctrine, i.e., a testimony at once Scriptural and apostolic.[190]

These three points critique matters of principle. With regard to the question of the apocrypha in detail, we wish to bring forward merely one example, concerning the influential apocryphum, the Gospel of Nicodemus: In his homily, "On Pascha," the second-century bishop St. Melito of Sardis writes in the person of Christ that

> I have freed the condemned,
> given life anew to the dead,
> raised up those in the grave;
> . . . .
> destroyed death,
> triumphed over the Enemy,
> trodden Hades under foot,
> bound the Strong Man,
> and led men into the heights of heaven.[191]

Something similar appears in the anaphora of St. Hippolytus of Rome's *Apostolic Tradition:*

> We thank You, God, through Your beloved servant Jesus Christ,
>   . . . the Logos coming from You . . . ,
> who, handed over to voluntary suffering,
> in order to abolish death,
> break the bonds of the devil,
> tread Hades under,
> enlighten the just,
> set a boundary,
> and announce the resurrection,
> took the bread, gave You thanks, and said. . . .[192]

The texts may themselves be related,[193] but in any case the likeness in thought is apparent. To these two texts, a third should be compared, namely, that of the Gospel of Nicodemus.[194] This famous apocryphum, widely regarded as having greatly influenced the *descensus* Tradition, shows similar features, even if highly dramatized: At the Descent of Christ, the gates and bars of the underworld are shattered,[195] and the bounds of the dead are broken. Hades is filled with light, while Satan is seized and ordered to be thrown in chains. It is specifically mentioned that Christ grasps Adam and raises him up, then leads all into paradise. The point of this comparison is to suggest that the general images found (and sometimes objected to) in the most influential apocryphum pre-existed in the Christian community, indeed in occasions of her public liturgy: St. Melito's text dates from c. 160[196] and the anaphora of St. Hippolytus from c. 218,[197] but the Gospel of Nicodemus from around 220.[198] Even if one were to suggest the apocryphal Gospel is much older, to show St. Melito and St. Hippolytus were dependent upon it or other apocrypha would be another thing, especially given that their restrained expressions can find adequate root in Sacred Scripture. Hence, given the presence of these images of redemption in Scripture and the works of early ecclesiastical writers (of whom only two have been mentioned here), it would have to be proven that the doctrine of Christ's triumphal descent is the result of these and later writers christianizing Greek and Jewish apocalyptic literature or depending primarily upon Christian apocrypha. The burden of proof rests with Balthasar.

In regard to specific sources and expressions of the traditional doctrine, we consider first the "rhetorical-popular theology" of the spiritual plays. In one place, Balthasar explains the dramatic structure of these plays in the following way:

> In this theatrical presentation of the mystery of Christ, the real peripeteia — Christ's suffering on our behalf — could not be portrayed at all; conse-

quently all the emphasis is on what is visible, namely defeat (the Cross) and victory (the Resurrection). So the opponents and enemies become stylized, the devil on one side and the Jews on the other.[199]

We note here four things: First, it is Christ's suffering that Balthasar sees as the heart of "the mystery of Christ." Second, the relevant agony is *not* that of the visible Cross, but that of Christ hidden in Sheol, which "could not be portrayed at all." Holy Saturday, not Good Friday, is the moment of the "real peripeteia." Third, in the disjunction between Cross and Resurrection as Balthasar states it, the possibility of a play for Holy Saturday is denied. Finally, no integration is made of those plays (by no means rare) that in fact depicted Christ's descent into hell — and with extraordinary unanimity depicted it as a triumph like that of the Resurrection.[200] Since the mystery of Holy Saturday is so central for Balthasar, this lacuna is striking — unless he has here misread or misrepresented as the Resurrection their portrayal of a victorious Descent. The lacuna is all the more striking given the regard he expresses elsewhere for the fruitfulness of the *descensus* plays and for the fact that "its perspective was centered in the eucharistic mystery and at the same time in the whole drama of salvation."[201] More specifically, we read,

> The Easter plays . . . are uniquely illuminating; naively portraying Christ's descent into the underworld, they mediate the awareness of an all-transforming action. Thus they continue the work of a theology that was alive in patristic preaching and in the frescoes and icons of the Eastern Church but which had been almost entirely stifled by the systematization of the scholastics.[202]

> As for these icons of a living theology, though generally one must

> guard against that theological busyness and religious impatience which insist on anticipating the moment of fruiting of the eternal redemption through the temporal passion — on dragging forward that moment from Easter to Holy Saturday,[203]

Balthasar concedes the *Anastasis* icon to the Eastern Church: It represents Holy Saturday as the moment of "supreme dramatic intensity"[204] and shows "the soteriological and social aspect of the redemptive work,"[205] albeit "by the transformation of a victory which was objective and passive into one that is subjective and active."[206] It is only on this basis of "dramatic intensity" that Balthasar can suggest a link between his soteriology and the Eastern tradition of the Church,[207] for which "the image of Redemption is the Descent of Christ into Hades."[208] According to Balthasar, this tradition was "lost to the West at an early stage,"[209] so that the corresponding image in the West is Christ's crucifixion.[210] He will interpret the icon, however, as a symbol of the redeeming character of Christ's descent (His "being dead"), rather than as a representation of its objective nature:

> The reality of the *poena damni* is spiritual and can be experienced only spiritually. . . . The descent of Jesus into the reality of death that preceded Redemption is part of his humiliations, even though this ultimate humiliation, beyond which no other is possible, is already shot through with the light of Easter night. . . . For this journey through Hades carries Redemption into it.[211]

The vivid portrayals of Christ's descent as triumphal in the icons, as well as in various other artistic media, can be explained by the fact that the event itself was not witnessed, but its decisive importance as the turning point from Good Friday to Easter Sunday required expression.[212]

As it was, the Descent's significance is shown in images exactly opposite of what Balthasar thinks its reality was. Thus Balthasar's interpretation seems forced and his dismissal of the traditional reading of the icon unsound, especially given the clear parallel between the representations of Christ in glory in the *Anastasis* icon and that of the Transfiguration. We recall the third canon of the Fourth Ecumenical Council of Constantinople:

> We decree that the sacred image of our Lord Jesus Christ . . . must be venerated with the same honor as is given the book of holy Gospels. . . . For, what speech conveys in words, pictures announce and bring out in colors.[213]

Balthasar overlooks that the *Anastasis* icon compacts the *entire* Triduum into one image *without* weighting one day or the other as the 'dramatic peak': Death, descent, and resurrection are all part of the essence of the icon. The *locus* imaged in the icon is the limbo of the Fathers, but the event shown is premised upon Christ's death on Good Friday. At the same time, it points ahead to His resurrection on Easter Sunday in the way only a visual image can do, that is, using the body as image of the soul. The dead but glorious Christ lifts the holy dead into His own glory, and thus the Body of the Church is conformed to her Head.

In addition, contrary to Balthasar's implied claim that the ancient Church in both East and West shared the Descent as the image of redemption, but that the West lost this focus early on, the Western artistic representation of Christ's harrowing of hell proliferated at least up until the Protestant Reformation and what it portrays is perfectly consistent with the Eastern icon, including showing the "soteriological and social aspect." As pointed out in Chapter Four, the decrease in artistic popularity of the subject matter in the West is not due to a change in doctrine, but appears to be the result of a shift in devotional emphasis.

The opposition Balthasar sets between the Church in East and West on the topic of the Descent is contrived.[214] Hence it results in untenable assertions, such as the following:

> We can, oversimplifying, distinguish two great lines of tradition: that of the East and that of the West. For the East, the icon of Christ's descent forms the main representation of our redemption. [A description of the icon follows.] This tradition reaches from very early preaching until the Easter mystery plays of the Middle Ages. . . . In the West, theology and liturgy mainly pay homage to the silence of death; the Church watches with silent Mary and prays at the grave.[215]

Here, Balthasar implicitly admits both the ancient origins of the traditional doctrine and its unbroken transmission until the late Middle Ages. He assigns these traditional expressions to "the East," although they flourished likewise in the West. His admission is not to be overlooked, since the entire Church is born from the East; 'the West' received the Faith as a whole from her roots in the East. The rest of his statement is simply erroneous historically: We have seen that the traditional doctrine of the Descent is expressed in the Western liturgy and, as for theology, one need only take St. Thomas Aquinas as an example of theologians who paid attention to the doctrinal content of the mystery beyond just "the silence of death." Balthasar himself frequently points to medieval discussions of whether Christ could be said to be a man while He was dead as impotent scholastic hairsplitting, but these same debates are evidence of a living interest in the mystery. As the Catholic Church in East and West is only one, her various traditions cannot have doctrines that conflict essentially about the locus of the redemption. In Part One, harmony or unanimity was seen on this matter. Markwart Herzog judges that, in the Catholic sphere, "through the centuries, one was too sure about the meaning and explanation of the Descent article for it to come to considerable controversy."[216] In any case, if one insists on two different images of the redemption, the two may easily be reconciled by observing that the Western emphasis on images of the crucifixion stresses the objective redemption, and the Eastern emphasis on the *Anastasis* icon highlights the subjective.

Unfortunately, the secondary literature on Balthasar all too frequently shows a blind acceptance of the opposition Balthasar claims to exist between East and West about the redemption and Christ's descent. What is yet more disturbing, because irresponsible, is that this opposition is often presented as a matter of accepted fact, i.e., without any acknowledgment of Balthasar as its source. We will not here embarrass specific authors.

As for the liturgy, Balthasar acknowledges its special importance as a *locus theologicus* when he turns to liturgical texts to discover the Church's mind and so to invoke her authority in support of his doctrine of hope for the salvation of all.[217] A like consideration of liturgical texts is conspicuously absent from Balthasar's treatments of the Descent, and he does not provide an account for the liturgical profession of a triumphal Descent, such as he did for the artistic representations.

As for the *descensus* theology of the saints, both scientific and homiletic (or "rhetorical"), it can generally be noted that the examples of Catholic saints Balthasar adduces in support of his thesis do not in themselves contradict the conclusions of Part One here. Indeed, if read on their own terms and without Balthasar's commentary, some clearly do not support his thesis about Christ's experience of abandonment in Sheol, and some even contradict it. Others do not support his thesis in any necessary sense, and are open to an interpretation consistent with the greater Tradition. If such an interpretation turned out to be impossible or unduly forced in some one case, it must be recalled first that saints only have authority as theologians insofar as they express the Faith of the Church; and second, that they themselves would likely be the first to give up a particular theological opinion if it contradicted the Church's Tradition.

Consequently, in this context of Balthasar's comportment to various *loci theologici,* it seems more appropriate to consider principles that are embedded in the work of many saints, rather than examining individual texts of individual saints. Recall that Balthasar's soteriology is heavily dependent upon the principle, "What is not *endured* is not healed," in contrast to the patristic principle, "What is not *assumed* is not healed." As seen in Chapter Five, the difference between the two is difficult to explain because Balthasar gives evidence he knows the original principle. He has another principle similar in origin and application to this one that uses "endured" rather than "assumed." Again Balthasar begins with St. Gregory Nazianzen, but ends up using him in a way inconsistent with his original text. In *ThDrIV,* Balthasar writes,

> Everywhere this formula, "me in my entirety and all that is mine," is similarly restricted to the consequences of sin and the punishment due to sin, whereas sin itself is *not* taken on by [Christ]. In this way the *admirabile commercium* comes up against an unconscious limit — unconscious because it is taken for granted. The Redeemer acting on the world stage does not completely fill out his role of representing the sinner before God.[218]

The interior quotation is from the sixth paragraph of St. Gregory's *Oration 30*. Balthasar here treats the Fathers in a way similar to how we earlier saw he treated the evangelists. Note what happens: First, one sentence by St. Gregory is elevated to an absolute principle to which redemption must conform. Second, this sentence is to be interpreted (and redemption consequently characterized) not in the way St. Gregory himself used it, or in the way the later Fathers understood it ("Everywhere this formula . . . is similarly restricted"[219]), but in the way Balthasar thinks it should be. If the principle has authority because it is patristic, to interpret it against the mind of the Fathers surely must dissolve this authority; taken in the way Balthasar understands it, it then becomes merely a principle of Balthasar's, like the principle, "What is not *endured* is not healed." If it has authority simply because it is true and if the truth of man's salvation is supposed to be securely passed on through Tradition, what can be said for Balthasar's regard for Tradition if he considers the unanimous consensus of the Fathers mistaken? And it is not only the Fathers whom he thinks are thus mistaken, for Balthasar points out that St. Anselm and St. Thomas Aquinas (at least) impose the same limit.[220]

Balthasar suggests, however, that there is a whole line of thought that supports his theology of a Descent to suffering. Luther's "teaching on Christ's penal suffering on our behalf (or his experience of hell)," he says, "was not his discovery but was known before his time."[221] Balthasar then attempts to show this history. Considering the examples he gives, however, the suggestion that there was a tradition *before Luther*, i.e., a *Catholic* tradition, according to which Christ suffered the punishment of hell is gravely misleading. For one, the received patristic and medieval tradition limited the assumption of 'punishment' to the natural πάθη consequent to the first sin, as he himself points out.[222] For another, the statements of some of the authors to whom he refers are open to an interpretation consistent with the received tradition, one they would likely appreciate, as already mentioned. The credibility of Balthasar's presentation of the 'tradition' he attempts to invoke is also weakened by missing citations and the presence of qualifiers that call into question how much the authors would really support Balthasar's position. Finally, the few authors whose texts do not fall into these first two categories have little, if any, weight compared to the others; their sparsity can hardly be called a Catholic tradition. Indeed, Markwart Herzog's focused study on *descensus* theologies indicates that, as late as 1457, Nicholas of Cusa was the first explicitly to make the suggestion for which Balthasar appreciates Luther — and that Nicholas' thought on this point, published in 1514, was known to both Luther and Calvin.[223]

Balthasar's objection to the received Catholic Tradition's limitation, and his clear intention to take the *admirabile commercium* beyond it, stand as sufficient caution against interpretations of his work that either would limit the Son's assumption of sin and the consequent God-abandonment to a subjective feeling, denying its status as also a real objective state, or would locate Christ's assumption of sin and His abandonment wholly in the economy, in order to avoid the implications of suffering in the immanent Trinity.[224] Balthasar himself claims the Incarnation affects the Son as such;[225] hence one must conclude that all that occurs to Him once incarnate must likewise affect Him as Son. Both proposed distinctions also overlook Balthasar's soteriology, which requires that the "distance" of all the world's sins be brought inside the "ever-greater distance" of the love between Father and Son. For this to occur only in the economy and not in the immanent Trinity, or only as felt by Christ without objectively happening, is of questionable significance, both as a statement and as an event.

Finally, this section cannot close without a look at Balthasar's clearest and most compact treatment of the traditional doctrine of the Descent, which is his essay, "The Descent into Hell" (*Chicago Studies* 23 [1984]: 223-36). His approach here could almost stand as a paradigm of his methodology on the topic. The essay has six parts: After his introduction, Balthasar considers the Old Testament and Judaic view of the underworld current at the time of Jesus, the Christian tradition regarding Christ's descent, and the New Testament foundation for that tradition. He goes on to present a theology of hell, and then closes the essay with certain conclusions about Christ's descent.

In the first section, on "The Old Testament and Judaism," Balthasar characterizes death not merely as the end of human life, but as separation from the living God and His promises; hence it carries connotations of human guilt and divine wrath. With the acknowledgment of God's dominion over death, however, comes the twofold hope for a bodily resurrection at the end of time and for the reward of good complemented by the punishment of evil. The image of the underworld here is not nearly as grim as those Balthasar presents elsewhere, and moreover it admits of distinct fates after death, unlike Balthasar's Sheol.

It appears this different presentation is necessary to establish a continuity between the Old Testament and Christian traditions, since Balthasar goes on first to mention the fourfold Christian differentiation of the underworld (the limbo of the Fathers, purgatory, the limbo of the children, and the hell of eternal punishment) and then to reduce it to the two he thinks relevant at the time of Jesus' death, namely, sheol and gehenna. "If we then ask, where the dead Jesus descended, according to Christian tradition, the answer is unequivocal: to *sheol*, if we understand by this term 'the realm of death.'"[226] This section of the essay cannot be read closely enough: In it, Balthasar acknowledges the existence *and* content of a unanimous Christian tradition, yet glosses his presentation such that it can be read in accord with the theology he himself explicates in other texts. Note first that, without Balthasar himself asserting it as such, the reader is given to understand *sheol* as the limbo of the Fathers due to the parallelism in Balthasar's presentation — and justly so, for sheol as *a* realm of the dead (as opposed to Balthasar's "*the* realm of death") is unambiguous in the *Christian* tradition. Secondly, after Balthasar's reduction (itself debatable), "what remains is *sheol (infernum)*, the classical 'hereafter' of the Old Testament and the gehenna of Judaism."[227] This phrase is reminiscent of his contrast, seen earlier, between sheol according to the earliest books of the Old Testament (its "classic theology"[228]) and that of "late Judaism under Persian and hellenistic influences."[229] In a likely unconscious echo of Adolf von Harnack's theory of Christianity as a hellenization of Judaism, Judaism itself has effectively become a hellenization of a yet more primitive religious experience.

We next find Balthasar himself stressing the unanimity and the authority of the *loci theologici* that teach Christ descended to sheol to liberate the dead. (His general omission of any specification of these dead as holy, however, will allow his summary to be read as compatible with his own theology of Christ's descent and with his hope for universal salvation.) Balthasar explicitly mentions Christ's parable of the strong man, authors of the patristic era, the medieval liturgy of Holy Saturday, and artistic representations from East and West. At this point, the crux of the article appears:

> This whole tradition hinges on an *a priori*: Jesus' descent to *sheol* is a triumphal entry of the already essentially resurrected Lord of Easter, [who conquered and emptied the underworld beforehand on Holy Saturday].[230]

(Note that, according to the received Tradition, Christ did not "empty the underworld," but only one part of it, namely, the limbo of the Fathers.) Here again, we see that Balthasar considers the traditional doctrine of the Descent as a projection of Easter Sunday back into Holy Saturday — and he thinks that this projection is an assumption *prior* to the authoritative sources of the Tradition. Hence, if the assumption is wrong, its embodiment in the theology of the Fathers and the saints, in the liturgy, and in art is also wrong. In other words, Tradition is wrong. More mildly put, it must be reinterpreted in light of a corrected doctrine, the one Balthasar proposes. It is precisely the error of this traditional *a priori* that Balthasar will attempt to establish in his section on the New Testament.

Before continuing, I must note that Balthasar is right that the Tradition hangs on an *a priori*. He is mistaken, however, as to both the nature of this *a priori* and its content. The content is not a projection of an "already essentially resurrected Lord," but rather the profession of the glorious descent into the underworld of Christ's immaculate soul united to His divine Person following His human death on the cross. This traditional doctrine is an *a priori* in the sense that it is a principle for theology, and so for liturgy, religious art, etc.; the principles of theology are necessarily the revealed truths of Faith. As such a principle, the doctrine is not *a priori* in the sense of being arbitrary, as if other options were (or are) available to the Church Christ established on His apostles and their successors, and which He promised to guide and preserve in the Holy Spirit. The traditional doctrine of Holy Saturday did not develop from a projection of Easter Sunday into Holy Saturday, but from reflection on the divine revelation in Christ and Scripture, and on the implications of death for One who is true God and true man. It is Balthasar who suggests the projection, thereby effectively calling into question the validity of the traditional doctrine.

This validity is further undermined in his section on Scripture, which was supposed to answer the question, "What foundation does the New Testament offer for this tradition?"[231] In actuality, Balthasar marshals his interpretations of Scripture *against* the Tradition, neglecting the use the Tradition itself made of the passages he references (the texts regarding Christ's burial; Eph 4:9; Mt 12:4; 27:51-53; Rev 1:17-18; Rom 10:6-8; and 1 Pet 3:18-20; 4:6). Christ's promise to the good thief (Lk 23:43) is dismissed with a placating condescension,

> Jesus might have had a moment of peace after his death when, as the Son of the Father, he felt the satisfaction of a mission fulfilled, before he began the last experience of being dead.[232]

The reader will recall Balthasar's extensive insistence on Jesus' experience — *precisely as Son* — of anguish, abandonment, and futility on the Cross, an experience that continues and intensifies in His descent. Such a concession can then only arouse wonder, about either Balthasar's consistency or his sincerity. Why does he pipe such different tunes?

The emphasis in Balthasar's section on the New Testament falls upon the reality of Jesus' being dead, i.e., His solidarity with the dead in death. In the section that follows, Balthasar shifts his focus to New Testament passages that establish the real possibility of hell (in the sense of gehenna). The superabundant merits of Christ and love of God form the additional premise necessary to suggest that Jesus' solidarity with the dead goes beyond sheol (in the traditional sense). Balthasar then concludes explicitly,

> Christ descended not merely to *sheol* but to *gehenna* in a purely objective victory [i.e., objectively victorious due to the washing of "the chaotic mass of sin . . . off humanity by the Cross"[233]], which he would experience subjectively in his final abandonment by God.[234]

The reader of Balthasar's essay has come a far way in a few pages: The theologian who opened his essay with a desire to clarify a credal article, after having asserted the existence of a unanimous Catholic Tradition concerning this article, sets Scripture against that very Tradition and ends up concluding something contrary to the Tradition he received and in which he claims to stand.

Conclusion

In this chapter, global concerns regarding the Person of Christ, His two natures, and specific instances of the use of Scripture and Tradition in Balthasar's theology of the Descent were discussed. Regarding the divine Persons, a tendency toward division between the divine nature and the divine attributes was seen, as well as one between the divine Persons and the divine nature. As a result, composition in God is implied: Either God is simple and the Son cannot "deposit" one attribute (e.g., the divine omniscience) without "depositing" the divine nature as a whole, or God's nature is composite. Again, either God is simple and the Son cannot deposit the divine nature without depositing His hypostasis and thereby ceasing to exist, or there is composition in God between Person and nature. In addition, the divine nature becomes a 'fourth thing' in the Trinity.

Regarding Christ's two natures, the failure seen to maintain the perfection of the divine and human natures results, first, in a failure to maintain their distinction. One might be tempted to add, "at least in language," but this qualification does not ultimately help: An idea is known through the words used to express it. The history of doctrinal development, and the role of heresies in that history, dictates that linguistic precision is not optional. Balthasar's Christology appears consequently to be a cross between Arianism and monophysitism in that Christ is not perfect God and perfect man, but some third thing. Second, the failure to maintain the perfection of natures leads necessarily to the effective diminishing of the importance of the role of human nature in the Person of Christ, and in the objective and subjective redemption. Among other manifestations, Balthasar's disproportionate emphasis on the divine will in Christ and its execution in human acts (what I have called the "hardwiring" of obedience in Him) ties the reduction of the role of human nature to His monophysite Christology. Finally, in virtue of the two foregoing effects, the same failure to maintain the natures' perfection ultimately results in the objective redemption being accomplished through what I have called the "physical mechanism" of sin-in-itself entering the Trinity through the Son's being "literally 'made sin'"; and in the subjective redemption becoming almost arbitrary in that it is dependent only upon God's choice, and He will not be restricted in His freedom by the negative choice of a creature against Him. In turn, God's absolute freedom coupled with His nature as self-gift (i.e., love) suggests universal salvation is necessary.

Finally, in the last section of this chapter, we examined Balthasar's reading of *Benedictus Deus*, his Scriptural foundation for his understanding of Sheol, and his regard for some of the sources and expressions of the traditional doctrine of Christ's descent. He evidently misread *Benedictus Deus*, there are reasons to have reservations about the soundness of his characterization of Sheol, and he discounted a number of *loci theologici* otherwise employed by the Church with considerable regard. Given the centrality of the theses Balthasar bases upon his use of these various *loci theologici* (e.g., his understanding of Sheol) or without their corrective (i.e., without *Benedictus Deus* and the liturgy, among others), these methodological concerns by themselves are sufficiently grave to call into question Balthasar's soteriology.

If all the difficulties raised throughout the course of our examination should be discarded because Balthasar's words are not to be taken as they stand, but are simply a mode of speaking, one could reasonably expect to find qualifications that make clear both the limitations of his expressions and his awareness of them. What are perhaps intended for such qualifications generally take the form of simple denials of what is implied in his language or simple reaffirmations of traditional doctrines, without explanation of the sense in which the affirmation (or the denial) and the rest of his texts can both stand. They also take the form of 'resolving' the apparent contradiction in the "ever-greater" mystery of God. But if we speak truths about God analogically based upon truths we know from creation, one must ask, for example, what meaning it has to assert that the incarnate Son believes in the Father "albeit in a unique sense that goes beyond all analogies";[235] or that suffering, obedience, and becoming exist in God — though not in the manner in which these are found in creatures?[236] Or again, since a conclusion exists in its premises albeit implicitly, to deny the conclusion or merely to refrain from drawing it out of 'respect for the mystery,' does not change the conclusion or its necessity; it merely demonstrates that human reasoning moves step by step and that one can stop oneself prematurely in that process.

It may be that an interpretation more consonant with the Catholic Tradition can be given to the texts we have discussed. For example, perhaps one might take "the execution [is] human" to mean "The task given was executed by God in the flesh." If this reinterpretation is what Balthasar meant, it is unfortunate he did not say it, for words mean what they say. Moreover, the justice of such interpretations is open to question: Texts are reinterpreted to preserve certain prior principles, and it is clear that Balthasar does not agree with all the principles of the patristic and Thomistic traditions, for example. It can happen then that his text is reinterpreted in accord with principles he himself rejected, which would be a misrepresentation. Thus, although I have attempted to interpret opaque or dubious passages of Balthasar in accord with the fixed points of Catholic doctrine and the greater theological tradition essentially linked to it, and to supply on his behalf responses to the concerns raised, I may have sometimes read him through an inappropriate lens. In the end, we ought to grant Balthasar to speak for himself sometimes, and not always to require strenuous interpretation.

On the basis then of what he says, the methodological issues regarding the use of Scripture and Tradition together with the concerns raised about Balthasar's Christology suggest again that the formal principle of redemption in Balthasar's soteriology is the Son's suffering of the *visio mortis* and of the Father's wrath *in virtue of His divinity*. The following factors come into play: the specific necessity of the Incarnation as a making good of finite freedom through God's self-gift unto Sheol; the way in which the Word is made man through the "depositing" of divine attributes; the lack of adequate distinction between the two natures of Christ, and hence between His two wills and His two acts; the way in which the Word made man is then "literally 'made sin'" through the "stripping" of the Incarnation; the quasi-physical mechanism of redemption in which sin-in-itself in the Person of the Son is brought into the Trinitarian love; the questionable role and efficacy of Christ's human nature in the redemption; the impossibility of Christians following Christ in His sacrificial act, and the immorality of their trying; Balthasar's principle, "What is not endured is not healed"; and finally, the need to question the soundness of some of his most central theses based on his use (or lack thereof) of important *loci theologici*. We have seen as well that Balthasar gives ample evidence of familiarity with many of the sources in which the traditional doctrine of the Descent is embodied. However, he thinks this doctrine is mistaken, and explicitly contrasts his own views with it. To these concerns, discussed in the present chapter, must be added Balthasar's rejection of Christ's possession of the beatific vision and his denial of the theological virtues to Christ in Sheol on the grounds that any of these would decrease His suffering. Similarly, since "'a suffering in community' 'would be an alleviation' for the Father and Son,"[237] the Son in Sheol is unaware that the Father also suffers abandonment, while the Father experiences His suffering as the ripping apart of the Trinity.

Suffering is the formal principle of redemption in Balthasar's soteriology. It is the suffering of sin-in-itself that redeems: the suffering of sin in Sheol by the Son in virtue of His divinity and, due to the Trinitarian character of that event, the 'suffering' of sin in the Trinity: God must endure the refusal of His love and this rebellious rejection on the part of creatures "causes him to suffer."[238] And yet "he cannot and will not suffer it";[239] He will not tolerate it. He must do something about it. And what does He do? If the annihilator can only be annihilated by itself, the death of sin that causes God to suffer must be brought within the "super-death" within the Trinity, which is accomplished through the Son's being "literally 'made sin.'" But the Trinitarian "super-death" is nothing other than the self-surrender of love among the divine Persons. *In this way,* sin is to be destroyed by love.

Yet because God's self-surrender is His bliss,[240] not only is the suffering of the incarnate Son a mode of His divine joy,[241] but His *divine* suffering (i.e., the embrace of sin-in-itself and the attendant God-abandonment within the Trinitarian "bracket") *is* the divine joy, the divine life of love. This equivalence is confirmed in three ways, and first by the utter simplicity of God, by which what are distinguished conceptually as His various attributes are in Him in reality the whole divine essence. Second, God endures sin by bringing it into His self-surrendering love, which is His bliss. Finally, the Son's suffering of the *visio mortis* in Sheol brings sin into the 'fire' of the Trinitarian love inasmuch as it is the *Son as such* who suffers — but not only the Son, for there is "reciprocal personal forsakenness on the part of Father and Son."[242] Hence the economic Descent event is itself the immanent Trinity's most intimate encounter with the rebellion of sin and the divine suffering it causes. However, the economic Trinity, especially in the Descent event, is the expression and revelation of the inner life of the immanent Trinity. Therefore *the real divine suffering of the economic Trinity is the divine joy of the immanent Trinity.*

This equivalence, together with the factors listed earlier and particularly the fact that they culminate to mean that a more-than-human (i.e., a divine) suffering is the formal principle of redemption, explain why Balthasar thinks speculation about whether God could have redeemed man in another way than He did is pointless, even harmful: The possible redemption of the world through a drop of Christ's blood is "free-wheeling speculation in empty space," caused by a "foolishness" that neglects God's "actual deeds."[243] If this evaluation is a conclusion of Balthasar's soteriology and hence also bears a necessary relation to his Christology, it is suggestive of a very different Christology and soteriology when Pope Clement VI in the bull *Unigenitus Dei Filius* writes, "A drop of His blood . . . would have sufficed for the redemption of the whole human race because of the union with the Word."[244]

CHAPTER ELEVEN

General Conclusion

The progress of our investigation of Christ's descent into hell has taken us from the breadth of the various Catholic expressions of this article of Faith to the central depths of Hans Urs von Balthasar's theology. One question in particular has accompanied this examination: In what sense was Christ's descent glorious? Is the glory of the Descent more like that of Easter Sunday as the traditional doctrine teaches, or is it rather more similar to Good Friday as Balthasar proposes?

Since the mystery of Holy Saturday is the bridge between those of the two other days, it has a necessary link to them both. In terms of the traditional doctrine, the effect of Good Friday is that Christ is dead, His body and soul separated, while the glorious foretaste of Easter Sunday is that He descends with power and authority to the souls of the holy dead, who behold the splendor of His divinity and His glorified soul. In terms of Balthasar's theological opinion, the glorious effects of Good Friday are that mankind is liberated from its sins through their transfer to Christ and that the profundity of the Trinitarian love is made as visible as possible; only once the perfect revelation of this love and the expiation of the punishment of mankind's sins are accomplished through the Son's being "literally 'made sin'" in Sheol can He be raised by the Father into the fullness of life, which Resurrection (as the utter opposite of the 'second death' of Sheol) is related to the Descent in its very discontinuity with it.

The extreme contrast between the traditional doctrine and Balthasar's extends the significance of the present investigation from a limited examination of one author's theological opinion to the more general question of whether a triumphal descent by Christ or a Descent to suffering is the true expression of the Catholic Faith. This question is of no mean importance, because the article's presence in the creeds suggests it uniquely reveals and safeguards something true about Christ and His saving work. The relevance of Tradition itself is also latently at stake: Is the content of a traditional doctrine binding, or may the verbal formulations be radically reinterpreted?

In Part One of the present work, a broad consultation of multiple objective repositories of the Faith was undertaken to ascertain whether an authoritative doctrine of Tradition on the Descent exists. The breadth of sources and wealth of material precluded any claim to exhaustion, but the consistency within each font and the consensus among them permitted a reasonable claim to adequate representation. These sources included creeds; universal catechisms of the Church; papal and conciliar statements; Scripture, with particular attention given to typological interpretation as well as to continuation of this typology in the relevant sacrament (baptism); theological writings of the saints, especially of the Fathers and Doctors, insofar as these manifest compatibility with the other *loci theologici* and consensus among themselves; liturgical texts (Roman and Byzantine) of Good Friday, Holy Saturday, and the Exaltation of the Cross; the Eastern liturgical icons for Good Friday and Holy Saturday; and non-iconic representations of the Descent in Western art taken as an expression of the *sensus fidelium* insofar as these works were compatible with the other expressions of the Faith. As a result of this investigation, it was concluded that a traditional doctrine of the Descent does indeed exist, one which then carries the weight of the authority of Tradition. This doctrine has been maintained with exceptional consistency from apostolic times. It is remarkably free from pointed controversy, though allowance is to be made for the normal refinement in the expressions used in the theology of the saints (notably more than in the other *loci theologici*), as well as their occasional differences of opinion on individual points. From the perspective of developed theology, this traditional doctrine was summarized in the following four points: First, Christ descended in His soul united to His divine Person only to the limbo of the Fathers. Second, His power and authority were made known throughout all of hell, taken generically. Third, He thereby accomplished the two purposes of the Descent, which were "to liberate the just" by conferring on them the glory of heaven and "to proclaim His power."[1] Finally, His descent was glorious, and Christ did not suffer the pain proper to any of the abodes of hell.

In Part Two, we turned to examine Hans Urs von Balthasar's theology of the Descent in some detail. Here we saw that the sins and guilt of all men are transferred to Christ in His passion and crucifixion such that men can truly be said to be freed from their sins by His cross. It is in this sense that Christ's words, *Consummatum est*, must be interpreted. Due to Christ's assumption of all guilt and sin, the Father abandons Him upon the cross, rejecting sin in His person. Christ's suffering does not end with His death, but continues in His descent and there far surpasses that of the cross. The God-abandonment of Christ *as Son* reaches its climax in Sheol when the Incarnation is "stripped" and He is "literally 'made sin'" through conformity to the *visio mortis*. Out of wrath against sin's abuse of His paternal love, the Father "crushes" sin in the Son, i.e., the Son as conformed to sin-in-itself. The Son thereby suffers *and discharges* the full penalty that mankind justly would have had to suffer without a Redeemer — indeed, worse, since His abandonment is proportionate to His filial relation to the Father. Despite the mutual God-abandonment between Father and Son (for the Father reciprocally experiences the loss of intimacy), they remain united by the bond of their love, which is the Holy Spirit. In this way, through mankind's sins being taken up into the Person of the Son, who still remains united to the Father in the Holy Spirit, sin is taken up into the Trinity. Because the Descent event is motivated by and expresses the love of the divine Persons for each other and for the world, God's love is shown to be "ever-greater" than sin. In this most extreme act of distinction-in-unity (or "love"), the Trinity has its fullest economic revelation. In short, Balthasar explicitly disagrees with the first and fourth points of the traditional doctrine as summarized, whereas at best one might say his theology would interpret the second and third points in a veiled sense. In addition, we saw that the distinction among the divine Persons appears to be dissolved by Balthasar's idea of "antecedent consent." In contrast, his ascription of proper acts to them in the economy results in tri-theism, and similarly the fact that the Holy Spirit is not love in the way the Father and Son are ends in bi-theism. Balthasar's theology of creation, sacramental theology, ecclesiology, eschatology, and Mariology all bear the clear impress of his Trinitarian and soteriological theology of the Descent.

In Part Three, issues of detail having been discussed as they arose in Part Two, selected global concerns with Balthasar's theology of the Descent were examined in Chapter Ten. Here, regarding the Person of Christ, it was argued that Balthasar's *descensus* theology manifests a tendency toward division between the divine nature and the divine attributes, as well as one between the divine Persons and the divine nature, both of which imply composition in God. Regarding Christ's two natures, it was argued that Balthasar's theology fails to maintain the perfection of the divine and human natures. It consequently fails to maintain their distinction, resulting in a sort of monophysitism, the devaluation of human nature in both objective and subjective redemption, the accomplishment of the objective redemption through a physical mechanism, and both an increased arbitrariness in subjective redemption and the apparent necessity of universal salvation. In addition, a tension was seen between Balthasar's assertion of the almost absolute necessity of an Incarnation unto Sheol and other principles of his that call into question both its necessity and its efficacy. Moreover, since Christians are called to follow the Lord who is their brother, a theologian's treatment of Christ's two natures has implications for those who follow Him: Our focus fell on the problem in Balthasar's theology that the Christian is left in alienation by his very Savior due to his inability to follow Christ in going into actual perdition for the salvation of others. The last global issue investigated concerned Balthasar's implementation of Tradition, as manifested in his use of the Constitution *Benedictus Deus,* his Scriptural foundation for his theology of Sheol, and his comportment to the *loci theologici* examined in Part One. Here, the evidence suggests his theology determined his usage of these sources, rather than the other way around. One might mention in particular Balthasar's change (intentional or not) of the patristic principle, "What is not *assumed* is not healed," to "What is not *endured* is not healed." Chapter Ten concluded with a summary of how the suffering of God is the formal principle of redemption in Balthasar's soteriology: In contrast to a soteriology of meritorious satisfaction operated through the humanity of Christ, redemption in Balthasar's theology turns on the suffering of the penalty of sin by the Son *as Son,* on the Father's suffering of the loss of the Son, and on the suffering of sin in the Trinitarian embrace closed by the Holy Spirit, in virtue of all of which sin is overcome.

The conclusions that Balthasar's theology of Christ's descent into hell neither represents the traditional Catholic doctrine nor is compatible with it hardly need be drawn. The contrast is not a matter of some subtlety of interpretation, but essential differences on the most central features of the doctrine. Balthasar himself makes explicit, if often subdued, contrasts of his theology with the traditional doctrine of the Descent. Generally, however, he does not identify his doctrine as his own but attempts to present it as a rereading of historical sources.[2] The secondary literature agrees on the discontinuity between Balthasar's theology and the traditional Catholic doctrine, and this generally on the basis of a much more limited examination than that undertaken here. Besides explicit or implicit acknowledgments that the traditional Catholic doctrine holds Christ's descent was glorious in the first imposition,[3] one finds that Balthasar's theology of Holy Saturday is observed in a straightforward manner to be new, different from the traditional Catholic doctrine, or incompatible with it.[4] The exceptions, i.e., those cases I have seen in which the Catholicity of Balthasar's position is assumed or suggested, do not manifest much, if any, acquaintance with the traditional doctrine of the Descent outside Balthasar's own presentations of it.

As for what is the truth of the matter, not to mention the authority and wealth of the material in support of the traditional doctrine, one notes the exertion necessary for Balthasar to connect his *descensus* theology even remotely

Plates

1. Lorenzo di Pietro "Il Vecchietta" (c. 1412–1480). Articles of the Creed, *Resurrection*. Fresco in the baptistery of the Duomo in Siena, Italy.   Photo: Scala, Florence.

In the Siena baptistery, in the very place where new members are joined to the Church by their profession of faith and baptism, a cycle of frescoes illustrates the articles of the creed. Here Christ's descent to the limbo of the Fathers is coupled with His resurrection, not His crucifixion. Dressed in the white of glory, Christ carries the standard of the victory of the cross and rays of light emanate from His figure in both halves of the image. In the limbo of the Fathers, Christ stands just inside the lintel of the broken portal to the underworld and grasps the wrist of Adam. St. John the Baptist holds a scroll with the words, "Ecce Agnus Dei" [Behold the Lamb of God], as he points to Christ. One demon lies beneath the door under Christ's feet, while Satan flees from the realm of death over which he previously held sway. The glory of Christ in His descent is similar to that of His resurrection on Easter Sunday, and the kneeling figure to the left professes *Credo,* "I believe."

2. Christ in Limbo. Ninth-century fresco in the church of San Clemente, Rome, Italy.

Photo: Alinari/Art Resource, New York

This image is among the oldest surviving representations of Christ's descent. From the artwork depicted on the following pages, one can see how the genre developed in distinct directions in the East and the West, all the while retaining the same central core: With the devil defeated, Christ draws Adam to Himself out of the realm of death in an act of power and glory.

Here, in His merciful love, the New Adam has gone down even into the realm of death to restore the first Adam. Christ and Adam are fully robed in similar garments, while the larger figure of Christ is surrounded by the graduated blues of the mandorla indicating His divine glory. Christ is both son of Adam and Adam's creator and archetype. He grasps the limp hand of Adam by the wrist. The devil is trodden underfoot, while he vainly attempts to prevent Adam's departure by hanging onto one of his feet. The devil's powerlessness is accentuated by his small size.

3. Christ descending into limbo taking Adam by the hand.
13th-century mosaic on the great central arch of the basilica of San Marco, Venice, Italy.

Photo: Cameraphoto/Art Resource, New York

This more-developed *Anastasis* mosaic is similar to the one on the cover, which is discussed in some detail in Chapter Four. Here Christ is dressed in the gold of divine glory and holds aloft the victorious cross. He lifts Adam by the wrist out and away from his tomb. The vigorous movement of their figures suggests the power of Christ's action. Impotently holding onto Adam's toes, Hades—who simultaneously represents in this genre of images not only that abode of the dead but also death itself and the devil—is portrayed chained in the posture of the defeated beneath the feet of the victor. On the left, Eve and a group of holy souls lift their hands to Christ in supplication. On the right, St. John the Baptist, King David, and King Solomon bear witness to the Messiah to whom they point.

Written in the Person of Christ, the inscription is addressed not only to Adam, Eve, and the others whom Christ is depicted as about to raise from the power of Hades, but also to the faithful reading the inscription in San Marco: "MORS ET ERO MORTIS SURGENTUM DUXQUE COHORTIS / MORSUS ET INFERNO VOS REGNO DONO SUPERNO" [I will be the death of Death and the leader of the company of those resurrecting. And I, the sting to Hell, give you to the heavenly kingdom]. Below this Latin text alluding to the prophecy in Hosea 13:14, there appears in Greek, "Ή ΆΓΙΑ ΑΝΑΣΤΑΣΙΣ" [The Holy Anastasis].

· MORS ET EROMRTISSVRGENTE DX CHRTS AVRSV SETTERNIVPG DNOS

HATARHAGTACIO ·

ANSEMENON SVRGENGEMSICVGEFUM CHOMASQVOTOQVERISIAACTVVINER

CREDIS :⁓

4. Dionysius (c. 1440 – c. 1508). Harrowing of Hell.   Photo: Archivo Iconografico, S.A./Corbis

In a yet more elaborate *Anastasis,* the number of the saved has swollen to a great multitude, which no one could count (Rev 7:9). Although still suggestive of action, Christ's posture is more tranquil. Taking Adam in one hand and Eve in the other, He raises them both into His glorious presence. Angels play a large role in this icon. From within Christ's mandorla of glory, some smite their fallen counterparts in the realm of the dead beneath the broken doors under Christ's feet. Still other angels hold the cross on high or bind Satan down below.

5. Christ's descent into limbo. Tiberius Psalter (1050).
British Library, MS. Cotton Tiberius C. 6, fol 14r.

This image is our first selection to represent the development in the West of the pictorial depiction of the doctrine of Christ's descent. Compared to the *Anastasis* icons of the Christian East, Western images of Christ's descent show greater variety in how they represent hell (in its generic sense), the limbo of the Fathers, or death. Here the mouth of a large beast is used to recall Scriptural images of death. Besides such "hellmouths," one most commonly finds a cave or a fortress used as the motif. The open door behind Christ conveys the idea of limbo (or hell) as an abode. Hence Christ's activity is two-fold: (1) He raises the holy souls to new life by saving them from being utterly swallowed by the hellmouth of death; and (2) He will liberate them from the place of their captivity, which was formerly controlled by the devil. Such salvation and liberation are identical to their passing into His company, i.e., to their reception of the beatific vision and their departure with Christ from the limbo of the Fathers.

Note that the core of this image is essentially the same as plate 2, the fresco in San Clemente. Standing upon the defeated figure of Satan, Christ grasps Adam's hand. Satan's consternation contrasts with Christ's tranquillity: The devil and the other powers of the netherworld present no obstacle to Christ, but in His presence Satan is bound and death yawns wide to release its prey as if it were dead itself. Meanwhile, Christ's attention is focused upon the holy souls, who are overjoyed to see Him. He extends His right hand in a sign of blessing and peace, while with His left He takes Adam in hand. Christ's face is paternal, both tender and strong, and the holy souls lift their hands to Him as children would. Other unique features of this image are highlighted in Chapter Four.

6. Nicolas of Verdun (c. 1150–1205). Christ's descent into hell. Enamel. Verdun altar, begun 1181. Sammlungen des Stiftes, Klosterneuburg Abbey, Austria.   Photo: Erich Lessing/Art Resource, New York

Powerful action is unmistakably attributed to Christ in this image. The doors through which Adam and Eve are drawn to Christ represent a Western version of the broken portels in the *Anastasis* icon. The scriptural and architectural element of the door and its lintel is developed in many ways in the West, sometimes as a gate over a cavern mouth, sometimes as the portal or even portcullis of a fortress. Although the door, whatever its form, usually lies torn off its hinges under Christ's feet, this image is an exception.

This enamel is one of fifty-one plaques making up the medieval masterpiece, the Altar of Verdun. The plaques are arranged in three rows representing the three stages of the history of salvation: The top row depicts the age "ante legem" [before the law], i.e., before Moses; the bottom row shows the period "sub lege" [under the law], i.e., between Moses and Christ; and the middle row represents the time "sub gratia" [under grace], i.e., the life of Christ and the Christian era. In fifteen of the Altar's seventeen columns, the plaques of the top and bottom rows depict prefigurations of the event in Christ's life represented in the middle row. The plaque "ante legem" that corresponds to the one illustrating Christ's descent depicts the tenth Egyptian plague (Ex 11:4-6; 12:1-30; see also Ezek 9:6). An Israelite marks a "T," that is, a cross, on the lintels of his door with the blood of the slain lamb visible in the background, while the angel of God passes his house by to slay the first-born son of the Pharaoh. Note how the two-fold fate of this prefiguration is consistent with the traditional doctrine of the Descent that similarly accords salvation to the faithful and eternal death to the wicked. The relevant plaque "sub lege" shows Samson defeating the lion with his bare hands (Judg 14:5-6), Samson being a type for Christ and the lion representing the devil (1 Pet 5:8).

Beneath the image stands its title, "DESTRUCTIO I[N]FERNI" [The Destruction of Hell], while the frame around it reads, "IUS DOMUIT MORTIS / TUA XPE POTENCIA FORTIS" [Your strong power, Christ, conquered Death's rule]. This latter acclamation makes clear that the "destruction" accomplished is not the utter annihilation of the netherworld, but rather the termination of its inescapable dominion. The dead will be resurrected body and soul, and God's faithful will be joined to Him in the fullness of communion.

7. The Harrowing of Hell. Holkham Bible Picture Book, 14th century. British Library, MS. Add. 47682, fol. 34r.

The artist here stresses the distinction between the abodes of the dead: As discussed in Chapter Four, the limbo of the Fathers is represented as a decorated gazebo of sorts. Christ has broken its door by the power of His cross; never again shall this limbo imprison anyone. The demons who had controlled the limbo of the Fathers *from the outside* scurry away before Christ, who is dressed in robes similar to those in depictions of His resurrection and the Last Judgment. Adam and Eve stand behind Him as part of His company. Those still within the limbo of the Fathers await Christ in prayerful expectation; only He can liberate them. Christ draws each holy soul forth individually. Christ's authority in the realm of the dead is contrasted with the impotence of all the other dead by the near-universal representation of Christ grasping the wrist, not the hand, of those whom He saves. This salvation does not extend to the group of souls being tormented in a distinctly separate furnace with no means of escape. The generic hellmouth here becomes a fiery maw that heats the cauldron of the damned.

With the abbreviations slightly expanded, the Old French inscription above Christ's head reads, "Coment la alme Ihesuss eut meyntenant aprees la mort descendist en enfer et deliverat Adam et Eve et tuz les bons qui estoyent dedenz en prison franche. Et tuz et tuttes les mauveyses yl lesat leynz domorer en peyne perpetuele" [How the soul of Jesus has now, after death, descended into Hell and set free Adam and Eve and all the good who were in the ultimate prison. And He leaves all the bad, male and female, therein to abide in perpetual pain]. Here, the author emphatically contrasts the liberation of the just with the continued imprisonment and punishment of the wicked. Note too how Christ's descent in soul is explicitly affirmed, as well as the identical spiritual responsibility of men and women.

I am indebted to Dr. Catherine Brown Tkacz for her help in transcribing and translating this inscription and those for images 3 and 6 above.

8. Duccio di Buoninsegna (c. 1260–1319). The Descent into Limbo.
Panel from the back of the Maestà altarpiece. Museo dell'Opera Metropolitana, Siena, Italy.

This painting is representative of an approach to portraying the doctrine of Christ's descent that, in my opinion, is near the peak of the genre in terms of clarity and depth of significance. The viewer is not distracted from the saving purpose of Christ's descent by the depiction of any warlike feats by Christ. As in Rufinus' analogy of the king, Christ enters tranquilly where He will: He is the creator of the universe and the redeemer of mankind, and the devil has already been defeated by His sacrifice on the cross. The limbo of the Fathers is represented as a cave, i.e., an enormous tomb. Christ stands both inside and outside limbo: He must be inside if He is to come to the holy souls and so grasp Adam's wrist, but He must also be outside, since He liberates them from limbo by drawing them to Himself. Christ is robed, not naked as on the cross, and He holds aloft the cross, which bears the standard of victory. Adam's stance before Christ is at once that of supplication and of homage to one's king. The souls behind Adam are those of identifiable individuals, all sinners who became saints by overcoming their various sins and failings through God's grace and friendship. Salvation is not conferred anonymously or generically; Christ calls us each by name.

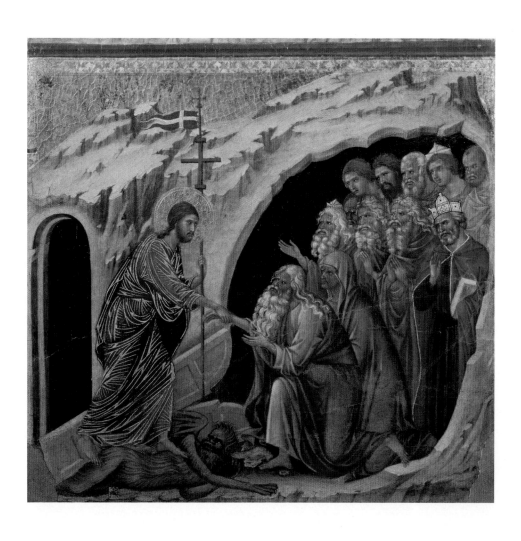

9. Jaime Serra. Descent into Limbo. Altarpiece of the Holy Sepulcher, 14th century.

Photo: The Art Archive/Corbis

This final image accentuates the salvific and liberating significance of Christ's descent into hell. Life itself sojourns in death, and those who died with the spark of that life unextinguished in their hearts are now to enter it fully. With Adam, Eve, and St. John the Baptist at the fore, the holy souls are led forth from the jaws of death, while the demons shrink as far away as possible. But where are the holy souls led? The background beyond the hellmouth is indistinct. Bathed in the gold of divine glory, its most distinguishing feature is the presence of Christ, who is dressed as at His imminent resurrection and surrounded by angels. Where Christ is, there is paradise.

to the larger Catholic theological traditions, including his citation of authors in a mode inconsistent with the context of their thought; his need to redefine terms radically; and his reliance on figures of questionable authority, often precisely with regard to positions of theirs not taken up or even rejected by the received tradition (e.g., Origen and Nicholas of Cusa). Other examples of problematic methodology were considered in detail in Chapter Ten. That Balthasar's positive arguments fail or involve self-contradictions has been seen throughout the present work. Regardless of whether Balthasar himself draws the conclusions embedded in his principles, the problems inherent in his Christology provide confirmation that the doctrine of the Descent uniquely safeguards something true of Christ and His redemptive work. To change one's doctrine of the Descent is to change one's doctrine of Christ. The importance of the issue demands that it be pressed home: If one does not believe in the Descent professed by the Church, does one still believe in the Christ professed by the Church?

That the *descensus* theology of a reputably *Catholic* theologian is openly acknowledged by himself and others to be incompatible with the traditional teaching of the Catholic Church on this central article of Faith sets before us the issue of Tradition, its role, and its authority. David Edward Lauber raises the question

> whether Balthasar's treatment of Holy Saturday, which stresses Jesus' solidarity with the passivity of human death, is inconsistent with the biblical witness and Christian tradition, which sees Christ descending as Victor — the harrower of hell.[5]

In an attempt to maintain some sort of *consistency* despite the *differences* in Balthasar's "rejection or radical revision of the traditionally dominant interpretation"[6] of the Descent, the (problematic) Balthasarian solution is to reread Christ's victory as a purely objective one, subjectively unapprehended by Jesus. That is, the Tradition is implicitly *acknowledged* to assert a victorious Descent, but is *reinterpreted* as a victory in seeming defeat, what has been described as the second imposition of *glory*. The formula is retained, so to speak, while its meaning is changed: The Descent was not glorious; it was 'glorious.' This methodology was seen in other elements of Balthasar's theology, e.g., in regard to his substitution of a *visio immediata* for Christ's beatific vision. Balthasar himself knows, however, that the allegiance of faith is due not only to the form of the profession of faith, but also to its material content:

> It is quite clear that anyone who practices theology as a member of the Church must profess the Church's Creed (and the theology implicit in it),

both formally and materially. This profession is made formally, by positing the ecclesial *act* of faith; materially, by accepting the ecclesial *contents* of the faith.[7]

Hence we come to the crux of the issue latent in discussions about the orthodoxy of a *descensus* doctrine, namely, the weight of the Tradition that specifies the contents of the act of faith. This issue is brought to the fore in theologies of Christ's descent, because, as has been said, the Descent occurred beyond the reach of the human eye and hence can only be approached on the basis of faith and its submission to *revealed* truth. There are then two possible repositories to consult: Scripture and Tradition. The most explicit Scriptural testimony is obscure, however, while the invocation of other passages to clarify and amplify these texts is already dependent upon a tradition of interpretation and belief. Hence, necessarily either we rely upon Tradition as an infallible guide to revealed truth and upon the ability of reason enlightened by faith to identify that Tradition under the magisterial guidance of the Church's hierarchy — or we *de facto* reject such Tradition in whole or in part. In the case of such rejection, theology becomes subjected to fallen reason's fancy, which inevitably leads to heresy, i.e., the picking and choosing of beliefs in which unaided reason cannot fail to err because the subject matter is beyond its capabilities.

As stated in the Introduction, I have deliberately eschewed the question of the origin of Balthasar's doctrine of the Descent, focusing instead on examining its doctrinal content in comparison with the traditional doctrine. Hence I do not draw conclusions about the nature of his personal rejection of that doctrine. What may be said, however, is this much: Insofar as the theology of the Descent proposed by Balthasar (as well as other areas of his theology dependent on it) is, in fact, incompatible with traditional Catholic doctrine; and insofar as his theology is, in fact, proposed specifically vis-à-vis the latter (i.e., he knew the traditional doctrine as such), there is a *de facto* rejection of the Catholic Tradition and its authority. In other words, Balthasar's *descensus* theology fails to adhere to the only sure guide and standard of truth in this matter; more, it contradicts it. For this reason alone — setting aside all the reasons of theological argumentation seen throughout this work — his *descensus* theology cannot be true, nor is it an expression of the Catholic Faith. By extension and notwithstanding differences in detail, any theology of a Descent to suffering may reasonably be approached with the assumption of incompatibility with the Catholic Faith, given the overwhelming support of the *loci theologici* for a Descent glorious in the first imposition.

The mystery of Christ's descent to hell, like all the mysteries of the Faith, is an endlessly rich source for theological reflection. Nonetheless, its character as a mystery does not preclude certain things being affirmed as true of it, and others being denied as false. Though the fullness of the mysteries of faith transcends human reasoning, God did not reveal them in order to confuse or confound the human intellect. Rather, "in Thy light, we shall see light" (Ps 35:10). That is, by the relatively dark light of faith, we can glimpse even now the supereminent Truth that the blessed behold clearly in the full day of glory. But God has given the safe-keeping of His mysteries to the Church, as a light is set within a lamp to protect it. Only with this lamp can any private theological opinion be adequately examined and, if a theologian would be illuminated by faith in his service, he must humbly submit himself to the voice of the Church resonating down the ages. The dangers are rife, for a thousand fall on the Church's left, and ten thousand on her right (Ps 90:7).

The traditional doctrine of the Descent then is anything but passé. It is essential to preserving and preaching the full truth of Christ and His redeeming work on our behalf — and this also specifically in the oh-so-mature and demythologized contemporary age. It was noted in the Introduction that the non-traditional *descensus* theologies of the present age appear heavily marked by the face of death in the twentieth century. Precisely this age needs to hear of Christ and the victory He offers to mankind over physical and spiritual death.[8] The truth of Christ's descent stands over against any 'tragic Christianity,' any seeking of redemption in God-abandonment as such, any attempt to breed the nihilism of the last century with holy death to selfishness: Who loses the life of the old man, *finds the life of the New* (see Mt 10:39); Christ has come that we might *have life*, not death, and that we might have it in its fullness (see Jn 10:10). It would be the worst betrayal of this age (not to mention of Christ) to offer it elaborate theological platitudes suggesting its wounds *are* its life, thereby remaking God in its image.

The redemption accomplished by Christ in His death on the cross and offered to us is fulfilled in an archetypal way in His own Person. In His resurrection, physical death as the separation of body and soul is overcome. His ascension affirms that man as a whole, not just his spiritual element, is ordered to fulfillment in God; the Blessed Virgin Mary's assumption body and soul into heaven confirms that this perfection of life is the destiny of the Church. In the union of Christ's entire humanity with God, the ultimate overcoming of all the effects of sin is prefigured for recreated man. Christ's victory over spiritual death, however, was operative already before His death in the flesh, through His freedom from sin in all its forms and His continuous possession of the beatific vision. These features of man's intended archetype — present freedom from sin and union with God through Christ, expectation of the glorified body's resurrection and communion in it with the heavenly company — as well as mankind's need for a savior and the certain hope of salvation provided by faith lived in charity all implicitly meet in an exceptionally vivid way in the proclamation of Christ's glorious descent. Redemption in Christ, its conditions, its sureness if one abides in His life, and its extent are found nowhere else so concentrated as in the traditional doctrine of the Descent and its expressions in Scriptural, liturgical, rhetorical, magisterial, and artistic works.[9]

The proclamation of Christ's descent hence must not be reduced to a mere reiteration of His death, and it certainly ought not be perverted in the image of mankind's sins. It should instead be the joyous avowal of Christ's authority and victory over death *in the realm of death itself.* Life is ultimately not conquered by death; we see this in Christ's Resurrection. But life is not even vanquished when it dies in human flesh. Christ's brothers in the flesh who live and die in Him in any age will live, and do live, the fullness of Life even when dead in the body. Hence those who are sons in the Son are free even now from the fear of death. Death has become for them the gate to perfect communion with God — and this even before the absolute liberation from death that will come with the awaited resurrection of the body. That, we see in Christ's Descent.

Bibliography

All cited works are included in the following bibliography. Selected other relevant works that were consulted but not cited are also listed, preceded by an asterisk (*).

A full bibliography of Balthasar's works may be found in Cornelia Capol, *Hans Urs von Balthasar: Bibliographie, 1925-1990* (Einsiedeln: Johannes, 1990). The editions and translations I used depended upon what was available to me at a particular time. When I had cause, translations were checked against the originals as I found them. The bibliography lists the version (original or translation) I primarily used.

For ease of identification, individual entries are provided both for cited essays by Balthasar and for the anthologies in which they appear. The essay title is followed only by the anthology title and the relevant page numbers; full bibliographic information may be found under the entry for the anthology itself. For the full title of those abbreviated here, see the list at the beginning of the book.

The reader should note that not all essays in different languages with equivalent titles are identical in content, even if by the same author.

Works by Hans Urs von Balthasar

"The Absences of Jesus," *New Elucidations*: 46-60.
"Abstieg zur Hölle," *Pneuma und Institution*: 387-400.
The Action. Vol. 4, *Theo-Drama*. Translated by Graham Harrison. San Francisco: Ignatius, 1994.
"Action and Contemplation," *Expl I*: 227-40.
*"Alle Wege führen zum Kreuz," *IKaZ Communio* 9 (1980) 4: 333-42.
"Although He was a Son, He Learned Obedience through Suffering," #49, *You Have Words*: 147-49.
"And the Sea of Being Lay Dry," #XI, *Heart*: 174-88.

Apokalypse der deutschen Seele: Studien zu einer Lehre von letzten Haltungen. Bd. 1, *Der deutsche Idealismus.* Einsiedeln: Johannes, 1998.

Das betrachtende Gebet. Einsiedeln: Johannes, 1955.

"Beyond Contemplation and Action?" *Expl IV:* 299-307.

"Bought at a Great Price," *Crown:* 76-81.

"The Broken Sun," #III, *Heart:* 58-72.

"La Chiesa e l'inferno," *La realtà e la gloria:* 61-66.

The Christian and Anxiety. Translated by Dennis D. Martin and Michael J. Miller. San Francisco: Ignatius, 2000.

"Christology and Ecclesial Obedience," *Expl IV:* 139-67.

Church and World. Translated by A. V. Littledale with Alexander Dru. New York: Herder & Herder, 1967.

"The Church as 'Caritas,'" *Elucidations:* 245-51.

Convergences: To the Source of Christian Mystery. Translated by E. A. Nelson. San Francisco: Ignatius, 1983.

Creator Spirit, Explorations in Theology, vol. 3. Translated by Brian McNeil. San Francisco: Ignatius, 1993.

Credo: Meditations on the Apostles' Creed. Translated by David Kipp. Edinburgh: T. & T. Clark, 1990.

"*Crucifixus etiam pro nobis,*" *IKaZ Communio* 9 (1980) 1: 26-35.

"Dare One Do Good on the Sabbath?" #51, *You Have Words:* 153-55.

Dare We Hope "That All Men Be Saved"? with "A Short Discourse on Hell." Translated by Lother Krauth and David Kipp. San Francisco: Ignatius, 1988.

"Death Is Swallowed Up by Life," *Communio ICR* 14 (1987) 2: 49-54.

"The Descent into Hell," *Chicago Studies* 23 (1984): 223-36.

"The Descent into Hell," *Expl IV:* 401-14.

"Dio e il dramma del mondo." Conference held in Milan 21 April 1983 by Centro Culturale San Carlo. Translated by Giovanni Mascetti. Edited by Paola Priori. Milan: Centro Culturale San Carlo, 1983.

"La discesa agli inferi," *RITC Communio* 55 (Gen/Feb 1981): 4-6.

Does Jesus Know Us — Do We Know Him? Translated by Graham Harrison. San Francisco: Ignatius, 1983.

The Dramatis Personae: Man in God. Vol. 2, *Theo-Drama.* Translated by Graham Harrison. San Francisco: Ignatius, 1990.

The Dramatis Personae: The Person in Christ. Vol. 3, *Theo-Drama.* Translated by Graham Harrison. San Francisco: Ignatius, 1992.

*"Earthly Beauty and Divine Glory." Translated by Andrée Emery. *Communio ICR* 11 (1983) 3: 203-6.

Elucidations. Translated by John Riches. San Francisco: Ignatius, 1975.

"Eschatology in Outline," *Expl IV:* 423-67.

"The Eye of the Peacock," #VI, *Heart:* 104-16.

"The Father's Vineyard," #IV, *Heart:* 73-88.

"*Fides Christi:* An Essay on the Consciousness of Christ," *Expl II:* 43-79.

The Final Act. Vol. 5, *Theo-Drama*. Translated by Graham Harrison. San Francisco: Ignatius, 1998.

"Fragments on Suffering and Healing," *New Elucidations*: 256-79.

Der Geist der Wahrheit. Bd. III, *Theo-Logik*. Einsiedeln: Johannes, 1987.

"Geist und Feuer: Ein Gespräch mit Hans Urs von Balthasar," *Herder Korrespondenz* 30 (Feb 1976) 2: 72-82.

"Gesù Cristo." Quattro meditazioni, 5-15.

"Glaube und Naherwartung," *Zuerst Gottes Reich: Zwei Skizzen zur biblischen Naherwartung,* 11-33. Neue Kriterien 4. Einsiedeln: Johannes, 2002.

"God Is 'Being With,'" *Crown:* 141-45.

*"God Is His Own Exegete." Translated by Stephen Wentworth. *Communio ICR* (1986) 4: 280-87.

"God Speaks as Man," *Expl I:* 69-93.

The God Question and Modern Man. Translated by Hilda Graef. New York: Seabury, 1967.

"Gott und das Leid," *Antwort des Glaubens* 34. Freiburg: Informationszentrum Berufe der Kirche, 1984.

Heart of the World. Translated by Erasmo S. Leiva. San Francisco: Ignatius, 1979.

"The Holy Spirit as Love," *Expl III:* 117-34.

Homo Creatus Est. Bd. V, *Skizzen zur Theologie*. Einsiedeln: Johannes, 1986.

"The Incarnation of God," *Elucidations:* 58-68.

In the Fullness of Faith: On the Centrality of the Distinctively Catholic. Translated by Graham Harrison. San Francisco: Ignatius, 1988.

"Ist der Gekreuzigte 'selig'?" *IKaZ Communio* 16 (1987) 2: 107-9.

"Jailhouse and Cocoon," #VIII, *Heart:* 133-44.

*"Jesus and Forgiveness." Translated by Josephine Koeppel. *Communio ICR* 11 (1984) 4: 322-34.

Karl Barth: Darstellung und Deutung seiner Theologie. Cologne: Jakob Hegner, 1951.

"Kenosis of the Church?" *Expl IV:* 125-38.

*"Kleine Katechese über die Hölle," *L'Osservatore Romano (Wochenausgabe in deutscher Sprache)* 14 (1984) 38: 1-2.

"Kommt und seht": Meditationen des Lebens Jesu. Freiburg: Informationszentrum Berufe der Kirche, 1983.

"The Last Five Stations of the Cross," *Theologians Today: Hans Urs von Balthasar.* No translator noted. Edited by Martin Redfern. London: Sheed & Ward, 1972: 117-26.

Leben aus dem Tod: Betrachtungen zum Ostermysterium. Einsiedeln: Johannes, 1997.

Light of the Word: Brief Reflections on the Sunday Readings. Translated by Dennis D. Martin. San Francisco: Ignatius, 1993.

"Loneliness in the Church," *Expl IV:* 261-98.

Love Alone: The Way of Revelation. No translator noted. London: Sheed & Ward, 1992.

"Martyrdom and Mission," *New Elucidations:* 279-305.

"Meeting God in Today's World," *Concilium* 6 (June 1965) 1: 14-22.

*"Der Mensch und das ewige Leben II: Der Auferstandene: Ichsein in Gott," *Konradsblatt Wochenzeitung f.d. Erzbistum Freiburg* 56 (April 16, 1972) 16.

"Der Mensch und das ewige Leben III: Der Auferstandene: Das Seligwerden des Leidens," *Konradsblatt Wochenzeitung f.d. Erzbistum Freiburg* 56 (April 23, 1972) 17:5.

*"Der Mensch und das ewige Leben VII: Geist von oben und von innen," *Konradsblatt Wochenzeitung f.d. Erzbistum Freiburg* 56 (May 21, 1972) 21:12.

"The Multitude of Biblical Theologies and the Spirit of Unity in the Church," *Convergences:* 75-110.

My Work: In Retrospect. No translator noted. San Francisco: Ignatius, 1993.

Mysterium Paschale: The Mystery of Easter. Translated by Aidan Nichols. Edinburgh: T. & T. Clark, 1990.

"Mysterium Paschale." In *Mysterium Salutis. Grundriss heilsgeschichtliche Dogmatik.* Bd. III/2: *Das Christusereignis,* 133-326. Hrsg. Johannes Feiner und Magnus Löhrer. Einsiedeln: Benzinger, 1969.

"The Mystery of the Eucharist," *New Elucidations:* 111-26.

Neuer Bund. Bd. III, teil 2, *Herrlichkeit. Eine theologische Ästhetik.* Einsiedeln: Johannes, 1969.

The New Covenant. Vol. 7, *The Glory of the Lord: A Theological Aesthetics.* Translated by Brian McNeil. Edited by John Riches. San Francisco: Ignatius, 1984.

New Elucidations. Translated by Mary Theresilde Skerry. San Francisco: Ignatius, 1986.

"Obedience in the Light of the Gospel," *New Elucidations:* 228-55.

"On Vicarious Representation," *Expl IV:* 415-22.

"Only If," *Convergences:* 135-53.

Origen: Spirit and Fire: A Thematic Anthology of His Writings. Translated by Robert J. Daly. Washington, DC: Catholic University of America Press, 1984.

The Old Covenant. Vol. 6, *The Glory of the Lord: A Theological Aesthetics.* Translated by Brian McNeil and Erasmo Leiva-Merikakis. Edited by John Riches. Edinburgh: T. & T. Clark, 1991.

"Our Love of Jesus Christ," *Elucidations:* 69-79.

Our Task: A Report and a Plan. Translated by John Saward. San Francisco: Ignatius, 1994.

Paul Struggles with His Congregation: The Pastoral Message of the Letters to the Corinthians. Translated by Brigitte L. Bojarska. San Francisco: Ignatius, 1992.

"The Personal God," *Elucidations:* 46-57.

Die Personen in Christ. Bd. II, teil 2, *Theodramatik.* Einsiedeln: Johannes, 1978.

"Pistis and gnosis." Translated by Seán O'hEarchaí. *Communio ICR* 5 (1978): 86-95.

Pneuma und Institution. Bd. IV, *Skizzen zur Theologie.* Einsiedeln: Johannes, 1974.

"Preghiera del Venerdì Santo," La realtà e la gloria: 91-93.

"Preliminary Remarks on the Discernment of Spirits," *Expl IV:* 337-51.

"Presenza della croce," *Monastica* 4 (1964): 21-23.

Prolegomena. Vol. 1, *Theo-Drama.* Translated by Graham Harrison. San Francisco: Ignatius, 1988.

**Quattro meditazioni. Esercizi spirituali per sacerdoti.* Conferenze a Colevalenza, 12-15 settembre 1983. Tradotte da Bruno Ognibeni. Supplemento al "Litterae communionis — CL," n. 6 (1984). 1. ristampa. Milan: Comunione e Liberazione, 1986.

La realtà e la gloria: Hans Urs von Balthasar articoli e interviste 1978-1988. Milan: EDIT Editoriale Italiana, 1988.

"Reflections on the Discernment of Spirits," *Communio ICR* 7 (1980) 3: 196-208.

"A Résumé of My Thought." In *Hans Urs von Balthasar: His Life and Work.* Translated by Kelly Hamilton. Edited by David L. Schindler. San Francisco: Ignatius, 1991.

"The Scapegoat and the Trinity," *Crown:* 82-86.

Seeing the Form. Vol. 1, *The Glory of the Lord: A Theological Aesthetics.* Translated by Erasmo Leiva-Merikakis. Edited by Joseph Fessio, S.J., and John Riches. Edinburgh: T. & T. Clark, 1982.

"Das Selbstbewußtsein Jesu," *IKaZ Communio* 8 (1979): 30-39.

"The Self-Consciousness of Jesus," *Crown:* 315-19.

"A Short Discourse on Hell." In *Dare We Hope "That All Men Be Saved"? with "A Short Discourse on Hell."* Translated by Lothar Krauth and David Kipp. San Francisco: Ignatius, 1988.

**A Short Primer for Unsettled Laymen.* Translated by Michael Waldstein. San Francisco: Ignatius, 1985.

"Some Points of Eschatology," *Expl I:* 255-77.

"Spirit and Institution," *Expl IV:* 209-43.

Spirit and Institution. Explorations in Theology, vol. 4. Translated by Edward T. Oakes. San Francisco: Ignatius, 1995.

Spouse of the Word. Explorations in Theology, vol. 2. No translator noted. San Francisco: Ignatius, 1991.

*"Stellvertretung: Schlüsselwort christlichen Lebens," *Leben im Geist,* 3-7. Anregungen für Priester 4. Freiburg: Informationszentrum Berufe der Kirche, 1976.

*"Sul significato della lettera enciclica," *Verso il terzo millennio sotto l'azione dello Spirito: Per una lettura della "Dominum et vivificantem,"* 34-38. Città del Vaticano: Libreria Editrice Vaticana, 1986.

Test Everything: Hold Fast to What Is Good. Interview by Angelo Scola. Translated by Maria Shrady. San Francisco: Ignatius, 1989.

A Theological Anthropology. No translator noted. New York: Sheed & Ward, 1967.

"Theologie des Abstiegs zur Hölle." In *Adrienne von Speyr und ihre kirchliche Sendung. Akten des römischen Symposiums 27-29 September 1985,* 138-46. Einsiedeln: Johannes, 1986.

"Theologische Besinnung auf das Mysterium des Höllenabstiegs." In „Hinabgestiegen in das Reich des Todes": Der Sinn dieses Satzes in Bekenntnis und Lehre. Dichtung und Kunst, 84-98. Hrsg. Hans Urs von Balthasar. Munich: Schnell & Steiner, 1982.

A Theology of History. No translator noted. San Francisco: Ignatius, 1994.

**Thérèse of Lisieux.* Translated by Donald Nicholl. New York: Sheed & Ward, 1954.

"The Three Evangelical Counsels," *Elucidations:* 207-22.

The Threefold Garland: The World's Salvation in Mary's Prayer. Translated by Erasmo Leiva-Merikakis. San Francisco: Ignatius, 1982.

"Der Tod im heutigen Denken," *Anima* 11 (1956): 292-99.

"Der Tod vom Leben verschlungen," *Homo Creatus Est:* 185-91.

*"Tragedy and Christian Faith," *Expl III:* 391-411.

*"La trasparenza del Mistero," *La realtà e la gloria:* 15-25.

*"La Trinità." *Quattro meditazioni*, 17-28.

"Trinity and Future," *Elucidations:* 80-90.

"The Unity of Our Lives," *Convergences:* 111-33.

"The Unknown God," *Elucidations:* 35-45.

"Von Balthasar antwortet Boros," *Orientierung* 34 (1970): 38-39.

Wahrheit Gottes. Bd. II, *Theo-Logik.* Einsiedeln: Johannes, 1985.

The Way of the Cross. Translated by John G. Cumming. Middlegreen, Slough, England: St. Paul, 1990.

* *The Way of the Cross.* Translated by Rodelinde Albrecht and Maureen Sullivan. London: Burns & Oates, 1969.

*"Why We Need Nicholas of Cusa." Translated by Maria Shrady. *Communio ICR* 28 (2001) 4: 854-59.

"With Him Two Others on Either Side, but Jesus in the Middle," #92, *You Have Words:* 251-53.

The Word Made Flesh. Explorations in Theology, vol. 1. Translated by A. V. Littledale and Alexander Dru. San Francisco: Ignatius, 1989.

*"Von Balthasar e Testori: quale fede, quale vita," *La realtà e la gloria:* 121-31.

You Crown the Year with Your Goodness. Translated by Graham Harrison. San Francisco: Ignatius, 1989.

You Have Words of Eternal Life: Scripture Meditations. Translated by Dennis Martin. San Francisco: Ignatius, 1991.

Zuerst Gottes Reich: Zwei Skizzen zur biblischen Naherwartung. Neue Kriterien 4. Einsiedeln: Johannes, 2002.

"Zur Frage: 'Hoffnung für alle.' Eine Antwort auf den Artikel von Pfr. Karl Besler," *Theologisches* 199 (1986): 7363-66.

Works by Other Authors

Aavv. *Adrienne von Speyr und ihre kirchliche Sendung. Akten des römischen Symposiums 27-29 September 1985.* Einsiedeln: Johannes, 1986.

Aavv. *Atti XIV Colloquio di Teologia di Lugano: Esperienza mistica e teologia. Ricerca epistemologica sulle proposte di Hans Urs von Balthasar = Rivista Teologica di Lugano* 6 (2001).

About the Harrowing of Hell: A Seventeenth-Century Ukrainian Play in Its European Context. Translated with introduction and notes by Irena R. Makaryk. Ottawa: Dovehouse Editions Canada, 1989.

Ambaum, Jan. "An Empty Hell? The Restoration of All Things?: Balthasar's Concept of Hope for Salvation." Translated by Michael J. Dodds. *Communio ICR* 18 (1991) 2: 35-52.

*Ambrose, St. *Of the Christian Faith.* Translated by H. De Romestin. Nicene and Post-Nicene Fathers, 2nd ser., vol. 10. Grand Rapids: Eerdmans, 1979.

*————. "The Sacrament of the Incarnation of Our Lord," *Theological and Dogmatic Works.* Translated by Roy J. Deferrari. The Fathers of the Church 44. Washington, DC: Catholic University of America Press, 1963.

*Ariès, Philippe. *Geschichte des Todes.* 5. Auflage. Übersetzt von Hans-Horst Henschen und Una Pfau. Munich: Carl Henser, 1980.

*Athanasius, St. "In Defence of the Nicene Definition," *Select Treatises of St. Athanasius, Archbishop of Alexandria, in controversy with the Arians,* 1-72. Translated by members of the English Church. Library of the Fathers of the Holy Catholic Church 8. Oxford: John Henry Parker, 1842.

*————. "Four Discourses Against the Arians," *Select Treatises of St. Athanasius, Archbishop of Alexandria, in controversy with the Arians,* 177-280. Translated by members of the English Church. Library of the Fathers of the Holy Catholic Church 8. Oxford: John Henry Parker, 1842.

Augustine, St. *Epis. ad Evodius.* PL 33:708-16.

————. Ep. 164. *Letters,* vol. 3 *(131-64).* Writings of St. Augustine 11. The Fathers of the Church 20. New York: Fathers of the Church, 1953.

*————. *The First Catechetical Instruction.* Translated by Joseph P. Christopher. Ancient Christian Writers 2. Edited by Johannes Quasten and Joseph C. Plumpe. Westminster, MD: Newman, 1946.

————. *Sermo de symbolo.* Cap. 5-7. PL 40:1193-94.

*————. *Sermons on the Liturgical Seasons.* Translated by Mary Sarah Muldowney. The Fathers of the Church 38; Writings of St. Augustine, vol. 17. Washington, DC: Catholic University of America Press with Consortium Books, 1959.

*————. *Expositions on the Book of Psalms.* Edited by A. Cleveland Coxe. Nicene and Post-Nicene Fathers, 1st ser., vol. 8. Grand Rapids: Eerdmans, 1983.

*————. "On the Creed: A Sermon to the Catechumens." Edited by Philip Schaff. Nicene and Post-Nicene Fathers, 1st ser., vol. 3. Grand Rapids: Eerdmans, 1980.

Bätzing, Georg. *Kirche im Werden: Ekklesiologische Aspekte des Läuterungsgedankens.* Trierer Theologische Studien 56. Trier: Paulinus, 1996.

*Beckwith, John. *Early Christian and Byzantine Art.* London: Yale University Press, 1979.

Berger, David. "Woher kommen die Thesen Hans Urs von Balthasars zur Hölle? Oder: hatte 'Theologisches' doch recht?" Book review of *Atti XIV Colloquio di Teologia di Lugano: Esperienza mistica e teologia. Ricerca epistemologica sulle proposte di Hans Urs von Balthasar* = *Rivista Teologica di Lugano* 6 (2001): 1-64. *Theologisches Katholische Monatsschrift* 31 (2001) 5/6: 265-68.

*Bertonière, Gabriel. *The Historical Development of the Easter Vigil and Related Ser-*

vices in the Greek Church. Orientalia Christiana Analecta 193. Rome: Pontifical Institute of Oriental Studies, 1972.

Bibleworks 95/NT release. Version 4.0.026e (3549) CD-ROM. Bibleworks. 1998.

Bieder, Werner. Die Vorstellung von der Höllenfahrt Jesu Christi. Beitrag zur Entstehungsgeschichte der Vorstellung vom sog. Descensus ad inferos. Abhandlungen zur Theologie des Alten und Neuen Testament 19. Zurich: Zwingli, 1949.

Boismard, M.-E. "La typologie baptismale dans la première épître de Saint Pierre," La Vie Spirituelle, no. 416 (1956): 339-52.

*Bonaventure, St. "Compendium Theologicae Veritatis," Opera omnia, T. VIII. Paris: Ludovicus Vives, Biblipola Editor, 1866.

Brambilla, Franco Giulio. "Salvezza e redenzione nella teologia di K. Rahner e H. U. von Balthasar," La Scuola Cattolica 108 (1980): 167-234.

Byzantine Daily Worship. Translated by Joseph Raya and Jose de Vinck. Allendale, NJ: Alleluia, 1969.

Cabrol, F. "Descente du Christ aux enfers d'après la liturgie," in Dictionnaire d'archéologie chrétienne et de liturgie, 1920 edition: 682-93.

Calvin, John. Institutes of the Christian Religion. Translated by Ford Lewis Battles. Edited by John T. McNeill. The Library of Christian Classics, vol. 20. Philadelphia: Westminster, 1960.

*Cantalamessa, Raniero. The Mystery of Easter. Translated by Alan Neame. Collegeville, MN: Liturgical Press, 1993.

————. La pasqua della nostra salvezza: Le tradizioni pasquali della bibbia e della primitiva chiesa. Casale Monferrato (AL), Italy: Marietti, 1971.

Cantate et Jubilate Deo: A Devotional and Liturgical Hymnal. Edited by James Socías. Princeton, NJ: Scepter, 1999.

Catechism of the Catholic Church, revised ed. London: Geoffrey Chapman, 1999.

Catechism of the Council of Trent. Translated by John A. McHugh and Charles J. Callan. New York: Joseph F. Wagner, 1923.

Chaine, J. "Descente du Christ aux Enfers," in Dictionnaire de la Bible Supplément, 1934 edition: 395-431.

The Christian Faith in the Doctrinal Documents of the Catholic Church, 6th ed. Edited by Jacques Dupuis. Staten Island, NY: Alba House, 1996.

Cipriani, Settimio. "Insegna la prima lettera di Pietro (3,19-29; 4,6) la 'discesa' di Cristo agli inferi?" RITC Communio 55 (Gen/Feb 1981): 7-19.

Cleasby, Richard, and Gudbrand Vigfusson. An Icelandic-English Dictionary, 2nd ed. Oxford: Clarendon, 1951. S.v. "hel."

*Clement of Alexandria, St. The Stromata, or Miscellanies. The Ante-Nicene Fathers, vol. 2. Grand Rapids: Eerdmans, 1979.

*Connell, Martin F. "Descensus Christi ad inferos: Christ's Descent to the Dead," Theological Studies 62 (2001) 2: 262-82.

Cooper, Alan. "Ps 24:7-10: Mythology and Exegesis," Journal of Biblical Literature 102 (1983) 1: 37-60.

Crehan, Joseph H. *A Catholic Dictionary of Theology.* New York: Thomas Nelson & Sons, 1962. S.v. "baptism."

Cross, F. L. *I Peter: A Paschal Liturgy.* London: A. R. Mowbray, 1954.

*Cullman, Oscar. *Baptism in the New Testament.* Translated by J. K. S. Reid. Studies in Biblical Theology 1. London: SCM, 1964.

*Cyril of Alexandria, St. "On the Symbol of the Faith by Blessed Cyril," *A Collection of Unpublished Syriac Letters of Cyril of Alexandria.* Translated by R. Y. Ebied and L. R. Wickham. Corpus Scriptorum Christianorum Orientalium 360; Scriptores Syri 158. Louvain: CSCO, 1975.

*————. *On the Unity of Christ.* Translated by John Anthony McGuckin. Crestwood, NY: St. Vladimir's Seminary Press, 1995.

*————. *Letters 1-50.* Translated by John I. McEnerney. Fathers of the Church 76. Washington, DC: Catholic University of America, 1987.

*Cyril of Jerusalem, St. "Lenten Lectures," *The Works of St. Cyril of Jerusalem,* vol. 2. Translated by Leo P. McCauley and Anthony A. Stephenson. The Fathers of the Church 64. Washington: Catholic University of America Press, 1969.

*————. "On the Ten Doctrines," *The Works of St. Cyril of Jerusalem,* vol. 1. Translated by Leo P. McCauley and Anthony A. Stephenson. The Fathers of the Church 61. Washington, DC: Catholic University of America Press, 1969.

Dalton, William Joseph. *Christ's Proclamation to the Spirits: A Study of 1 Peter 3:18–4:6.* Analecta Biblica 23. Rome: Pontifical Biblical Institute, 1965.

Daniélou, Jean. "Déluge, Baptême, Jugement," *Dieu Vivant* 8 (1947): 97-111.

————. "Le Symbolisme des Rites Baptismaux," *Dieu Vivant* 1 (1945): 17-43.

————. Review of *Die Vorstellung von der Höllenfahrt Jesus Christi* by Werner Bieder. *Recherches de Science Religieuse* 37 (1950): 594-601.

Dante. *The Divine Comedy.* Translated by Mark Musa. New York: Penguin, 1971.

Davidson, Clifford. "The Fate of the Damned in English Art and Drama," *The Iconography of Hell.* Edited by Clifford Davidson and Thomas H. Seiler. Early Drama, Art, and Music Monograph Series 17. Kalamazoo, MI: Medieval Institute Publications, Western Michigan University, 1992.

Delaune, Etienne (follower of). Print #571. 16th century or later. Ashmolean Museum, Oxford.

de Meester, A. "Descente du Christ aux enfers dans les liturgies orientales," in *Dictionnaire d'archéologie chrétienne et de liturgie,* 1920 edition: 693-97.

Denifle, Henricus. *Chartularium Universitatis Parisensis.* Paris: Delalain, 1891.

Denzinger, H., and A. Schönmetzer, eds. *Enchiridion Symbolorum. Definitionum et Declarationum de Rebus Fidei et Morum,* 36 ed. Freiburg: Herder, 1976.

Dieser, Helmut. *Der gottähnliche Mensch und die Gottlosigkeit der Sünde: Zur Theologie des* Descensus Christi *bei Hans Urs von Balthasar.* Trierer Theologische Studien 62. Trier: Paulinus, 1998.

The Divine Office: The Liturgy of the Hours according to the Roman Rite. Vol. 2: Lent and Eastertide. London: Collins, 1974.

Dold, Alban. "Ein einzigartiges Dokument der Karsamstagsliturgie," *Paschatis*

Sollemnia: Studien zu Osterfeier und Osterfrömmingkeit, 179-87. Vienna: Herder, 1959.

Dölger, F. J. *Sol Salutis,* 3. Auflage. Liturgiewissenschaftliche Quellen und Forschungen Heft 16/17. Munster: Aschendorff, 1972.

Duden Oxford Kompaktwörterbuch Englisch, 1992 ed. S.v. "entblössen."

Duquoc, Christian. "La descente du Christ aux enfers: Problématique théologique," *Lumière et Vie* 17 (1968) 87: 45-62.

Ephraim Syrus, St. *The Nisibene Hymns.* Translated by J. T. Sarsfield Stopford. Nicene and Post-Nicene Fathers, 2nd ser., vol. 13. Grand Rapids: Eerdmans, 1976.

*————. "Homily on Our Lord," *Selected Prose Works: Commentary on Genesis, Commentary on Exodus, Homily on Our Lord, Letter to Publius,* 273-332. Translated by Edward S. Mathews, Jr., and Joseph P. Amar. Edited by Kathleen McVey. The Fathers of the Church 91. Washington, DC: Catholic University of America Press, 1994.

Espezel, Alberto. *El Misterio Pascual en Hans Urs von Balthasar.* Buenos Aires: Impreso en Grafideas, 1987.

Evdokimov, Paul. *The Art of the Icon: A Theology of Beauty.* Translated by Steven Bigham. Redondo Beach, CA: Oakwood, 1996.

The Faith of the Early Fathers. Vols. 1-3. Edited and translated by William A. Jurgens. Collegeville, MN: Liturgical Press, 1970-79.

*Farrell, Bertin. "The Descent into Hell." Proceedings of the Nineteenth Annual Convention of the Catholic Theological Society of America, held in New York 22-25 June 1964, 73-79.

*Faulkner, Ann. "The Harrowing of Hell at Barking Abbey and in Modern Production," *The Iconography of Hell.* Edited by Clifford Davidson and Thomas H. Seiler. Early Drama, Art, and Music Monograph Series, 17. Kalamazoo, MI: Medieval Institute Publications, Western Michigan University, 1992. 141-57.

The Festal Menaion. Translated by Mother Mary and Kallistos Ware. South Canaan, PA: St. Tikhon's, 1998.

Frohnhofen, Herbert. *APATHEIA TOU THEOU: Über die Affektlosigkeit Gottes in der griechischen Antike und bei den griechischsprachigen Kirchenväter bis zu Gregorios Thaumaturgos.* European University Studies. Series XXIII Theology, vol. 318. Frankfurt: Peter Lang, 1987.

Galot, Jean. "Christ's Descent into Hell," *Theology Digest* 13 (1965) 2: 89-94.

*Gardiner, Eileen. *Medieval Visions of Heaven and Hell: A Sourcebook.* New York: Garland Publishing, 1993.

Garrigou-Lagrange, Reginald. *Our Savior and His Love for Us.* Translated by A. Bouchard. London: B. Herder, 1951.

The Gospel of Nicodemus. In Edgar Hennecke, *New Testament Apocrypha,* vol. 1. Edited by Wilhelm Schneemelcher. English translation edited by R. McL. Wilson. Philadelphia: Westminster Press, 1963.

The Greek New Testament, 4th ed. Edited by Kurt Aland, Matthew Black, Carlo M. Martini, Bruce M. Metzger, and Allen Wikgren, in cooperation with the Institute for

New Testament Textual Research. Stuttgart: Deutsche Bibelgesellschaft, 1994. In *Bibleworks 95/NT release,* Version 4.0.026e (3549) CD-ROM. Bibleworks, 1998.

Gregory Nazianzen, St. *Ep. 101. Ad Cledonium presbyterum contra Apollinariue.* PG 37:181.

*———. *La passione di Cristo.* Traduzione, introduzione, e note a cura di Francesco Trisoglio. Rome: Città Nuova, 1979.

*Gregory of Nyssa, St. *Ascetical Works.* Translated by Virginia Woods Callahan. The Fathers of the Church 58. Washington, DC: Catholic University of America Press, 1967.

———. *The Great Catechism.* Translated by William Moore and Henry Austin Wilson. Nicene and Post-Nicene Fathers. 2nd ser., vol. 5. Grand Rapids: Eerdmans, 1954.

*———. "On the Three-Day Period of the Resurrection of our Lord Jesus Christ" and "The Holy and Saving Pascha." Translated by S. G. Hall. In *The Easter Sermons of Gregory of Nyssa: Translation and Commentary,* 31-53. Edited by Andreas Spira and Christoph Klock. Patristic Monograph Series, vol. 9. Cambridge, MA: Philadelphia Patristic Foundation, 1981.

*———. "Against Eunomius." Translated by Philip Schaff and Henry Wace. Nicene and Post-Nicene Fathers, 2nd ser., vol. 5. Grand Rapids: Eerdmans, 1954.

Gregory the Great, St. *Epis. XV. Ad Georgium presbyterum.* PL 77:869-70.

Grillmeier, Alois. "Der Gottessohn im Totenreich: Soteriologische und christologische Motivierung der Descensuslehre in der älteren christlichen Überlieferung," *Mit ihm und in ihm: Christologische Forschungen und Perspektiven,* 2. Auflage, 76-174. Freiburg: Herder, 1975.

Gschwind, Karl. *Die Niederfahrt Christi in die Unterwelt.* Neutestamentliche Abhandlungen 2. Band, 3./5. Heft. Munster: Aschendorff, 1911.

The Harrowing of Hell: A Miracle-Play Written in the Reign of Edward the Second. Translated by James Orchard Hallwell. London: John Russell Smith, 1840.

Herzog, Markwart. "Descensus ad inferos": *Eine religionsphilosophische Untersuchung der Motive und Interpretationen mit besonderer Berücksichtigung der monographischen Literatur seit dem 16. Jahrhundert.* Frankfurter Theologische Studien 53. Frankfurt: Josef Knecht, 1997.

*———, and Markus von Hagen. "Descent into the Kingdom of the Dead." *Theology Digest* 37 (1990) 2: 123-25.

Hippolytus of Rome, St. *Commentaire sur Daniel.* Translated by Maurice Lefévre. Sources Chrétiennes, vol. 14. Edited by H. de Lubac and J. Daniélou. Paris: Éditions du Cerf, 1947.

*———. "On Psalm CIX or CX," in "The Extant Works and Fragments of Hippolytus." Translated by S. D. F. Salmud. The Ante-Nicene Fathers, vol. 5. Grand Rapids: Eerdmans, 1978.

*———. "Treatise on Christ and Antichrist." Translated by S. D. F. Salmud. The Ante-Nicene Fathers, vol. 5. Grand Rapids: Eerdmans, 1978.

*———. *La tradition apostolique,* 2nd ed. Translated, with introduction and notes, by Bernard Botte. Paris: Éditions du Cerf, 1968.

The Holy Bible. Douay-Rheims Version, 1899 American ed. In Bibleworks 95/NT release. Version 4.0.026e (3549) CD-ROM. Bibleworks, 1998.

The Holy Bible. Revised Standard Version, 1952 ed. Division of Christian Education of the National Council of Churches of Christ in the United States of America, 1973. In Bibleworks 95/NT release. Version 4.0.026e (3549) CD-ROM. Bibleworks, 1998.

*Hughes, Robert. Heaven and Hell in Western Art. London: Weidenfeld & Nicolson, 1968.

Hunt, Anne. The Trinity and the Paschal Mystery: A Development in Recent Catholic Theology. New Theological Studies 5. Collegeville, MN: Liturgical Press, 1997.

*Ignatius of Antioch, St. The Epistles of St. Clement of Rome and St. Ignatius of Antioch. Translated by James A. Kleist. Ancient Christian Writers 1. Edited by Johannes Quasten and Joseph C. Plumpe. Westminster, MD: Newman, 1946.

*Ingold, A. "Descente de Jésus aux enfers," in Dictionnaire de théologie catholique, 1939 edition: 565-620.

International Theological Commission. "The Consciousness of Christ Concerning Himself and His Mission," Texts and Documents, 1969-1985, 305-15. Edited by Michael Sharkey. San Francisco: Ignatius, 1989.

*———. "Select Questions on Christology," Texts and Documents, 1969-1985, 185-205. Edited by Michael Sharkey. San Francisco: Ignatius, 1989.

*———. "Theology, Christology, Anthropology," Texts and Documents, 1969-1985, 207-23. Edited by Michael Sharkey. San Francisco: Ignatius, 1989.

*Irenaeus, St. Against Heresies. The Apostolic Fathers with Justin Martyr and Irenaeus, American Edition. The Ante-Nicene Fathers, vol. 1. Grand Rapids: Eerdmans, reprint 1985.

*———. Proof of the Apostolic Preaching. Translated by Joseph P. Smith. Ancient Christian Writers 16. Edited by Johannes Quasten and Joseph C. Plumpe. Westminster, MD: Newman, 1952.

Jacquemont, Patrick. "La Descente aux Enfers dans la Tradition Orientale," Lumière et Vie 17 (1968) 87: 31-44.

Jeremias, Joachim. "Zwischen Karfreitag und Ostern: Descensus und Ascensus in der Karfreitagstheologie des Neuen Testamentes," Zeitschrift für die Neutestamentliche Wissenschaft 42 (1949): 194-201.

*John Chrysostom, St. Baptismal Instructions. Translated by Paul W. Harkins. Ancient Christian Writers 31. Westminster, MD: Newman, 1963.

*———. The Homilies of St. John Chrysostom, Archbishop of Constantinople, on the Gospel of St. John. Translated by members of the English Church. Library of the Fathers of the Holy Catholic Church. Oxford: John Henry Parker, 1852.

*———. The Homilies of St. John Chrysostom, Archbishop of Constantinople, on the Gospel of St. Matthew. Translated by members of the English Church. Library of the Fathers of the Holy Catholic Church. Oxford: John Henry Parker, 1843.

*———. "Homily VII" on Philippians, Homilies on the Epistles of St. Paul the Apostle to the Philippians, Colossians, and Thessalonians. Oxford Translation. Nicene and Post-Nicene Fathers, 1st ser., vol. 13. Grand Rapids: Eerdmans, 1979.

*————. "Homily XI" on Ephesians. Edited by Philip Schaff. Nicene and Post-Nicene Fathers, 1st ser., vol. 8. Grand Rapids: Eerdmans, 1979.

*————. "Homily on the Passage (Mt 26:29), 'Father if it be possible,' etc., and Against the Marcionists and Manichaeans." Translated by W. R. W. Stephens. Nicene and Post-Nicene Fathers, 1st ser., vol. 9. Grand Rapids: Eerdmans, 1978.

John Damascene, St. *De fide orthodoxa.* Translated by S. D. F. Salmond. Nicene and Post-Nicene Fathers, 2nd ser., vol. 9. Grand Rapids: Eerdmans, 1983.

*————. *On the Divine Images.* Translated by David Anderson. Crestwood, NY: St. Vladimir's Seminary Press, 1997.

John of the Cross, St. *Ascent of Mt. Carmel.* Translated by Kieran Kavanaugh and Otilio Rodriguez. In *The Collected Works of St. John of the Cross.* Washington, DC: ICS, 1979.

*John Paul II. *Dominum et vivificantem.* Encyclical letter, 1986.

*————. *Duodecimum saeculum.* Apostolic letter, 1987.

————. "He Descended into Hell," General Audience, January 11, 1989.

————. *Novo millennio ineunte.* Apostolic letter, 2000.

————. "Perennial Philosophy of St. Thomas Aquinas for the Youth of Our Times." Address to an International Congress on St. Thomas Aquinas, 1979.

Jöhri, Mauro. "Descensus Dei": *Teologia della croce nell'opera di Hans Urs von Balthasar.* Corona Lateranensis 30. Rome: Libreria Editrice della Pontificia Università Lateranense, 1981.

Kartsonis, Anna D. *Anastasis: The Making of an Image.* Princeton, NJ: Princeton University Press, 1986.

Kehl, Medard. "Höllenabstieg Christi," in *Lexikon für Theologie und Kirche,* 3rd ed: 238. Hrsg. Walter Kasper. Freiburg: Herder, 1996.

Kelley, Bennet. *Spiritual Direction According to St. Paul of the Cross.* New York: Alba House, 1993.

*Kelly, J. N. D. *The Athanasian Creed.* The Paddock Lectures, 1962-63. London: Adam & Charles Black, 1964.

————. *A Commentary on the Epistles of Peter and of Jude.* Black's New Testament Commentaries. London: Adam & Charles Black, 1969.

————. *Early Christian Creeds.* London: Longmans, Green, 1950.

*————. *Early Christian Doctrines.* London: Adam & Charles Black, 1968.

Kenny, J. P. *A Catholic Dictionary of Theology.* London: Thomas Nelson & Sons, 1971. S.v. "hell."

Kerezty, Roch. "Response to Professor Scola," *Communio ICR* 18 (1991) 3: 227-36.

Kirkland, James Hampton. *A Study of the Anglo-Saxon Poem. The Harrowing of Hell (Grein's Höllenfahrt Christi).* Halle: Ehrhardt Karras, 1885.

*Klaghofen, Wolfgang. *Karfreitag: Auseinandersetzung mit Hans Urs von Balthasars Theologik.* Salzburger Theologische Studien 4. Innsbruck: Tyrolia, 1997.

Knox, Ronald. *The Creed in Slow Motion.* London: Sheed & Ward, 1949.

*Krenski, Thomas Rudolph. Passio Caritatis: *Trinitarische Passiologie im Werk Hans*

Urs von Balthasars. Sammlung Horizonte. Neue Folge 28. Einsiedeln: Johannes, 1990.

Lauber, David Edward. *Towards a Theology of Holy Saturday: Karl Barth and Hans Urs von Balthasar on the* Descensus ad inferna. Ann Arbor, MI: UMI Dissertation Services, 1999.

The Lenten Triodion. Translated by Mother Mary and Kallistos Ware. South Canaan, PA: St. Tikhon's, 1999.

Leo XIII. *Aeterni Patris.* Encyclical letter, 1879.

Léon-Dufour, Xavier, ed. *Dictionary of Biblical Theology.* Translated by P. Joseph Cahill. Revised and translated by E. M. Stewart. Boston: St. Paul, 1988. S.v. "death," "hell."

*Levering, Matthew. "Balthasar on Christ's Consciousness on the Cross," *The Thomist* 65 (2001): 567-81.

**Lexikon für Theologie und Kirche,* 2. Auflage. Hrsg. Josef Höfer and Karl Rahner. Freiburg: Herder, 1960.

Lexikon für Theologie und Kirche, 3. Auflage. Hrsg. Walter Kasper. Freiburg: Herder, 1996.

Lochbrunner, Manfred. "Das Ineinander von Schau und Theologie in der Lehre vom Karsamstag bei Hans Urs von Balthasar," *Rivista Teologica di Lugano* 6 (2001) 1: 171-93.

*Ludlow, Morwenna. "Universal Salvation and a Soteriology of Divine Punishment," *Scottish Journal of Theology* 53 (2000) 4: 449-71.

Lundberg, Per. *La typologie baptismale dans l'ancienne Eglise.* Acta Seminarii Neotestamentici Upsaliensis 10. Leipzig: Alfred Lorentz, 1942.

Lyonnet, Stanislas, and Léopold Sabourin. *Sin, Redemption, and Sacrifice: A Biblical and Patristic Study.* Analecta Biblica 48. Rome: Biblical Institute Press, 1970.

Maas, Wilhelm. "Abgestiegen zur Hölle. Aspekte eines vergessenen Glaubensartikels," *IKaZ Communio* 10 (1981) 1: 1-18.

*————. *Das Geheimnis des Karsamstags.* In *Adrienne von Speyr und ihre kirchliche Sendung. Akten des römischen Syposiums 27-29 September 1985,* 128-37. Einsiedeln: Johannes, 1986.

————. *Gott und die Hölle: Studien zum* Descensus Christi. Einsiedeln: Johannes, 1979.

MacCulloch, J. A. *The Harrowing of Hell: A Comparative Study of an Early Christian Doctrine.* Edinburgh: T. & T. Clark, 1930.

Mansi, Giovanni Domenico. *Sacrorum Conciliorum nova, et amplissima collectio.* . . . 59 vols. Paris: H. Welter, 1901-27.

Mansini, Guy. "Balthasar and the Theodramatic Enrichment of the Trinity," *The Thomist* 64 (2000): 499-519.

Marchesi, Giovanni. *La cristologia trinitaria di Hans Urs von Balthasar: Gesù Cristo pienezza della rivelazione e della salvezza,* 2 ed. Biblioteca di Teologia Contemporanea 94. Brescia: Queriniana, 2003.

Maritain, Jacques. *St. Thomas Aquinas: Angel of the Schools.* London: Sheed & Ward, 1942.

Martin, Regis. *The Suffering of Love: Christ's Descent into Hell and Human Hopelessness, with Particular Reference to the Holocaust of the Jews.* STD diss., Pontificia Università S. Tommaso d'Aquino, 1988.

———. "The Suffering of Love: Christ's Descent into the Hell of Human Hopelessness." Steubenville, OH: Franciscan University, 1990.

Martinelli, Paolo. *Il mistero della morte in Hans Urs von Balthasar: Il mistero pasquale come rivelazione dell'amore Trinitario di Dio.* STD diss., Pontificia Università Gregoriana, 1996.

Maximus the Confessor, St. *The Disputation with Pyrrhus of Our Father Among the Saints, Maximus the Confessor.* Translated by Joseph P. Farrell. D.Phil (Oxon).

*McDade, John. "The Trinity and the Paschal Mystery," *The Heythrop Journal* 29 (1988) 2: 175-91.

*McDonnell, Kilian. "The Baptism of Jesus in the Jordan and the Descent into Hell," *Worship* 69 (1995) 2: 98-109.

McGuckin, Terence. "The Eschatology of the Cross," *New Blackfriars* 75 (1994): 364-77.

Melito of Sardis, St. *Melito of Sardis:* On Pascha *and Fragments.* Texts and translations edited by Stuart George Hall. Oxford: Oxford University Press, 1979.

*Meredith, Peter. "The Iconography in the English Cycles: A Practical Perspective," *The Iconography of Hell,* 158-86. Edited by Clifford Davidson and Thomas H. Seiler. Early Drama, Art, and Music Monograph Series 17. Kalamazoo, MI: Medieval Institute Publications, Western Michigan University, 1992.

Migne, J.-P, ed. *Patrologia . . . : Series graeca.* 166 vols. Paris: Garnier, 1857-66.

———. *Patrologia . . . : Series latina.* 219 vols. Paris: Garnier, 1878-90.

*Millgram, Abraham E. *Sabbath: The Day of Delight.* Philadelphia: Jewish Publication Society of America, 1965.

*Moda, Aldo. *Hans Urs von Balthasar: un' esposizione critica del suo pensiero.* Bari: Ecumenica, 1976.

———. *La gloria della croce: Un dialogo con Hans Urs von Balthasar.* Padua: Messaggero di S. Antonio, 1998.

*Molsdorf, Wilhelm. *Christliche Symbolik der Mittelalterlichen Kunst.* Leipzig: Karl W. Hiersemann, 1926.

Müller, Gerhard L. "Höllenabstieg Christi," in *Lexikon der katholischen Dogmatik,* 271-73. Hrsg. Wolfgang Beinert. Freiburg: Herder, 1987.

Nandkisore, Robert. *Hoffnung auf Erlösung: Die Eschatologie im Werk Hans Urs von Balthasars.* Tesi Gregoriana Serie Teologia No. 22. Rome: Editrice Pontificia Università Gregoriana, 1997.

Nichols, Aidan. *Introduction to Hans Urs von Balthasar: No Bloodless Myth: A Guide Through Balthasar's Dramatics.* Washington, DC: Catholic University of America, 2000.

———. Introduction to *Mysterium Paschale: The Mystery of Easter,* by Hans Urs von Balthasar. Edinburgh: T. & T. Clark, 1990.

————. *Introduction to Hans Urs von Balthasar: Say It Is Pentecost: A Guide Through Balthasar's Logic.* Washington, DC: Catholic University of America, 2001.

Oakes, Edward T. *Pattern of Redemption: The Theology of Hans Urs von Balthasar.* New York: Continuum, 1994.

O'Connor, James T. "Von Balthasar and Salvation," *Homiletic & Pastoral Review* (July 1989): 10-21.

The Odes of Solomon. Edited and translated by James Hamilton Charlesworth. Oxford: Clarendon, 1973.

O'Donnell, John. *Hans Urs von Balthasar.* New York: Continuum, 1991.

O'Hanlon, Gerard F. *The Immutability of God in the Theology of Hans Urs von Balthasar.* Cambridge: Cambridge University Press, 1990.

The Ordinary and *The Anaphora of the Apostles.* Edited by Tesiamoriam Baraki. Washington, DC: privately printed, no date.

*Origen. "Against Celsus." Translated by Frederick Crombie. The Ante-Nicene Fathers, vol. 4. Grand Rapids: Eerdmans, 1979.

*————. *Commentary on the Gospel According to John, Books 1–10.* Translated by Ronald E. Heine. The Fathers of the Church 80. Washington, DC: Catholic University of America Press, 1989.

*————. "Dialogue of Origen with Heraclides," *Treatise on the Passover* (Peri Pascha). Translated and annotated by Robert J. Daly. Ancient Christian Writers 54. New York: Paulist, 1992.

————. *On First Principles.* Koetschau's text, translated by G. W. Butterworth. Gloucester, MA: Peter Smith, 1973.

*————. "Sul primo libro dei 'Re.'" *La Maga di Endor.* A cura di Manlio Simonetti. Biblioteca Patristica 15. Florence: Nardini, 1989.

*————. *Treatise on the Passover* (Peri Pascha). Translated and annotated by Robert J. Daly. Ancient Christian Writers 54. New York: Paulist, 1992.

Ott, Ludwig. *Fundamentals of Catholic Dogma.* Translated by Patrick Lynch. Rockford, IL: Tan, 1974.

Ouspensky, Leonid, and Vladimir Lossky. *The Meaning of Icons.* Translated by G. E. H. Palmer and E. Kadloubovsky. Crestwood, NY: St. Vladimir's Seminary Press, 1999.

Oxford Dictionary of the Christian Church, 3rd ed. S.v. "hades," "gehenna," and "sheol."

Oxford English Dictionary. 2nd ed. S.v. "harrow."

Pächt, Otto, and J. J. G. Alexander. *Illuminated Manuscripts in the Bodleian Library Oxford.* Vol. 1: German, Dutch, Flemish, French, and Spanish Schools. Oxford: Clarendon, 1966.

————. *Illuminated Manuscripts in the Bodleian Library Oxford.* Vol. 2: Italian School. Oxford: Clarendon, 1970.

————. *Illuminated Manuscripts in the Bodleian Library Oxford.* Vol. 3: British, Irish, and Icelandic Schools. Oxford: Clarendon, 1973.

Palli, Elisabetta L. "Der syrisch-palästinensische Darstellungstypus der Höllenfahrt Christi," Festschrift Engelbert Kirschbaum. *Römische Quartalschrift für*

Christliche Altertumskunde und Kirchengeschichte 58. Teil 1-2, 250-67. Freiburg: Herder, 1963.

A Patristic Greek Lexicon. Edited by G. W. H. Lampe. Oxford: Clarendon, 1961. S.v. προσλαμβάνω and relatives.

Perrot, Charles. "La Descente du Christ aux Enfers dans le Nouveau Testament," *Lumière et Vie* 17 (1968) 87: 5-29.

*Peter Canisius, St. *Catechismi latini et germanici.* Rome: Pontificia Universitas Gregoriana, 1933.

*———. St. *Kurzer Inbegriff der christlichen Lehre oder Katechismus.* Landshut: Joseph Thomann, 1826.

*Picca, Salvatore. "La discesa agli inferi e la salvezza dei non cristiani. Linee teologiche per una soluzione del problema." Dissertation defense held 4 June 2004 at Pontificia Università Santa Croce, Rome.

*Pius XII, *Sempiternus Rex Christus.* Encyclical letter, 1951.

*Plastaras, J. "Abraham's Bosom," in *New Catholic Encyclopedia,* 2nd edition: 39. Washington, DC: Catholic University of America, 2003.

*Prestige, Leonard. "Hades in the Greek Fathers," *Lexicon of Patristic Greek.* Journal of Theological Studies 24. Oxford: Clarendon, 1923.

Pseudo-Epiphanius. *Sancto et magno Sabbato.* PG 43:439A-464D.

Pseudo-Hippolytus. *In sanctum pascha.* Studio edizione commento da Giuseppe Visonà. Studio Patristica Mediolanensia 15. Milan: Vita e Pensiero, 1988.

Pyc, Marek. "L'obbedienza di Cristo nelle opera di Hans Urs von Balthasar," excerpt from STD diss., Pontificia Università Gregoriana, 1987.

*Quasten, Johannes. *The Beginnings of Patristic Literature.* Patrology, vol. 1. Utrecht: Spectrum, 1950.

Quillet, H. "Descente de Jésus aux enfers," in *Dictionnaire de théologie catholique,* 1939 edition: 565-619.

*Rahner, Karl. "Dogmatische Fragen zur Osterfrömmigkeit," *Paschatis Sollemnia: Studien zu Osterfeier und Osterfrömmigkeit,* 1-12. Vienna: Herder, 1959.

*———. "Hidden Victory," *Further Theology of the Spiritual Life I.* Theological Investigations, vol. 7. Translated by David Bourke. London: Darton, Longman, & Todd; New York: Herder & Herder, 1971.

———. "Karsamstag," *Geist und Leben* 30 (1957): 81-84.

Ramirez, Santiago. "The Authority of St. Thomas Aquinas," *The Thomist* 15 (January 1952) 1: 1-109.

*Ratzinger, Joseph. "Abgestiegen zu der Hölle," *Einführung in das Christentum: Vorlesungen über das apostolische Glaubensbekenntnis,* 276-84. Munich: Kösel, 2000.

*———. *Eschatology: Death and Eternal Life.* Translated by Michael Waldstein. Edited by Aidan Nichols. Washington, DC: Catholic University of America Press, 1988.

*———. "Five Meditations," *The Sabbath of History.* Washington, DC: William G. Congdon Foundation, 1998.

*The Redentin Easter Play. Translated with introduction and notes by A. E. Zucker. New York: Columbia University Press, 1941.

Reymond, Philippe. L'Eau, sa vie, et sa signification dans l'Ancien Testament. Supplements to Vetus Testamentum, vol. 6. Leiden: Brill, 1958.

Robert Bellarmine, St. De controversiis Christianae Fidei adversus hujus temporis haereticos. Mediolani: Edente Natale Battezzati, 1857.

*————. De septem verbis a Christo in cruce prolatus libri duo. Rome: Zannetti, 1618.

*Romano the Melode, St. Inni. Introduzione, traduzione e note a cura di Georges Gharib. Rome: Edizioni Paoline, 1981.

Rousseau, Olivier. "La Descente aux Enfers. Fondement Sotériologique du Baptême Chrétien," Mélanges Jules Lebreton II. Recherches de Science Religieuse 40 (1951-52): 273-97.

Rothkranz, Johannes. Die Kardinalfehler des Hans Urs von Balthasar. Durach: Anton Schmid, 1989.

Rufinus. A Commentary on the Apostles' Creed. Translated by W. H. Fremantle. Nicene and Post-Nicene Fathers, 2nd ser., vol. 3. Grand Rapids: Eerdmans, 1979.

Rushforth, G. McN. "S. Maria Antiqua," Papers of the British School at Rome 1 (1902) 1: 1-119.

Sacramentum Mundi, 1969 English edition. S.v. "hell."

Sales, Michel. "The Fulfillment of the Sabbath: From the Holiness of the Seventh Day to God's Resting in God." Translated by Mark Sebanc. Communio ICR 21 (1994) 1: 27-48.

*Schlier, Heinrich. Il mistero pasquale e la Passione secondo Marco. Tradotto da Luigi Geninazzi e Gianni Poletti. Milan: Jaca, 2002.

*Schmidt, Carl. Gespäche Jesu mit seinen Jüngern nach der Auferstehung: Ein katholisch-apostolisches Sendschreiben des 2. Jahrhunderts. Texte und Untersuchungen zur Geschichte der altchristlichen Literatur 3. Reihe, 13. Band. Leipzig: Hinrich, 1919.

Schmidt, Gary D. The Iconography of the Mouth of Hell: Eighth-Century Britain to the Fifteenth Century. London: Associated University Presses, 1995.

Schmidt, Herman. "Paschalibus initiati mysteriis," Gregorianum 39 (1958): 463-80.

*Schongauer, Martin. Print (Douce Bequest #1863.1664). 15th century. Ashmolean Museum, Oxford.

*Schumacher, Michele M. "The Concept of Representation in the Theology of Hans Urs von Balthasar," Theological Studies 60 (1999): 53-71.

Schulz, Hans-Joachim. "Die 'Höllenfahrt' als 'Anastasis,'" Zeitschrift für Katholische Theologie 81 (1959): 1-66.

*————. "Der österliche Zug im Erscheinungsbild Byzantinischer Liturgie," Paschatis Sollemnia: Studien zu Osterfeier und Osterfrömmigkeit, 239-46. Vienna: Herder, 1959.

*Schwank, Benedikt. The First and Second Epistles of Peter. Translated by Walter Kruppa. Edited by John L. McKenzie. London: Burns & Oates, 1969.

*Scola, Angelo. "Nature and Grace in Hans Urs von Balthasar," Communio ICR 18 (1991) 3: 207-26.

Scotus anonymous. *Commentarius in epistulas catholicas. In epistula Petri I* in CLCLT-3-Cetedoc. Louanii Noui CD-ROM. January 2002.

*Service Book of the Holy Orthodox-Catholic Apostolic Church, 3rd ed. Translated by Isabel Florence Hapgood. Brooklyn, NY: Syrian Antiochan Orthodox Archdiocese, 1956.

*Sophocles, E. A. *Greek Lexicon of the Roman and Byzantine Periods (From b.c. 146 to a.d. 1100).* New York: Charles Scribner's Sons, 1900. S.v. προσλαμβάνω and relatives.

Spicq, C. "La Révélation de l'Enfer dans la Sainte Écriture," *L'Enfer,* 89-143. Foi Vivante 52. Paris: Les Éditions de la Revue des Jeunes, 1950.

*Spira, Andreas. "Der *Descensus ad inferos* in der Osterpredigt Gregors von Nyssa *De tridui spatio (De tridui spatio* pp. 280,14–286,12)," *The Easter Sermons of Gregory of Nyssa: Translation and Commentary,* 195-261. Edited by Andreas Spira and Christoph Klock. Patristic Monograph Series, vol. 9. Cambridge, MA: Philadelphia Patristic Foundation, 1981.

Stadelmann, Luis I. J. *The Hebrew Conception of the World: A Philological and Literary Study.* Analecta Biblica 39. Rome: Pontifical Biblical Institute, 1970.

Strynkowski, John. "The Descent of Christ among the Dead." STD diss., Pontificia Università Gregoriana, 1972.

———. *The Descent of Christ among the Dead.* Excerpt from STD diss., Pontificia Università Gregoriana, 1971.

*Theologische Realenzyklopädie (TRE). Hrsg. Gerhard Muller. Berlin: Walter de Gruyter, 1986. S.v. "Hölle I," "Hölle II," "Höllenfahrt Christi."

*Thérèse of Lisieux, St. *Story of a Soul: The Autobiography of St. Therese of Lisieux,* 3rd ed. Translated by John Clarke. Washington, DC: ICS Publications, 1996.

Thomas Aquinas, St. *Catena Aurea: Commentary on the Four Gospels Collected out of the Works of the Fathers.* Edited by John Henry Newman. Southampton, UK: Saint Austin, 1997.

*——. *Commentaria in omnes D. Pauli Apostoli Epistolas.* Editio nova, sedulo recognita et mendis expurgata, II (Leodii, Sumptibus et typis H. Dessain, 1857).

———. *Commentary on Ephesians.* Translated by Matthew L. Lamb. Albany, NY: Magi Books, 1966.

———. *The Sermon-Conferences of St. Thomas Aquinas on the Apostles' Creed.* Translated from Leonine edition and edited by Nicholas Ayo. Notre Dame, IN: University of Notre Dame Press, 1988.

———. *Summa Theologiae.* Translated by Fathers of the English Dominican Province. Allen, TX: Christian Classics, 1981.

———. *Super Epistolas. Lectiones ad II Cor.*

*Thomas More, St. *De tristitia Christi.* Edited and translated by Clarence H. Miller. The Complete Works of St. Thomas More, vol. 14, part 1. New Haven, CT: Yale University Press, 1976.

*——. "A Treatise upon the Passion." Edited by Garry E. Haupt. The Complete Works of St. Thomas More, vol. 13. New Haven, CT: Yale University Press, 1976.

Tossou, Kossi K. Joseph. *Streben nach Vollendung: Zur Pneumatologie im Werk Hans Urs von Balthasars*. Freiburg: Herder, 1983.

*Tromp, Nicholas J. *Primitive Conceptions of Death and the Nether World in the Old Testament*. Biblica et Orientalia 21. Rome: Pontifical Biblical Institute, 1969.

Turek, Margaret. *Towards a Theology of God the Father: Hans Urs von Balthasar's Theodramatic Approach*. American University Studies. Series VII, vol. 212. New York: Peter Lang, 2001.

Turner, Ralph. "*Descendit ad inferos*: Medieval Views on Christ's Descent into Hell and the Salvation of the Ancient Just," *Journal of the History of Ideas* 27 (1966): 181.

Vatican II. *Dei Verbum*. Dogmatic constitution, 1965.

———. *Gaudium et spes*. Pastoral constitution, 1965.

———. *Lumen Gentium*. Dogmatic constitution, 1964.

Vogels, Heinz-Jürgen. *Christi Abstieg ins Totenreich und das Läuterungsgericht an den Toten*. Freiburger Theologische Studien 120. Freiburg: Herder, 1976.

*Vorgrimler, Herbert. "Fragen zum Höllenabstieg Christi," *Concilium* 2 (1966) 1: 70-75.

———. *Geschichte der Hölle*. Munich: Wilhelm Fink, 1993.

*———. "Vorfragen zum Theologie des Karsamstags." *Paschatis Sollemnia: Studien zu Osterfeier und Osterfrömmigkeit*, 13-22. Vienna: Herder, 1959.

Wallner, Karl Josef. *Gott als Eschaton: Trinitarische Dramatik als Voraussetzung göttlicher Universalität bei Hans Urs von Balthasar*. Heiligenkreuzer Studienreihe Bd. 7. Heiligenkreuz: Heiligenkreuzer, 1992.

Walshe, M. O'C. *A Concise German Etymological Dictionary*. London: Routledge & Kegan Paul, 1951. S.v. "Hölle."

Wilpert, Joseph. *Die römischen Mosaiken und Malereien der kirchlichen Bauten vom IV. bis XIII. Jahrhundert*. Freiburg: Herder, 1917.

Worthen, Thomas Fletcher. *The Harrowing of Hell in the Art of the Italian Renaissance*. Vols. I & II. Ann Arbor, MI: University Microfilms, 1981.

*Zucker, Mark J. *The Illustrated Bartsch: Early Italian Masters*, vol. 25. New York: Albais Books, 1984.

Other Relevant Works

I append here a bibliography of relevant works that I found after the substantial completion of my own text in 2004. Some texts published earlier than that were not available to me, while new texts have doubtless been published in the meantime.

*Birot, Antoine. "Le Mystère Pascal, expression supreme de l'Amour trinitaire selon Adrienne von Speyr et Hans Urs von Balthasar," *Communio Revue Catholique Internationale* 24 (1999): 127-38.

*Biser, Eugen. "Abgestiegen zu der Hölle: Versuch einer aktuellen Sinndeutung." *Münchener Theologische Zeitschrift* 9 (1958) 3: 205-12; 9 (1958) 4: 283-93.

*Bousset, Wilhelm. "Zur Hadesfahrt Christi." *Zeitschrift für die Neutestamentliche Wissenschaft* 19 (20): 50-66.

*De Margerie, Bertrand. "Note on Balthasar's Trinitarian Theology," *The Thomist* 64 (2000): 127-30.

*Dol, P. Jean-Noël. "L'inversion trinitaire chez Hans Urs von Balthasar," *Revue Thomiste* 100 (2000) 2: 205-38.

*Goodall, Lawrence D. "Hans Urs von Balthasar: A Respectful Critique," *Pro Ecclesia* 8 (1999) 4: 423-36.

*Guerriero, Elio. "L'estremo amore di Dio nella gloria del suo morire: la Teodrammatica," *RITC Communio* 120 (1991): 60-71.

*Lafontaine, René. "'Arrivés a Jésus, ils le trouvèrent mort' (Jo. xix,39): Hans Urs von Balthasar, théologien du samedi saint," *Revue Thomiste* 86 (1986) 4: 635-43.

*Lippi, Adolfo. "La croce nella Trinità: La theologia crucis di Hans Urs von Balthasar," *La Sapienza della Croce* 10 (1995) 3: 225-53.

*Lochbrunner, Manfred. "Descensus ad inferos: Aspekte und Aporien eines vergessenen Glaubensartikels," *Forum katholische Theologie* 9 (1993) 1: 161-77.

*————. "Rahner and Balthasar on the Efficacy of the Cross," *Irish Theological Quarterly* 63 (1998) 3: 232-49.

*Moscow, Miriam. "Passion et action de Dieu au samedi saint," *Revue Thomiste* 86 (1986) 4: 629-35.

*Philips, G. "La descente du Christ aux enfers." *Revue Ecclésiastique de Liège* 24 (1932-33): 144-56.

*————. "L'oeuvre du Christ aux enfers." *Revue Ecclésiastique de Liège* 24 (1932-33): 273-86.

*Prümm, Karl. "Die Darstellungsform der Hadesfahrt des Herrn in der Literatur der alten Kirche. Kritische Bemerkungen zum ersten Kapitel des Werkes von Jos. Kroll: *Gott und Hölle.*" *Scholastik* 10 (1935): 55-77.

*Simmel, Oskar. "Abgestiegen zu der Hölle." *Stimmen der Zeit* 156 (1954-55): 1-6.

*Salvati, Giuseppe Marco. "Trinità e croce: Tematiche e bibliografia," *Sapienza* 39 (1986) 4: 435-65.

*Vorgrimler, Herbert. "Christ's Descent into Hell — Is It Important?" *Concilium* 1(1966) 2: 75-81.

Endnotes

Notes to Chapter One

1. Vatican II, *Gaudium et spes,* #62.

2. Christian Duquoc, "La descente du Christ aux enfers: Problématique théologique," *Lumière et Vie* 17 (1968) 87: 49.

3. John Strynkowski, "The Descent of Christ among the Dead" (STD diss., Pontificia Università Gregoriana, 1971). I am indebted to Strynkowski for drawing my attention to some of the papal and conciliar material that appears here in my section, "Other Magisterial Statements."

4. For a brief history of Balthasar's major treatments of Holy Saturday, see Manfred Lochbrunner, "Das Ineinander von Schau und Theologie in der Lehre vom Karsamstag bei Hans Urs von Balthasar," *Rivista Teologica di Lugano* 6 (2001) 1: 184-88. For a more general treatment of the historical development in Balthasar's thought, see Mauro Jöhri, "Descensus Dei": *Teologia della croce nell'opera di Hans Urs von Balthasar,* Corona Lateranensis 30 (Rome: Libreria Editrice della Pontificia Università Lateranense, 1981).

5. "Descensus ad inferos": *Eine religionsphilosophische Untersuchung der Motive und Interpretationen mit besonderer Berücksichtigung der monographischen Literatur seit dem 16. Jahrhundert,* Frankfurter Theologische Studien 53 (Frankfurt: Josef Knecht, 1997), 244: "Zu einer wirklichen Veränderung in der römisch-katholischen Lehre ist es unter dem Einfluß von Hans Urs von Balthasars »Theologie des Karsamstags« gekommen."

6. Herzog, "Descensus," 14.

7. "The Descent into Hell," *Spirit and Institution,* Explorations in Theology, vol. 4, trans. Edward T. Oakes (San Francisco: Ignatius, 1995), 412; this anthology is hereinafter referred to as *Expl IV,* and the specific essay as "Desc."

Notes to Chapter Two

1. See, e.g., *Catechism of the Catholic Church,* revised ed. (London: Geoffrey Chapman, 1999), #632, 637.

2. J. N. D. Kelly, *Early Christian Creeds* (London: Longmans, Green, 1950), 172-73.

3. PL 21:356, quoted in Strynkowski, "Descent," 20: "Vis tamen verbi eadem videtur esse in eo, quod sepultus dicitur."

4. See Rufinus, *A Commentary on the Apostles' Creed,* trans. W. H. Fremantle, Nicene and Post-Nicene Fathers, 2nd ser., vol. 3. (Grand Rapids: Eerdmans, 1979), #27-28, pp. 60-61.

5. Kelly, *Early Christian Creeds,* 379.

6. The point is stressed by F. Cabrol, "Descente du Christ aux enfers d'après la liturgie," in *Dictionnaire d'archéologie chrétienne et de liturgie,* 1920 ed., 683-85. See also Alois Grillmeier, "Der Gottessohn im Totenreich: Soteriologische und christologische Motivierung der Descensuslehre in der älteren christlichen Überlieferung," *Mit ihm und in ihm: Christologische Forschungen und Perspektiven,* 2. Auflage (Freiburg: Herder, 1975), in particular 90.

7. καὶ ἀναστάντα τῇ τρίτῃ ἡμέρᾳ κατὰ τὰς γραφάς, or *Et resurrexit tertia die, secundum Scripturas.* Greek and Latin texts are from DS 150. Similar examples include DS 42, 44, 46, 48, 55, 62-64, 72, and 125.

8. *CCC* #626.

9. See St. Thomas Aquinas, *Summa Theologiae,* trans. Fathers of the English Dominican Province (Allen, TX: Christian Classics, 1981), Ia q. 52, a. 1. This text is hereinafter cited as *ST.*

10. See St. Thomas Aquinas, *ST,* Ia q. 52, a. 2.

11. See, e.g., "Some Points of Eschatology," *The Word Made Flesh,* Explorations in Theology, vol. 1, trans. A. V. Littledale and Alexander Dru (San Francisco: Ignatius, 1989), 264; this anthology is hereinafter referred to as *Expl I.*

12. E.g., the "Apostolic Tradition of Hippolytus," reproduced in *The Christian Faith in the Doctrinal Documents of the Catholic Church,* ed. Jacques Dupuis, 6th ed. (Staten Island, NY: Alba House, 1996), #2 (DS 10). This anthology is hereinafter cited as *CF,* followed by the relevant paragraph number and, in parentheses, the corresponding reference to H. Denzinger–A. Schönmetzer, eds., *Enchiridion Symbolorum, Definitionum et Declarationum de Rebus Fidei et Morum,* 36th ed. (Freiburg: Herder, 1976), when provided by Dupuis. Other creeds like this one are DS 11-15, 25, 40, 41, 60, and 61.

13. E.g., the "Symbol of Rufinus," *CF* #4 (DS 16), as also DS 23, 27, 28, and 30.

14. E.g., the Fourth Ecumenical Lateran Council, "Symbol of Lateran," *CF* #19 (DS 801). *CF* #17 represents DS 76 as saying "ad infernos," but DS 76 itself says "ad inferos."

15. E.g., the Pseudo-Athanasian creed "Quicumque," DS 76; the "Profession of Faith of Michael Palaeologus," *CF* #23 (DS 852); and the Apostles' Creed, as reproduced in St. Thomas Aquinas, *The Sermon-Conferences of St. Thomas Aquinas on the Apostles' Creed,* trans. from Leonine edition and ed. Nicholas Ayo (Notre Dame, IN: University of Notre Dame Press, 1988), 78 (compare *CF* #5 [DS 30]). Other creeds in this group include DS 29 and 485. The notes to DS 30 (DS, p. 28) point out that the *inferna* of the Roman Order of Baptism (DS 30) was changed to *inferos* in both the *Catechism of the Council of Trent* and, in order to eliminate

371

differences in prayer, the *Roman Breviary*. The same source notes the result was that the form of the creed with *inferos* was established as the standard in the entire Latin Church.

16. *Catechism of the Council of Trent*, trans. John A. McHugh and Charles J. Callan (New York: Joseph F. Wagner, 1923), 63; *CCC* #632.

17. J. P. Kenny, *A Catholic Dictionary of Theology* (London: Thomas Nelson & Sons, 1971), s.v. "hell"; *Oxford Dictionary of the Christian Church*, 3rd ed., s.v. "gehenna." See also C. Spicq, "La Révélation de l'Enfer dans la Sainte Écriture," *L'Enfer*, Foi Vivante 52 (Paris: Les Éditions de la Revue des Jeunes, 1950), 119-22.

18. *CCC* #1030.

19. *Catechism of the Council of Trent*, 63.

20. M. O'C. Walshe, *A Concise German Etymological Dictionary* (London: Routledge & Kegan Paul, 1951), s.v. "Hölle"; and Richard Cleasby and Gudbrand Vigfusson, *An Icelandic-English Dictionary*, 2nd ed. (Oxford: Clarendon, 1951), s.v. "hel."

21. Kelly, *A Catholic Dictionary of Theology*, s.v. "sheol"; *Oxford Dictionary of the Christian Church*, s.v. "sheol" and "hades."

22. C. Spicq, "La Révélation de l'Enfer dans la Sainte Écriture," *L'Enfer*, Foi Vivante 52 (Paris: Les Éditions de la Revue des Jeunes, 1950), 89-143; Charles Perrot, "La Descente du Christ aux Enfers dans le Nouveau Testament," *Lumière et Vie* 17 (1968) 87: 7-14; J. Chaine, "Descente du Christ aux Enfers," *Dictionnaire de la Bible Supplément*, 1934 ed., 403-4.

23. Perrot, "La Descente du Christ," 8-12.

24. Perrot, "La Descente du Christ," 11: *"Le mot Shéol deviant alors tres ambigu et, dans certains cas, «descendre aux enfers» correspond finalement à «monter au paradis»!"*

25. Perrot, "La Descente du Christ," 12. See also Joachim Jeremias, "Zwischen Karfreitag und Ostern: Descensus und Ascensus in der Karfreitagstheologie des Neuen Testamentes," *Zeitschrift für die Neutestamentliche Wissenschaft* 42 (1949): 199-200; Chaine, "Descente du Christ aux Enfers," 414; Karl Rahner, "Karsamstag," *Geist und Leben* 30 (1957): 82.

26. See, e.g., Fourth Lateran Ecumenical Council, "Symbol of Lateran," *CF* #20 (DS 801); Second Ecumenical Council of Lyon, "Profession of Faith of Michael Palaeologus," *CF* #26 (DS 858); Innocent III, letter to Humbert, Archbishop of Arles, *CF* #506 (DS 780); and Ecumenical Council of Florence, "Decree for the Greeks," *CF* #2309 (DS 1306). See also Ludwig Ott, *Fundamentals of Catholic Dogma*, trans. Patrick Lynch (Rockford, IL: Tan, 1974), 113-14.

27. Second Ecumenical Council of Lyons, *CF* #26 (DS 855-58); Ecumenical Council of Florence, *CF* #2308-09 (DS 1304-6).

28. *CCC* #633, citing the *Roman Catechism*, I.6.3.

29. *CCC* #632, 633.

30. Lk 16:22ff.; Mt 27:52-53; *Catechism of the Council of Trent*, 63; Council of Toledo IV (DS 485); Council of Rome (DS 587); Benedict XII, *Cum dudum* (DS 1011); and Clement VI, *Super quibusdam* (DS 1077).

31. *CCC* #635, 637; bracketed text is in the original. Bracketed Scripture citations are in footnotes in the original.

32. *Catechism of the Council of Trent*, 64.

33. *Catechism of the Council of Trent*, 64.

34. *Catechism of the Council of Trent*, 64.

35. *Catechism of the Council of Trent*, 64-65.

36. See, e.g., Leo XIII's encyclical, *Aeterni Patris* (1879), and John Paul II, "Perennial Philosophy of St. Thomas Aquinas for the Youth of Our Times," address to an International Congress on St. Thomas Aquinas (1979). See also Jacques Maritain, *St. Thomas Aquinas: Angel of the Schools* (London: Sheed & Ward, 1942), 184-88, and Santiago Ramirez, "The Authority of St. Thomas Aquinas," *The Thomist* 15 (January 1952) 1: 1-109.

37. St. Thomas Aquinas, *ST*, IIIa q. 52, a. 2, emphasis in edition.

38. *Catechism of the Council of Trent*, 64, 65.

39. In keeping with the dogmatic, rather than historical, focus of the present work, patristic theologies of the Descent will not be set forth separately here. An introduction to the presence of these elements, together with some of the individual Fathers' differences with it, may be seen, e.g., in Grillmeier, "Der Gottessohn im Totenreich"; J. A. MacCulloch, *The Harrowing of Hell: A Comparative Study of an Early Christian Doctrine* (Edinburgh: T. & T. Clark, 1930), 67-83, 253-60; and *The Faith of the Early Fathers*, ed. and trans. William A. Jurgens (Collegeville, MN: Liturgical Press, 1970), #45, 238, 818, 1103-4, 2210.

40. "Miror cujusquam catholici intelligentiam laborare, tanquam incertum sit, an descendente ad inferna Christo, caro ejus requieverit in sepulcro: quae sicut vere et mortua est et sepulta, ita vere est tertio die suscitata," *Epis. XV, Ad Turribium Asturicensem episcopum*, c. 17, PL 54:690; quoted in H. Quillet, "Descente de Jésus aux enfers," *Dictionnaire de théologie catholique*, 1939 edition: 573.

41. DS 369: "Idem enim Deus et homo, non, ut ab infidelibus dicitur, sub quartae introductione personae, sed ipse Dei Filius Deus et homo, idem virtus et infirmitas, humilitas et maiestas, redimens et venditus, in cruce positus et caeli regna largitus, ita nostrae infirmitatis ut posit interimi, ita ingenitae potentiae ne posset morte consume. Sepultus est iuxta id, quod homo voluit nasci, et iuxta id, quod Patri erat similis, resurrexit: patiens vulnerum et salvator aegrorum, unus defunctorum et vivificator obeuntium, ad inferna descendens et a Patris gremio non recedens. Unde et animam, quam pro communi condicione posuit, pro singulari virtue et admirabili potentia mox resumpsit." That *animam* is not to be understood here in the sense of *soul*, but in the sense of *breath* or *life*, would be supported by Grillmeier, "Der Gottessohn im Totenreich," who argues that it became clear between the second and fifth centuries that Christ's soul remained united to the Word during His death according to the flesh, i.e., well before the pope's letter.

42. "Christus itaque, Deus veraciter totus, et totus homo est, sic conceptus, sic conversatus in saeculo, sic passus, sic apud inferos, sic resuscitatus . . . ," *Epis. ad Anastasium imper.*, Mansi 8:214; PL 62:66sq; quoted in Quillet, "Descente de Jésus aux enfers," 573.

43. DS 741: "Quod anima Christi per se non descendit ad inferos, sed per potentiam tantum."

44. DS 801: "Descendit ad infernos, resurrexit a mortuis et ascendit in caelum: sed descendit in anima, et resurrexit in carne: ascenditque pariter in utroque" [He descended to those below, resurrected from the dead, and ascended into heaven: but He descended in soul, and rose in the flesh, and ascended equally in both].

45. Following Strynkowski, "Descent," 32-33.

46. See Strynkowski, "Descent," 33-34; and Ralph Turner, "*Descendit ad inferos*: Medieval Views on Christ's Descent into Hell and the Salvation of the Ancient Just," *Journal of the History of Ideas* 27 (1966): 181.

47. DS 852: "Mortuum et sepultum, descendisse ad inferos, ac tertia die resurrexisse a mortuis vera carnis resurrectione" [Dead and buried, He descended to those below, and on the third day rose from the dead in a true resurrection of the flesh].

48. Fourth Council (DS 485): "Perferens passionem et mortem pro nostra salute, non in virtute divinitatis, sed in infirmitate humanitatis, descendit ad inferos ut sanctos, qui ibidem tenebantur, erueret, devictoque mortis imperio resurrexit . . ." [Suffering through His passion and death for the sake of our salvation, not in virtue of the divinity but in that of the infirmity of humanity, He descended to those below in order that He might lead out the holy ones, who were being held there, and having conquered the realm of death, He rose]. Sixteenth Council (Mansi 12:67): "Effusione sui cruoris totum mundum a paedoribus abluit, ac ne potestatem mors fecunda in Dei haberet electis, eam usquequaque impassibilis divinitatis sua iaculo perculit ac peremit, dicente propheta: O mors, ero mors tua: tartara penetravit in anima, et sanctorum animas, quas illic hostis vinctas tenebat, morsu potentiae suae exemit, ut prophetale vaticinium inqui: O inferne, ero morsus tuus . . ." [Through the outpouring of His blood, He washed the whole world from its filth, and lest fertile death have power over God's elect, He struck it with His lance of impassible divinity and thoroughly destroyed it, as the prophet said: O death, I will be your death: in His soul, He penetrated hell, and withdrew the souls of the holy, whom death was holding as a captive host, from the sting of its power, as the prophet said: O hell, I will be your sting]. Both texts I have originally from Strynkowski, "Descent," 24-25, who also rightly notes that the rather dramatic language used by the Sixteenth Council "stands in sharp contrast" to that of other councils.

49. Conc. Arelatense VI, in Hardouin, vol. 4, col. 1003, cited in Quillet, "Descente de Jésus aux enfers," 574; see Mansi 14:59.

50. PL 77:870: "Nihil aliud teneatis nisi quod vera fides per catholicam Ecclesiam docet: quia descendens ad inferos Dominus solummodo ab inferni claustris eripuit quos viventes in carne per suam gratiam in fide et bona operatione servavit. . . . Nam trahi ad Deum post mortem non potuit, qui se a Deo male vivendo separavit."

51. The council anathematizes Clement for preaching (among other things) that "Dominum Iesum Christum descendentem ad inferos omnes pios et impios exinde praedicat [simul inde] abstraxisse" [the Lord Jesus Christ, descending to those below, preaches to all the pious and the impious and likewise led them out] (DS 587).

52. Regarding the history of the communication concerning the errors of the Armenians, I here follow Strynkowski, "Descent," 36-40, who provides additional references. I differ from him somewhat in the conclusions I draw from the episode, however; compare his pages 39-40.

53. DS 1011. See also DS 1006.

54. "Illos . . . qui dicunt, quod peccatores, qui damnati errant in aeternum, crediderunt in Christum et justificati sunt in inferno, reprobamus et despicimus." [We condemn and despise those who say that the sinners who had been eternally damned, believed in Christ in hell and were justified.] (Mansi 25:1200, quoted in Strynkowski, "Descent," 38.)

55. DS 1077: "Quod Christus non destruxit descendendo ad inferos inferiorem infernum." See also DS 1072.

56. Henricus Denifle, Chartularium Universitatis Parisensis, t. II, 1 (Paris: Delalain, 1891), #975, p. 419: "Quod in limbo sanctorum patrum non fuerit pena nisi pena dampni, que

est carentia visionis divine"; "Quod Christus non potuit liberare animas sanctorum de lacu inferni et de vinculis, nisi dando eis claram visionem divine essentie." For the papal confirmation, see Denifle, *Chartularium*, t. II, 1, #976, p. 425.

57. Denifle, *Chartularium*, t. II, 1, #975, p. 422: "Negat captivitatem, detentionem localem et privationem libertatis."

58. Denifle, *Chartularium*, t. II, 1, #975, p. 419.

59. Johannes Rothkranz, *Die Kardinalfehler des Hans Urs von Balthasar* (Durach: Anton Schmid, 1989), 372, highlights this distinction and its significance in the context of the Descent.

60. *CF* #2307 (DS 1002).

61. Balthasar's clearest presentation of his understanding of the traditional doctrine of the Descent is found on pages 226-28 of his "The Descent into Hell," *Chicago Studies* 23 (1984): 223-36, originally published as "Theologische Besinnung auf das Mysterium des Höllenabstiegs," *„Hinabgestiegen in das Reich des Todes": Der Sinn dieses Satzes in Bekenntnis und Lehre, Dichtung und Kunst*, hrsg. Hans Urs von Balthasar (Munich: Schnell & Steiner, 1982), 84-98. The English translation of this essay is hereinafter referred to as "DescHell."

62. "DescHell," 227.

63. "DescHell," 227.

64. On prime analogates, especially that of fatherhood, see St. Thomas Aquinas, *ST,* Ia q. 13, a. 6.

65. See, e.g., Balthasar, *The New Covenant*, vol. 7, *The Glory of the Lord: A Theological Aesthetics*, trans. Brian McNeil, ed. John Riches (San Francisco: Ignatius, 1984), 265, 269, 271, 279, 287. This work is hereinafter referred to as *GloryVII*. In *GloryVII*, in his chapter "2. The Substance of Glory," subsection 1 (pp. 273-80) corresponds to reality, subsection 2 (pp. 280-86) to appearance, subsections 3a and 3b (pp. 286-92) to recognition, and subsection 3c (pp. 293-95) to the fourth element Balthasar adds, attraction. On this last, see also *GloryVII*, 291-92. It is worth noting that Balthasar does not appear to have considered much, if at all, the problem of false glory, or of false beauty, perhaps because he describes glory as dependent upon truth; see *GloryVII*, 243.

66. *GloryVII*, 241-42.

67. *GloryVII*, 242.

68. *GloryVII*, 242-43.

69. *GloryVII*, 243.

70. *GloryVII*, 242.

71. *GloryVII*, 243, emphasis in original.

72. *GloryVII*, 243.

73. *GloryVII*, 293-317; also Balthasar, *The Final Act*, vol. 5, *Theo-Drama*, trans. Graham Harrison (San Francisco: Ignatius, 1998), 507; this work is hereinafter referred to as *ThDrV.* Compare also the likeness between beauty and glory in *GloryVII*, 287, 315; and Balthasar, *Seeing the Form*, vol. 1, *The Glory of the Lord: A Theological Aesthetics* (Edinburgh: T. & T. Clark, 1982), ii-iii; this last work is hereinafter referred to as *GloryI*. For examples of other texts linking glory and action, see *GloryVII*, 265, 269, 271, 289, 290-92, 396; Balthasar, *Prolegomena*, vol. 1, *Theo-Drama*, trans. Graham Harrison (San Francisco: Ignatius, 1988), 16; this work is hereinafter referred to as *ThDrI.* On the uptake, or involvement, of the beholder in glory, see Jöhri, *"Descensus Dei,"* 350-51; and Margaret Turek, *Towards a Theology of God the*

Father: Hans Urs von Balthasar's Theodramatic Approach, American University Studies Series VII, vol. 212 (New York: Peter Lang, 2001), 45, 176-77.

74. Exceptions to his usual causal order may be noted. For example, he says (*GloryVII,* 291) God's love in Jesus "is seen to be what it is, only when one is oneself seized by it," which reverses the causal order of recognition and configuration, but leaves appearance untouched.

75. See *GloryVII,* 268-69, 304-17.

76. See *GloryVII,* 308-17.

77. *GloryVII,* 304.

78. *GloryVII,* 305.

79. See, e.g., *ThDrV,* "The Serious Possibility of Refusal," 285-91.

80. *ThDrV,* 85-88.

81. *ThDrV,* 245.

82. *ThDrV,* 515-16, emphasis added.

83. *ThDrV,* 515-16.

84. *ThDrV,* 521; see also "The Incarnation of God," *Elucidations,* trans. John Riches (San Francisco: Ignatius, 1975), 67.

85. References for the first case are reserved until Chapter Six, when more will be said about wrath as love. Regarding the second case, the relevant text is *ThDrV,* 506-21. See also Balthasar, *The Dramatis Personae: The Person in Christ,* vol. 3, *Theo-Drama,* trans. Graham Harrison (San Francisco: Ignatius, 1992), 523; this work is hereinafter referred to as *ThDrIII.* See also "The Incarnation of God," 67.

86. *ThDrV,* 514. Guy Mansini offers a very to-the-point analysis of this position in his "Balthasar and the Theodramatic Enrichment of the Trinity," *The Thomist* 64 (2000): 499-519.

87. *Catechism of the Council of Trent,* 64, 65.

Notes to Chapter Three

1. On the authority of the Fathers, see, e.g., Second Ecumenical Council of Constantinople, *Profession of Faith, CF* #204. See also the Lateran Council, canon 17, *CF* #205 (DS 517); Leo XIII, *Providentissimus Deus, CF* #222 (DS 3284); and the Congregation for Catholic Education, *Instruction on the Study of the Fathers of the Church in the Formation of Priests, CF* #266a and b.

2. An example of such a clarification in doctrine regarding Christ's descent into hell may be found in Grillmeier, "Der Gottessohn im Totenreich," 76-174. See also Duquoc, "La descente du Christ aux enfers," 51-52.

3. St. Thomas Aquinas, *ST,* Ia q. 1, a. 8.

4. The treatment of Scriptural *themes* in relation to the Descent unfortunately has not attracted the attention it deserves; Strynkowski, "Descent," 12-17, 41-132, provides an important contribution in this area.

5. See St. Thomas Aquinas, *ST,* IIIa q. 28, q. 2 ad 2.

6. *CCC* #632.

7. St. Gregory of Nyssa, *The Great Catechism,* trans. William Moore and Henry Austin

Wilson, Nicene and Post-Nicene Fathers, 2nd ser., vol. 5 (Grand Rapids: Eerdmans, 1954), ch. 32, p. 500, emphasis in edition. "Anxious" might also have been translated "be inquisitive for" or "search out."

8. St. Thomas Aquinas, Sermo VII, *The Sermon-Conferences,* 78-79. See also the commentaries on the Gospel passages about the death and burial of Christ in St. Thomas Aquinas, *Catena Aurea: Commentary on the Four Gospels Collected out of the Works of the Fathers,* ed. John Henry Newman (Southampton, UK: Saint Austin, 1997), where the theological principle under consideration is applied frequently. Particularly pertinent are Theophylact on Mk 15:33-37; St. John Chrysostom on Jn 19:28-30; and St. Bede on Lk 23:50-56.

9. Rufinus, *Commentary,* #17, p. 550.

10. Ecumenical Council of Trent, Sixth Session, *Decree on Justification,* cap. VII, *CF* #1932 (DS 1529).

11. St. Bede on Mk 15:33-37, *Catena Aurea,* p. 325. See also Rufinus, *Commentary,* #16, p. 550.

12. Although this interpretation (found, e.g., in Rufinus, *Commentary,* #28) does not go uncontested in contemporary exegesis, it is also not without possible supporters. Contrast, e.g., William Joseph Dalton, *Christ's Proclamation to the Spirits: A Study of 1 Peter 3:18–4:6,* Analecta Biblica 23 (Rome: Pontifical Biblical Institute, 1965), 126, who holds that the verse refers to Christ's resurrection, with John J. Strynkowski, *The Descent of Christ among the Dead* (Rome: Pontificia Università Gregoriana, 1972), 26, who would support the interpretation given here. This latter work is a published excerpt of Strynkowski's unpublished dissertation. The excerpt focuses on 1 Pet 3:18–4:6, whereas the dissertation is much broader. To distinguish the two more easily, the excerpt is hereinafter referred to as Strynkowski, *The Descent (excerpt),* while the dissertation continues to be referred to as Strynkowski, "Descent."

13. St. Augustine, *Sermo de symbolo,* cap. 5, PL 40:1193: "Mors Domini nostri Jesu Christi non fuit in anima, sed in sola carne: mors vero nostra non solum in carne, sed etiam in anima: in anima propter peccatum, in carne propter poenam peccati. Ille vero quia peccatum non fecit, nec habuit in anima; non est mortuus, nisi in carne tantum: et hoc per similitudinem carnis peccati quam de Adam traxit. . . . [E]t suam unam mortem carnis detulit, duasque nostras solvit."

14. Unless quoted within the text of another author, Scriptural quotations regardless of version are from *Bibleworks 95/NT release,* Version 4.0.026e (3549) [CD-ROM], Bibleworks, 1998. The Douay-Rheims text given there is the 1899 American Version.

15. I substitute *sting* here for what the Douay-Rheims version renders as *bite.* The Latin word is *morsus,* and can have either meaning. *Sting* is perhaps the more familiar English translation, and carries more direct connotations of paralysis that are relevant in some of the commentaries.

16. St. Thomas Aquinas, Sermo VII, *The Sermon-Conferences,* 81. See also Pope St. Gregory the Great, *Homil. in Evang.* 22, n. 6, PL 76:1177, cited in Quillet, "Descente de Jésus aux enfers," 576; and St. Augustine, *Sermo de symbolo,* cap. VII, PL 40:1194.

17. St. Bede on Mk 15:42-47, quoted in *Catena Aurea.* See also his comment on Lk 23:50-56. See also Alban Dold, "Ein einzigartiges Dokument der Karsamstagsliturgie," *Paschatis Sollemnia: Studien zu Osterfeier und Osterfrömmigkeit* (Vienna: Herder, 1959), 180-

84. Dold considers a liturgical book from the end of the fifth, or beginning of the sixth, century, which contains a threefold Scriptural petition for the Lord to arise from His rest.

18. With respect to water as the realm of death and the devil, see Per Lundberg, *La typologie baptismale dans l'ancienne Eglise,* Acta Seminarii Neotestamentici Upsaliensis 10 (Leipzig: Alfred Lorentz, 1942), 64-72.

19. See St. Hippolytus of Rome, *Commentaire sur Daniel,* bk. III, ch. 29, trans. Maurice Lefévre, Sources Chrétiennes, vol. 14, ed. H. de Lubac and J. Daniélou (Paris: Éditions du Cerf, 1947), p. 255. See also ch. 30, p. 257; and ch. 33, p. 331.

20. *CCC* #624, emphasis added.

21. Michel Sales, "The Fulfillment of the Sabbath: From the Holiness of the Seventh Day to God's Resting in God," trans. Mark Sebanc, *Communio ICR* 21 (1994) 1:28.

22. Sales, "The Fulfillment of the Sabbath," 28-29.

23. Sales, "The Fulfillment of the Sabbath," 44. Balthasar has a meditation on the nature of the Sabbath rest in Christian terms, "Dare One Do Good on the Sabbath?" *You Have Words of Eternal Life: Scripture Meditations,* trans. Dennis Martin (San Francisco: Ignatius, 1991), 153-55. It is striking, however, that he does not apply it to Holy Saturday.

24. Balthasar, *The Old Covenant,* vol. 6, *The Glory of the Lord: A Theological Aesthetics,* trans. Brian McNeil and Erasmo Leiva-Merikakis, ed. John Riches (Edinburgh: T. & T. Clark, 1991), 218; this book is hereinafter referred to as *GloryVI.*

25. *GloryVI,* 219.

26. *GloryVI,* 216, 218-19.

27. See, e.g., Jean Daniélou, "Déluge, Baptême, Jugement," *Dieu Vivant* 8 (1947): 97-111; Lundberg, *La typologie baptismale,* 109-13.

28. On Christ's universal power of judgment and of giving life manifested in His descent, see also Strynkowski, *The Descent (excerpt),* 43-47.

29. A focused treatment is Lundberg, *La typologie baptismale.*

30. St. Melito of Sardis, "Über das Taufbad" ["On the Bath of Baptism"], #4, in F. J. Dölger, *Sol Salutis,* 3. Auflage, Liturgiewissenschaftliche Quellen und Forschungen Heft 16/17 (Munster: Aschendorff, 1972), 345. Dölger notes he bases his text upon that of E. J. Goodspeed, *Die ältesten Apologeten* (Göttingen 1914), 310f. He also draws attention to St. Melito's use of baptismal terminology in his description of the setting sun; p. 343, n. 1.

31. Dölger, *Sol Salutis,* 337.

32. Dölger, *Sol Salutis,* 357.

33. St. Melito, #3-4, in Dölger, *Sol Salutis,* 343-45. Note the similar Greek and Egyptian conception, pp. 357-59.

34. St. John Chrysostom, *In coemeterii appellationem,* PG 49:395, quoted in Dölger, *Sol Salutis,* 349, my translation. See also St. Melito, #4, in Dölger, *Sol Salutis,* 345. The "Sun of Righteousness" is a scriptural Messianic title; see Mal 4:2. Compare Lk 1:78-79.

35. *The Holy Bible, Revised Standard Version,* 1952 ed. (Division of Christian Education of the National Council of Churches of Christ in the United States of America, 1973), in *Bibleworks 95/NT release,* Version 4.0.026e (3549) [CD-ROM], Bibleworks, 1998.

36. Dölger, *Sol Salutis,* 336-53. Dölger begins with the image's Scriptural foundation (Ps 67:5, 34), notes the use of this psalm in Eph 4:8-10, and cites numerous texts of the Fathers and early ecclesiastical writers.

37. Dölger, *Sol Salutis,* 352, n. 3.

38. Herman Schmidt, "Paschalibus initiati mysteriis," *Gregorianum* 39 (1958): 472-78.

39. Schmidt, "Paschalibus initiati mysteriis," 473.

40. On the unity of the paschal mystery itself and that of its liturgical commemoration, see, e.g., Schmidt, "Paschalibus initiati mysteriis," 463-71; and Raniero Cantalamessa, *La pasqua della nostra salvezza: Le tradizioni pasquali della bibbia e della primitiva chiesa* (Casale Monferrato [AL], Italy: Marietti, 1971), 142 (n. 9), 160-61, 174-75.

41. On paradise being the presence of Christ, see Perrot, "La Descente du Christ," 11-15. See also the quotation of St. John Chrysostom marked with n. 34 above.

42. Patrick Jacquemont, "La Descente aux Enfers dans la Tradition Orientale," *Lumière et Vie* 17 (1968) 87: 39-41. On the return to paradise, see also Jean Daniélou, "Le Symbolisme des Rites Baptismaux," *Dieu Vivant* 1 (1945): 20-31; and Lundberg, *La typologie baptismale,* 183-84.

43. Jacquemont, "La Descente aux Enfers," 41.

44. Lundberg, *La typologie baptismale,* 211; see also Philippe Reymond, *L'Eau, sa vie, et sa signification dans l'Ancien Testament,* Supplements to *Vetus Testamentum,* vol. 6 (Leiden: Brill, 1958), 243-44.

45. With regard to the cross as the efficient cause of the saving effect of baptism, and this specifically in relation to baptism as a descent, see Lundberg, *La typologie baptismale,* 187, 190, 193, 200, 225.

46. Cantalamessa, *La pasqua della nostra salvezza,* 171-74, 194. Cantalamessa draws out this bath-theology from the second century, noting that the Greek practice of the nuptial bath was called "iniziazione alle nozze" [the initiation of the wedding]; p. 173, n. 36.

47. This mystagogical exegesis is particularly well established for the patristic view and the perspective of early Christianity. See, e.g., the exceptional article of Olivier Rousseau, "La Descente aux Enfers, Fondement Sotériologique du Baptême Chrétien," *Mélanges Jules Lebreton* II, *Recherches de Science Religieuse* 40 (1951-52): 273-97; and Jean Daniélou, review of *Die Vorstellung von der Höllenfahrt Jesus Christi* by Werner Bieder, *Recherches de Science Religieuse* 37 (1950): 596-99. The fact that this participation occurs in virtue of Christ's cross is not to be forgotten; see Lundberg, *La typologie baptismale,* 178-200, 225.

48. Cantalamessa, *La pasqua della nostra salvezza,* 171; see also pp. 112-13; Schmidt, "Paschalibus initiati mysteriis," 470-71; Dold, "Ein einzigartiges Dokument," 183; Rousseau, "La Descente aux Enfers" 285-86; Lundberg, *La typologie baptismale,* 116-35; and M.-E. Boismard, "La typologie baptismale dans la première épître de saint Pierre," *La Vie Spirituelle,* no. 416 (1956): 339-52.

49. S.v. "baptism," Joseph H. Crehan, *A Catholic Dictionary of Theology* (New York: Thomas Nelson & Sons, 1962); and Lundberg, *La typologie baptismale,* 146-66. See also the Fourth Council of Toledo (633), can. 6 (Mansi 10:618-19), which links the crossing of the Jordan by the people of God in the company of the ark of the covenant with Christ's baptism, His descent into hell, and sacramental baptism.

50. Cantalamessa, *La pasqua della nostra salvezza,* 171-74, 194-95; Dold, "Ein einzigartiges Dokument," 185; and Daniélou, "Le Symbolisme," 31.

51. Rousseau, "La Descente aux Enfers," 285-97. Rousseau's choice of the word *echo* (p. 285) captures admirably how the one baptized is dependent upon the reality accomplished in Christ, but also really participates in it.

52. See s.v. "baptism," Crehan, *A Catholic Dictionary of Theology*; Rousseau, "La Descente aux Enfers," 293; and Daniélou, "Le Symbolisme," 36. See also *CCC* #1214-16.

53. Regarding the Exultet [*"Nox ut dies illuminabitur"*] and the Easter candle: Rousseau, "La Descente aux Enfers," 287. On Christ as light in connection with the rite of baptism, see also Daniélou, "Le Symbolisme," 20-31.

54. Thomas Fletcher Worthen, *The Harrowing of Hell in the Art of the Italian Renaissance*, vols. 1 & 2 (Ann Arbor, MI: University Microfilms, 1981), 308.

55. See Rousseau, "La Descente aux Enfers," 296.

56. See Daniélou, "Le Symbolisme," 20-31.

57. See Rousseau, "La Descente aux Enfers," 279-80, 288, 293-94.

58. See Rousseau, "La Descente aux Enfers," 295-96. On the renunciation and the arming for combat, see also Daniélou, "Le Symbolisme," 18-20, 28-34.

59. See Rousseau, "La Descente aux Enfers," 296-97.

60. Following Jacquemont, "La Descente aux Enfers," 41-42. On the triple immersion, see also Daniélou, "Le Symbolisme," 36.

61. *The Ordinary and The Anaphora of the Apostles*, ed. Tesiamoriam Baraki (Washington, DC: privately printed, no date), 21, parenthetical content in edition.

62. See Daniélou, "Le Symbolisme," 36-40.

63. *The Ordinary and The Anaphora of the Apostles*, 14.

64. See Jacquemont, "La Descente aux Enfers," 44.

65. St. Augustine on Lk 16:22-26 in *Catena Aurea*.

66. See St. Gregory the Great on Lk 16:22-26 in *Catena Aurea*; and Heb 9:6-14; 10:19-20; and 11:39-40. See also Strynkowski, *The Descent (excerpt)*, 40-42.

67. See n. 15 above regarding the substitution of *sting* for *bite*, to render the Latin *morsus*.

68. Acts 2:24: "Whom God hath raised up, having loosed the sorrows of hell [more literally, *death*], as it was impossible that he should be holden by it." Phil 2:8-10: "He humbled himself, becoming obedient unto death, even to the death of the cross. For which cause, God also hath exalted him and hath given him a name which is above all names: That in the name of Jesus every knee should bow, of those that are in heaven, on earth, and under the earth." Rev 1:18: "I am living for ever and ever and have the keys of death and of hell." Is 49:24-25a: "Shall the prey be taken from the strong? or can that which was taken by the mighty, be delivered? For thus saith the Lord: Yea verily, even the captivity shall be taken away from the strong: and that which was taken by the mighty, shall be delivered."

69. St. John Chrysostom on Mt 12:29 in *Catena Aurea*.

70. St. Jerome on Mt 12:29 in *Catena Aurea*.

71. St. Augustine on Mt 12:29 in *Catena Aurea*.

72. Besides noting in an appendix the passage's prevalence in early Christian exegesis, Alan Cooper argues from the perspective of a linguistic and cultural exegesis in favor of interpreting it in accord with a *descensus* theme; see "Ps 24:7-10: Mythology and Exegesis," *Journal of Biblical Literature* 102 (1983) 1: 37-60.

73. "1 Pet 3:18 Because Christ also died once for our sins, the just for the unjust: that he might offer us to God, being put to death indeed in the flesh, but enlivened in the spirit, 19In which also coming he preached to those spirits that were in prison: 20Which had been some time incredulous, when they waited for the patience of God in the days of Noe, when the ark

was a building: wherein a few, that is, eight souls, were saved by water. 21Whereunto baptism, being of the like form, now saveth you also: not the putting away of the filth of the flesh, but, the examination of a good conscience towards God by the resurrection of Jesus Christ. 22Who is on the right hand of God, swallowing down death that we might be made heirs of life everlasting: being gone into heaven, the angels and powers and virtues being made subject to him. 4:1Christ therefore having suffered in the flesh, be you also armed with the same thought: for he that hath suffered in the flesh hath ceased from sins: 2That now he may live the rest of his time in the flesh, not after the desires of men but according to the will of God. 3For the time past is sufficient to have fulfilled the will of the Gentiles, for them who have walked in riotousness, lusts, excess of wine, revellings, banquetings and unlawful worshipping of idols. 4Wherein they think it strange that you run not with them into the same confusion of riotousness: speaking evil of you. 5Who shall render account to him who is ready to judge the living and the dead. 6For, for this cause was the gospel preached also to the dead: That they might be judged indeed according to men, in the flesh: but may live according to God, in the Spirit."

74. See, for example, J. N. D. Kelly, *A Commentary on the Epistles of Peter and of Jude*, Black's New Testament Commentaries (London: Adam & Charles Black, 1969); and MacCulloch, *The Harrowing of Hell.* Strynkowski, *The Descent (excerpt),* is a more recent study particularly to be recommended.

75. From among the extensive historical-critical literature, e.g., the work of Dalton, *Christ's Proclamation to the Spirits,* received particular attention in the last century.

76. PL 33:708-16; hereinafter cited according to St. Augustine, Ep. 164, *Letters,* vol. 3 (131-64), Writings of St. Augustine 11, The Fathers of the Church: A New Translation 20 (New York: Fathers of the Church, 1953).

77. St. Augustine, Ep. 164, *Letters,* 383.

78. St. Augustine, Ep. 164, *Letters,* 392.

79. St. Robert Bellarmine, *De controversiis Christianae Fidei adversus hujus temporis haereticos,* t. 1, contro. 2, l. 3, cap. 8 (Mediolani: Edente Natale Battezzati, 1857), 281. St. Robert refers to St. Jerome's *In quaest. Hebr. in Genes.,* cap. 6.

80. I here apply in a parallel way the argument St. Robert makes in support of Christ fulfilling Sir 24:45 ("I will penetrate to all the lower parts of the earth, and will behold all that sleep, and will enlighten all that hope in the Lord") though, in contrast to St. Robert, without Christ's descending in soul to every region of hell. See St. Robert Bellarmine, *De controversiis,* t. 1, contro. 2, l. 3, cap. 16, 286. The Neo-Vulgate preserves this verse of the Vulgate, but many modern versions lack it.

81. St. Robert Bellarmine, *De controversiis,* t. 1, contro. 2, l. 3, cap. 8, 281. See also Spicq, "La Révélation de l'Enfer dans la Sainte Écriture," 115-16; Daniélou, "Déluge, Baptême, Jugement," 100-101; and Chaine, "Descente du Christ aux Enfers," 420-23. Strynkowski, *The Descent (excerpt),* 52-53, extends the 'preaching' beyond a communication of a state of events to the revelation of the Father to the elect; see also pp. 38-47, 52-54.

82. See Jean Galot, "Christ's Descent into Hell," *Theology Digest* 13 (1965) 2: 91-93.

83. As St. Thomas Aquinas put it, *ST,* IIIa q. 52, a. 2.

84. On the theology of baptism in the context of 1 Peter, see, e.g., F. L. Cross, *I Peter: A Paschal Liturgy* (London: A. R. Mowbray, 1954), 28-31, 39.

85. Daniélou, "Déluge, Baptême, Jugement," 97-111; see also Lundberg, *La typologie*

baptismale, 109-13. If Daniélou is right about this typology — and he makes a strong case for it — then it would be another reason why the Petrine epistles may not be so dependent on the Book of Enoch, an apocryphal Jewish apocalyptic, as proposed by some authors (and as accepted by Daniélou at least to some extent). This parallel has been a widespread theory since 1890, but the more recent work of Heinz-Jürgen Vogels, *Christi Abstieg ins Totenreich und das Läuterungsgericht an den Toten,* Freiburger Theologische Studien 120. Band (Freiburg: Herder, 1976), 5, 74-87, would indicate it is ultimately untenable.

86. The *RSV* translation is the English version closest to the French Daniélou presents, except in the case of the text in brackets, which is from the Douay-Rheims. As the bracketed text stands at the heart of Daniélou's treatment, the replacement here was necessary.

87. In what follows, I have extended the conclusion of Daniélou's typological argument. He takes the imprisoned spirits to be the fallen angels, whereas I have also included all human souls already in hell at the time of Christ's descent.

88. Cantalamessa, *La pasqua della nostra salvezza,* 112. Boismard, "La typologie baptismale," 339-40, specifies the homiletic portion is 1 Pet 1:3–4:11.

89. St. Augustine, Ep. 164, *Letters,* 389.

90. St. Augustine, Ep. 164, *Letters,* 390-91; Dalton, *Christ's Proclamation to the Spirits,* 20, n. 32; p. 46. Dalton, however, points out that those of the Alexandrian school who consider the possibility of conversion after death use 1 Pet 3:19, but not 4:6 (p. 43).

91. St. Augustine, Ep. 164, *Letters,* 392.

92. St. Augustine, Ep. 164, *Letters,* 385.

93. St. Augustine, Ep. 164, *Letters,* 391.

94. Ronald Knox, *The Creed in Slow Motion* (London: Sheed & Ward, 1949), 113.

95. Dalton, *Christ's Proclamation,* 44.

96. See Scotus anonymous, *Commentarius in epistulas catholicas, In epistula Petri I* in CLCLT-3-Cetedoc, Louanii Noui [CD-ROM]; January 2002.

97. Dalton, *Christ's Proclamation,* 46.

98. St. Augustine, Ep. 164, *Letters,* 395-96.

99. Dalton, *Christ's Proclamation,* 55. See also J. N. D. Kelly, *Epistles of Peter and of Jude,* 151-53.

100. I here adapt Strynkowski, *The Descent (excerpt),* 31-32. To represent Strynkowski accurately, I note that he holds Christ receives the beatific vision in His descent, a position with which I disagree. Pope John Paul II speaks of the glorification of Christ's soul after His death, but does not specify it further; see his General Audience of January 11, 1989, #5. As he holds Christ possessed the beatific vision during His life (idem, Apostolic Letter *Novo millennio ineunte,* #26), however, the pope must have in mind the glorification of Christ's *entire* soul along the lines I have suggested, i.e., as the extension of the effects of the beatific vision to all the powers of His soul, as well as the open manifestation of His glory.

101. Spicq, "La Révélation de l'Enfer dans la Sainte Écriture," 93, 105-6, 108. See also Vogels, *Christi Abstieg ins Totenreich,* 106-7. Passages such as Gen 2:7 and Ezek 37:6, 8 provide a basis within Jewish culture for an anthropological distinction similar to the 'Greek' one.

102. Knox, *The Creed in Slow Motion,* 111-12.

103. Knox, *The Creed in Slow Motion,* 113-15.

104. *CCC* #634. See also Pope John Paul II, General Audience, January 11, 1989, #5-7.

105. St. Augustine, Ep. 164, *Letters,* 382, 397.

106. On the substitution of *sting,* see n. 15 above.

Notes to Chapter Four

1. See Vatican II, Dogmatic Constitution *Dei Verbum,* #9.

2. "Obsecrationum quoque sacerdotalium sacramenta respiciamus, quae ab Apostolis tradita in toto mundo atque in omni Ecclesia catholica uniformiter celebrantur, ut legem credendi lex statuat supplicandi" [Let us respect the prayer and likewise the priestly sacraments, which handed on from the apostles are celebrated uniformly in the whole world and in every catholic church, since the law of supplication establishes the law of belief], cap. 8 of the "Pseudo-Celestine Chapters," or the *Indiculus,* DS 246. See also *CCC* #1124, with additional references; and *CF* #1212 and, with introduction, *CF* #1913.

3. For a compact introduction to some of these other texts, see the articles of F. Cabrol, "Descente du Christ aux enfers d'après la liturgie," and A. de Meester, "Descente du Christ aux enfers dans les liturgies orientales," in *Dictionnaire d'archéologie chrétienne et de liturgie,* 1920 ed. See also Grillmeier, "Der Gottessohn im Totenreich," 90-100.

4. *The Lenten Triodion,* trans. Mother Mary and Kallistos Ware (South Canaan, PA: St. Tikhon's, 1999), 600. When necessary, the more readily available Orthodox translations of the Byzantine liturgies are used here. The services of the Orthodox Churches do not differ significantly from those of the Byzantine Catholic Churches in their doctrine of Christ's descent.

5. For a discussion of the redemptive significance of blood in Scripture according to biblical theology, see Stanislas Lyonnet and Léopold Sabourin, *Sin, Redemption, and Sacrifice: A Biblical and Patristic Study,* Analecta Biblica 48 (Rome: Biblical Institute Press, 1970), particularly ch. 7, "The Sacrificial Function of Blood," 167-81, as also 258-61. See also Ecumenical Council of Trent, Fifth Session, *Decree on Original Sin, CF* #510 (DS 1513).

6. *Cantate et Jubilate Deo: A Devotional and Liturgical Hymnal,* ed. James Socías (Princeton, NJ: Scepter, 1999), 129.

7. *CF* #1409 (DS 780).

8. *CF* #643 (DS 1025).

9. *The Lenten Triodion,* 595.

10. Ecumenical Council of Trent, Sixth Session, *Decree on Justification,* cap. III, IV, VII, XIII, and XIV, *CF* #1927, 1928, 1932-34, 1942, 1943 (DS 1523, 1524, 1528-31, 1541, 1542); Fourteenth Session, *Doctrine on the Sacrament of Penance,* cap. I, *CF* #1615-17 (DS 1668-70).

11. *The Festal Menaion,* trans. Mother Mary and Kallistos Ware (South Canaan, PA: St. Tikhon's, 1998), 131-63; the text marked by "Tone Five," 139-40, is particularly succinct.

12. See, e.g., *The Festal Menaion,* 153, 156.

13. See, e.g., the Creed of the Fourth Ecumenical Lateran Council, *CF* #20 (DS 801); the Constitution *Benedictus Deus, CF* #2305-7 (DS 1000-1002); and the Decree for the Greeks of the Ecumenical Council of Florence, *CF* #2308-9 (DS 1304-5). *Benedictus Deus* explicitly quotes 2 Cor 5:10, "So that each one may receive good or evil, according to what one has done in the body."

14. St. Thomas, *Sermo VII*, *The Sermon-Conferences*, 78: "ut sustineret totam poenam peccati, et sic totam culpam expiaret."

15. *Byzantine Daily Worship*, trans. Joseph Raya and Jose de Vinck (Allendale, NJ: Alleluia, 1969), 836.

16. *Byzantine Daily Worship*, 836.

17. St. Thomas Aquinas, *ST*, IIIa q. 52, a. 1. See also Chaine, "Descente du Christ aux Enfers," 423, 427; Strynkowski, *The Descent (excerpt)*, 43-47.

18. "Third Stasis," *Lenten Triodion*, 642.

19. "Canticle Three," *Lenten Triodion*, 647.

20. "First Stasis," *Lenten Triodion*, 628.

21. "First Stasis," *Lenten Triodion*, 623.

22. *Lenten Triodion*, 652 and 656. See also 648, 649, 652-53.

23. *The Divine Office: The Liturgy of the Hours according to the Roman Rite*, vol. 2: Lent and Eastertide (London: Collins, 1974), 319. Note especially verses 4, 5, and 10 of Heb 4:1-13 *(RSV):* "1Therefore, while the promise of entering his rest remains, let us fear lest any of you be judged to have failed to reach it. 2For good news came to us just as to them; but the message which they heard did not benefit them, because it did not meet with faith in the hearers. 3For we who have believed enter that rest, as he has said, 'As I swore in my wrath, "They shall never enter my rest,"' although his works were finished from the foundation of the world. 4For he has somewhere spoken of the seventh day in this way, 'And God rested on the seventh day from all his works.' 5And again in this place he said, 'They shall never enter my rest.' 6Since therefore it remains for some to enter it, and those who formerly received the good news failed to enter because of disobedience, 7again he sets a certain day, 'Today,' saying through David so long afterward, in the words already quoted, 'Today, when you hear his voice, do not harden your hearts.' 8For if Joshua had given them rest, God would not speak later of another day. 9So then, there remains a Sabbath rest for the people of God; 10for whoever enters God's rest also ceases from his labors as God did from his. 11Let us therefore strive to enter that rest, that no one fall by the same sort of disobedience. 12For the word of God is living and active, sharper than any two-edged sword, piercing to the division of soul and spirit, of joints and marrow, and discerning the thoughts and intentions of the heart. 13And before him no creature is hidden, but all are open and laid bare to the eyes of him with whom we have to do."

24. "First Stasis," *Lenten Triodion*, 629.

25. *Lenten Triodion*, e.g., 622, 624, 628.

26. *Lenten Triodion*, 626, 635.

27. *Lenten Triodion*, 632.

28. *Lenten Triodion*, 597, 598, 601, 632-39.

29. "Second Stasis," *Lenten Triodion*, 632-39.

30. "Second Stasis," *Lenten Triodion*, 632-39.

31. *Lenten Triodion*, 646.

32. *The Divine Office*, vol. 2, 320. The entire homily may be found in PG 43:439A-464D.

33. *The Divine Office*, vol. 2, 321.

34. *The Divine Office*, vol. 2, 321.

35. *The Divine Office*, vol. 2, 321.

36. Lk 4:18-19 *(DRA):* "18 The spirit of the Lord is upon me. Wherefore he hath

anointed me to preach the gospel to the poor, he hath sent me to heal the contrite of heart, 19 To preach deliverance to the captives and sight to the blind, to set at liberty them that are bruised, to preach the acceptable year of the Lord and the day of reward." Is 61:1-2 *(DRA):* "₁The spirit of the Lord is upon me, because the Lord hath anointed me: he hath sent me to preach to the meek, to heal the contrite of heart, and to preach a release to the captives, and deliverance to them that are shut up. ₂To proclaim the acceptable year of the Lord, and the day of vengeance of our God: to comfort all that mourn."

37. *The Divine Office,* vol. 2, 322.

38. *The Divine Office,* vol. 2, 322.

39. *Cantate et Jubilate,* 38-39.

40. *Cantate et Jubilate,* 96.

41. *Cantate et Jubilate,* 150.

42. *CCC* #632; Pope John Paul II, General Audience January 11, 1989, #4; Kelly, *Early Christian Creeds,* 380; Rousseau, "La Descente aux Enfers," 284; the references could be multiplied.

43. Byzantine Matins of Holy Saturday, as in "First Stasis," *Lenten Triodion,* 625.

44. St. Thomas Aquinas, Sermo VII, *The Sermon-Conferences,* 78-79.

45. St. Melito of Sardis, New Fragment II, 12, in *Melito of Sardis:* On Pascha *and Fragments,* texts and translation ed. Stuart George Hall (Oxford: Oxford University Press, 1979), 90.

46. Paul Evdokimov, *The Art of the Icon: A Theology of Beauty,* trans. Steven Bigham (Redondo Beach, CA: Oakwood, 1996), 323.

47. See Leonid Ouspensky and Vladimir Lossky, *The Meaning of Icons,* trans. G. E. H. Palmer and E. Kadloubovsky (Crestwood, NY: St. Vladimir's Seminary Press, 1999), 96.

48. *CCC* #889. See also Vatican II, Dogmatic Constitution on the Church *Lumen Gentium,* #12, 35.

49. *CF* #1253 (DS 653-54).

50. Anna D. Kartsonis, *Anastasis: The Making of an Image* (Princeton, NJ: Princeton University Press, 1986), 4, stresses the "resurrection" aspect of the icon, and thinks it is misleading to translate the Greek name of the icon as "The Descent into Hell." See also the vigorous protest of Hans-Joachim Schulz, "Die „Höllenfahrt" als „Anastasis"," *Zeitschrift für Katholische Theologie* 81 (1959): 1-66. Kartsonis is correct about the literal meaning of the word, but since the image itself is polyvalent as reflected in the liturgical texts that provide its context, her exclusion seems overly strict to me. Likewise, in my opinion, the arguments by which Schulz would exclude the icon's being read as an image of Christ's descent fail, while his positive arguments for its depiction of the resurrection may be extended to the Descent. This being said, an adequate discussion of his multiple arguments must be postponed for a different occasion. Here I would merely give as a counterexample to his thesis Joseph Wilpert, *Die römischen Mosaiken und Malereien der kirchlichen Bauten vom IV. bis XIII. Jahrhundert,* 1. Band, 2. Buch (Freiburg: Herder, 1917), 202. Wilpert argues that an image with the basic features of the *Anastasis* icon was paired in the *Constantinian* Lateran basilica of the fourth century with the passage of the Israelites through the Red Sea. If Wilpert is right, this typological prefiguration would be more akin to the Descent than to the Resurrection.

51. Kartsonis, *Anastasis,* 21-22; see also pp. 227, 229, and 233 regarding the essential reference to Christ's descent in the icon of the *Anastasis* and its forebears.

52. St. John Damascene, *De fide orthodoxa,* IV, PG 94:1101, cited in Kartsonis, *Anastasis,* 22, n. 16. See also St. John Damascene, *De fide orthodoxa,* trans. S. D. F. Salmond, Nicene and Post-Nicene Fathers, 2nd ser., vol. 9 (Grand Rapids: Eerdmans, 1983), ch. 29, pp. 72-73.

53. St. Athanasius, *De incarnatione. Contra Apollinarium,* I, PG 26:1117, cited in Kartsonis, *Anastasis,* 21 (n. 15).

54. Kartsonis, *Anastasis,* 69. See also Wilpert's suggestion in n. 50 above; and idem, *Die römischen Mosaiken,* 2. Band, 3. Buch, 895. For the earliest known *extant* objects illustrating the subject, see Elisabetta L. Palli, "Der syrisch-palästinensische Darstellungstypus der Höllenfahrt Christi," Festschrift Engelbert Kirschbaum, *Römische Quartalschrift für Christliche Altertumskunde und Kirchengeschichte* 58, Teil 1-2 (Freiburg: Herder, 1963), 250-67, especially 261; and G. McN. Rushforth, "S. Maria Antiqua," *Papers of the British School at Rome* 1 (1902) 1: 116.

55. Ouspensky and Lossky, *The Meaning of Icons,* 188.

56. According to *The Oxford English Dictionary,* 2nd ed., a *harrow* is a heavy toothed frame that "is dragged over ploughed land to break clods, pulverize and stir the soil, root up weeds, or cover in the seed." The verb *to harrow* indicates primarily the use of this instrument or, derivatively, *to tear, to wound,* or even *to castrate.*

57. Worthen, *The Harrowing of Hell,* 44.

58. Reproduced in Clifford Davidson, "The Fate of the Damned in English Art and Drama," *The Iconography of Hell,* ed. Clifford Davidson and Thomas H. Seiler, Early Drama, Art, and Music Monograph Series 17 (Kalamazoo, MI: Medieval Institute Publications, Western Michigan University, 1992), fig. 18.

59. British Library, London, MS. Cotton Tiberius C.6, fol. 14 r, reproduced in Gary D. Schmidt, *The Iconography of the Mouth of Hell: Eighth-Century Britain to the Fifteenth Century* (London: Associated University Presses, 1995), 74.

60. Wilpert, *Die römischen Mosaiken,* 2. Band, 3. Buch, 895.

61. St. Ephraim Syrus, *The Nisibene Hymns,* trans. J. T. Sarsfield Stopford, Nicene and Post-Nicene Fathers, 2nd ser., vol. 13 (Grand Rapids: Eerdmans, 1976), Hymns 37, 38, and 66.

62. St. Ephraim Syrus, *The Nisibene Hymns,* Hymn 60, #31.

63. St. Ephraim Syrus, *The Nisibene Hymns,* Hymn 65.

64. James Hampton Kirkland, *A Study of the Anglo-Saxon Poem, The Harrowing of Hell (Grein's Höllenfahrt Christi)* (Halle: Ehrhardt Karras, 1885). Dante, *The Divine Comedy,* vol. 1: Inferno, trans. Mark Musa (New York: Penguin, 1971), cantos IV.46-63, VIII.125-26, XII.38-39; see also Musa's notes to cantos VIII and IX. *About the Harrowing of Hell: A Seventeenth-Century Ukrainian Play in Its European Context,* trans. with introduction and notes by Irena R. Makaryk (Ottawa: Dovehouse Editions Canada, 1989); this outstanding work not only discusses liturgical, apocryphal, and patristic sources for the Ukrainian play, but also similar dramas in France, England, Spain, Italy, Germany, Austria, Bohemia, and Poland.

65. Strynkowski, *The Descent (excerpt),* 55. See also Chaine, "Descente du Christ aux Enfers," 428-31; Vogels, *Christi Abstieg ins Totenreich,* 221-23, 229-31; and Karl Gschwind, *Die Niederfahrt Christi in die Unterwelt,* Neutestamentliche Abhandlungen 2. Band, 3./5. Heft. (Munster: Aschendorff, 1911), 6-13.

66. Worthen, *The Harrowing of Hell,* 7. Worthen describes the first as narration, and the second as (symbolic) signification.

67. Worthen, *The Harrowing of Hell*, 18; see also pp. 314-25 on the use of the image to indicate salvation.

68. Worthen, *The Harrowing of Hell*, 58-59. Compare St. John Chrysostom, cited above with n. 34 in Chapter Three.

69. Worthen, *The Harrowing of Hell*, 330. He also suggests a decrease in the publication of literary works concerning Christ's descent contributed to the change in the subject's popularity, but the converse seems more likely to me. Herzog, *Descensus*, 458-85, provides a bibliography of monographs on the Descent, with an emphasis on works since the sixteenth century.

70. Worthen, *The Harrowing of Hell*, 331-33.

71. See Worthen, *The Harrowing of Hell*, 332. See also Gerhard L. Müller, "Höllenabstieg Christi," *Lexikon der katholischen Dogmatik,* hrsg. Wolfgang Beinert (Freiburg: Herder, 1987), 272.

Notes to Chapter Five

1. *Mysterium Paschale: The Mystery of Easter,* trans. Aidan Nichols (Edinburgh: T. & T. Clark, 1990), 151. This text is the English translation of Balthasar's *Theologie der drei Tage* (Einsiedeln: Benzinger, 1969), which in turn is the independent publication of "Mysterium Paschale," his contribution to *Mysterium Salutis. Grundriss heilsgeschichtliche Dogmatik. Bd. III/2: Das Christusereignis,* hrsg. Johannes Feiner und Magnus Löhrer (Einsiedeln: Benzinger, 1969), 133-326. *Mysterium Paschale* is hereinafter referred to as *MP.*

2. *MP*, 172.

3. *MP*, 172. See also p. 180; "Desc," 411; and *Wahrheit Gottes*, Bd. II, *Theo-Logik* (Einsiedeln: Johannes, 1985), 319; this last work is hereinafter referred to as *ThLogII.*

4. *MP*, 148.

5. *MP*, 148; see also p. 149. See also *GloryVII*, 225 and 234.

6. *MP*, 172.

7. *MP*, 148-49, 161, 172.

8. *MP*, 149.

9. *MP*, 150-51.

10. *MP*, 150.

11. *MP*, 150. See also p. 164; *GloryVII*, 209.

12. *MP*, 150, emphasis added.

13. *GloryVII*, 230. The Descent is also described as "passivity" in *God Question*, 138.

14. *GloryVII*, 250.

15. See "The Mystery of the Eucharist," *New Elucidations*, trans. Mary Theresilde Skerry (San Francisco: Ignatius, 1986), 114.

16. "Obedience in the Light of the Gospel," *New Elucidations*, 231; see also pp. 233-34.

17. See "Death Is Swallowed Up by Life," *Communio ICR* 14 (1987) 2: 50.

18. "Desc," 407-8.

19. "Desc," 407-8.

20. "Desc," 408.

21. *MP*, 152.

22. See, e.g., "Desc," 407-8.

23. See, e.g., *ThDrI*, 370-400.

24. "Desc," 411.

25. *CCC* #1016. See also *CCC* #624; the *Symbol* of the Fourth Lateran Ecumenical Council, *CF* #20 (DS 801); the *Profession of Faith* of Pope Paul VI, *CF* #39/21; Canon 1 of the 16th Council of Carthage, *CF* #501 (DS 222); and Pope John Paul II, General Audience of January 11, 1989.

26. "Desc," 408.

27. "Desc," 411.

28. On the important role of death as the separation of body and soul in the development of Christology and this specifically in relation to Christ's descent, see Grillmeier, "Der Gottessohn im Totenreich," 100-174.

29. Positive assertions are in *Leben,* 50; and *ThDrV,* 339.

30. *MP,* 161. On Balthasar's understanding of Sheol, see "Trinity and Future," *Elucidations,* 81; *The God Question and Modern Man,* trans. Hilda Graef (New York: Seabury, 1967), 132-33; and "Desc," 408. In regard to influences from outside Judaism, see also *GloryVII,* 229, including n. 3. In *The Action,* vol. 4, *Theo-Drama,* trans. Graham Harrison (San Francisco: Ignatius, 1994), 119-20 (this book is hereinafter referred to as *ThDrIV*), Balthasar extends the results of this pagan influence even to the Chosen People's desire or hope for an afterlife at all. There is some inconsistency in what he claims was the Jewish or Old Testament expectation of the afterlife; compare *ThDrV,* 143, with the texts previously mentioned.

31. *MP,* 177.

32. *MP,* 174, 178.

33. *MP,* 178-79, and n. 110 to that chapter; "Desc," 406; "Some Points of Eschatology," 264; *ThDrV,* 362-64.

34. *MP,* 173-74, 177; "Desc," 406; *GloryVII,* 233-34; "DescHell," 229.

35. On the suggestion that the Sheol experienced by those who died before Christ might have been mitigated, see *MP,* 167; *GloryVII,* 231-32; and "Some Points of Eschatology," 264. Perhaps because there is no consistent place for an abode of the just dead in his theology, Balthasar does not mention the limbo of the Fathers in his chapter on Holy Saturday in *MP,* a silence that is striking given the presence of the doctrine in theological sources.

36. *MP,* 161, 172; "Desc," 408; "On Vicarious Representation," *Expl IV.*

37. *MP,* 165.

38. Balthasar, "Der Tod im heutigen Denken," *Anima* 11 (1956): 299. See also *GloryVII,* 229; "La Chiesa e l'inferno," *La realtà e la gloria: Hans Urs von Balthasar articoli e interviste 1978 1988* (Milan: EDIT Editoriale Italiana, 1988).

39. *MP,* 149, 161, 165. See also the references in n. 30 above; *Credo: Meditations on the Apostles' Creed,* trans. David Kipp (Edinburgh: T. & T. Clark, 1990), 54; *GloryVII,* 209.

40. "La discesa agli inferi," *RITC Communio* 55 [1981]: 4: "Nella morte termina ogni comunicazione non solo con gli uomini ma anche con Dio."

41. "Desc," 411. To be precise, Balthasar says "the triad of death-Hades-Satan" is this "summation." He had introduced these three as characters in the popular dramatic representations of the Descent (p. 409), then moved on to unite them as referring to "the reality" that "Christ existentially experiences and encounters" (p. 410). This single "reality" is called *Sheol* in Balthasar's theological vocabulary.

42. *MP*, 173.

43. On sheol in the Old Testament, see also Luis I. J. Stadelmann, *The Hebrew Conception of the World: A Philological and Literary Study*, Analecta Biblica 39 (Rome: Pontifical Biblical Institute, 1970), 171-76; Herbert Vorgrimler, *Geschichte der Hölle* (Munich: Wilhelm Fink, 1993), 62-63; and Herzog, *Descensus*, 220-31.

44. *MP*, 162.

45. *MP*, 162-63.

46. *MP*, 163, NB his n. 47. See also *ThDrV*, 302, including n. 3; *Dare We Hope "That All Men Be Saved"? with "A Short Discourse on Hell,"* trans. Lothar Krauth and David Kipp (San Francisco: Ignatius, 1988), 51-53, 127, including n. 7; and "Short Discourse," 242; "Some Points of Eschatology," 264.

47. *MP*, 150, 162-63; see also "Some Points of Eschatology," 259.

48. "Some Points of Eschatology," 264, parenthetical content is Balthasar's.

49. *MP*, 148. See also "Vicarious," 422; "Desc," 408; as well as places where Balthasar speaks of Christ taking upon Himself "our fate" (*ThDrIV*, 495, 493) or experiencing our death from the "inside" (*ThDrIII*, 241; *ThDrIV*, 132; and *God Question*, 133).

50. *MP*, 149. See also "DescHell," 224, 229. On solidarity with the dead, see also *MP*, 160-61, 164, 168; *GloryVII*, 229; and "Desc," 408.

In *ThLogII*, 315, n. 1, Balthasar notes that *MP* "den Versuch darstellt, der kühneren Lehre Adriennes von Speyr einen Weg zu bahnen. Der Begriff «Solidarität mit den Toten» war ein Kompromiß, er kommt im Folgenden nicht mehr vor" (represented an attempt to prepare the way for the bolder teaching of Adrienne von Speyr. The concept 'solidarity with the dead' was a compromise, which does not appear any more in [*Theo-Logik*]). On the one hand, Balthasar distances himself here somewhat from his concept of solidarity, though only to develop Speyr's "bolder teaching." On the other hand, the concept's function as a bridge to her thought remains undenied. After all, *MP* was written *after* Balthasar's private publication of *Kreuz und Hölle*, Speyr's principal account of her descent experiences. Given the concept's role as bridge and the repeated centrality it plays in most of Balthasar's own treatments of Christ's descent (one notes the relatively late date of *ThLogII*), it remains here as a key element of his theology of Holy Saturday. In contrast, Robert Nandkisore, *Hoffnung auf Erlösung: Die Eschatologie im Werk Hans Urs von Balthasars*, Tesi Gregoriana Serie Teologia No. 22 (Rome: Editrice Pontificia Università Gregoriana, 1997), 230-37, holds that Balthasar's comment in *ThLogII* means he "ganz auf[gibt]" [wholly gives up] the idea of solidarity. I think Nandkisore goes a bit too far on this point, but he rightly shows a shift in accent in Balthasar's theology from the anthropological perspective to the theological, i.e., from Christ's experience in Sheol as solidarity with the other human dead to it as insight into the personal mystery of the Father.

51. *MP*, 168. Compare *GloryVII*, 140. See also *Leben*, 38, 69.

52. "Desc," 410.

53. *MP*, 150. Compare the expression in *ThLogII*, 322, emphasis added: "wenn alles mit dem Kreuz doch schon «vollbracht» *scheint*" [when all *seems* already 'finished' with the cross].

54. Balthasar's reference here is to St. Thomas Aquinas, "*Expositio Symboli* 5 (Spiazzi 926): Descenditque cum illo in foveam' (p. 930)." The quotation marks are missing in the English *MP*.

55. *MP*, 164-65. These last two sentences are Balthasar's, but he attributes the final one to St. Irenaeus, giving a footnote to his "*Adversus Haereses* III.23, 2 (PG 7, 961)."

56. *ThDrIII*, 238; Balthasar's citation is "*To gar aproslepton atherapeuton* (PG 37, 181)."

57. St. Gregory Nazianzen, *Ep. 101, Ad Cledonium presbyterum contra Apollinariue*, PG 37:181.

58. *Mysterium Salutis*, III/2, 240.

59. On suffering as the formal principle in Balthasar's theology of the Descent, consider, e.g., his attempt to show support for this principle (*MP*, 164-65), his treatment of St. Bonaventure (*MP*, 103-4), and the development of his theology of Holy Saturday in light of both of these; see also *ThDrI*, 106. See also Jöhri, *Descensus Dei*, 281, n. 181.

60. See St. Thomas Aquinas, *ST*, IIIa q. 19, a. 3, 4; IaIIae q. 5, a. 4; IIIa q. 14, a. 1 ad 1.

61. See, e.g., *CF* #15, 17, 20, 23, 39/5, and 39/10 (DS 72, 76, 801, 852).

62. *ThDrV*, 266.

63. *ThDrV*, 314. See also *MP*, 173; *GloryVII*, 233; Balthasar, "Zur Frage: 'Hoffnung für alle' Eine Antwort auf den Artikel von Pfr. Karl Besler," *Theologisches* 199 (1986): 7365, emphasis in original: "Wenn die Sünde, wie platonisierende Denker sagen, einfach ein Nichtsein wäre dann bräuchte es im Grunde keine Beichte. Sie *ist* etwas. . . ." [If sin, as platonizing thinkers say, were simply a non-being, then there would basically be no need for confession. Sin *is* something . . .]. This argument clearly depends on what one thinks confession does.

64. On the "load" of sin, see, e.g., *GloryVII*, 208-9; and *Leben*, 36. Contrast St. Thomas Aquinas, who characterizes sin as a reality insofar as it is an act, but holds that a specific act is a sin insofar as this real act lacks something it should have (*ST*, IaIIae q. 79, a. 2). Sin, according to Balthasar, however, is something in itself, as opposed to a defect in something; consequently, it may be separated both from the one who commits it and from the act of commission.

65. *ThDrV*, 285.

66. *ThDrV*, 314. See also pp. 285, 321; *MP*, 50, 173; *GloryVII*, 233; and "DescHell," 235.

67. *MP*, 101; *Leben*, 36; *ThDrIV*, 345. See also "The Eye of the Peacock," *Heart of the World*, trans. Erasmo S. Leiva (San Francisco: Ignatius, 1979), 104-16.

68. *ThDrIV*, 334, emphasis in original.

69. "Meeting God in Today's World," *Concilium* 6 (June 1965) 1: 20.

70. *GloryVII*, 208-9.

71. *GloryVII*, 203.

72. *GloryVII*, 204.

73. *GloryVII*, 290, emphasis added.

74. *GloryVII*, 149.

75. In contradistinction to Easter Sunday and Ascension Thursday; Leben, 79: "Karfreitag mit dem Karsamstag des Todes in sich — und Ostern mit der Richtung der Himmelfahrt zum Vater hin."

76. *ThDrIV*, 319.

77. On the "hour," see, e.g., *ThDrIV*, 231-40, 343; and *A Theological Anthropology*, no trans. noted (New York: Sheed & Ward, 1967), 275. See also *ThDrIV*, 334.

78. This is often the case even when "the Cross" is mentioned in isolation; see, e.g.,

ThDrV, 260, and *GloryVII*, 279. Sometimes, however, "the Cross" refers to the Crucifixion as distinct from the Descent; see, e.g., *MP*, 150; *ThDrV*, 266.

79. *GloryVII*, 277.

80. Thus, even as "the Cross" may include the Descent, sometimes "Cross and Hell" refers to a *single* concept. See, e.g., *GloryVII*, 243, 316; and "La Chiesa e l'inferno," 65, emphasis added, where Balthasar speaks repeatedly of the saints' participation in Christ's "abandonment on the *cross*" while treating of "the mystery of this *descent*" of Christ's to hell.

81. *MP*, 155.

82. *GloryVII*, 230.

83. *MP*, 155, with interior quotation of Col 2:13. See also *Leben*, 50-51; and "Some Points of Eschatology," 264.

84. *ThDrV*, 477.

85. *God Question*, 133.

86. *MP*, 165.

87. *MP*, 165-66. See also *God Question*, 132-33. For Balthasar, time requires hope, and so a lack of hope must imply a sense of timelessness; see "The Unity of Our Lives," *Convergences: To the Source of Christian Mystery*, trans. E. A. Nelson (San Francisco: Ignatius, 1983), 114.

88. "Desc," 408.

89. *MP*, 165.

90. *MP*, 165, 166. Balthasar gives St. Thomas Aquinas as an example of someone who "naively" does so.

91. *MP*, 167. See also *GloryVII*, 231-32; and "Some Points of Eschatology," 264.

92. *MP*, 164-65.

93. *MP*, 167. See also *GloryVII*, 225, 231-33; *God Question*, 132, 137; "Desc," 408. The general denial of the theological virtues to any of the dead is applied to Christ in "The Multitude of Biblical Theologies and the Spirit of Unity in the Church," *Convergences*, 98. Balthasar apparently thinks the presence of any one theological virtue implies the presence of the others. While this is true of charity, traditionally it has not been held with regard to faith and hope, which may be present, but not "living." See, e.g., Jas 2:17 and St. Thomas Aquinas, *ST*, IaIIae q. 62, a. 3; IIaIIae q. 4, a. 3, 4.

On Christ's exclusive experience of Sheol, see *GloryVII*, 214, 233; "And the Sea of Being Lay Dry," *Heart*, 175; *Th'l Anth*, 242, 285; "The Last Five Stations of the Cross," *Theologians Today: Hans Urs von Balthasar*, ed. Martin Redfern, no trans. noted (London: Sheed & Ward, 1972), 121; *ThDrIV*, 132, 495. See also *Leben*, 40, 49; "Only If," *Convergences*, 136-37.

94. Franco Giulio Brambilla, "Salvezza e redenzione nella teologia di K. Rahner e H. U. von Balthasar," *La Scuola Cattolica* 108 (1980): 205-6: "Ma tale movimento per cui la discesa di uno solo nell'abisso, si trasforma nell'ascesa di tutti, presuppone il «per tutti» della discesa, perché Egli sia il prototipo della resurrezione: e proprio per questo è salvifico."

95. "Desc," 408. See also *Th'l Anth*, 242; "The Broken Sun," *Heart*, 70-71; "The Eye," 109-10, 115. See also Balthasar, "La Chiesa e l'inferno," 61-66; and "Desc," 408. Balthasar is more cautious in the late work *ThLogII*, 319; note that there Jesus' faith is not denied — logically enough, because Balthasar understands faith as fidelity (see "*Fides Christi*: An Essay on the Consciousness of Christ," *Spouse of the Word*, Explorations in Theology, vol. 2, no trans. noted [San Francisco: Ignatius, 1991]), which would be required for obedience.

96. *MP*, 122. One familiar with Balthasar's work should hear overtones here of his in-

sistence that God take "seriously" the possibility and consequence of finite freedom's rejection of Him, that He not remain aloof from His creation in His transcendence (e.g., "Only If," 136-37) or "play around" in how He redeems the world (e.g., *Th'l Anth*, 242; see also *ThDrIV*, 325; *ThDrV*, 127, 259; *GloryI*, 474; and "Trinity and Future," 82). Balthasar's desires to affirm the possibility of a real created freedom, and to avoid deism and docetism are legitimate, but his rejection of Christ's beatific vision as the 'solution' is debatable. This topic will be treated in detail in Chapter Seven.

97. *MP*, 164.

98. *MP*, 174; see also p. 167. According to Balthasar, Holy Saturday is the "definitive, eschatological turn" ("Desc," 402). See also *MP*, 174: "That the Redeemer is solidary . . . with this death . . . — this is the final consequence of the redemptive mission he has received from the Father"; *Th'l Anth*, 285: "the gulf between death and Resurrection . . . reaches to the bottom of hell"; *GloryVII*, 395, Balthasar freely interprets Ephesians: "He alone 'descended' ([Eph.] 4:9) into our condition below, i.e., into the condition we all shared of 'being dead' through our 'transgressions and sins ([Eph.] 2:1)"; as also "Desc," 407; *GloryI*, 473; *GloryVII*, 228-29, 233, 248; *ThDrV*, 139, 486; "The Multitude of Biblical Theologies," 97; "Mystery," 116; "Only If," 136-37; *Leben*, 49; and "DescHell," 234.

99. *MP*, 172-74. See also *GloryVII*, 233; and the texts in n. 98 above.

100. *MP*, 172.

101. *MP*, 172.

102. *MP*, 170. Balthasar quotes much more. His citation is "*Excitationes* 10 (Basle 1565), p. 659." The Latin text (and excerpts of other relevant texts of Cusanus) may be more readily found in Herzog, *Descensus*, 170, who identifies it as marginalia to part ("*Ex sermone. Qui per spiritum sanctum semetipsum obtulit.*") of a sermon from April 3, 1457. Herzog, pp. 166, 169, 173, 340, reiterates that Nicholas of Cusa is the first to hold that Christ suffered the pains of the damned in hell after His death, and that his text stands at the head of the various *descensus* doctrines (including those of Luther and Calvin) in which Christ suffers the pains of hell as part of His atoning work.

Balthasar's theology has strong Lutheran and Calvinistic tones and content in this regard, although he attempts to distinguish his doctrine from Calvin's. On the other hand, Balthasar's admiration of Luther is unmistakable: In regard to an understanding of soteriology in terms of substitution, e.g., he says, "It is as if Luther's thought, right from its very beginnings, was bent upon filling precisely the gap that patristic theology had left open in the *admirabile commercium*" (*ThDrIV*, 284). Luther's theology of redemption "must be taken seriously," he says, then quotes several of Luther's characterizations of Christ's redemptive work, including this one: "Christ is more damned and forsaken than all the saints; . . . In all reality and truth, he submitted to God the Father's eternal damnation for us" (*ThDrIV*, 285). The synopsis of Luther's *descensus* doctrines in Herzog, *Descensus*, 247-48, 307-11, could almost serve as a summary for Balthasar's position, except it lacks Balthasar's Trinitarian focus and his emphasis on Christ's "ever-greater" God-abandonment after death; otherwise, most of his major points are there.

It is true that Balthasar sees certain defects in Luther (see, e.g., *ThDrIV*, 290), but these it seems he intends to correct in his own work; see his use of Adrienne von Speyr in exactly this way in the closing sections of *ThLogII*. If John O'Donnell has rightly summarized Balthasar's main concern with Luther as to whether there can be contradiction in God (idem,

Hans Urs von Balthasar [New York: Continuum, 1991], 103), then it seems Balthasar answers by arguing that the contradictory opposites are, in a manner of speaking, identical. The extremes (of wrath and love, death and life) touch.

103. Represented, e.g., by *God Question*, 132-34.

104. As seen, e.g., in *MP*, 168-74.

105. See "Desc," 409.

106. *God Question*, 133.

107. *God Question*, 133.

108. *God Question*, 133. See also "Desc," 408; *GloryI*, 475; and "Death Is Swallowed," 51.

109. "Trinity and Future," 82.

110. "Mystery," 116.

111. *MP*, 172.

112. *MP*, 161, 172.

113. *MP*, 148; see also "Desc," 407-8.

114. "Vicarious," 422.

115. "The Eye," 107: "The leprosy of millions covers you, and you go down into a nameless sewer." His "mortal flesh" is passive like "an alphabet or a keyboard" (*GloryVII*, 143). On "Gehenna," see *ThDrV*, 314-16.

116. "DescHell," 236.

117. See, for example, *GloryVII*, 207.

118. *GloryVII*, 209.

119. *GloryVII*, 208-9; see also, e.g., *Leben*, 36. "Load" should raise echoes of Balthasar's use of *momentum* and *crushing* in his theology.

120. *MP*, 163. Balthasar's treatment points to these images as products of the imagination, or at least as residing therein. However, the passage serves only to prepare the way for his exposition of the *visio mortis*. Hence it is in the full sense of this *visio*, which does not appear to be limited in its informative effect to the imagination, that the soul's subjection to images should be taken.

121. See, e.g., "Desc," where Balthasar both conflates (409) and distinguishes (411) Christ's subjective experience of Sheol with what (i.e., the object) He experiences. Note also nn. 46 and 120 above, and 136 below.

122. *God Question*, 133.

123. St. Thomas Aquinas, *ST*, Ia q. 12, a. 4, 9.

124. *MP*, 173. On the anonymity of sin in Sheol, see *ThLogII*, 318, 324-25. We note here that Balthasar's identification of the 'second death' with Sheol may be questioned on the basis of Rev 20:14 *RSV*, in which hades (i.e., sheol) is distinct from the 'second death': "Then Death and Hades were thrown into the lake of fire. This is the second death, the lake of fire."

125. See *ThDrV*, 288: "Christ's work 'must not turn into some sort of blurred collective redemption.'" The interior quote is from Adrienne von Speyr, *Katholische Briefe*, vol. 1 (Einsiedeln: Johannes, no date given), 161. See also *Th'l Anth*, 121.

126. *MP*, 173. See also *GloryVII*, 233.

127. *MP*, 173.

128. "Desc," 409.

129. *Leben*, 36: "buchstäblich «zur Sünde gemacht» wird (2 Cor 5:21)."

130. *ThDrIII*, 517, emphasis in original. See also *ThDrIV*, 336.

131. *ThDrIV*, 334. See also "The Eye," 107.

132. *ThDrV*, 263, with reliance on Speyr.

133. See *ThDrV*, 261, 268. Regarding God as fire, see *ThDrV*, 268 (with respect to the Trinitarian relations); *ThDrIV*, 59-61; *ThDrV*, 301 (with respect to hell); and *ThDrV*, 360-69 (with respect to purgatory). See also "Fragments on Suffering and Healing," *New Elucidations*, 278; and "And the Sea," 185.

134. *ThDrIV*, 334, emphasis in original. On the alienation of sin and Christ's assumption of it, see also "Loneliness in the Church," *Expl IV*, 269.

135. "Desc," 409. See also *GloryVII*, 223; "The Eye," 115-16; "And the Sea," 181; *ThDrIII*, 530; *ThDrV*, 486; and p. 267: He enters "into the pure essence of sin that has been separated from the world, into what has been condemned by God, in which God cannot be found."

136. "Desc," 409. See also "Desc," 411; *ThLogII*, 319-21. The pairing of the contraries *in* and *out*, and the meaning Balthasar attributes to them illuminates his frequent description of sin or the human condition (including death) being taken up "from within," "upon himself," "*pro nobis*." See, e.g., *ThDrIII*, 241, 530; *ThDrIV*, 356; *ThDrV*, 257; "Vicarious," 422; "The Eye," 105; and *Leben*, 36.

137. *MP*, 169.

138. *MP*, 104, with reference to St. Bonaventure, *In III Sententiarum Libros*, d. 16, a. 2, p. 2, conclusio (Quaracchi III., p. 356) One must ask whether St. Bonaventure and Balthasar understand *spiritual* in the same way in this matter, because, for Balthasar, this spiritual suffering will ultimately refer to Christ's divinity.

139. *MP*, 104.

140. *MP*, 103-5. What he says here about Christ's experience of the "entrance of sin" during His agony in the garden is *a fortiori* relevant to His definitive experience of sin in Sheol.

141. See, e.g., *MP*, 104-5, 138.

142. *MP*, 103.

143. Hans Urs von Balthasar, *Does Jesus Know Us — Do We Know Him?* trans. Graham Harrison (San Francisco: Ignatius, 1983), 32. Text in brackets is a correction to the translation, which simply had "it." See also "Vicarious," 422.

144. For an explicit statement, see *ThDrIV*, 345. For explicit statements about Christ's assumption of the guilt of all individuals, see "The Church as 'Caritas,'" *Elucidations*, 246, 247, and "The Personal God," 54. See also "The Unknown God," 42; and "Only If," 139.

145. See *The Threefold Garland: The World's Salvation in Mary's Prayer*, trans. Erasmo Leiva-Merikakis (San Francisco: Ignatius, 1982), 79. Contrast St. Thomas Aquinas, *Super Epistolas, Lectiones ad II Cor.*, cap. 5, lec. 5. St. Thomas writes that Christ is said to be "made sin" in three ways: as a sacrifice for sin, as sharing a likeness to the punishments of passibility and mortality for sin, and as He was thought to be a sinner.

146. *GloryVII*, 208; see also p. 209.

147. *GloryVII*, 206.

148. *GloryVII*, 300.

149. See *ThDrV*, 261. See also "The Broken Sun," 71; and *God Question*, 133.

150. *MP*, 168.

151. *ThDrIII*, 517, emphasis in original.

152. *GloryVII*, 211.

153. *Leben,* 36.

154. See *Th'l Anth,* 231. See also "Von Balthasar antwortet Boros," *Orientierung* 34 (1970): 38-39. In *ThLogII,* 324-24, Balthasar explains a little more about sin separated from sinners: A man loans something of his own reality to his sins; hence, they are not a 'nothing.' Christ's spousal (!) encounter in Sheol with these individual sins, called *effigies* by Speyr, removes their personal character by the gift of grace to the sinner. The sum total of now-anonymous sins constitute sin as such. Although "sin in itself" is a central theological tool for Balthasar, Speyr's effigies play little role in his theology, so I will not discuss or critique them.

Alberto Espezel, *El Misterio Pascual en Hans Urs von Balthasar* (Buenos Aires: Impreso en Grafideas, 1987), 192, straightforwardly rejects the concept of sin-in-itself on the grounds that it lacks sufficient foundation in Scripture and Tradition. Although I have reservations about a number of his other conclusions, it is noteworthy of Espezel's treatment that the majority of his concerns about Balthasar's theology of Holy Saturday relate to Scriptural exegesis; see his Chapter 2.

155. *ThDrV,* 321.

156. *ThDrIV,* 501. See also p. 496; and *Th'l Anth,* 280.

157. *GloryVII,* 205.

158. *Th'l Anth,* 231.

159. *GloryVII,* 232.

160. *GloryVII,* 206; *ThDrIV,* 339, 341.

161. *ThDrIV,* 341.

162. See *ThDrIV,* 500.

163. See *GloryVII,* 208.

164. *MP,* 104.

165. *MP,* 105.

166. *MP,* 137. Compare *Does Jesus Know Us?* 32.

167. See also *ThDrIII,* 350: "God does nothing anti-divine — the sinner does — but he can experience it within his own reality. This is Christ's descent into hell. . . ."

168. See the references in n. 144 above. See also "Only If," 139; and "The Personal God," 54.

169. "The Church as 'Caritas,'" 246. Compare the stress on the personal pronouns or their role in "Meeting God," 20; "Jailhouse and Cocoon," *Heart,* 143; "Mystery," 116; *GloryVII,* 307, n. 15; *Leben,* 38; and compare *Leben,* 66-67, where the pronouns (and the sin) switch from being "ours" to being "his."

170. "The Church as 'Caritas,'" 247.

171. *GloryVII,* 136-41; see also pp. 229-35.

172. For Balthasar's more clear, complete, and succinct presentations of Christ's existence *pro nobis,* see *ThDrIV,* 238-43; "With Him Two Others on Either Side, But Jesus in the Middle," *You Have Words,* 251-53; "Meeting God," 20; and "Bought at a Great Price," *You Crown the Year with Your Goodness,* trans. Graham Harrison (San Francisco: Ignatius, 1989), 78. Pyc, *L'obbedienza,* 80-91, presents five ways in which Christ identifies Himself with sinners out of obedience, and these serve well to summarize Balthasar's use of the *pro nobis:* being with sinners, being for sinners (i.e., He acts for their good), making the place of sinners His own so as not to distinguish Himself from them, being "made [their] sin," and letting Him-

self be judged for their sins in place of them. The relevant features also appear in the person of St. Paul (Rom 9:3); see *Test Everything: Hold Fast to What Is Good,* interview with Hans Urs von Balthasar by Angelo Scola, trans. Maria Shrady (San Francisco: Ignatius, 1989), 35.

173. *ThDrIV,* 338. See also "The Eye," 105; and "And the Sea," 185; but contrast *ThDrV,* 140. The distinction between these aspects is overlooked by those who hold that Balthasar rejects any idea of Christ's suffering as punishment; e.g., Nandkisore, *Hoffnung auf Erlösung,* 235, n. 121. From the complexity of the penal character of Christ's suffering in Balthasar's theology, one can understand why he writes in *ThDrIV,* 337, "Whether or not the concept of 'punishment' is to be applied to Christ's suffering on the Cross is largely a matter of language."

174. *Does Jesus Know Us?* 35.

175. "Vicarious," 415. See also "Martyrdom and Mission," *New Elucidations,* 287; and n. 169 above. Note especially the change from *my* to *his* in *Leben,* 66-67; and "Mystery," 116.

176. "Vicarious," 420. The "physical solidarity" of a shared nature is subordinate to the preeminent characteristic of the *pro nobis* (*Glory VII,* 208), which is nonetheless also described in "Spirit and Institution," *Expl IV,* 227, as being "in a certain way 'physical'" in that it is the real assumption of the death (bodily death and the 'second death') deserved by all sinners.

177. See *ThDrV,* 140: "True, according to Paul (Rom 8:10), death remains a punishment for sin: this was seen most graphically in Christ's Cross. . . . But death's penal character is experienced on behalf of sinners, and so it is changed into love." See also *ThDrIV,* 345, in n. 144 above. Compare Calvin: "Christ was put in place of evildoers as surety and pledge — submitting himself even as the accused — to bear and suffer all the punishments that they ought to have sustained. All — with this one exception: 'He could not be held by the pangs of death' (Acts 2:24)." John Calvin, *Institutes of the Christian Religion,* ed. John T. McNeill, trans. Ford Lewis Battles, The Library of Christian Classics, vol. 20 (Philadelphia: Westminster, 1960), Book II, Ch. XVI, #10, pp. 515-16.

178. See, e.g., St. Thomas Aquinas, *ST,* IIIa q. 48, a. 2.

179. "Vicarious," 421-22.

180. "Vicarious," 421.

181. "Vicarious," 422. His descent must be in "nontime" that it may embrace sinners of all times.

182. See, e.g., *ThDrIV,* 338, 342, 350, 433-52; *ThDrV,* 199-205, 285.

183. *ThDrIV,* 496, emphasis in original. See also, e.g., *ThDrV,* 326-27.

184. *ThDrV,* 308.

185. *Th'l Anth,* 121.

186. *Glory VII,* 208.

187. *Glory VII,* 208.

188. *Glory VII,* 208. See also *ThDrV,* 272, 277.

189. *Glory VII,* 208-9, emphasis added. Balthasar's original emphasis is only on the *not* of "not by himself."

190. Compare *MP,* 169, where Balthasar says Calvin "defends himself . . . against the charge of interpreting the abandonment by God in Hell as the 'despair of not believing': 'The weakness of Christ was pure of all stain, since it was enclosed within obedience to God.'" Balthasar's reference here for Calvin is "*Institutio* II.16, 10-12."

191. *Catechism of the Council of Trent,* 64, 65.

192. "Desc," 405.

193. "Desc," 405. On p. 414 (emphasis added), he says such "folk myths . . . do not *in any way* anticipate the answer to that riddle" of human death, and in particular, of Christ's descent. He also indicates (p. 407) that he is aware of the testimony of the theological sources (in his words, the "liturgical, speculative and rhetorical-popular theology") discussed in the first two chapters of this thesis; he does not mention the magisterial sources.

Notes to Chapter Six

1. See DS 3326.

2. See the Nicene-Constantinopolitan creed. See also *ST,* Ia q. 45, a. 6 ad 2; *ST,* IIIa q. 32, a. 1; and *Summa contra gentiles* IV, ch. 19, 20, for some other reasons given by St. Thomas.

3. See, e.g., "The Holy Spirit as Love," *Creator Spirit,* Explorations in Theology, vol. 3, trans. Brian McNeil (San Francisco: Ignatius, 1993), 118-19; this anthology is hereinafter referred to as *Expl III.*

4. *ThDrIV,* 327.

5. On creation and the Trinity, see *ThDrIV,* 333; *ThDrV,* 81, 100, 245, 257, 516; *Leben,* 70; "Trinity and Future," 81. See also *ThDrIV,* 329; *ThDrV,* 395.

6. *ThDrIII,* 183-84; "The Holy Spirit as Love," 118-19. Balthasar's arguments on this point and the difficulties associated with them will be treated in Part Three.

7. See, e.g., *ThDrIII,* 188, 200, 520.

8. See Edward T. Oakes, *Pattern of Redemption: The Theology of Hans Urs von Balthasar* (New York: Continuum, 1994), 236, with quotation from Balthasar, "The Work and Suffering of Jesus," *Faith in Christ and the Worship of Christ: New Approaches to Devotion to Christ,* ed. Leo Scheffczyk, trans. Graham Harrison (San Francisco: Ignatius, 1982), 17, n. 14.

9. See, e.g., *ThDrIV,* 493-94.

10. *GloryVII,* 216.

11. *GloryVII,* 209.

12. *GloryVII,* 208.

13. Except for the women, no one wants anything to do with the condemned Christ: See "The Eye," 108; *GloryVII,* 224; and *MP,* 112-18.

14. See the texts referenced in n. 108 in Chapter Five.

15. See *ThLogII,* 294-98; Balthasar uses *hell,* not *Sheol,* here. See also *ThDrIV,* 329.

16. See *ThDrIV,* 356; "Desc," 408; *GloryVII,* 209, 224; and "The Eye," 108.

17. *GloryVII,* 216.

18. *Leben,* 40, regarding Jesus Christ and the Father, and p. 48, with respect to Him and the Holy Spirit.

19. *GloryVII,* 224. Balthasar ends the sentence with a reference to 1 Sam 24:5. This verse does not seem relevant. If he intended 1 Sam 24:4, it requires a questionable Scriptural interpretation: The unjust Saul becomes a type for Jesus whereas David becomes a type for the arch-"enemy" of God, sin.

20. Treating of Christ's abandonment "by God" in *GloryVII,* 224, Balthasar refers to Mk 9:31; 10:33; 10:45; and their parallels. The English translator has accurately rendered

Balthasar's German *preisgeben* as *abandon*, but the German does not render the Greek as closely as possible, and even less so does the English. Regarding the first two verses Balthasar references, the relevant verb in the prophecies of Mk 9:31, 10:33, and parallels (Mt 20:18, Lk 18:32; Mt 17:22, Lk 9:44) are all derived from παραδίδωμι, as are the verbs describing the prophecies' fulfillment in Jesus' being "handed over" or "delivered" by the chief priests to Pilate, and by Pilate to crucifixion (Mt 27:2, 18, 26; Mk 15:1, 10, 15; Lk 23:25; 24:20; see also Lk 21:16). None of these passages use ἐγκαταλείπω, which appears in Christ's cry of abandonment on the cross (Mt 27:46; Mk 15:34). Hence German translations of the Bible commonly render the Greek in the passages to which Balthasar refers as *überantworten*, not as *preisgeben*. Balthasar is more careful in *MP*, 107-12, where the same passages are discussed in terms of Christ's being "handed over" [*überliefert*]. Regarding Balthasar's reference to Mk 10:45, which appears in both *GloryVII* and *MP*, one observes that it does not refer either to Christ's being handed over or abandoned, but rather to His own giving up (from δίδωμι) of Himself.

21. *GloryI*, 475.

22. *GloryVII*, 148. See also p. 207.

23. *ThDrIV*, 495. See also "Death Is Swallowed," 51; "Mystery," 116; *The Christian and Anxiety*, trans. Dennis D. Martin and Michael J. Miller (San Francisco: Ignatius, 2000), 107; "Spirit and Institution," 228; and *ThDrV*, 256

24. *GloryVII*, 208.

25. *ThDrV*, 272.

26. *ThDrV*, 277, emphasis added.

27. See *GloryVII*, 216. See also "The Eye," 115-16.

28. *ThDrIII*, 530, emphasis in original.

29. An alternative reading of the text is possible: It may be a reassertion that Christ is abandoned not only with respect to His human nature, but also with respect to His divine. I think the reading about the Father experiencing reciprocal abandonment is the more correct, but the ambiguity of the context does not rule out the alternative, which is consistent with Balthasar's thought elsewhere.

30. See "The Multitude of Biblical Theologies," 93; and *ThDrV*, 516, quoting Speyr.

31. See "The Personal God," 54; "The Three Evangelical Counsels," *Elucidations*, 220; *ThDrIII*, 514, 518-19, 530, 535; *ThDrIV*, 325-29; and *ThDrV*, 327, 483, 516. See also *GloryVII*, 227. The "self-surrender of Christ" and "the Father's surrender of the Son for us" (see "Obedience," 232) should be read in light of this abandonment of the Son: It is not surrender merely as permitting something to occur (see, e.g., St. Thomas Aquinas, *ST*, IIIa, q. 47, a. 3.), but surrender as the giving away of something (see *ThDrIII*, 515-16).

32. See *ThDrV*, 263: "There must be reciprocal personal forsakenness on the part of the Father and Son." See also *ThDrIII*, 515-16; and *ThDrV*, 327, 516.

33. *ThLogII*, 294-98.

34. See, e.g., *GloryVII*, 249.

35. *GloryVII*, 249, n. 5.

36. *ThDrIV*, 325. See also Balthasar, *The Dramatis Personae: Man in God*, vol. 2, *Theo-Drama*, trans. Graham Harrison (San Francisco: Ignatius, 1990), 256, 268; this work is hereinafter referred to as *ThDrII*.

37. *ThDrV*, 91, emphases in original.

38. *ThDrV*, 92. See also *ThDrV*, 131, with use of Speyr and keeping in mind the discussion in *ThDrV*, 66-109; 512, 515, also with use of Speyr; and, in relation to the Son, *GloryVII*, 397. Balthasar himself says once that *becoming* should not be used to describe the divine life, precisely due to the implication of imperfection (*ThDrV*, 77; see also the quotation of Speyr's denial of change in God in *ThDrV*, 514), but this caution does not reflect his normal *modus operandi*, judging by the texts cited in this footnote, *inter alia*.

39. *ThDrV*, 67. Thus, the eternal Being is "an equally eternal (that is, not temporal) happening" (p. 67). See the entire extended discussion of *ThDrV*, 66-109; and also p. 120.

40. *ThDrIV*, 323-27; *ThDrV*, 245.

41. *ThDrIV*, 325-27, 331.

42. *ThDrIV*, 324.

43. *ThDrV*, 245. See also *Leben*, 69-70.

44. See *ThDrIV*, 324-26.

45. See *ThDrV*, 93-94, 98.

46. *ThDrV*, 245.

47. *ThDrV*, 98, quoting Speyr about love in the context of Trinitarian "distance."

48. "Death Is Swallowed," 51.

49. See "Meeting God," 20.

50. *ThDrIV*, 324.

51. *ThDrIV*, 332.

52. *ThDrIV*, 328.

53. *ThDrIV*, 323-33. See also *GloryVII*, 213-14, 268.

54. *ThDrIV*, 325-26, 329-31.

55. *ThDrIV*, 323, emphasis added. See also *ThDrIV*, 362; *ThDrV*, 257; "Trinity and Future," 81-82; and "The Incarnation of God," 67. Also compare "Meeting God," 20, with *GloryI*, 479-80.

56. *ThDrIV*, 325, emphasis in original.

57. *ThDrIV*, 325, emphasis in original.

58. *ThDrIV*, 324.

59. *ThDrIV*, 323.

60. *ThDrIV*, 324.

61. *ThDrIV*, 324-26, 333. See also *ThDrV*, 216, 242-46, 268; and *Th'l Anth*, 278.

62. *ThDrV*, 99. See also pp. 100, 245.

63. *ThDrV*, 100.

64. *ThDrV*, 100. See also "Trinity and Future," 81.

65. *ThDrV*, 245, emphasis in original. See also *ThDrV*, 131; and *ThDrIV*, 333.

66. Contrast St. Thomas Aquinas, *ST*, Ia q. 45, a. 6.

67. *GloryI*, 328; see also pp. 480, 613.

68. See, e.g., *ThDrV*, 327.

69. *MP*, 174.

70. See "Death Is Swallowed," 51.

71. *ThDrIV*, 324, 329.

72. See, e.g., *ThDrV*, 256-57.

73. On the Son's offer: *ThDrIV*, 500. On the Father's letting Him go: *ThDrV*, 90 (quoting Speyr).

74. Adrienne von Speyr, *The Word Becomes Flesh* (San Francisco: Ignatius, 1987), 42-43.

75. Balthasar does not give a citation for this quotation.

76. *ThDrV*, 251. Note that it is carefully said that death "as an end" is not in God. Inasmuch as God's "sacrifice of life" is eternal and without end, He may be called "the ever-dying God" just as well as "the ever-living God." See also *GloryI*, 616.

77. *ThDrIV*, 362; *ThDrV*, 261, 263; "Death Is Swallowed," 51; *GloryVII*, 214.

78. "Fragments," 268; *ThDrIII*, 186, 188; *ThDrV*, 262; *GloryVII*, 214. See also *GloryVII*, 262.

79. *GloryVII*, 234, 292; *ThDrIV*, 356, 362; *MP*, 175; *GloryI*, 323.

80. See *GloryVII*, 214.

81. *ThDrV*, 327.

82. *GloryI*, 613. See also *ThDrV*, 66, 94, 258.

83. *ThDrV*, 263. Balthasar illustrates the unity of this love in abandonment in "The Father's Vineyard," *Heart*, 87.

84. *ThDrIV*, 320, emphasis added.

85. In contrast, Karl Josef Wallner, *Gott als Eschaton: Trinitarische Dramatik als Voraussetzung göttlicher Universalität bei Hans Urs von Balthasar*, Heiligenkreuzer Studienreihe Bd. 7 (Heiligenkreuz: Heiligenkreuzer, 1992), 181-82, reads similar passages as implying that the Father and Son can never really be separated, but only appear thus in the economy. I think he is right to say they are never really separated, but we must ask *in what way*, for there are manifold ways in which the two may be said to be united, but which also preserve Balthasar's stress on the separation's reality, as I have summazized here.

86. *GloryVII*, 211.

87. *ThDrV*, 517. Compare *GloryI*, 611.

88. See the discussion of *ThDrV*, 85-88. See also "Mystery," 114-15; "Obedience," 233-34.

89. All three preceding quotations are from *ThDrV*, 86.

90. *ThDrV*, 87, emphasis in original, with use of Adrienne von Speyr, *Die Welt des Gebetes* (*The World of Prayer* [San Francisco: Ignatius, 1985]), 65.

91. *ThDrV*, 245.

92. *ThDrV*, 86-87.

93. *ThDrV*, 87.

94. *ThDrIII*, 518-19.

95. *ThDrIV*, 332.

96. *ThDrV*, 84; see also *ThDrIV*, 498; *ThDrV*, 245; *The Way of the Cross*, trans. John G. Cumming (Middlegreen, Slough, England: St. Paul, 1990), 60-61; and *Der Geist der Wahrheit*, Bd. III, *Theo-Logik* (Einsiedeln: Johannes, 1987), 222-23; but contrast *Leben*, 70. Balthasar's notion of the archetype of death being essential to God would be illustrated by his frequent reference to the "lamb slain from the beginning of the world"; see *Leben*, 52, with references to Rev 5:6, 9, 12; and 13:8.

97. See, e.g., *ThDrIV*, 331; and *ThDrV*, 76, 85, 250.

98. *ThDrV*, 255.

99. *ThDrV*, 254-55.

100. *ThDrV*, 94. See also *GloryVII*, 229.

101. *ThDrV*, 95, emphasis added. "Divine economy" means the intra-Trinitarian relations as *event*. As elsewhere throughout *ThDrV*, Balthasar refers here to the work of Speyr.

102. Oakes, *Pattern of Redemption*, 282, my emphasis; Oakes emphasizes the entire sentence.

103. On the Father's primacy, see, e.g., *CF* #19, 308, 325-26 (DS 800, 525, 1330-31).

104. The interpretation as proposed on Balthasar's behalf seems implied by Turek, *Towards a Theology*, 158-63.

105. St. Thomas, *ST*, Ia q. 28, a. 2 c.

106. Balthasar here has a reference to Speyr, *The World of Prayer*, 45.

107. Balthasar's reference here is to Speyr, *The World of Prayer*, 48.

108. Balthasar's reference here is to Speyr, *The World of Prayer*, 59. The entire block quotation is from *ThDrV*, 517.

109. The same problem is raised by Balthasar's doctrine that God is essentially free gift of self or, in his terms, love (e.g., "The Incarnation of God," 62). The only way a deduction of the Trinity can be avoided in this latter case is if revelation is necessary to know either that God is love or that love is free gift of self, which would be debatable on the ground of the philosophical position that God is the supreme good and *bonum diffusivum sui est*.

110. E.g., St. Thomas Aquinas, *ST*, Ia q. 8.

111. Brambilla, "Salvezza e redenzione," 227, expresses concern that Balthasar equivocates in his use of *kenosis* for this reason.

112. *ThDrV*, 250-52, 502, with heavy use of Speyr, but contrast *ThDrV*, 327-28. See also *Leben*, 70.

113. *ThDrV*, 314.

114. *Leben*, 70-71. Contrast *ThDrV*, 245.

115. *ThDrV*, 84; and the other texts referenced in n. 96 above. Balthasar also says (*Leben*, 70-71) that the "natürliche Tod der Geschöpfe" (the natural death of the created), but not the death of sin, has a likeness to the self-giving within the Trinity; this too is problematic: Did God make this "natural death" then, or did it enter the world through sin (Rom 5:12; see also *ThDrIV*, 120)?

116. On this forsakenness, consider *ThDrIV*, 324. On sin as death, see *MP*, 155.

117. E.g., *ThDrIV*, 333; and *ThDrV*, 245, 395.

118. *ThDrV*, 257.

119. *ThDrIV*, 362.

120. *ThDrIV*, 324.

121. *ThDrIV*, 323.

122. See *ThDrIV*, 329.

123. *ThDrIV*, 328.

124. *ThDrV*, 94.

125. *ThDrV*, 502.

126. *ThDrV*, 516.

127. *MP*, 155; *GloryVII*, 230.

128. On sin 'in' God, see also *ThLogII*, 294-98, 331; *ThDrIV*, 384; *ThDrV*, 250-68, 280-84, in particular 258, 261, 268, 283, and his n. 23; "The Incarnation of God," 67-68.

129. *MP*, 119-25; *ThDrIV*, 338-51.

130. See texts in the previous note.

131. *GloryVII*, 207; and *ThDrV*, 266 (with use of Speyr), 348-49.

132. See *ThDrIV*, 341-49; *ThDrV*, 267; and *GloryVII*, 205-7.

133. See "Fragments," 268, 275; *GloryVII*, 205.

134. See *GloryVII*, 209. See also "The Broken Sun," 71; and "The Eye," 109-11.

135. See nn. 93 and 95 in Chapter Five for texts where Balthasar denies hope and the other theological virtues to those in Sheol.

136. See, e.g., *GloryVII*, 216; and *God Question*, 133.

137. *GloryVII*, 211. See also p. 223; "The Eye," 111; "Sea," 187.

138. *GloryVII*, 204. I would suggest that in Balthasar's use of "hidden" here is an echo of "The Eye," especially p. 116. It would be difficult to believe that the *leitmotifs* throughout his theology are accidental. To gather the red thread of their themes is to unwind the labyrinth of his doctrine. Such links need not dissolve into personal hermeneutic, if their meaning is determined by the more extended expositions Balthasar provides. In the present work, I have tried to refrain from citing such links made through keywords, so that the exposition of Balthasar's thought may be more clearly seen, and with more justification, to the reader who makes use of the citations. I have also avoided founding presentations of Balthasar's thoughts and arguments upon the imaginative reflections published as *Heart*, intending references to that work by way of illustration.

139. *GloryVII*, 208.

140. *ThDrIV*, 341-44; and *GloryVII*, 206.

141. Abraham J. Heschel, *The Prophets* (New York: Harper & Row, 1955), 295.

142. *ThDrIV*, 344.

143. *ThDrIV*, 344, with reference given to Heschel, *The Prophets*, "271, cf. 234: unlike that of other gods."

144. Heschel, *The Prophets*, 231.

145. *ThDrIV*, 344.

146. See *ThDrV*, 212-46. See also *GloryVII*, 213.

147. *ThDrV*, 214-15.

148. *ThDrV*, 215-16.

149. *ThDrV*, 216-18.

150. *ThDrV*, 218.

151. *ThDrV*, 219.

152. *ThDrV*, 219-20.

153. *ThDrV*, 222. Hence it is that "God *allows* himself to be thoroughly affected by [the guilt of the world], *not only in the humanity* of Christ but also in Christ's trinitarian mission" (*ThDrIV*, 335, emphasis added). It was pointed out earlier that the Father is also 'affected' in the Descent event.

154. *ThDrV*, 221.

155. *GloryVII*, 213, emphasis added. It is noteworthy that Balthasar relies only upon his reading of Origen for his extension of πάθος to God as such in virtue of His freedom; see *ThDrV*, 221; *Th'l Anth*, 275-78. His other patristic sections draw on a larger base (if still somewhat limited, and occasionally lacking citations). Balthasar gives no indication how Origen himself integrated his views on God's πάθος of love with other assertions of his such as the following, taken from Balthasar's own anthology of Origen: "Christ suffers, but in the flesh; and he undergoes death, but this is the flesh, whose image here is the ram, as John said: 'Behold the lamb of God, who takes away the sin of the world' (Jn 1:29). But the WORD abides 'in incorruption' (cf. 1 Cor 15:42), the WORD which is Christ according to the Spirit, the im-

age of whom is Isaac" (Balthasar, *Origen: Spirit and Fire: A Thematic Anthology of His Writings*, trans. Robert J. Daly [Washington, DC: Catholic University of America Press, 1984], 134). It should also be noted that historically Origen is not counted among the authoritative Fathers; that, even if he were, a single Father's weight in the face of a differing consensus among the others is questionable; and that the text of his invoked by Balthasar in the referenced texts is open to interpretation.

156. *ThDrV*, 242. The interior quote lacks a reference. Compare *ThDrIV*, 324.

157. St. Thomas Aquinas, *ST*, Ia, q. 13, a. 6.

158. *CF* #613 (DS 300).

159. Herbert Frohnhofen, *APATHEIA TOU THEOU: Über die Affektlosigkeit Gottes in der griechischen Antike und bei den griechischsprachigen Kirchenväter bis zu Gregorios Thaumaturgos*, European University Studies, Series XXIII Theology, vol. 318 (Frankfurt: Peter Lang, 1987), 27-42. Although the speculative theological conclusions in the second half of his work are debatable, the first half of Frohnhofen's work is a very careful analysis of the ancient and early patristic sense of ἀπάθεια.

160. Frohnhofen, *APATHEIA TOU THEOU*, 48.

161. It is noteworthy that the same limitation on the patristic sense of ἀπάθεια appears in the 1981 document of the International Theological Commission, "Theology, Christology, Anthropology," section II, B, 3, although the document also has clear denials of suffering and change in God as such (e.g., section II, B, 3 and 4.1). Balthasar, who was a member of the ITC at the time, may have had a major hand in writing the patristic section. Suggestive in this regard is his lack of citation of the ITC document for the similar conclusions in *ThDrV*, 218-23, published two years later in the German original.

162. See *GloryVII*, 208.

163. See in particular *GloryVII*, 209; and *ThDrIV*, 494.

164. *GloryVII*, 245.

165. Both quotations in this sentence are from *GloryVII*, 225.

166. See "The Personal God," 54.

167. See *ThDrIV*, 319; and also "Meeting God," 20; *ThDrIV*, 243; and "The Unity of Our Lives," 122-23, which must be read in light of how Balthasar elaborates on the judgment of sin in the Person of Christ. See also the texts cited in n. 168 below.

168. On the "double love" at work in the Incarnation-Descent (either the love of Father and Son, or the love of one for the other and for the world), see *ThDrIV*, 500-1; *GloryI*, 616; *GloryVII*, 205, 207, 290-91; "Death Is Swallowed," 54; and "Our Love of Jesus Christ," *Elucidations*, 75. The "double love" for the Trinitarian other and for the world can be a 'single love' due to the correspondence between the Father's generation of the Son and His "crushing" Him, and due to the identity of the Son's procession and mission.

169. See *ThDrIV*, 500-501; "Vicarious," 422; "Our Love of Jesus Christ," 75; and *GloryI*, 475.

170. *ThDrIV*, 500, emphasis in original. The "'for' us" should be read with the full weight Balthasar gives to *pro nobis*, i.e., out of love for us, on our behalf, and in the place that was ours.

171. *ThDrIV*, 501, emphasis in original.

172. This conclusion is implicit in *ThDrV*, 265-69, and especially in *ThLogII*, 321-22. The fact that Balthasar sees creation as the proper work of the Father lies in the background here. Helmut Dieser, *Der gottähnliche Mensch und die Gottlosigkeit der Sünde: Zur Theologie*

des Descensus Christi *bei Hans Urs von Balthasar,* Trierer Theologische Studien 62 (Trier: Paulinus, 1998), 217-18, 292-95, 323, 428-30, repeatedly highlights the analogy between the filial procession and the Descent.

173. Nandkisore, *Hoffnung auf Erlösung,* 230-37.

174. See *ThDrV,* 265-69.

175. *GloryVII,* 230. See also the comparison with Job, "crushed by suffering," in "Fragments," 267.

176. *GloryVII,* 256.

177. See *GloryVII,* 260, in which "the *kabod*-momentum of the Cross of Jesus" is identified with "*kabod*-glory."

178. See Meditation #44 in Balthasar, *You Have Words,* 133-35. The metaphor of the hammer continues in Meditation #67, pp. 193-95.

179. See Balthasar, *Love Alone: The Way of Revelation,* no trans. noted (London: Sheed & Ward, 1992), 47-49. On p. 48, Balthasar points out this weight can only be endured when it is understood as love. It appears he here falls back upon the classic signification of love as desire for the good (instead of as self-gift), since his observation suggests the act of self-giving (which he otherwise considers the fundamental notion of love and which is another way to describe the Father's "crushing") would be a destructive outrage unless it aims at the good of its object.

180. The raising of Jesus is not an act of the Trinity, but a proper work of the Father on behalf of the Son, who remains passive until this point and, in the Eucharist, even after it. See, e.g., *GloryVII,* 211, 248-50, 255, 270; and "Death Is Swallowed," 54.

181. See, e.g., *GloryVII,* 250-55.

182. *GloryVII,* 255-59.

183. *GloryVII,* 260.

184. *GloryVII,* 203: "*kabod,* as the momentum of God."

185. *GloryVII,* 205.

186. *GloryVII,* 211.

187. *ThDrIV,* 325-26, 331.

188. *GloryVII,* 233, emphasis added.

189. *GloryI,* 329.

190. *GloryVII,* 269-70, emphasis added.

191. *ThDrV,* 501.

192. *GloryVII,* 398-99.

193. See "Vicarious," 422. See also *ThDrII,* 259; *ThDrIV,* 328-32; *ThDrV,* 103, 105; *GloryVII,* 396; and the concern about a "Deus ex machina" in *Leben,* 22.

194. *GloryVII,* 146.

195. *GloryVII,* 147.

196. *GloryVII,* 147. See also "Death Is Swallowed," 54; and *GloryVII,* 391.

197. On the once-beloved Father, see "The Eye," 115; on the once-loving Father, see *ThDrIV,* 344, with interior quotation from Abraham J. Heschel, *The Prophets* (New York: Harper & Row, 1955), 295: "the 'suspended love' that is anger."

198. See *GloryVII,* 209.

199. *GloryVII,* 209.

200. See *GloryVII,* 209. See also "The Broken Sun," 71; and "The Eye," 109-11.

201. See St. Thomas Aquinas, *ST,* IIIa, q. 47, a. 1 c; a. 3 c, a. 3, ad 1, 2.

Notes to Chapter Seven

1. *Credo*, 46.

2. "Desc," 412.

3. "Obedience," 235. There are many related texts: Balthasar, *A Theology of History*, no trans. noted (San Francisco: Ignatius, 1994), 29-32, is particularly clear. Other relevant passages include *ThDrII*, 646; *ThDrIII*, 201, 230, 509, 511, 516-20, 533; *ThDrIV*, 326; *ThDrV*, 63, 80-81; *GloryVII*, 397. See also *ThDrIII*, 165, 508, in relation to *ThDrI*, 252-54, 281-97, 628, 645-46.

4. "Death Is Swallowed," 52; *GloryI*, 323.

5. See "Obedience," 235-36. See also *GloryI*, 479; *GloryVII*, 214; *ThDrIII*, 183; *ThDrIV*, 494; *ThDrV*, 123, 247-48.

6. See *GloryI*, 480. See also "God Speaks as Man," *Expl I*, 92.

7. See, e.g., *ThDrII*, 267-68; *ThDrIII*, 199. See also *GloryVII*, 395-96.

8. See *GloryI*, 469. See also *GloryVII*, 468-69.

9. See *GloryI*, 474.

10. For texts linking glory and action, see *GloryVII*, 265, 269, 271, 289, 290-92, 396; *ThDrI*, 16.

11. See *GloryI*, 322-23, 327, 615, 617.

12. *GloryVII*, 211. See also *GloryI*, 323, 614-15.

13. *GloryI*, 479. See also p. 609.

14. For Balthasar's discussion of this dilemma, see *ThDrIII*, 166-72. See also p. 510. On the problem of heteronomy, see also "God Speaks as Man," 93; *ThDrIII*, 198, 225-26; "Obedience," 234.

15. *ThDrIII*, 169.

16. *ThDrIII*, 227.

17. See St. Maximus the Confessor, *The Disputation with Pyrrhus of Our Father Among the Saints, Maximus the Confessor*, trans. Joseph P. Farrell, D.Phil (Oxon).

18. *GloryVII*, 143-44.

19. *ThDrIII*, 199.

20. "God Speaks as Man," 93. See also the texts regarding heteronomy referenced in n. 14 above.

21. *ThDrIII*, 198; "Obedience," 234.

22. See *ThDrIII*, 168, 199, 516; "Fragments," 275; *ThDrV*, 95, 485-86. He is more careful in "Fragments," 268, and "Death Is Swallowed," 51, but there is still difficulty in understanding how "room" is provided "within the perfect unity of the essential will of Father, Son, and Spirit" by the "distance" between the divine Persons, as he says in "Death Is Swallowed."

23. On the Incarnation being ordered to the Descent, see, e.g., *GloryVII*, 22. See also *GloryI*, 468-75.

24. "Trinity and Future," 82-83. See the similar arguments made in "The Incarnation of God," 65-68; *ThDrIV*, 328-32. See also "Desc," 410-12; *GloryI*, 479-80; *GloryVII*, 214; "Fragments," 278; and "Meeting God," 20.

25. Another solution is possible, namely, that He gathers lost creatures anew into His immutable justice through bringing that justice into their lostness rather than bringing their God-estrangement into Himself.

26. It would seem that salvation in the mode Balthasar proposes would be similarly impossible for a three-personed God with a single will.

27. *GloryVII*, 283. See also "The Unknown God," 42; *ThDrV*, 495-96. This incomprehensibility, like His omnipotence and sovereignty, reflects His being absolute freedom; see *ThDrII*, 244.

28. See *GloryVII*, 242.

29. *GloryI*, 609, emphasis in original.

30. See *GloryVII*, 161.

31. One of Balthasar's clearest statements on the identity of the Son's procession and His mission in virtue of their kenotic character is in "Dio e il dramma del mondo," trans. Giovanni Mascetti, ed. Paola Priori, conference held in Milan 21 April 1983 by Centro Culturale San Carlo (Milan: Centro Culturale San Carlo, 1983), 16-17.

32. *ThDrV*, 120.

33. *ThDrIV*, 132, emphasis in original.

34. *GloryVII*, 143-44.

35. *ThDrV*, 257-59, 326.

36. *Credo*, 46. See also "The Self-Consciousness of Jesus," *Crown*, 319. These attributes remain with the Father during the economy (see, e.g., *ThDrV*, 328, with use of Speyr), but the Son will receive them back when the Father raises Him from being dead (see, e.g., *ThDrII*, 299). Given these two features, the English word *deposit* conveys the full significance of Balthasar's concept.

37. *Church and World*, trans. A. V. Littledale with Alexander Dru (New York: Herder & Herder, 1967), 107.

38. *Church and World*, 107. This statement directly continues the preceding quotation.

39. *GloryVII*, 213.

40. *GloryVII*, 213, emphasis added.

41. *GloryVII*, 213. Balthasar finds God's infinite freedom to be sufficient ground for the apparent resolution of his most pressing difficulties. See also n. 27 above.

42. *ThDrII*, 256. In context, Balthasar is referring to the surrender of the divine nature in the Trinitarian processions. But this surrender occurs also in the mission, because it continues the procession.

43. See *GloryI*, 616, on the fulfillment of the *bonum diffusivum sui* in the surrender of the divine love's essence; and, e.g., *GloryVII*, 391, on the nature of being as giving.

44. See *GloryVII*, 215.

45. St. Thomas Aquinas, *ST*, Ia, q. 25, a. 1 ad 1, a. 3.

46. As I infer from St. Thomas Aquinas, *ST*, Ia, q. 25, a. 1, 2, 5, and 6, together with *ST*, Ia, q. 12, a. 7, et al.

47. See *GloryVII*, 215, including Balthasar's use of Karl Barth; see also "The Incarnation of God," 67-68; "Desc," 413; "The Multitude of Biblical Theologies," 93; and *GloryVII*, 242-43.

48. For the interdependence of glory, freedom, power, abandonment, and powerlessness, see *GloryVII*, 211, 269; "Trinity and Future," 80-84; *ThDrIV*, 325-26, 331; *ThDrV*, 74; "Eschatology in Outline," *Expl IV*, 435. The interested reader would also make a good beginning by tracking Balthasar's descriptions of God as "ever-greater."

49. On God's being "ever greater," see *ThDrV*, 78-79, 509-21; more extensive references

are provided in n. 102 of Chapter 8. On His going to the "end" or the "extreme," see *GloryI*, 616; *ThDrV*, 94, 98, 326, 427; *Leben*, 34; "Desc," 413. See also "Trinity and Future," 81; *GloryVII*, 148, 248; "Meeting God," 21; *ThDrIII*, 518 (with respect to the Father); and *ThDrIV*, 495.

50. *ThDrIV*, 132.

51. *ThDrIV*, 338. See also p. 495; and *ThDrV*, 193.

52. *ThDrII*, 268. See also *GloryVII*, 160, 211; *ThDrIII*, 518-19; *ThDrIV*, 325-26.

53. *GloryI*, 670.

54. See *ThDrV*, 212-246, 257-59, 326, 513-14; and also *ThDrIII*, 226; *ThDrIV*, 324, 328; "Spirit and Institution," 233-34; "Loneliness in the Church," 273; *MP*, 208. It is thus a simplification for a more popular audience when Balthasar says explicitly, "Gewiß ist die geschaffene Welt, die da leidet, nicht Gott" [Certainly it is the created world that suffers, not God], in "Gott und das Leid," *Antwort des Glaubens* 34 (Freiburg: Informationszentrum Berufe der Kirche, 1984), 14. As he explains there (pp. 9, 11, 15), the world was made in light of the (suffering) Christ, who suffered more than all, in place of all, in order to undergird and make potentially fruitful all suffering. As we have seen, however, Christ's mission unto Sheol is His procession, the perfect expression of the Father, and the ultimate revelation of the Trinitarian life. Hence, the accommodation he makes in "Gott und das Leid" seems somewhat disingenuous when read in light of his corpus with respect to God's life as the archetype of suffering, and with respect to the Father and Son suffering mutual abandonment.

Other examples of Balthasar's ambiguous denial of suffering in God can be found in his *Das betrachtende Gebet* (Einsiedeln: Johannes, 1955), 144; and, when read in light of his developed doctrine of the Incarnation, *Th'l Anth*, 275.

55. *ThDrIII*, 533, emphasis in original. Here, I would stress "identical" also. See also the related texts in n. 3 above. Balthasar explicitly says this identification "is the main conclusion" of *ThDrIII*.

56. *ThDrIV*, 494. "Becoming" is to be taken as a continuing action, like the "eternal event" of the Trinity.

57. *GloryVII*, 397. "Becoming" is to be taken as described in the previous note.

58. Balthasar gives a footnote here: "*Theo-Drama* III, 183-202." The "Trinitarian inversion" will be discussed in the next chapter.

59. *ThDrIV*, 356, emphasis in original. See also *ThDrIV*, 361-62.

60. See "*Crucifixus etiam pro nobis*," *IKaZ Communio*, 9 (1/1980): 33-35.

61. *Th'l Anth*, 279, emphasis added. See also "Death Is Swallowed," 50.

62. *ThDrIII*, 228, with extended footnote. See also *Church and World*, 106-7, in which the Incarnation is stressed as "a real movement" by the reiteration of the Word's passing "from" the form of God "into" the form of man. Compare "Kenosis of the Church?" *Expl IV*, 138: "In the *kenosis* of the Son, it is true that his innate 'form of God' stays back with the Father, is 'left behind' with him. . . ." Note that Phil 2:6-7 does not use the terminology "from" and "to": "Who being in the form of God, thought it not robbery to be equal with God: But emptied himself, taking the form of a servant, being made in the likeness of men, and in habit found as a man."

63. See *ThDrV*, 508-9.

64. Balthasar treats the "distance" between God and creatures, and that between God

and sinful creatures, as 'less' than that between Father and Son when he uses the imagery of the former distances being taken into the latter in the Incarnation and the redemption of the world. It is not clear why the former distances are 'less' than the latter, however: On the one hand, the 'lesser' "distance" seems suggested by the analogical likeness between God and creatures (i.e., they are closer), which contrasts to the absolutely opposite relations of Father and Son; on the other hand, Father and Son are more perfectly united in the divine nature than God and creatures are through the analogy of being. Balthasar (*ThDrIV*, 380) invokes the greater dissimilitude that persists in every analogical likeness between God and creatures (DS 806) against equating the intra-Trinitarian "distance" with the "distance" between God and creatures in implicit support of the former "distance" being 'greater' than the latter. In fact, however, the conciliar text cannot help him, since it teaches that the difference between God and creatures is greater than the similarity *between the same*, making no comparison to the relations among the divine Persons.

65. *GloryVII*, 274. "Freedom" refers to the divine essence as self-surrender, and "personality" to the hypostasis of the Word. Together these two fully characterize the Son of God. Hence I have glossed the quotation with the bracketed text to bring out the significance of Balthasar's choice of words.

66. *ThDrIV*, 343, emphasis added. Contrast *ThDrV*, 266, where Balthasar, quoting Speyr, makes it explicit that Christ is not the one treading the wine press of God's wrath, but is the one *crushed* in it. The most relevant biblical texts concerning the wine press are found in Is 63:1-6 and Rev 19:15. On the cup of God's wrath, see *ThDrIV*, 338-39, 343, 345, 348.

The image of the slain Lamb is a favorite of Balthasar's. Read in light of his theology, it dramatically shows the "super-death" of the Son, i.e., His sacrifice of life in self-surrender within the Trinity. In that He *is slain*, His receptive passivity is also shown. I surmise Balthasar would take the fact that He is said to be slain "since the beginning of the world" (Rev 13:8) and not "since eternity" (as would seem to be necessary to refer the slain lamb to the Son as such) to refer to the eternal decision to create the world.

67. For the terminology of *pure relation*, see *GloryVII*, 160. On the abandonment of the divine nature, see "Mystery," 126; *GloryI*, 616; *Th'l Anth*, 284; and "And the Sea," 178.

68. *GloryVII*, 305. The context is identifying "the 'means of atonement' (Rom 3:25)." It thus makes clear that Balthasar, in calling this obedience "hypostatic," does not have in mind just the intra-Trinitarian "distance," but also the form of Jesus' existence throughout His mission, even (or especially) in Sheol.

69. *GloryVII*, 143-44.

70. See *Th'l Anth*, 279.

71. See *ThDrIV*, 325-26, 331.

72. *ThDrV*, 74: "Absolute self-giving is beyond 'power' and 'powerlessness': its ability to 'let be' embraces both."

73. See, e.g., St. Thomas Aquinas, *ST*, Ia, q. 28, in particular a. 2; q. 29, a. 4; q. 33, a. 3 ad 1.

74. Another example of division being made between the *esse* and the *ratio* of the divine relation of the Son may be seen in *Th'l Anth*, 275.

75. *GloryVII*, 160.

76. *GloryVII*, 305.

77. *Church and World*, 107.

78. See *GloryVII*, 391: "'Being = giving.'"

79. *ThDrV*, 85.

80. *ThDrV*, 86.

81. *ThDrIV*, 325.

82. As indicated in *ThDrV*, 267-68, with the revelation of the Father's "personal mystery."

83. *ThDrIII*, 518.

84. See, e.g., *ThDrIII*, 518; *ThDrV*, 516.

85. *ThDrIII*, 523. See also *ThDrIII*, 228; and *ThDrV*, 508-9.

86. *ThDrIII*, 228; see also *ThDrIII*, 523.

87. *ThDrIII*, 523.

88. *ThDrV*, 247.

89. On this "image," see *GloryI*, 613: The "personal opposition" of Father and Son "is expressed in the opposition of God and man." See also n. 64 above.

90. *ThDrII*, 268, emphasis added.

91. *ThDrII*, 256.

92. "Death Is Swallowed," 54.

93. *ThDrV*, 261, emphasis added, quoting Speyr, *Passion nach Matthäus* (Einsiedeln: Johannes, no date given), 154. See also "And the Sea," 178.

94. *ThDrV*, 262.

95. *ThDrIII*, 183-84.

96. *ThDrIII*, 186.

97. *ThDrIII*, 166.

98. See *GloryVII*, 150.

99. *ThDrIII*, 170, 172.

100. See *ThDrV*, 123; and *ThDrIII*, 182. See also Chapter Eight on the Holy Spirit.

101. *ThDrIII*, 200, 510-11, 533.

102. *ThDrIII*, 511, emphasis added.

103. "Fides," 53.

104. "Fides," 53.

105. *ThDrIII*, 194-96, 226.

106. *ThDrIII*, 182-83, 188, 196, 226-27; *ThDrV*, 124.

107. *ThDrIII*, 166. See also pp. 196; 197, n. 60.

108. *ThDrIII*, 195.

109. *ThDrIII*, 166, 227. See also *GloryVII*, 246, n. 4.

110. *ThDrIII*, 196.

111. *ThDrIII*, 196-97, including p. 197, n. 60.

112. *GloryVII*, 143.

113. *ThDrIII*, 194-96, 226. Regarding the mission as the measure of His knowledge, see also *A Theology of History*, 36-38.

114. *ThDrIII*, 166. See also pp. 182, 196-97. Jöhri, "Descensus Dei," 356-57, seems to understand Christ's knowledge and its limitation as similar to the difference between habitual and actual knowledge. If so, I am not sure this reading does justice to Balthasar's stress on the Holy Spirit's role in revealing Christ's mission to Him.

115. *ThDrIII*, 522.

116. *ThDrIII*, 171.

117. *ThDrIII*, 196-97, 511, 522.

118. See *Th'l Anth*, 246, 269. See also *ThDrIII*, 166.

119. *Th'l Anth*, 258; *ThDrIII*, 182.

120. On Jesus' not anticipating the 'hour,' see "Fides," 53; *GloryVII*, 145, 216; *ThDrIII*, 170; *ThDrIV*, 493; *ThDrV*, 325; *MP*, 93-94, 106; "The Self-Consciousness of Jesus," 317-19; *A Theology of History*, 36-40. Contrast *CF* #619/4 (DS 419), 624-26 (DS 474-76), and 651/1-3 (DS 3645-47).

121. *ThDrIII*, 170-71.

122. "Desc," 408.

123. *GloryI*, 325; *ThDrIII*, 166, 227-28; and *ThDrV*, 125-28, where, quoting from Speyr, Balthasar argues that Christ must experience growth in knowledge of His divinity if He is to provide a path for other men to participation in the divine life. In other words, in order to make a path for us, Jesus must show us the way without Himself knowing it, because we will also have to go that way without fully knowing it. Indeed, this very going without knowing (faith) is the way itself.

124. *GloryI*, 325, 328. Just how Christ comes to know His divinity through His humility is unclear. One surmises that, as a person knows himself in his acts, the acts of Christ's humility are supposed to reveal His kenotic Trinitarian personality to Him. Because His humility is the human parallel to His divine kenosis, He knows His human experience is the experience of a divine Person, and participates in the Son's divine consciousness, to the extent granted Him by the Spirit in accord with the needs of His mission. He thus intuitively experiences Himself as begotten and incarnated.

125. *ThDrIII*, 182. See also *ThDrII*, 297, and "La Chiesa e l'inferno," 65.

126. *GloryVII*, 145. See also *ThDrII*, 297; *ThDrIV*, 356-57; *Th'l Anth*, 279; "The Father's Vineyard," 87.

127. See *Leben*, 40 (quoted on the frontispiece) and 87; *ThDrIV*, 496. Even if Balthasar intends to speak only metaphorically when he says the dead Son feels the Father's hands no more (*ThDrV*, 327) and wonders if God exists ("The Eye," 110), he elsewhere makes clear the real abandonment and ignorance these metaphors are meant to represent.

128. "The Incarnation of God," 65; *GloryVII*, 143-44; *ThDrIII*, 162; *ThDrIV*, 356-57, 496; *ThLogII*, 317; "Dio e il dramma del mondo," 12; "The Broken Sun," 71; and "And the Sea," 175.

129. "Dio e il dramma del mondo," 12.

130. See texts in n. 128 above.

131. See "The Scapegoat and the Trinity," *Crown*, 84, and the texts in n. 128 above.

132. "The Self-Consciousness of Jesus," 318.

133. Balthasar, "Crucifixus etiam pro nobis," 30.

134. "Dio e il dramma del mondo," 12.

135. See *A Theology of History*, 34.

136. Kossi K. Joseph Tossou, *Streben nach Vollendung: Zur Pneumatologie im Werk Hans Urs von Balthasars* (Freiburg: Herder, 1983), 257-58.

137. "Fides," 43, 51, 53; *GloryVII*, 135-36; *ThDrIII*, 170; *ThDrV*, 272-73.

138. *ThDrIII*, 171.

139. *GloryVII*, 218.

140. "Fides," 62.

141. See *Church and World*, 61-62. See also *A Theology of History*, 42, 47-50.

142. "Fides," 43, 78.

143. See *ThDrV,* 125, with use of Speyr. See also *ThDrV,* 259.

144. *ThDrV,* 263. See also the discussion in Chapter Six of the ways in which the Son remains united to the Father despite being abandoned by Him.

145. See *ThDrV,* 495-96.

146. "Desc," 408; "The Multitude of Biblical Theologies," 98. See also the texts referenced in nn. 87 and 93 in Chapter Five. Contrast "The Self-Consciousness of Jesus," 319.

147. See *Th'l Anth,* 242-43, where Balthasar says that human fidelity involves hope: If Christ in Sheol does not have hope, because hope would contradict His sense of futility and of Sheol's timelessness, then He also could not have had faith, nor, indeed, have been faithful, i.e., obedient.

148. See *ThDrIV,* 493. See also *ThDrV,* 125-28.

149. "Fides," 50-51.

150. "Fides," 73.

151. "Fides," 43, 51, 53.

152. "Fides," 51.

153. "Fides," 51.

154. "Fides," 52, in Balthasar's use of the quotation from Romano Guardini.

155. *ThDrIII,* 171.

156. *GloryVII,* 143-44.

157. "Fides," 70. See also *GloryVII,* 145, 229; *God Question,* 133.

158. The allusion is explicit in *Does Jesus Know Us?* 23, but note that Heb 4:15 runs slightly differently, emphasis added: "For we have not a high priest who cannot have compassion on our infirmities: but one *tempted* in all things like as we are, without sin."

159. "Fides," 70; *ThDrIII,* 192, 522; "The Self-Consciousness of Jesus," 317-19. See also *ThDrV,* 127; and *A Theology of History,* 36-37.

160. "God Speaks as Man," 93. See also *ThDrIII,* 175, 196.

161. See *ThDrIII,* 171, and compare *GloryVII,* 217-18. What is said there of obedience can be said as well of faith; obedience's receptive openness to God's will and fulfillment of it parallel exactly faith's fidelity in not seeing. See *GloryVII,* 304.

162. *ThDrIII,* 198.

163. *ThDrIII,* 198.

164. *ThDrIII,* 167.

165. *GloryI,* 325.

166. *ThDrIII,* 198. See also p. 168; and "Glaube und Naherwartung," *Zuerst Gottes Reich: Zwei Skizzen zur biblischen Naherwartung,* Neue Kriterien 4 (Einsiedeln: Johannes, 2002), 13.

167. *ThDrIII,* 170.

168. "Fides," 74, emphasis in original. See also Balthasar's use of Speyr in *ThDrV,* 125-28, 258-59.

169. "Fides," 69, 73; *ThDrV,* 96-97, 485-86.

170. *ThDrII,* 258. See also *ThDrV,* 79, 486; and Balthasar's use of Speyr in *ThDrV,* 95-96.

171. *ThDrII,* 257.

172. *ThDrII,* 258.

173. *ThDrII,* 287. See also *ThDrV,* 83, 89-90, and 515 (quoting Speyr). Wallner, *Gott als*

Eschaton, 141-42, 175, explains this "surprise" as indicating that the Son (and we may extend his exposition to the Holy Spirit) is a real other and not, so to speak, a mere product intended to serve selfish ends of the Father. Here and throughout *Gott als Eschaton,* Wallner points out Balthasar's anti-Hegelian intention. This intention would also explain much of Balthasar's concern to avoid a *system* that limits God to the conclusions of finite reason. There are texts (e.g., *ThDrII,* 257, quoted above, marked by n. 171), however, that make one ask whether Balthasar's anti-scientific concern gets applied to the Trinity itself (i.e., that God's knowledge of Himself would limit Himself) and hence whether explanations such as Wallner's, helpful as they are, are perhaps not comprehensive of Balthasar's ideas. See also Wallner's discussion of God as mystery in *Gott als Eschaton,* 355-63, especially 359-60.

174. See *ThDrV,* 89-98; and *ThDrII,* 256-59, on this unpredictability and surprise in the Trinitarian love.

175. *ThDrV,* 124.

176. "Dio e il dramma del mondo," 13.

177. Balthasar says Christ has knowledge of the success of His mission and an "unshakable hope" in "The Self-Consciousness of Jesus," 319.

178. *The Christian and Anxiety,* 95-96.

179. *The Christian and Anxiety,* 107, emphasis in original.

180. *ThDrIII,* 196.

181. *ThDrIII,* 197.

182. *ThDrIII,* 522.

183. *ThDrV,* 508-9, emphasis in original; see also *ThDrIII,* 228.

184. The obstacle presented by the beatific vision as traditionally understood is explicitly mentioned by Balthasar in *MP,* 101. As for what appears in Scripture and Tradition to be the timelessly preordained or, better, foreknown events of Christ's life, Balthasar will deny it is "inherent in the real character of his existence in the world" (*A Theology of History,* 40). Nevertheless, Balthasar admits (see his reference to the work of Riedlinger in *ThDrIII,* 174) that the theology to which he objects is biblically based.

185. *ThDrV,* 514, emphasis added.

186. This statement is a direct quotation of Speyr made by Balthasar in *ThDrV,* 259. The footnote given is to her work, *Isaias* (Einsiedeln: Johannes, no date), 91-92. Balthasar expresses a similar concern himself in *GloryVII,* 223. In the context of Balthasar's thought, "human suffering" includes the penalty mankind would have had to suffer if Christ had not undergone the *visio mortis* in Sheol. The concern in this quotation about "suffering to the limit" illustrates Balthasar's emphasis on the quantitative nature of Christ's suffering. Whether Speyr thinks likewise is a question outside the present scope, which aims to present his thought, and not to determine whether his use of Speyr is faithful to the context of her corpus.

187. "Some Points of Eschatology," 264.

188. "Some Points of Eschatology," 264, n. 20.

189. *GloryVII,* 216.

190. *GloryVII,* 229.

191. *ThDrIII,* 195.

192. *ThDrIII,* 200. Balthasar will later assert, "The Spirit does not prevent the Son from receiving his mission directly but makes it possible for him to receive it obediently" (*ThDrIII,* 522). The Son receives His mission "directly" from the Father insofar as He is always immedi-

ately generated by Him; after all, the mission is the procession. "His *awareness* of his mission is only indirect" (p. 200, emphasis added) in that Jesus knows His mission, *and His procession*, only to the (always limited) extent that the Spirit mediates this self- and mission-consciousness to Him — and sometimes the mission requires that He be ignorant of it. Such utter dependence on the Spirit, even for self-knowledge, manifests His utter kenotic receptivity.

193. *God Question,* 133, emphasis added.

194. *GloryI,* 329.

195. *ThDrV,* 123.

196. *ThDrV,* 123.

197. *ThDrV,* 124.

198. *ThDrV,* 124.

199. *ThDrV,* 123.

200. *ThDrV,* 124. After the comma, Balthasar gives a reference to Speyr, *The Letter to the Ephesians* (San Francisco: Ignatius, 1996), 61. For the quotation of the word "faith," he gives a citation to Speyr, *Katholische Briefe,* vol. 1 (Einsiedeln: Johannes, no date), 140, and to "radiant faith" from Speyr, *The Passion from Within* (San Francisco: Ignatius, 1998), 17.

201. On the loss of His understanding of His self-identity, see *Leben,* 40, 87; and *ThDrIV,* 496.

202. *GloryVII,* 223. See also *ThDrV,* 140.

203. See especially "The Father's Vineyard," 87; "The Eye," 109-10, 115; and *ThDrIV,* 356-57.

204. *GloryVII,* 143. Balthasar is here speaking in general of the Word's existence in the flesh; hence, what he says applies also to the particular case of His abandoning the divine knowledge, a kenosis which characterizes His incarnation.

205. *ThDrIII,* 166.

206. *ThDrIII,* 172; see also pp. 166, 192, 195.

207. *ThDrIII,* 166. It is in light of passages such as this one and the others discussed in this exposition of Balthasar's Christology that apparent contradictions (e.g., *ThDrV,* 513) are to be taken, as evident from the wider context Balthasar provides (e.g., *ThDrV,* 514).

208. *ThDrIII,* 168, emphasis added.

209. *ThDrIII,* 168, emphasis added.

210. See "Beyond Contemplation and Action?" *Expl IV,* 302.

211. *ThDrV,* 255, emphasis in original.

212. *ThDrV,* 254; see also p. 268.

213. *ThDrV,* 254-55.

214. *ThDrV,* 254-55. See also the texts referenced in n. 202 above.

215. *ThDrV,* 254. In arguing for a sort of co-penetration between joy and pain (*ThDrV,* 253-54), Balthasar fails to take adequate account of the role of time and of the order between joy and pain in the examples he brings forward. His examples all fall into one of two categories: either they relate to the temporal replacement of pain by joy, or they touch on the simultaneity of joy with pain *despite* (and not because of) the painful situation.

216. *GloryVII,* 209, 216.

217. St. Thomas Aquinas, *ST,* IIIa q. 34, a. 4; q. 46, a. 8.

218. St. Thomas Aquinas, *ST,* IIIa q. 10, a. 1.

219. St. Thomas Aquinas, *ST,* IIIa q. 10, a. 2.

220. *ThDrIII*, 195, with citation "'Baptême et esprit' in *Lumen vitae* 16 (March 26, 1956), 95-96."

221. *CF* #2305 (DS 1000).

222. *GloryI*, 326.

223. *GloryI*, 325.

224. *GloryVII*, 291.

225. *ThDrV*, 425. See also pp. 402-10, which provides context and implicitly introduces a contrast between "eternal life" and the beatific vision. See also *GloryI*, 330: As His disciples, in whom Christ lives, cannot experience ministry to God as "an object of self-gratifying contemplation" because such ministry is a selfless "service even unto death on the Cross," it is implied neither should Christ Himself.

226. See also *Leben*, 42; and *ThDrV*, 402-10.

227. *ThDrV*, 486.

228. See *ThDrV*, 402-10, especially 404.

229. See *ThDrV*, 96-97.

230. Certain limits are placed upon this freedom, however: The utter self-surrender in the Trinitarian processions occurs without "inbuilt securities or guarantees," but is prevented from being "an absolute 'risk'" by the "eternal infinite gratitude" of the Person proceeding (*ThDrV*, 245), while finite freedom "is bound — precisely because it is oriented to the Prototype and Origin of all freedom — to assimilate itself to whatever decisions are uttered by the triune God" (p. 485). These boundaries on the exercise of infinite and finite freedom are necessitated by two *a priori* commitments, namely, to prevent sin from being "a possibility in the Son's relationship with the Father" (p. 502) while maintaining the possibility that sin and redemption exist at all and are to be identified with the rejection of God's will or assimilation to it. With respect to the denial of sin in God, other principles of Balthasar's theology make it difficult for him to maintain this position, as will be seen.

231. See the texts referenced earlier in nn. 169-174 above concerning surprise among the divine Persons. See also *Dare*, 130-33, but we note that it is misleading of Balthasar there to use St. Irenaeus to represent "the Thomistic teaching that we will never have a comprehensive vision of God." As Balthasar presents him, St. Irenaeus thought the blessed (NB, not the divine Persons, as Balthasar himself suggests in his corpus) would have a progression in knowledge in heaven, but this is not St. Thomas's view. Contrast *ST*, Ia, q. 7, 10.

232. *GloryI*, 328.

233. *GloryI*, 328, n. 141. On the basis of this text, we could question Balthasar's use of a human psychology of prayer (*ThDrIII*, 510-11) to characterize Jesus' experience of prayer.

234. *ThDrIII*, 196. See also *ThDrV*, 501. This argument also takes the form of "unless a child is awakened to I-consciousness through the instrumentality of a Thou, it cannot become a human child at all" (*ThDrIII*, 175). Balthasar is arguing for ignorance in Christ; the latent concern is Christ's perfect knowledge, hence His beatific vision. This anthropological argument is the only objection Balthasar brings to bear against his own admission that the traditional doctrine of Christ's beatific vision is solidly based in Scripture, and runs from there through the patristic and scholastic periods; see his treatment and use of H. Riedlinger's work in *ThDrIII*, 174. Balthasar's citations are to Riedlinger, "*Geschichtlichkeit und Vollendung des Wissens Christi*, QD 32 (Herder, 1966)," 58-71, 65 (note), 148-53. Contrary to Balthasar's conclusion, one could argue that if Christ had the beatific vision from His con-

ception, He as a human child could be "awakened" by the "Thou" of the Father, with whom He as man would be in a knowing and loving personal relationship through that very vision. Balthasar himself has recourse to the relationship between the Father and Jesus as His Son that exists from His conception in order to prevent Jesus coming to know He was God, which would contradict His unity with the Father and the unity of His own consciousness.

235. *Does Jesus Know Us?* 36.

236. *Does Jesus Know Us?* 36.

237. *Does Jesus Know Us?* 36.

238. See *Does Jesus Know Us?* 40.

239. *Does Jesus Know Us?* 38.

240. See the texts referenced in n. 157 above, and also Balthasar, "Ist der Gekreuzigte >>selig<<?" *IKaZ Communio* 16 (1987): 108-9.

241. "Fides," 70.

242. *Does Jesus Know Us?* 38.

243. *Does Jesus Know Us?* 38.

244. *MP,* 72-75. Though Balthasar discusses the suffering of abandonment in connection with Christ's agony in the garden, this context does not prevent application of what he says there to the Crucifixion and the Descent, since these latter mysteries are intensifications of the abandonment Balthasar sees in the garden; see *MP,* 72. St. Thomas Aquinas differs from Balthasar in his understanding of God's "turn" from the sinner: God would be said to turn from a sinner only in that the sinner turns away from God. See St. Thomas Aquinas, *ST,* IaIIae q. 79, a. 1 ad 1; q. 79, a. 3 and 4; IIaIIae q. 24, a. 10.

245. *MP,* 73-75.

246. The content of this sentence, with its quotations, is from *MP,* 75.

247. *Does Jesus Know Us?* 33.

248. See Hans Urs von Balthasar, *The Way of the Cross,* trans. John G. Cumming (Middlegreen, Slough, England: St. Paul, 1990), 52.

249. *Does Jesus Know Us?* 33, emphasis added. See also *ThDrV,* 261: "On the Cross, God's final judgment is pronounced upon this sin [i.e., "the whole reality of the world's sin"], which the Son now embodies (*cf.* 2 Cor 5:21)." See also *Does Jesus Know Us?* 32, and Balthasar's admiring exposition of Luther on this topic in *ThDrIV,* 284-85.

250. *MP,* 72.

251. *MP,* 74.

252. On the 'dark night' as a "descent into hell," see *God Question,* 134; *ThDrV,* 308; *Does Jesus Know Us?* 37-38.

253. *Does Jesus Know Us?* 38.

254. *MP,* 79. Contrast *God Question,* 134.

255. See in particular those texts where Balthasar gives specific examples, e.g., *MP,* 71-79; *ThDrV,* 308-14, especially n. 21; *Dare,* 106-22; "Short Discourse," 204-18; *Does Jesus Know Us?* 37-38. Not all the features mentioned here are present in each case. *God Question,* 134-35, is an informative summary.

256. *MP,* 77.

257. *Does Jesus Know Us?* 3; *MP,* 78; "Short Discourse," 216.

258. Direct quotation of Speyr, *Isaias* (Einsiedeln: Johannes, no date), 91-92, made by Balthasar in *ThDrV,* 259. See also *GloryVII,* 223.

259. See St. Thomas Aquinas, *ST,* IIIa q. 46, a. 7.

260. Reginald Garrigou-Lagrange, *Our Savior and His Love for Us,* trans. A. Bouchard (London: B. Herder, 1951), 271.

261. See St. Thomas Aquinas, *ST,* IIIa q. 14, a. 1 ad 2. That it did not, shows His love.

262. Ott, *Fundamentals,* 164, with reference to St. Thomas Aquinas, *ST,* IIIa q. 46, a. 8.

263. St. John Damascene, *De fide orthodoxa,* iii, quoted in St. Thomas Aquinas, *ST,* IIIa q. 46, a. 6. See also *ST,* IIIa q. 46, a. 8 ad 2; and St. Maximus the Confessor, *Disputation with Pyrrhus,* 72.

264. See "Ist der Gekreuzigte >>selig<<?," 108-9.

265. "Ist der Gekreuzigte >>selig<<?," 108.

266. On the fulfillment of one power at the same time as another suffers, see St. Thomas Aquinas, *ST,* IIIa q. 46, a. 8 ad 1. Consider also *ST,* IaIIae q. 23, a. 2.

267. *MP,* 108, 138.

268. See *Glory VII,* 217-18.

269. *MP,* 137. Contrast the bull *Unigenitus Dei Filius, CF* #643 (DS 1025), seen earlier in Chapter Four, in which Pope Clement VI says, "A drop of His blood . . . would have sufficed for the redemption of the whole human race because of the union with the Word."

270. St. Thomas Aquinas, *ST,* IIIa q. 46, a. 3.

271. St. Thomas Aquinas, *ST,* IIIa q. 46, a. 6.

272. St. Thomas Aquinas, *ST,* IIIa q. 46, a. 5.

273. See St. Thomas Aquinas, *ST* IIIa, q. 9, a. 3 ad 2.

274. *Does Jesus Know Us?* 23.

275. *CF* #614 (DS 301).

276. See St. Thomas Aquinas, *ST,* IIIa, q. 10, a. 1, 2.

277. St. Thomas Aquinas, *ST,* IIIa q. 46, a. 6 ad 3.

278. St. John of the Cross, *Ascent of Mt. Carmel,* trans. Kieran Kavanaugh and Otilio Rodriguez, in *The Collected Works of St. John of the Cross* (Washington, DC: ICS, 1979), I.2.1.

279. St. John of the Cross, *Ascent of Mt. Carmel,* I.2.1, II.3.1, II.8.6, II.9, etc.

280. St. John of the Cross, *Ascent of Mt. Carmel,* II.9.

281. See, e.g., St. John of the Cross, *Ascent of Mt. Carmel,* III.1.1.

282. See John Paul II, *Novo millennio ineunte,* #26-27.

283. Bennet Kelley, *Spiritual Direction According to St. Paul of the Cross* (New York: Alba House, 1993), 42-45. Given that the charism of the Passionists, the community founded by St. Paul of the Cross, is to renew within themselves Christ's Passion, St. Paul's spiritual direction seems particularly relevant to the context of the present work.

284. John Paul II, *Novo millennio ineunte,* #26.

285. John Paul II, *Novo millennio ineunte,* #27, quoting St. Catherine of Siena, *Dialogue of Divine Providence,* with citation, "Cf. n. 78."

286. John Paul II, *Novo millennio ineunte,* #27, quoting St. Thérèse of Lisieux, with citation, "*Last Conversations.* Yellow Booklet (July 6, 1897): *Œuvres complètes* (Paris, 1996), p. 1025."

287. St. Thomas Aquinas, *ST,* IaIIae, q. 67, a. 2 c.

288. See St. Thomas Aquinas, *ST,* Ia q. 3, a. 7; q. 14, a. 4; q. 28, a. 2; and q. 29, a. 4.

289. Pope Pius XII, Encyclical Letter *Sempiternus Rex* (1951), #29, reproduced in *CF* #662.

290. *CF* #611 (DS 293).

291. Rothkranz, *Die Kardinalfehler,* 190-91, similarly objects to the Son's "depositing," noting the division introduced within the divine omniscience in general, between the divine knowledge and the divine essence, and between the Son's knowledge (and essence) and the Father's.

292. As seen earlier, but see also, e.g., "Trinity and Future," 84; and "The Three Evangelical Counsels," 220.

293. *GloryVII,* 129-42. See also *Church and World,* 61-62, regarding the Christ-ian form of life.

294. "Desc," 412.

295. See *GloryVII,* 141, 147.

296. See *GloryVII,* 142.

297. See *GloryVII,* 143. See also *GloryVII,* 208; and *MP,* 107-19.

298. *GloryVII,* 150; *ThDrI,* 375-77; *ThDrIV,* 489-92, 497-98.

299. *GloryVII,* 147.

300. *GloryVII,* 291.

301. *GloryVII,* 211.

302. *ThDrI,* 375-77; *ThDrIV,* 487-503, especially 489, 494, and 497-98.

303. *GloryVII,* 148.

304. This quotation is an example of the difficulties raised for Balthasar's reader by his use of quotation marks. Here they are intended to indicate a paraphrase, but the reader could be misled into thinking otherwise, because the same marks are used also for direct quotations.

305. Greek texts from the New Testament are taken from *The Greek New Testament,* 4th ed., ed. Kurt Aland, Matthew Black, Carlo M. Martini, Bruce M. Metzger, and Allen Wikgren, in cooperation with the Institute for New Testament Textual Research (Stuttgart: Deutsche Bibelgesellschaft, 1994), in *Bibleworks 95/NT release,* Version 4.0.026e (3549) CD-ROM. Bibleworks, 1998.

306. *ThDrII,* 256.

307. "Desc," 411-12, emphasis in original.

308. Hans Urs von Balthasar, "Abstieg zur Hölle," *Pneuma und Institution,* bd. IV, *Skizzen zur Theologie* (Einsiedeln: Johannes, 1974), 397.

309. *Duden Oxford Kompaktwörterbuch Englisch,* 1992 ed., s.v. "entblößen."

310. *Duden Oxford Kompaktwörterbuch Englisch,* 1992 ed., s.v. "entblößen."

311. "Stripping away," as opposed to just *stripping,* is the reasonable translation into English here. If the Logos strips itself, we must ask, "Of what?" Balthasar has answered clearly by saying "Jesus has gone to the end of his being man and his having been man." "Stripping away" makes clear in English that the genitive that follows is objective, rather than subjective.

312. It may be that Balthasar was inclined to this conclusion not only by his view of the divine essence as self-gift, but also by extending the idea that Christ was no longer man after His death to the position that He was then no longer human: If one comes to the end of one's having become man (or having become human; the German admits both), one is no longer man (or human). But this extension would be in error, since it is not essential to human nature that the soul and body be united. Otherwise man would be naturally immortal in his body as well as in his soul. Thus, though Christ may be said not to be a man after His death,

yet He is still human, for both the body and soul remained subsisting in the Person of the Word. After all, the Son of God takes on a human nature, not a man, in the Incarnation, and the Incarnation was not interrupted by Christ's death.

313. See texts referenced in n. 49 above.

314. *GloryVII*, 150.

315. "Desc," 412.

316. "Desc," 411, my corrected translation. I wish here to note *ThLogII*, 323, where Balthasar says something that apparently both contradicts and confirms the foregoing presentation. He writes there that Christ can only be obedient in Sheol, "als reine «Funktion», wobei der Sohn sosehr bloßer Mensch wird, daß sein menschlicher Gehorsam nur noch von seinem göttlichen her erklärbar ist" [as pure 'function,' such that, however much the Son might be mere man, His human obedience is still only explicable from His divine obedience]. The interior quotation is from Speyr, *Kreuz und Hölle*, 215, and Balthasar gives a footnote at the end of the sentence with an additional quotation from the same page. The point of confirmation is that the only explanation for Christ's obedience in Sheol is His divinity, i.e., His Trinitarian personality (already suggested by "pure 'function'"). The point of apparent contradiction is that the Son is referenced as "mere man" ("bloßer Mensch"). This description should be taken in reference to the Son's "depositing" of divine attributes in order to become man, and not as an increased emphasis on His human nature in the Descent event; the latter interpretation is ruled out by Balthasar's having explained Christ's redemptive obedience with His divinity. As we will say later, the Son passes *through* human nature on His way back to the Father via Sheol.

I note here also the differing interpretation of the same passage made by Rothkranz, *Die Kardinalfehler*, 285-86. He rightly understands it to indicate the end of the hypostatic union, but sees the result as Jesus being only man in His descent, i.e., some other person than the Son. The difference in our two interpretations stems from the fact that Rothkranz treats it in a context concerning the *soul* of Christ and *its* descent (pp. 275-84), whereas I have followed the passage from the wider perspective of Balthasar's Christology, in which he avoids speaking about Christ's distinct natures or about the separation of body and soul in death, preferring instead to treat of the Descent of the *Son*. Consequently, I think Rothkranz misinterprets Balthasar on this point.

317. *GloryI*, 673.

318. *GloryI*, 673. Compare *ThDrV*, 495-96.

319. *GloryI*, 673.

320. "Death Is Swallowed," 50.

321. *GloryVII*, 223.

322. *GloryVII*, 231, with German inserted from Balthasar, *Neuer Bund*, bd. III *Theologie*, teil 2, *Herrlichkeit, Eine theologische Ästhetik* (Einsiedeln: Johannes, 1969), 214. At the end of the last sentence, Balthasar gives a footnote: "On this terminology, *cf.* P. Althaus, 'Das Kreuz Christi,' in: *Theologische Aufsätze* I (1929), p. 41."

323. *GloryVII*, 231.

324. *GloryVII*, 211.

325. "Desc," 411.

326. *MP*, 149.

327. Balthasar, *Apokalypse der deutschen Seele: Studien zu einer Lehre von letzten*

Haltungen. Bd. 1. Der deutsche Idealismus (Einsiedeln: Johannes, 1998), 335: "ein Schritt, ein Fall durch die Höllentiefe hindurch in den Vaterschoß."

328. Pyc, *L'obbedienza,* 79, 93 (Pyc's references to Balthasar are here omitted): "Gesù è anzitutto colui che è stato consegnato da Dio, gli uomini invece sono solo strumenti all'interno di questo agire di Dio. . . . Dio lo spinge in braccio alle potenze della corruzione. . . . Si rivela davanti a noi una supertragedia di estremo abbandono di Dio, di caduta nell'inferno della perdizione di Dio. Da una parte il Padre, che fa cadere il Figlio nell'abisso dell'inferno . . . , e, dall'altra, il Figlio che, spinto dallo Spirito, si lascia cadere in questo abisso senza fondo, si rimette nelle mani del Padre. . . ."

329. "Death Is Swallowed," 50.

330. *Glory VII,* 223. See also "Mystery," 126.

331. *Leben,* 36.

332. See references in n. 136 in Chapter Five.

333. "Desc," 411.

334. "Desc," 411, emphasis added. See also p. 410.

335. *God Question,* 133. See also the texts referenced in n. 136 in Chapter Five; "Desc," 408-9, 411; *MP,* 173; *ThDrIV,* 337-38, 349; et al.

336. "Desc," 411.

337. The Son is God also in relation to the Holy Spirit, but observe that He is not alienated from Him, because, according to Balthasar's theology, the Holy Spirit functions as the bond of love both in the Trinity and in the Descent.

338. "Desc," 413. See also *ThDrIV,* 320, 335-36.

339. "Vicarious," 416.

340. "Desc," 412.

341. See "Desc," 409. See also "The Incarnation of God," 67-68.

342. *ThDrIV,* 336.

343. *ThDrV,* 513-14.

344. See "The Incarnation of God," 67-68.

345. *Glory VII,* 391.

346. See *Glory VII,* 146-47.

347. Consider the formula of Chalcedon, *CF* #615 (DS 302).

348. "Desc," 412, emphasis added.

349. "Death Is Swallowed," 54: In the Resurrection, "the Son receives himself — with body and soul, with divinity and humanity — back from the Father."

350. *Leben,* 51: "in sein göttliches Leben." See also *ThDrV,* 330.

351. See the use of Speyr in *ThDrV,* 513-14. See also n. 35 above.

352. See *ThDrIV,* 336, 366. See also *ThDrV,* 301-2, 513-14.

353. See *ThDrV,* 328, n. 18, with use of Speyr.

354. See "Beyond Contemplation and Action?" 302; and compare *ThDrIII,* 168.

355. "Death Is Swallowed," 50.

356. *Glory VII,* 231.

357. *Glory VII,* 283; *ThDrV,* 267.

358. "Desc," 407.

359. "Desc," 414. In this essay Balthasar sets the Catholic Tradition concerning the Descent within the context of pagan and apocryphal myths. Not to mention his neglect of im-

portant differences and his representation of the Catholic Tradition largely with Christian apocrypha, the fact that Balthasar has in view with this "folk myths" primarily the traditional doctrine rather than the pagan myths is clear from the shifts in focus toward the Catholic Tradition on pp. 405, 407, and his statement that, with his proposal, "the false triumphalism of the early Christian (and in fact of almost all of the theology of the *descensus*) is both overcome as well as critically distinguished . . ." (p. 411).

360. "Desc," 405.

361. "Desc," 412.

362. *GloryVII*, 150. See also pp. 142-61, 202, 207; *ThDrIV*, 489; and "And the Sea," 176. Other texts to be considered include those that refer to the Word's becoming a "not-word," such as *GloryVII*, 143, 202, 234; texts regarding His "self-alienation," e.g., "Desc," 409, 411; and texts that refer to the "wordless" or "silent" character of His descent, such as *Th'l Anth*, 283-84.

363. *ThDrIII*, 530.

364. See *ThDrIV*, 325.

365. See *ThDrV*, 310.

366. "Desc," 409.

367. *GloryVII*, 160.

368. *GloryI*, 616.

369. *ThDrIV*, 489, emphasis in original.

370. In regard to the foregoing briefest of summaries of elements of Balthasar's understanding of death, see *ThDrI*, "The Theme of Death," 369-413; and *ThDrIV*, "A Duel between Two Deaths," 487-503. The latter is an application of the former to the death of Christ. Curiously absent from Balthasar's treatments of death is an adequate analysis of the act of suicide and its sterility.

371. See *Leben*, 24-27.

372. *ThDrIV*, 491-92.

373. *ThDrIV*, 493; *GloryVII*, 229.

374. See "The Incarnation of God," 65; *GloryVII*, 143-44; *ThDrIV*, 356-57; "The Broken Sun," 71; "And the Sea," 175.

375. *ThDrIV*, 493. On Jesus' not anticipating the hour, see "Fides," 53; *GloryVII*, 145, 216; *ThDrIII*, 170; and *ThDrV*, 325.

376. See *MP*, 100-5; *ThDrIV*, 335, 345; and "The Eye," 104-16.

377. "Death Is Swallowed," 50. See also *Th'l Anth*, 279.

378. See, e.g., "Desc," 411; *MP*, 149, 160-61, 164, 168; and *ThDrIV*, 348.

379. *ThDrIV*, 487.

380. See *ThDrIV*, 491-93.

381. See "The Incarnation of God," 65, 68; *ThDrV*, 276, 327.

382. *ThDrIV*, 132. See also *GloryVII*, 397; *Leben*, 70; and see also Balthasar, "Der Mensch und das ewige Leben III: Der Auferstandene: Das Seligwerden des Leidens," *Konradsblatt Wochenzeitung f.d. Erzbistum Freiburg*, 56 (April 23, 1972) 17: 5.

383. *MP*, 155. Rom 14:9: "For to this end Christ died and lived again, that he might be Lord both of the dead and of the living." They are also not to be distinguished in 1 Pet 3:18-20. The echoes of this lack of distinction are also to be heard in "Meeting God," 20: Jesus Christ

"gives his life for my eternal salvation, and by dying buries what was evil in me with himself in hell. 'In this we have come to know his love, that he laid down his life for us . . .' (1 Jn 3:16)."

384. *ThDrIV*, 493; see also p. 495. His obedience, and hence His death, is "qualitatively different" from that of other free creatures; see *GloryVII*, 217-18, 304. It is conformity to sin-in-itself in virtue of the Son's divinity.

385. *ThDrIV*, 498.

386. *GloryI*, 470.

387. "Der Mensch und das ewige Leben III," 5: "Jenseits von Tod und Hölle — das heißt von endgültiger Gottferne — taucht er mit diesen Wundmalen im Licht auf. Das Ausgangslose hat einen Ausgang. Und nicht nur das: das Ausgangslose . . . , erweist sich am Ende gerade als der Weg. . . . Die Gestalt des Nein, das Leiden, durch ein tieferes Ja zu untergreifen und zu einem Ausdruck der Liebe umzuwerten."

388. *ThDrIV*, 489, emphasis added.

389. See *ThDrIV*, 494-98; *ThDrV*, 500-502.

390. *ThDrIV*, 495. See also *MP*, 174.

391. See *ThDrV*, 139. See also *GloryVII*, 305-6; and *ThDrIV*, 495.

392. See "Vicarious," 421-22.

393. *ThDrIV*, 500.

394. See *ThDrV*, 314. See also "Only If," 136-42.

395. *ThDrIV*, 487.

396. *ThDrIV*, 495.

397. *ThDrIV*, 494-95.

398. *ThDrIV*, 498. See also the contrast made by Nandkisore, *Hoffnung auf Erlösung*, 234, between self-gift and Christ's suffering God-abandonment in Sheol.

399. *GloryVII*, 208, emphasis only on "not" in original, other emphases added.

400. "Vicarious," 421-22.

401. "Vicarious," 421-22.

402. *Th'l Anth*, 117.

403. *ThDrIV*, 487.

404. *ThDrIV*, 495, emphasis added. See also *GloryVII*, 216; ThDrV, 272, 277; *God Question*, 133.

405. *ThDrIV*, 492-93.

406. *ThDrV*, 251, quoting Speyr.

407. This comes out explicitly in what follows the extended quotation above; see *ThDrIV*, 495-98.

408. See, e.g., *ThDrV*, 311-14.

409. *ThDrIV*, 494, emphasis in original, with paragraph break before final sentence.

410. *MP*, 137. Contrast the bull *Unigenitus Dei Filius*, *CF* #643 (DS 1025), seen earlier in Chapter Four, in which Pope Clement VI says, "A drop of His blood . . . would have sufficed for the redemption of the whole human race because of the union with the Word."

411. *GloryVII*, 208.

412. *GloryVII*, 305.

413. *ThDrIV*, 493, emphasis added.

414. *MP*, 165.

415. *ThDrV*, 123.

416. See the relevant section in Chapter Six for details on the Father's abandonment of the Son. For abandonment by men, see *GloryVII*, 224-26; *MP*, 100-119; "The Eye," 108. See also "Loneliness in the Church," 271: "One man, 'for the sake of the many,' becomes the ultimate individual of all, utterly abandoned by God and man alike." The faithfulness of Mary is overlooked in these passages.

417. "The Absences of Jesus," *New Elucidations*, 56; *ThDrIV*, 356-57, 501.

418. See *GloryVII*, 208, 231.

419. See "The Incarnation of God," 62, 67; "The Personal God," 54; "Meeting God," 20; *GloryI*, 616; *GloryVII*, 278, 391, 393; *ThDrI*, 18; *ThDrII*, 205, 256, 286; and *ThDrV*, 82-85, 245, 326-28, 521.

420. See *GloryI*, 605-6, 614; *GloryVII*, 213, 278, 391; "Preliminary Remarks on the Discernment of Spirits," *Expl IV*, 340.

421. *GloryI*, 479, 613; *GloryVII*, 208-9, 211, 223, 290-91, 262; "Mystery," 126.

422. *GloryVII*, 282-83.

423. See *Th'l Anth*, 275.

424. See *ThDrV*, 90, 255.

425. *ThDrIII*, 518-19.

426. *ThDrIII*, 163-229, with explicit statements on, e.g., pp. 187, 224; see also *Leben* 33-34.

427. *ThDrIII*, 226.

428. See *GloryI*, 609.

429. *ThLogII*, 288.

430. See Nandkisore, *Hoffnung auf Erlösung*, 236. The anthropomorphic petulancy of requiring such a guarantee calls into question the infinitude and self-sufficiency of God.

431. Here, I build upon the insightful treatment of Nandkisore, *Hoffnung auf Erlösung*, 235-37, who succinctly sets forth the connection Balthasar makes between creation, redemption's guarantee, and the Descent as an induction of Christ into the personal mystery of the Father.

432. On this "reserved" darkness, which is the Father's "personal mystery," see *ThDrV*, 265-69.

433. See, e.g., *ThDrI*, 18; and also Balthasar, *My Work: In Retrospect*, no trans. noted (San Francisco: Ignatius, 1993), 114-17.

434. See, e.g., Aidan Nichols, *Introduction to Hans Urs von Balthasar: No Bloodless Myth: A Guide Through Balthasar's Dramatics* (Washington, DC: Catholic University of America, 2000), 212, 215.

435. See also n. 3 above.

436. St. Thomas Aquinas, *ST*, Ia q. 43, a. 2.

437. Anne Hunt, *The Trinity and the Paschal Mystery: A Development in Recent Catholic Theology*, New Theological Studies 5 (Collegeville, MN: Liturgical Press, 1997), 86.

438. Hunt, *The Trinity and the Paschal Mystery*, 81.

439. St. Thomas Aquinas, *ST*, IIIa, q. 16, a. 6 ad 2.

440. *GloryI*, 327, emphasis added. See also *Das betrachtende Gebet*, 144.

Notes to Chapter Eight

1. "The Incarnation of God," 67. See also *GloryI*, 613.

2. *GloryVII*, 205-6.

3. *GloryVII*, 206.

4. See *ThDrV*, 262.

5. *GloryVII*, 291, with footnote, "On this, and on the formulae of mutual indwelling, *cf.* F. Mussner, ZΩH [*Die Anschauung vom 'Leben' im vierten Evangelium*, in: Münch. Theol. St. I, 5 (1952)], pp. 151ff."

6. *ThDrIII*, 511; *ThDrII*, 256; *ThDrIV*, 320, 324, 326, 329; *ThDrV*, 245; "The Holy Spirit as Love," 126-28. See also *GloryVII*, 263; and "God Is 'Being With,'" *Crown*, 144. Compare *ThDrIII*, 526, for a general description of the "we" that is the transcendent fruit of an "I" and a "thou." See also Kossi K. Joseph Tossou, *Streben nach Vollendung: Zur Pneumatologie im Werk Hans Urs von Balthasars* (Freiburg: Herder, 1983), 326-28.

7. *ThDrIV*, 326.

8. *GloryVII*, 291.

9. *GloryVII*, 395.

10. Tossou, *Streben nach Vollendung*, 316, 322. See also Wallner, *Gott als Eschaton*, 179.

11. *GloryVII*, 291; see also p. 394 with its like emphasis on participation.

12. *GloryVII*, 390-99.

13. *ThDrV*, 91. Balthasar emphasizes "event" in the original.

14. *GloryVII*, 267, emphasis added. Balthasar gives a reference to "J. Huby, *Mystiques johannique et paulinienne* (1946)."

15. All three foregoing terms are from *ThDrIV*, 324. On the Holy Spirit as "seal," see also Balthasar, "Reflections on the Discernment of Spirits," *Communio ICR* 7 (1980): 200. On the Spirit as the "bond" between Father and Son, see "Trinity and Future," 82.

16. *ThDrIV*, 333.

17. See *ThDrV*, 96-98; see also nn. 170-174 in Chapter Seven regarding surprise within the Godhead. Compare *ThDrV*, 105.

18. See "Dio e il dramma del mondo," 16.

19. Wallner, *Gott als Eschaton*, 200-203.

20. *GloryVII*, 391.

21. *ThDrII*, 286, emphasis added.

22. On the eternal unity of Father and Son in the Holy Spirit, see *ThDrII*, 286-87.

23. St. Thomas Aquinas, *ST*, Ia, q. 37, a. 1.

24. The Holy Spirit's proper act of incarnating the Son will be discussed in more detail in Chapter Ten.

25. See in particular the section with that title, *ThDrIII*, 183-91.

26. "Spirit and Institution," 231.

27. See *Credo*, 45-46.

28. "Obedience," 234.

29. *ThDrIII*, 171, 522.

30. "Obedience," 234.

31. *ThDrIII*, 182. Its not being "given once for all" may reasonably be read as a denial of Christ's perpetual possession of universal knowledge through the beatific vision, while His

not possessing it as "his own property" points to the depositing of His filial knowledge of the Trinitarian plan.

32. *ThDrIII*, 187; see also pp. 183, 186. See also *A Theology of History*, 39.

33. *ThDrIII*, 196-97, 511, 522.

34. *ThDrIII*, 171. See also *ThDrIII*, 521.

35. *ThDrIII*, 188, emphasis in original. See also "Obedience," 234; and "The Holy Spirit as Love," 120.

36. *ThDrIII*, 521.

37. Balthasar gives a footnote here to "Felix Malmberg, *Über den Gottmenschen*, QD 9 (Herder, 1960), 115-22."

38. *ThDrIII*, 200.

39. *ThDrIII*, 166.

40. *ThDrIII*, 166.

41. *ThDrIII*, 198.

42. *ThDrIII*, 199.

43. *ThDrIII*, 225.

44. *ThDrIII*, 168.

45. *ThDrIII*, 522; see also *ThDrIII*, 196-97.

46. See, e.g., *ThDrIII*, 188.

47. In contrast to the foregoing objections, Tossou, *Streben nach Vollendung*, 268, holds that Balthasar's pneumatic Christology sets especially high value on Christ's human freedom. Christ fulfills the Father's will, not so much as a law, but as free exercise of His own subjectivity: Since the Father is origin of both His mission and His person, the more perfectly He fulfills the one in obedience, the more perfectly He possesses Himself (pp. 250, 267-68); there is no heteronomy between Christ and the Father. Christ's freedom is not so much in choosing between possibilities (p. 260) — the Father's will appears to Him as a decision already-preferred (p. 248) — but in grasping and pursuing the desired option with the full force of His personality (p. 260). Analogous to the inspiration of the artist, the Holy Spirit reveals this object to Jesus and 'drives' Him to fulfill it. Since the Holy Spirit is the Spirit not only of the Father, but of the Son, however, there is also no heteronomy between Christ and the Holy Spirit (see p. 261).

Tossou's exposition goes far, yet tensions remain. First, the inspiration of Jesus similar to that of the artist is contrasted (p. 260) with views that regard those inspired as if "mehr oder weniger in die Funktion passiver Instrumente in der Hand des Heiligen Geistes verdrängt wurden" [they would be more or less repressed in the function of passive instruments in the hand of the Holy Spirit]. But one could hardly stress more than Balthasar the passivity of Jesus in the reception of His mission. If the "more or less . . . passive instruments" were not actually coerced by the Holy Spirit *against their will*, then the difference between their passivity and that of Balthasar's Jesus is unclear, and the question of the objective relationship between Holy Spirit and the person inspired remains unanswered. Does one feel hemmed in or liberated by the revealed will of God? Does one comply with it due to a stick or a carrot? To experience the desire of God always as the route of perfect self-fulfillment and self-expression (as do the artist and Jesus?) is precisely such a carrot. In contrast, temptation may include experiencing what is expected by God as more difficult, more constraining, and undesirable from a certain perspective. Balthasar insists upon the reality of Jesus' temptations, and also that the will of God appears to Him as the more difficult thing to do in a particular situation. Does *He* then feel "repressed" by the Holy Spirit at times? Does His unfailing obedience make *Him* a "passive instrument"? In addition, one observes that the artist may betray his inspiration, but an explanation of why Christ never did sin, if He could have (as Tossou holds, pp. 250, 267-69), or why He could not have sinned (as Balthasar holds) is lacking. The mere invocation of the *factual* identification of the Person with the mission (i.e., the hypostatic union) is insufficient. In addition, the explanation of the lack of heteronomy between Spirit and Son depends on the communication of idioms and neglects the distinction in natures: As man, the Spirit is not Jesus' in the way He is His as God. Balthasar makes this clear by indicating that Jesus as man receives power over the Spirit only after the fulfillment of His mission and His return to the Father; see *ThDrIII,* 189; *ThDrIV,* 364; and Tossou, p. 296.

48. *ThDrIII,* 168, emphasis added.

49. See n. 297 in Chapter Seven and the related discussion in the main body of the text. See also "God Speaks as Man," 92. Given Balthasar's particular doctrine of the Incarnation, it is more precise to say "in the human" than to use the broader phrase, "through the human."

50. *ThDrIII,* 200.

51. "DescHell," 231-32. Compare *MP,* 169, emphasis added, regarding how Calvin "defends himself . . . against the charge of interpreting the abandonment by God in Hell as the 'despair of not believing': 'The weakness of Christ was pure of all stain, *since it was enclosed within obedience* to God.'" After this quotation of Calvin, Balthasar continues, "And precisely in that did his mortal anguish and God-abandonment differ radically from the habitual anxiety of the sinner." Balthasar's citation for Calvin is "*Institutio* II.16, 10-12."

52. *ThDrIII,* 200. Balthasar's footnote here reads "'Nec libertas nec pars libertatis est potestas peccandi': Anselm, *De libertate arbitrii* I (Schmitt I, 208, 11), following Augustine: 'Multo quippe liberius erit arbitrium quod omnino non poterit servire peccato': *Enchir.* 105 (PL 40:281). So in St. Thomas: 'Unde maior libertas est in angelis qui peccare non possunt quam in nobis qui peccare possumus': *S. Th.* I, 62, 8 ad 3."

53. See St. Thomas Aquinas, *ST,* Ia, q. 62, a. 8; IIIa, q. 7, a. 9; q. 9, a. 2, especially ad 2; q. 15, a. 3. Consider also *ST,* IaIIae, q. 1, 3. Christ's freedom in His human nature from ignorance, error, and sin does not jeopardize the truth of that nature, but reveals its perfection. Freedom from ignorance and error parallels His freedom from concupiscence and sin.

54. *ThDrV,* 300.

55. Here I draw upon Tossou, *Streben nach Vollendung,* 316-22, who discusses the Holy Spirit as freedom in Person.

56. Tossou, *Streben nach Vollendung,* 319.

57. Tossou, *Streben nach Vollendung,* 321.

58. Tossou, *Streben nach Vollendung,* 322.

59. See Tossou, *Streben nach Vollendung,* 322, 324, 330.

60. See Tossou, *Streben nach Vollendung,* 322.

61. Compare Tossou, *Streben nach Vollendung,* 310, who describes what is most proper to God as "das Offensein über sich hinaus" [the being open beyond Himself].

62. See Tossou, *Streben nach Vollendung,* 324.

63. Tossou, *Streben nach Vollendung,* 316, 460.

64. Tossou, *Streben nach Vollendung,* 309-30.

65. See Tossou, *Streben nach Vollendung*, 213, 460.

66. Consider the nexus of perfection, the good, power, and beatitude among St. Thomas Aquinas, *ST,* Ia, q. 4, a. 1 c; q. 5, a. 4 ad 2; q. 6, a. 1 c; q. 25, a. 1 c, a. 2 c; q. 26, a. 1 c, a. 2 c; and IaIIae q. 79, a. 1 c.

67. *Dare,* 93.

68. *ThDrIII,* 188. See also the wider context, pp. 187-88.

69. *ThDrIII,* 188.

70. *ThDrIII,* 190.

71. *ThDrIII,* 190.

72. *ThDrIII,* 523, emphasis added. See also pp. 228, 508-9.

73. *ThDrV,* 66, emphasis added.

74. See St. Thomas Aquinas, *ST,* Ia, q. 41, a. 2, c and ad 5.

75. *ThDrIII,* 520, emphasis in original.

76. *ThDrIII,* 522. Note the comment in n. 192 in Chapter Seven.

77. *ThDrIII,* 521, emphasis added.

78. *ThDrIII,* 191, emphasis added.

79. E.g., *GloryVII,* 389-99, especially 391; *ThDrV,* 66-98.

80. Balthasar gives a footnote here: "In the terminology of *The Glory of the Lord* VII, 115-61."

81. Hans Urs von Balthasar, *Theodramatik,* 2. Band, Teil 2: *Die Personen in Christus* (Einsiedeln: Johannes, 1978), 174.

82. *ThDrIII,* 189, emphasis added.

83. See *CF* #612 (DS 294).

84. *ThDrIV,* 364; see also "Spirit and Institution," 236. This position would seem to call into question the continuation of Jesus' character as obedient and receptive of the Father's will.

85. "Spirit and Institution," 236.

86. "Christology and Ecclesial Obedience," *Expl IV,* 144, emphasis added.

87. *ThDrIII,* 523.

88. *ThDrIII,* 189. See also "Spirit and Institution," 236.

89. "Trinity and Future," 83.

90. "Trinity and Future," 82.

91. *GloryI,* 613.

92. *ThDrV,* 261.

93. "The Incarnation of God," 67.

94. "Trinity and Future," 82.

95. "Trinity and Future," 82-83. See also "The Incarnation of God," 65-68; "Desc," 410-11; and *GloryVII,* 214, 396-97.

96. See "Vicarious," 422. See also *ThDrII,* 259; *ThDrIV,* 328-32; *ThDrV,* 103, 105; *GloryVII,* 396; and the concern about a "Deus ex machina" in *Leben,* 22.

97. *God Question,* 134. See also p. 138.

98. *ThDrIII,* 531. See also *ThDrIV,* 329.

99. *ThDrIV,* 501.

100. See *ThDrIV,* 501.

101. *ThDrV,* 261-63. As I understand Balthasar, he keeps in mind the Holy Spirit's char-

acter in the immanent Trinity even when he discusses the economy; i.e., the Spirit acts in the economy in accord with His eternal personal property. Hence, even at the moment of greatest soteriological abandonment, the Holy Spirit remains a substantial bond between Father and Son, i.e., unites them as true God proceeding from them both. Contrast Wilhelm Maas, *Gott und die Hölle: Studien zum Descensus Christi* (Einsiedeln: Johannes, 1979), 251. See also idem, *"Abgestiegen zur Holle. Aspekte eines vergessenen Glaubensartikels," IKaZ Communio* 10 (1981) 1:14-15.

102. Particularly pertinent references are *ThDrIV*, 349, 362, 384; *ThDrV*, 55, 78-79, 89-90, 102, 245, 261, 265-69, 282-84, 395, 509-14. It may be that Balthasar has St. Anselm's *id quo majus cogitari non potest* in mind. See *Th'l Anth*, 265, together with *ThDrV*, 78; *Dare*, 149. St. Anselm, however, did not refer this "greater" to what God could know of Himself, but only to what man could think of Him. Balthasar's use of Matthew of Aquasparta in the important essay "Fides" (p. 69) is also suggestive, although the passage of Matthew of Aquasparta quoted by Balthasar likewise refers only to God being "ever greater than what [the blessed] see," and not to God's own self-knowledge. ThDrV, 78, with its footnotes suggests Speyr had the weightiest influence on Balthasar in this regard.

103. See *ThDrII*, 259; and *ThDrV*, 78.

104. Balthasar's clearest and most succinct statement is in "The Scapegoat and the Trinity," 85.

105. See "Vicarious," 421; "Death Is Swallowed," 50-51. See also *GloryVII*, 205.

106. See *ThDrIV*, 328-29.

107. *ThDrV*, 268; *ThDrIV*, 349; "And the Sea," 175.

108. On the world existing within the Trinity, see n. 5 in Chapter Six.

109. "Death Is Swallowed," 50.

110. *GloryVII*, 160.

111. *GloryVII*, 223.

112. *GloryVII*, 305, emphasis added to "hypostatic." See also p. 249, n. 5.

113. *GloryVII*, 152, emphasis added. See also pp. 97-99 above; and *ThDrV*, 314-15, with use of Speyr.

114. "Vicarious," 421-22; *ThDrIV*, 324-27, 329, 496-97; *ThDrV*, 283, 325-27.

115. See "Some Points of Eschatology," 262; "Fragments," 277-78; "Only If," 139-42.

116. See, e.g., *ThDrIV*, 384: In the 'hour,' "the sinful world, alienated from God, is taken into the infinite Father/Son relationship (which is now 'economic'). . . ." See also *ThLogII*, 294-98, 331; "The Scapegoat and the Trinity," 85; *ThDrIV*, 329, 384; *ThDrV*, 250-68, 280-84, in particular 258, 261, 268, 283, and his n. 23. See also *ThDrV*, 329.

117. *ThDrV*, 502, emphasis in original.

118. *ThDrII*, 268-70; *ThDrIV*, 332. See also *ThDrIII*, 199.

119. *ThDrV*, 245.

120. See, e.g., "Trinity and Future," 82; *ThDrV*, 285-90; and "The Incarnation of God," 65.

121. See p. 227 above.

122. *Leben*, 36.

123. See *ThDrIII*, 228; see also *ThDrV*, 508.

124. "Eschatology in Outline," 434.

125. All three quotations are from *ThDrIV*, 336, emphasis added.

126. See the texts referenced in nn. 49, 55, 61, and 97 in Chapter Six.

127. See *ThDrIV*, 329; *ThDrV*, 261; and *ThLogII*, 294-98, 331.

128. See "The Incarnation of God," 67-68.

129. "Desc," 413, 416; "The Multitude of Biblical Theologies," 93; *GloryVII*, 215, including Balthasar's use of Karl Barth; *GloryVII*, 242-43; *ThDrII*, 244; *ThDrIII*, 228, 530-31; *ThDrV*, 268, 508-9; "And the Sea," 179-81; and "The Incarnation of God," 67-68.

130. For an explicit statement on the Person's being affected, see *ThDrIV*, 501. Again, since "true freedom is . . . in self-giving" (*ThDrIV*, 147) and the essence of the divine nature is self-gift (*ThDrV*, 255), the essence of being God is to have perfect freedom.

131. Balthasar's basic argument is presented in the main text, at n. 428 and just thereafter in Chapter Seven. See also n. 24 in Chapter Seven; *GloryVII*, 243-63, especially 243, 248, 251, 260; "The Personal God," 54; "The Incarnation of God," 67-68; "Only If," 136-37, 142; "Death Is Swallowed," 51-53; "Trinity and Future," 83; *Th'l Anth*, 240; "The Last Five Stations," 122; "Mystery," 119; "Vicarious," 415-16; *GloryI*, 609, 613-16; *ThDrIII*, 507-8, 530; *ThDrIV*, 319-28, 349; *ThDrV*, 121, 252, 260, 262-63 (with use of Speyr), 496; *GloryVII*, 277, 289. Less explicit references are made in *GloryVII*, 144, 211, 215, 231, 282-83; *ThDrV*, 94, 98, 516-17. See also *ThDrIII*, 518-19.

132. See n. 49 in Chapter Seven for God's going to the "end" or to the "extreme."

133. "Death Is Swallowed," 51; and, with extensive use of Speyr, *ThDrV*, 262.

134. *ThDrIII*, 228, with an extensive footnote. See also, in particular, *ThDrIV*, 323-26.

135. "Trinity and Future," 82. See also "The Incarnation of God," 67.

136. "Trinity and Future," 81.

137. Balthasar here gives a footnote with ten *New* Testament citations linking glory and power, and a reference to another source for Old Testament citations. The footnote is curious in that, in the quoted text, Balthasar represents such a link as expressive of an "*Old* Testament" sense of glory. In other words, in admirable honesty, but with a somewhat unclear purpose, he takes pains to point out the existence of such a link also in the New Testament, but does not provide even examples of the usage in the Old Testament. Moreover, he gives three additional New Testament citations in *GloryVII*, 269, n. 7, where he says "Glory and power are close to each other," and here precisely in a *New* Testament context.

138. *GloryVII*, 147. See also p. 146, which likewise points to a new ideal of δόξα as "the renunciation of one's own δόξα." That this new *glory* must be seen as the *renunciation of glory* again indicates Balthasar does not take *glory* in the sense of its first imposition.

Notes to Chapter Nine

1. See Balthasar, "Presenza della croce," *Monastica* 4 (1964): 22; "Trinity and Future," 84; "Some Points of Eschatology," 263; *GloryVII*, 397; "Only If," 135-53; *ThDrV*, 483-84; and "Our Love of Jesus Christ," 79.

2. Maas, *Gott und die Hölle*, 245: "die Mitte und eigentlich der ganze wesentliche Inhalt seiner Theologie." Compare also Lochbrunner, "*Das Ineinander*," 188.

3. See, e.g., Aidan Nichols's introduction to Balthasar, *MP*, 7; Aidan Nichols, *Introduction to Hans Urs von Balthasar: Say It Is Pentecost: A Guide Through Balthasar's Logic* (Washington, DC: Catholic University of America, 2001), 120-21; and Dieser, *Der gottähnliche Mensch*, 442.

4. "The Multitude of Biblical Theologies," 93, emphasis in original. See also p. 98; and "Our Love of Jesus Christ," 79.

5. "Trinity and Future," 82-83. See the similar arguments made in *ThDrIV*, 328-32; "The Incarnation of God," 65-68; "Only If," 151-52; and "Der Mensch und das ewige Leben III," 5: "Gott selber muß seine Theodizee erfinden" [God must invent his own theodicy]. Part of Balthasar's concern seems to be how God could be a God of love if He created beings that can damn themselves but did not provide a means of salvation.

6. See *GloryVII*, 217.

7. *GloryVII*, 217. See also p. 132.

8. *GloryVII*, 217-18.

9. See the texts referenced in n. 5 in Chapter Six.

10. "Trinity and Future," 80.

11. "Trinity and Future," 80.

12. "Trinity and Future," 81-82.

13. "Trinity and Future," 81-84. On the world "in" God, see also the texts of n. 5 in Chapter Six.

14. Reiterated three times, "Trinity and Future," 81-82. Balthasar very frequently insists upon the necessity of his theological positions. See, e.g., "Only If," 135-53; *ThDrIV*, 345 and 348 with regard to God's wrath; pp. 357, 495; *GloryVII*, 228-30; "The Incarnation of God," 65; "The Eye," 116; *Th'l Anth*, 282; *ThDrIII*, 530; *ThDrV*, 486. To the extent that these statements of certainty may be equivalently expressed as "if and only if" formulations, they will fall if either antecedent or consequent is shown to be mistaken. Given the interdependence of Balthasar's theological positions, his entire theology is made vulnerable by the frequency of such assertions of necessity: The fall of only one antecedent or consequent will have a domino effect throughout his doctrines.

15. Balthasar's two presentations of his argument in "Trinity and Future," 81-82, are here combined, as each sheds light on the other. For his related arguments about the Trinity, see n. 24 in Chapter Seven. On the deduction of the Trinity, see the text in the main body associated with n. 109 in Chapter Six.

16. See texts referenced in n. 10 in Chapter Seven.

17. See "The Incarnation of God," 62. Balthasar's conclusion that God is Trinitarian is not supposed to be a deduction from natural reason, but rather is seen as founded on God's revelation of His own nature. Whether he avoids the deduction is debatable; see n. 109 in Chapter Six.

18. *ThDrV*, 516.

19. *ThDrV*, 245.

20. For the content of the entire sentence, see *ThDrIV*, 333; *ThDrV*, 81, 245, 257, 516; *Leben*, 70.

21. See *ThDrV*, 216, 242-46; and also *ThDrIV*, 324-26; *Th'l Anth*, 278.

22. *GloryVII*, 268.

23. This conclusion is reasonable enough given Balthasar's stress on being as event, but see also *GloryVII*, 289.

24. *ThDrIV*, 494.

25. See, e.g., *GloryVII*, 304-9.

26. Wallner, *Gott als Eschaton*, 221, 319, 369-73, argues that the possible loss of creatures does not imply an eternal tragedy for God: Creation, and so likewise its redemption, is mod-

eled on the eternal form of the Son in the Holy Spirit, i.e., receptive freedom ordered to union in love with its principle. Since the transcendent (divine) model has always already achieved fulfillment in the "seal" of love that is the Holy Spirit, however, God is in Himself the Eschaton and there can be no ultimate tragedy for Him.

I agree with Wallner insofar as the Trinity is the model that has always achieved fulfillment. However, I would have to ask whether this intra-Trinitarian solution adequately takes into account Balthasar's indications of God's relation to the world He creates, including the fact that He gains something from the inclusion of saved creatures in the Trinitarian life (see *ThDrV*, 521). If the immanent Trinity expresses itself in the economy, i.e., is the model of God's relation to the world and His action in it, are not the Descent and universal salvation necessary, because only in them are "distances" of sin and of sinful creatures brought into unity with God? In other words, does Wallner's solution take into account its own implications: If creation's *model* has always achieved fulfillment despite the greatest opposition (between Father and Son), is it possible for creation *not* to do so?

27. *ThDrIV*, 324. See also "Mystery," 111-26; *Leben* 69; *ThDrIV*, 330-31.

28. See *Leben*, 70. Consider also *ThDrV*, 86-87; "Death Is Swallowed," 52.

29. See *Leben*, 70; *ThDrV*, 86-87; and the texts of n. 31 in Chapter Six.

30. *GloryVII*, 226.

31. *GloryVII*, 150.

32. *ThDrV*, 510. See also p. 483.

33. See also "Mystery," 115.

34. See n. 66 in Chapter Seven.

35. *ThDrIV*, 348. See also *ThDrV*, 477, in which the Eucharist is described in terms exactly parallel to those Balthasar uses of the Incarnation and Descent.

36. *GloryVII*, 148-52. See also p. 226.

37. *GloryVII*, 304-6.

38. "Death Is Swallowed," 50.

39. "Mystery," 117. Due to Balthasar's theology of the Incarnation, "earthly substance" does not refer only to the elements of His human nature, but also to the Word as having become these. This conceptual content is perhaps clearer in his use of "creaturely structure" (p. 119). Thus, Christ's body and blood, soul *and divinity* can be understood to be intended by Balthasar in these passages.

40. "Mystery," 117.

41. "Mystery," 119. Compare p. 122; and *GloryVII*, 160.

42. See *ThDrV*, 477-78. See also the texts on sacramental participation in the death of Christ in *ThDrV*, 333, 344-46.

43. See *ThDrV*, 134, with use of Speyr.

44. *Leben*, 66: "Der Glaubende glaubt für die Nichtglaubenden, er kommuniziert für die Nichtkommunizierenden, weil der Leib, den er empfängt, die Sünden aller getragen hat." See also *ThDrIV*, 406-23, on the Church's participation in Christ's *pro nobis* through the communion of saints.

45. See Vatican II, *Lumen gentium*, #1, 7, 17; and *Gaudium et spes*, #45, 92.

46. *Leben*, 61: "Ostergnade."

47. *Leben*, 63: "Leben aus dem Tod."

48. *ThDrIV*, 386. The traditional doctrine of Christ's descent would see such a "liberat-

ing summons to come forth from darkness" as issued by Him to the souls in the limbo of the Fathers. Balthasar intends rather a link with Easter Sunday, as made explicit in the quotation's original context; i.e., the "summons" are addressed to *Christ* to come forth from the darkness of Sheol.

49. *Leben,* 63: "Der für Gott tote Sünder durch den vom Tod der Sünder auferstanden Herrn in ein Leben durch Gott und für Gott zuruckgeholt."

50. See *ThDrV,* 136.

51. See, e.g., *ThDrV,* 120-22.

52. "The Incarnation of God," 67; *Church and World,* 72; *GloryI,* 480, 618; *GloryVII,* 253, 292-94, 396; *ThDrII,* 302; and "The Father's Vineyard," 87.

53. On the Son's work of "finishing," not much elaborated by Balthasar, see *GloryVII,* 233; consider also "The Unity of Our Lives," 120-21; *Leben,* 37-38, 42; *ThDrV,* 316, 329.

54. See *ThDrV,* 131-32. See also *GloryVII,* 152, 394, 397; *ThDrIV,* 384. If this sonship is that of grace, as suggested by the context of *ThDrV,* 131-32, it seems the objective redemption would necessarily accomplish universal subjective redemption.

55. *ThDrV,* 250-68, 280-84, 329, in particular 258, 261, 268, 283 with its n. 23, with use of Speyr, and 329.

56. See *GloryVII,* 301; and also consider Balthasar's general emphasis on event (e.g., within the Trinity) and act (e.g., glory as act) in opposition to 'static' representations (e.g., seeing God as *nunc stans,* the 'cosmological' view of the world, a beatific vision that makes God an object).

57. *GloryVII,* 296. See also *GloryVII,* 305-11.

58. See *GloryVII,* 309, 395, 398-99.

59. "The Church as 'Caritas,'" 246; "Mystery," 121; *GloryVII,* 254-60; *Th'l Anth,* 269; *ThDrII,* 268; *ThDrIII,* 199, 201; *ThDrII,* 267; and "God Speaks as Man," 93.

60. "Mystery," 121; *Church and World,* 60-61.

61. "Mystery," 121.

62. *Church and World,* 61-64, 69-73; *GloryVII,* 160; *ThDrIII,* 528.

63. *GloryVII,* 257. See also *Church and World,* 64-74; *GloryI,* 330; *GloryVII,* 293, 304-6; *ThDrV,* 483-85.

64. "Mystery," 122. See also "Obedience," 238, *Church and World,* 64-87; *GloryVII,* 160.

65. "Obedience," 237-38. See also *Church and World,* 64-68, 73, 92-94; *GloryVII,* 132-33, 294; *ThDrII,* 259, 270-71, 298-99; *ThDrIII,* 527-28; *ThDrV,* 76; and the texts of n. 59 above.

66. *ThDrIII,* 247.

67. On the content of this paragraph, otherwise without footnotes, see *GloryVII,* 304-12. I have drawn out the parallels between the Christian and Christ, his archetype, implicit in Balthasar's text.

68. "Mystery," 126; "Death Is Swallowed," 52-53; *Church and World,* 83-87; *ThDrII,* 259.

69. *GloryVII,* 256-61. See also *ThDrV,* 334; *ThDrIII,* 526.

70. See n. 67 above.

71. On the Christian's participation in Christ, see, e.g., *ThDrIII,* 247-49, 535; *ThDrIV,* 384; "The Eye," 115; "And the Sea," 186-188. On the "communicable" death of Christ, see *ThDrIV,* 133. On participation in the death of Christ through the sacraments, see the texts of the previous section, as well as *ThDrV,* 333, 344-46.

72. *ThDrIV,* 366.

73. *ThDrIV,* 388. See also the texts referenced in n. 71 above. Balthasar does not here (*ThDrIV,* 388) say explicitly that this selfless bearing of fruit is like Christ's, but such likeness is indicated by the context and by Christ's status as exemplar.

74. See *ThDrV,* 139.

75. "Martyrdom and Mission," 286-90.

76. *GloryVII,* 390.

77. *GloryVII,* 390-91.

78. *GloryVII,* 391.

79. Regarding this interior disposition, see the texts of n. 63 above.

80. See "Short Discourse," 205-7. Note, however, that Balthasar had said a person's spiritual director should forbid similar acts; see *Dare,* 106.

81. *God Question,* 134-38. See also "Martyrdom and Mission," 282-85; *Dare,* 106-11; "Short Discourse," 217. In *Th'l Anth,* 282; *ThDrIV,* 337; and *ThDrV,* 308-10, the 'dark night' is linked to the Cross, but one must recall the Cross is the gate to Sheol, and "Cross and Hell" form a single event that has its climax in the abyss. This reading is made explicit as *Th'l Anth* continues; see pp. 283-85. See also *Leben,* 24-26, 40-41.

82. *ThDrV,* 495.

83. *ThDrV,* 495.

84. On nearness despite apparent absence, see *ThDrV,* 150, 327. See also "Loneliness in the Church," 266-98.

85. See, e.g., *ThDrV,* 484; and compare *GloryVII,* 309, with p. 389.

86. See n. 381 in Chapter Seven for texts on the endowment of death with meaning.

87. Balthasar, "Beyond Contemplation and Action?" 302-7.

88. *ThDrIII,* 197, with extended footnote. On the experiences of dark contemplation by Christ and the Christian, see also *The Christian and Anxiety,* 107; and "Action and Contemplation," *Expl I,* 227-40, especially 236. In the text of *The Christian and Anxiety,* Balthasar characterizes this contemplation as the privation of God's light, whereas in the second, it is due to a prevalence of God's presence. The apparent contradiction can be explained consistently with Balthasar's more detailed expositions in one of two ways: either the closer God actually is to a person, the more He abandons him, with this abandonment itself revealing something of God; or, only Christ ever experienced the full reality of this abandonment and He did so that we might be spared it. In the latter case, the mystics' participation in Christ's abandonment is only an apparent abandonment, because only a participation, whereas Christ's abandonment was complete.

89. "Fides," 77, emphasis in original.

90. "Fides," 77-78.

91. To coin a Balthasarian-like term on the basis of *ThDrV,* 124: "primal faith within the Trinity."

92. *God Question,* 134-39.

93. See also St. Thomas Aquinas, *ST,* Ia q. 12, a. 2; and *ST,* Supp. q. 92, a. 1.

94. See *God Question,* 135; *MP,* 77. *ThDrV,* 484, can be taken in reference to this personal purification, although it is not specifically tied to mystical experience.

95. See *Dare,* 105-11; "Short Discourse," 204-10, 214-18.

96. *Dare,* 106.

97. See *The Threefold Garland,* 93.

98. "The Multitude of Biblical Theologies," 100.

99. "The Multitude of Biblical Theologies," 100. See also *ThDrV*, 346-69.

100. "The Multitude of Biblical Theologies," 98.

101. "The Multitude of Biblical Theologies," 97-99.

102. *MP*, 174. For texts relevant to Christ's descent establishing Him as judge, see *MP*, 177; *GloryVII*, 152, 233-34; "Mystery," 116; *ThDrIV*, 363-64; and *Leben*, 75.

103. Balthasar draws on Rev 1:18 in varying contexts, e.g., "Death Is Swallowed," 54; *Does Jesus Know Us?* 38; *MP*, 156.

104. See *MP*, 175, in its context of pp. 168-81. On the connection between Christ's experience in Sheol and His becoming judge, see also Pyc, *L'obbedienza*, 91; Nandkisore, *Hoffnung auf Erlösung*, 234-35, 240.

105. *MP*, 175. See also *GloryVII*, 233-34.

106. *MP*, 174, emphasis in original. See also *GloryVII*, 233-34; "Vicarious," 422; *Dio e il dramma del mondo*, 18; *ThDrV*, 362-64; and "Desc," 412.

107. *MP*, 177.

108. E.g., "Vicarious," 422; *Dio e il dramma del mondo*, 18.

109. See "Vicarious," 422; *ThDrV*, 311-14, 326-27.

110. See Nandkisore, *Hoffnung auf Erlösung*, 233-34, 248-52.

111. "Desc," 412.

112. See "DescHell," 229, 236.

113. Rothkranz, *Die Kardinalfehler*, 372.

114. *CF* #2307 (DS 1002).

115. "Some Points of Eschatology," 264-65; Nandkisore, *Hoffnung auf Erlösung*, 242-47. See also *ThDrV*, 362-63.

116. See the texts referenced in the previous note.

117. Nandkisore, *Hoffnung auf Erlösung*, 252-53.

118. See Nandkisore, *Hoffnung auf Erlösung*, 253.

119. "Some Points of Eschatology," 264.

120. *ThDrV*, 515-16, with interior quotation of Speyr, *The Discourses of Controversy* (San Francisco: Ignatius, unspecified date between 1987 and 1994), 161.

121. *ThDrV*, 518.

122. See Balthasar's use of Speyr, *ThDrV*, 509-10, including his quotation on p. 510, of Speyr, *Objektive Mystik* (Einsiedeln: Johannes, no date given), 90-92: "Now the Father need no longer regard his world as something *extra muros*, since it is embedded in the relationship of love between Son and Spirit and shares in the triune love."

123. *ThDrV*, 514, quoting Speyr, *The Discourses of Controversy*, 292.

124. *ThDrV*, 521.

125. *ThDrV*, 507. Nonetheless, creation is gratuitous: "Both in the trinitarian self-communication and again in the decision to create the world, [absolute freedom] is *its own necessity*" (*ThDrV*, 508, emphasis in original).

126. See Wallner, *Gott als Eschaton*, 348-53.

127. *ThDrIII*, 189, emphasis added; see also *Leben*, 56-57.

128. On understanding "in His humanity" to mean "from His humanity," see the earlier treatment of this passage, marked with n. 82 in Chapter Eight. Jöhri, *Descensus Dei*, 278, also understands Balthasar in this way: "L'umanità del Figlio entra definitivamente a far parte della

spirazione attiva dello Spirito da parte del Padre e del Figlio" [The humanity of the Son enters definitively to take part in the active spiration of the Spirit by the Father and Son].

129. *ThDrIII*, 523. See also *ThDrIII*, 228.

130. *ThDrV*, 482-83.

131. *ThDrV*, 483.

132. Mansini, "Balthasar and the Theodramatic Enrichment of the Trinity," *The Thomist* 64 (2000): 499-519. His analysis indicates, however, that this position either must indicate real change in God, with the implication that there is potentiality, temporality, complexity, and imperfection in God, or that it is a merely verbal assertion without any corresponding reality.

133. *ThDrV*, 483. Instead of "to," the English translation has "through," apparently a typographical error.

134. *ThDrIII*, 522.

135. *ThDrIII*, 189.

136. On the return of Christ's divine attributes in His resurrection, see *ThDrII*, 299; *Leben*, 51; "Death Is Swallowed," 54.

137. *ThDrV*, 520. This block quotation appears set off from Balthasar's main text, indented and in slightly smaller print, but without reference or footnote. In consequence, conflicting indications are given as to the authorship, and the reader cannot identify securely if it is Balthasar's original work, a quotation from another book of his, or the writing of another author whom he is quoting.

138. *ThDrV*, 521. Despite the identification of the Son's mission in the flesh and His procession, this sentence should not be taken to mean that either the Son's Incarnation or procession cease. "The Son's mission attains its end . . ." would perhaps have expressed more clearly the necessary intention. On the close of the Son's mission with the reconciliation of all, see the use of Speyr in *ThDrV*, 282-83, especially n. 23, and the similar texts of p. 329.

139. *ThDrV*, 521, using Speyr, *I Korinther* (Einsiedeln: Johannes, no date given), 506.

140. Consider "Short Discourse," 211-21; *GloryVII*, 297; the extension of the *communio sanctorum* in *Leben*, 65-66, 85. In "An Empty Hell? The Restoration of All Things?: Balthasar's Concept of Hope for Salvation," trans. Michael J. Dodds, *Communio ICR* 18 (1991) 2: 35-52, Jan Ambaum argues that Balthasar's hope for universal salvation depends on a peculiarity in his concept of (theological) hope, namely, that he takes it as referring more to God as bringing history to fulfillment than to man relying on the promises of God.

141. *Test Everything*, 85-86; *ThDrV*, 316-21, 285-90. This contrast also runs throughout *Dare*, 13-28, 44-45, 65, 72, 87, 93-94, 113; and "Short Discourse," 166, 178, 183, 221, 251. Hence Balthasar emphasizes the speculative tone of Origen's writings on the topic (*Dare*, 59-63; "Short Discourse," 232, 238).

142. Balthasar's most-extended, and certainly best-known, treatment is *Dare*, with the accompanying "Short Discourse." The larger context of these works is a preceding debate in the journals *Der Fels* and *Theologisches*. The reader interested specifically in this aspect of Balthasar's theology is consequently referred to texts more narrowly focused on it, including the *Atti XIV Colloquio di Teologia di Lugano: Esperienza mistica e teologia. Ricerca epistemologica sulle proposte di Hans Urs von Balthasar* [= *Rivista Teologica di Lugano* 6 (2001)]; and James T. O'Connor, "Von Balthasar and Salvation," *Homiletic & Pastoral Review* (July 1989): 10-21. To call this last article "accessible" would be to compliment the author on

its clarity and succinctness, but not to downplay in any way its theological strength: With a clear eye for the importance of Tradition (which we have seen to be a recurring question on these topics), O'Connor not only considers Balthasar's arguments, but examines the sources he claims for support.

143. *Th'l Anth,* 240.

144. On protests against hell for others, see, e.g., *God Question,* 127-29, 136-39 (though note well pp. 141-42); "Some Points of Eschatology," 266-69; as well as Balthasar's own in *Dare,* in particular 188-97.

145. "Some Points of Eschatology," 268-69.

146. See "Some Points of Eschatology," 268-69. See also *God Question,* 138. What Balthasar says in this latter text about the works of Gertrud von le Fort and Georges Bernanos can be taken as a summary of his own conclusions for this section of *God Question,* 119-42.

147. On the communion of saints, see also *ThDrIV,* 406-23; *ThDrV,* 482-87; *Leben,* 66.

148. *ThDrV,* 140, direct quotation of Speyr, with footnote: "*Der grenzenlose Gott* (Einsiedeln: Johannes Verlag, no date given), 19; *cf. I Korinther,* 181. On these various aspects of death, *cf.* J. A. Fischer, *Studien zum Todesgedanken in der alten Kirche* (Munich: Huber, 1954)." On Balthasar's positive appraisal of death, see "Der Tod vom Leben verschlungen," *Homo Creatus Est.* Bd. V, *Skizzen zur Theologie,* (Einsiedeln: Johannes, 1986), 190-91. The last three paragraphs of the German essay are missing from the English translation, which was published as "Death Is Swallowed."

149. See *ThDrV,* 139-41.

150. *ThDrV,* 341.

151. *ThDrV,* 341. If the "new value" of death is found in its characterization by faith, as Balthasar suggests in how he continues (p. 342), his extension of this value to the death of sinners "who die turned away from God" is puzzling — unless one takes into account his ideas that a complete rejection of God is impossible without perfect freedom, that Christ's being dead can disturb the sinner's self-imposed isolation even after death, and that (as he says in *Leben,* 66) "the believer believes for the non-believer." On the "new value" death *objectively* has, see also "The Father's Vineyard," 78: "What can still be called death after I have died my death? Does not every dying from now on receive the meaning and the seal of my death?"

152. *ThDrV,* 285-90.

153. See what has been said about the Son as archetype of creatures in this chapter and Chapter Seven, as well as texts such as *ThDrII,* 259; *ThDrIII,* 199; *GloryVII,* 217; *ThDrV,* 301.

154. *ThDrV,* 301.

155. *ThDrV,* 299.

156. *ThDrV,* 302.

157. See *ThDrV,* 299; 302, n. 3. Compare also the situation of Christ in "Some Points of Eschatology," 264.

158. "The Scapegoat and the Trinity," 85.

159. *ThDrV,* 301-3.

160. "Vicarious," 421. See also *GloryVII,* 228.

161. *ThDrV,* 295. This reason is the same as implied in Balthasar's use of Edith Stein, *Welt und Person. Beitrag zum christlichen Wahrheitsstreben,* ed. L. Gelber and Romaeus

Leuven (Freiburg: Herder, 1962), 158ff., in "Short Discourse," 218-21. See Balthasar's own similar treatment, "Short Discourse," 208-10. The basic argument running throughout *Dare* and "Short Discourse" is that not to have hope for the salvation of all (where *all* is taken collectively, rather than partitively) is to doubt God's omnipotence, which is to doubt His love, as well: God's love in Christ "is stronger than any resistance that it encounters and . . . hope for all men is therefore permitted" (*Dare*, 97). See also "Short Discourse," 178.

162. See *ThDrV*, 314, with use of Speyr.

163. See the references of n. 24 in Chapter Seven.

164. As treated in association with n. 381 in Chapter Seven.

165. Pointed out in n. 151 above and the text in the main body associated with it.

166. "Vicarious," 422, emphasis added.

167. *ThDrIV*, 338, 495; and *ThDrV*, 193.

168. *ThDrV*, 360.

169. The eternity of the experience of Sheol is touched upon in, e.g., *God Question*, 132; "The Multitude of Biblical Theologies," 97-100; *GloryVII*, 229, 232.

170. See, e.g., *Dio e il dramma del mondo*, 18.

171. "Some Points of Eschatology," 264-65; *Dare*, 141, 147.

172. "Vicarious," 422.

173. *ThDrV*, 313.

174. *ThDrV*, 313-14.

175. *GloryVII*, 305-6.

176. *ThDrV*, 295. See also "Vicarious," 421; *Dare*, 24, 26-27, and Balthasar's use in *Dare* of quotations from Gustave Martelet (p. 53, n. 10), Karl Rahner (p. 80, n. 9), Erich Przywara (p. 86, n. 1), Maurice Blondel (p. 115), and Adrienne von Speyr (p. 141). Note that Balthasar does in fact describe God's creation as restricting Him; see, e.g., *ThDrIV*, 328.

177. *ThDrV*, 302.

178. *GloryVII*, 233-34, emphases added. Contrast Balthasar's "Hell *was* necessarily the fate of man" if he rejected salvation in full knowledge, with how he continues, "Purgatory *must be* a possibility for man. . . . Heaven *must be* a possibility for man. . . ."

179. *ThDrV*, 321. Balthasar does not give an attribution for the interior quotation.

180. *ThDrV*, 321, emphases added.

181. *ThDrV*, 298.

182. *ThDrV*, 296. See also the stress on the complete nature of this rejection in Balthasar's quotation of Speyr in *Dare*, 141, n. 5.

183. *ThDrIV*, 350. This assertion calls into question the divine love's being "ever-greater" and implies a restriction of God's omnipotence and infinite freedom, one apparently unnoticed by Balthasar.

184. *ThDrIV*, 350, emphasis added.

185. *ThDrIV*, 350, with reference to Mt 12:31, "Whoever speaks against the Holy Spirit will not be forgiven, either in this age or in the age to come."

186. See in particular "Short Discourse," 208-10.

187. See, e.g., *ThDrI*, 46, 628, 645-46; *ThDrIII*, 165-67, 201, 207-8, 220.

188. *ThDrV*, 287, 301.

189. *ThDrV*, 295-96.

190. Since the fire of the divine love consuming sin in the Person of the Son is not dis-

tinct from the fire of the divine wrath, i.e., of judgment, the sinner's entrance into the fire of judgment is simultaneously an embrace by the Trinitarian love; see especially *ThDrV*, 268-69. Bätzing, *Kirche im Werden*, 238; and Nandkisore, *Hoffnung auf Erlösung*, 234, also understand Balthasar to think Christ's expiatory suffering *pro nobis* embraces the sin of final impenitence. Bätzing considers this expiation as the foundation for Balthasar's hope for universal salvation. Given the context of the text they have in mind (*MP*, 172), I read the passage as intended to characterize Christ's experience in Sheol, rather than to indicate its redemptive value. As the two cannot be separated drastically in Balthasar's theology, however, I agree with Bätzing's conclusion, also for the reasons I have given in the main body here.

191. "The Incarnation of God," 68.

192. "Short Discourse," 182. Compare DS 411, 838.

193. See *Dare*, 94, with quotation of W. Kreck, *Die Zukunft des Gekommenen* (Munich: Kaiser-Verlag, 1961), 144; see also p. 154, and "Short Discourse," 197, in which Balthasar is concerned just by Barth's coming "dangerously near" or "too close" to the doctrine of apokatastasis.

194. O'Connor, "Von Balthasar and Salvation," 12, emphasis in original. Roch Kerezty, "Response to Professor Scola," *Communio ICR* 18 (Summer 1991): 229, also makes this point.

195. For an explicit statement regarding a descent to gehenna, see "DescHell," 236.

196. *ThDrV*, 301; see also pp. 268-69, with use of Speyr.

197. *ThLogII*, 296.

198. *ThDrV*, 299.

199. "Desc," 408; *Does Jesus Know Us?* 38.

200. "DescHell," 234.

201. Roch Kerezty, "Response to Professor Scola," 228-31.

202. See n. 5 above for references.

203. *ThDrV*, 288, with internal quotation of Speyr, *I Korinther*, 283.

204. Speyr, *I Korinther*, 348, quoted in *ThDrV*, 288. As the thought of Adrienne von Speyr deserves the justice of being treated in the context of her own corpus, I have largely avoided quoting or representing Balthasar on the basis of his quotations of her. In his later works, this policy becomes more difficult to maintain, due to his heavy dependence on her and the seamless way he integrates quotations from her work into the presentation of his thought; i.e., he does not make a distinction between his thought and hers. Whether such an identification is admissible on the basis of her own works, and not only his, remains to be demonstrated.

205. *ThDrIV*, 352.

206. *ThDrIV*, 354.

207. *ThDrIV*, 352, 354.

208. *ThDrIV*, 355.

209. *ThDrIV*, 354, emphasis in original.

210. *ThDrIV*, 354.

211. "The Absences of Jesus," 56. See also *ThDrV*, 346.

212. *ThDrIV*, 357.

213. *ThDrIV*, 356, emphasis in original.

214. *ThDrIV*, 501.

215. *ThDrIV*, 359.

216. *ThDrIV*, 358.

217. *ThDrIV*, 359.

218. *ThDrIV*, 361.

219. *ThDrIV*, 355.

220. *ThDrIV*, 361.

221. In *GloryVII*, 160, Balthasar objects to "the so-called 'transcendental christology'" of B. Welte, K. Rahner, J. Ratzinger, and others on the grounds of the following problem: "If we follow this christology, what is to prevent the wholly and immaculately transcendent human being Mary from becoming likewise a 'God-human being' *(Gottmensch)*" like Christ? As the same question can reasonably be raised with respect to Balthasar's Mariology, I have provided a response on the basis of his theological principles.

Notes to Chapter Ten

1. *ThDrII*, 268.

2. See *ThDrIV*, 325-26. See also *ThDrIII*, 530.

3. More will be said on the Holy Spirit's proper act of incarnating the Son later in this subsection.

4. This Christology suggests why, at one point, Balthasar carefully says that the economic Trinity cannot be identified with the immanent Trinity, since the latter is the ground for the former (*ThDrIII*, 508). Balthasar here wishes to deny that the immanent Trinity realizes itself through its economic manifestation. However, the two 'trinities' also cannot be identified because the immanent Trinity is 'inverted' in the economy, because the Son does not possess the divine attributes in both, and because He allows the Incarnation (and hence necessarily His experiences in the flesh) to affect Him as Son. See *ThDrIII*, 228, 239-40; *Th'l Anth*, 275; these three passages to be read with *ThDrV*, 212-46, especially 222.

5. *ThDrV*, 66; see also p. 76.

6. *ThDrV*, 66, bracketed text in original, no reference given for inner quotation.

7. *ThDrII*, 259, emphasis added.

8. On the "area of freedom" each Person has vis-à-vis the others, see *ThDrII*, 257. See also *ThDrV*, 96, in which Balthasar quotes Speyr speaking about the Father concealing something from the Son in His love.

9. *Th'l Anth*, 275-76, emphasis added.

10. Gerard F. O'Hanlon, *The Immutability of God in the Theology of Hans Urs von Balthasar* (Cambridge: Cambridge University Press, 1990), 43.

11. *ThDrIV*, 325.

12. *ThDrV*, 468.

13. "Death Is Swallowed," 54.

14. *Th'l Anth*, 280; see also *GloryI*, 616; and *GloryVII*, 226.

15. *ThDrII*, 257.

16. *ThDrII*, 257-58; *ThDrV*, 90.

17. "The Holy Spirit as Love," 118. Balthasar's argument here hinges not so much upon Scripture (he only invokes the passage under debate, Lk 1:35), but upon his premise that a divine mission is to make evident the distinction of Persons.

18. *ThDrIII*, 183-84.

19. *ThDrIII*, 184.

20. See *MP*, 149.

21. See *ThDrIII*, 184, n. 31.

22. See also Grillmeier, "Der Gottessohn im Totenreich," which indicates the importance of the Son's divine omnipresence with respect to the Descent for the development of Christology.

23. Letter *Inter ea quae* (DS 369): "Unus defunctorum et vivificator obeuntium, ad inferna descendens et a Patris gremio non recedens."

24. Canticle Seven, Mattins of Holy Saturday, *Lenten Triodion,* 650.

25. *ST,* IIIa, q. 7, a. 13; quoted in *ThDrIII,* 184.

26. *GloryVII,* 390, emphasis added.

27. *GloryVII,* 390.

28. *GloryVII,* 390.

29. *ThDrIII,* 530.

30. *ThDrIII,* 530, emphasis added.

31. See *ThDrV,* 95.

32. *ThDrII,* 267.

33. *ThDrIII,* 226.

34. See, e.g., *ThDrV,* 212-69, 516.

35. *MP,* 150.

36. "Death Is Swallowed," 54; see also *Leben,* 51; *GloryVII,* 211, 270.

37. *MP,* 204. See also p. 175.

38. See, e.g., Vatican II, *Dei Verbum,* #8, 9, 12; as also *CF* #215 (DS 1507) and, in connection with it, *CF* #206 (DS 609).

39. *CF* #20, 19 (DS 801, 800); see also DS 415, 441, 501, and 542 regarding the single operation of the three Persons, as also DS 545, 571, 573, 1330-31, 3326-27.

40. *ThDrV,* 95, Balthasar's text but with a reference to Speyr, *The Farewell Discourses* (San Francisco: Ignatius, unspecified date between 1987 and 1994), 232.

41. *ThDrIV,* 325.

42. *ThDrIV,* 326; *ThDrII,* 268.

43. *ThDrV,* 91.

44. "Preliminary Remarks on the Discernment of Spirits," 341.

45. On the Spirit and deification, see, e.g., "Spirit and Institution," 234-35.

46. See the texts referenced in n. 22 in Chapter Seven.

47. *ThDrII,* 257-58. I note here that the mutual petition within the Trinity is imaged in the prayer of Jesus, who must pray as Son even as He obeys as Son.

48. *ThDrIII,* 187.

49. *ThDrV,* 123.

50. *ThDrIII,* 168.

51. *ThDrIII,* 187.

52. *ThDrV,* 485, emphasis in original.

53. *ThDrV,* 88.

54. Speyr, *The World of Prayer,* 57f.

55. *ThDrV,* 89.

56. *ThDrV*, 89, emphasis added, with reference at the end of the sentence to Speyr, *The World of Prayer*, 60-65.

57. See, e.g., *ThDrII*, 257-58.

58. *ThDrII*, 188.

59. *CF* #615 (DS 302).

60. *CF* #613 (DS 300): The Council "excludes from the sacred assembly those who dare to declare subject to suffering the divinity of the Only-begotten."

61. *CF* #612 (DS 294).

62. See *CF* #635-37 (DS 556-58).

63. See, e.g., *ThDrIII*, 228, n. 68: "We cannot enter into a detailed discussion for the appropriate categories for thinking about the unity of the person of Christ in the analogy of his natures." Because Balthasar does not pursue this issue, it is not clear why he calls the Son's possession of two natures an "analogy."

64. *GloryI*, 606.

65. "Trinity and Future," 82-83.

66. *The Christian and Anxiety*, 75; see also *Th'l Anth*, 275.

67. *Church and World*, 107. The discussion is associated with the text marked by n. 37 in Chapter Seven.

68. *ThDrIII*, 226.

69. *ThDrIII*, 226. The remark of O'Hanlon, *The Immutability of God*, 43, is helpful: Balthasar "will refuse to limit that change and suffering which Christ experiences to his human nature alone. This is the advance on Chalcedon and its traditional interpretation which Balthasar proposes. . . . [H]e is anxious to insist on a more than merely logical *communicatio idiomatum*," and yet also avoid attributing suffering univocally to God. To my mind, this move is really the destruction of Chalcedon.

70. Balthasar, *The Christian and Anxiety*, 74-75, is one passage in which appropriate specifications regarding human nature appear with uncharacteristic frequency. Compare *Th'l Anth*, 275. Nonetheless, these texts cannot be read in isolation from Balthasar's later works, particularly as they also contain elements that connect them to his wider Christology.

71. *MP*, 138, emphasis in original.

72. See "Vicarious," 415-16.

73. "The Unity of Our Lives," 121.

74. *GloryI*, 605-6.

75. *GloryI*, 606.

76. *GloryI*, 469.

77. "Desc," 411. Balthasar rejects the aid of philosophy in characterizing Christ's death in "Von Balthasar antwortet Boros," *Orientierung* 34 (1970): 38-39. His hesitation or neglect to consider the metaphysical nature of death raises the question of the relationship he sees between reason and faith. His desire to ground himself in Scripture is evident in his heavy use of it (though his interpretations remain open to debate), but the other sciences have their proper sphere, even if all are ultimately subordinated to the science of the Word of God.

78. *MP*, 56.

79. See "Desc," 411.

80. *MP*, 56, n. 9.

81. See the summary about Durandus de S. Porciano (c. 1275-1334) in Herzog, *Descensus*, 292.

82. *MP*, 203, emphasis added.

83. *ThDrIII*, 227.

84. *ThDrIII*, 510. See also *ThDrIII*, 522, 533.

85. "God Speaks as Man," 93.

86. See pp. 152-53 above.

87. *ThDrIII*, 199.

88. *ThDrIII*, 199.

89. *GloryI*, 469. The "attunement" here refers to the agreement between the task received and the living out of it.

90. *ThDrIII*, 510.

91. *ThDrIII*, 200.

92. *ThDrIV*, 132, emphasis in original.

93. "Geist und Feuer: Ein Gespräch mit Hans Urs von Balthasar," *Herder Korrespondenz*, 30 (Feb 1976) 2: 76. His intention was expressed generally, although he gives the Church as an example.

94. *ThDrV*, 99-100, 245, 395; "Trinity and Future," 81; *ThDrIV*, 329, 333.

95. See, e.g., *GloryVII*, 214.

96. See, e.g., *The Threefold Garland*, 79-80.

97. See "The Incarnation of God," 65, with p. 62; the entire essay, "Only If"; "Trinity and Future," 81-83. In the first two of these texts, it would seem the Incarnation unto Sheol is necessary (and hence also sin would be); in the last, Balthasar is more careful.

98. See "Trinity and Future," 81-83; "The Incarnation of God," 65; "Only If," 135-53; *GloryVII*, 218, 229-30; *ThDrIV*, 487-88, 495. Compare also *MP*, 137, on theories about whether redemption in another way was possible.

99. *ThDrII*, 269.

100. *GloryVII*, 211.

101. *ThDrIV*, 495-96. See also *ThDrV*, 277; *God Question*, 133; *GloryVII*, 216.

102. *ThDrIV*, 495, emphasis added. See also *The Threefold Garland*, 73.

103. "Loneliness in the Church," 274.

104. "Loneliness in the Church," 274.

105. *Th'l Anth*, 275.

106. "Vicarious," 415-16, emphasis in original. Similar problems are also found in "Obedience," 230; *GloryI*, 617.

107. See, e.g., *GloryVII*, 217-18, 231; *ThDrIV*, 494-95; *ThDrV*, 261 (with Speyr).

108. *GloryI*, 327, emphasis added; see also *GloryVII*, 143-44.

109. See *ThDrV*, 261: God's judgment is pronounced upon all the world's sin, "which the Son now embodies."

110. *ThDrIII*, 239-40. On why anthropology might present limiting conditions for "enter[ing] into the desperate situation," compare "Vicarious," 415-16 (see n. 106 above).

111. *MP*, 203, emphasis added. In contrast to my assessment of the minimal importance of Christ's human nature in Balthasar's Christology, Giovanni Marchesi, *La cristologia trinitaria di Hans Urs von Balthasar: Gesù Cristo pienezza della rivelazione e della salvezza*, 2nd ed., Biblioteca di Teologia Contemporanea 94 (Brescia: Queriniana, 2003), 24-45, 448-57, 508,

543-45, thinks a very high value is given to it. It is to be noted, however, that he attributes this value precisely due to the *expressive* role of Christ's human nature in revealing God, and not to a soteriological function. Though Christ's human nature is preeminently expressive in the soteriological moments, this is not the same as ascribing a soteriological value to that human nature.

112. *ThDrIV*, 132.

113. *ThDrIV*, 132.

114. *God Question*, 133.

115. *GloryVII*, 257.

116. "Mystery," 121.

117. "Martyrdom and Mission," 286-91, has been taken into account. Balthasar states explicitly in *ThLogII*, 319, that no following is possible; see also pp. 325-27.

118. *GloryVII*, 390.

119. See, e.g., *Church and World*, 65.

120. *MP*, 121; *GloryVII*, 316; contrast "Meeting God," 20: "God in human form died the death of a redeemer (that is, of a sinner)."

121. "Mystery," 117; *ThDrIV*, 487, 495.

122. *MP*, 121, emphasis in original.

123. In itself, faith is more certain than the knowledge of God had through human reason (St. Thomas Aquinas, *ST* IIaIIae q. 4, a. 8 c), because the object it knows is more certain.

124. E.g., Marchesi, *La cristologia trinitaria*; Brambilla, "Salvezza e redenzione"; Wallner, *Gott als Eschaton*; Aldo Moda, *La gloria della croce: Un dialogo con Hans Urs von Balthasar* (Padua: Messaggero di S. Antonio, 1998); and Terence McGuckin, "The Eschatology of the Cross," *New Blackfriars* 75 (1994): 364-77. Helmut Dieser, *Der gottähnliche Mensch*, 463, emphasis added, rightly captures the Balthasarian usage when he describes the cross "als *Symbol* des Passionsmysteriums insgesamt" [as a *symbol* of the mystery of the Passion as a whole]. The authors who use *cross* to include the Descent without being much attentive to Balthasar's radical valuation of the latter appear to share as well an *a priori* interest in relating his theology to a *theologia crucis*.

125. *Dare*, 106.

126. *Dare*, 106.

127. *Dare*, 106.

128. *CF* #2305 (DS 1000), emphasis added.

129. It may be that some, or all, of the holy dead were bodily resurrected with Christ and hence were taken up to heaven body and soul. One may draw this conclusion on the basis of Mt 27:52-53, as well as on the fact that Christ's liberation of the souls through His descent is both their liberation *into* the beatific vision and their liberation *from* limbo. Their bodily resurrection from the tombs thus would manifest their souls' liberation.

130. See Worthen, *The Harrowing of Hell*, 58-59.

131. *Commentary*, #31, p. 61.

132. *ST*, IIIa q. 57, a. 6; and St. Thomas Aquinas, *Commentary on Ephesians*, c. 4, l. 3.

133. Fragment XIII, lines 775-86, quoted in Grillmeier, "*Der Gottessohn im Totenreich*," 82.

134. On this reading of the thousand years, see Daniélou, "*Déluge, Baptême, Jugement*," 112.

135. *ThDrV*, 357, emphasis added.

136. *ThDrV*, 405, emphasis added.

137. For indications of the abruptness of the change from Christ's being dead to His resurrection, see, e.g., *GloryVII*, 234; *ThDrIV*, 361.

138. *MP*, 161; "Desc," 408; "Vicarious," 422.

139. *MP*, 165.

140. "Desc," 411.

141. *MP*, 173.

142. Cooper, "Ps 24:7-10," 53-54.

143. Descriptions such as the one marked by n. 138 above would be supported by, e.g., the work of C. Spicq, "La Révélation de l'Enfer dans la Sainte Écriture," 93-96; and Perrot, *"La Descente du Christ,"* 7-8.

144. *GloryVII*, 229, n. 3. Compare Balthasar's discussion of methodology on this point in *ThDrIV*, 117-21. There he first decides it is wrong to start from a Christian standpoint, then considers the Old Testament as the correct perspective with which to begin, finds an obstacle, and ends by concluding that the Christian point of view is indeed the essential one. Nonetheless, in practice, he uses his reading of the Old Testament sheol.

145. "Geist und Feuer: Ein Gespräch," 75: "Das gesamte Evangelium ist inspiriert."

146. I highly recommend C. Spicq, "La Révélation de l'Enfer dans la Sainte Écriture." Also noteworthy is Chaine, "Descente du Christ aux Enfers," who sets his consideration of the New Testament doctrine of Christ's descent in the context of the theology of sheol of the whole Old Testament (not just a part), as well as that of the intertestamental literature; this approach is more adequate to the material than Balthasar's. See also Strynkowski, "Descent," and Cooper, "Ps 24:7-10," 53-54.

147. *ThDrII*, 114. See also Stadelmann, *The Hebrew Conception of the World*, 176, who stresses that "a full and balanced view [of the Hebrew conception of the world] may be attained only by combining in a single account the insights gathered from several...." This observation reasonably applies to the part (sheol) as well as the whole (the universe).

148. See also Spicq, "La Révélation de l'Enfer dans la Sainte Écriture," 97.

149. "DescHell," 225-26.

150. Consider *ThDrV*, 256-65.

151. Balthasar does not mention Ruth nor 1 and 2 Samuel, which fall between Judges and Kings. It is not clear whether he is deliberately excluding them, or including Ruth with Judges, and the books of Samuel with those of Kings.

152. *ThDrIV*, 120. See also "Desc," 408, and his treatment of "Jewish hope" in *ThDrV*, 143-44.

153. *MP*, 161.

154. See Spicq, "La Révélation de l'Enfer dans la Sainte Écriture," 89-112.

155. "Das Selbstbewußtsein Jesu," *IKaZ Communio*, 8 (1979): 34.

156. "Der Tod im heutigen Denken," 299. Balthasar's word for such theologians is "töricht" [foolish]. See the similar comment in "Geist und Feuer: Ein Gespräch," 74.

157. See, e.g., *MP*, 172, 177.

158. See also *Th'l Anth*, 283.

159. See Balthasar's own statement in *ThDrIII*, 167.

160. "Some Points of Eschatology," 270.

161. The arguments are in *ThDrIII*, 184, n. 31. See also the discussion in n. 6 in Chapter Six.

162. *GloryVII*, 230, n. 7.

163. Espezel, *El Misterio Pascual*, 68.

164. See *MP*, 153, 160-68.

165. See, e.g., "Geist und Feuer: Ein Gespräch," 75; *ThDrII*, 114; and *The Threefold Garland*, 102, with regard to the Gospels.

166. See, e.g., *MP*, 137, regarding Heb 4:15; and *ThLogII*, 322, with implicit reference to Jn 19:30.

167. See, e.g., *GloryVII*, 223, on the Passion according to St. John.

168. See, e.g., *GloryVII*, 210, on the words from the cross.

169. This omission is particularly notable in his use of only selected Psalms to characterize Sheol. We find more complete treatments of the Psalms, and consequently a different view of Sheol, in the works of Strynkowski, "Descent," 41-70; s.v. "death," in Xavier Léon-Dufour, ed., *Dictionary of Biblical Theology*, 2nd ed., trans. P. Joseph Cahill, rev. and trans. E. M. Stewart (Boston: St. Paul, 1988); and Spicq, "La Révélation de l'Enfer dans la Sainte Écriture," 91-112, to take a few examples.

170. *Credo*, 51, emphasis added.

171. *MP*, 50, emphasis added.

172. *MP*, 173-74; "DescHell," 233.

173. *ThDrV*, 314-16.

174. *ThDrV*, 314.

175. *ThDrV*, 314.

176. See, e.g., *MP*, 173.

177. *Leben*, 36.

178. *ThDrV*, 261.

179. *MP*, 50.

180. *ThDrV*, 321. In "Loneliness in the Church," 273, the same comparison is made with respect to Rev 17:16 and 18:17, though more cautiously.

181. "Desc," 407.

182. "Desc," 405, 407.

183. "Desc," 405.

184. "Desc," 405. He similarly groups Catholic and apocryphal works together on p. 407.

185. "Desc," 414, emphasis added.

186. Nn. 115 and 116 to his chapter on Holy Saturday in *MP*.

187. Grillmeier, *"Der Gottessohn im Totenreich,"* 87: "Hinter allen Bildern . . . steht die eine Idee von der Erlösung durch Christus und der Überwindung der feindlichen Mächte des Bösen."

188. In contrast, see Grillmeier, *"Der Gottessohn im Totenreich,"* 94, 97.

189. See, e.g., Lundberg, *La typologie baptismale*, 109-10, 215-16; Wilpert, *Die römischen Mosaiken*, 2. Band, 3. Buch, 889; Perrot, *"La Descente du Christ aux Enfers,"* 27-28; Chaine, *"Descente du Christ aux Enfers,"* 429-31; F. Loofs, "Christ's Descent into Hell," *Transactions of the Third International Congress for the History of Religions,* vol. 2 (Oxford: Clarendon Press: 1908), 290-301, cited in Cabrol, *"Descente du Christ aux enfers d'après la liturgie,"* 692.

Chaine's work is particularly noteworthy in this context because he examines both Scripture and the myths that are supposed to have influenced the Judeo-Christian Tradition so heavily.

190. Grillmeier, *"Der Gottessohn im Totenreich,"* 79; see also p. 80 with n. 11.

191. My translation of Fragment XIII, lines 775-77, 780-85, quoted in Grillmeier, *"Der Gottessohn im Totenreich,"* 82: "Ich habe den Verurteilten befreit,/ich habe den Toten wieder belebt,/ich richte den Begrabenen wieder auf;/. . . ich habe den Tod zunichte gemacht/und über den Feind triumphiert/und den Hades mit Füßen getreten/und den Starken gebunden/ und den Menschen/zu den Höhen des Himmels geführt." Clear boundaries are not always drawn in the fragment between Christ's death, descent, resurrection, and ascension, which reflects a vision of the unity of the mystery of redemption. Grillmeier holds that the text "destroyed death, triumphed over the Enemy," etc., refers to Christ's descent.

192. My translation of the text as quoted in Grillmeier, *"Der Gottessohn im Totenreich,"* 91: "Wir danken dir, Gott, durch deinen geliebten Knecht Jesus Christus, . . . den von dir stammenden Logos . . ./der, freiwilligen Leiden überantwortet,/um den Tod aufzuheben, die Bande des Teufels zu zerbrechen,/den Hades (Unterwelt) niederzutreten,/die Gerechten zu erleuchten,/eine Grenze zu stecken,/Und die Auferstehung kundzutun,/das Brot nahm, dir dankte und sprach. . . ."

193. Grillmeier, *"Der Gottessohn im Totenreich,"* 90-92.

194. See, e.g., *Gospel of Nicodemus,* sec. 17-27, in Edgar Hennecke, *New Testament Apocrypha,* ed. Wilhelm Schneemelcher, Eng. trans. ed. R. McL. Wilson, vol. 1 (Philadelphia: Westminster Press, 1963), 470-76.

195. On the biblical description of the underworld in terms of gates and bars, see Stadelmann, *The Hebrew Conception of the World,* 171-72; see also, in particular, Ps 106 (107):16.

196. Vorgrimler, *Geschichte der Hölle,* 339.

197. Grillmeier, *"Der Gottessohn im Totenreich,"* 91.

198. Vorgrimler, *Geschichte der Hölle,* 339.

199. *ThDrI,* 106-7.

200. An outstanding work on this topic is *About the Harrowing of Hell: A Seventeenth-Century Ukrainian Play in Its European Context,* trans. with introduction and notes by Irena R. Makaryk (Ottawa: Dovehouse Editions Canada, 1989). Liturgical, apocryphal, and patristic sources for the play are discussed, as also similar plays in France, England, Spain, Italy, Germany, Austria, Bohemia, and Poland.

201. *ThDrI,* 114.

202. *ThDrI,* 113, with reference "K. W. Schmidt, *Die Darstellung von Christi Höllenfahrt in den deutschen und ihnen verwandten Spielen des Mittelalters* (Marburg, 1915). J. Kroll, *Zur Geschichte des Spiels von Christi Höllenfahrt* (Vorträge der Bibl.: Warburg, Teubner, Leipzig, 1932). For editions of the many plays, with bibliography: W. Kosch, *Dt. Lit. Lex III* (1956), s.v. 'Osterspiele.'"

203. *MP,* 179. See also *Credo,* 53.

204. *MP,* 179-80.

205. *MP,* 180.

206. *MP,* 180.

207. *God Question,* 129-42.

208. *God Question,* 130.

209. *God Question*, 129.

210. *God Question*, 129.

211. *God Question*, 133-34.

212. See *God Question*, 132; *ThDrI*, 106; *MP*, 151-52.

213. *CF* #1253 (DS 653-54).

214. It is most unfortunate that Balthasar's presentations of the *Anastasis* icon seem to have convinced Manfred Lochbrunner, "Das Ineinander von Schau und Theologie in der Lehre vom Karsamstag bei Hans Urs von Balthasar," *Rivista Teologica di Lugano* 6 (2001) 1: 171-93. In an exceptionally fine article summarizing both the traditional doctrine and Balthasar's position, Lochbrunner distinguishes three fundamental types of doctrines on the Descent (his page 177): the Eastern Church ("ostkirchlichen"), the Protestant, and the Catholic. His description of the Eastern Church's doctrine is pure Balthasar: "Hier wird das Triduum mortis als eine einzige Bewegung gesehen, die im Abstieg am Karsamstag ihre höchste dramatische Intensität erreicht. . . . Während die westlichen Osterbilder Christus immer nur einsam auferstehend zeigen, lässt der Osten die soteriologisch-soziale Seite der Erlösungstat sehen. . . . Das antezipierende, triumphalistische Moment gilt als Charakteristikum des östlichen Typs." ["Here the *Triduum mortis* is seen as a single movement, which reaches its highest dramatic intensity in the Descent on Holy Saturday. . . . While the Western images of Easter always show Christ rising alone, the Eastern image lets the soteriologico-social side of the act of redemption be seen. . . . The anticipating, triumphalistic moment serves as the characteristic of the Eastern type."] Both Balthasar and, following Balthasar, Lochbrunner set in opposition the Catholic doctrine and that of the Eastern Church. But who is this Eastern Church? If it is the Orthodox, it remains to be shown that the Orthodox and Catholic doctrines of the Descent differ. If it is those Catholics of the Eastern rites, to whom the icon belongs as much as to the Orthodox, it is unjust to oppose "Eastern" and "Catholic." Indeed, the dichotomy is seen to be false from the fact that the so-called "Eastern Church" doctrine and the "Catholic" one are wholly compatible: All the features Lochbrunner summarizes as the "Catholic" doctrine are imaged in the icon: that the Descent regards the glorification of Christ's soul, that His soul united to the Word descended only to the Limbo of the Fathers, and that the Descent does not pertain to the redemptive satisfaction of Christ, which is "consummated" (Jn 19:30) on the cross, but (I add in clarification) to the salvific application of His redemptive work. Finally, the reduction of the icon to an anticipation of Easter has inclined Lochbrunner to compare it to Western images of Easter, thereby overlooking the Western 'soteriologico-social' images of Holy Saturday, i.e., of the harrowing of hell.

The "Eastern Church" is even worse mishandled by Maas, *Gott und die Hölle*, 253. After a presentation that follows close on the heels of Balthasar, Maas concedes that "Für die fromme Meditation gibt es durchaus eine legitime Ausmalung des erlebten Triumphes, der freudigen Begegnung zwischen Jesus und den Gefangenen, zwischen dem neuen und alten Adam. Aber dies alles überschreitet die Aussagemöglichkeiten der *Theologie*" [For pious meditation, there is a legitimate depiction of the experienced triumph, of the joyful meeting between Jesus and those imprisoned, between the New Adam and the Old. But all this oversteps the possibilities of what *theology* can say]; the emphasis is in the original. First, the icon is dismissed as "pious meditation" and denied its character as a theological statement. I do not think St. John Damascene would sit quietly to hear that; nor the other iconophiles who saw the "Triumph of Orthodoxy" with the defeat of the iconoclasts at Nicaea II; nor the fathers of Constantinople IV and Trent; nor, to indicate contemporary continuity, John Paul II (Apostolic Letter *Duodecimum saeculum*). Secondly, the division between what is legitimate for piety and what for theology suggests there is a sort of religious 'double truth,' as if piety can run around saying all sorts of things that theology has no capability or responsibility to confirm as true or correct as false. In other words, the *lex orandi, lex credendi* is sundered.

In Part One, I argued for a single Catholic doctrine of the Descent, and showed evidence from both East and West for it. Wilpert, *Die römischen Mosaiken*, 1. Band, 2. Buch, 202-5; and 2. Band, 3. Buch, 887-95, points out that those who treat images of a triumphal descent as proper only to the East have overlooked something, since such representations appear early and often in Rome. He goes on to make the provocative argument that the similarity of extant representations suggests they had a common archetype. The archetype, he argues, could only have been a particular mosaic cycle in the Lateran Basilica of Rome, one *from the time of Constantine* that *predated* monumental Byzantine productions. In other words, notwithstanding the spread of the *doctrine* of the Descent from the East as the birthplace of Christianity, Wilpert argues the archetypal *image* of the Descent spread from the West, from Rome. (If so, it would be an interesting coincidence, for the Lateran Basilica, cathedral of the bishop of Rome, is the station church for Holy Saturday.) I cannot judge this question of art history — Wilpert is the only one I have seen set forth such an idea — but I point out his text to indicate that a position on the far extreme from Balthasar's can be held and argued, not just asserted, by a specialist in art history.

215. My translation of Balthasar, "Theologie des Abstiegs zur Hölle," *Adrienne von Speyr und ihre kirchliche Sendung, Akten des römischen Symposiums 27-29 September 1985* (Einsiedeln: Johannes, 1986), 140-41: "Wir können, vereinfachend, zwei große Traditionsstränge unterscheiden: den des Ostens und den des Westens. Fur den Osten bildet die Ikone vom Abstieg Christi die Hauptdarstellung unserer Erlösung. . . . Von ganz frühen Predigten reicht diese Tradition bis zu den im Mittelalter gespielten Ostermysterien. . . . Im Westen, ehren Theologie und Liturgie vorwiegend das Schweigen des Todes, die Kirche wacht mit Maria schweigend und betend am Grab."

216. Herzog, *Descensus*, 243: "Durch die Jahrhunderte war man sich über Sinn und Bedeutung des Descensusartikels zu sicher, als daß es zu erheblichen Kontroversen hätte kommen können."

217. *Dare*, 35, n. 3; 47.

218. *ThDrIV*, 253-54, emphasis in original. Balthasar's reference for the interior quotation is given on p. 250: "*Or.* 30, PG 36, 108C-109C."

219. *ThDrIV*, 253. See also the discussion of other Fathers, pp. 250-54.

220. *ThDrIV*, 263.

221. *ThDrIV*, 290.

222. *ThDrIV*, 253-54, 263.

223. Herzog, *Descensus*, 166, 169, 173, 340. Although Balthasar could not have known Herzog's work (it was published well after Balthasar's death), he was certainly familiar both with Nicholas of Cusa and with the traditional doctrine of the Descent.

224. Balthasar's position is softened by the readings, for example, of David Edward Lauber, *Towards a Theology of Holy Saturday: Karl Barth and Hans Urs von Balthasar on the Descensus ad inferna* (Ann Arbor, MI: UMI Dissertation Services, 1999), 200-201; Marchesi,

La cristologia trinitaria, 551, 560, 566-68; Regis Martin, *The Suffering of Love: Christ's Descent into Hell and Human Hopelessness, with Particular Reference to the Holocaust of the Jews* (STD diss., Pontificia Università S. Tommaso d'Aquino, 1988), 127, 162 (n. 28); and Dieser, *Der gottähnliche Mensch*, 291-92, 298, 300, 311-25, 473. They do so despite indications of the objective reality Christ experiences elsewhere in their own texts (in Lauber, pp. 176, 274; in Marchesi, e.g., pp. 246-48, 337; in Martin, e.g., pp. 190-92, 237; in Dieser, given his argument that the Son's descent images His procession, the one should be as real the other, if one considers, e.g., pp. 429-30, 446). The softened readings turn on the ambiguity of such concepts as *experience, undergo,* and *suffer,* as well as *state,* which can refer to events or conditions that are wholly objective, wholly subjective, or mixed. Also at play is the equivocation possible with the concept *not-godly,* which is open to being employed as the morally neutral *finite* or as *anti-divine* (i.e., *sinful*).

225. *ThDrIII*, 228.

226. "DescHell," 227.

227. "DescHell," 227.

228. *GloryVII*, 229.

229. *GloryVII*, 229, n. 3.

230. "DescHell," 228. See also *MP*, 179. The bracketed text is a correction to the translation, which read instead, "in anticipation of the Holy Saturday's conquest and emptying of the underworld." Balthasar's original reads, "der vorweg am Karsamstag die Unterwelt besiegt und entleert."

231. "DescHell," 224.

232. "DescHell," 231. In *ThLogII*, 317, Balthasar writes, "From his death . . . , before the passage through hell, there is possibly something like a pause, in which he sets down the thief in the promised Paradise. . . ." This idea contradicts Balthasar's position that Christ's experience in Sheol is necessary to constitute all other realms of the afterworld. The description of "a moment of peace" bears striking resemblance to Speyr's experience of such a pause; see "Theologie des Abstiegs," 143. The suggestion that Christ goes first to paradise, and then to hades, is also made by Origen; the citations in Grillmeier, *"Der Gottessohn im Totenreich,"* 157, n. 167, are *"Matthäuserklärung XII 3* = GCS Orig. 10, Klostermann-Benz, 72,33–73,3 (*zu* Mt 16,1ff.)" and "*Johanneskommentar XXXII* (395f.) = GCS Orig. 4, Preuschen 479,29–480,12 (*zu* Joh 13,33)," where GCS stands for *Die griechischen christlichen Schriftsteller der ersten drei Jahrhunderte* (Leipzig, 1897ff.).

233. "DescHell," 235; see also p. 228.

234. "DescHell," 236. See also "Der Tod im heutigen Denken," 299, where Balthasar also explicitly identifies Sheol with what the New Testament calls "Hölle" [hell], i.e., gehenna.

235. *ThDrIII*, 522.

236. *GloryVII*, 313.

237. *ThLogII*, 296, with interior quotations from Speyr, *Erde und Himmel,* Bd. 2 (Einsiedeln: Johannes, 1976), 157.

238. *ThDrIV*, 329.

239. *ThDrIV*, 329.

240. *ThDrV*, 255.

241. *ThDrV*, 252-56, 257, 268.

242. *ThDrV*, 263. See also *ThDrIII*, 530.

243. *MP,* 137.

244. *CF* #643 (DS 1025).

Notes to Chapter Eleven

1. *Catechism of the Council of Trent,* 64, 65.

2. This mode of presentation lasts up until *ThDrIV,* in which the determining influence of Adrienne von Speyr becomes overt; see Lochbrunner, *"Das Ineinander,"* 186-88.

3. E.g., Herzog, *Descensus,* 7, 240-44 especially, 335, 340, 352-53, *inter alia;* the article, "Hell," in *Dictionary of Biblical Theology,* ed. Xavier Léon-Dufour; Kelly, *Early Christian Creeds,* 380-81; and Espezel, *El Misterio Pascual,* 70.

4. E.g., Herzog, *Descensus,* 242-44, 350-51; Medard Kehl, "Höllenabstieg Christi," *Lexikon für Theologie und Kirche* (LTK) 5. Band, 3d ed., hrsg. Walter Kasper (Freiburg: Herder, 1996), 238; Aidan Nichols in his introduction to Balthasar, *MP,* 7; Lochbrunner, *"Das Ineinander,"* 178; Maas, *Gott und die Hölle,* 248; Hunt, *The Trinity and the Pascal Mystery,* 69, n. 60; David Berger, "Woher kommen die Thesen Hans Urs von Balthasars zur Hölle? Oder: hatte „Theologisches" doch recht? Book review of *Atti XIV Colloquio di Teologia di Lugano: Esperienza mistica e teologia. Ricerca epistemologica sulle proposte di Hans Urs von Balthasar* [= *Rivista Teologica di Lugano* 6 (2001): 1-64], *Theologisches Katholische Monatsscrift* 31 (2001) 5/6: 267-68; Roch Kerezty, "Response to Professor Scola," 230-31; Vorgrimler, *Geschichte der Hölle,* 342; Lauber (*Towards a Theology of Holy Saturday,* 17; see also pp. 34, 58, 186), who notes the same conclusion drawn for varying reasons by John Saward and Fergus Kerr (pp. 258-59); and Rothkranz, *Die Kardinalfehler,* 273 (see also pp. 47-50, 273-75, 379-81). Rothkranz is among the few authors actually to examine the sources Balthasar invokes and, on this account alone, whatever one thinks of the tone of Rothkranz's book, his arguments should be considered seriously.

5. Lauber, *Towards a Theology of Holy Saturday,* 17.

6. Lauber, *Towards a Theology of Holy Saturday,* 258; see also pp. 260-61.

7. Balthasar, "From the Theology of God to Theology in the Church," *Communio ICR* 9 (1982): 213.

8. On pastoral issues, either in terms of the present need or the relevance of the Descent, see, e.g., Strynkowski, *The Descent (excerpt),* 51-55; idem, "The Descent," 249-69; Herzog, *Descensus,* 240; Cantalamessa, *The Mystery of Easter,* 111-26; s.v. "hell," no trans. noted, *Sacramentum Mundi,* 1969 ed., 9-10; s.v. "death," *Dictionary of Biblical Theology,* 118-19. See also Grillmeier, *"Der Gottessohn im Totenreich,"* 79; and Herzog, *Descensus,* 396-98, on the universality of Christ's mission made evident in His descent.

9. See Grillmeier, *"Der Gottessohn im Totenreich,"* 80, 94, 97-98, 100, 158, 174.

Index